ALEKSANDR SOLZHENITSYN:

Critical Essays
and
Documentary Materials

Contributors:

Dorothy Atkinson
Heinrich Böll
Thompson Bradley
Vera Carpovich
Terrence Des Pres
Milovan Djilas
John B. Dunlop
Milton Ehre
Victor Erlich
Donald Fanger
Kathryn B. Feuer
Xenia Gasiorowska
David M. Halperin
Richard Haugh
Irving Howe
Roman Jakobson
Alexis Klimoff
Rosette Lamont
Vadim Liapunov
Mary McCarthy
Czeslaw Milosz
Helen Muchnic
Michael Nicholson
Philip Rahv
Alexander Schmemann
Gleb Struve
Nikita Struve
Boris O. Unbegaun
Hélène Zamoyska
Gleb Zekulin

ALEKSANDR SOLZHENITSYN:
Critical Essays and Documentary Materials

Edited by:
John B. Dunlop
Richard Haugh
Alexis Klimoff

NORDLAND PUBLISHING COMPANY
Belmont, Massachusetts 02178

Library of Congress Catalog Card Number 73-88869
ISBN 0-913124-03-6

PRINTED IN THE UNITED STATES OF AMERICA

Notes on Contributors and Editors

DOROTHY ATKINSON, a National Fellow at the Hoover Institution, teaches Russian History at Stanford University. Her publications on Solzhenitsyn have appeared in *The Russian Review*.

HEINRICH BÖLL, recipient of the Nobel Prize for Literature in 1972 and President of the International P.E.N., is one of the most prolific and popular of postwar German writers. Mr. Böll's latest novel is *Group Portrait with Lady*.

THOMPSON BRADLEY, Assistant Professor of Russian at Swarthmore College, has published extensively on Solzhenitsyn. At present he is completing a lengthy work tentatively entitled *Aleksandr Solzhenitsyn and the Rebirth of Slavophilism*.

VERA CARPOVICH, Assistant Professor of Russian at Vassar College, is co-editor of the *Russian-English Chemical Dictionary*. She is working on a dictionary of Solzhenitsyn's language.

TERRENCE DES PRES, Junior Fellow in the Harvard Society of Fellows, holds the Crawshaw Chair in English Literature at Colgate University. He is presently completing a book on the ethos of survival, to be published by Oxford University Press, entitled *The Survivor*.

MILOVAN DJILAS, renowned Yugoslav writer and dissident, is the author of *Conversations with Stalin* and *The New Class*.

JOHN B. DUNLOP, co-editor of this volume, is Assistant Professor of Russian at Oberlin College. He is the author of *Staretz Amvrosy* and is presently completing a volume entitled *The New Russian Revolutionaries*.

MILTON EHRE, Associate Professor of Russian Literature at the University of Chicago, is the author of *Oblomov and His Creator: Life and Art*.

VICTOR ERLICH, Bensinger Professor of Slavic Languages and Literatures at Yale University, has written extensively in the field of Russian literature. His books include *Russian Formalism, The Double Image,* and *Gogol*.

DONALD FANGER, Professor of Slavic and Comparative Literature and Chairman of the Slavic Department at Harvard University, is the author of *Dostoevsky and Romantic Realism* and numerous essays and articles. He is currently at work on a book about Gogol and the rise of Russian fiction.

KATHRYN B. FEUER, Professor of Slavic Languages and Literatures at the University of Toronto, is the author of several works on the 19th and 20th-century novel.

XENIA GASIOROWSKA, Professor of Slavic Languages and Literatures at the University of Wisconsin, has published numerous articles in American and European scholarly journals and is the author of *Women in Soviet Fiction: 1917-1964*.

DAVID M. HALPERIN is currently a graduate student in Classics and Humanities at Stanford University.

RICHARD HAUGH, co-editor of this volume, is Assistant Professor of Religious

Studies at Iona College and an editor of *Transactions of the Association of Russian-American Scholars.* He is the author of a forthcoming volume on comparative Byzantine and Carolingian thought and is completing a book on Dostoevsky.

IRVING HOWE, Professor of Literature at CUNY Graduate Center, is editor of *Dissent.* His many books on literature include *William Faulkner: A Critical Study* and *Sherwood Anderson.*

ROMAN JAKOBSON, Cross Professor of Slavic Languages and Literatures at Harvard University and Institute Professor of Linguistics at M.I.T., has published a vast number of studies in linguistics, poetics, and literary theory.

ALEXIS KLIMOFF, co-editor of this volume, is Instructor of Russian at Vassar College. He has had an abiding interest in the problem of translation.

ROSETTE C. LAMONT, Professor of Comparative Literature at CUNY Graduate Center, has written widely on French and Russian symbolist poetry, contemporary European and American theater, Marcel Proust and Boris Pasternak.

VADIM LIAPUNOV is Assistant Professor of Slavic Languages and Literatures at Yale University.

MARY MCCARTHY is a novelist, essayist, and critic. Her latest novel is *Birds of America* and her most recent book of literary criticism is *The Writing on the Wall.*

CZESLAW MILOSZ, Professor of Slavic Languages and Literatures at the University of California at Berkeley, received the *Prix Littéraire Européan* in 1953. His many books and essays include *Postwar Polish Poetry, The Captive Mind,* and *The History of Polish Literature.*

HELEN MUCHNIC, Professor Emeritus of Russian Literature at Smith College, has written widely on Russian literature. Her books include *Introduction to Russian Literature, From Gorky to Pasternak,* and *Russian Writers.*

MICHAEL NICHOLSON, author of several studies on Solzhenitsyn, teaches Russian and Soviet Literature at the University of Lancaster, England.

PHILIP RAHV, editor of *Partisan Review* and *Modern Occasions,* is Professor of English at Brandeis University. He is the author of *Literature and the Sixth Sense, Image and Idea,* and *The Myth and the Powerhouse,* as well as many other books and articles. His latest work, a book on Dostoevsky, is soon to be published.

ALEXANDER SCHMEMANN, Dean of St. Vladimir's Theological School, has written and edited numerous works in theology and literature, including *Ultimate Questions: An Anthology of Modern Russian Religious Thought.*

GLEB STRUVE, Professor Emeritus of Slavic Languages and Literatures at the University of California at Berkeley, is the author of numerous works, including *Russian Literature under Lenin and Stalin* and a history of Russian émigré literature, and co-editor of the only complete editions of Mandel'shtam, Akhmatova, Gumilev, and Pasternak.

NIKITA STRUVE, Professor of Russian Literature at the University of Paris, is the editor of *Vestnik RSKhD* and the author of several studies, including *Christians in Contemporary Russia.*

BORIS O. UNBEGAUN (d. March 4, 1973), Fellow of Brasenose College, Oxford, was the author of hundreds of works, including *La Langue russe au* XVIe *siècle, Russian Versification,* and a recently published monograph, *Russian Surnames.* At the time of his death, he was Visiting Professor at New York University.

HÉLÈNE ZAMOYSKA, Professor of Slavic Literatures at the University of Toulouse, France, has written widely on Russian literature.

GLEB ZEKULIN, Associate Professor of Slavic Languages and Literatures at the University of Toronto, has written extensively on 19th and 20th-century Russian literature.

Contents

Preface

A little more than a decade ago an unknown physics teacher from the Soviet city of Riazan' attained instant celebrity with the publication of his short novel *One Day in the Life of Ivan Denisovich.* In the years that followed—and especially since 1970, when he was awarded the Nobel Prize in Literature—Aleksandr Solzhenitsyn has repeatedly attracted the spotlight of world attention. The admiration for his fearless public statements has been closely followed by a growing recognition of his stature as an outstanding master of Russian prose. Today Solzhenitsyn's words are circulated with astonishing rapidity and are accorded a degree of respect given to few other living writers.[1]

Due to Solzhenitsyn's immense historical and political significance, readers in the West have been understandably uneasy about the proper criteria to use in assessing his fiction. The principal aim of this volume is to supply the English reader with a broad and informed range of critical opinion on Solzhenitsyn's art. To this end, the editors have solicited, translated, and reprinted essays which focus on a number of important aspects of the writer's work. No single point of view is urged in this collection. The editors prefer to think that the individual emphases and divergent viewpoints of the

---

[1]Three major new statements by Solzhenitsyn came to light as this volume was in press: "Not One Step Further," *The New York Review of Books,* 4 October 1973 (a more complete version appeared in *The Times* [London], 29 August 1973); "Dissident Cites KGB in Suicide," *The Washington Post,* 7 September 1973; and "Peace and Violence," *The New York Times,* 15 September 1973.

critical responses gathered here will serve to illuminate the many dimensions of Solzhenitsyn's art.

The "Critical Essays" section of this volume has been divided into two parts: the first consists of essays of a general nature which treat the entire corpus of Solzhenitsyn's writings; the second contains analyses of specific works. The large selection of criticism devoted to *August 1914* is justified, the editors believe, by the controversial reception of this novel in the West and by the fact that Solzhenitsyn is currently writing a two-volume sequel to it.

Four important statements by Solzhenitsyn, published here with copious notes, have been included to assist the reader in understanding Solzhenitsyn's views on literature and on the writer's responsibility toward society. Annotated bibliographies of Soviet and Western responses to Solzhenitsyn's writings and activities have been appended, as well as a critical evaluation of the major English translations of Solzhenitsyn's fiction.

The editing of this volume has not been an easy task and the editors gratefully acknowledge the helpful counsel or technical assistance provided by the following individuals: Eugene Carpovich, Vera Carpovich, Marjorie L. Hoover, Serge Kryzytski, Joan Mussoff, Sergei Pushkarev, Peter Reddaway, Thomas Remington, and Louise Sheehan. A special debt is owed to Michael Nicholson of the University of Lancaster whose impressive expertise in all matters relating to Solzhenitsyn was generously and repeatedly placed at the editors' disposal. Finally, it is our pleasant duty to thank our wives for their unflagging support of a project that has absorbed our time for a longer period than any of us thought possible.

J.B.D.
R.H.
A.K.

NOTE: With the sole exception of "Tolstoy" and "Dostoevsky," Russian names and words have been transcribed according to the Library of Congress system of transliteration.

CRITICAL ESSAYS
I

Heinrich Böll on Solzhenitsyn

KOCH: We think of him [Solzhenitsyn] in connection with Dostoevsky and with Tolstoy.

BÖLL: And rightly so in the sense of the humanistic tradition. I think that is quite right. The most surprising thing for me about Solzhenitsyn is the sequence of his works. His first book, I believe, after his release from imprisonment was *The First Circle.* Then came *One Day in the Life of Ivan Denisovich* and then *Cancer Ward.* Now this volume of short prose pieces has come out, *For the Good of the Cause;* it contains, however, pieces scattered over the years. The surprising and, for me, astonishing thing was that along with the magnificent epic tradition of the Russian 19th century he used methods of socialist realism and found—you cannot call it a combination, but a unity and also a transition to very, very modern forms of the novel in the West. *The First Circle* is a voluminous, complicated book with many allusions and relationships, including religious ones. I believe that Solzhenitsyn has not yet been recognized as a religious writer. He has not been recognized as taking his departure from the 19th century, then overcoming the weaknesses of socialist realism to become a wholly contemporary writer—I use "contemporary" here for "modern."

KOCH: Solzhenitsyn once wrote that, though he does not know

Heinrich Böll interviewed by Werner Koch. Copyright: West German Radio, Third Program, and *Sonntags Journal,* No. 42, 17-18 (October 1970), 27. Excerpts. Reprinted by permission. Translated from the German by Marjorie L. Hoover.

world literature, above all, Western literature, and knows only Russian literature, he believes that Western literature must be quite ephemeral because Western authors are not engaged in a struggle for existence.

BÖLL: I too have seen it this way and have said something like this in a long book review. I believe this is the problem of the resistance which one feels today not outwardly from police and censorship, but as resistance against our age and the spirit of the age. In the Soviet Union during Solzhenitsyn's lifetime this was Stalinism with its horrors and the resistance against such horror. Solzhenitsyn is, properly speaking, an author concerned with suffering.

KOCH: . . . yes, but concerned with compulsory suffering.

BÖLL: Yes. You're not asked there whether you want to undergo suffering or not; suffering overtakes you as a consequence of your place in history. There is such a thing as a writer's biography being inextricably set in his time. Solzhenitsyn was born in 1918 in the Soviet Union and has lived there 50 years. It was not for him to decide whether he might withdraw from suffering; he had merely to endure it, and this one must accept as a reality. And he probably feels that the West, to put it bluntly, is quite decadent with its literature essentially deprived of problems—human ones—and cares.

KOCH: Though the [Soviet] Writers' Union expelled him, Mr. Böll, it did tell him, as it told Pasternak, that he could leave the Soviet Union at any time. Now assuming that this case should lead to political consequences, I mean the award of the Nobel Prize, do you think (a) that the Writers' Union will keep its word, and (b) that Solzhenitsyn will even consider leaving?

BÖLL: That is very hard to say. I cannot speak for Solzhenitsyn. I can attempt to get close to his point of view and to put that into words. The Soviet Writers' Union probably adopts the attitude of Soviet authorities toward petitions. I do not believe that Solzhenitsyn would voluntarily leave the Soviet Union. I simply cannot imagine that. That sounds very presumptuous, but I do not think so. Pasternak too did not leave; he could have and he would have lived well and so on. This is something we probably cannot understand. I have used for that the word "to be imprisoned," imprisoned in two, three or four meanings. Probably that too is a presumptuous designation, but I have no other word for it. I do not think Solzhenitsyn would leave voluntarily. And if they forced him to, threw him out, so to speak, I would find that terrible both for the Soviet Union and for him personally.

KOCH: To return to the Nobel Prize. Nobel Prizes do not come to one by chance. A committee searches and hears opinions before making its decision. You who are yourself a candidate for the Nobel Prize[1]—were you able to do something for Solzhenitsyn in the matter of this award, and did you do something?

BÖLL: I did do something, empowered by the presiding board of the German PEN Club. As President at that time, I proposed Solzhenitsyn in the name of the German PEN Club. Three or four months ago, I am not sure exactly when, I also wrote as a private citizen to a gentleman I know in Sweden: "There is a proper candidate for you." Whether I accomplished something for him or against him in so doing, I do not know. I can only say if someone asks me: "Did he deserve the Nobel Prize literarily?"—Yes, without reservation. The consequences? I don't know what will happen. I hope the Soviet Union and the Soviet authorities accept him as one of their own, publish him in the Soviet Union despite all his criticisms of the Soviet past and present—I hope they accept him as their own great son descended from their great humanistic tradition.

Translated by Marjorie L. Hoover

[1]Böll received the Nobel Prize in 1973.—Tr.

The Writer as Witness: The Achievement of Aleksandr Solzhenitsyn

BY VICTOR ERLICH

A recent visitor to the Soviet Union, fortunate enough to meet and befriend some nonconformist Russian intellectuals, will almost invariably find in the homes of his hosts three literary icons. These are Anna Akhmatova, Boris Pasternak, and Aleksandr Solzhenitsyn.

Solzhenitsyn is the only surviving member of the trinity and the only representative of prose-fiction in this heterodox literary pantheon. For thousands of literate men and women all over Russia he is the conscience of modern Russian literature, a moral force, a culture hero. More than a mere writer, one may be tempted to say. The phrase, however, would be misleading: Solzhenitsyn's moral authority derives primarily from his being a writer, more exactly from being the kind of writer he chose and dared to be.

An attempt to assess the literary accomplishment of a novelist of such stature and resonance is inevitably a humbling and precarious task. As is so often the case in dealing with recent Soviet literature, literary and moral-political considerations are

"The Writer as Witness: The Achievement of Aleksandr Solzhenitsyn." From *Slavic Forum: Studies in Language and Literature* (Mouton, 1973).

so closely intertwined here as to be virtually inseparable. When, as readers of *One Day in the Life of Ivan Denisovich,* we confront the belated revelation of a long-denied nightmare, no sane person, to paraphrase Irving Howe, can be expected to register a "purely" literary response.[1]

What is called for, I submit, is not literary purism, but respect for the autonomy of literary criteria. Our admiration for the man and our affinity for his stance need not determine our considered judgment of the scope and the texture of the writer's achievement. A moving human testimony couched in fictional terms may or may not be a literary masterpiece. At the same time, we would do well to beware of the opposite danger, that of inhibiting our literary response, of underestimating the heroic writer's actual effectiveness out of an excessive distrust of our own motives, an inordinate fear of being or appearing to be swayed by extra-literary considerations.

Let me mention another difficulty which seems to beset a Western critic of fiction in dealing with Solzhenitsyn. His conceptual apparatus, attuned as it is to the post-modern sophistication of Nabokov and Borges, John Barth and Nathalie Sarraute, is likely to grind to a halt in the face of a novelist so sturdily and expansively old-fashioned, so steeped in the 19th-century realistic tradition, so unself-conscious about the "point of view" as to insert casually into a section of his major novel which reconstructs a protagonist's past largely in his own terms an unabashedly explicit authorial generalization: "He [Rubin, V.E.] was all-in-all a tragic figure."[2]

This uneasiness, this uncertainty of criteria, may account in part for a freakishly wide range of response to Solzhenitsyn in American criticism. In an early reaction,[3] Franklin D. Reeve hailed *One Day in the Life of Ivan Denisovich* as one of the greatest works of 20th-century European literature, more accomplished than Thomas Mann's *Death in Venice* or André Gide's *The Counterfeiters.* Several years later, in discussing Solzhenitsyn's longest and most ambitious novel, *The First Circle,* Robert Garis adjudged him a mediocre if honorable

[1]Irving Howe, "Predicaments of Soviet Writing," I, *The New Republic,* May 11, 1963, p. 19.

[2]*V kruge pervom* (Paris: YMCA Press, 1969), p. 477.

[3]"The House of the Living," *The Kenyon Review,* Spring 1963, pp. 356-360.

writer.[4] Strangely enough, both Reeve and Garis went out of their way to play down the topicality of Solzhenitsyn's work. Mr. Reeve contended that *One Day* was "really" not about a Soviet forced labor camp, but about a man's search for his self. Mr. Garis claimed that Solzhenitsyn's social criticism could have been directed with equal force against "any" society. I am tempted to suggest that this curious convergence between otherwise so disparate assessments points to another pitfall of modern criticism—notably its occasional preference for the fanciful over the "obvious." The latter, in this case, might be couched in an unexciting, but, I believe, correct proposition that, while the import of Solzhenitsyn's fiction clearly transcends its immediate setting, much of his authority and persuasiveness derives from his immersion in Soviet reality, his unerring sense of the characteristically, if not always uniquely, Soviet institutional patterns, of the characteristically, if not always uniquely, Russian modes of repression and protest, of depravity and integrity.

But I am getting ahead of my story. It is high time that we stop worrying about the critics' dilemmas, whether real or imaginary, and confront our subject.

It is symbolic of Solzhenitsyn's place in modern Russian literature that he should have begun his career as a taboo-breaker. In his momentous debut, *One Day in the Life of Ivan Denisovich* (1962), a dread institution whose existence had hitherto been ignored or timidly hinted at by an Ehrenburg, a Dudintsev, or a Viktor Nekrasov, was suddenly catapulted into public view. The grim routine of what a French writer, David Rousset, had called "l'univers concentrationnaire," the unspeakable squalor and misery, the backbreaking labor, the animal scrounging for food, is authenticated here by a wealth of detail and made more credible by the author's quiet, undramatic manner. *One Day* is not a horror story. Physical violence appears in the novel not as a central actuality, but as an everpresent threat. When the shivering, hungry inmates start their forced march, the guards load their rifles: any false step will mean death.

The long, grueling sequence from reveille to "lights-out" chronicled in Solzhenitsyn's unhurried narrative represents an ordinary, in fact, a relatively "lucky" day in the life of the

[4] "Fiction Chronicle," *The Hudson Review,* April 1969, pp. 148-154.

tale's good-natured protagonist who, even in the forced labor camp inferno, takes pride in a job well done. As the story draws to its close, Ivan Denisovich muses thus: "He had had a lot of luck today... they hadn't put him in the cooler. He had finagled an extra bowl of mush at noon... nothing had spoiled the day, and it had been almost happy..."[5]

Though technically, *One Day* is a third-person narrative, the point of view is provided here by a "simple" peasant whose potential for survival is greater than his ratiocinative powers. This device, skillfully and consistently employed, is both a strength and a built-in limitation. The language of *One Day*—an effective blend of the earthy peasant vernacular with the harsh camp jargon which occasionally lapses into profanity—is a far cry from the colorless, timidly puritan prose of "socialist-realist" fiction. It is also testimony to Solzhenitsyn's sturdy sense of style—a quality which, of late, has not been much in evidence in Soviet fiction. Yet the sustained "folksy" stylization which lends solidity and color to the verbal texture of *One Day* constricts the story's scope and import and obviates the need for, indeed eliminates the possibility of, an articulate judgment on the life presented.

Solzhenitsyn's keen ear for the leisurely rhythms of the Russian folk speech stands him in good stead in a story which, to my mind, is his most accomplished work to date, "Matrena's Home" (1963). The narrator, who, not unlike the author, is a former political prisoner and a teacher, decides to "cut loose and get lost in the innermost heart of Russia, if there is any such thing."[6] The phrase seems to suggest a hankering for some traditional Russian ambience. In fact, both the language and the moral tenor of "Matrena's Home" have a strikingly old-fashioned quality. The central figure of the story, a selfless, gentle, pure-of-heart peasant woman, makes one think of the quiet radiance of that chastened village belle, Luker'ia, in Turgenev's "The Living Relics." When Matrena dies, a victim, symbolically, of her neighbor's brutal, unthinking acquisitiveness, the narrator is moved to comment: "We all lived beside her and never understood that she was the righteous one, without

[5] *One Day in the Life of Ivan Denisovich,* trans. by Max Hayward and Ronald Hingley, (New York: Frederick A. Praeger, 1963), pp. 209-210.

[6] "Matrenin dvor," in Solzhenitsyn, *Sobranie sochinenii,* (Frankfurt: Posev, 1970), I, p. 195.

whom no village can stand, nor any city. Nor our homeland."[7]

None of this was likely to please the official critics. Owing to Khrushchev's personal *imprimatur, One Day* enjoyed initially a measure of immunity, but "Matrena's Home" was fair game. The story was promptly attacked for offering a distorted picture of the Soviet village. Did the author fail to realize that such "capitalistic" attitudes as competitiveness and greed had long ago disappeared from the Soviet countryside? Nor was Solzhenitsyn's positive message—clearly at odds with the "struggle-oriented" and stridently public Soviet ethos—any less objectionable.

It is a matter of record that neither of Solzhenitsyn's full-length novels was allowed publication in his native land. The writer whom many Russians regard, in Evtushenko's phrase, as "our only living classic," has been forced underground. Was this due to the deterioration of the Soviet cultural climate since Khrushchev? While the fact itself is undeniable, in all fairness to present-day Russia's dour-faced bosses, there is little reason to assume that either *Cancer Ward* or *The First Circle* would have received a nod from the more ebullient Nikita Khrushchev.

A Western critic, mindful of the larger thrust of Solzhenitsyn's fiction and conditioned to symbol-hunting, may be tempted to construe *Cancer Ward* as a parable for a deadly disease which had eaten its way into the Soviet body politic.[8] This temptation ought to be resisted. *Cancer Ward* is a sturdily realistic novel rather than an allegory. It appears to be a thoroughly reliable and accurate portrayal of a "real" cancer ward in a "real" hospital in Soviet Central Asia. Characteristically, the impression of authenticity owes at least as much to the apparent mastery of the *realia*—the density of relevant medical detail—as it does to the biographical fact of Solzhenitsyn's actually having had a bout with cancer of the stomach. Yet it is hardly necessary to insist that the novel has wider, non-medical implications. The motif of an incurable or seemingly incurable illness serves here as a mode of revealing character and impelling a verdict over the meaning or meaninglessness of a doomed life. The nearly

[7] *Ibid.*, p. 231.

[8] For obvious reasons, the above interpretation was eagerly adopted by some of Solzhenitsyn's Soviet detractors. At a November 17, 1966 meeting of the Artistic Prose Division of the Soviet Writers' Union, one N. Asanov meandered ominously: "Cancerous growth, incurability of cancer... suppose what is meant here is not an individual, but [our] society?" See *Novyi zhurnal* [New York], No. 93 (1968), p. 229.

inescapable parallel with Lev Tolstoy's masterly "Death of Ivan Il'ich" has already been drawn.[9] While the affinity between the two works is undeniable, one of the significant differences is that while in Tolstoy the moment of truth dramatizes the terrible emptiness of an "ordinary" life—Ivan Il'ich is Everyman—in Solzhenitsyn the ultimate confrontation is a *sui generis* projective test designed to elicit a variety of character-and-status determined responses.

Already in this, the less ambitious of his two major novels, Solzhenitsyn demonstrates his remarkable ability to encompass within a confining institutional framework a galaxy of richly differentiated character studies. Here is a successful Stalinist bureaucrat Rusanov, appalled at being thrown together with the "common people" whom he presumably serves, blithely assuming that each morning he ought to be the first to get the newspaper, not only because he is an important person, but because he alone is able to decipher the arcane language of the Party edicts; a smug dignitary whose arrogance is visibly eroded by the inexorable progress of his illness and his mounting dependency on the hospital staff and his fellow patients. Here is a dedicated young geologist, racing against time for the sake of the only thing that matters to him—a scientific breakthrough which he feels he alone is capable of effecting; a tough, unscrupulous operator, deeply stirred by the reading of Lev Tolstoy's parable "What Do Men Live By?" and, characteristically, unable to share his excitement and his belated soul-searching either with the cliche-ridden Party hack or the single-track-minded scientist. A former labor camp inmate Kostoglotov, intransigent and blunt to the point of rudeness, who in a heated exchange with Rusanov, calls him a "racist" for judging people by their social origins rather than by what they are or do. Finally there is a haggard ex-academician whose physical misery is compounded by a crushing sense of guilt over having been silent while the best of his contemporaries were vilified, tortured and annihilated.

In his relentless integrity, his past ordeals and his current difficulties of "readjustment," Oleg Kostoglotov comes closest to being the author's counterpart as well as the hero of the novel. His intimate entanglements—a timid yet urgent romance,

[9]See especially Deming Brown, "*Cancer Ward* and *The First Circle*," *Slavic Review*, Vol. 28. No. 2 (June 1969), pp. 304-313.

poignantly undercut by medical treatment which threatens his sexual potency—are handled with empathy and tact. Yet interestingly enough, it is the guilt-ridden ex-conformist Shulubin who is entrusted with articulating as positive a moral-political vision as any found in the Solzhenitsyn *oeuvre*—a vision of "ethical socialism,"[10] of a "society in which all relationships, principles and laws would be based on morality and on nothing else."[11]

The attribution of what can be assumed to be the author's own social ideals to—if I may paraphrase a current cliche—a member of Stalinist Russia's "silent majority," a man, who unlike Solzhenitsyn or Kostoglotov, had failed the test of courage, is a singularly compassionate, non-vindictive gesture. Moreover, Shulubin's credo suggests an important Solzhenitsyn theme—that of a man's ability to think heterodox thoughts while bowing to outward pressures, an ability which no amount of repression, short of one's actual annihilation, can totally inhibit or destroy. "Tell me," asks Kostoglotov, "did you think of this during those twenty-five years when you were bowing low and renouncing your beliefs?" "Yes, I did," answers Shulubin, "I renounced everything and kept on thinking. I stuffed the books into the stove and I kept thinking. Why not? Haven't I earned the right to a few thoughts my sufferings, through my betrayal?"[12]

The motif of inward freedom which "they" cannot take away from you reappears in a different key in Solzhenitsyn's most broadly conceived work, whose title is drawn from Dante's "Inferno," *The First Circle*. In Solzhenitsyn's fictional universe "hell" is the Soviet forced labor camp system. Its "first circle," its upper stratum, is the technical research institute on the outskirts of Moscow, whose employees—top-flight scientists, engineers, and mechanics—are brought from the lower circles

[10]Characteristically, Shulubin insists on labeling his brand of socialism as ethical or moral [*nravstvennyi*] rather than "Christian" or "democratic." Though the good society that he envisions is to be built on love rather than on hate, the slogan of "Christian Socialism" strikes him as too pat and "too far removed from reality." By the same token, the phrase "democratic socialism" is discarded as overly procedural and essentially negative. The word "democratic," maintains Shulubin, "does not describe the nature of socialism, but its form, a kind of institutional set-up. But this is just a declaration . . . that heads won't roll, but nothing is said about what this socialism will be built on." *Rakovyi korpus* (Paris: YMCA Press, 1968), p. 370.

[11]*Rakovyi korpus,* p. 371.

[12]*Rakovyi korpus,* p. 372.

of the inferno in order to work feverishly on high-priority security assignments. The "project" which provides the core of the bulky narrative is a concerted effort to evolve a technique whereby a minute acoustic analysis of a tapped telephone conversation could yield the speaker's identity. The "privileged" victims of a totalitarian regime are compelled thus to strain their intelligence and skills in order to entrap others into the fatal net. The tragic irony of the situation is compounded by the fact that some of the more dedicated researchers-inmates are propelled not merely by a fear of returning to the pit, but also by a misplaced intellectual zest and residual Party loyalty.

The central plot of this wide-ranging novel, encased in three frenzied and fateful days, is that of a chilling technological suspense story. On December 24, 1949, Innokentii Volodin, an up-and-coming young Soviet diplomat, makes a call from a public booth: he is trying to warn an eminent Soviet physician whom he has known since childhood against sharing a medical discovery with his French colleagues and thus walking into a trap laid for him. The conversation is intercepted. Two days later, an enthusiastic philologist turned acoustician in the elite prison-institute breathlessly announces a breakthrough on the voice-identification "front." In a matter of hours, Volodin lands in the dread Moscow Lubianka jail: a dignitary is reduced to an un-person. . .

It is a tribute to Solzhenitsyn's novelistic skill that working out of so narrow a base, he manages, by making full use of the inmates' links with the outside world, to bring into the compass of his narrative various strata of Soviet society—security officials, diplomats, writers, students. The cumulative effect is as panoramic a vision of Stalinist Russia as any found in recent Soviet literature.

The picture of the Soviet system which emerges from Solzhenitsyn's narrative is as credible as it is terrifying.[13] It is a bureaucratic spiral of fear: everybody, from the boss of the secret police through the head of the "research institute" and its divisional directors down to the prison guard, is terrorized, for everybody's career and life are literally "on the line." A blunder, a failure to meet a typically unrealistic deadline, can easily prove irreversible.

[13]In a lecture delivered at Yale, Hannah Arendt maintained that *The First Circle* ought to be required reading for students of totalitarianism.

This pyramid of terror is capped by the Leader, a devious, vindictive, pathologically suspicious and grubbily lonely tyrant. The Stalin sequence in *The First Circle* has come in for vigorous criticism. It has been found jarring, if not self-indulgent, a lapse into pamphleteering, an obtrusion of loaded speculation upon a well-authenticated testimony. These strictures have some validity. Solzhenitsyn's Stalin—though, to my mind, credible enough—lacks the authority and the depth of his best characterizations. Occasional intrusion of heavy sarcasm, of *de facto* editorializing, into a reconstruction of Stalin's nighttime thoughts, represents a discernible shift in tone and style. (The importance of this "lapse" can be easily overestimated. A vaster and more resonant work than *One Day, The First Circle* fails to achieve, or for that matter, to aim at, the degree of stylistic unity which characterized Solzhenitsyn's compact debut.) Yet the implication that the Stalin chapters are a foreign body in Solzhenitsyn's fictional universe, strikes me as totally false. Whatever their shortcomings, they represent an organic, perhaps an indispensable, element of the novel's structure not only because the picture of the system would not have been complete without its pivot, but, and more importantly, because Solzhenitsyn's conception of Stalin is an essential aspect of the moral dialectics which informs *The First Circle.*

Though the theme of incarceration dominates the world of Solzhenitsyn, the rather platitudinous, if not altogether erroneous, notion of Stalin's Russia as one big prison is *not* the central, let alone the distinctive, insight here. What confronts us is a seeming moral paradox: only in prison can one be really free. Only those who like Nerzhin, Bobynin, Khorobrov, have nothing to lose since they have already lost everything—influence, power, material possessions, often their loved ones—can maintain their basic humanity, their personal dignity, their ability to act upon the dictates of their consciences.[14] But if only the powerless can be brave, it stands to reason that the Omnipotent Leader should be the most fearful of them all. Thus, rather than being a gratuitous discharge of the author's pent-up rage, the image

[14]Bobynin states the matter forcefully in the course of a confrontation with the sinister Man of Power, the head of the MGB, Abakumov: "I have nothing, you understand, nothing! You can't get my wife or child—a bomb got them first. My parents are already dead. All I own is my handkerchief . . . you took my freedom away long ago. What else can you threaten me with? What else can you deprive me of?. . ." See *V kruge pervom,* p. 183.

of Stalin's free-floating paranoia completes the moral equation which is central to the novel. It eminently belongs in the picture.

Though not a flawless work, *The First Circle* is a compelling literary performance. To have launched a multi-level and many-voiced novel through the medium of a fateful phone call, and, having plausibly and dramatically intertwined so many individual destinies, to have brought the narrative back to its starting point in the powerful scene of Volodin's arrest, one of the most memorable passages in modern Russian literature, is eloquent testimony to Solzhenitsyn's compositional resources and narrative gifts. By the same token, it is a tribute to Solzhenitsyn's powers of characterization that both the novel's chief protagonist, Gleb Nerzhin, and his loving adversary, Lev Rubin, should be so thoroughly convincing, so richly credible.

Solzhenitsyn succeeds where many creditable novelists have failed. In Nerzhin he has created a "positive hero" who dispenses with false heroics, an author's *alter ego* who is not an ideological vehicle but a fully realized human being. A humanist who, in his journey through hell, has jettisoned his illusions but not his values, a thinking man who sets more store by experience than by ideology, an intellectual who is free of intellectual pride,[15] a mathematician who, in a quixotic gesture, foregoes the rewards of the relative security of a strenuous cryptographic project in order to keep himself available to reflection, to "learning about life" on one of the lowest rungs of the labor camp inferno, Nerzhin is one of the few truly satisfying portrayals of an honorable man in modern literature.

If Nerzhin is a triumph of objectified introspection, Lev Rubin is a feat of empathy for the "Other." A life-loving doctrinaire, a brilliant and erudite scholar who, after all his ordeals, persists in speaking about Stalin in terms of uncritical

[15]Therein lies a significant difference between Nerzhin and another appealing protagonist of *The First Circle,* Sologdin. A brilliant and proud man, a relentless challenger of orthodox pieties which Rubin seeks to uphold, Sologdin is the most articulate non-conformist in *The First Circle.* In one of his confrontations with Rubin he clearly speaks for the author as he exclaims: "The higher the ends the higher must be the means!... Morality shouldn't lose force as it increases its scope!" (p. 469). And yet it is at least arguable that in the end Sologdin's intellectual pride subverts his intransigence. Since his superiors desperately need Sologdin's problem-solving talents, he turns the tables on them! Instead of grovelling and begging for favors the powerless prisoner confronts the powers-that-be with an ultimatum. He wins, but only at the cost of agreeing to play the game which the less flamboyant Nerzhin firmly refuses to do.

adulation, an honest and warm-hearted man betrayed by a mixture of intellectual exuberance and misguided patriotism into tightening a noose on the neck of an unsuspecting victim, Lev Rubin as a fictional creation bears witness to Solzhenitsyn's compassion and to his keen awareness of the tragic complexity of human motives.

As one surveys Solzhenitsyn's fictional universe, from Ivan Denisovich's struggle for "an extra bowl of mush" down to Nerzhin's brief and tense prison meeting with his wife, the overarching impression, the salient quality is that of relentless veracity. No other living Russian writer has earned as fully as did Solzhenitsyn the right to echo the young Tolstoy's famous credo and battlecry: "The real hero of my tale, whom I love with all the force of my soul. . . is Truth."[16]

Yet, one might interpose, is not the parallel with one of the world's literary giants precisely the kind of extravagant overestimate against which I was cautioning in my opening remarks? Not necessarily. It is a legitimate tribute to the moral force and the literary solidity of Solzhenitsyn's *oeuvre* that the parallel should suggest itself so readily. By the same token, it is no reflection on the import and the genuineness of his attainment to urge that the analogy be not pressed too far. (How many distinguished novelists could stand this comparison without being diminished by it?) A standard reaction to a Solzhenitsyn character or incident is "yes, that's the way it must have been," "yes, that's the way people—or this particular kind of person—act under stress." Yet when Tolstoy describes Levin's and Kitty's honeymoon, the "truth" about personal relations acquires the force of a moral jolt, of an unsettling epiphany. To put it differently, it is obvious, at least to me, that Solzhenitsyn is a *major* writer. Yet if "greatness" in literature spells transcendent moral illumination and/or an esthetic breakthrough, this quality may have to be denied to Solzhenitsyn as it would have to be denied, I believe, to any other living novelist.

A final distinction: in Solzhenitsyn, like in Tolstoy, "truth" is both an avowed ideal and a polemical strategy, a challenge to the *idées reçues*. Yet their lines of attack are different. An iconoclast of genius, Tolstoy had set out to dislodge the extant

[16] "Sevastopol' v mae," L. Tolstoi, *Sobranie sochinenii* (Moscow, 1958), Vol. 2, p. 158.

fictional modes of seeing and portraying reality. His leitmotif, to quote the brilliant Formalist critic Boris Eikhenbaum,[17] was "it is not what you think [*ne to*]." War is not what you think ("The Sebastopol Stories," *War and Peace*). Love is not what you think (*Family Happiness*). History is not what you think (*War and Peace*).

Solzhenitsyn's immediate targets are not literary conventions grown stale, but externally imposed and enforced taboos and cliches. The task that fell to him, at the peak of the post-Stalin literary thaw, was no less significant for being more "elementary." In a situation where, to paraphrase his own words, "many an author who saw and touched the truth... lied with cold glassy eyes,"[18] calling a spade a spade, naming the unnameable, was a liberating act. To establish a reliable connection between words and things, between language and the facts of experience, is to recreate the essential conditions of a genuine literary enterprise, to restore to Russian literature mired in ready-made formulae, in melodramatic stereotypes, its proper role, its natural function, that of search, exploration, and above all, testimony.

Let me cite in closing a poignant passage from *Cancer Ward,* a conversation between Kostoglotov and another former labor camp inmate, a cultivated, middle-aged woman reduced to the status of a hospital orderly. She speaks with bitterness about her daughter's shedding tears over *Anna Karenina.* To Elizaveta Anatol'evna Anna's fate is almost enviable: she made her choice and paid the price. "How about us?" she asks in an anguished whisper. "How about millions whose lives were destroyed or maimed by police arbitrariness? Where can I read about us? In a hundred years?"[19]

Thanks to Solzhenitsyn, she did not have to wait that long. In his fiction, the speechless have found a voice; the dispossessed a home. To have borne witness to the truth in the teeth of mounting persecution is an act of moral courage unsurpassed in this or any other era. To have done so on a scale and in a manner commensurate with the magnitude of the subject, is one of the major literary achievements of our time.

[17]*Molodoi Tolstoi* (Petrograd-Berlin, 1922).
[18]*V kruge pervom,* p. 198.
[19]*Rakovyi korpus,* p. 402.

On Solzhenitsyn

BY ALEXANDER SCHMEMANN

> . . . the whole meaning of existence—his own and of everyone in the world—came to his mind. The image he saw did not seem to be embodied in the work or activity which occupied them, which they believed was central in their lives, and by which they were known to others. The meaning of existence was to preserve unspoiled, undisturbed, and undistorted the image of eternity with which each person is born. . .
>
> *Cancer Ward,* Chapter 30

I

That Solzhenitsyn represents a phenomenon of major importance is, I think, no longer disputable. For this very reason it is all the more imperative to ask what is, in fact, the nature of this importance. More than once during the past decades the world has been excited and agitated by events which could not be patly fitted into the conventional pattern of Soviet reality. Certainly everyone will recall the arguments, the emotions, and the hopes evoked in the fifties by Dudintsev's *Not by Bread Alone,* the subsequent shock of *Doctor Zhivago,* the emotional wave generated by the poetry of Evtushenko and Voznesenskii, and more recently still—the trial of Siniavskii and Daniel'. Is Solzhenitsyn—beginning with *One Day in the Life of Ivan Denisovich*—a phenomenon of the same order? One

First published in Russian in *Vestnik RSKhD* (Paris), No. 98 (1970), 72-87. Authorized translation by Serge Schmemann.

more brave voice breaking through the deafening silence of Soviet conformism? To identify him as such, however, would not yet determine his place in and significance for Russian literature, nor, for that matter, would it acknowledge that he is a phenomenon of any literary significance at all. One would hardly include Chernyshevskii's *What Is To Be Done?*, for example, in the "golden fund" of Russian literature, even though no one would deny that the work played a tremendous part in Russian social history.

That Solzhenitsyn is a hero, a martyr, and a victim, that his works are "documents" of staggering importance—all this is indisputable and accepted by everyone, including the Swedish Academy. But the question remains: what is his place and significance in Russian literature? Do we experience trepidation, joy and elation when we read Solzhenitsyn because his themes are so agonizing for us? Or is it because something very significant, very profound has occurred in Russian literature when he appeared?

These questions are important not only from a purely literary point of view; indeed, the very fate of Russia has been, in an ultimate and profound sense, inseparable from the fate of Russian literature. If this is partly true for all nations, it is entirely true for Russia. Russian culture either failed or was unable to amass a "golden store" of anything other than her literature; all that was best and eternal in her she expressed and embodied in her saints and in her writers.

Saints, however, cannot be contained by a "cultural" frame of reference. If, in the expression of St. Paul, there are "celestial bodies and terrestrial bodies" (I Cor. 15:40), then Russian saints are the creators of the "celestial body" of Russia in which all that which is *merely* culture, and therefore mortal, is consumed and transfigured; the "perishable" is "sown" and is only called to be raised in imperishability (I Cor. 15:42). Russia's writers and her great literature, however, are the creators of the "terrestrial body" of Russia—that image, calling, and content by which, despite all her "terrible sins" (Khomiakov), Russia is absolved and made worthy of pure love and loyalty. What occurs in Russian literature occurs not only *in* Russia but *with* Russia. That is why it is so important to determine the literary significance of Solzhenitsyn, not only in relation to the "Soviet scene," but in relation to Russian literature as a whole.

II

I am certain that the primary significance of Solzhenitsyn lies beyond the fact that he is a courageous voice of protest and of searching: he is, above all, an infinitely important and genuinely fateful event in Russian literature. With his appearance something *new* happened to Russian literature, a new literary era began, even if he should remain an isolated case. No one else, not even Pasternak with his *Doctor Zhivago*—despite all his significance—could compare in this respect. Why? This is the first question, the answer to which will determine all subsequent evaluations of Solzhenitsyn.

I mentioned Pasternak. He alone can be placed alongside Solzhenitsyn if the criterion is the "repercussions" they evoked. But the creativity of Pasternak, including *Doctor Zhivago, culminated* rather than initiated a defined period of Russian literary history. Spiritually, psychologically and literarily, Pasternak belonged in the already waning, twilight atmosphere of the "Silver Age." The terrible experience of the Soviet years, of course, deepened his consciousness, placed new themes before him and compelled him to look into areas he had not known when he poured forth the "shower of light" of his early poetry. But even these new themes he posited and developed in the spiritual perspective of the Silver Age. *Doctor Zhivago* is still an echo—after the tragic events of the twenties and thirties—of Blok's "The Twelve." It is an attempt to respond to the tortured, seductive affirmation which overwhelmed Blok himself in the last line of his famous poem: ". . .at the fore is Jesus Christ."

Akhmatova, too, concluded and crowned the Silver Age. Perhaps she even purified it from within and atoned for all that which was partially frivolous and irresponsible and made the age precisely "silver," and not "golden"; all that was burned and purged, redeemed and forgiven in "A Poem Without a Hero" and *Requiem.* Such a conclusion was essential and in itself highly significant, and only those who themselves breathed the air of those years could have given it to us. But the conclusion, the epilogue, even if it is included in the subsequent chapter of literary history by virtue of the continuity of culture, cannot itself become a new chapter or even a new "beginning."

Such a "beginning" may have glimmered among the writers who worked in that period of time which ended with the final enthronement of Stalin and the official imposition of "socialist realism." Something, it seemed sure, was beginning or could have begun then, but it was abruptly crushed not only by force, not only by murder and suicide, but also by the spiritual ambiguity so apparent in the literature of those years. The ambiguity consisted of the fact that literature had continued to live in some measure by the romance of the revolution which had earlier seduced both Blok and Esenin, and had destroyed both. Chaos and blood was still seen by many as that "primeval chaos" from which, they believed, something would be born, would grow and would blossom.

This same ambiguity was in "The Twelve," except that Blok himself was the one who first understood, by virtue of his integrity, that the music of the revolution—which he himself had called men to hear—really did not exist, and that everything he had sought to proclaim as the prophetic dawn of a new age was really only narrow fanaticism, and nothing more. But those who despite everything continued for two more decades to listen for that "music" could not help but reach a dead end, even had that end not been the torture chambers of Stalin or his decree to sing the glories of Five-Year Plans, tractors, and the *Dneprostroi.* This false "beginning" could not have been the way for continuing the tradition of genuine Russian literature. In its place there came the conventionalized and orthodox "Soviet" literature.

III

Only in the light of what has been said does it seem possible to understand why the creativity of Solzhenitsyn is really a new phenomenon, changing at its very source the spirit of Russian literature.

First of all, Solzhenitsyn does not belong, either spiritually or biographically, among the representatives or imitators of the Silver Age. He is neither a grandson of Vladimir Solov'ev, a son of Blok nor a brother to Pasternak. Furthermore, the Revolution, as an abrupt break in the fate of man and nation, was outside his personal experience. Finally, he is not an "internal émigré" in the sense that the older generation of writers became despite everything; they had known pre-revolutionary Russia and could not help becoming spiritual "exiles" in Soviet Russia.

By flesh and blood Solzhenitsyn *belongs* to that Russia which now alone exists—not pre-revolutionary or revolutionary Russia, but precisely Soviet Russia. And the uniqueness of Solzhenitsyn the writer is that while he belongs completely to that Soviet reality, he is just as fully and completely *free* of it.

Solzhenitsyn's "freedom" demands explanation. The older generation of writers—Akhmatova, Mandel'shtam, and Pasternak—always remained free "within," however enslaved from without. The enslavement of culture occurred at a time when their experience of freedom had made a full personal enslavement impossible. At the same time, many Soviet men passed through the experience M. M. Koriakov called the "liberation of the soul" in the course of the long Soviet half-century. But this liberation was usually an escape from Soviet reality, either physical or spiritual and entire categories could be made of these escapes: emigration to the West, escape into ancient Russian art, into history, into the past or into the future. . . .

Solzhenitsyn's freedom—or rather his uniqueness—is that none of these categories of escape is applicable to him. He did not "depart" anywhere, he demanded no "compensation" from foreign cultures, he romanticized neither the past nor the future, he did not seek to breathe any other air. The Soviet world is so organically and wholly his world, his reality, that it is possible to say he is free not *from* Soviet reality, but *within* Soviet reality. And this creates a very special relationship between him and that world. On a creative level, it makes him uniquely capable of *revealing* that world from within, of creatively *explaining* it, and finally of *overcoming* it.

All this is so because the "liberation" of Solzhenitsyn occurred not on a personal, intimate plane, but on what cannot be termed other than a "national" plane—through the triune experience of *war, imprisonment* and *return to life.*

Solzhenitsyn's generation was too young to be scarred by the Revolution or even by the nightmare of the Stalinist 'thirties. Its first crisis, its first moral awakening was World War II, which gave it the experience of suffering, fervor, friendship and patriotism, and allowed a free "reflection" on the theretofore habitual, almost organic fear before the ubiquitous regime. The war made this generation look anew on its former life and to want change. This was the first "liberation."

After the war came the second trial, the terrible betrayal by the regime which decided to enslave again those freed by war, and threw into prison all those who had survived the trenches and the German camps. And finally came the third trial, the return from prisons and from labor camps to life, to the world which had ceased to belong to them: "In the summer of 1953 I was returning from a hot, dusty desert," writes Solzhenitsyn in the beginning of "Matrena's Home," "simply back to Russia. There was nobody waiting for me, no one to welcome me, because I'd been delayed on the way home . . . by some ten years. . . ."

The storm of the war, that ten-year "delay," the return to a life from which they had become estranged, the painfully clear awareness of truth, the conscience forged in suffering on which they could weigh everything anew, freely; all this, again, was the experience of an entire generation. But Solzhenitsyn the writer expressed and embodied it with remarkable depth, recreating it from within and illumining it with the light of that moral truth, without which there can be talented writers, but no great writer and no major literature.

IV

All this makes Solzhenitsyn the first *national* writer of the Soviet period of Russian literature, and in this lies his fundamental newness. By "national" I do not mean to imply some specific interrelation between the writer and "national" themes, but rather the acceptance of that spiritual responsibility for his people, his age and his world, that a great writer accepts freely, as something natural and self-evident. This responsibility does not mean the writer is somehow shackled to "current events"; it is not what Sartre christened with that specious and essentially meaningless term "littérature engagée." On the contrary, only inasmuch as he is spiritually free of "current events" and true to that "image of eternity" which, as Solzhenitsyn himself said, is implanted in every man, can the writer discharge his responsibility properly, for the responsibility is precisely an inner referral of art to some higher judgment, to something which surpasses all "issues," to that "image of eternity" which alone can put all things in their proper place "in time" and therefore alone can reveal the truth about them.

Before Solzhenitsyn there was no national writer in this sense in Soviet literature. There were some who in the name of their individual creativity and spiritual survival declined this responsibility and *escaped* into another "world" of their choice. There were also those who betrayed the responsibility by accomodation, silence, or lies. Solzhenitsyn went nowhere, and by a conscious, irreversible, spiritual and creative choice accepted his entire responsibility. With his gifts he obviously could have become a major *Soviet* writer, but he became instead, I am sure, a *great* Russian writer. He became one precisely because he accepted the "Soviet" as the inalienable fate of his art, as the chalice which he could not leave unemptied, as that experience which art is obliged to embody, reveal and illumine with the light of truth.

Let this appear in paradox: Solzhenitsyn actually fulfills in his works the "order" that the regime hypocritically and falsely gave to art; but he carries it out neither hypocritically nor falsely. He does not oppose that order with some other theory of art, he does not shout about the artist's freedom to write about whatever he pleases, he does not defend "art for art's sake," he does not debate the writer's obligation to become "involved in his age" and in the life of his people, and so on. Rather, it is as if he accepts all the "orders" completely and seriously, but precisely by this seriousness and freedom reveals their lies and their triteness. Precisely because he is *part* of Soviet literature and not outside it, he can bring it out into the open air through his creativity, and the "Soviet" period ends. His truth exposes the lie of Soviet literature, but because he is totally a part of it, he converts the "Soviet" into Russian. Having brought forth a national writer, Soviet literature ends, but it also acquires in itself the principle for its rebirth as Russian literature.

V

All this brings us back to the question with which we began these musings, the question of the literary merit of Solzhenitsyn's art. One refined connoisseur of Russian literature wrote me recently that Solzhenitsyn is a "major event, but a bad writer. . . ." What does this mean? Conceding my lack of competence as a literary scholar, I will still make bold to assert that there exist no absolute scientific criteria for the categorization of writers as "good" and "bad." After all, it is still being said of Dostoevsky that though he is a "brilliant thinker," he is a "bad writer." On the Olympian heights of literary expertise, in the small circles where a constant muted rumble betrays mighty passions, is it not true that one occasionally hears affirmations of the sort that "Bunin and Nabokov write better than Tolstoy," or that X or Y is "better than Blok"? And the critic *par excellence,* Sainte-Beuve, failed to "recognize" Baudelaire, while André Gide failed to recognize Marcel Proust. In short, the ordinary reader may perhaps be forgiven for not taking too seriously the contradictory verdicts of specialists.

It could be argued that a "good writer" is one whose art has been integrated by some mysterious "reception" into the "golden fund" of a given literature, where it remains forever as an inalienable part. The critic, specialist and literary historian indisputably can and must assist in this reception, but equally indisputably, they are not gifted with infallibility. Therefore my assertion, as neither a critic nor a specialist, that Solzhenitsyn is not only "good" but a major writer, is, of necessity, subjective. Who is right, the specialist who wrote me or I, only the future can show. I cannot prove I am right. All I can do is to present in defense of my assertion a few suggestions and observations, however incomplete and fragmented.

First of all, *language.* Solzhenitsyn's language is "Soviet," which is most probably one of the reasons he is not appreciated as a writer by certain purists. But for me, the miracle of Solzhenitsyn is that this Soviet language, which more than anything else had expressed and embodied the fall not only of literature, but of Russia herself, which was corrupted and corroded by the unctious Soviet deceit, intrusiveness, and lies, and the alteration and subversion of all meanings; that this language became in Solzhenitsyn for the first time so clearly and so completely the language of *truth.* If we were to use a religious image, we could say that Solzhenitsyn *exorcised* the language, driving out of it the "seven evil spirits." He did this not as a sort of conscious linguistic experiment, but by virtue of that same inner responsibility of which we spoke before.

Solzhenitsyn's criterion of language is Tolstoyan—the criterion of truth, not "literature." He is not enticed or tempted, like many of his contemporaries, to take junkets into archaisms or linguistic innovation. Alien to him is that obsession with language and its "problems" which is so characteristic of our time and in which, I deeply believe, it is far more accurate to see signs not of health, but symptoms of a profound illness in art. If the language of Solzhenitsyn is "worse" than the language of Bunin or Nabokov, it is because such is the living language of Russia—but then in the final analysis this comparison is meaningless, because Solzhenitsyn could not have created in any other language. Russian literature cannot artificially return to the glorious language which died with Bunin without severing its organic tie to Russia and her language, and it is as fruitless to mourn this as it is to join Remizov in mourning the loss to Russian literature of the language of the archpriest Avvakum after Peter the Great. Solzhenitsyn *transformed* the "Soviet" language into his own, into the language of his art and his creative truth. This is his linguistic achievement, and I am sure "specialists" will carefully study it in the future, because, in the final analysis, it is precisely this achievement that makes possible the continued life of Russian literature, and returns to her the tools that had seemed hopelessly rusted.

Solzhenitsyn's *world.* It is hardly necessary to repeat here the familiar truism that the mark of a good writer is his ability to create his *own* world; a living and real world, "convincing" not because it resembles the world we perceive—it may or may not resemble it—but because of its inner truth and vitality; because even though it was created and imagined by the author, it lives its *own* life, independent ultimately even of the author himself. It is precisely the fulness of its *own* life that sets major literature apart from a "document" or from "mere literature," however brilliant, ingenious, or profound these may be. There are writers—Nabokov, for example—who despite an almost limitless, near-miraculous literary gift are still incapable of creating such a world. In his most recent work, *Ada,* Nabokov, to escape the boredom and restraints that he finds so oppressive in this world, leads us at last to another world, one apparently wholly imaginary: an "anti-terra." And yet no new "non-Nabokovian" world arises which is free of his limitless creative dictatorship. As everywhere and always in his art, behind every line, behind every movement stands Nabokov, his brilliant mind, his acute insight and his ironical smile. Never, not for one second does he set his heroes free; he knows three hundred pages in advance precisely what is to happen to them; their exact possibilities and limitations are transparent to his all-knowing, all-understanding, and almighty mind. A Nabokovian Adam could not even long for a forbidden fruit. Everything is foreseen, guessed, prepared, and orchestrated to the end; everything is noted, noticed, seen, named and presented as never before—but nothing is created, nothing is living or eternal, like the worlds created by Tolstoy, Dostoevsky, and—I am not afraid to add—Solzhenitsyn.

Slipping into Iakonov's office behind the prisoner Gerasimovich, we do not know until the last second—as, probably, Solzhenitsyn himself did not know—whether Gerasimovich would find in himself the strength to reject with that "resounding squeak" the offer of freedom, of his wife, of life. Nor do we know, following the arrested Volodin into prison, whether the "liberation of the soul" that has begun within him will be completed. We do not know, because the works of Solzhenitsyn, however "historical," "autobiographical" or even "ideological," are the result, above all, of a mysterious *transformation* of these elements into a spiritual reality; a transformation which is, ultimately, the essence of art. What makes a writer a creator, or where his imagination and his world spring from, can long be argued (V.V. Weidlé speaks to this in his *The Dilemma of the Arts*). But it can scarcely be denied that there *is* a Solzhenitsyn *world* (and not merely a gripping "documentary"), just as there is a Tolstoyan world and a Dostoevskian world.

I would not say that everything in Solzhenitsyn's world is "embodied" in equal measure or with equal clarity. Future critics will doubtlessly show that he was an uneven writer, sometimes soaring and sometimes drifting, but I do not think they will be able to deny the reality of his world. And if Russia—as something whole, as an experience and a continuity, as an object of philosophic speculation and not merely of academic study—exists above all in her literary "incarnations," then to the Russias of Pushkin, of Gogol', of Tolstoy and of Chekhov, we must now add the Russia of Solzhenitsyn.

Solzhenitsyn's *heroes*. I will limit myself here to an assertion based on one bold comparison: Tolstoy's Napoleon and Solzhenitsyn's Stalin. The Napoleon of *War and Peace,* for all the minute, painstaking detail of his image, remains a caricature drawn by Tolstoy to illustrate his rather incomprehensible and unconvincing "philosophy of history." The "philosophy" needed an example, a proof, and Tolstoy accordingly drew an image of Napoleon with the traits the theory required. When reading passages on Napoleon (or on the Liturgy in *Resurrection* or on the theater), one is always sorry that Tolstoy wrote them, for they are in such tortured dissonance with Tolstoy's own profound criterion of "truth"—not "realistic" or "descriptive," but inner and spiritual truth.

Solzhenitsyn's Stalin, on the other hand, is not a caricature. He may not be the whole Stalin—certainly the whole truth about him is not made known here—yet he is *true* and we owe this truth to more than Solzhenitsyn's integrity; we owe it to his "creative conscience." Yes, everything is "invented," but nothing is artificially concocted or added on.

Tolstoy's Napoleon is entirely "appearances"—a projection totally of Tolstoy's *idea* of Napoleon—and because of this, despite the abundance of detail (the fleshy back, the heavy thighs), he does not come to life as does the lowliest "invented" soldier on that same terrible Borodino plain. Solzhenitsyn's Stalin is drawn entirely from within. Yes, he *is* "invented"—as are the night, the cell, the lethargy, the conversation with Abakumov, the writing, the anguish, the fear and hatred. But they are invented with creative conscience, for which I cannot find a better term. This creative conscience is the force which transforms invention into life, into the life *we* live during those several unforgettable hours in Stalin's cell, where we not only learn something *about* Stalin ("documentation"), but mysteriously come to know Stalin himself (art). The same is true for Solzhenitsyn's other heroes, both "positive" and "negative." And perhaps the main point is that these familiar categories do not apply to Solzhenitsyn's heroes; that this writer, who more than any writer in the history of literature has the right to a "settling of moral accounts," to the separation of everything into "positive" and "negative," "black" and "white" categories, precisely does not use this right, but rather creates and crafts his own world on totally different principles. This brings me to the concluding, and for me the most important part of these fragmentary thoughts about Solzhenitsyn.

VI

I would not have dared to write about Solzhenitsyn at all, not being a literary critic, had I not been so astonished by what I can only call the Christian inspiration of his writing. For me the most important, the most joyful news in the "miracle" of Solzhenitsyn was that the first national writer of the Soviet period of Russian literature was at the same time a Christian writer. I would like to conclude with a few words on this, even though it is very complex.

Let me emphasize at the outset that when I say "Christian writer" I do not have in mind whether Solzhenitsyn is a "believer" or a "non-believer"—whether he accepts or rejects Christian dogma, ecclesiastical ritual, or the Church herself—nor do I mean specific "religious problematics," which I do not consider central to Solzhenitsyn. I humbly assert that the official declaration by an author that he is a "believer" or a "non-believer" cannot be considered a trustworthy test to qualify his work as essentially Christian or non-Christian. There have been writers who proclaimed themselves believers and even wrote profusely about religion and "religious problems," who nonetheless could not and should not be considered Christian writers. And there have been writers who proclaimed themselves non-believers, though their entire artistic output could and should have been recognized as Christian. Thus the late G.P. Fedotov called Pushkin's *The Captain's Daughter* "the most Christian work in Russian literature," which is especially noteworthy because the "God-seeking" of so many Russian writers, the long "infatuation with God" in our literature began not with Pushkin, but after him. To Rozanov and to others, Pushkin appeared rather insipid from this point of view, insufficiently "religiously problematic." I am convinced, however, that Fedotov was quite right, and that Russian literature was Christian to the extent that it remained essentially faithful to Pushkin; that far from everything in its celebrated "infatuation with God," especially during the Silver Age, was of Christian origin or inspiration. But what do I mean when I speak of Solzhenitsyn or of his art as Christian?

When I speak of a "Christian writer" and of Solzhenitsyn in particular, I have in mind a deep and all-embracing, although possibly unconscious perception of the world, man, and life, which, historically, was born and grew from Biblical and Christian revelation, and only from it. Human culture as a whole may have had other sources, but only Christianity, only the revelation of the Old and New Testaments contains that perception of the world which, incorporated into human culture, revealed in it the potential, and indeed the reality of a Christian culture. I shall call this perception, for lack of a better term, the *triune intuition of creation, fall, and redemption.* I am convinced that it is precisely this intuition that lies at the bottom of Solzhenitsyn's art, and that renders his art Christian. I will try to briefly explain my thought.

The intuition of *creation.* The Christian vision is rooted in a perception and acceptance of the original goodness of the world and life; of their fulness with that joyful and positive sanction of His creation by God which resounds in the very first chapter of the Bible: "And God saw everything that he had made, and behold *it was very good*" (Gen. 1:31). Therefore to view the world as meaningless and absurd, to adopt an ontological pessimism, to reject life and to surrender to Manichean dualism in any of its shades, inevitably places one outside of Christianity. No matter how real the ugliness, suffering and evil in the world, no matter how fallen it is—and Christianity firmly maintains that it "lies in evil"—fundamentally, originally the world is light and not dark, meaningful and not meaningless, good and not bad. This "cosmic" source of the Christian perception may be obscured or distorted, but as long as it exists as even a remote "point of reference" in art, that art remains Christian.

Solzhenitsyn's writings are almost entirely about ugliness, suffering and evil. His world truly "lies in evil;" not in an abstract, metaphysical sense, but in a very real one: the nightmare reality of the labor camp, the Mavrino sharashka, and the cancer ward. Yet nowhere, never, not once (and let the reader check my assertion) do we find or even sense in all his works that ontological *blasphemy* about the world, man, and life, the poisonous whisper of which can be heard so clearly in so much of "contemporary art." I could cite examples of this, but specific instances, of course, are not proof. The proof, rather, is in the overall tonality of the art, in its inner "music," which eludes formal analysis alone. And in Solzhenitsyn this music, though seemingly spun so entirely from the cries of suffering, mystically admits and reveals that very *praise* which constitutes the ultimate depth of the Biblical vision of the world. For through all the writing of Solzhenitsyn there shines that "morning of creation" into which Kostoglotov steps, and about which he rejoices upon quitting the cancer ward:

> This was the morning of Creation! The world was being created anew for this alone, to be given back to Oleg: Go! Live!. . .
>
> And radiating happiness in his face, smiling at no one, just at the sky and the trees, filled with that early-springtime, early-morning joy that floods the old and the sick, Oleg walked along familiar lanes. . .

> Who could act rationally on the first morning of Creation? Discarding all his plans, Oleg conceived a zany idea, to go immediately to the Old City to see the apricot tree in bloom in the early morning. . . .

The intuition of *fall.* While it is obvious that evil and suffering are central in Solzhenitsyn's writing, it is essential to note that they stem from the Christian intuition and experience of the "mystery of evil." Nowhere, indeed, does Christianity differ as markedly from non-Christian religions, philosophies, or ideologies, as in its intuition of evil. All other religions and philosophies are directed essentially toward *explaining* and thereby *neutralizing* evil, since explaining it renders it somehow legitimate and, consequently, justified; a *phenomenon bene fundatum.* Christianity alone, notwithstanding the assertions of self-confident scholastics throughout all the ages, does not explain away evil; yet Christianity alone reveals it. This, indeed, is the whole point, that for Christianity evil is not a kind of independently formed "essence," not "evil in itself," as it appears to those, some of them Christians, who expose "dark forces." But evil is at the same time not merely a negation, an absence of good, as affirmed by rationalists of all kinds in their utopian optimism.

For Christianity, evil is first and always a *fall.* Only that which is raised on high can fall, and the higher, the more brilliant, and the more precious it is, the stronger the horror, grief and suffering. Evil is this fall from on high and the horror, grief and suffering it evokes. Horror at how unnecessary the fall, how contrary to the nature of the fallen; the grief and suffering because that which was originally "very good" is irreparably broken. Therefore no matter what the reasons for the fall, no matter how "legitimate" and "justified" it appears, it can have no explanation, no justification, and no excuse. There can be only horror, grief, and suffering. But to experience and to recognize evil as fall and to be horrified by it is precisely to *reveal evil as evil,* for this means to experience evil as the terrible presence, reality and efficacy of that which has no "essence," and yet exists. Evil is not reduced to a cause, a reason, or a deficiency which, once "explained," would be justified and fitted into the rational order. The horror is precisely that it does exist, and cannot be disregarded, dismissed, or neutralized by any "explanations."

This is precisely what evil means in Solzhenitsyn. It is always real, unique and concrete, rather than a manifestation of some universal Evil Essence suspended in the atmosphere, and because of this it is always horrible, grievous and irreparable. The Mavrino *sharashka* and the cancer ward are images not of the world, but of the *fallen* world, which by its very fall bears testimony to freedom, health and life. Reading Nerzhin's conversation with his wife before their final separation ("...only then he noticed that the wedding band from which she never parted was not on her finger..."), we know with our whole being that no explanation will help, just as we need no explanation when on Good Friday we hear once again: "...he began to be sorrowful and very troubled" (Mt. 26:37).

Evil in Solzhenitsyn is real because it is always *personal.* It is not found in impersonal "systems" or "structures," it is always found in and caused by man. Even in the *sharashka* and in the cancer ward evil does not appear as some elemental force and fate to which man is absolutely subjugated and for which he is in no way responsible, and to which, after it is "explained" and "accepted," it remains only to stoically resign oneself. Above all and always, evil is *men* who have opted and continue to opt for evil, men who have truly chosen to serve evil. And therefore evil is always a fall, and always a choice. The horror of Kafka's *The Trial* is that there is no escape from the anonymous, faceless, and absurd evil; the horror of Mavrino, however, is precisely the opposite: men—living, concrete, "personal" men—torture other men; even more, the horror is that they could, if they so chose, *not* torture. This is the Christian intuition of Evil. Christ was not crucified by impersonal *moira* or by "dark forces," but by men who had the choice not to crucify Him, and yet freely condemned Him rather than Barabbas to death. Evil in Solzhenitsyn always remains on a *moral,* and therefore *personal* plane; it is always related to the conscience which is in every man. It is not a failing, an absence of something, a blindness or a lack of responsibility; it is man's betrayal of his humanity; it is his *fall.*

And finally, the intuition of *redemption.* This intuition is not, of course, a humanistic optimism, a faith in "progress," a "bright tomorrow" or a "triumph of reason." All this is alien to the Christian gospel of rebirth and salvation, as it is alien to Solzhenitsyn. Yet in his works, as in Christianity, there is an indestructible faith in the possibility of *regeneration* for man, a refusal to "write off" anyone or anything forever. All is possible, he seems to say, if only man finds his conscience, as did the debased and self-centered State Counsellor Second Rank Innokentii Volodin or the inmates of the *sharashka,* who found their conscience in their "immortal zek souls." What moved Volodin on that festal Christmas eve, what induced him to phone a warning to the condemned doctor? And what made several zeks prefer the hopelessness of hard labor to the relative comfort of Mavrino? In Solzhenitsyn's art there are answers to these questions, and they come, in the final analysis, from the conscience of Solzhenitsyn himself.

Conscience invisibly rules, triumphs over and illumines the horror, ugliness and evil of the "fallen" world. As on the Cross, defeat is transformed into victory: at the end, Volodin gazes down "from those heights of struggle and suffering to which he had been lifted. . . ," and the last words about those in the *sharashka* are ". . .there was peace in their souls." And if it is so, then nothing is closed, condemned or damned. Everything is open, everything remains possible.

VII

Much more could and should be said about all this. What has been said may sound somewhat schematic, and Solzhenitsyn is a phenomenon of far too great significance to be reduced to a diagram. His creative path, besides, has not yet ended. Writing these lines which may be unworthy of him I have only one justification: "out of the abundance of the heart the mouth speaks" (Mt. 12:34). Solzhenitsyn is a joy, and joy always begs to be shared.

A final point. Ours is the time of the obvious collapse of Christian culture. This collapse is related, first of all, to the decomposition of that *triune intuition* from which that culture grew and in which it lived. Around us ardent efforts are being made to find new soil, new roots for culture and art, and it is clear that both the ardor and the efforts are filled with an irrational hatred for the Christian roots of culture, for its *triune intuition.* This is the time of an apostate culture! And even more frightening is that one fails to see hardly any resistance left on the Christian side. Some Christians are ready to withdraw to the catacombs, and to renounce any responsibility for culture. Others are ready, even zealous, to cross over into the opposite camp, certain that Christianity itself calls them to this—writers about the "death of God" or about the Christian justification for "secular society" are most often, alas, themselves Christians. Either to leave culture to the Devil, who "from the beginning was a liar" about the world, man and life, or to benignly see him as an "angel of light"; such is the nightmarish dilemma in which we find ourselves.

But then, in this dark night, in a country which more than half a century ago officially renounced its Christian name and calling, there arises a lone man who through his art reveals the lie and the sin of that dilemma and liberates us from it. A writer. A Russian writer. A Christian writer. For this liberation, for this witness, and for its coming from Russia, making Russia herself again and again ours; for preserving "unspoiled, undisturbed and undistorted the image of eternity with which each person is born," our joyful gratitude to Aleksandr Solzhenitsyn.

Translated by Serge Schmemann

EDITORS' NOTE. *In the summer of 1972 an interesting response by Solzhenitsyn to the above essay became known in the West. It was contained in a letter to the editors of* VESTNIK RSKHD, *the Paris-based journal in which the article had appeared. The major part of the letter deals with the moral support which Father Schmemann gave to Solzhenitsyn's "Lenten Letter" in a sermon broadcast over Radio Liberty. (Solzhenitsyn had been criticized for his views by several clerics of the Moscow Patriarchate.) Solzhenitsyn expresses his appreciation and adds:*

> . . . his article about me in [*Vestnik RSKhD*] No. 98 was also very valuable to me. It explained me to myself and explained Pushkin, as well as the reason why I have always felt such close affinity with him in tone and in my perception of the world. It also formulated important traits of Christianity which I could not have formulated myself. . . (*Novoe Russkoe Slovo,* 9 August 1972).

The Heroism of Survival

BY TERRENCE DES PRES

Resistance and Spiritual Growth

Since World War II the idea of "survival value" has gained a currency in our judgments about institutions, about persons and human works in general that even a few years earlier would have caused alarm and denial. To consider survival in this way signals a change in consciousness, a shift to limits and foundations, to care and a new humility, which is rooted in the weakening and sporadic failure of civilization as an efficient mechanism. It is rooted also in the climate of atrocity and the rhythm of destruction which have characterized our century; and in the unveiling of death for what it is, something simply and implacably before us, impervious to the myths and rationalizations which had for millennia served men against dread and hopelessness. Facing grim events and grimmer possibilities, we begin to arrive at the kind of awareness that, in his analysis of survival in the Nazi camps, David Rousset describes as the positive outcome of his ordeal:

> Dynamic awareness of the strength and beauty of the sheer fact of living, in itself, brutal, entirely stripped of all superstructures—living through even the worst cataclysms and most disastrous setbacks. A cool, sensuous thrill of joy founded on the most complete understanding of the

"The Heroism of Survival." Selected from "The Survivor: On the Ethos of Survival in Extremity," *Encounter*, XXXVII, no. 3 (September, 1971), 10-19.

wreckage, and consequently incisiveness in action and firmness in decisions, in short, a broader and more intensely creative vigour.[1]

In a different context a statement like Rousset's might be the propaganda of yet another barbarism. But as the insight of a remarkable survivor (Rousset helped organize resistance groups within the German camps), it is a profoundly human response to the blessing and wonder of being alive. It is, in fact, a kind of observation that the rapacious survivor could never make; and it is something too which Rousset shares with other survivors like himself.

Survival, as we are defining it, is an act of refusal and resistance; and the survivor's capacity to bear inhuman hardship, his small victories against the monolith of destruction, are the forms of life-inspired stubbornness. From this point of view the survivor's struggle is largely negative. It may have a positive outcome; by living through a situation he may alter it, but this end the survivor will not count on. And there are situations, like those of Solzhenitsyn's heroes, entirely beyond the individual's influence. But this circumstance need not set a limit to the survivor's significance. As Rousset's comment suggests, there is something, a form of accomplishment, still to be considered; something found when a man is driven down past aid and hope, down through humiliation and helpless suffering to a state of complete nakedness. Here, precisely because it does not die or give up, the surviving self comes upon itself and the ground itself, as it could never begin to do while enjoying the delicate, efflorescing manifestations of selfhood which civilization creates and supports.

The value here is in the act itself, and becomes visible as soon as the struggle to survive is recognized as also a struggle to preserve the living seeds of existence as a human being. The survivor is a hero in that by staying alive he becomes an effective agent in the fight against extremity. But just as much, the survivor is a hero because as soon as he chooses not only to live, but to live humanly, he takes upon himself the burden of an extraordinary enterprise, an action requiring enormous will, courage, capacity to bear pain, and an unshakable faith in the value of life and human decency—requiring, in fact, an assertion of the self that by any standard ought to be considered heroic.

[1]David Rousset, *The Other Kingdom* (tr. Guthrie, 1947).

From this experience comes a special integrity and clarity of vision, and more, something close to what we speak of as the religious experience, that unique liberation and concentrated fulfilment of the saint—of those who, having passed in pain beyond family, possessions and self-will, find themselves face to face, in joy and in peace, with the numinous power of life in itself. This, or something close to it, is what Rousset discovered, and this is also what holds Solzhenitsyn's deepest attention: the spiritual and transcendent dimensions of the survivor's experience; the unexpected, invaluable return.

Solzhenitsyn's survivor is the man ardently in love with his people and their cause; the man who stood against the Nazi onslaught only to find himself thrown into a Siberian labour camp; this same man, helpless but fiercely unreconciled to victimhood, who is determined to remain a human being, innocent and unbroken, under conditions specifically devised to crush out life and spirit. His energies burn with the pointed fury of an extreme tension between the will to live and the will to remain pure—between an almost mystical appreciation of life, on the one hand, and on the other an unwavering refusal to capitulate, sell out, or in any way become accessory to a system which reduces men to puppets and meat. This is the survivor's predicament, and from it, with the intimate authority of one who has fully suffered his subject, Solzhenitsyn draws an image of man for whom the struggle to keep a living soul in a living body becomes the *sine qua non* of moral being—and in this stark sense the definitively human act.

Solzhenitsyn's world has all the marks of extremity, with the concentration camp, terror's source and reference point, as the navel of the totalitarian nightmare. It will not do, either, to say that the camps and prisons are metaphors for society; they are the reality behind appearance, the dark heart within the body of life's business, just as, in *The First Circle,* the trucks in which the *zeks* are shipped are painted to appear as grocery vans. The practice of terror connects surfaces with the thing itself, and a man may fall—one day a diplomat, the next a prisoner—as easily as picking up the phone. In this world, ways of life and the moral attitudes which attend them are measured against a standard that derives from the experience of the survivor. Solzhenitsyn's heroes have undergone the "apprenticeship" of the camps, and their authority comes straight from the fact that they survived. And when human beings are made to accept and service an order maintained by murder and deliberate dehumanization, the survivor's uncompromising moral vision is no more extreme than the conditions he opposes. In extremity there is a point after which compromise becomes complicity; after which irony becomes duplicity; and after which the survivor's purity takes precedence over other claims to moral authority.

The intention of totalitarian methods is control of man in the mass, and therefore destruction of individual autonomy, which is to say, elimination of the intractable human element from social organization. Men are to live on schedule, and if the human spirit will not be programmed—not for the good of the cause, the war effort, or increased production—well then, it will have to be removed. Russia is not unique in this respect, but only, after Nazi Germany, the worst example of a universal practice.

For everywhere men set as their goal the systematic intensification of a tendency, as old as the human condition, to subordinate human ends to technical means, which in our time becomes the attempt of governments to subject whole populations to kinds of super-organization which more efficiently serve the means (not ends) of war, production, and organization itself. The rapid progress of this eminently 20th-century enterprise makes increasingly possible the destruction of individual persons, and in the end, of man as a human being; for whatever its methods, control aims at totality and demands, therefore, an end to freedom and integrity, to the private moral vision of self-directed men. It seems possible that a new world condition is taking shape, in which the whole of mankind is being pulled, with enormous pain, under the control of two or three governments—all of us, that is, in the hands of a few men who, whether we call them evil or well-intended, stupid or the pawns of ungovernable power, are in any case the agents of policies fatal to such human essentials as respect for life and the dignity a man creates by preserving his innocence and making significant choices. As Hannah Arendt has remarked:

> It is as though mankind had divided itself between those who believe in human omnipotence (who think that everything is possible if one knows how to organize masses for it) and those for whom powerlessness has become the major experience of their lives.[2]

[2]Hannah Arendt, *The Origins of Totalitarianism* (1951).

The ethos of the survivor applies only to the latter, for a powerless man may still refuse to accept his place as victim; he may reject the benefits of abdication and, powerless, choose not to compromise—and by the fact that he exists become a reproach to the system, a sliver in the throat of power. Given the gigantic forces he confronts, his act will be painful and on a very small scale, but thereby he becomes, in his own body and person, the indispensable and life-giving proof that the human spirit will not be broken. He acts to keep faith in himself, but like the saint his example is invested with a power that moves other men to thought and inspiration.

The Move Beyond Despair

Shukhov, the simple-hearted hero of *One Day in the Life of Ivan Denisovich*[3] is this kind of man. He has been unjustly imprisoned, and has lived years of days of sub-zero weather without decent clothing or a warm place to sleep, rising each day before the sun to twelve hours of heavy labor on a starvation diet. He steers his life through sickness and exhaustion, through the random cruelty of camp procedure and the betrayal of fellow prisoners ready to sell their souls or another's life for a few ounces of bread. And yet he is not broken: "even eight years as a convict hadn't turned him into a jackal—and the longer he spent at the camp the stronger he made himself."

Shukhov is willing to give way to other *zeks,* to perform services for men he respects, but will not make a deal with power or authority, never inform, never do a favor for the cooks or ask one of them. He has developed the *zek's* special ability to cheat the officials and camp regulations, by which he saves his strength and now and then gets an extra bowl of soup (these are major victories), but he will not cheat others in the same situation as himself. And through it all he maintains an elementary sense of self-respect:

> Every nerve in his body was taut, all his longing was concentrated in that cigarette butt—which meant more to him now, it seemed, than freedom itself—but he would never lower himself like that Fetiukov, he would never look at a man's mouth.

Due to his situation as much as to his character, Shukhov

[3]Alexander Solzhenitsyn, *One Day in the Life of Ivan Denisovich* (tr. Ralph Parker, 1963).

has come a long way in the wisdom of simplicity. He has learned to extract immense satisfaction—a sense of animal well-being which saves him from self-pity and despair—from slight and infrequent moments of pleasure. Working with his squad to build a wall (the temperature is —17°), Shukhov is inspired to delight by the rhythm of the work and the interplay of skills; he enjoys the warmth which spreads through his body, and later, the deeper joy of a job well done. He has, in short, learned to fully appreciate every inch of life that transcends pain and hopelessness. In this respect, by far the most important event in his life is food, and like all of Solzhenitsyn's heroes, Shukhov has developed an extraordinary attitude toward the watered-down soup and black bread which sustain him. To eat becomes a ritualized experience in which the resurrection of bodily joy—or rather, since he never gets enough, the heightened tension of desire on the verge of fulfilment—becomes the physical ground of faith in the value of life. Soup-time becomes a "sacred moment," a revelation deep in the body's pleasure that, at bottom and in spite of everything, life is strong and worth its pain:

> Shukhov took off his hat and laid it on his knee. He tasted one bowl, he tasted the other. Not bad—there was some fish in it. . . .
>
> He dug in. First he only drank the broth, drank and drank. As it went down, filling his whole body with warmth, all of his guts began to flutter inside him at their meeting with that stew. Goo-ood!
>
> And now Shukhov complained about nothing; neither about the length of his stretch, nor about the length of the day, nor about their swiping another Sunday. This was all he thought about now: we'll survive. We'll stick it out, God willing, till it's over.

Extremity intensifies experience, purifies it, forces men to the essence of their encounters with reality. Only sex (and how like sexual climax Shukhov's ritual is) comes close in that it too may issue in the physical intuition of a goodness at life's core. Shukhov eats his soup, and bliss wells up like a visitation, like an extravagant blessing, as though this second bowl, tricked from the cooks, were the fullest beneficence of God. Like some of Tolstoy's characters—Pierre, Levin—Shukhov attains that rarest of moments, when a man is simply, and against all evidence, happy to be alive.

What Solzhenitsyn means is clear: *You have not beaten us down.* The whole point of *Ivan Denisovich* is that yes, such a man exists in such a place. If we miss this we miss everything the survivor is about. Surrounded by the combined inhumanity of man and nature, this small simple man has made a life for himself, with its grossly handicapped balance of pain and pleasure, risk and victory, deprivation and fulfilment. And to a slight but all-important degree, it is *his* life; each act in violation of camp regulations, each moment of pleasure, lifts him anew above the sheer necessity which the agents of dehumanization thought to impose upon him. We may find it difficult to comprehend, but Solzhenitsyn's hero lives on the edge of happiness. Of course Shukhov suffers; we cannot forget that *this* day was uncommon for luck, and that pain is the substantial element in which he lives, as present and cruelly persistent as the Siberian winter. But he has come to terms with it, transcended his situation by refusing self-pity or despair or the temptation to hope for anything but life itself, and then gone on to find what goodness he can in the life he has. Deprived of ordinary possibilities, he is also free from the tangle of responsibility and failure which yokes and bends other men. And unlike those of us who enjoy the benefits of civilization, Shukhov has only one problem, essential and clear-cut: how to survive without losing his innocence.

Man's Choice

Innocence is a definitive condition of the human survivor. Of course there have always been innocent victims; God's four horsemen see to that. But the large-scale and systematic victimization of innocent populations—from Babii Iar and the Baltic resettlement to Viet Nam and Biafra—is new, if only in the speed, range, and precision of its means. It is new as a planned contingency in the political decisions of governments possessing a sufficient technology. And as Frederick Hoffman has pointed out,[4] there is no longer a rational or affective relation between victim and aggressor: victimization is abstract, impersonal, *en masse*. What the victim himself experiences is an encompassing violence, beyond comprehension or human measure, merely "the landscape as assailant." Innocence within a landscape of total violence has been the condition of millions of people in our century, and to withstand this condition without betraying his innocence is the survivor's particular job.

[4]Frederick Hoffman, *Death and the Modern Imagination* (1964).

Most of the convicts in Dostoevsky's *House of the Dead* are victims, but they are not innocent. They may be more sinned against than sinning, but still, each has directly violated another person. Solzhenitsyn's convicts, on the other hand, are political prisoners; theirs is an abstract guilt, defined and made official by "Section 58." They have not hurt anyone, and they do not, like the tragic hero, help to bring about their fate through some failure of moral awareness. Like Solzhenitsyn himself, they suffer because more than most men they think and judge for themselves. This, for example, is the fate of Kostoglotov in *Cancer Ward*,[5] who along with his fellow students got seven years plus exile:

> We used to come together, court the girls, dance; but the boys also talked about politics. And about HIM. . . . Two of us had fought at the front and had expected something else after the war. In May, just before the examinations, we were arrested, the girls too.

Solzhenitsyn's *zeks* end up in the camps *because* they are innocent; because, that is, control by terror is based on random selection and because their integrity is incompatible with the system in which they are trapped, causing them to become visible as individuals in contradiction to the logic of their environment. *The First Circle* is an inventory of the victimization of innocence: Gerasimovich for "intent to commit treason"; Kagan for "failure to inform"; Dyrsin for "a denunciation cooked up by some neighbors who wanted his apartment and afterwards got it."[6] It is the same in *Ivan Denisovich;* Shukhov fought at the front, was captured by the Germans, and escaped back to his own lines where he was promptly arrested for the following crime: "Yes, he'd surrendered to the Germans with the intention of betraying his country and he'd returned from captivity to carry out a mission for German intelligence. What sort of mission neither Shukhov nor the interrogator could say." No matter. From the totalitarian point of view, guilt is "historical" and "objective"; in other words, a matter of form and theory, or at best of circumstantial evidence. From the same point of view, anyone whom chance or decision singles out automatically sins against an order in which the individual person, by the very fact that he exists as such, is subversive. And Shukhov's story was in fact the fate of thousands of Russian

[5]Alexander Solzhenitsyn, *Cancer Ward* (tr. Rebecca Frank, 1967).
[6]*The First Circle* (tr. T. P. Whitney, 1968).

POWs—victims of war and the criminal unpreparedness of Russian defences, of Stalin in particular, the system in general.

A totalitarian order based on terror is the clearest example of an extreme situation in which the survivor's refusal to part with his innocence is why he became a survivor in the first place. Prolonged extremity becomes for most men a slow, despairing abdication of courage and self-respect; a readiness to condone and remain silent, to look away while others die. Under Stalin this process was widespread, including (this is noted without claiming anything better to be expected from ourselves, should a reign of terror descend) just about everyone in some degree—everyone except the *zeks.* And this is Solzhenitsyn's highest claim for the men in the camps: they alone did not bow down. In *Cancer Ward* Shulubin, bitter because he too saw and remained silent, quotes Pushkin:

In this our age of infamy,
Man's choice is but to be
A tyrant, traitor, prisoner;
No other choice has he.

No choice, surely, is more bitter, and yet a choice that cannot, in extremity, be avoided. When terror and massive injustice become the policies of power, when people are murdered in great numbers, when the prisons are full of men that anyone can tell are innocent, then the claims of civilization—irony, ambiguity, compromise—lose their validity. To escape involvement becomes impossible: being *in* it, one either implements evil, allows it, or suffers it. And in a totalitarian order especially, to condone evil, to evade and rationalize, to watch and fail to speak, is precisely the mark of its victory over the human spirit. In this case only the survivor, by being thrown into the camps and by running a higher risk of death, comes through (if he comes through) with innocence intact. In extremity, that is, if a man is determined to remain a human being he must be ready to take upon himself the survivor's risk and suffering.

We can always uncover legitimate reasons—social, psychological, economic—to explain why one man violates another. But the fact that good and sufficient reasons exist does not account for the separate fact that a man must choose, whatever his reasons, to act on them; he chooses to accept or resist the conditions which make violence a logical outcome of his situation. This may not be clear in the classroom, but in the concentration camps, where a man has every reason to justify Darwinian behaviour, there are yet some men—David Rousset was one, Solzhenitsyn another—who simply will not allow themselves to violate their sense of elemental decency. They make compromises; they are ruthless with themselves and others up to a point; but beyond that point they will not go, for to do so would be to destroy within themselves that deep innocence which makes faith in human value possible. Judging from the documents of the camps, the number of such men was small and yet, given the circumstances, miraculously large.

We might say, invoking myth, that man fell from the garden of God's will into the world of pain and death. He fell, that is, from innocence to victimhood, from divine grace to the condition of original sin. But this second necessity, by negating the first, opens the way to a third condition. The cycle of humanity is a movement of the spirit from ignorant innocence through the sorrow of experience toward that higher innocence of sainthood. Original sin is the condition of experience, of existence as a world of cannibalism, in which life lives at the expense of other life. Here survival itself is original sin—the grim theme of William Golding's novels. To accept as final the ways of the cannibal is to live as victim and victimizer, and to greater or lesser degree, most of us remain within this limit. But there is, at least sometimes, the possibility for another kind of survival. To be in the world, as one must, and yet not of it, as one may choose, is to claim that higher innocence which is most difficult and, for some men, most ardently desired.

The Way Down and the Way Up

This desire, and the possibility of this choice, is the axis of concern in *The First Circle.* Foremost among Solzhenitsyn's band of survivors, and the center of moral intelligence in the novel, is Gleb Nerzhin, "a prisoner in his fifth year of harness who never hurries because he expects only worse from what lies ahead." Like Solzhenitsyn himself, Nerzhin was arrested at the front for private criticism of Stalin, and given a ten-year sentence. He is a mathematician, brought to the special prison at Mavrino after four years in the camps. Mavrino is a godsend for most of the *zeks*: "Meat at dinner. Butter in the morning. Hands not flayed with work. Fingers not frozen." Here the *zeks* are scientists and technicians, and they are forced to work on the refinement of a special technology—devices which will increase the power of totalitarian control. Most of them only pretend to work, but anyone who directly refuses to co-operate is certain to be in the next transport, which means—

> Perhaps he will not arrive at his destination. In a cattle car he may die either of dysentery or of hunger, because the *zeks* will be hauled along for six days without bread. Or the guard may beat him with a hammer because someone has tried to escape. Or, at the end of the journey in an unheated car, they may toss out the frozen corpses of the *zeks* like logs.

On the other hand, the *zek* who invents a new device may earn his release. But as Gerasimovich says, "the trouble is that the inventions . . . are—well, extremely undesirable."

People outside must decide how much their "freedom" is worth: how many lies they will live by, how far they will acquiesce while their neighbors are destroyed. "If one is forever cautious, can one remain a human being?" So thinks Innokentii Volodin, the young diplomat whose simple act of humanity will send him to prison. To remain human in such a world is to become a *zek* but the *zek* too has his moments of decision. Khorobrov was arrested for defacing an election ballot, and after years in the camps he comes, at Mavrino, to this crisis:

> At the *sharashka* good sense demanded that he lose himself in the activity of Number Seven and assure himself, if not of liberation, at least of a decent existence. But nausea at all the injustices aside from his own case rose inside him until he had reached the point where a man no longer wants to live.

In extremity this may become any man's crisis. Each must decide how he will reconcile the desire for life and comfort with the desire for purity and self-respect. And in relation to this choice, each character in Solzhenitsyn's world takes his place on a scale of moral being that runs from monstrosity to sainthood.

The low end is occupied by men in positions of authority and power: petty bureaucrats, state ministers, Stalin first of all. Minister of State Security Abakumov, for example, is the model of official success. Beginning as a mere NKVD courier, "it turned out that Abakumov conducted interrogations effectively; his long arms were an asset when it came to smashing people in the face." Success has brought him close to Stalin, increasing the chance of a bullet in the neck, and his dread filters down through the official hierarchy, each man beneath the heel of the man above him. All the ministers, bureaucrats, jailors, etc., that serve the system comprise the "They" to which the *zeks* refer, men without character or depth, the product of the machine they service. There is immense cruelty, suffering without end, but the brutality of the "They" is not, for example, a matter of sadism. Mainly it is institutionalized evil, carried out by men who have abdicated their humanity, men who have made the decision—from fear, from the desire for safety and comfort—to work with the system. The same may be said of those *zeks* who sell out. Siromakha, king of the informers, is the kind of man whose survival capacity is legendary: "Those who, as camp guards, could club their countrymen in the face; those who, as bread-cutters and cooks, could eat the bread of others who were starving." Plainly, there is more than one kind of survivor, and a point after which the heroism of survival turns into its opposite. "The wolfhound is right and the cannibal is wrong."

At Mavrino, Nerzhin is forced to work, but he does not give himself to the purpose imposed upon him. His desk is piled with books and folders, but "in fact it was all a false front." His real work is a collection of notes in which he analyses the failure of the Revolution—how, that is, history purifying itself came to result in concentration camps. But then he is called before the officials and asked to volunteer for a special project, and this, to willingly offer his service, he will not do. If he were to agree he might earn his release, but on the other hand, his refusal "was certain to result, perhaps very soon, in a long and arduous journey to Siberia or the Arctic, to death or to a hard victory over death." Other *zeks,* like Rubin and Sologdin, decide to work for their freedom (and Solzhenitsyn allows them a sympathetic understanding). But Nerzhin is uncompromising; he will keep himself pure and take his chances. As soon as the decision is made his spirit begins to shore its strength, drawing on the survivor's special wisdom:

> Nerzhin . . . was now thinking that only the first year of camp could finish him, that he had achieved a completely different tempo, that he would not try to scramble into the ranks of the goldbrickers, that he would not be afraid of camp labour, but would slowly, with an understanding of life's depths, go out for morning line-up in his

padded jacket smeared with plaster and fuel oil and tenaciously drag through the twelve-hour day—and so on, for the whole five years remaining until the end of his term. Five years is not ten. One can last five.

The odd thing is that Nerzhin prefers the camps to Mavrino. As long as he must exist in the lower depths he would rather go all the way; for there, at the absolute limit of soul and body, life is forced to its irreducible elements, truths on which, should he survive, a man may firmly build. "Camp life," Solzhenitsyn tells us, "exceeds in its ruthlessness anything known of the lives of cannibals and rats." But at the same time he speaks of "the harsh apprenticeship of camp." To what can this refer, if not to the apprenticeship of one's own soul, to the crystallization—as under immense pressure carbon turns to diamond—of that essence all men share but seldom realize or even acknowledge. As Nerzhin puts it, "one must try to temper, to cut, to polish one's soul so as to become a *human being*" (Solzhenitsyn's italics). This recalls Shukhov: "the longer he spent at the camp the stronger he made himself."

It seems clear that the ordeal of survival becomes, at least for some men, an experience of growth and purification. By virtue of the extraordinary demands made upon the man in extremity, his struggle to remain human is in fact a process of becoming more—essentially, purely—human. Not, perhaps, the humanness of refinement and proliferation, but of fundamental moral vision, of the knowledge of good and evil, on which the value of everything else depends. Nerzhin says: "I had no idea what good and evil were, and whatever was allowed seemed fine to me. But the lower I sink into this inhumanly cruel world, the more I respond to those who, even in such a world, speak to my conscience." For the survivor too, the way down is the way up.

The way down is a passage through loss and risk and endless suffering, a process of concentration and self-knowledge issuing, for those who come through, in the stark fulfilment of spiritual intensification and authentic selfhood. The survivor's pain is always there, in the body, in the heart and in the soul, a seamless chamber which holds him caught, and yet the condition which shears the self down to what is essential and irreducible. In extremity a man's strength is inversely proportionate to the number of his needs, a point made by Bruno

Bettelheim, when he attacks "business as usual."[7] The survivor has no business as usual, neither family nor position, neither possessions nor opportunity to pursue ordinary satisfactions. For better and worse he is free of the needs which keep other men trapped in self-alienating activities. He has only the purity of a self which exists beyond all save the need to live, and this condition, painful though it is, is also a position of power. State Minister Abakumov can make his subordinates tremble in nervous terror (as he himself does in front of Stalin), but his power does not penetrate the iron soul of *zek* Bobynin. "Shout at your colonels and generals," Bobynin tells him, "they have too much in life they're afraid of losing."

In all of Stalin's Russia, none but the lowly *zeks* can speak without fear. And this, as Bobynin points out, is the crack in totalitarian perfection:

> . . . you are strong only as long as you don't deprive people of *everything*. For a person you've taken everything from is no longer in your power. He's free all over again.

Like other types of the hero, the survivor takes his stand directly on the line, but he is unique in that he stays there. And it is there, where life meets death as an equal, that his peculiar freedom and power become real and effective. His vision is not clouded by the protective illusions which civilization fosters, and he sees, with acute lucidity, that existence is a wager between life and death, that spirit thrives in the balance of being and non-being. He does not suddenly, in the ambush of crisis, discover his mortality, for in order to remain alive he must at every moment acknowledge the centrality of death. And this familiarity has not failed to breed its proper contempt; he may be killed, but so long as he lives he will not be intimidated.

And closer to death, the survivor is closer to life than other men. His will to survive is one with the thrust of life in itself, numinous and inexhaustible, severely joyful and as stubborn as the upsurge of spring. In this state a strange exultation fills the soul, a sense of being equal to the worst (and so long as he lives, the survivor *is* equal to the worst). This is the attitude of those *zeks*—Nerzhin, Gerasimovich, Khorobrov—who at the end of *The First Circle* are shipped off to the transport:

> Concentrating on the turns the van was making. the *zeks* fell silent. Yes, the taiga and the tundra awaited them, the record cold of

[7]Bruno Bettelheim, *The Informed Heart* (1960).

> Oymyakon and the copper excavations of Dzhezkazgan; pick and barrow; starvation rations of soggy bread; the hospital; death. The very worst.
>
> But there was peace in their hearts.
>
> They were filled with the fearlessness of those who have lost *everything*, the fearlessness which is not easy to come by but which endures.

This is a state of mind such as few of us might expect to know; but embroiled as we are in the lesser symmetries of life and death, it is something felt to be invaluable, a courage beyond hope which reveals the unexpected and even joyous strength of man at the limits of life.

The Presence of Life

Having fought against the Nazi invasion, Solzhenitsyn's survivors are also soldiers, and this is how they think of themselves as day by day they withstand extremity with the modest tactics that keep them going. "A soldier gets along best on the defensive," says Kostoglotov in *Cancer Ward,* and indeed the survivor's struggle is very much like guerrilla warfare—as Mao defines it, "tactical offensives within a strategy of defense." In *The First Circle* Nerzhin succeeds in retrieving his copy of Esenin from the security officer, a pitched battle executed with surprise and speed, a tactic in the strategy of spiritual self-preservation. As Nerzhin says, "It's not so much the book . . . as the principle: they must not beat us down." But the survivor's enemy is death, and in the end he is a soldier who can never hope for more than small and temporary victories.

The cancer ward is death's home ground, and those who find themselves there have no thought but to survive, to employ any medical tactic which may strengthen their defensive; and, since death will not retreat, to come to terms with their situation so as to live beyond fear and despair. "In the face of death, in the face of the striped panther of death who had already lain down beside him, in the same bed, Vadim, as a man of intellect, had to find a formula for living." Kostoglotov's answer is to live as the soldier lives: aware of danger and ready to die, yet putting up the longest fight possible, and regarding all men kindly but without pity as brothers in a losing war—"This bullet was yours; the next may be mine."

This hardness of the living heart is something a man like

Kostoglotov cannot do without. After the War he entered the university, but before his life could begin to take shape, he was arrested and sent to the camps. After that, exile, and then cancer, so we cannot avoid the impression that Kostoglotov, still in his thirties, is an old man. The extreme pathos of his situation is that, on the verge of death, he is a man who never had a life, "a river that doesn't go anywhere, that haphazardly gives away its best water and power along the way." He has survived years of incredible hardship, missed death by a hair's breadth, only to find, not the tree of life flaming with blossoms, with promise and budding fruits, but this implacable cancer which will soon shut him from life. Kostoglotov thirsts for fulfilment with a fierceness only equalled by his despair of attaining it, and having acquired in the camps "the ability to shake off all but the main thing," he comes at last to the humblest kind of hope: "I want to live for a bit without guards and without pain, and that's the limit of my dreams."

This is as much as he can hope for from treatment in the cancer ward:

> not for a complete new life, but for an extra portion, like the makeweight end of a loaf fastened onto the main part of the ration, a twig stuck through the two to hold them together—part of the same ration, but a separate piece.

This image is drawn from life in the camps, and what it suggests is that when men die in millions, the myth of rebirth dies too. The survivor only lasts; what he achieves is some "small, additional, added-on life." And even this has its price, for in extremity, every moment of life is purchased at exorbitant cost, forcing the survivor to repeatedly consider the balance of values. As Kostoglotov puts it:

> I have often wondered before, and now particularly I wonder: What, after all, is the highest price one should pay for life? How much should one pay, how much is too much?

This question is always present, and each turn of the situation requires a new answer. So it is when Kostoglotov enters the cancer ward. Very nearly dead, his chance for a bit more of life depends on a hormone treatment which will deprive him of his virility, and this is the decision he must face: "To become a walking husk of a man—isn't that an exorbitant price? It would be a mockery. Should I pay it?" And if he pays, what then?

Whom shall I seek, with whom share
The heavy-hearted joy of my survival?

He would share it with a woman, Vega Gangart, and come to the fullness of life in love and a home. But to live at all is to give up this chance. We can suppose that this lusty man would once have led a simple fruitful life. But now he must continue to live against encroaching cancer with the knowledge that he has lost everything, that love and work, children, life ripening within, will not be his to try. And this solitude, beyond resolve or answer, is surely the ultimate pain of the surviving self.

But he does choose to live, as if, given the man he is, there were no alternative, or as if life itself were final judge of what price is worth paying. Once more Kostoglotov sacrifices a part of himself in order to preserve what he calls "the main thing." He will not give up, because after the camps he cannot, in this last extremity, negate the only meaning his life has had; and because to continue to live, even for a few months, is absolutely worth it. This is clear from the happiness of his walk through the city: his rapport with the teeming life and motion, the intense relish with which he eats some roasted meat, the tender gratefulness he feels toward Vega for her love. It is a wonderful day, and the wisdom of Kostoglotov's deep delight is apparent: "Even if next spring never came, even if this was the last, it was one *extra* spring! And thanks be for that!" Like Shukhov and like Nerzhin, Kostoglotov is able to respond to life's least gift with a fullness of gratitude that is, finally, greater and more powerful than hope.

This is the survivor's small but priceless inheritance. In this state of mind Kostoglotov leaves the hospital in search of a flowering apricot tree, not to possess it of course, but only, for a moment's time, to behold it, to rest his joy on this delicate, enduring emblem of life. Then he will board the train, find a place to lie in the baggage rack, and settle himself for the journey back into exile:

> Others had not survived. He had survived.... It was good to stretch out.... Only when the train jolted and started to move did he feel a stab of pain around his heart, around his soul—somewhere in the most crucial part of his chest. He turned over, lay face downward on the trench coat, shut his eyes and nuzzled his face into the knapsack, lumpy with loaves of bread.... The train moved, and Kostoglotov's boots, as if dead, dangled over the passageway, toes down.

The pathos of his final condition is very great, yet tempered by his will to bear it. Kostoglotov is a man without hope, but even so he has lived as long as he could, without damage to his innocence, without harm to his fellowmen.

And in this effort—to carry on when ordinary avenues of fulfilment are closed and death lies visible ahead—the heroism of survival reaches its limit. In the end Kostoglotov has nothing, nothing at all but this short reprieve, this extra life free and his own. But for the survivor this is everything. Pathos dissolves in the liberation of total loss, and renunciation of life's particulars opens on the glory and power of the main thing, the presence of life in itself.

Solzhenitsyn's celebration of life is the outcome of his own apprenticeship. It owes nothing to the abstractly-conceived vitalism of the last century, and is something hardly to be known by thought alone. And yet, since the survivor loses everything except life, life and his capacity to see an absolute value therein, we cannot but wonder what it is he finds, what is *there* to hold and sustain him. Why one man survives and another does not, is not fully explicable; chance and character play their part, but something else as well, a sort of grace. And what the survivor arrives at by reaching past despair *and* hope would seem to be similarly unnameable. But surely he comes on something, an entrance to the heart of being, the furious purity of an endless energy, of life in itself, something unexpectedly uncovered when the spirit is driven down to its roots, all insolence lost, and through its pain brought to a pristine concentration, and to a sense of finality and quietude that, once again, surpasses understanding. In another age we might have called it God, God the bleak, the rush, the final point of a vibrant, unshakable peace.

Whatever it is, the survivor is driven to embrace it, aware of its power and holiness. And whatever it is—to call it life will have to do—it is the fundament of flesh and the soul, the ground on which the survivor stands, upright in innocence and in the will to continue as a human being.

Solzhenitsyn and *Samizdat**

BY MICHAEL NICHOLSON

In September 1967 Solzhenitsyn appeared before the Secretariat of the Board of the Soviet Writers' Union for a discussion of mutual grievances. Towards the close of what proved to be a hostile encounter, he was involved in the following exchange with Aleksei Surkov, an established poet of the older generation:

> Surkov: You should tell us whether you disassociate yourself from the role ascribed to you in the West, the role of leader of the political opposition in our country.
> Solzhenitsyn: Aleksei Aleksandrovich, it's sickening to hear such a thing, and from you of all people. A creative writer and a leader of the political opposition! How do they fit together? (VI, 57)[1]

This incredulous question could usefully stand as a cautionary epigraph to any discussion of Solzhenitsyn's links with manifestations of dissidence in the Soviet Union. Neither his literary credo, nor his civic, publicistic utterances could, in good faith, be interpreted as the program of a political oppositionist, and any attempt to depict him as the underground demagogue of Russia's disaffected minorities would be patently absurd. The

*I am most grateful to Dr. Zhores Medvedev for correcting several of my misapprehensions during the preparation of this essay.

[1]References given in this form are to the appropriate volume and page number of Aleksandr Solzhenitsyn, *Sobranie sochinenii v shesti tomakh* (Frankfurt am Main: Posev, 1969).

fact that Solzhenitsyn's photograph frequently occupies a place of honor in the homes of men and women whose conscience and convictions have brought them into conflict with aspects of Soviet society and its political administration should not lead us glibly to translate an act of moral identification into political terms, to seek programs, platforms and organizational structure where none are to be found.

Such a caveat in no way detracts from the importance of Solzhenitsyn's place in the development of *samizdat,* that comparatively recent episode in Russia's long history of "unofficial" publishing. Indeed, it will be shown in the course of this survey that his participation in the ethos of *samizdat* has been increasingly conscious and deliberate. Yet, whether as the author of stories and novels spontaneously adopted by the reader-distributors of *samizdat,* or as an orator availing himself of the only medium open to him, Solzhenitsyn has endeavored to distinguish between political intervention and the defense of supra-political values and beliefs. Thus, earlier in the session already referred to, he defined the writer's obligations in terms which, given the occasion and the composition of his audience, were breathtakingly a-political:

> And besides, the tasks of the writer cannot be reduced to a defense or criticism of one or another means of distributing the social product, to a defense or criticism of one form of state system or another. The tasks of the writer are concerned with more general and universal questions: the secrets of the human heart and conscience, the confrontation of life and death, the triumph over spiritual grief, and those laws of mankind's long history which were born in the depths of time immemorial and which will not cease until the sun itself is extinguished. (VI, 53)

The ultimate repository of such laws and secrets is the individual and not the collective, party or "Opposition." Moral self-assertion in the face of falsehood or evil is of greater moment than the victories won and defeats sustained in the practical arena. Solzhenitsyn's firm belief in the social responsibilities of the writer, his alleged statement that "the basis of literature is a profound experience of social processes,"[2] must be considered in this light. He is no more a politician than he is a quietist.

Five years ago the word *samizdat* (translated approximately

[2]Pavel Licko, "Jednêho Dna u Alexandra Isajevica Solzenicyna," *Kulturny Zivot* (Bratislava), 31 March 1967, p. 10. Russian in *Posev,* 23 June 1967, p. 4.

as "do-it-yourself publishing") was virtually unknown in the West outside specialist circles. By now there can be few newspaper readers for whom it does not have at least vague associations of dissidence, typescripts and official displeasure.[3] Stripped of its historical and cultural specificity, *samizdat* may be tentatively defined as a process of duplicating and disseminating written works independently of the state-controlled press and publishing-houses, and without legal access to means of mass duplication beyond the typewriter. Such a working definition emphasizes the traditions and continuity which lie behind the new name. With all due acknowledgement of the relative technical sophistication of the typewriter and carbon paper, this remains in essence a "neo-scribal" process of copying and recopying, a fact which has not escaped attention in the Soviet Union. In his letter of May 1967 to the Fourth Congress of the Soviet Writers' Union Solzhenitsyn complains that "simply giving someone a manuscript to 'read and copy' is now forbidden by law in our country (the ancient Russian scribes of five centuries ago were permitted to do this!)" (VI, 13). One of the best known songs by the unofficial chansonnier Aleksandr

[3]For further discussion of the history, mechanics and background of *samizdat* see, e.g., *Aspects of Intellectual Ferment and Dissent in the Soviet Union,* a study by the Legislative Reference Service of the Library of Congress, prepared for a Senate Sub-Committee (Washington: US Government Printing Office, 1968); Albert Boiter, "Samisdat in der UdSSR," *Osteuropa,* 22 (1972), 645-654; Abraham Brumberg, ed., *In Quest of Justice: Protest and Dissent in the Soviet Union Today* (New York: Praeger, 1970); L. Donatov, "Tamizdat—literatura v izgnanii," *Posev,* 28 (Feb. 1972), 47-51; *The Future of Samizdat: Its Significance and Prospects,* transcript of a conference held in London on 23 April 1971 (Information Division, Radio Liberty); M. Osharov, "Iubilei Samizdata," *Russkaia mysl',* 12 March 1970, p. 4; Albert Parry, "Samizdat Is Russia's Underground Press," *NYT Magazine,* 15 March 1970, pp. 64-77; Peter Reddaway, ed., *Uncensored Russia: The Human Rights Movement in the Soviet Union: The Annotated Text of the Unofficial Moscow Journal* A Chronicle of Current Events [Nos. 1-11] (London: Jonathan Cape, 1972); Abraham Rothberg, *The Heirs of Stalin: Dissidence and the Soviet Regime 1953-1970* (Ithaca and London: Cornell Univ. Press, 1972); L. Sergeeva, "Samizdat: vozniknovenie i budushchee," *Posev,* 25 (Oct. 1969), 38-47; and Alan Wood, "The Resurgent Russian Intelligentsia," in *Dissent and Disorder: Essays in Social Theory,* ed. Bhikhu Parekh (Toronto: World University Service of Canada, 1971), pp. 81-95. Of particular interest are the following articles, whose authors were until recently closely involved with the phenomenon of *samizdat:* Julius Telesin, "Inside 'Samizdat,'" *Encounter,* 40 (Feb. 1973), pp. 25-33; and Iurii Glazov, "Background to Dissent," *Survey,* 19, No. 1 (86) [Winter 1973], pp. 75-91. For information concerning the most comprehensive collection of *samizdat* materials in the West, Radio Liberty's *Arkhiv Samizdata,* see Albert Boiter, "Samizdat: Primary Source Material in the Study of Current Soviet Affairs," *Russian Review,* 31 (1972), 282-285.

Galich, "We're No Worse than Horace,"[4] describes the elegant life of privileged, conformist intellectuals, ironically comparing them with the "good" Kievan knight of the Russian oral folk tradition, Dobrynia Nikitich. But among the Dobrynias walk "those parasites, the Nestors and Pimens," modest chroniclers and scribes of Russia's ancient past, an allusion to the maligned heroes of the new uncensored Soviet literature, whose "names are not syrupped forth from the stage." The stanza ends:

> An "Erika" [typewriter] can take four copies,
> That's all, and it's sufficient!
> We'll make do for now with just four copies,
> That's sufficient!

There is nothing uniquely Russian about censorship evasion. Aleksandr Radishchev, who was himself to suffer after outwitting Catherine the Great's censors, pointed out in his *Journey from Petersburg to Moscow* (1790) that "printing begat censorship."[5] Some forty years after the first printed book came off Johann Gutenburg's press in Mainz around 1445, the Archbishop of that city promulgated the first recorded preventive censorship decree, availing himself of the centralization and controllability of the printing trade. But preventive censorship swiftly stimulated methods of bypassing it, and the ingenuity expended in the process increased in direct proportion to the intellectual ferment which the censor was anxious to check. Thus Paul Hazard's account of the illicit publication and distribution of banned works in Europe during the Enlightenment[6] reveals many parallels with the more recent Russian experience. Fits of fanatical severity alternated with spells of near-anarchy, producing an atmosphere of uncertainty which eroded the efficacy of the censorship. Apart from the proliferation of underground printing presses and a brisk trade in manuscript copies of unpublishable works, the eighteenth century had its own forerunner of *tamizdat* (publication "over there," i.e. in the West, often leading to reimportation in one form or another). Manuscripts would be smuggled out of France, usually to Holland, where they were printed on presses specializing in

[4]"My ne khuzhe Goratsiia" in Aleksandr Galich, *Pesni* (Frankfurt am Main: Posev, 1969), pp. 115-116.

[5]*Puteshestvie iz Peterburga v Moskvu* (Leningrad: Khudozhestvennaia literatura, 1969), p. 137.

[6]*European Thought in the Eighteenth Century* (London: Penguin, 1965), pp. 107-113.

this trade. The finished product would return to its country of origin, often concealed amongst the cargo of a river barge.

Whatever the method used, be it pen, typewriter, camera, tape-recorder or even the human memory, Soviet Russia has had its share of men and women who took a similar pride in "overcoming Gutenburg."[7] At a meeting in memory of the poet Osip Mandel'shtam, liquidated in the purges of the 1930's, which was held at Moscow University on 13 May 1965, Varlam Shalamov recalled the tenacity with which Mandel'shtam's verses had survived: "In fact, it has turned out that we need him now more than ever, even though he has made scarcely any use of Gutenburg's press."[8] On the debit side, dispensing with the services of Gutenburg can lead to the proliferation of "scribal errors," the intrusion of *loci spurii,* and the circulation on an equal footing of revised and superseded variants. The canon of Solzhenitsyn's works is still affected by factors of this sort, despite his recent efforts to control the fate of his manuscripts at least beyond the frontiers of the Soviet Union.

Inevitably some aspects of the struggle for independent publication in the Soviet Union have precedents in other lands and other ages. Nevertheless, it may be argued that Russian history, particularly in the past 150 years, has been so fraught with confrontations between writers and authority as to establish a living tradition of clandestine circulation which has become an organic part of the Russian literary heritage, and which even the bleakest years of Stalin's Terror could not wholly extinguish. Perhaps the most famous comedy in the Russian language is Griboedov's *Gore ot uma* [*The Misfortunes of Being Clever*] (1824). Its unrestrained satire ensured that only extracts appeared in the poet's life-time, and some forty years were to elapse before an integral version could be printed. Meanwhile, the play led an independent existence, circulating "in copies" [*v spiskakh*] in an "edition" which some scholars have estimated at as many as 40,000 copies. One Soviet scholar, N. K. Piksanov, is satisfied that "no book was published at that time in as many copies as there were manuscript copies of *The Misfortunes of Being Clever* in circulation."[9] Many of Pushkin's blasphemous or

[7]Marina Tsvetaeva, cited in Telesin, p. 25.

[8]"Vecher pamiati Mandel'shtama v Moskovskom Universitete: 13 maia 1965 g. mekhmat. Predsedatel'—Erenburg" (handwritten *samizdat* transcript), repr. in *Grani,* 25, No. 77 (1970), p. 86.

[9]A. S. Griboedov, *Gore ot uma,* ed. N. K. Piksanov and A. L. Grishunina (Moscow: Nauka, 1969), p. 332.

subversive poems reached a wide audience in the same manner: such were the ode "Liberty" (1817), the notorious "Gabrieliad" (1821), and "Fairy Tales: A Noel" (1818), of which a contemporary, Ivan Iakushin, could write: "Everyone knew the poem by heart and sang it almost in the streets."[10]

The nineteenth century is rich in examples of this kind, ranging from the indiscretions of established writers, to the systematic preparation and proliferation of verse, prose and pamphlets as propaganda for one radical cause or another. Since any efforts to frustrate the tsarist censors are regarded in the Soviet Union as, by definition, healthy and progressive, scholarly research in this field has continued uninterrupted.[11] However, while meticulously documenting the evolution of the "free Russian uncensored press," Soviet scholars apparently develop a certain imperviousness to historical irony. Thus, A. Bikhter, in his introduction to a collection of underground Populist poetry, writes: "It is also known that there existed among the student youth of that epoch a tradition of circulating in manuscript form the most popular works of the uncensored press."[12] Bikhter's words were published in 1967, several years after the dramatic revival of that same student tradition in a new, Soviet setting. Needless to say, the resurgence was officially regarded as anything but "progressive."

Information regarding censorship and its evasion is as scant for the Soviet period as it is voluminous for the preceding century. The late Arkadii Belinkov drew a distinction between Soviet censorship and that of any previous era: "Before it emerged, dictatorial societies, from antiquity onwards, had been concerned merely to repress heretical opinions, whereas the Soviet Communist Party has introduced a system so thorough that it not only censors a writer but dictates what he shall say." Belinkov provides a graphic illustration of the baneful effects of such prescriptive censorship. Referring to recent achievements by Soviet scholars engaged in restoring censored Russian literary classics, he emphasizes the fact that such developments have not led to any substantial alteration in our view of nine-

[10]Cited in David Magarshack, *Pushkin: A Biography* (London: Chapman and Hall, 1967), p. 86.

[11]See Martin Dewhirst's valuable introduction and bibliographical annotation to *The Soviet Censorship,* publ. as one issue of *Studies on the Soviet Union,* NS 11, No. 2 (1971), especially pp. i-vii.

[12]*Poety revoliutsionnogo narodnichestva* (Leningrad: Khudozhestvennaia literatura, 1967), p. 11.

teenth century Russian literature. "If, however, the same painstaking method of correcting the censor's distortions were to be applied to Soviet literature, different works would emerge, because Soviet censorship has consistently mutilated manuscripts to such a degree that it has transformed them into works quite opposed to their authors' intentions." Accordingly, the result of Soviet censorship has been, in Belinkov's words, "that the great Russian literary tradition has all but been destroyed."[13] The works of Solzhenitsyn and others are living proof that the tradition has survived in its essentials, but alternative literature under Stalin was an altogether grimmer and sparser province than ever Griboedov or Pushkin had known.

Apart from writing "for the desk drawer," there was beyond a doubt limited and cautious "publication" of the *samizdat* type during the 1930's and 1940's. For obvious reasons, poetry lent itself more readily than prose to clandestine transmission and retention. Towards the end of his life Maksimilian Voloshin (1877-1932) was barred from publishing his verse, yet, despite the material hardship which this caused him, he could still follow with pride the secret life of his banned works:

> But my own lips have long been sealed. No matter!
> There's greater honour still in being learned by heart
> And copied out in secret, furtively,
> In this life being not a volume but—a notebook.[14]

In an article in the Soviet press in 1957 A. Kovalenkov recalled how poems by Nikolai Gumilev were still being circulated in duplicated form in the early 1930's, some ten years after the poet's execution for allegedly subversive activities.[15] It was during the same decade that Nikolai Kliuev, Mikhail Kuzmin and Osip Mandel'shtam read their unpublished works at private gatherings. "Many of them," writes Boris Filippov, "frequently unbeknown to their authors, were copied out by hand, multiplied, also by hand, and circulated throughout the Soviet Union."[16] In some cases, at least, poems were deliberately committed to the vagaries of manuscript and oral transmission in the belief that, in Mandel'shtam's words, "people will preserve

[13]*The Soviet Censorship*, pp. 1 and 4.

[14]Cited in Boris Filippov, "Maksimilian Voloshin," *Russkaia mysl'*, 11 Jan. 1973, p. 6.

[15]A. Kovalenkov, "Pis'mo staromu drugu," *Znamia*, No. 7 (1957), p. 167.

[16]In the introduction to his anthology *Sovetskaia potaennaia muza: Iz stikhov sovetskikh poetov, napisannykh ne dlia pechati* (Munich: I. Baschkirzew Verlag, 1961), pp. 6-7.

them."[17] And, indeed, unpublished poems by Mandel'shtam, Kliuev and Voloshin did survive, to reemerge in *samizdat* after the death of Stalin.

In their own way, Stalin's prisons and labor camps came to be the country's main bastions of unofficial literary expression. As one imprisoned communist, Evgeniia Ginzburg, discovered, recalling and composing verse provided some relief during the long hours of solitary confinement: "My memory, cut off from all impressions from outside, unfolded like a chrysalis transformed into a butterfly."[18] Another survivor, Varlam Shalamov, devotes one of his harrowing "Kolyma Stories" to the function of the *rasskazchik* [story-teller] in camp society.[19] The intellectual Platonov keeps himself alive in a particularly harsh camp by paraphrasing Dumas and Conan Doyle from memory for the delectation of the common criminals whose law is absolute within the barracks.

Two lighter examples of the creative powers of the story-teller are given in *The First Circle,* in the episodes "The Traitor Prince" (Ch. 50) and "The Smile of Buddha" (Ch. 54). But the preeminence of poetry in this setting is perhaps best expressed in a poem by Boris Slutskii written in 1951, which begins with the stanza:

> When Russian prose went off to the camps,
> Some to be shovellers, and smarter ones—medics,
> Some to be wood-cutters, sharper ones—drivers,
> Or barbers, or actors;
>   All of you forgot your own craft straight away.
>   What comfort is prose in moments of grief?
>   Like frail little splinters
>   the ocean of poetry
>   Drew you and rocked you and bore you away.[20]

Later in the poem Slutskii describes how "the iambus was born out of the steady pounding of shovels . . . And the trochee was commissioned by a thief in exchange for sugar . . ." Not surprisingly, Solzhenitsyn shared something of this experience.

[17]Nadezhda Mandel'shtam, *Vospominaniia* (New York: Chekhov Publishing Corporation, 1970), p. 289.

[18]*Krutoi marshrut* (Milan: Mondadori, 1967); this translation from Evgenia S. Ginzburg, *Into the Whirlwind,* trans. Paul Stevenson and Manya Harari (Harmondsworth: Penguin, 1967), p. 157.

[19]"Zaklinatel' zmei," *Novyi zhurnal,* No. 86 (1967), pp. 10-16.

[20]Printed anonymously in *Sovetskaia potaennaia muza,* p. 127. On Slutskii's authorship see L. Donatov, "Kogda russkaia proza ushla v lageria . . . ," *Posev,* 24 (Sept. 1968), 45.

He too created and memorized poems and plays in verse during his years in the camps. The most sombre of these works to reach the West has as its refrain Pushkin's line, "God, Do Not Let Me Lose My Mind!"[21] In it Solzhenitsyn describes how dearly he has bought his right to be a poet: he writes of his mother, who died alone and destitute, of the years of marriage stolen from him, of the cries of children he will never father. To this price he adds the deaths and ruined lives of countless fellow-prisoners. His poem is a precious burden, "the dripping of fragrant resin in a chopped-down forest," and he looks forward to the moment when he will at last release his memory and commit the lines to paper in the seclusion of his place of exile.

During his three years of "exile in perpetuity" in Southern Kazakhstan Solzhenitsyn fulfilled his pledge, leading a dual existence, as school-teacher and writer "for the desk-drawer." This continued after the Twentieth Party Congress of 1956, when he was permitted to return to Central Russia. The factual and speculative aspects of his literary debut in 1962 need not be repeated here.[22] Suffice to say that Solzhenitsyn effected the transition from surreptitious to officially recognized writer with dramatic suddenness, and apparently without involvement in the nascent *samizdat* of those years. For the late 1950's saw the growth of a new phase in the uncensored literary life of the Soviet Union. Although the name itself would not gain currency until after 1966, that year marked a coming-of-age rather than a beginning.

Samizdat was born out of the spasmodic easing of literary controls which followed the death of Stalin and the public criticism of his dictatorship initiated by Khrushchev. This is not to say, of course, that the Party abdicated its responsibility for the ideological content of literary output. It did mean, however, that a measure of genuine debate was to be tolerated here as in other walks of life, and that miscreant writers would henceforth be disciplined as writers rather than as political offenders,

[21]"Pust' b'iutsia stroki—ne shepni . . ." (1948-1950), one of three poems or excerpts cited in D. Blagov (pseud. of Veniamin Teush), "A. Solzhenitsyn i dukhovnaia missiia pisatelia" (not publ. in the Soviet Union, dated "autumn 1963"), *Sobr. soch.* (VI, 308-309).

[22]See, e.g., Michel Tatu, *Power in the Kremlin: From Khrushchev's Decline to Collective Leadership* (London: Collins, 1969), pp. 247-248; Peter Benno, "The Political Aspect," in *Soviet Literature in the Sixties: An International Symposium*, eds. Max Hayward and Edward L. Crowley (London: Methuen, 1965), pp. 191-192; and David Burg and George Feifer, *Solzhenitsyn* (New York: Stein and Day, 1972), Chs. XX and XXI.

to be swept away at the first sign of heterodoxy. As it became clear that some kind of "sincerity in literature"[23] was once again compatible with physical survival, any attempt to stem the tide was likely to lead to the opening of alternative channels. Thus in the latter part of the 1950's the desk-drawers gradually yielded up their well-guarded contents, and manuscripts circulated privately on a scale which had been impossible for decades. Evtushenko recalls how Boris Slutskii once showed him drawers bulging with unpublished verse and reassured him that: "Our day will come. All we have to do is wait for that day and have something ready for it in our desks and in our hearts."[24] That day appeared to be dawning, although many examples of "camp" and "purge" literature, such as Lidiia Chukovskaia's *Opustelyi dom* [*Deserted House*] and Evgeniia Ginzburg's memoirs, would be submitted for publication in the wake of Solzhenitsyn's first triumph only to find that the breach had already been stemmed. Controversial works by Dudintsev, Iashin and Tendriakov appeared, as did the anthologies *Literaturnaia Moskva* [*Literary Moscow*] and *Tarusskie stranitsy* [*Pages from Tarusa*], thanks, in part at least, to censorship "irregularities." Other works which could not find a publisher, or which were, of their essence, unpublishable, found their way abroad and were published there. These ranged from Pasternak's *Dr. Zhivago* and the works of Siniavskii and Daniel' to comparatively obscure items such as Mikhail Naritsa's novel *Nespetaia pesnia* [*An Unsung Song*]. The uncertainties of Khrushchev's cultural policies did at least permit a degree of creative friction in the arts.

Moscow's Maiakovskii Square was the crucible from which emerged an amalgam characteristic of the early *samizdat*. In the summer of 1958, at a time when Solzhenitsyn was working on his *One Day in the Life of Ivan Denisovich* and *The First Circle*, the first spontaneous meetings were held at the foot of the newly erected statue to Maiakovskii. Thanks to eyewitness accounts, notably that of Vladimir Osipov,[25] we have an excellent picture, both of the events which lay behind the open-air *maiaki*, as they came to be called, and of the mood and atmo-

[23]The title of an article by V. Pomerantsev, "Ob iskrennosti v literature," *Novyi mir*, No. 12 (1953), pp. 218-245.

[24]Yevgeny Yevtushenko [Evgenii Evtushenko], *A Precocious Autobiography* (London: Collins and Harvill, 1963), p. 80.

[25]Vladimir Osipov, "Ploshchad' Maiakovskogo; stat'ia 70-aia" (Samizdat, 1970), *Grani*, 26, No. 80 (1971), 107-162.

sphere which dominated the gatherings up to their dispersal in 1961. These were amateur poetry-readings, accompanied by discussions, primarily of a literary nature. Apart from the works of established poets, the young people who assembled in the square on Saturday and Sunday evenings would recite their own unpublished verse, and it was but a short step from here to the creation of the first typewritten journal, *Sintaksis* [*Syntax*]. The existence of various unofficial student journals had been mentioned in the press as early as 1955, but they appear to have been mainly handwritten, and of extremely limited circulation.[26] *Syntax* was in a different category altogether. In 1960 a disapproving Soviet journalist noted: "Judging by the different type-faces, it has not just been printed in four or five copies to adorn the book-shelf of a poetry lover, but was intended to reach a significantly wider circle of readers."[27] In the winter and spring of 1959 and 1960 three issues appeared, under the editorship of Aleksandr Ginzburg. They were devoted almost exclusively to poetry of all shades, "formalistic, religious, frankly pro-Soviet, 'decadent,' anti-Stalinist, etc." (Osipov, p. 112). Other journals soon followed: *Bumerang* [*Boomerang*] in November 1960, edited by Osipov himself, and Iurii Galanskov's *Feniks* [*Phoenix*] in spring of the following year.

Although journals such as *Syntax* and *Phoenix* were, in L. Sergeeva's words, "created in an epoch when intellectual and spiritual searching was chiefly reflected in poetry,"[28] and as such were close to the spirit of the mass poetry-readings and Days of Poetry held in this period, the seeds of the later, socio-political phase of *samizdat* were already discernible in the preoccupations of at least some of the *maiakovtsy*. "Nineteen fifty-six had been the spring of hope," writes one of them, "but the spring had turned in its tracks, and in 1958 we found ourselves at a dead-end. It was this chaos of doubts and searchings which we brought into the spontaneous open-air club" (Osipov, p. 111). From mid-1960 the political aspect loomed ever larger. In 1961 Iurii Galanskov wrote that the authorities regarded

[26]See Alexander Steininger, *Literatur und Politik in der Sowjetunion nach Stalins Tod* (Wiesbaden: Otto Harrassowitz, 1965), pp. 99-100.

[27]Iu. Ivashchenko in *Izvestiia,* 2 Sept. 1960, cited in M. Osharov, "Iubilei Samizdata." Iosif Brodskii regards the term "journal" as inappropriate and estimates the number of copies of *Syntax* at 100 or less, see "Interview with Iosif Brodsky," *Index,* 1, Nos. 3/4 (1972), 151.

[28]"Samizdat: Vozniknovenie i budushchee," p. 42.

Maiakovskii Square as "a hotbed of anti-Sovietism,"[29] and another, unidentified *maiakovets* appealed to the Central Committee to set up a discussion club for young people, arguing that: "Full independence, free initiative—these are the demands of the young, and then they will show some concern for laws and ethics."[30] By the end of 1961 the unique public forum which the Square provided had been destroyed in a wave of press attacks, arrests, interrogations and reprisals. Henceforth the successors to *Syntax* and *Phoenix* would move increasingly towards the type of the mixed literary and socio-political journal, already discussed in the early 1960's. Such ventures were *Kolokol* [*The Bell*], *Russkoe slovo* [*The Russian Word*] and *Phoenix-66,* all of which appeared between 1965 and 1966. In the December 1965 issue of another such journal, *Tetrad'* [*The Notebook*], a poem by Iosif Brodskii and one of Solzhenitsyn's prose poems, "Ozero Segden" ["Lake Segden"] appear between the same covers as an article entitled "Who Killed Trotskii?" and other publicistic materials.[31] By the late 1960's this tendency would culminate in the appearance of *samizdat* journals with little or no literary content, including the celebrated *Khronika tekushchikh sobytii* [*Chronicle of Current Events*], Valerii Chalidze's *Obshchestvennye problemy* [*Social Problems*], and *Ukrainskii vestnik* [*The Ukrainian Herald*].

Thus, at the turn of the decade and on the eve of Solzhenitsyn's emergence as a public figure, some of the outstanding names in the later history of *samizdat,* Galanskov, Ginzburg, Vladimir Bukovskii et al., were already undergoing their baptism of fire. These years saw a marked hardening in what had been relatively fluid official attitudes towards spontaneous expression and publication. Moreover, they gave a number of idealistic young people a firsthand insight into the way in which the provisions of the Soviet Constitution could be vitiated by the official countenancing of procedural "irregularities" and by a mechanical interpretation and application of the article of the Criminal Code intended to combat "anti-Soviet agitation and propaganda." Osipov writes of how the baton borne by the *maiakovtsy* would, some years later, "be taken up by the 'constitutionalists,' who

[29]"Pis'mo Iuriia Galanskova v Komitet Gosudarstvennoi Bezopasnosti," *Russkaia mysl',* 20 April 1968.

[30]E. A., "Pis'mo v TsK KPSS po povodu publichnogo chteniia i diskussii na ploshchadi Maiakovskogo," *ibid.*

[31]For a facsimile of the list of contents see L. Sergeeva, "Samizdat: Vozniknovenie i budushchee," p. 43.

chose the statue of Pushkin as the site of their meetings" (p. 136). He is referring to the period following the arrest of Siniavskii and Daniel in the autumn of 1965, a date which marks the beginning of a new intensity and a new spirit in *samizdat.* As will be seen, Solzhenitsyn's own experiences closely parallel the events of these years.

Solzhenitsyn's attitude towards the phenomenon of *samizdat* publication develops perceptibly from a passive curiosity to a feeling of protectiveness and sympathy. It is singularly apt that even his first published work, *One Day in the Life of Ivan Denisovich,* which appeared with the explicit support of the First Secretary of the Communist Party, should have enjoyed a brief unofficial circulation prior to its publication in *Novyi mir* in November 1962. D. Blagov alleges that the story was privately duplicated despite stringent precautions to prevent copies from leaving the *Novyi mir* offices, and speaks of it "whistling," as through the chinks in a vacuum chamber, and finding its way to "thousands of readers."[32] Reviewing *One Day* . . . in the official press in January 1963, I. Drutse confirms that its fame had spread before even the awaited issue of *Novyi mir* appeared on the newsstands; rumors had given way to detailed paraphrase even before the advance distribution of proof copies to reviewers.[33] It has been observed that submission of a talented, but ideologically eccentric work to a publishing house or editorial board in those years almost guaranteed "quasi-publication" or "crypto-publication" of the *samizdat* sort.[34] In Solzhenitsyn's case, however, this appeared, initially at least, to be an "accidental" occurrence, which the availability of authorized editions made irrelevant. With the benefit of hindsight it is clear that, in fact, the *official* publication, rather than the crypto-publication, was historically aberrant.

Some insight into Solzhenitsyn's reaction to the *samizdat* dissemination of his writings in the first half of the decade is afforded by the transcript of his meeting with the Writers' Union Secretariat in September 1967. Asked to explain the ap-

[32]D. Blagov, "Dukhovnaia missiia," pp. 311-312.

[33]I. Drutse, "O muzhestve i dostoinstve cheloveka," *Druzhba narodov,* No. 1 (1963), pp. 272-274, repr. in *Slovo probivaet sebe dorogu* (USSR: Samizdat, n.d.), p. 31.

[34]Peter Benno, "The Political Aspect," p. 193.

pearance of hundreds of typewritten copies of *Cancer Ward,* he replied:

> Well, it turns out that my works have some strange quality. People insistently ask to read them, and once they've taken them to read they re-type them in their own time, or at their own expense, and pass them on to others to read . . . Three years ago my "micro-stories" or poems in prose were circulated just as rapidly. I'd no sooner begun to let people read them, than they had flown from one Soviet city to the next. (VI, 38)

Solzhenitsyn's tone combined irony, directed at his interlocutors, with something resembling amused surprise at the industry shown by the *samizdatchiki.* The scene has strong historical echoes. In a letter of June 1825 to S. N. Begichev, Griboedov complained that: "Everyone is pestering me with requests for the manuscript [of *The Misfortune of Being Clever*]."[35] Twelve years later an obscure young cornet in the Life-Guards, Mikhail Lermontov, was called upon to account for his behaviour in composing and disseminating a "seditious" poem, "Death of a Poet" (1837). His statement reads, in part: "When I wrote my poem on the death of Pushkin (which I unfortunately did precipitously), my good friend Raevskii, not finding anything illegal in my verses, asked if he could copy them; he probably showed them to someone else as a novelty, and in this way they passed around."[36]

Such allusions to Russia's literary past are by no means irrelevant to the present discussion. One of the most intriguing features of Solzhenitsyn's works is their relationship to earlier literary traditions, and above all to aspects of the nineteenth century Russian literary heritage which were "discontinued" after 1917 or during the literary *Gleichschaltung* of the early 1930's. His deliberate practice of citing or evoking the words, themes, and ethical preoccupations of Pushkin, Turgenev, Dostoevsky and Tolstoy adds a rich dimension to works which are still all too often regarded as mere fictionalized autobiography. When the official Soviet attitude towards Solzhenitsyn began to change from 1963 onwards, and particularly after his unsuccessful candidacy for the Lenin Prize in Literature, it was precisely the alleged archaism, inertia and "Karataevism" (after

[35]Cited in A. S. Griboedov, *Gore ot uma,* ed. N. K. Piksanov and A. L. Grishunina (Moscow: Nauka, 1969), p. 331.

[36]"Ob"iasnenie korneta leib-gvardii Gusarskogo polka Lermantova," cited in V. Manuilov, *Letopis' zhizni i tvorchestva M. Iu. Lermontova* (Moscow-Leningrad: Nauka, 1964), p. 73.

the God-fearing peasant, Platon Karataev, in Tolstoy's *War and Peace*) of Ivan Denisovich and Matrena Vasil'evna which were seized upon by his critics. They endeavored to depict Solzhenitsyn as a writer locked in the stifling atmosphere of nineteenth-century "abstract" humanism, a mystical, pessimistic world-view, unalleviated by that capacity to comprehend reality in its revolutionary development which is expected of the creators of Socialist Realism. The frequent remoteness of such assessments from the texts on which they were ostensibly based did not prevent them from being canonized and from contributing substantially to Solzhenitsyn's progressive disfranchisement as a Soviet writer. Ironically, this process could not but force his works into the realm of Russia's alternative literary life, thereby establishing him in another of Russia's venerable literary lineages, that of the writer beset by officialdom, but read in spite of it.

The essentially passive phase of Solzhenitsyn's experiences with *samizdat* came to an end during the critical period from autumn 1965 to summer 1968. In these years he fought and lost a campaign to secure publication of his works, notably *Cancer Ward,* through official channels, falling foul, in the process, of the KGB, the Soviet Writers' Union and virtually the whole of the Soviet press. By summer 1968 his position within his homeland had changed dramatically; circumstances had for the first time forced him actively to seek the support of public opinion; his unpublished works were circulating in an astounding number of copies (Tvardovskii speaks of thousands)[37] and had appeared abroad, providing the Writers' Union with a welcome pretext for a *de facto* expulsion, which was formalized the following year. A more detailed consideration of some of these events may help to explain the particular warmth with which Solzhenitsyn was later to recall the achievements of "our noble *samizdat.*"[38]

A tragi-comic finale to the period of predominantly literary and cultural dissidence epitomized by the Maiakovskii Square readings was the brief heyday of SMOG, an abbreviation which may be deciphered in at least three different ways. Composed

[37] In his letter of 7-15 January 1968 to Konstantin Fedin (VI, 73).

[38] "Interv'iu A. Solzhenitsyna zapadnym korrespondentam 30 marta 1972," *Vestnik Russkogo Studencheskogo Khristianskogo Dvizheniia,* No. 103 (1, 1972), p. 191. Contrast the reference to "the notorious *samizdat*" in one of the most recent Soviet articles to attack Solzhenitsyn: V. Ozerov, " 'Dukhovnaia elita' ili boitsy partii?" *Znamia,* No. 4 (1973), p. 199.

almost entirely of amateur poets at Moscow's various institutes of higher learning, the group asserted its right to read and publish its own verse and to disavow the hallowed tenets of Socialist Realism. The SMOG-ists did not eschew confrontation in the cause of freedom of expression. After organizing readings and discussions during 1964 with a bravado reminiscent of the "yellow-blouse" iconoclasm of Maiakovskii's early Futurist days, they held a well-publicized meeting and demonstration in April 1965 which was duly attended by plain-clothes KGB operatives and *druzhinniki* ["vigilantes"]. One observer of the SMOG episode and the reprisals taken after its disintegration has attempted to locate it in the cultural and political currents of that time: "Now, after some ten years have elapsed, I personally see SMOG as nothing less than a natural manifestation of the troubled background to the last . . . months of Khrushchev's 'thaw,' when the country's intellectuals lived in nervous anticipation of the position which the authorities would finally adopt with regard to questions of artistic creativity."[39] Uncertainty came to an end with the arrest of Siniavskii and Daniel' in September 1965, and the almost simultaneous confiscation of typescripts of Solzhenitsyn's *The First Circle,* together with his literary archive, from the home of one of his acquaintances. The arrest and trial of the two lesser known writers marks a watershed, and is widely accepted as the prelude to the appearance of *samizdat* proper. By intimation and example the KGB made it known that the unofficial preparation and dissemination of written materials was henceforth to be regarded as reprehensible *per se,* and new legislation introduced in September 1966 put teeth into this threat.[40] Such terms as "slanderous fabrications" and "anti-Soviet" content acquired a corresponding elasticity, and the scene was set for the best-known and best-documented *causes célèbres* in the recent history of dissent in Russia: Ginzburg's compilation of a transcript and other materials on the Siniavskii-Daniel' trial led to his own arrest in January 1967

[39]A. Dror, "Samoe molodoe obshchestvo . . . ," *Posev,* 29 (April 1973), 33.

[40]Article 190-1 of the Criminal Code was directed against "the systematic dissemination by word of mouth of deliberate fabrications discrediting the Soviet political and social system, or the manufacture or dissemination in written, printed or other form of works of the same content." It provided a more versatile weapon against *samizdat* than the existing article 70, which dealt specifically with "fabrications" manufactured and disseminated "*for the purpose of* subverting or weakening Soviet power, or of committing particular especially dangerous crimes against the state" (Emphasis added—M.N.). See Peter Reddaway, ed., *Uncensored Russia,* p. 11.

along with others who had engaged in comparable "anti-Soviet agitation and propaganda"; Bukovskii, Delone, and a group of companions who protested in Pushkin Square against these latest arrests were detained in their turn and eventually brought to trial on a variety of charges, from "hooliganism" to unlawful assembly.[41]

In these momentous years a pattern was established of kangaroo courts, calling forth protests, open letters and "white books" of otherwise inaccessible documentation, and, inevitably, generating further arrests and repression. The uncensored typewritten "press" reduplicated hundreds of appeals against closed or blatantly biased hearings. *Glasnost'* [publicity] and *zakonnost'* [legality] became unifying slogans, and the rapid adoption of the name *samizdat* itself testifies eloquently to a growing sense of identity. For the editors of the *Chronicle of Current Events* 1968 was a year of transition: "In this year *samizdat* has not been enriched by a single major prose work, as it was in past years by such works as the novels of Solzhenitsyn, the memoirs of Evgeniia Ginzburg, the collections of stories by Shalamov . . . ; during the year no literary miscellany such as *Syntax* or *Phoenix* has appeared. On the other hand, the readers of *samizdat* (they are also its volunteer publishers) have received during the year a regular flow of documents, open letters, speeches, commentaries, articles, news items, etc."[42] From 1968 dates the feeling, among sections of the intelligentsia, that *samizdat* is reporting on and chronicling a process or "movement." Whether any such coherent dissident movement actually exists, and whether Solzhenitsyn is a participant in it, are questions which must be considered in due course.

Solzhenitsyn's struggle during the mid-1960's was distinct, yet by no means unrelated. He has been ever loath to tolerate distractions from his consuming vocation, as more than one would-be interviewer has learned to his cost. Yet the confiscation

[41]A number of collections of materials relating to these and other trials are available in English: Leopold Labedz and Max Hayward, eds., *On Trial. The Case of Sinyavsky (Tertz) and Daniel (Arzhak)* (London: Collins and Harvill, 1967); *The Trial of the Four. A Collection of Materials on the Case of Galanskov, Ginzburg, Dobrovolsky and Lashkova 1967-68,* compiled by Pavel Litvinov, ed. Peter Reddaway (London: Longman, 1972); Pavel Litvinov, ed., *The Demonstration on Pushkin Square* (London: Collins and Harvill, 1969); and Natalia Gorbanevskaya, *Red Square at Noon* (London: Andre Deutsch, 1972).

[42]*Chronicle of Current Events,* No. 5 (December 1968) in Peter Reddaway, ed., *Uncensored Russia,* p. 350.

of his manuscripts and the mounting pressure of which it was symptomatic could not go unanswered. Private letters proved ineffective. Meanwhile, public readings from his works planned for 1966 were cancelled, and, in spite of the somewhat anachronistic appearance of "Zakhar-Kalita" in January of that year, it was soon evident that *Novyi mir* would be no more able to honor its agreement to publish *Cancer Ward* than it had been in the case of *The First Circle.* Accordingly, Solzhenitsyn cast about for a wider audience. A meeting of rank-and-file members of the Moscow Writers' Organization, convened at his request in November 1966, discussed *Cancer Ward,* expressing itself overwhelmingly in support of publication, and directing its officials to assist the passage of the book. The euphoric atmosphere which prevailed at the meeting had little or nothing to do with the realities of the day, and *Cancer Ward* was blocked again, even though it had been partially set up in type. At the same time, Solzhenitsyn's pilfered manuscripts, far from being returned to him, were circulating in the very antipole of *samizdat,* a secret limited edition officially distributed as ammunition in the campaign to discredit and silence him. It was against this background that Solzhenitsyn laboriously typed out his appeal to the Fourth Writers' Congress in May 1967, sending a copy to each of the several hundred delegates. The letter was concerned with the fate of Russian literature, with the baneful consequences of censorship, that "relic of the middle ages" (VI, 7), and with the abject failure of the Writers' Union to defend its members against victimization. Only limited success attended this venture. Despite letters of support from over 100 of Solzhenitsyn's fellow-writers, the presidium allowed no discussion of the appeal. Needless to say, it circulated widely in *samizdat,* earning for Solzhenitsyn the enduring hatred of certain members of the Board of the Soviet Writers' Union, who regarded the public washing of dirty linen and the resulting "clamor" in the West as far greater evils than any which exercised Solzhenitsyn.

There was no question of Solzhenitsyn deliberately and demonstratively scorning the use of accepted channels in favor of *samizdat,* as had certainly been the case with some of the young poets of earlier years. Indeed, in 1967 and 1968, *samizdat* revealed itself as something of a double-edged weapon. Uncontrollable proliferation within the country meant that sooner or later copies would fall into the hands of Western journalists, diplomats or tourists and find their way into print beyond the borders of the Soviet Union. In the case of an open letter, or the transcript of a meeting held *in camera,* foreign publication might increase the possibility of repercussions. At the same time, those who circulated such materials did so in order to overcome a communications barrier and the added resonance of foreign publication could actually help to achieve this aim. However, seeing his stories and novels surface in Western Europe was a far more disturbing experience for Solzhenitsyn. As has so often been emphasized, he regards himself above all as a Russian writer, and addresses himself in the first instance to his fellow-countrymen. Where *samizdat* provided a makeshift substitute for, and in certain cases might even stimulate, a more desirable form of mass-publication, foreign publication could so incense the authorities as to seriously damage the chances of the work ever reaching more than a fraction of the Russian reading public. It was considerations such as these which led Solzhenitsyn to exercise rigorous control over manuscript copies of *August 1914* until all hope of official publication had passed. The importance of distinguishing between literary and non-literary writings when discussing Solzhenitsyn's attitude towards *samizdat* is illustrated by his position in early 1968, when he was obliged to employ the *samizdat* network in an attempt to avert a danger to which *samizdat* itself had inadvertently contributed: *Cancer Ward* had passed out of his control and might soon be published abroad without his approval if the competent authorities continued to hold up its scheduled appearance at home.

A similar warning sent to *Literaturnaia gazeta* in April 1968 was published some three months later when Solzhenitsyn's fears had already become reality.[43] The accompanying editorial comment gave a very clear picture of the official view of Solzhenitsyn's relationship to *samizdat* during those years. It was a sharply worded and wide-ranging attack on the whole spectrum of dissent among Soviet intellectuals and on its external manifestation, *samizdat.* Galanskov and Ginzburg were two of the targets identified by name, and mention was made of those irresponsible writers who had signed letters in support of them and their ilk. Solzhenitsyn's behaviour was then presented as part and parcel of this wider malaise: he had left

[43]*Literaturnaia gazeta,* 26 June 1968. The editorial commentary, "Otvetstvennost' pisatelia," is reprinted in *Sobr. soch.* (VI, 104-115).

typescript copies of his works in the care of a man known to have delivered anti-Soviet materials abroad, thus effectively relinquishing control of them; he had sent his letter to the Fourth Writers' Congress, "obviously calculating that it would be even further duplicated, but this time in an uncontrolled manner, and would pass from hand to hand, becoming a literary sensation" (VI, 110); furthermore, he had circulated two letters in which he expressed "feigned alarm" at the prospect of *Cancer Ward* being published in the West, together with a "tendentious, extremely unobjective" transcript of his meeting with the secretaries of the Writers' Union (VI, 113). Lest the point be missed, *Literaturnaia gazeta* rewrote Solzhenitsyn's biography in order to insinuate that he was *justly* punished in 1945 for anti-Soviet activity (criticizing Stalin!), and confined its analysis of his works to a single play, written in a labour camp some twenty years before and purloined in its only extant copy by the KGB.

This is the point at which discussion, or indeed any pretense of discussion, disappears once and for all from official Soviet coverage of Solzhenitsyn's life and works. Henceforth his works are by definition "anti-Soviet" (even when they are set in tsarist Russia), the channels by which he transmits them are by definition "illicit," and any of his statements which cannot be ignored altogether are by definition "fabrications" or "distortions." None the less, *Literaturnaia gazeta's* blanket condemnation of *samizdat,* dissidence and Solzhenitsyn does invite comment. Certainly Solzhenitsyn was, as has been seen, "involved" willy-nilly with *samizdat.* It had adopted his works, and helped to ventilate his grievances. Nor is *Literaturnaia gazeta's* decision to mention him in the same breath as Galanskov and Ginzburg entirely inappropriate. For several of the many letters of protest which found their way into *samizdat* during and after the "Trial of the Four," as it has come to be known, ranged far beyond the case in point. They touched upon all manner of "Stalinist" illegalities in contemporary Soviet society, the treatment of minorities, the stifling of all forms of intellectual creativity, and a number of them mentioned Solzhenitsyn specifically: "What were our homegrown bosses thinking of, shutting Solzhenitsyn's mouth . . . ?" (I. Iakhimovich); "There is room in our literature for the paltry works of Kochetov . . . But only the fortunate few have been able to read Solzhenitsyn's *Cancer Ward*" (I. Gabai, Iu. Kim and P. Iakir); "I pity those readers who do not know that there is a great Russian writer living and working in the land of Russia, Solzhenitsyn, the author of the novels *Cancer Ward* and *The First Circle,* and the plays *Candle in the Wind* and *The Love-Girl and the Innocent*" (L. Pliushch).[44] The crucial distinction is that Solzhenitsyn has never been a "joiner," a "signer," or a "demonstrator." His understanding of the potential of true literature is such as to make literary creation itself a profoundly social act. "Beauty will save the world," he says in his Nobel Lecture,[45] echoing Dostoevsky, and it is at this level that the active dissidents appear most often to respond to him. Certainly, he is respected as a man who has demonstrated his readiness to speak out on matters of public concern. But it is as the author of works which combine talent with integrity that Solzhenitsyn is perhaps closest to Iakhimovich, Gabai or Galanskov and Ginzburg themselves. For the world of Solzhenitsyn's fiction offers amplification and confirmation of the individual act of conscience, and his personal example of dedication and fortitude is felt in every line he writes.

While preferring not to become embroiled in the politics of dissent, Solzhenitsyn has lent his strong support to individuals and "causes" on more than one occasion since 1968. Do these actions constitute some kind of affiliation with an identifiable "Democratic Movement" in the Soviet Union? Probably nobody would claim that the many hundreds of *samizdat* items known in the West, and including a vast body of documents prepared by representatives of national and religious minorities, reflect an identity of interests, grievances and goals. On the other hand, many observers, both within the Soviet Union and without, have discerned what they feel to be a common denominator in the various dissident factions. Naoum Odnopozov, a former "underground poet," writes: "democratization is a common platform, but on the forms which it should take, a discussion is in progress."[46] Among the best-known contributions to that discussion is Andrei Amal'rik's essay, "Will the Soviet Union Survive Until 1984?" In it he distinguishes between the earlier period of unofficial publishing, which he terms the "Cultural Opposition," and the *samizdat* which developed after 1965:

[44]*The Trial of the Four,* compiled by Pavel Litvinov, pp. 236, 245 and 335.
[45]*Les Prix Nobel en 1971* (Stockholm: Nobel Foundation, 1972), pp. 130-131.
[46]Naoum Odnopozov, "Life in the Soviet Underground," *Sunday Times,* 14 Jan. 1968.

"Nevertheless, *samizdat,* like the Cultural Opposition, gradually gave birth to a new independent force which can already be regarded as a real political opposition to the regime, or, at least, as a political opposition in embryo."[47] Although it lacks organizational form, it has a sense of cohesion, a body of activists or "leaders," and a number of common aims and traditions. Moreover, Amal'rik argues, the movement desires and actively seeks legal status and full publicity for its activities. Peter Reddaway gives cautious support to the notion that a Democratic Movement is indeed in the making:

> . . . the Democratic Movement is essentially middle and upper-middle class. Launched partly through the unification of groups in the natural sciences and the humanities, it has yet to make any serious appeal to "the people" or "*narod*." Not surprisingly, therefore, its adherents are few in number: only about two thousand mainstream members have so far dared to identify themselves deliberately by name. Clearly, however, these people receive support from many thousands of sympathizers who, while reading and circulating *samizdat,* prefer for various reasons to stop short of signing protests, forming groups or demonstrating.[48]

Added authority for this view would appear to have come in the form of a new *samizdat* journal, *Svobodnaia mysl'* [*Free Thought*], the first issue of which is dated 20 December 1971. *Free Thought* sets itself the goal of "promoting the exchange of opinions on pressing theoretical and practical questions of the Democratic Movement,"[49] and assumes throughout that the existence of such a movement is self-evident. However, it must be emphasized at once that *Free Thought* has yet to establish its credentials as an organ of dissident opinion in the Soviet Union, and at this stage only the most tentative conclusions may be drawn from its appearance. This new socio-political journal pays considerable attention to the minutiae of arranging subscriptions, contributions and delivery in such a way as to protect the identities of those involved, and its first article discusses the desirability of moving more swiftly from the amateurish and wasteful methods of *samizdat* towards a new concept of *kolizdat* ["collective publishing"].[50] *Kolizdat* is used to designate a far more rationalized and better organized form of *samizdat* activity, in which the gap between type-

[47]Andrei Amalrik, *Will the Soviet Union Survive Until 1984?* (New York and Evanston: Harper and Row, 1970), pp. 9-10.

[48]Peter Reddaway, *Uncensored Russia,* p. 23.

[49]*Svobodnaia mysl'. Obshchestvenno-politicheskii zhurnal,* Vypusk 1 (20 Dec. 1971), repr. in *Vol'noe slovo* (Frankfurt am Main), No. 7 (1973), p. 5.

[50]S. Topolev, "Ot samizdata k kolizdatu," *ibid.,* pp. 10-27.

writer and printing-press would be bridged by wider use of hectographs, mimeographs and a variety of other mechanical duplicating processes. Whether the term and the ideas behind it will gain currency remains to be seen. The strongest warning against overestimating the incipient Democratic Movement has come from the late Tibor Szamuely, who regards the title itself as a misnomer.[51] According to Szamuely, the mainstream of *samizdat* could more accurately be called a "civil rights movement" and is essentially "a movement of the intelligentsia, by the intelligentsia and for the intelligentsia." Liberal appeals for freedom to hold and express opinions not shared by those in power, for creative freedom in the arts and freedom of research and consultation in the sciences, have no appeal in the country at the grass-roots level, and are politically an irritant rather than a threat: "An unbridgeable abyss divides *samizdat* from the Soviet population," writes Szamuely, and even within *samizdat* the alliance between the liberal civil rights wing and such radical factions as the Ukrainian nationalists is temporary, if not illusory. Whatever conclusion is reached as to the nature and effectiveness of the Democratic Movement, the concept exists, and it is appropriate that Solzhenitsyn's public commitment in recent years should be considered in the light of the foregoing discussion.

In general such selective gestures of identification as Solzhenitsyn has chosen to make have been with the civil rights mainstream, an assertion which requires immediate qualification. Solzhenitsyn is not insensitive to the suffering of persecuted national and religious minorities and evidence of this fact may be found in his earliest published works. The composition of Ivan Denisovich's labor camp accurately reflects the treatment of the smaller nations under Stalin. In *Cancer Ward* they are represented by such figures as Federau, a Volga German, and Sibgatov, a Crimean Tatar. Forcibly deported to Central Asia in 1944 for their alleged collective betrayal of the Soviet Union, the Crimean Tatars have been campaigning since 1956 for the right to return. By 1968, when contact was made with Russian civil-rights dissidents, the Crimean Tatars had already collected more than three million signatures on countless letters and petitions. Apart from nominal rehabilitation in 1967 they achieved nothing. This lends particular poignancy to the scene in which

[51]Tibor Szamuely, "The Future of Soviet Dissent," *Spectator,* 22 July 1972, pp. 132-133. Quotations in this paragraph are from p. 133 of Szamuely's article.

Sibgatov, called upon to answer Tolstoy's question "What do men live by?", utters a single word, *rodinoi* [homeland] (II, 121). An even greater qualification must be made in the case of Solzhenitsyn's concern for the fate of oppressed religious believers. One need only recall the sympathetic portrayal of Alesha the Baptist in *One Day in the Life of Ivan Denisovich* or of the ethereal Agniia in *The First Circle*. Further evidence of his involvement in the Russian Orthodox Church's struggle for survival in an officially atheistic society is provided by his "Lenten Letter" to the Patriarch, and the subsequent exchange with Father Sergii Zheludkov.[52]

The cause of civil and human rights in the Soviet Union derived a considerable impetus from the foundation of the *Chronicle of Current Events* in 1968, International Human Rights Year. The journal appropriately took as its epigraph a quotation from the Universal Declaration of Human Rights, and after 1968 issues bore the heading "Human Rights Year in the Soviet Union Continues." Solzhenitsyn's sympathy with this cause is deeply rooted in his personal experiences and reflected in a variety of ways in his writings and thought. Thus, in his insistence upon the need for openness and publicity, he speaks not simply as a writer but as a trained scientist and a member of that scientific and cultural intelligentsia which has so influenced the *samizdat* era. In *Candle in the Wind* the scientist Terbol'm uses a model of the human brain to illustrate the flow of information within a healthy society. Threads of light are seen constantly darting to and fro between all the individual cells of the organism, demonstrating the cybernetic principles of "information, co-ordination and feedback" (V, 173). The alternative presented is that of an organically inert paradigm, a pyramidic structure in which information flows only from the apex downwards. Years later Solzhenitsyn would return to scientific comparisons when composing his Nobel Lecture: "Contemporary science knows that suppression of information leads to entropy and universal destruction."[53] Similar warnings are expressed throughout his literary and publicistic writings. Thus, in "For the Good of the Cause" Lidiia Georgievna reminds the secretary of the *partbiuro* of Lenin's words: "Lenin taught us:

[52]Solzhenitsyn's "Velikopostnoe pis'mo" appeared in *Russkaia mysl'*, 30 March 1972, Zheludkov's reply *ibid.*, 22 June 1972, and both, together with Solzhenitsyn's response to Zheludkov, in *Vestnik RSKhD*, No. 103 (1, 1973), pp. 145-149, 156-159.

[53]*Les Prix Nobel en 1971*, p. 137.

Do not be afraid of publicity! Publicity is a healing sword!" (I, 277). In an open letter to the Secretariat of the Soviet Writers' Union following his expulsion in November 1969 Solzhenitsyn wrote that mankind is set apart from the animal world by the power of thought and speech: "But if these are fettered, then we revert to the animal state. *Publicity,* full and honest *publicity*—this is the first condition of health in any society, including our own" (VI, 149-150).

Solzhenitsyn has not confined himself to broad statements of principle. He has protested against the political persecution of those who share his attachment to freedom of expression and to *samizdat* as one means of attaining it. The year 1970 provides two instances. On 29 May Zhores Medvedev, an outstanding genetecist and close acquaintance of Solzhenitsyn, was forcibly interned in a psychiatric hospital. The details of this incident are set out in a book which Zhores wrote in collaboration with his brother Roy.[54] The fact that a typescript copy of an unfinished work on international scientific co-operation, which Medvedev had hoped eventually to publish, had fallen into the hands of the KGB no doubt played a part, as also did his open letter on the occasion of Solzhenitsyn's expulsion from the Writers' Union some six months previously. When, after two weeks, Medvedev's relatives, friends and colleagues had been unable to effect his release, Solzhenitsyn contacted Medvedev's brother and told him of his desire to make a statement in defence of Medvedev and "all others imprisoned in psychiatric hospitals."[55] The offer was accepted and Solzhenitsyn's declaration, dated 14 June 1970 circulated widely and rapidly.

Though primarily a bid to help a friend in distress, the statement "This Is the Way We Live!" may be set in a wider context. Solzhenitsyn's abhorrence of the abuse of psychiatry is of long standing. The play, *Candle in the Wind,* was written in the early 1960's at a time when such practices were not yet systematically applied against Soviet citizens who declined to conform. A central theme of the play is scientific interference with the human personality. Set in an indeterminate country at some time in the future, it shows the threat from an irresponsible branch of cybernetics which proposes to "neurostabilize" people

[54]Zhores A. Medvedev and Roy A. Medvedev, *Kto sumasshedshii?* (London: Macmillan, 1971). An English translation, *A Case of Madness,* was brought out in the same year and by the same publisher.

[55]*Kto sumasshedshii?*, p. 99.

who fall short of rigid criteria of normality. Soon the military authorities recognize the project's potential and guarantee to fund its development. The "candle" of the title is the flickering flame of the human soul threatened by the "terrible wind" (V, 167) of a science which has chosen to disregard the voice of conscience. Some years later the editor-in-chief of *Pravda* would publicly describe Solzhenitsyn himself as a "schizophrenic" and "a psychologically abnormal person" (VI, 58), and anonymous *agitatory* would echo the charge at closed meetings of party activists throughout the country. All of this can be felt in Solzhenitsyn's appeal: "This may happen tomorrow to any one of us . . . seizing free-thinking healthy people and locking them in mental homes is *spiritual murder* . . . It is short-sighted to think that you can live by constantly relying on force alone, constantly ignoring the objections of conscience."[56]

When he wrote that: "Some of the victims are widely known, many more are unknown,"[57] Solzhenitsyn may have had at least one such "unknown" man in mind. In October 1969, shortly before Solzhenitsyn was expelled from the Writers' Union, Vladimir Gershuni was arrested. He had been a supporter of the Action Group for the Defence of Civil Rights in the Soviet Union, a body formed in May 1969 after the arrest of Petr Grigorenko, a leading civil rights campaigner. The *Chronicle of Current Events* writes: "Gershuni is a man with an unusually highly developed instinct for justice. For him the struggle against lies is not a part of life, but the whole of it."[58] The *Chronicle* further reveals that Gershuni had been imprisoned for political offences some twenty years earlier and had served his sentence in the same labour camp as Solzhenitsyn and at the same time. In March 1970 Gershuni was judged to be a schizophrenic and was sentenced *in absentia* to detention in a psychiatric prison hospital for an unspecified time.

By the time it became known in October 1970 that Solzhenitsyn had been awarded the year's Nobel Prize for Literature, Medvedev was a free man once more. Gershuni, on the other hand, had been moved to Butyrki prison and was

[56]Cited *ibid.*, pp. 99-100.

[57]*Ibid.*, p. 100.

[58]*Chronicle of Current Events,* No. 11 (October 1969) in Peter Reddaway, ed., *Uncensored Russia,* p. 169. For further evidence that Solzhenitsyn was thinking of Gershuni see Per Egil Hegge, *Mellommann i Moskva* (Oslo: Cappelen, 1971), p. 100.

awaiting transfer to a special psychiatric prison.[59] This did not prevent him from adding his signature, by proxy, to a letter from thirty-seven Soviet intellectuals congratulating Solzhenitsyn upon the award.[60] Many of the names it bore are inseparable from the history of *samizdat,* such as those of Iakir, Bukovskii, Chalidze and Lashkova. Equally prominent among the signers were Zinaida Grigorenko, whose husband, Petr, had already been confined for over a year in a prison psychiatric hospital, and the mother of Aleksandr Ginzburg, still serving his sentence in a labour camp. At about the same time Solzhenitsyn must have been particularly moved to receive a message of congratulations smuggled out of the Pot'ma camp complex and signed by a group of prisoners, including Iurii Galanskov, who by then had only two more years to live. The text reads in part: "Barbed wire and automatic weapons prevent us from expressing to you personally the depth of our admiration for your courageous creative work, upholding the sense of human dignity and exposing the trampling down of the human soul and the destruction of human values."[61]

All of this must have been in Solzhenitsyn's mind as he sat down to compose his message to the Nobel Banquet in Stockholm. The ceremony was to be held on 10 December, International Human Rights Day, when Gershuni, Galanskov and scores of other prisoners would declare the now traditional hunger-strike. Thus it came about that Solzhenitsyn's message of greetings not only drew the attention of those present to the significance of the date, but, in a line which was not read out, urged: "Let us, at this richly laden table, not forget the political prisoners

[59]For further details see *Uncensored Russia,* pp. 169-170; *Khronika tekushchikh sobytii,* No. 2 (13), 30 April 1970, repr. in *Posev. Chetvertyi spetsial'nyi vypusk* (June 1970), p. 24; *Khronika,* No. 18 (5 March 1971), repr. in *Posev. Vos'moi spets. vyp.* (June 1971), pp. 41-42; Gershuni's notes from Orel special psychiatric prison appeared in *Khronika,* No. 19 (30 April 1971), repr. in *Posev. Deviatyi spets. vyp.* (Oct. 1971), pp. 4-6. Issues of the *Chronicle* from No. 16 onwards have been published in English by Amnesty International Publications (London).

[60]English in Leopold Labedz, ed., *Solzhenitsyn. A Documentary Record* (New York, Evanston, etc.: Harper and Row, 1971), pp. 214-215. For the Russian text, with a full list of signatures, see Radio Liberty *Arkhiv Samizdata,* No. 516.

[61]For this extract see Labedz, *Solzhenitsyn,* p. 219. The full text appeared in *Khronika,* No. 16 (31 Oct. 1970), repr. in *Posev. Shestoi spets. vyp.* (Feb. 1971), p. 29.

who are today on hunger strike for restitution of their limited rights, which have been completely trampled underfoot."[62]

It would be precipitate to interpret the events of December 1970 as a major new departure for Solzhenitsyn. The Nobel citation had referred to "the ethical force with which he has pursued the indispensable traditions of Russian literature,"[63] and one of these is undoubtedly the "civic" tradition. The idea that the writer's vocation brings with it obligations to the society in which he lives has never been lastingly challenged in Russia, although such commitment is by no means synonymous with political partisanship. Solzhenitsyn emphasized his adherence to this tradition in his Nobel Lecture: "Indeed, Russian literature has for decades tended to avoid losing itself in self-contemplation or blithe frivolity, and I am not ashamed to continue this tradition to the best of my powers. Russian literature has long fostered the innate idea that a writer can, and *ought* to do much for his people."[64] Under the circumstances, it would have been unthinkable for Solzhenitsyn to have allowed a banquet to be held in his honor on Human Rights Day without so much as an allusion to the suffering of the new generation of Soviet political prisoners. In *The First Circle* Gleb Nerzhin recalls with abhorrence the behavior of Soviet men of letters in the years following the murder of Kirov. Confronted on all hands with palpable falsehood, "Russian writers who dared to trace their lineage back to Pushkin and Tolstoy were composing nauseating, sugary eulogies on the tyrant" (III, 285). How could the author of these words, representing in the eyes of the whole world the "indispensable traditions of Russian literature," ignore the special meaning of Human Rights Day in his homeland?

Some eight years before the Nobel festivities in his honor Solzhenitsyn, the otherwise obscure author of a sensational first novel, had begun to receive letters from readers throughout the Soviet Union, many of them former and present labour camp inmates. These responses impressed him so deeply that he compiled and edited a collection of excerpts from them. When it became clear to even the most sanguine that *One Day in the Life of Ivan Denisovich* had not, after all, ushered in an era

[62]English in Labedz, *Solzhenitsyn,* p. 225. Russian in *Khronika,* No. 17 (31 Dec. 1970), repr. in *Posev. Vos'moi spets. vyp.* (June 1971), p. 7.

[63]See the facsimile of Solzhenitsyn's Nobel-Diploma in *Svenska Dagbladet,* 5 April 1972, p. 1.

[64]*Les Prix Nobel en 1971,* p. 135.

of truth and justice, the collection, which bore the title "They Are Reading *Ivan Denisovich*,"[65] began to circulate in *samizdat*. No clearer evidence of the inner consistency of Solzhenitsyn's literary and public career can be found than his introduction to the letters sent by present-day political prisoners. Dismissing the official enthusiasm for his novel, expressed in countless headlines to the effect that "it happened, but will never happen again,"[66] Solzhenitsyn writes: "As always, they have lied about the main thing. They make it sound as if we are now out of the mire. But we are still in it, even today. And this has particularly annoyed the present-day *zeks*" (V, 247). For them the story of Ivan Denisovich is a continuing saga; they await the sequel which will reveal how little things have improved. "Let the truth be told, and let things be changed! If words aren't concerned with deeds and don't lead to deeds, then what good are they? They're no more use than the barking of village dogs in the night" (V, 247).

Reaffirming this commitment in December 1970, Solzhenitsyn was not abandoning the pen in favor of the tribune. As at the beginning of his career, he spoke first and foremost as a writer intent on producing works which would not simply engender glib headlines, but, in the words of one of Ivan Denisovich's fellow-prisoners, would "arouse good feelings" (I, 64). Later, in his Nobel Lecture, Solzhenitsyn would declare his concern with the individual ethical sensibility as the touch-stone of a just, "organic" social order, and, at the same time, his faith in the ability of art to transform the world. As ever in Solzhenitsyn's writings, social commitment is ultimately subsumed under literary commitment, the endeavor to create works "which might express the mature thinking of the people, which might have a timely and salutory influence in the realm of the spirit or upon the development of social conscience . . ." (VI, 7).

Since the days when Solzhenitsyn's admirers first undertook the labor of copying out works, some of which ran to many hundreds of pages, *samizdat* has developed into a much-needed alternative medium for discussion and exchange of information. Far from competing with the official press, it has become, at least in Solzhenitsyn's case, the only source of reliable information and balanced comment available to a Soviet citizen. Where

[65]"Chitaiut *Ivana Denisovicha*" (V, 241-260).

[66]For examples see the bibliography of Soviet responses appended to this volume.

else can he find documented case after case in which Solzhenitsyn's works, public appeals and even his photograph have been confiscated during house-searches?[67] Where else can he read a 40,000-word compilation of reviews of *August 1914*[68] unconnected with the orchestrated "responses" to the novel with which *Literaturnaia gazeta* has regaled its readers? However tiny may be the percentage of the Soviet population which has access to *samizdat* channels, the value of any effort to retard the process of "entropy" may not be assessed exclusively in terms of statistics. At present *samizdat* is threatened as never before, and not simply by the latest wave of arrests and investigations, apparently aimed at suppressing the *Chronicle of Current Events* and breaking the back of the civil rights movement. A further threat has come in the form of the Soviet Union's accession to the International Copyright Convention, something which Solzhenitsyn could never have anticipated when, in 1968, he urged just such a move to protect the authors of *samizdat* works pirated by Western publishers (VI, 101). In April 1973 the text of a letter addressed to UNESCO became known, in which a group of Soviet citizens, including three full members of the Human Rights Committee, warned that the agreement might, in effect, lead to the *suppression* of authors' rights.[69]

Samizdat, in one form or another, is as old as the "Great Tradition" of Russian literature itself. It is hard to believe that it will prove less enduring. In March 1971, not long before his arrest, Petr Iakir wrote to the Presidium of the Twenty-Fourth Congress of the Soviet Communist Party in the following words: "*Samizdat* has appeared and stubbornly continues to exist. Surely this is a sign that the spiritual needs of society are not being properly satisfied? And surely imprisonment for *samizdat* publishing is no way to satisfy a spiritual hunger?"[70] It is for the spiritual sustenance which his works offer that Solzhenitsyn is revered in the world of *samizdat,* and not as a "leader of the political opposition." It seems appropriate to close this survey with the words which Petr Grigorenko wrote to Solzhenitsyn on the

[67]Since its creation, the *Chronicle of Current Events* has repeatedly provided such details.

[68]"*Avgust Chetyrnadtsatogo" chitaiut na rodine* (Moscow: Samizdat, 1972), repr. in Radio Liberty *Arkhiv Samizdata,* No. 1199, and published by the YMCA-Press (Paris), 1973.

[69]Peter Reddaway, "Russians Send Plea to West on Copyright," *Sunday Times,* 15 April 1973, p. 9.

[70]*Khronika,* No. 19 (reference as in note 59), p. 22.

occasion of his fiftieth birthday. Grigorenko, who now seems likely to end his life in a prison psychiatric hospital, typifies the "democratic" or civil rights movement which has grown up in direct association with *samizdat.* His message, unpublished except in *samizdat,* indicates the sense in which Solzhenitsyn and *samizdat* may be said to belong together. A great people, reaffirming its greatness in moments of moral extremity, brings forth titans, writes Grigorenko: "I am proud that my people has also shown itself capable of this. I bow before your titanic talent and wish, on this your fiftieth birthday, that it may continue to flourish and bear fruit for many, many years to come."[71]

[71] *Slovo probivaet sebe dorogu* (USSR: Samizdat, n.d.), p. 482.

Solzhenitsyn's Nationalism

BY ROSETTE C. LAMONT

The Roots of Nationalism

A young man is sitting in a railway station, waiting for a train to take him north from the Caucasus to Moscow. It is summer. On the platform, he is hailed by a plain-looking girl wearing a sensible, ugly hat, the kind supposed to protect you from the sun without adding to attractiveness. Isaakii—the youth—recognizes a Piatigorsk acquaintance, a school friend who harbored a crush on him. Varia, an orphan whose education was financed by a generous but remote guardian, had found in the serious gymnasium student an intellectual mentor. She had adopted as her own his Tolstoyan beliefs: pacifism, chastity—a rather extreme form that precluded holding hands and dancing at student balls—and vegetarianism. When Isaakii left for the university the two young people corresponded, always keeping in their letters the lofty moral tone that characterized their relationship. Though Varia met many cultured people in Petersburg, she never forgot her first friend, and it is clear as they meet that she still feels deep affection for him.

Now that fate has brought them together, Varia questions Isaakii as to his plans. Why is he leaving for Moscow three

"Solzhenitsyn's Nationalism.' Abridged from "Solzhenitsyn's 'Maimed Oak.'" From *Review of National Literatures,* III, No. 1 (Spring, 1972), 153-182.

weeks before the start of the academic year? War has been declared, yet it is unlikely, she points out, that a student at the end of his studies will be drafted. Isaakii avoids giving direct answers; he looks away. Varia, horrified, wonders: Could it be? He, the Tolstoyan, the liberal who taught her not to be in awe of the tsar, of unkempt priests, could he be volunteering? Isaakii meekly parries: This isn't the Russo-Japanese War! The Slavs, their brothers, have been attacked. Varia, shocked by her mentor's change of mind, will not listen. Logically she is right, but there are sentiments that transcend logic. Had Isaakii studied Pascal he might have quoted the *pensée:* "The heart has reasons reason does not know." Smiling apologetically, he can only venture: "My heart aches for Russia!"[1]

The first chapter of Solzhenitsyn's *August 1914* sets the tone for the rest of that first volume of what promises to be a trilogy. Nationalism, for this Russian novelist, is not an idea, an intellectual fabrication, but an affective reaction, deeply rooted in the subconscious. It has something to do with the soil, the ever-changing scenery—the high mountains of the Caucasus, the wooded, gently hilly country around Voronezh, "the spot where real Russia starts";[2] it has everything to do with the people, particularly country folk, and their profound faith in God and in their saints; it is connected to the full-bodied languages spoken in Georgia, the Ukraine, Belorussia, and the dialects of the various sections of this immense land. Divorced from political ideologies, from the transient rule of inept tsars or ruthless bureaucratic dictators, Solzhenitsyn's nationalism is as natural as a tree, deeply rooted in the subsoil of a culture and rising toward the heavens in a desire to transcend the immediate situation.

It is in this sense rather than on account of a controversial realism that Solzhenitsyn can be called the heir of both Tolstoy and Dostoevsky. National feeling for him, as for his predecessors, has little to do with patriotism. The latter is a political emotion, whereas Solzhenitsyn's is a spiritual one. It paradoxically transcends boundaries, being closer to Christian teaching than to geographical demarcations. To be, or to make oneself, deeply Russian is for Solzhenitsyn a way of reaching out beyond

[1]Aleksandr Solzhenitsyn. *Avgust chetyrnadtsatogo* (Paris: YMCA, 1971), p. 17. All quotations from *August 1914* in this essay have been translated by the present writer.

[2]*Ibid.*, p. 20.

Oriental Europe both to the West and to the East. As to Russia, it is not a place on a map, but an image shaped by the Russians in the way artists give form to their autonomous universes by means of words, colors, sounds. Dipping his language into the sphere of his characters, Solzhenitsyn re-creates Russia—symbol and deep spiritual reality. For those characters whose intertwined existences compose the polyphonic structure of the novels, the feeling for Russia constitutes a principle of regeneration.

In Chapter 21 of *August 1914,* two men meet on a battlefield. They exchange some thoughts in the course of a tense night of waiting for the German attack. The two are Major General Nechvolodov, and Artillery Colonel Smyslovskii. The latter knows that the general is the author of a Slavophile, patriotic book, and of a compilation of *Legends of the Russian Land* put together for the education of the people. More sophisticated than this traditionalist, the colonel does not esteem these works. "But, as the whole war seemed paltry before the greatness of the night sky, so did their differences pale accordingly."[3]

The mention of the oppressed Serbians leads into metaphysical speculations: How can one account for life on this small, accidental planet? Science yields to mystery. Life is the result of unknown forces. The general is pleased by the turn in the discussion since he holds there is more to life than the one-sidedness of military life. He raises a slight objection to the colonel's cosmological meditation: "Yes . . . you have a wide view . . . As for myself I cannot see wider than Russia."[4] Without replying, the colonel reflects inwardly that this is not a good thing. Indeed, he attributes this limitation to the fact that a man who is a fine military man wastes time on the writing of bad books, preferring this avocation to the exercise of his true talent.

As the conversation shifts, Colonel Smyslovskii gives up the subject of metaphysics, which is his great interest, to discuss something less abstract: "But our people don't understand what Russia means. FATHERLAND—nineteen out of twenty have no concept of what it is. Soldiers fight only for their faith and their tsar. That's what keeps an army going."[5] Not only the people, but the officers also have strict orders not to enter into

[3]*Ibid.,* p. 188.
[4]*Ibid.,* p. 189.
[5]*Ibid.*

political controversy. The general knows that these are the directives issuing from the highest authority. Thus, he contents himself with enlarging on his interlocutor's statement: "That's what makes it all the more important to maintain the concept of fatherland as a universal, heart-felt sentiment."[6] The colonel is aware that Nechvolodov is alluding to his own book, hoping to elicit discussion of it, but he avoids this trap. Solzhenitsyn writes: "Aleksei Smyslovskii, through education, had by-passed tsar and faith, but as to one's native land, this he understood completely, yes, this he understood."[7]

The educated young officer and the seasoned traditionalist share a similar attachment to Russia. At the level of national feeling there is no argument between them. Love of country transcends intellectual discussion and even political realities. Solzhenitsyn sketches out the two men's respective positions as he lets us know that Nechvolodov, who as a young officer suggested possible reforms in the organization of the officers' corps, is now willing to "swim with the current."[8] As Smyslovskii questions the older man about what happened to this erstwhile project, the colonel reveals his own liberal tendencies, advanced for their time. In this way Solzhenitsyn uncovers the ferment that brought about the Revolution.

But, on that day in August, 1914, ideological differences must be set aside for the task at hand: the decision to face the enemy attack with insufficient ammunition or to retreat. The colonel awaits respectfully the general's decision, deferring to his rank and experience. Suddenly, coming from the German side, the light of projectors begins, as the novelist says, to feel out the Russian position, like an exploring hand. The truce of night is broken. The experienced leader of men knows what must be done, though he hates doing it. As further news of the breakup along the Russian front reaches him, he orders the retreat. Smyslovskii must see to the dismantling of the artillery and join Nechvolodov's forces later. All intellectual speculation is washed away by the tragic reality of the onset of defeat, but it is with Roman courage that the young colonel takes his leave of the general, tossing at him a gallant quota-

[6]*Ibid.*
[7]*Ibid.*
[8]*Ibid.*, p. 190.

tion: "Feci quod potui, faciant meliora potentes." ["I did what I could, let those who can do better."][9]

"The Solzhenitsyn universe is a reinvention of Christian culture,"[10] declares Georges Nivat the critic and goes on to say that though the chain of history seems broken in the particular society presented to us in these novels, History will be reborn out of the sacrifice of a Nerzhin, a Volodin. The spiritual climate of this *oeuvre* does indeed bring it close, as Nivat claims, to that century when mystical values were affirmed in Europe, the twelfth. In that sense we can suggest that the Tolstoyan love ethic is integrated into that great vision of renunciation and oneness that links Plotinus and Solov'ev.

What Men Live By

At the beginning of *August 1914,* as we follow Isaakii in his journey by train, we are told by means of a flashback that four years earlier, under the pretext of wishing to visit the place of origin of their family, the young man had received his father's permission to travel north of Voronezh. His pilgrimage was not wholly familial; he wanted to view a place he considered holy, the Tolstoy estate at Iasnaia Poliana.

That day, early in August, at six in the morning, the young man gets off the train at Kozlova Zaseka. After asking for directions, he starts out on foot in the direction of "The Ash Tree Clearing." The meaning of Iasnaia Poliana (*iasnyi* means luminous, but *iasen'* is the word for ash tree, and so the name is ambiguous) is the occasion of the young man's first mistake. Finding himself in a deep forest of ash trees and pines, he assumes he is already on the grounds of the private estate. The description of these woods is a paean to the richness of Russian nature, symbolic of the spirit of the "prophet" who walked through the sylvan tract:

> Clambering down a gully and climbing up a slope, Isaakii found himself in such a forest—wide, fecund, thick-trunked, formal, parklike—as, living in the South, he could never have envisioned, never having seen anything approaching it in pictures. Covered with dew, milky at first, then rainbow-hued, these woods beckoned, not to be crossed, but to be

[9] *Ibid.,* p. 194.

[10] Georges Nivat, "Essai sur la Symbolique de Soljénitsyne," *L'Herne,* XVI (1971), 364. All quotations from *L'Herne* in this essay have been translated by the present writer.

> lingered in for sitting, lying down, for infinite, endless retreat. And what made them truly exceptional was the feeling that the prophet's spirit hovered there: after all, Tolstoy walked or rode to the station, and thus could not avoid crossing these parts. This forest was already the beginning of his estate.[11]

As the young man continues walking in the direction pointed out to him at the station, he reaches the end of the forest. From there a broad expanse meets his eyes: Tolstoy's estate. A ditch separates the latter from the rest of the land. A little farther on a wide gate and a road lead into the property, but the shy young man, though eager to meet the writer, does not dare enter. It seems simpler to jump over the ditch, make his way through the brambles, and simply wander through that other forest, Tolstoy's private park. All Isaakii, as the prophet's disciple, wishes to do is to tread lightly on sacred soil. Solzhenitsyn presents with tender amusement the veneration of a student brought up in a tradition of respect for his elders, and in particular for a great artist and a great teacher of ethics.

For Solzhenitsyn, who believes that the Soviet elite has appropriated Nature for itself, an untouched forest, an untroubled lake become symbols of an ancient freedom. Linden and birch trees evoke the essence of Russia, awaken deeply nationalistic responses. For Isaakii, Tolstoy and his woods are one, and he seeks in his contact with one or the other or both a reaffirmation of his integrity. As the youth wanders down a narrow path he reaches a clearing and spies among the trees someone approaching, a man with a snowy beard, white hair, so familiar from the pictures Isaakii has been shown that he seems to be a concretization of a dream rather than a reality. Afraid to approach him, Isaakii watches the seer from behind the trunk of a thick linden tree.

Though the young student cannot know it, the man he sees in August, 1910, is close to his death at eighty-two, on November 7 of the same year. Solzhenitsyn describes him as still vigorous, which indeed he was, despite numerous attacks of phlebitis and weakened lungs. Tolstoy is also depicted as wearing the peasant shirt he liked to use in order to imitate the simple habits of his farmers. As for Isaakii, he has not come to question the author of *War and Peace* as much as to elicit some kind of response from the writer of "What Men Live By."

The student has reached that point in his life when, despite

[11]Solzhenitsyn, *Avgust chetyrnadtsatogo,* pp. 20-21.

his admiration for the teachings of Tolstoy, he has doubts as to whether human society can live by love alone. Magnificent as it is, the parable of Simon, the Bootmaker, and Michael, the Angel, does not seem to apply to the dealings of men in modern society. Standing before the old man, who looks at the boy benevolently, not surprised at having been sought out, Isaakii asks: "What is the goal of human existence?" The answer is the one expected from his reading of the master's religious works: "To serve God, and in so doing to establish his reign on earth." At the risk of angering the thinker, the student ventures: "Lev Nikolaevich, are you sure you are not overestimating the power of love in the human being? Or, at least, whatever part of it remains in contemporary man? What if love is not so strong or necessary after all that it can triumph—then your whole teaching will prove . . . fruitless? Or perhaps very, very premature? Shouldn't one plan for some intermediate step, with more limited requirements? . . . For, as I have observed, Lev Nikolaevich, in our South, universal good will does not exist; no, it does not exist." The aging seer, who interpreted the Epistle of St. John by writing that God does not wish men to live apart but united, and by love alone, merely reiterates: "Only by love! Only. No one has invented a more foolproof method."[12]

Lev Tolstoy's teachings are also discussed by the patients of "Wing 13," the cancer ward. For them the question of "what men live by" and thus how men die is of the essence. It is Kostoglotov who "palms off" on Podduev, "one wretched evening," a blue book with a "gold signature."[13] From the titles of the tales in this thin volume one can see that the author and his book "mean business": "Work, Illness and Death," "The Chief Law," "The Source," "Neglect a Fire and It Will Overmaster Thee," "Three Old Men," "Go into the Light While Light There Is."[14] The man into whose hand this book has been placed is no reader. Efrem Podduev, an individual who could have been in the prime of life had he not been struck down by cancer, once worked on barges and did construction work, moving wherever opportunity took him, feeling the whole body of Russia like that of a woman, taking wives and mistresses along the way and leaving them since women for him were not "fully

[12] *Ibid.*, p. 23.

[13] Solzhenitsyn, *Cancer Ward,* trans. by N. Bethell and D. Burg (New York: Farrar, Straus, & Giroux, 1969), p. 101.

[14] *Ibid.*

fledged people"[15] despite all the talk of equality. This man who liked two things—"a free life and money in his pockets"[16]—has been "prepared . . . for living . . . not for dying."[17] Now cancer has lodged itself in his loud, lying tongue and from there traveled into his neck and up to his head. Podduev can no longer ignore the fact of his near death, and he is looking for some answers. This "calm, quiet book"[18] is "talking to him."[19]

Podduev is the typical modern Russian, the uprooted Soviet man adrift in this epoch of the broken chain of history. The optimistic slogans of a regime that has turned its back on the metaphysical are of no assistance now that he feels the progress of disintegration within his very flesh. Rusanov's advice that he ought to read Nikolai Ostrovskii, the author of a book in which a character attempts to be of use to the Party from his deathbed, is tactless and stupid. Rusanov, who refuses to acknowledge that he has cancer, who will leave the hospital to die at home, blind to his condition, feels that Lev Tolstoy is a "namby-pamby" writer, inferior to Aleksei Tolstoi and to other patriotic scribes who teach one to "resist evil" and "fight against it."[20] Kostoglotov answers Rusanov's objections with the statement: "If we can't talk about death *here,* where on earth can we?"

A cancer ward is a political no-man's-land. Former prisoners, political dissidents, and government bureaucrats occupy adjoining beds, brought to this favor, as Hamlet says to the gravediggers, by the leveling of a common malady. By describing a hospital, and in particular a ward where the contest between life and death is played out dramatically, Solzhenitsyn forces a regime to look at the very fact they refuse to recognize: all men are equal because all men die. A regime that tears down churches and neglects graveyards, thinking only of material progress, would like to forget the human condition. When Kostoglotov shouts at Rusanov, we are aware that Solzhenitsyn is shouting to Russia to open its eyes and see reality:

> What do we keep telling a man all his life: "You're a member of the collective!" That's right. But only while he's alive. When the time comes for him to die, we release him from the collective. He may be

[15] *Ibid.,* p. 104.
[16] *Ibid.,* p. 98.
[17] *Ibid.,* p. 97.
[18] *Ibid.,* p. 102.
[19] *Ibid.*
[20] *Ibid.,* p. 108.

> a member, but he has to die alone. It's only he who is saddled with the tumor, not the whole collective. Now you, you, you . . . come on, tell us, what are you most afraid of in the world now? Of dying! What are you most afraid of talking about? Of death! And what do we call that? Hypocrisy![21]

The geologist with a pleasant face adds: "We're so afraid of death, we drive away all thoughts of those who have died. We don't even look after their graves."[22] Rusanov, the party hack, seems to agree: "Monuments to heroes should be properly maintained."[23] But the geologist makes a strong point: "Not only heroes, everyone."[24] There is no social elite in the other world. The geologist reminds his companions that in Russia there used to be respect for cemeteries, and, as Kostoglotov echoes, even reverence.

What is the deep meaning of this conversation? It has to do with Solzhenitsyn's feelings that fine old values are being destroyed. Above all, there is no room left for contemplation, for sentiment, in a culture intent on happiness, material gain. Once simple Russian peasants accepted death as a fact, an intimate part of their lives and their rituals. There was dignity in that and a kind of serenity. Podduev recalls "how the old folk used to die back home on the Kama—Russians, Tartars, Votiaks or whatever they were. They didn't puff themselves up or fight against it or brag that they weren't going to die—they took death calmly. They didn't stall squandering things away, they prepared themselves quietly and in good time, deciding who should have the mare, who the foal, who the coat and who the boots. And they departed easily, as if they were moving into a new house."[25]

For these simple people, as for the characters of Tolstoy's parables, death is the unavoidable end; it holds no fear but it must be planned for. After their death, life will continue for others, and these others, modest heirs of the humble belongings of their relatives, will take up the tasks at hand where they have been left off. Like Shulubin who will express it fully in Part II of *Cancer Ward,* the geologist is aware that one "can't build socialism on an abundance of material goods."[26] Shulubin is

[21] *Ibid.,* p. 140.
[22] *Ibid.*
[23] *Ibid.*
[24] *Ibid.*
[25] *Ibid.,* p. 100.
[26] *Ibid.,* p. 445.

also a Tolstoyan when he preaches "ethical socialism"[27] and states: "One should never direct people toward happiness, because happiness too is an idol of the market place. One should direct them toward mutual affection. A beast gnawing at its prey can be happy too, but only human beings can feel affection for each other, and this is the highest achievement they can aspire to."[28]

The Sacred Past

Nationalism is that feeling of affection which binds together people of a common culture. It encloses the living in a spiritual substance as palpable as matter. It establishes connections between the living and the dead, buried under their feet. To abandon cemeteries until "cattle wander through them, and pigs dig them up,"[29] to allow churches to go to ruin, or be pillaged by kolkhozniks who use the tiles of the floors, the metal of the cupolas, the wood of the iconostases as building material for their homes, is not, according to the geologist of *Cancer Ward,* and no doubt the author himself, part of the Russian "national character."[30] Nor does it seem right to him as he describes it in "A Poet's Ashes," one of the sketches in his collection *Studies and Miniatures,* that churches spared by the grandson of Genghis Khan should have been sold to kolkhozes to build stables from the bricks. Monasteries have been replaced by the miradors of slave-labor camps, barbed wire spells out a more recent past, and on the door of an ancient retreat one can see a billboard depicting a Russian workingman holding in his arms an African child. The caption reads: "Peace Among Nations." This pious slogan is a disguise for a more pernicious form of imperialism. It does not hide, however, the sacking of an entire area. As the narrator asks to see the grave of the lyric poet Iakov Polonskii, he is told that it is in an off-limits zone and that, besides, the poet's remains have been removed to Riazan'. Neither the great dead nor their wishes are respected in the Soviet Society. Stalin, who declared: "All Georgia must

[27] *Ibid.,* p. 446.
[28] *Ibid.,* p. 447
[29] *Ibid.,* p. 140.
[30] *Ibid.,* p. 141.

be plowed under," had no reason to be gentle with the defenseless dead. Like the quick they could be moved at will, resettled. They are the "Dead Souls" of the U.S.S.R.

The living prefer to forget the dead who do not let them "live." In a second sketch, "No, We Will Not Die," Solzhenitsyn decries the fact that in Russia there is no feast day to recall and honor the dead, not even those who perished in the wars. The piece evokes the past, when people used to spend part of Sunday walking through verdant cemeteries, singing hymns and swinging censers until it appeared to them that their dead whispered consolingly from below the green mounds: "It's all right, it's not so bad." The dead and the living were united by this ritual, and a continuity was established. Now, says Solzhenitsyn, bulldozers level the burial ground to make way for stadia. "We will not die" is the philosophy of the technological society of the twentieth century.

The last time one of Solzhenitsyn's stories was published in his country was in 1966, when *Novyi mir* came out with "Zakhar-Kalita." This short tale is one of the most complete statements we have by Solzhenitsyn on the theme of nationalism. It describes the author's pilgrimage to one of the holy places of Russia's glorious past, the battlefield of Kulikovo. There, in 1380, two hundred thousand Russian soldiers assembled to fight Mamai, one of the pretenders to the throne of the khans, his Tartar fighters, and his ally, Oleg, prince of Riazan'. The enemy was defeated by Dimitrii, grand duke of Moscow, who was surnamed thereafter Donskoi (of the Don). Nine out of ten blond warriors fell on this battleground. Solzhenitsyn says that they dissolved in this earth to their very skeletons so that the Russian land might shake off the yoke of the infidel.

The man who has cycled with a friend to visit a place unmarked on maps despite the fact that its cost in lives and spirit was greater than that of the bloody battle of Borodino, envisions the death struggle between continents that was played out on this dry heath back in 1380. His imagination is further stirred, as is most natural for a writer, by the obsessive rhythm of a cavalcade of warriors captured by one of Solzhenitsyn's great literary ancestors in his poem "On the Battlefield of Kulikovo." Aleksandr Blok's lyric evocation of Russia, the bard's "spouse," her heart pierced by the flying arrow of a Mongol attacker, reflects the Symbolist's concept of his country as a long-suffering, patient, peasant maiden filled with a life force, a life wish, which, in the poet's view, should inform the self-destructive intelligentsia. Blok's view of Russian history bears traces of Dostoevsky's Slavophile-Christian teachings. Plunging deeper into Russia's historical past one can trace a linear literary progression linking *The Lay of Igor,* the medieval epic of the defeat of a Russian prince by Asian invaders, the Polovetsians, to the clash between the khans and Dimitrii's armies, finally to the barbaric hordes covering with graffiti the memorial monument of Kulikovo visited by Solzhenitsyn and his friend.

In the course of the night the two young people spend in Zakhar's guard hut, they imagine they can hear the swans of Blok's poem singing from the waters of the Nepriadva. Since the Symbolist poet's swans echo the song of those in the ancient epic, what is suggested here is a continuity of feeling dependent on poetic passion and literary tradition. Literary memory, in this sense, is more trustworthy than the recordings of chroniclers. The young writer claims that in order to understand the battle in its integrity, its profound irreversibility, as an event that shaped the essence of Russia, one must erase from one's mind the reservations of historians who remind us that Mamai was overthrown by Tokhtamysh, who, strengthened by Timur's patronage, undertook a campaign against Moscow, forcing the hero of Kulikovo Meadow, Dimitrii Donskoi, to retreat north to Kostroma while Moscow was being sacked and pillaged only two years after the Russian victory. We know, however, that the Golden Horde eventually fell apart, ingested by that great wilderness it occupied. For the observer of the meanders of history, says Solzhenitsyn, the winding passage through centuries tends to fade, or rather alter, until it appears to resemble the taut measuring line of the topographer. Perhaps we can deduce from this statement that poets and scientists scan the past and future detecting an order, a superior harmony of purpose, where social historians only see the wavering graph of change.

Zakhar-Kalita, the eccentric guard of the Kulikovo memorial, is a reincarnation of Blok's Russian folk hero. Redheaded, unshaven, powerful, his shirt unbuttoned to the waist, Zakhar looks like a knight of old, the resurrected ghost of one of the slain heroes. With his officer's trousers dating from a couple of wars back and his star of Lenin's "October Children," he does not seem to belong to the Stalinist or, as in this case, the post-Stalinist era. Like a pilgrim, he carries a sack with the modest provisions he requires for a day's sustenance. Under his jacket, against his chest, hangs a pouch or satchel made from the same rough cloth as the sack; it is of a size to hold the guest book. The guard is proud of his functions. Clearly he would protect the guest book and the entire site with his life. He decries the fact that the government has refused him a gun to fulfill his duties, for with the vandalism that takes place he would need, says he, at least a machine gun.

Indeed, the hordes of tourists have defaced the memorial. Solzhenitsyn states that "fools" armed with nails carved their names into the metal. Delegates of district assemblies and committee members are not ashamed of seeking destructive immortality for their paltry beings; they are the new proprietors of the Russian past. Nor has ownership awakened in them a sense of responsibility or respect. The neglected church is torn to shreds, as though stone were cloth. A plaque commemorating Dimitrii Donskoi is missing, stolen by a villager who keeps it in his hut. As the guard informs the visitors of his problems, we see a simple, uneducated man, so devoted to the past that it would seem that those who perished on the battlefield had fallen only yesterday and were his brothers, brothers-in-law, or sons whose life-sustaining presence has now been taken from him.

Little by little the two friends find out all there is to know about Zakhar's life. He is paid less than a minimum rate of thirty rubles, has no day off, spends all day and all night on the site. He just takes a fraction of time to run to his village of Kulikovo to grab a bit of supper, and then returns to sleep in a tiny shelter on the field. It is the latter he offers his new friends and their bicycles when they say they would like to stay in this deserted spot overnight. As he replaces the guest book in the satchel, the writer notices a short ax under his cloak. "That's all I'm allowed to have," explains the fanatic defender of the battleground.

Left to themselves, the friends walk about, trying to recapture the spirit of the epic struggle and identify the heather tramped by the horses of Blok's poem. All they see is dry, tough grass, but at night, under the stars, this turning point of Russia's destiny acquires magic. The centuries come to a stop, whirl back; the earth and moon become again the earth and moon of 1380. In the darkness of the field, reciting to themselves and to one another Blok's great poem, the companions experience that participation in communion which, according to Alan Tate, is the essence of a work of literature. So close do they feel to Dimitrii's soldiers that Solzhenitsyn can write: "We fall as wheat cut down. We die under the horse's hoofs." The iambic dimeter and pentameter of Blok's rushing cavalcade runs through their minds and over their bodies with an overwhelming physical presence.

In the years preceding the Revolution, the Symbolist poet Aleksandr Blok looked forward to a reconciliation between the intellectuals and the peasants. In his article "The People and the Intelligentsia," he explained that the battle of Kulikovo served as a symbol for the struggle between these two classes. Blok hoped to bring them together, and feared also that this was impossible. His poem, written in 1908, is tinged with the tragic knowledge that Russia, his "bride," is calling to him, and that he may be powerless to come to her assistance. Yet, in Solzhenitsyn's magnificent short tale such a reconciliation seems to have taken place. Zakhar-Kalita, "the Russet Spirit of the Battlefield," and the two young men become friends because they share the same reverence for a plot of land, a place in history. What unites them is a deep, almost subconscious form of national feeling, one that can never arise in the vulgar, materialistic new elite of the bureaucrats-technocrats. Because modern man is in frantic motion, he cannot penetrate to the essence of things. Zakhar, the true representative of the people [*narod*], and the narrator of the tale communicate above the heads of the new invaders, the disrespectful hordes.

After their night excursion, the companions fall soundly asleep. The following morning, as they step out of the shelter, they see their "host" rise from the haystack, "like a watchful faun." He explains that he had not dared disturb their sleep by knocking on the little door. This extraordinary regard for others, so natural in this new friend, is characteristic of the Russian man. Solzhenitsyn suggests that Zakhar-Kalita is one of the Just, like Matrena, another true Russian. The Keeper of the Book, the Defender of the Place, does what he must without questioning it. As the companions take their leave of this touching, antiquated figure, this relic of old warriors, armed as they were only with an ax, we realize that this self-appointed knight of nationalistic faith will hold back the vandals, as perhaps the story "Zakhar-Kalita" will awaken some people to greater consciousness.

The Man of the People

Solzhenitsyn's mystical nationalism renders him particularly dangerous to the present regime. It is obvious that in his turning away from the proletariat—an anti-Marxist attitude—and the cultivated bureaucrats, in his Tolstoyan, Blokian return to the man of the people, he is, not unlike the hero of *August 1914,* Isaakii, a throwback to a group of social thinkers long gone, the populists [*narodniki*]. Isaakii, though he does not dare define himself in this manner, believes in his heart of hearts that one must go to the people with "the book, the word and love."[31] In turn, the man of the people, even when ignorant or illiterate, becomes in Solzhenitsyn's novels the keeper of the written word.

How else can we understand the mysterious gift of Nerzhin to the blind janitor, Spiridon? We know with what difficulty Nerzhin was able to wrest from major Shikin, by means of tightly argued legalities, the volume of Esenin's poetry given to him by his wife, with the inscription: "And so it will be that everything lost will return to you!" Now the prisoner reminds the major that the book was published in the Soviet Union in 1940, that it is not "in the forbidden period between 1917 and 1938."[32] He insists therefore that, "in accordance with item 7 in Section B of the prison rules,"[33] the book taken illegally from him be now returned. Since the major still hesitates, unwilling to let this suspicious literature slip from his grasp, Nerzhin exclaims with grandiose folly: "I warn you: I will not give up that book to you. I will die in the Kolyma—but from the other side of death I'll tear it away from you! I will fill the mailboxes of all the Central Committee and the Council of Ministers with complaints against you."[34] This mad discourse, uttered just before his departure from the Limbo of the First Circle to the Inferno of the slave labor camp, is clearly metaphysical in character. There is a Gogol' touch of black humor in the project of reaching out to wreak vengeance from "the other side of death." Since Nerzhin is aware that the officer will not allow him to take the book out of the sharashka, his fight is logically absurd, futile, yet, walking out of the office,

[31]Solzhenitsyn, *Avgust chetyrnadtsatogo,* p. 11.
[32]Alexander Solzhenitsyn, *The First Circle,* trans. by Thomas P. Whitney (New York: Harper & Row, 1968), p. 560.
[33]*Ibid.*
[34]*Ibid.,* p. 562.

book in hand, the *zek* savors this brief moment of spiritual triumph at the instant when "everything was in ruins."[35]

A great writer is "a second government,"[36] states one of the characters in *The First Circle,* undoubtedly voicing the author's opinion. Born in a modest village of the province of Riazan', marked by a tragic destiny—he committed suicide on December 28, 1925—the peasant poet Sergei Esenin depicts with deep sorrow the ruined churches, the devastated hamlets of his homeland. One of the recurrent themes of his last poems is the relentless encroachment of expanding cities on the villages that to him are the true centers of Russian life. Returning to his own village after an absence of eight years, the youthful admirer of that "austere genius,"[37] Lenin, who, having guided his people toward new life, left it to be "immured in concrete"[38] by his somber followers, is shocked to find the cross removed from the church, the graveyard abandoned, chaotic. On the road Esenin meets but fails to recognize his own aged grandfather. The old man tells him about life in the hamlet: the poet's sisters have become *komsomolki;* they mouth clichés from their newly acquired, ill-digested readings of Marx and Engels. They have thrown away the icons that used to hang in their little house, and the commissar ordered the cross taken out of the church. Now the old man must sneak into the woods to pray "to the aspen trees."[39] The "sixth part of the earth"[40] is no longer the Russia the poet remembers, and one feels that Solzhenitsyn, who describes his own pilgrimage to Esenin's village in one of the most moving sketches in *Studies and Miniatures,* shares this sadness. On the banks of the Oka, the Russian novelist recalls the mysterious line—"Haystacks of sunlight in watery hollows"—and meditates on the fact that a great poet issued from this crumbling *izba* to sing about a countryside trampled and scorned.

Esenin, the poetic genius, belongs to the human family that has produced the generous, respectful Matrena who shelters the writer-teacher during his year of enforced residence following

[35]*Ibid.*

[36]*Ibid.,* p. 358.

[37]Sergei Esenin, "Lenin," *Izbrannoe* [*A Selection of Poems*] (Moscow, 1946), p. 302. All quotations from Esenin have been translated by the present writer.

[38]*Ibid.,* p. 305.

[39]Esenin, "Vozvrashchenie na Rodinu" ("Return to the Fatherland"), in *Izbrannoe,* p. 308.

[40]Esenin, "Rus' sovetskaia" ["Soviet Russia"], *Izbrannoe,* p. 314.

his release from camp, the modern knight of Kulikovo battlefield, Zakhar-Kalita, and the janitor Spiridon. The latter, whose country, religion, and ideals are his family, is a peasant who once loved his land. Through the vagaries of wars and political upheavals, he has been forced to cross and recross "from one warring side to another."[41] Yet what moves him is something beyond self-preservation. Nerzhin wonders: "Didn't it somehow relate to the Tolstoyan teaching that no one in the world is just and no one guilty? Wasn't there a whole system of philosophical skepticism in the almost instinctive acts of the redheaded peasant?"[42] This man, who knows unshakably what he smells, sees, hears, and understands, challenges at moments of crisis "the most rational pages of Montaigne and Charron."[43] Thus, it is he who will come out with the clearest moral pronouncement in the novel. He answers the question: "Is it conceivable that any human being on earth can really tell who is right and who is wrong?" with the expressive statement, the result of his intimate acquaintance with the natural order of our planet: "The wolfhound is right and the cannibal is wrong."[44]

It is not surprising then that when Nerzhin has to leave his volume of Esenin in someone's safekeeping he should turn to Spiridon. Though the latter will never be able to read the poems, being both half blind and illiterate, he is the keeper and the transmitter of a profound wisdom. This long-suffering man, deprived of family, of his beloved daughter whom he protected through all the exoduses but who has now been seduced or raped in the forests near Perm' where she has been condemned to forced labor, is a symbol of the Russian people. As Nerzhin leaves him, he places the heartbreaking letter of Spiridon's daughter, the letter he has just had to read to the janitor, into the volume of Esenin's poems. They form a single statement of tragic destruction—the rape of a girl, the desecration of the land—yet we are made to feel that the truth of this revelation will lie dormant in the great, silent hands of Spiridon to emerge from the darkness of the age and reach a new generation. Nerzhin's gift is an act of faith.

The end of *The First Circle* explains fully the peculiar

[41]Solzhenitsyn, *The First Circle*, p. 400.
[42]*Ibid.*
[43]*Ibid.*, p. 396.
[44]*Ibid.*, p. 401.

friendship between Nerzhin and the janitor. It is referred to by the Marxist Rubin, the Aquinas of Dialectic Materialism, and by his antagonist, the elitist Sologdin, a Faustian figure, as "going to the people." Solzhenitsyn writes: "In their view, Nerzhin was seeking that same great homespun truth which before his time had been sought in vain by Gogol', Nekrasov, Herzen, the Slavophiles, the 'People's will' revolutionaries, Dostoevsky, Lev Tolstoy, and, last of all, Vasisualii Lokhankin."[45] These two intellectuals, in firm possession of "absolute truth,"[46] mock their companion's Romantic pursuit. Rubin believes in the collectivism of the proletariat, Sologdin in "unique personalities."[47] Both are convinced that they are pure Russians, Rubin because he has remained a Communist even in prison, Sologdin, the Hegelian Mephistopheles with the Aleksandr Nevskii beard, on account of his avoidance of words of foreign origin, "bird words," and his espousal of what he calls "The Language of Maximum Clarity." In reality it is clear that the two men live by abstractions, and that they are far removed from whatever gives Russia its particular flavor. Only Nerzhin educates himself to know what "the People" truly means.

A driver on transport wagons during the war, Nerzhin, probably like the author himself, is at first clumsy, and the skilled workers who operate by his side laugh at him. At that stage he finds the People disagreeable. Having reached the rank of artillery officer, Nerzhin becomes a leader of "the obedient, loyal, industrious, and, consequently, pleasant People."[48] He belongs at this stage of his life to an elite. After his arrest, however, the young man discovers the cowardice of members of this so-called elite in circumstances "where firmness of character, strength of will, and loyalty to one's friends were vital to a prisoner."[49] Amid the wreckage of his life, Nerzhin discovers the importance of manual labor. He comes to believe that the only people who mattered were "those who planed wood, worked metal, plowed land, and cast iron with their own hands."[50] Solzhenitsyn tells us that Nerzhin has come back full circle to the fashion of the nineteenth century, except that he has one advantage over a Tolstoy; he does not have to

[45]*Ibid.*, p. 386.
[46]*Ibid.*
[47]*Ibid.*, p. 387.
[48]*Ibid.*, p. 388.
[49]*Ibid.*
[50]*Ibid.*

sneak down a staircase "to go to the people," or invite, as did the author of *Anna Karenina,* a cobbler to come to his apartment to give him private lessons in making shoes; he is already among the people. Thus he discovers that he is neither superior to them by virtue of being an "educated gentleman," nor inferior because he was not born into the homespun truth. He is "an equal among equals."[51]

To be a true Nationalist, a man who loves the People without romanticizing it or himself, one must go through the apprenticeship of Nerzhin. Having come to full maturity, the young man realizes that to become part of the people he must forge his own personality. This is the key to Solzhenitsyn's own nationalist feelings. Indeed, one can say that the novelist's nationalism is a form of humanism. Solzhenitsyn redefines the concept when he writes about Nerzhin that the young man "understood the people in a new way, a way he had not read about anywhere: the people is not everyone who speaks our language, nor yet the elect marked by the fiery stamp of genius. Not by birth, not by the work of one's hands, not by the wings of education is one elected into the people. But by one's inner self. . . . One must try to temper, to cut, to polish one's soul so as to become a human being."[52]

Ivan Denisovich Shukhov is that man of the people who, like the educated *zek* Nerzhin, makes his own being. He forges his inner self within the cold fires of the Inferno of the slave-labor camp to which he is condemned. "It has been the particular achievement of Solzhenitsyn," writes Michel Aucouturier, "to have made of the concentration camp experience the privileged *locus* of meditation of Russia, on the world and on ourselves."[53]

As we see the prisoners struggle against an alien environment and their own exhaustion, we are made sharply aware of the biological myth that is played out here at every moment of everyday existence. Things ordinarily taken for granted—warm socks, a bed to sleep in, a bowl of hot soup, a drag from a cigarette, a moment of rest—become infinitely precious commodities. At the same time, paradoxically, the physical realm is vested with spirituality. It becomes a holy act, a form of prayer and respect, to worship one's body as the vessel of the soul, to attempt to ensure its survival. A man of the people becomes thus

[51] *Ibid.*
[52] *Ibid.*, p. 389.
[53] Michel Aucouturier, "L'Art de Soljénitsyne," *L'Herne, XVI (1971)* 347.

his own church, and the bodies the regime attempts to use up until their dying breaths seem not unlike the ravaged churches of Stalin's era.

In *The First Circle,* Agniia tries to explain to her fiancé, the future colonel of engineers of the State Security Service, Iakonov, that the Church of St. John the Baptist, standing alone on a hill above Moscow, is one of the most beautiful places in the world, one of the few that contain "all the music"[54] of the world. The same music sings within that paltry thing, a man who tries to remain human. As one reads *One Day in the Life of Ivan Denisovich,* some lines from William Butler Yeats's "Sailing to Byzantium" come to mind:

> An aged man is but a paltry thing,
> A tattered coat upon a stick, unless
> Soul clap its hands and sing, and louder sing
> For every tatter in its mortal dress . . .[55]

A regime that destroyed "the gold mosaic of a wall"[56] could not silence this quiet song. The living men of the camp are "sages standing in God's holy fire,"[57] and thus "the singing-masters of [our] soul."[58]

When Ivan Denisovich and his companions erect a wall, working in forgetfulness of self as though they were building a Gothic cathedral to the glory of the Lord rather than an electric plant, they affirm by deed the medieval values of grace and courage. And when, at the end of an exhausting day's work, Ivan Denisovich and Sen'ka the Deaf—the survivor of Buchenwald condemned for that very survival to its Soviet equivalent—linger on after their companions have begun to put away their tools, they affirm in their tacit agreement to complete a portion of the wall their individual human values: pride in a task well done, in craftsmanship, solidarity, self-respect. Thus, the men who are forced to work for a system are, in effect, at such a moment, subverting that system's values, or altering them to make them serve spiritual goals. Ivan and Sen'ka demonstrate that the camp system, which wastes both individual talent and collective effort, starves potentially productive work-

[54]Solzhenitsyn, *The First Circle,* p. 91.

[55]William Butler Yeats, "Sailing to Byzantium," *The Collected Poems* (New York, 1945), p. 223.

[56]*Ibid.*

[57]*Ibid.*

[58]*Ibid.*

ers, and provides technologically inadequate means to carry out projects, has also failed in its declared purpose of re-educating "political dissidents." Unwilling to allow themselves to be made into robots, the prisoners retain that honesty which characterizes the Russian *muzhik* and impart meaning to the absurd and inhumanly arduous labor they are required to perform. This caricature of the socialist ideal, camp teamwork, is redeemed by Ivan Denisovich when, risking punishment for lateness, he stops to cast a long, loving glance at his handiwork: "Not bad. . . . His eyes were true as a level. The wall was straight as a die. His hands were still good for something!"[59] We recognize in this modest self-appraisal a new form of heroism.

Interviewed in March, 1967, by the Slovak journalist Pavel Licko for *Kulturny zivot,* Solzhenitsyn explained that, though it might be simpler for a writer to speak of himself, his own desire had always been to depict Russia's destiny. Tolstoy taught him that the subject of a novel could be a century of European life or one day in a *muzhik's* existence. He chose the latter, attracted by the artless truth of a simple man of faith. Ivan Denisovich is that man, miraculously uncorrupted by the manner in which he is made to live. His optimism, his inherent goodness and vitality, are symbolized by the belief he holds that a brand-new moon rises every month and that the old moon, unwasted by a provident God, is broken up into stars.

The Maimed Oak

Few great writers or artists appear in the pages of Solzhenitsyn's novels. There is, however, one notable exception. In *The First Circle* we are introduced to an original, a profoundly mystical painter. Because he is already in the *sharashka,* Kondrashev-Ivanov is paradoxically free not to use the Socialist-Realist style he abhors. To Rubin, who believes in "objectivity," the painter declares with violent passion: "Yes, I am nonobjective, and I am proud of it."[60] Kondrashev-Ivanov tries to capture through color the emotional totality of nature in its ungainliness, exaggeration, incongruity. "Every act of perception has an emotional coloring,"[61] explains this man for whom

[59]Alexander Solzhenitsyn, *One Day in the Life of Ivan Denisovich,* trans. by Max Hayward and Ronald Hingley (New York: Praeger, 1963), p. 129.
[60]Solzhenitsyn, *The First Circle,* p. 325.
[61]*Ibid.,* p. 324.

art "was the only possible way of life."[62] Those who claim that the tormented representations of mountains, trees, and rivers are not Russia but the Caucasus, fail to realize that Kondrashev sees Russian nature as one that "exults and rages and doesn't give way before the Tartar hoofs."[63] It is as though Blok had tried to paint the Kulikovo battlefield. To his friend Nerzhin, who concedes that there may well be such places in Russia,[64] the painter addresses a whole discourse on aesthetics:

> There not only *may* be such places in Russia, but, there are. I'd like to take you to some places near Moscow—without an escort guard. What's more they can't be the Caucasus. Understand one thing: the public has been fooled by Levitan. After Levitan we've come to think of our Russian nature as low key, impoverished, pleasant in a modest way. But if that's all our nature is, then tell me where all those rebels in our history come from: the self-immolators, the mutineers, Peter the Great, the Decembrists, the "People's Will" revolutionaries?[65]

To depict Russian nature whether on canvas or in a novel, one can not be confined by Socialist Realism; one must seek the deeper reality of passionate rage, the wider truth of passionate action.

The symbolic representation Kondrashev-Ivanov has chosen is of a maimed oak. This six-foot-tall picture has found no customer.

> It showed a solitary oak which grew with mysterious power on the naked face of a cliff, where a perilous trail wound upward along the crag. What hurricanes had blown here! How they had bent that oak! And the skies behind the tree and all around were eternally storm-swept. These skies could never have known the sun. This stubborn, angular tree with its clawing roots, with its branches broken and twisted, deformed by combat with the tireless winds trying to tear it from the cliff, refused to quit the battle and perilously clung to its place over the abyss.[66]

This tree is both Russia itself and the Russian man. Like the tree, Solzhenitsyn has refused to be uprooted, to risk the danger of exile by going to Sweden to receive the Nobel Prize. Like the oak, the Russian artist needs his soil, his storm-swept mountainside. Foreign critics, such as Edmund Wilson, claim to be bewildered by the peculiar "masochism" of this most Russian of Russian writers. Can one speak of the masochism of a

[62] *Ibid.*
[63] *Ibid.*, p. 256.
[64] *Ibid.*
[65] *Ibid.*
[66] *Ibid.*, p. 251.

"maimed oak" that chooses to endure? Does it not seem to convey instead obstinate courage, utter lack of sentimentality, and a noble need? The character of Kondrashev-Ivanov is as much a self-portrait of Solzhenitsyn the artist as Elstir in *A la recherche du temps perdu.* Solzhenitsyn's novels are his "Maimed Oak." Yet, we must not forget that the wounded, threatened tree is not the only great work of the imprisoned painter. There is also a study for the "principal painting" of his life. The artist doubts that he will ever paint it, but he is willing to show the first sketch to his friend Nerzhin. It shows a rider skirting an abyss. His steed is unafraid, and the horseman looks "into the distance where a reddish-gold light coming perhaps from the sun, perhaps from something purer than the sun, flooded the sky behind a castle . . . the aureate-violet castle of the Holy Grail."[67]

In Kondrashev-Ivanov's work the sunless gorge of the "Maimed Oak" gives way to the paradisiacal light of the holy castle. Great Russian literature has always inscribed itself under the sign of a spiritual quest. Solzhenitsyn's Russian "scenes" bathe in a mysterious light, one whose source is purer than the sun. It is the light that touches the face of Ivan Denisovich when he sits at table at the end of a long day. It envelops the healing cancerous flesh of Kostoglotov when, sacrificing the hope of life with Doctor Vera Gangart, he leaves on a train for Oriental Russia, stretched out on the baggage rack, a paltry thing perhaps, and yet a knight of the absurd renunciation, setting out with his lady's image in his heart, like some distant white constellation. It shines within the humble heart of Matrena and in the eyes of Zakhar-Kalita. Perhaps, unlike the painter of *The First Circle,* the Russian novelist has already given us a number of finished versions of his *Parsifal.*

[67]*Ibid.,* p. 258.

Solzhenitsyn's Women

BY XENIA GASIOROWSKA

The climate is harsh in the world of Solzhenitsyn's fiction: scorching summers alternate with freezing winters, with scarcely a ray of spring sunshine or autumn breeze. Under a leaden sky, most of the inhabitants, isolated from normal life by the walls of hospital or prison or by the barbed wire of a labor camp, painfully drag out their grim existence. This is what constitutes the subject and the plot of three of Solzhenitsyn's major works, *Cancer Ward, The First Circle,* and *A Day in the Life of Ivan Denisovich:* the process of living through the days and years of imprisonment, or the process of dying of cancer. Nobody regains freedom or finds release in death in the course of the narrative.

Those of the characters who are neither moribund nor serving a time for imaginary crimes fare little better. Families of prisoners and patients, men fighting in the two World Wars, refugees escaping Hitler's advancing army, peasants who a decade later still barely scratch out a living in their *kolkhozes*—all live in an atmosphere of uncertainty and frustration. Even the privileged—top bureaucrats, diplomats, the MGB executives—while living in comparative opulence know no peace and no safety, jailers one day, jailed the next. The luxurious life of the rich on the eve of the First World War in *August 1914* is darkened by a feeling of impending doom. Even the captive animals in the zoo in *Cancer Ward* suffer like people and, like them, lose the very capacity of enjoying freedom: "With the loss of their motherland they also lost the sense of decent freedom, and sudden liberation could only make things more frightening for them,"[1] explains the narrator.

Thus, Kostoglotov, reprieved from the cancer ward and the camp, cannot resume life at the point where it had been interrupted by sixteen years of war, imprisonment, and illness. Nor will the protagonist of "Matrena's Home," having suffered a similar fate, desire anything in life except peace and obscurity. Nor, finally, will the rhesus monkey regain its sight destroyed by an evil man "for no reason—just like that." No children are born into Solzhenitsyn's gloomy world where there is no laughter, no home, no pets. However, there are, of course, women.

At the unique birthday party which also proves to be a farewell party on the eve of his deportation to a labor camp, Nerzhin proposes a toast to all the prisoners' wives tormented, frightened, and persecuted.

Indeed, in Solzhenitsyn's world of the insulted, humiliated, and suffering, the prisoners' wives have the sad distinction of occupying a prominent place. These "brightfaced Isoldes, mates of the Vikings," as Sologdin calls them,[2] continue the noble tradition of faith and devotion established by the wives of the Decembrists. But they cannot even follow it exactly: Soviet wives are not allowed to accompany their husbands to the place of their imprisonment. Just as the lot of Soviet "zeks"[3] cannot be easily compared to that of political prisoners in the nineteenth century,[4] so the sacrifice of the Soviet wives is not comparable to that of the Decembrists' ladies.

[1]A. Solzhenitsyn, *Rakovyi korpus* [*Cancer Ward*] in *Sobranie sochinenii,* 6 vols. (Frankfurt, 1969-1970), II, 560. All subsequent references will be made to this edition, unless otherwise stated. Abbreviations used in the text are *F.C.* for *The First Circle* and *C.W.* for *Cancer Ward.*

[2]*V kruge pervom* [*The First Circle*], *Sobranie,* III, 256.

[3]Slang term for "prisoner," (*z/k,* short for *zakliuchennyi*).

[4]The subject obviously cannot be adequately discussed in a footnote, but some comparisons based on Dostoevsky's *Notes from a Dead House* and Chekhov's *Sakhalin Island* can be made. The Soviet "zeks" are not fettered, nor flogged as nineteenth century convicts were. The latter, however, did not starve, were released from work in case of illness, could have purchases made for them outside, celebrated official holidays and even their own birthdays. Moreover, while sadistic officers abound in both cases, convicts were supervised by good-natured invalid veterans, while the "zeks" are subjected to the vigilance of MGB-MVD personnel of all ranks. As to women, while the "dead house," like Ivan Denisovich's camp, has an all-male cast, their lot on Sakhalin was comparable to that shown in Solzhenitsyn's play *The Simpleton and the Strumpet* (also translated as *The Love-Girl and the Innocent*).

It is not only physical hardships that sap the life and youth of these women: having in most cases lived through the war and its aftermath, they are used to them. It is the atmosphere of hostility and persecution that they find so hard to bear. They are ostracized and harassed by neighbors in their communal apartments, endlessly interrogated by the MGB, deprived of scholarships and jobs. They are being punished for their double crime of having married a man capable of becoming an "enemy of the people" and of refusing to divorce him even after he has been unmasked and sentenced.

It was so easy to divorce a "socially noxious element" convicted on the basis of Section 58/10 of the Criminal Code for unexpressed but potentially dangerous thoughts. A husband needed not even be asked to give his consent for divorce nor was he informed when it was granted. His wife, having resumed her maiden name, could now omit mentioning her marriage in application forms for a job, admission to the university or for an apartment. She could start life anew. Instead, these women chose to endure and wait for their husbands' return—forever. "What force has chained her with such hopeless obstinacy to a man whom she will not see for years to come and who is only ruining her whole life?"—wonders Colonel Kliment'ev of the MGB (*F.C.*, III, 216).

They wait—losing their youth, health and good looks—sexless, comfortless, alone. They are either left childless like Nadia Nerzhin; or raise their fatherless children as best they can, like the wives of Sologdin and Ivan Denisovich. Or they bury them, like Natasha Gerasimovich; Elizaveta Anatol'evna, in *Cancer Ward,* has done both. Maltreated and impoverished, they wait and try to conceal their tragedy in order not to aggravate it still further.

They realize that precedents whether in life or in fiction do not apply to their situation. "What heroic deeds did the wives of the Decembrists accomplish? . . . accompanied by a murmur of admiration from elegant society . . . leaving for Siberia in their private expensive carriages," asks Natasha (*F.C.*, III, 301-2). And Elizaveta Anatol'evna says bitterly: "Anna Karenina chose passionate love and paid for it—that's happiness! She was a free and proud human being." (*C.W.*, II, 530). She, her husband, and children, deprived of all their possessions, were exiled to Siberia where several years later her husband was sent to a labor camp and now letters from him had stopped coming.

"Give her a chance to live!" advises the prison informer, Larisa, trying (successfully) to seduce the husband of one such "brightfaced Isolde." But the latter do not want to be set free to live. As women, they treasure the bitter joy of sacrifice, the warm feeling of being the only mainstay of their helpless, suffering mates. Still, a nagging doubt persists. Are their men really helpless, do they need that loving concern for their health, food, laundry, all that practical "clinging feminine care which causes a family to *be* a family and sustains the human race" (*F.C.*, III, 298)?

Occasionally, the inmates of the "sharashka"[5] were accorded visits with their families. During such a visit, lasting thirty minutes and rigidly supervised, the Nerzhins and the Gerasimoviches avidly probe their mate's feelings and appearance. Both the husbands notice with helpless pity that their wives have become worn, tired, and plain. Both wives see their men's good suits (specially issued for the occasion), healthy looks and, most of all the serene, smiling, confident expression. And Natasha realizes sharply that Gerasimovich does not fully appreciate the misery of her daily existence while Nadia is looking—unconsciously and in vain—for some sign of weakness in Nerzhin. "A sign of tiredness, illness, an appeal for help, things for which a woman could sacrifice the rest of her life" (*F.C.*, III, 311). And they wonder whether their devotion and sacrifice are not superfluous.

The couples' mutual love, and faith, and the terrible community of their suffering is genuine. But, separated by the prison walls, they no longer think in the same categories or treasure the same values. Moreover, while aggravated by circumstances this difference is even more basic at its source: Solzhenitsyn's men are guided by intellect and ethics, his women—by instinct and emotions. Thus, Nerzhin's heart bleeds for Nadia who after nine years has been finally goaded into contemplating divorce—fictitious, she assures him, but he knows that eventually he may lose her for ever. Yet, when offered participation in a project in cryptography with the prospect of being freed in recompense—he refuses. Firstly, because he will not accept forgiveness for his crime of harboring unexpressed

[5]Slang term for a scientific institute staffed by specialists brought from various Soviet labor camps and prisons.

thoughts, secondly because he prefers his clandestine historical research to sterile work on cryptography. His answer to the "accursed question" about what is the most important thing in life obviously is not personal happiness. Not even with Nadia.

Gerasimovich weeps when Natasha after a twenty-year ordeal sobs out that she has reached the limit of her endurance. Yet, offered the same reward as Nerzhin for developing a miniature camera which would serve to catch unsuspecting "criminals" like himself—he too refuses. Like another protagonist in *The First Circle,* Volodin, he acts on the principle that while it is true that we have only one life, we also have only one conscience.[6] And conscience wins against Natasha.

It is not that Solzhenitsyn's women have no understanding of higher ideals and noble principles. It is just that to them the men they love are more important than ideals, however noble. And it is not that Solzhenitsyn's best men do not value their women: indeed, women evoke in them not only desire but ecstatic admiration, such as inspires pious poets with litanies to the Virgin Mary (*F.C.,* III, 181). Yet, as Colonel Vorotyntsev sees it, women are too possessive, tend to exaggerate the importance of love, while "a feeling worthy of a man's breast can only be civic, patriotic or universal."[7] Men on a lower spiritual level adopt the attitude of the good-natured and merry Chalyi who readily accepts the devotion of his numerous wives. "Why should a woman lead a lonely life?" he queries. "Let her have somebody at least who would visit her if only once a year! Moreover, it is convenient for a man travelling on business: a room and a chicken leg in every town" (*C.W.,* II, 353). And, still more bluntly, Efrem, who as a matter of self-respect has always been the first to end an amour, without openly denying women's right to equality, does not consider them complete human beings (*C.W.,* II, 120). Even the sixteen-year-old Demka, while fully appreciating the skill of his excellent, attentive doctor, Evgeniia Ustinovna, prefers to be operated on by a male surgeon. For some reason he feels sure that a man would do the job better (*C.W.,* II, 337).

Solzhenitsyn's favorite device is to have an omniscient narrator tell the story and let the characters express their feelings

[6]The principle, a basic one with Solzhenitsyn's heroes, is repeated by the author's double, Aleks, in the play *Svecha na vetru* [*A Candle in the Wind*], *Sobranie sochineii,* V, 159.

[7]A. Solzhenitsyn, *Avgust chetyrnadtsatogo* [*August 1914*] (Paris, 1971), p. 117.

in indirect monologue. But he comments on these feelings and in so doing takes sides. Moreover, it is he, the author, who directs the events, chooses the cast and distributes the roles. And the roles allotted to women are secondary to men's. Except for the central characters in "Matrena's Home" and *The Simpleton and the Strumpet,* only Nadia Nerzhin and the two doctors in *Cancer Ward,* Vera Gangart and Lud'mila Dontsova, can be regarded as protagonists. It is, of course, impossible at this stage to tell how important the role of women will be in the future parts of the multi-volume novel on World War I, a project which Solzhenitsyn himself considers his *opus magnum* (*August 1914,* 572). But judging from *August 1914,* it is not likely to be very significant.

True, Solzhenitsyn's cast is always large: his method is to present several protagonists, a number of episodic characters, and a multitude of extras, many even without lines. But even so, the majority of *dramatis personae* are men and it is their fate that the story is about. There are no women scientists in the "sharashka" though they do exist in real life as well as in Soviet fiction.[8] So, the reader is not told whether they are capable of personal sacrifice in the name of ideals higher than faithful love. Or, whether they could ever have experienced in prison the heady feeling of freedom from family cares and the ecstasies and agonies of love. Or could feel the lofty presence of the spirit of masculine [that is genuine] friendship and philosophy (*F.C.,* IV, 412).

Except for in *The Simpleton and the Strumpet,* a play less about people in a labor camp than about conditions there, Solzhenitsyn's labor-camp inmates are men. Readers, therefore, are spared a painful acquaintance with the life of a feminine counterpart of Ivan Denisovich and denied the masterly insight into her mind. As for *August 1914,* the novel is wholly a soldier's world and is no place for women and their sensibilities. And *Cancer Ward* is the ward for men patients.

Patients in the women's ward are extras: a faceless crowd, unruly and chattering, a nuisance for nurse Zoia, and a challenge for Doctor Vera Gangart who is handling it with particular tact. Unlike the male patients, they do not spend their time in discussing politics, medicine, and the mysteries of life

[8]For example, the heroines of *Elena* (1955) by K. L'vova, *Doctor Vlasenkova* (1953) by V. Kaverin, *The Brothers Ershov* [*Brat'ia Ershovy*] (1958) by V. Kochetov, *The Battle on the Way* [*Bitva v puti*] (1957) by G. Nikolaeva.

and death. Clad in shapeless grey hospital robes, deprived of every vestige of attractiveness, they drift onto the staircase and fan out into the hospital to gaze at the windows of the surgery room, buy extra cream and milk from peddlers, wash something in the sink, visit another patient. Two apparitions from that "lair of sick women" materialize for Demka. One is old Aunt Stefa bringing him words of comfort and homemade pies, and the other, the youthful Asia, full of zest of life, who in the end tempestuously mourns the loss of a breast, "today's miracle destined for a slop pail tomorrow." Both women serve to characterize Demka by opening for him the vistas of religion and of love. In general, women characters are introduced for that purpose and if developed subsequently, then chiefly in relation to men.

It would, of course, be absurd to suggest that Solzhenitsyn considers the lot of Soviet women (and for that matter, children) unimportant, or that he is unsympathetic to the suffering they share with men. But Solzhenitsyn, like most talented writers, prefers to describe the environment he knows best. In his own tragic life this means the front in wartime, a labor camp, prison, and a cancer ward in a hospital—all of them isolating men from women. Moreover—and this a limitation of his creative scope—he prefers to portray the sensations and thoughts he had, or could have experienced himself.[9] He does not readily venture into the domain of feminine psychology, for him purely imaginative, and never into that of feminine sensations. Thus, he does apprehend Nadia's all-enduring devotion to her doomed "zek" husband, Vera's faithful memory of her fiancé killed in the war, Doctor Dontsova's agony in facing a mortal illness. These are universal human feelings. But he could not, like Chekhov in "The Namesday," record the sensations of pregnancy and miscarriage or, like Tolstoy, convey Natasha's helpless infatuation with a philanderer, or the all-consuming passion of Anna Karenina.

Solzhenitsyn's women are faithful wives, skillful doctors, efficient nurses, even conscientious employees of the MGB (though as informers only). However, with him feminine

[9]To cite just one of many possible examples. In 1953, sentenced to "eternal" (rather than "lifelong") exile, Solzhenitsyn was deeply vexed by the legal wording which seemed to make captivity reach beyond death. He voiced this resentment personally at a writers' meeting in 1968 (*Sobranie sochinenii*, VI, 40) and through his characters in "The Right Hand" (V, 209), *Cancer Ward* (II, 188), and *The First Circle* (III, 30 and IV, 751).

behavior is determined by feelings and runs a gamut from boundless devotion in the face of the harshest realities to dereliction of duty when its performance interferes with love. Thus, nurse Zoia agrees to omit hormone injections threatening the virility of Oleg Kostoglotov whom she might consider marrying; and the MGB informers, Simochka and Larisa, consent respectively to hide secret notes for, and to write biased reports on, the "zeks" with whom they have fallen in love.

There are several complete women characters in Solzhenitsyn's fictional world. Complete, in that they have a three-dimensional characterization: a prehistory, a physical portraiture, and a measure of insight allowed the reader into their thoughts and feelings.

Zoia and Vera represent the sensual and the spiritual side of Kostoglotov's attitude towards women.[10] Zoia, whose golden eyelashes and shapely breasts are rather overemphasized, is a coquette, but basically a kind-hearted, compassionate girl, a medical student who makes her own clothes and is kind to her grandmother. Vera's coffee-brown eyes and slim legs are repeatedly mentioned, but there is an aura of light and freshness which seems to surround her. Her affection for Doctor Dontsova, her grave, sympathetic manner with patients, the emptiness of her personal life—all contribute to her attractive personality. Would she be happier married to Oleg as his wife just in name? Or was he right in dismissing such a marriage with a bitter: "a bird does not live without a nest, a woman without a bed" (*C.W.*, 569)? The decision was his to make.

It is also up to Nerzhin to decide on the future of tiny, plain Simochka, brainwashed by the MGB but blossoming under the first kiss in her life. She was ready to become Nerzhin's mistress, bear his child, wait for his release from prison—if only he would let her. But, faithful to Nadia, he does not. Klara Makarygin is another MGB employee who falls in love with a "zek" she is supposed to watch. She is better educated and more intelligent as well as prettier than Simochka, but her romance is also doomed. There are no happy endings in Solzhenitsyn's world and Klara will eventually marry a suitable young careerist. She has more immortal soul than is good for

[10]Generally, Solzhenitsyn's women who appeal primarily to men's senses—Zoia, Larisa, coarse-mannered Nellia—are plump. Those evoking nobler emotions—ethereal Vera, soulful Agniia—are slim. Practically all are of small stature, except Agniia whose elongated, bony figure resembles an icon.

a daughter of a "prosecutor for special cases," but at times she is unbelievably naive.[11] Liuba, the camp prostitute, is the most tragic among Solzhenitsyn's women. Early orphaned, she had suffered all kinds of privations, was twice unhappily married, finally was sent to a succession of labor camps. She still is capable of falling in love with an honorable man, but loses him too.

There are two women who can be considered characters in their own right in that their fate is not dependent on any man: Doctor Dontsova and Matrena. Matrena—elderly, sickly and, except for her radiant smile, unattractive, possesses great virtues: Christian, traditionally Russian, and reportedly Soviet. A dedicated worker [*truzhenitsa*], indifferent to money [*besserebrenitsa*], she is kind to people, fond of animals and plants, patiently bears loneliness and poverty. In a way, she qualifies both as the prerevolutionary heroine, the long-suffering peasant woman [*mnogostradal'naia baba*] and in certain respects as a *kolkhoznitsa* required under Socialist Realism. Solzhenitsyn considers her a righteous person [*pravednitsa*] though her record of piousness is incomplete and she is given to superstitions.[12] But she is much more alive than Khristina in *A Candle in the Wind* who resembles her closely.[13]

Doctor Dontsova is a righteous person too. Like Matrena, she has all the requisite saintly qualities, even more occasions for doing good, and as hard a life. After a long exhausting day at the hospital, full of bureaucratic harassments, she has to queue for groceries, do the family laundry and cooking. A talented scientist, she has been denied the opportunity for further research. Moreover, unlike Matrena, she does not die swiftly in an accident but undergoes the agony of several times rejecting and accepting her own diagnosis of terminal cancer. And Solzhenitsyn denies her the fortitude of his male characters: she is afraid of suffering and death.

Solzhenitsyn's feminine episodic characters are numerous and play a considerable role in his works. They serve to illustrate Soviet conditions, especially those outside the terrain to which

[11]She is capable, for instance, of wondering whether her papa might ever have contributed to convicting an innocent person (*F.C.*, III, 342).

[12]So apparently is Solzhenitsyn. Matrena, like Anna Karenina, has a compulsive fear of locomotives, one of which eventually brings her death.

[13]Because of the allegoric and fantastic features in the play itself, the characters are largely symbolic, including the heroine, Al'da, whose personality is changed in a cybernetic experiment.

men protagonists are confined; or help explain the protagonists in depth, since they reveal themselves best by their attitudes to episodic situations.

There is therefore the teeming hospital personnel in *Cancer Ward:* chain-smoking, "sorrowfully elegant" Doctor Evgeniia Ustinovna; nurses—icon-like Maria,[14] sexy Anzhelika, plain Mita; aides—tragic Elizaveta Anatol'evna and loud, robust Nellia. There are the six students crowded into a narrow, rat-infested dormitory room with one window and one perpetually failing electric light at the ceiling. Like the unfortunate Nadia Nerzhin hiding the dangerous secret of her husband's whereabouts, all the students belong to the "doomed generation" of girls whose contemporaries—and thus prospective husbands—perished in the Second World War. The roommates are Erzhika, a Hungarian, naively puzzled by the realities of Soviet life; Dasha, hopelessly longing for marriage and motherhood; promiscuous Liudka; Olia, who still believes that happiness is possible for a "learned female," and Muza who had just been invited to start informing the MGB on them all, or else.

In the short stories, which themselves are based on an episode, women still play supporting roles. In "Incident at Krechetovka Station," a wartime story, several lonely women—the grass widow Polina, flirtatious Valia, sex-hungry Antonina, help establish lieutenant Zotov's psychological makeup before the author exposes him to his dilemma. In "For the Good of the Cause" instructor Lidiia Georgievna[15] offsets the cynicism of the bureaucrats who appropriate the new school building after the students had helped complete its construction.

Members of the Soviet elite, rather prominent in post-Stalinist literature,[16] are also represented. Kapitolina Rusanov, wife of an official who had made his career on false denunciations, and Alevtina Makarygin, wife of "the prosecutor for special cases," are typical of the older generation. They are plump and overdressed, and enjoy the comforts of their husbands' privileged positions with all the aplomb and gusto of the *nouveaux riches.* Their daughters, Alla Rusanov, and Dinera

[14]Maria has a twin in nurse Tania in *August 1914.*

[15]Professor Ol'da Andozerskaia in *August 1914* resembles Lidiia Georgievna. Generally, episodic characters in Solzhenitsyn's world tend to develop into certain standard types.

[16]For instance, Ganicheva in V. Dudintsev's *Not by Bread Alone* [*Ne khlebom edinym*] (1956) and Nadezhda Bartoshevich in V. Panova's *The Seasons* [*Vremena goda*] (1953).

and Dotnara Makarygin,[17] are amoral, sophisticated and, brought up to trust the Party's judgment, are sure of the excellence of their own. In contrast to this social group and equally representative of theirs, are the women of the prerevolutionary leisured class in *August 1914:* gentle Irina and effervescent Ksen'ia Tomchak,[18] thoughtful Veronika, decadent Ela, and the school principal, Aglaida Kharitonova who believes that "the main goal of education is to produce a CITIZEN—that is a person hostile to the authorities" (*August 1914,* 50).

A role is reserved for a group of women who perform the same function as episodic characters and extras without, however, appearing on the stage. Such are the wives of "zeks": Ivan Denisovich's and Dyrsin's, who write tear-stained letters about conditions at home, and Sologdin's wife who had stopped writing in order to keep her job. Such is Doctor Anna Zatsyrko, desperately trying to obtain a rare medication for her dying son; or young Demka's disreputable mother. Some of these women are only memories—like Kostoglotov's girl arrested for associating with boys who disapproved of Stalin. Or Agniia, former fiancée of MGB Colonel Iakonov, the personification of his youth and the ideals he had lost pursuing his career. Or they are thoughts, like lawyer Rusanov's about the case of two office girls who were stealing stamps to supplement their miserable salaries. Or even dreams, like "She"—happiness, love incarnate—appearing to Vorotyntsev on the eve of a battle.

Solzhenitsyn does not adhere to the Russian literary tradition of juxtaposing strong-willed heroines and weak heroes. But he does follow another: his heroes forever seek only good and justice. Moreover, they are strong. In a world where even the words manly [*muzhestvennyi*] and masculine [*muzhskoi*] are terms of high praise, women, whatever their personal worth and social significance, do not affect the human condition, or the destiny of individual men, or even their own. Their virtues are endurance, faith, and love and they value them as highly as life itself. But for men there are values more precious than life: personal integrity, freedom of individual choice, independent abstract thought, to which they are ready to sacrifice

[17]Dinera for "Child of New Era" [*Ditia Novoi Ery*]; Dotnara for "Daughter of Laboring People" [*Doch Trudovogo Naroda*]. In general, Solzhenitsyn likes names with a meaning fitting the bearer—for instance, Zoia (life), Vera (faith), Nadia (hope), Klara (luminous), Irina (peaceful), etc.

[18]Ksen'ia apparently has for a prototype Solzhenitsyn's mother.

everything, and that is what makes them strong. Zoia and Vera can *feel* in Kostoglotov—destitute as he is, barely recovered from cancer, deprived of civil rights—this quality of stability and strength tested by all the hardships he had endured.

"Women," says Vera, "seek in men attentive tenderness and a feeling of being safe in his presence, secure, sheltered." (*C.W.*, II, 382.) But Solzhenitsyn's women have a strength men do not possess: they are never evil, never inflict suffering, or destroy life—"just like that."

Solzhenitsyn and the Legacy of Tolstoy

BY KATHRYN B. FEUER

The recent, almost simultaneous, appearance of Solzhenitsyn's two long novels, *The First Circle* and *Cancer Ward*,[1] the news of the forthcoming *Arkhipelag Gulag*,[2] the publication of various stories and sketches—this sudden emergence of a voluminous mass of new fiction, by a writer of extraordinary ability, creates an unusual situation for literary criticism, which is accustomed to great works more deliberately spaced. Views proposed now must inevitably be subject to later revision, while the novels are so masterly that judicious silence is difficult. In a new situation one looks for familiar guideposts; in the terra incognita of the Solzhenitsyn novel the traces of Tolstoy create constantly recurring moments of recognition. One approach to Solzhenitsyn then is to survey his "Tolstoyanism" with the

[1]Aleksandr Solzhenitsyn, *V kruge pervom* (New York: Harper and Row, 1968). A. Solzhenitsyn, *Rakovyi korpus* (Paris: YMCA Press, 1968). All references in this study are to these editions, abbreviated as VKP and RK respectively. I have consulted and sometimes followed *The First Circle*, translated by Thomas P. Whitney (New York: Harper and Row, 1968), *Cancer Ward*, translated by Rebecca Frank (New York: Dial Press, 1968) and *Cancer Ward*, translated by Nicholas Bethell and David Burg (New York: Bantam Books, 1969). References to Tolstoy are to volume and page of L. N. Tolstoi, *Sobranie sochinenii v dvadtsati tomakh* (Moscow, 1960-1965).

[2]*Time Magazine* (March 21, 1969), p. 40.

secondary aim of defining an influence but primarily to point up by this narrow light some features of his own literary landscape.

I

In several ways Tolstoy seems to have provided models for Solzhenitsyn's fiction. Since a writer's first published work is usually significant of his elective affinities, it is worth noting that the account of a day in the life of Ivan Denisovich recalls Tolstoy's "The Woodfelling" in its chief organizing devices: men of various class and attitude, caught in a common situation of stress which belongs to and is yet outside the ordinary life of their society, joined together by membership in a group within the larger whole, conducted through a day which begins before dawn and ends in moonlight, with the position and heat of the sun used to define forward movement and also to demarcate shifts in mood or focus.

In Solzhenitsyn's novels some Tolstoyan structural features are also apparent. Both use extremely large casts of characters whose coming together, however unlikely, is made to seem natural and believable—in Tolstoy by an intricate system of family relationships, in Solzhenitsyn by the common extraordinary situation of sharashka and cancer ward. Like Tolstoy, Solzhenitsyn involves the reader in the destinies of both primary and secondary protagonists among these characters, although in this respect Solzhenitsyn is more "egalitarian" than Tolstoy, who tends to reserve important spiritual development for his major heroes and heroines. Moreover both writers incline toward the expansive *roman-fleuve,* in which external action has only a minor role. Both the minimalization of plot events and their openendedness are particularly notable in Solzhenitsyn because they are unusual features in novels whose time structures are so rigorously controlled—four days for *The First Circle,* about six weeks for *Cancer Ward.*[3] In this respect Solzhenitsyn

[3]*The First Circle* begins at 4:05 P.M., December 24, 1949, and ends in the early afternoon (after lunch) of December 27. Midnight of the 24 probably comes around the division between chaps. 15 and 16; midnight of the 25 probably comes in chaps. 65 and 66; midnight of the 26 in chap. 83 or 84. Part I of *Cancer Ward* goes from Thursday, February 3, 1955, to Thursday, February 10. Part II can be dated exactly from Thursday, March 3, to Friday, March 11 (Chaps. 22-26). Thereafter dating is not entirely clear. The novel

may seem to resemble his other great predecessor, Dostoevsky, but there is this important difference. When finishing, for example, *The Brothers Karamazov,* the careful student who adds up how much time has passed is astonished at the result of his calculations. Time sequence in Dostoevsky is usually correct, but the illusion of temporal realism is sacrificed to dramatic unity. Both Solzhenitsyn and Tolstoy, on the other hand, manifest strong concern for the sequential treatment of depicted time. They like to provide the reader with internal temporal references, and they find it hard to elide, to break out of continuous time—indeed the depiction of the four "days" of *First Circle* continues through the three intervening nights. Occasionally minor timetable errors even occur in their novels, but never to the reader who does not track them down. Rather, the reader's impression is that time has been carefully accounted for and that the duration of hours or days or weeks has been experientially sustained.

As to narrative structure, the similarities between the two authors are perhaps outweighed by the differences. Solzhenitsyn's use of the first person in "The Right Hand"[4] a story which seems in all other respects a rejected fragment of *Cancer Ward,* suggests that he may have worked his way from *Ich* to *Er* by the same kind of meticulous experimentation as the young Tolstoy. Neither writer explicitly abjures omniscience yet both prefer to narrate within the specified points of view of their characters, shifting easily from one to another but adhering faithfully, while with a particular character, to his experience, attitudes, and limitations. Perhaps because their heroes are so recognizably "autobiographical" both Tolstoy and Solzhenitsyn tend to mark clearly their own authorial appearances as uncharacterized narrators or commentators. Solzhenitsyn, of course, does not reason with the reader about causes or meanings, but both writers make themselves felt as constantly hovering presences of critical intelligence, and both make frequent injections of biting social irony, more massive in Tolstoy, more mordant in Solzhenitsyn—the irony of the observer, perhaps, versus that of the participant. And it can be noted also that both authors'

ends (Chaps. 35-36) on a Saturday which seems to be March 26, but could be the 19. The latter is more likely since Kostoglotov arrived at the hospital on January 23 and is said (several times) to have been there eight weeks and Rusanov, who arrived on February 3, is said to have stayed six weeks.

[4]Aleksandr Solzhenitsyn, "The Right Hand," *The Atlantic Monthly* (April, 1969), pp. 45-49.

voices are primarily those of moralists, with the great difference that Solzhenitsyn's modesty and compassion rarely acquire the insistently didactic Tolstoyan accent.

Whatever the tone, both Solzhenitsyn and Tolstoy know well the effectiveness of flat interjections in their own voice. When Solzhenitsyn begins a chapter with the statement: "Strange are the relationships between a man and a woman: they cannot be predicted, they possess no direction, they have no laws" (VKP, 361) he is surely recalling the opening of ***Anna Karenina*** (and note the typically Tolstoyan concreteness in generalizations: "*a* man and *a* woman"). But far more often, as in his notable chapter endings, or in the passage near the end of *The First Circle* when he suddenly addresses the reader as "you," Solzhenitsyn achieves an immediacy and force which is strikingly his own—for reference in the latter case to "Sevastopol in December" would probably be more pedantic than true:

> And so . . . the zek puts his hands behind his back, and . . . surrounded by dogs and convoy guards, he goes to the railroad car.
>
> You have all seen him at that moment in our railroad stations—but you have hastened to look down at the ground like a coward, to turn away like a loyal subject, so that the convoy lieutenant will not suspect you of something and arrest you.
>
> The zek goes into the car . . . [VKP, 491-492]

Potapov's highly stylized narration of "Buddha's Smile" is a sustained mock epic brilliantly evocative of both "Graf Nulin" and "Istoriia sela Goriukhina" (after all Potapov is the camp Pushkinist) and the tale's most effective point comes at its only interruption:

> "But the next thing—not one of you could guess! They brought in potatoes—not frozen, not rotten, not black—simply, what one might call ordinary potatoes."
>
> "That's impossible!" the listeners protested. "Now that's not true to life!"
>
> "But that's just what happened!" [VKP, 295]

Such moments in Solzhenitsyn owe nothing to Tolstoy. They are, however, reminiscent of Tolstoy's power to manipulate his own realistic surface with a twist of narrational change-of-pace.

Solzhenitsyn has adapted and put his own stamp on many other traits of the Tolstoyan novel. Both portray real historical men of power and introduce current public events, with a similar awareness of the havoc they can bring to individuals and a similar refusal to accept them as determinative of men's ultimate moral choices. There is a like desensationalization of inherently dramatic situations and at the same time the ability to renew the commonplace, to make the petty concerns and familiar sentiments of ordinary people vital, fresh, and extraordinary. Tolstoy's and Solzhenitsyn's protagonists are genuinely comparable: unheroic heroes, whose adventures are in the realms of conscience and thought; wonderfully individualized heroines who nevertheless exist most powerfully in the novels as objects of temptation or tenderness or saving love for the men. This kinship is all the more striking when one considers that two important aspects of Solzhenitsyn's feminine portrayals derive from conditions inconceivable to Tolstoy: the theme, developed with sensitivity and compassion, of an entire generation of women "widowed" by the war and the terror; and the custodial role (nurses, doctors, MGB officers) of almost all the loved women.

Finally, Tolstoy was a significant exemplar for Solzhenitsyn in a number of important secondary characterizations. A detailed comparison could be made, for example, of Solzhenitsyn's security officers and those of *Resurrection*. Kondrashev-Ivanov in *First Circle* recalls Mikhailov in *Anna Karenina*, by the function and the very construction of their scenes. The two authors' diffident, even humble, yet mystically idealized conceptions of art are expressed by an interplay of three elements: what the visitors see, what the paintings show, what the artists think. Most interesting, however, are the characterizations in which Solzhenitsyn not only uses but deliberately recalls a Tolstoyan model. Three notable examples are Rusanov and Ivan Il'ich, the Makarygin family and the Rostovs, Stalin and Nicholas I.

Solzhenitsyn has emphasized the Tolstoyan source of these characterizations by supplementing their numerous parallel passages and motifs with a detail taken from another, related Tolstoy character. Thus Rusanov, the Soviet true believer, follows each step trod by Ivan Il'ich, yet in his encounter with the unknown he also recalls Tolstoy's other great bureaucrat, Karenin:

> Aleksei Aleksandrovich was confronted with life . . . and this seemed meaningless and incomprehensible to him, because it was life itself. All his life he had lived and worked in official spheres, which deal only with reflections of life. [VIII, 170]
>
> And Rusanov, caught unaware by this stealthy approach of death, not only could not fight it but he could not in general think or decide about it or pronounce on it in any way.
>
> It came illegally, and there were no rules, no instructions to defend Pavel Nikolaevich. [RK, 223]

Thus the Makarygin family dinner party is so reminiscent of the Rostov nameday party that the prosecutor takes his male guests to his study to see his "tobacco-altar" (VKP, 318) as the count takes the men to his study to see his "choice collection of Turkish pipes" (IV, 80), and Natasha's cry, "Mama! What will there be for dessert?" (IV, 89) is echoed by Klara's, "Mama! Can't our table have an intermission till tea?" (VKP, 314). In addition to such Rostov details, however, there is Klara's sister Dotty whose English nickname recalls Tolstoy's other daughters of the nobility—Kitty, Dolly, and Missy. And Stalin, seen on (Western) Christmas day, while Nicholas I was seen on New Year's day, is like Nicholas in his senility, gloom, intellectual pretensions, capriciousness, sensuality, malice, and above all in his egomania:

> "Yes, what would Russia be without me," he said to himself, sensing again the approach of a feeling of discontent. "Yes not Russia alone, but what would Europe be without me . . ."
>
> Returning . . . he saw the carriages of Elena Pavlovna . . . [who] was to him the personification of those futile people who discussed not only science and poetry but also the governance of men, imagining that they could rule themselves better than he, Nicholas, ruled them. He knew that however much he crushed these people they would again come to the surface, they would keep crawling out. . . . And a vexed and gloomy feeling gripped him. [XVI, 94]
>
> Vexation which nothing could overcome burned inside him. Like a legendary bogatyr Stalin had all his life been chopping and cutting off the sprouting heads of the hydra . . . [but still they] kept proposing some kind of new, better socialism.
>
> Better socialism! *Different* from Stalin's! Snot! Who could build socialism *without Stalin?*
>
> The collected works of Lenin had already been revised three times, and those of the Founding Fathers twice. They had all been asleep for a long time now, those who had disagreed, who had been cited in old footnotes, all who had thought of building socialism *in some other way.* And now when even in the rustling of the taiga there were no critics, no doubts to be heard—Josef Tito crawls out . . . and says that things should be done differently. [VKP, 84-85]

Solzhenitsyn's Tolstoyan emphasis is double in Stalin's portrait. "Even to his intimates, he must appear as he would to history" (VKP, 86) is a clear recollection of the Napoleon of *War and Peace,* while "He must be a mountain eagle always, always" (VKP, 91) is an echo of Nicholas I's alter ego in tyranny, Shamil'.[5]

[5]Compare from *War and Peace:* "With the characteristically Italian ability to change the expression of his face at will . . . [Napoleon] assumed a look of reflective tenderness. He felt that what he said and did now would be history" (VI, 245). And from *Hadji Murad,* the description of Shamil' as "a mountain-man. And in those mountains eagles live" (XIV, 77).

With these underlined prototypes Solzhenitsyn is not so much labeling a literary influence as he is creatively reshaping a literary influence. Rusanov emerges as a Soviet Ivan Il'ich whose life is indeed "most simple, most ordinary and therefore most terrible." The Makarygins are not only a Soviet family of privilege; they enjoy their prerogatives less gracefully and more hypocritically than their predecessors. And although it is not "easy to be the Greatest of All the Great," Stalin, when measured against a favorite Soviet image of evil despotism, overtakes and surpasses.

II

In language and style Solzhenitsyn is a descendant of Tolstoy, but a living creative descendant whose voice is distinctively his own. The extraordinary pathos which Solzhenitsyn achieves in Spiridon does derive something from the Tolstoyan method (in his novels) of portraying peasants as they look and sound to educated men, without entering into their consciousness, without reporting their admirable or petty ambitions, their touching or unworthy fears. The language of Ivan Denisovich and of Spiridon, however, is more subtle than that of Tolstoy's peasants, whose speech seems always stylized to externalize their simple virtues, while in Solzhenitsyn's usage of peasant speech it is the complexity of the inarticulate which is revealed.

Solzhenitsyn's short sentences contrast with Tolstoy's complex ones as sharply as his use of conversation contrasts with Tolstoy's avoidance of it. Indeed, Solzhenitsyn's colloquial mastery is remarkable. As he moves from one to another character's consciousness, the language becomes unmistakably Nerzhin's or Rubin's or Kostoglotov's or Rusanov's. Tolstoy only occasionally achieved this; in his novels the content of a character's thought and speech is adapted to his consciousness with such massive and precise detail that each is definitively individualized, but Nikolai and Pierre think their different thoughts in a common vocabulary, Dolly and Anna conceive their different worlds in the same sentence structures. Solzhenitsyn has learned from Tolstoy, but he has also incorporated into his style the delicacy of Chekhov's language of nuance and the achievements of the great practitioners of *skaz.* Vinogradov's notable study of Tolstoy's language was based on his works of the fifties and sixties; the Solzhenitsyn oeuvre is already sufficient to make a similar study rewarding.

The two features of Solzhenitsyn's style which seem specifically Tolstoyan are his powerful physical language and, stemming from this, his ability to present external objects and settings in such a manner that without losing their existential integrity they irradiate the novel with meaning. Solzhenitsyn is not a Tolstoyan poet of the healthy body, and indeed only a few of his characters have sharp corporeal immediacy: red-haired Nerzhin's wrinkled face; the almost translucent two triangles of Vega; Shikin with his globular head and tiny feet in boys' shoes; shaggy Rubin in his underwear. Yet from the Tolstoy who created Vronskii's toothache, Serpukhovskoi's "putrescent worm-infested body in its new uniform and polished boots" (XII, 44) and Ivan Il'ich's gnawing pain, Solzhenitsyn is a remarkable inheritor. Both use healthy flesh to convey the horror of diseased flesh: as the doctors prepared to amputate Anatole Kuragin's shattered leg, his *other* "large, white plump leg kept rapidly, constantly twitching with febrile tremors" (VI, 290). "And Federau . . . with his still smooth, white but already condemned neck lay curled up on his side . . ." (RK, 122-123). But Solzhenitsyn eschews Tolstoy's relentless visual detail (such as Nikolai Levin's emaciated hand and arm "like a huge rake . . . attached to a long, thin, untapering spindle" IX, 70) for images which are just as stark, even more concentrated, but dynamic rather than descriptive: through five weeks of his life Rusanov had been "pulled along by his tumor like a hooked fish" (RK, 316); Vadim's "leg was caught in a trap—and his whole life with it" (RK, 320); Innokentii, reading on the warrant for arrest his own name, "was pierced throughout the whole length of his body as if by a single, huge needle" (VKP, 460).

It was not necessary for one translator of *Cancer Ward* to "Tolstoyanize" Solzhenitsyn's language by having Shulubin call his cancer "it,"[6] in echo of chapter VI of "The Death of Ivan Il'ich." Although this tale provided a major theme for the novel, Solzhenitsyn found his own methods for conveying what Tolstoy achieved with his pronoun—the personalized malice and mindlessly impersonal menace of cancer:

[6]Rebecca Frank, p. 359.

> [Kostoglotov] immediately felt how that toad inside him, his life's companion, burrowed itself deep within him and pressed down. [RK, 54]

> [Perhaps even as a child Vadim] was already striving to outdistance the future tumor, but he was racing into darkness, not seeing where his enemy was—while it saw everything and at the most ardent moment of his life it struck and bit! Not a sickness—a snake! And its snakish name—melanoblastoma! [RK, 216]

> the striped panther of death which had settled down in the same bed beside him . . . [RK, 217]

> Death had already made her nest in him—and he would not believe it! [VKP, 106]

It should be noted that Solzhenitsyn's animal imagery (which is only one of many varieties of his physical language) is by no means confined to disease. Indeed in this realm he is as vivid as Leskov and as versatile as Tolstoy (although far less knowledgeable—one is not sure that he has ever really watched a panther). Tolstoy's constant observation of real animals in human settings imbues his fiction with the sense of man's moral strivings as part of the world of nature, while Solzhenitsyn's animals, metaphoric in hospital and prison, remind us that the spiritual aspirations and sufferings which are his prime concern are borne not by moral abstractions but by men of flesh and blood.

The use of a recurrent and unifying symbol in *Anna Karenina* was exceptional for Tolstoy, and similarly, the bird symbolism of *First Circle* seems unusual for Solzhenitsyn.[7] When they do employ it however, both writers use sustained symbolism in the same way. In *Anna Karenina* the railroad has a primary meaning, the destruction of natural good by man's devisement, and the symbolization does not transform the railroad image or expand the meaning, but rather introduces the meaning into various contexts, through different manifestations of the image: an important locale for Anna's and Vronskii's fatal passion; an intrusive children's game in the "upset" Oblonskii and Karenin households; the focus of Levin's study of the land and peasant; the profession of a man named Malthus. The birds of *First Circle* have a primary meaning of human freedom, physical freedom from captivity and spiritual freedom within captivity. Like Tolstoy's railroad, Solzhenitsyn's birds are not transmuted

[7]At the end of *First Circle* the departing zeks are compared to Christ at Gethsemane, and Nerzhin's birthday is December 25. Nevertheless, the novel does not seem to me to contain *sustained* Christian symbolism.

or distorted as images, but are rather presented in many guises, introducing the idea of freedom into different situations: the bird plumage robe of the Hungarian partisan girl, caged in a Moscow dormitory; Sologdin's "bird-words," bearers of alien concepts; "the great beating wings" of true intellect and the "winged language of allusion" which can speak freely even in prison; courageous Gerasimovich, "puny as a sparrow, . . . the sparrow in the proverb, whose heart was as brave as a cat's" (VKP, 416); Shchevronok, who will be arrested because of Rubin's eagerness for "scientific" success and whose name makes Rubin think of a skylark [*zhavoronok* (VKP, 174)]; Innokentii's green enamel Lubianka mug on which a cat (in reading glasses) menaces a bird; Simochka, shy as a quail, whose heart liberates her mind from MGB indoctrination; Innokentii, who has learned to distinguish between good and evil, going to his interrogation "with his head thrust back, as a bird drinks water" (VKP, 488).

Far more than he used single, unifying symbols, Tolstoy developed the device of endowing individual scenes or particular physical objects with human meanings which infuse the entire novel, and through them giving simple, concrete expression to complex and ambiguous emotions or reflections: Dolly's visit to Anna, Katiusha at the railroad station, Karenin's ears, Pierre's bare feet, Liza Bolkonskaia's tombstone, etc. Solzhenitsyn has made these techniques his own and such scenes as the mock trial of Prince Igor, the visit of Gleb and Nadia, the blood transfusion, Kostoglotov's letter to the Kadmins and his "day" in Tashkent should soon be competing with Frou Frou's last ride as subjects for "intrinsic and extrinsic analysis." And for Solzhenitsyn's readers a whole host of material objects will never again be merely themselves: Zoia's *moulinet* (recalling Dolly's and Kitty's embroidery); Kostoglotov's army belt; the oxygen bag; the clothes of casual lovers strewn around a bedroom; a skewer of smoking shashlik; the blossoming apricot tree (which Vega seeks and Kostoglotov finds, and which unites them as their common dream united Anna and Vronskii); the blinded rhesus monkey; a black imitation-caracul coat; fluffy pink bath towels and a cake of "Lilac Fairy" soap; a parquet floor; a book of poetry with oak leaves on the cover; a neatly labeled "Meat" truck, and many more.

Solzhenitsyn has even invented his own special categories of meaningful objects. First, those which are empty or absent or simply not there: the rhesus monkey is not in its cage and is never seen; there is a sliver of moon but no bird in the cage which Ivan the glassblower spins (for the New Year's tree which is barely glimpsed by the departing zeks as it is being delivered); the spot on the stairs over which Klara cannot walk is invisible; the music which Agniia strives to make Iakonov hear comes after the church bell has ceased to ring, while the bell to whose tolling Nerzhin listens is "mute." And Solzhenitsyn has a special sensitivity for the pathos and meaning which can be transmitted to objects by the human bodies which have touched them: the cancer ward's "tarnished door handles, rubbed by the hands of the sick" (RK, 14) and its veranda "polished by thousands of feet" (RK, 92); the little table behind which generations of prisoners have sat, its surface warped and marked "with strange wavy or angular figures, unconsciously drawn, which in some mysterious way preserved the secret twistings of the soul, . . . the little table which had seen many tears" (VKP, 199, 202); the stairs in Lubianka which Innokentii notices: "From the edge to the middle they were worn down in oval hollows to half their depth. He shuddered: in thirty years how many feet! how many times! must have shuffled across here, to so wear down the stone!" (VKP, 482). In Solzhenitsyn's novels these worn objects embody the accumulated suffering of those who have touched them while the absent objects signify the non-material reality of such moral entities as freedom, guilt, injustice, truth.

Even in the realm of the physical language of bodies and objects Solzhenitsyn's accomplishments cannot, of course, always be related to Tolstoy's. Pondering his recovery from cancer, which threatens him with impotence, Kostoglotov reflects: "The honey in the barrel was equally mixed with grease, and now it was no good, either to eat or to oil a wheel" (RK, 382). Both the coarseness of the imagery and the second explanatory clause are reminiscent of Tolstoy, but such is not always the case. For example, Chalyi's explanation of why bigamy is convenient for traveling men: "in every city there's a room with a chicken leg" (RK, 270). Or the portrayal of the marriage of Innokentii's Bolshevik father to his gentle mother who lived in a world of symbolist poetry and idealistic ethics, "that world into which his father, in a black raincoat, his belt hung with grenades, entered with a search warrant" (VKP, 306). For such expressions as these no useful specific comparison to Tolstoy can be drawn. What can be concluded is that in ways sometimes similar, sometimes different, Tolstoy and Solzhenitsyn are probably the two greatest practitioners of that variety of Russian realism which uses the concrete, physical, everyday entities of the external world to represent the intangible, spiritual, personal yet universal phenomena of the inner world. A realism in which the puddle not only reflects but is the cloud:

> The strange, palely-sunshiny spot on the ceiling suddenly rippled, sparkled in brightly silver dots, and then disappeared. And with this running rippling, with these tiny wavelets, Oleg finally understood that the mysterious, lofty cloud on the ceiling was simply the reflection of a puddle which had not dried up, near the fence outside the window. A transformation of a simple puddle. [RK, 286]

III

> School children write compositions: On the Unhappy, Tragic... Life of Anna Karenina. But was Anna really unhappy? She chose passion—and paid for passion, that's happiness! She was free and proud! But what if, in peacetime, men in caps and overcoats come into the house where you were born, where you've lived all your life, and order the whole family to leave the house and the city in twenty-four hours, taking only what your weak hands can carry?... And nosy speculators... shamelessly offer you a hundredth of its value for your mother's piano,—and your little daughter in a hair-ribbon sits down to play Mozart for the last time, but bursts out crying and runs away,—why should I re-read *Anna Karenina?* Where can I read about *us, about us?* [RK, 401-402]

The closest kinship between Tolstoy and Solzhenitsyn is philosophic, and when significant differences appear they seem to stem from two sources, one temperamental and one biographical. Where instinctive pride made Tolstoy an answerer, intrinsic modesty casts Solzhenitsyn as a questioner, but the terms of his queries are Tolstoyan. The questions which preoccupy Solzhenitsyn have arisen from realities which he has experienced and Tolstoy never dreamed of: prison camp, cancer, lives cruelly disrupted, helpless people unjustly tormented—not by war or by "society" but "just simply so."

First one may note how many favorite Tolstoyan attitudes, even quirks of thought, Solzhenitsyn assumes or assigns to his characters. Sologdin reminds us of Tolstoy of the diaries when he punishes himself with "fault-marks" for transgressions of his private intellectual or sexual rules. And there is still another bond between the two, for although Tolstoy frequently used not only the language but even the syntax of "Apparent Clarity" he sounds very much like Sologdin when he argues in *What Is Art?* that beauty [*krasota*] should not be used for words or sounds or deeds because its old Russian meaning was purely visual (XV, 56-57). With regard to doctors and medicine the realities of his own experience have led Solzhenitsyn to a reasoned and reasonable acceptance: gratitude for the relief of pain and sympathetic indignation at the persecution to which dedicated, overworked physicians are subject in the Soviet Union. But his instinctive attitude is very much like Tolstoy's, as in the description of Klara's illness, which recalls both Natasha's and Kitty's, or in Kostoglotov's plea that his recovery be left to "the defensive forces of the organism" (RK, 56). Another shared attitude is their uncompromising insistence that whatever the circumstances love cannot survive the violation of a woman's faithfulness and purity. Thus Kostoglotov cannot return to the girl he had loved. Thus Prince Andrei's bitter paradox—"I said that a fallen woman ought to be forgiven, but I didn't say that I could forgive her. I can't"—is echoed by Rubin and Nerzhin: "Theoretically Glebka is right," Rubin comments on Nerzhin's former belief that if a husband can be forgiven for unfaithfulness, so can a wife. "But to make love to your wife after someone else has made love to her? Brrr! Biologically, I can't!" (VKP, 287).

Other, perhaps more fundamental views are also shared by Solzhenitsyn and Tolstoy. Kostoglotov's idyll of the Kadmins' simple life in Ush-Terek produced his most Tolstoyan animal, the dog Zhuk, and even recalls Tolstoy's tender description of another exiled, elderly husband and wife as "Baucis and Philemon."[8] The wood-chopping scenes of *The First Circle,* with their expression of the elementary pleasure of physical labor, recall Levin mowing with his peasants, despite Solzhenitsyn's remark in another context that war correspondents are as different from front line soldiers "as a count who plows the soil is different from a real *muzhik*" (VKP, 334). When Kostoglotov advises Demka that "education doesn't make you smart.... Trust your own eyes, not what you hear [from others]" (RK, 30) he is warning him of the morally stultifying effect of received doctrine, a basic Tolstoyan tenet. The same point is made through Vadim, who partly from reverence for his father and

[8]L. N. Tolstoi, *Polnoe sobranie sochinenii,* LX, 113. The reference is to the exiled Decembrist, M. I. Pushchin, and his wife, whom Tolstoy visited in Switzerland in the spring of 1857.

partly from his scientific ambition (as selfless yet egoistic as Andrei's quest for glory) has refused the wisdom of his own insight into Stalin. (It is striking how Solzhenitsyn the writer shows through—recognition of Stalin's turgid literary style is a revelatory experience for several of his characters, and distaste for poor quality paper and ink is one of the rare complaints about material hardships repeated in the novels.)

Nothing is more basic to Tolstoy's thought and art than the conviction that only one's own experience can be trusted and that the inner voice of conscience must be trusted. But no single character in Tolstoy exemplifies this principle as perfectly as Lev Rubin of *The First Circle*. Generous, kind, honorable, selfless, Rubin is a figure of tragic stature, blinded by political dedication. Rising above his personal suffering "for the good of the cause," he betrays the humanity he has sacrificed all to serve, and it is a measure of Solzhenitsyn's artistry that Rubin is never more appealing than when entrapping Innokentii for his decent impulse, scorning food and sleep in his enthusiastic pursuit of "the fountainhead of science." Although Rubin's first reaction on hearing Innokentii's tape was to like the "simple fellow" who tried to warn the philanthropic doctor, he then suppressed his own inner voice: "But *objectively*—objectively that fellow, wanting to do good, had in fact acted against the progressive forces of history" (VKP, 173).

The terms of Rubin's fatal self-delusion are pure Leninism: *objectively* humanity is the working class, the working class is the party, the party is its vanguard, the vanguard is Stalin; objectively sadism and injustice are progressive if they serve Stalin's will, decency and honor must be crushed if they impede it. Solzhenitsyn's fundamental counter-premise—trust your own eyes, your own experience, your own inner feelings—has led him to other beliefs to which Tolstoy also proceeded from the same starting point. First is ultimate reliance on the private, individual conscience, not because it is perfect but because it is the least faulty of men's governors. From this follows the ardent, personal quest for truth through sincerity. To Elizaveta Anatol'evna's question as to how to bring up her son: "to hide the truth or to reconcile him with life?" Kostoglotov's reply is staunch: "Burden him with the truth!" (RK, 400). And it is notable that except in his portrayal of Stalin, Solzhenitsyn's sarcasm is most devastating in his treatment of writers who have betrayed this great Russian literary tradition. As Alla Rusanova triumphantly proclaims:

> [Writers adjust smoothly to a change in the official literary line]—it's one of those sharp reversals life is so full of.... If there were disharmony, if some said the old things and some the new, then you would notice that something has changed. But as it is, right away, everyone starts saying the new thing together.... Sincerity cannot possibly be the chief criterion in literature. When there are untrue ideas or alien tendencies it only strengthens the harmful effect of a work; sincerity is *harmful!* Subjective sincerity can detract from the truthfulness of the portrayal of life—that's dialectics. [RK, 245-246]

Subjective sincerity in the quest for truth, reliance on one's own experience and conscience, are doctrines which exalt the individual but circumscribe the self. Both Tolstoy and Solzhenitsyn value the healing humility which comes from the acceptance of compassion to oneself, and Solzhenitsyn's attempts to "rehabilitate" pity provide several of his most moving passages. And both stress the presumptuous egoism of judging for others: "A circle of wrongs! A circle of wrongs!... Where should one begin to set the world right? With others? Or with oneself?" (VKP, 377). Between trust in oneself and humility toward oneself the link is a conception of man as not merely a physical organism but as the possessor of a soul. Kostoglotov repeatedly protests the idea that life is man's highest value, "at any price," and in this Solzhenitsyn joins himself to Tolstoy in opposition to Russian literature's chorus of life-worshipping yea-sayers. Indeed Solzhenitsyn's first mention of the soul comes with a characteristically ironic reference to Tolstoy: "It is well known that when a French soldier would not permit Pierre to cross the road, Pierre roared out laughing: 'The soldier did not let me across. Who—me? It's my immortal soul he did not let across!' " (VKP, 152). As Solzhenitsyn moves forward in *First Circle,* and then in *Cancer Ward,* this affirmation loses its touch of self-consciousness and becomes strong and explicit.

Tolstoy told Gorkii:

> about the soul I know one thing: the soul desires nearness to God. And what is God? That of which my soul is a particle.

Kondrashev reflects to Nerzhin:

> In a human being, from birth, there is instilled a certain Essence! And no one knows which forms what: life may shape man or man with his strong spirit may shape life! Because... man has something

> with which to compare himself. Something to *look to*. For there is in him an image of Perfection, which in rare moments suddenly emerges. Before the spiritual gaze. [VKP, 228]

And Dr. Oreshchenkov muses that the meaning of existence lies in the extent to which men

> succeed in preserving—undimmed, uncongealed and undistorted—that image of eternity which is given to every person.
>
> Like a silver moon in a peaceful pond. [RK, 361]

Pierre tells Andrei:

> We must live, we must love and we must believe . . . that we live not only in the present on this patch of earth, but that we have lived and will live eternally, there, in the whole (and he pointed to the sky). [V, 133]

Shulubin tells Oleg:

> But sometimes I feel so clearly: what is in me—that's not the whole "I." There is still something else, quite indestructible, something very lofty! Some fragment of the World Spirit. [RK, 405]

Tolstoy explains Pierre's decision to set out against Napoleon:

> It was the feeling . . . which impels a man to perform actions which are (from a commonplace point of view) insane, as if he were measuring his personal power and strength and affirming the existence of a higher, non-human judgment of life. [VI, 404]

And Nerzhin gives up the relative security of the sharashka for "death or a hard victory over death" in the camps:

> You know what they say: "It's not the sea that drowns you but the puddle." [VKP, 501]

Despite such congruences, Solzhenitsyn's philosophic relationship to Tolstoy is most interesting where he is powerfully attracted yet not entirely convinced. The life story which Nerzhin hears from Spiridon embodies all of Tolstoy's accumulated wisdom about the peasant—"What Spiridon loved was the land. What Spiridon had was a family." So that Nerzhin wonders: "Did not Spiridon's complicated life . . . somehow correspond to the Tolstoyan teaching that there are no just and no guilty in the world? Was there not revealed in these almost instinctive acts . . . a universal system of philosophic skepticism?" But Spiridon says no: "The wolf-hound is right but the cannibal is not" (VKP, 352, 355, 356), and in this rejection of the

Tolstoyan view one hears Solzhenitsyn's voice also. However deep his response to the idea that "God Sees the Truth" but men cannot judge, Solzhenitsyn has experienced (and his conscience has compelled him to depict) too much injustice to himself and others to assume so lofty and in some ways comforting a detachment. And yet he remains aware of the "circle of wrongs" which can issue from righteous judgment, and of how easily consciousness of just intentions can muffle the conscience. With painful irony he ascribes his own doubts about the Tolstoyan position to Rusanov, Rusanov whose whole life has been a history of non-resistance to evil and active compromise with it: "He's a namby-pamby, your Tolstoy! . . . Evil must be resisted, my boy, evil must be fought!" (RK, 99).

These words end the chapter of *Cancer Ward* called "What Men Live By" but the question reverberates throughout the novel. Just as Solzhenitsyn introduced the vital theme of man's soul into *The First Circle* in a humorously deprecatory Tolstoyan citation ("It is well known"), so the problem which dominates *Cancer Ward* first appears with a concealed Tolstoyan joke, for Demka, who has brought the book into the ward has dismissed it as useless in the words of Tolstoy's famous disdainment of historians in *War and Peace:* "It completely missed the point, like a deaf interlocutor who answers questions you have not asked" (RK, 97 and see VII, 335). When men begin to ask what people live by, they have rejected the traditional formulations of state, church, and "common sense," and so it is with Tolstoy and Solzhenitsyn. In his youth Tolstoy experimented with rational epicureanism and through Innokentii, Solzhenitsyn pursues this answer to its hollow ending. Love of the most immediate neighbor, one's family, was for a time the answer which satisfied Tolstoy, and it is a solution to which Solzhenitsyn gives serious consideration and shattering refutation through the Makarygins, the Rusanovs, and above all through Shulubin. Solzhenitsyn's extraordinary accomplishments as a moral philosopher-artist, however, are to be found not in his rejections nor even in his affirmations but in the delicately sustained subtlety and profundity of his explorations.

Thus in *Cancer Ward* the question, What do men live by? inheres in the separate stories of a dozen patients and doctors, provides a silent accompaniment to Oleg's encounters with Zoia and Vega, pinpoints his dilemmas—to accept hope with its risk of pain? to survive at the expense of manhood?—and skeins through the whole novel in speculations on how far the physician has the right to preserve life at any price, how far any man has the right to decide for others, when at stake is that great unknown, the thing by which men should live. Thus in *First Circle,* the fabric of the novel interweaves a multitude of stories of past revelation and dawning insight, while embroidered on this fabric are the present dramatizations of men and women at moments of moral decision. Three of these protagonists are women, and so delicate is Solzhenitsyn's treatment that one cannot say which path each will ultimately elect. Nor, even if some Belinskii ex machina could reveal that Serafima would show Nerzhin's notes to a future husband, that Klara will become a suitable mate for Lanskii, that Nadia will divorce Gleb, has Solzhenitsyn prepared the way for their condemnation. The six men make their choices, at least this day's choices. The reader admires Ruska and Innokentii for the courage with which they arrive at an initial commitment and rejoices at the more long-fought and hard-won spiritual victories of Nerzhin and Gerasimovich. What is astonishing, however, is that Solzhenitsyn has so arranged matters that while the reader deplores the choices made by Rubin and Sologdin, he does so with the judgment which hates the sin but loves the sinner.

Solzhenitsyn has said that "the task of the writer is to select . . . universal and eternal questions, the secrets of the human heart and conscience."[9] In turning his teacher's answers into eternal questions, Solzhenitsyn is at once most truly Tolstoyan and most uniquely himself.

[9]See "Appendix" to *Cancer Ward* (Bantam Books edition), p. 554.

Lukacs and Solzhenitsyn

BY IRVING HOWE

For most of his life Georg Lukacs, the intellectual heresiarch of Communism, was unable to write freely. During the years he spent under Stalin in Russia and Rakosi in Hungary he had no freedom at all; more recently, under Kadar in Hungary, he was granted a measure of intellectual independence but only in a cautious, limited way. Lukacs made one major bolt from the bounds of political orthodoxy by joining the Nagy government of 1956, but once the Russian troops destroyed it he gradually came back into the fold. He had always to keep looking over his shoulder, sometimes literally and more often figuratively, so as to measure the latitude allowed him by the Party. Long ago he had chosen the role of the (at times) semi-dissident Communist, but never an openly oppositionist Communist and certainly not a public opponent of the party-state dictatorship.

Lukacs's reasons for this choice were clear: the locomotive of history had gone badly astray, the best passengers had been killed, the engineer had turned out to be a homicidal maniac, yet somehow that locomotive chugged in the direction of progress. To have declared himself in clear opposition to totalitarianism, he believed, would have meant to isolate himself from History. It was a choice like that of the old Bolshevik

"Lukacs and Solzhenitsyn." From *Dissent* (December, 1971), 643-647

Nikolai Bukharin, who in the early thirties paid a secret visit to some Mensheviks in Paris, trembling with fright and horror at the excesses of Stalin yet unable to face the prospect of exile. For Bukharin the result was death; for Lukacs a captivity sometimes grating, sometimes silken. The course they chose, whatever its political merits, was not likely to encourage moral strength or forthrightness, since "if you always look over your shoulder," as a character in Solzhenitsyn's *The First Circle* remarks, "how can you still remain a human being?" Not a good Communist or adept dialectician, but "a human being." That these words should now be cited with seeming approval by Lukacs, a man who knew his way around his shoulder, is a matter of high intellectual drama.

The small book Lukacs wrote about Solzhenitsyn at the very end of his life is a remarkable work, certainly far more so than the theoretical writings of his early years, which in their recent translations have given rise to a wavelet of Marxist scholasticism. In his study of Solzhenitsyn—perhaps because he found it easier or more prudent to express his deepest convictions through the mediated discourse of literary criticism than through the directness of political speech—Lukacs expresses fervently, as perhaps never before, the disgust he felt for Stalinism, at least Stalinism as the terrorist phase of the party-state dictatorship, if not as an integral sociopolitical system.

In *One Day in the Life of Ivan Denisovich,* writes Lukacs, "*the concentration camp is a symbol of everyday Stalinist life.*" Remarkable; especially when one remembers a little wryly the rebukes from Left and Right delivered to those of us who have been saying exactly the same thing. Still more remarkable is Lukacs's reference, obviously made with an eye toward the Khrushchev and Brezhnev regimes, to "the new era with all its changes which preserve *the essential methods of Stalinism* with only superficial modifications" (emphasis added—I.H.). Such passages, and there are a number of them, are at least as revealing of Lukacs's inner thoughts as of Solzhenitsyn's well-known books.

Lukacs's admiration for Solzhenitsyn clearly went beyond the latter's literary achievement; it had much to do with his moral stature. At a number of points Lukacs writes with approval of Solzhenitsyn's independence and courage.[1] And it is precisely here that we encounter a painful problem. For between the absolute candor of Solzhenitsyn's work and the deviousness of Lukacs's career there is a startling difference, so much so that one senses in this little book a measure of discomfort and defensiveness. A man as intelligent as Lukacs could hardly have been unaware that he kept praising Solzhenitsyn for precisely the virtues he himself had rarely shown.

Completely fascinating in this respect is Lukacs's attitude toward one of the characters in *The First Circle,* the prisoner Rubin who is portrayed by Solzhenitsyn as a very decent man but intellectually still in the grip of Communist orthodoxy. For Rubin, writes Lukacs,

> friendship . . . is an indispensable part of life, and here [in the special camp for scientists] he cannot befriend like-minded persons, while all his friends reject his views. . . . In order to be able to exist accordingly, he repeatedly recites humorous parodies of poems . . . the only effect of which is that he must subsequently be ashamed of the role he has played.

Yet what have been a good many of Lukacs's own writings during the last few decades but parodies of Marxism composed under the pressures of the Party, for which he must subsequently have felt ashamed? One source, then, of his admiration for Solzhenitsyn seems to be the Russian novelist's deliberate refusal of "tactics," the whole stale jumble of "dialectics" by which thinkers like Lukacs have persisted in justifying their submission to the dictatorship of the Party.

Precisely this uncomfortable mixture of responses may account for the fact that in discussing Solzhenitsyn's novels Lukacs turns

[1]How admirable, even overwhelming, that courage is we can learn from the recently published collection of documents concerning the Solzhenitsyn "case" that has been edited by Leopold Labedz. In chronological order, these documents show the emergence of Solzhenitsyn as a new Russian writer welcomed by the more open-minded of his colleagues; then the mounting struggle between the Soviet bureaucracy and the independent-minded intellectuals over Solzhenitsyn's work; and finally the brutal clamping-down of the regime upon Solzhenitsyn and his supporters. There are two remarkable transcripts, the first of a group of Moscow writers discussing with Solzhenitsyn in 1966 his then uncompleted novel *Cancer Ward*—by and large, the discussion is serious, fraternal, in good faith; and second, of a meeting held a year later with the Secretariat of the Union of Soviet Writers—here the discussion consists of a disgraceful badgering of Solzhenitsyn by party hacks. Also included are articles by Russian writers, interviews, documents, letters, etc. An indispensable book.

See *Solzhenitsyn: A Documentary Record,* Leopold Labedz, ed., New York: Harper & Row, 1971, 229 pp.

to a theme that has long preoccupied independent critics in the West (and secretly, no doubt, in the East) but has hardly figured in Lukacs's own work. I refer to the problem of integrity, as a trait independent of and not reducible to political opinion or class status. It is the problem of how men under an absolute tyranny struggle, as Lukacs well puts it, "to preserve their own human integrity even here." And still more striking is Lukacs's remark that "in the camps"—which you will remember he has described as "a symbol of everyday Stalinist life" such as he himself experienced for years—"a refusal to compromise in all human and social essentials thus forms a prerequisite for anyone wishing to remain really human." Strong words!

Stronger still is the remark of Nerzhin, the central character of *The First Circle,* which Lukacs quotes with evident approval: there "is no better place" than prison "to understand the part of good and evil in human life." Good and evil! What is Lukacs doing with his praise of these "trans-historical," these quite undialectical, these perhaps neo-Kantian categories? Not "progressive and reactionary," but "good and evil." Something, one can only surmise, must have been fermenting in Lukacs's mind during his last years that the appearance of Solzhenitsyn's novels helped bring to fruition, something more heretical than he ever dared express in his own right.

Writing about the social world portrayed by Solzhenitsyn, Lukacs comments:

> Should bureaucracy become the dominant mode of life of those participating in it, should the decisions dictated by it determine their way of life, entirely, then inevitably the tactics of the apparatus, dictated by its day-to-day needs, become the ultimate judge of all decisions between good and evil.

It really begins to look as if, in the end, Lukacs was badly torn between such entirely admirable sentiments, elicited and brought to sharp articulation by Solzhenitsyn's books, and his continuing persuasion, part canniness and part habitual abjectness, that he had to remain faithful to the Party.

One reason Lukacs admires Solzhenitsyn the novelist is that he sees him as a realist in the nineteenth-century tradition who does not fiddle about with experimental techniques, clearly has large moral-historical scope, and puts a programmatically antimodernist critic like himself at ease. To some extent—I can't pretend to exactitude—this seems to me a misunderstanding of Solzhenitsyn's fiction, just as some years ago there was a similar misunderstanding of Pasternak's novel. Each of these writers chose to go back to the capacious forms of the nineteenth-century realistic novel, with its interweaving of themes, narrative elements, and characters, but not, I think, because of a deliberate or ideological rejection of literary modernism. Their decisions rested, instead, on moral-political grounds as these can be inferred from their novels themselves, namely, a persuasion that genuinely to return to the Tolstoyan novel, which the Stalinist dogma of "socialist realism" had celebrated in words but caricatured in performance, would constitute a revolutionary act of the spirit. It would signify a struggle for human renewal, for the reaffirmation of the image of a free man as that image can excite our minds beyond all ideological decrees. Pasternak had already been for many years a modernist poet, and Solzhenitsyn, forced by circumstances to live apart from all literary tendencies or groups, seems not to have been interested in the dispute over modernism. He had apparently reached the "instinctive" conclusion that in an authoritarian society the role of the writer is to recover fundamental supports of moral existence, direct intuitions of human fraternity, encompassing moments of truth. A writer seized by such a vision—which in some sense must be regarded as religious in urgency and depth—is not likely to think first of all about innovations of technique, though there is reason to suppose that he may nevertheless achieve them.

The first task of such a writer, as he takes upon himself the heavy and uncomfortable mantle of moral spokesman, is to remember, to record, to insist upon the sanctity of simple fact and uncontaminated memory. That is why Solzhenitsyn's apparent indifference to literary modernism which so pleases Lukacs would seem to be less a deliberate repudiation than a step beyond the circumstances that had first led to modernism. It is a step that prompted Solzhenitsyn to revive—though with significant modifications—the Tolstoyan novel, a step taken out of the conviction that in our time the claim for freedom is inseparable from the resurrection of history. To be free means in our century, first of all, to remember.

Simply as a literary critic, Lukacs often writes well in this book. He compares *One Day in the Life of Ivan Denisovich* with by-now classical novellas by Conrad and Hemingway in order to work out a rough schema for the novella, or short novel, as a form:

> It does not claim to shape the whole of social reality, nor even to depict that whole as it appears from the vantage point of a fundamental and topical problem. Its truth rests on the fact that an individual situation—usually an extreme one [but has not modernism just entered here, through the back door?—I.H.]—is possible in a certain society at a certain level of development, and just because it is possible, is characteristic of this society and this level.

If not quite original, this is very keen. More original and illuminating is Lukacs's notion that in the twentieth century there has appeared a kind of novel that enlarges upon the central structure of the novella. Lukacs notices this, first of all, in *The Magic Mountain,* whose "compositional innovation"

> may be described . . . in a purely formal way, namely that the uniformity of the setting is made the immediate foundation of the narrative. The characters of this novel are removed from the "natural" location of their lives and movements, and are transplanted into new and artificial surroundings (here the sanatorium for consumptives). The major consequence of this is that the characters do not come into contact with each other, as so often in life and even more frequently in art, in "normal" ways . . . ; rather this "chance" common terrain of their present existence creates new fundamental forms of their human, intellectual and moral relations with each other.

What such a literary structure then does is to sustain a prolonged interval of crisis in which the characters are put to a test. In *The Magic Mountain* Thomas Mann enforces the test through a confrontation with the reality of the characters' own death. In *The First Circle* Solzhenitsyn has the prisoners confronted "not only by the slender hope of liberation, but by a very real threat of a more infernal region of hell" (that is, shipment to the worst camps in Siberia).

Clearly this is the kind of analysis that serious readers can respect, since it makes an effort to see works of literature in their own realm of being and ventures upon comparisons in regard to structure and technique that leap across the dull hurdles of "socialist realism." Yet it seems utterly characteristic of Lukacs that just as he shows his mind at its liveliest he should also show it still unfree. Having analyzed the relation of the structural principle in Solzhenitsyn's novels to that which he locates in the work of Mann, Lukacs must then come up with a preposterous remark that "Solzhenitsyn's works appear as a rebirth of the noble beginnings of socialist realism." But this is sheer nonsense. Whatever Solzhenitsyn's novels may be, they really have nothing in common with "socialist realism," not even with the one, rather frayed instance offered by Lukacs of its "noble beginnings," the fiction of the Soviet writer Makarenko which he overrates simply in order to show that he does, still, adhere to a version of "socialist realism."[2]

The central criticism Lukacs makes of Solzhenitsyn is that the Russian novelist writes from the strong but limiting perspective of the plebeian mind, rather than from a socialist consciousness. Lukacs grants that Solzhenitsyn's criticism of Soviet society is "rooted in a genuine plebeian hatred of social privilege"; it is tied by numerous filaments of attitude to the "plebeian social view" of such Tolstoyan characters as Platon Karataev in *War and Peace;* but it lacks, as it must, the historical perspective, the theoretical coherence that can alone be provided by the "socialist" outlook.

This point is of considerable literary and political interest, since it marks quite clearly the limits within which Lukacs, for all his on-again, off-again hatred of Stalinist society and the "new era" which "preserves the essential methods of Stalinism," nevertheless continues to function.

Lukacs refers to a striking phrase of Marx, the "ignorant perfection" of ordinary people, a perfection of healthy social impulse, a moral rightness that can spontaneously arise among the masses. It is "perfection" because it immediately sniffs out frauds and tyrants, but "ignorant" because it has not been raised to a level of generality or fortified with "dialectics." It remains a healthy reaction to what exists, but by itself cannot lead to action in behalf of what might be. The vocabulary of Leninism made a parallel distinction between ordinary trade-union consciousness, which the masses can reach by themselves,

[2]Not one in a hundred of Lukacs's readers are likely to have read Makarenko, and that may lend his claim plausibility. But having struggled with an English translation of Makarenko's *The Road to Life,* which Lukacs praises so highly, even to the point of linking it with *The Magic Mountain,* I can only testify that it is a characteristic exercise in agit-prop, though perhaps a shade better than most Soviet writing. Perhaps Lukacs was indulging in some sort of inside joke, with those in Eastern Europe who do know Makarenko being tipped off not to take this standard reference very seriously.

and revolutionary consciousness, which the vanguard party must bring to (or impose upon) the masses.

Now, historically Lukacs is being more than a little ingenuous in confining the dominant vision of Solzhenitsyn's work, as well as that in Tolstoy best represented by the character Platon Karataev, to the level of the "plebeian." Plebeian these certainly are, as in the wonderful remark of Solzhenitsyn's character Spiridon who, when asked to describe the difference between the guilty and the innocent, answers, "Sheepdogs are right and cannibals are wrong." But in reality, as any student of Russian literature must know, the plebeian stress in Tolstoy and Dostoevsky, which one hears again in Solzhenitsyn, draws upon a strand of Christian belief very powerful in Russian culture, a strand that favors egalitarianism and ascetic humility, as if to take the word of Jesus at face value. Platon Karataev may himself be an example of "ignorant perfection," but Tolstoy's act in creating him is anything but that. It follows from a major world-view,[3] in its own way at least as comprehensive as that of Marxism. And the same might hold in regard to Solzhenitsyn's "plebeian" sentiments.

Furthermore, it should be stressed that at a time when the "socialist" vocabulary is used for oppressive ends, the "plebeian" response, even if undecorated with ideology and world views, takes on a liberating, indeed a revolutionary character. And the same, I would say, holds for certain religious responses. That Lukacs could, however, write a book about Solzhenitsyn without so much as mentioning the problem of his religious inclinations, let alone those of the Tolstoy to whom he links Solzhenitsyn, is indeed a "dialectical" feat.

Let us nevertheless stay with Lukacs's argument for a moment, even granting, for the sake of that argument, the evident justice in his remark that "the inner 'ignorant perfection' of the common people is not sufficient to develop in man a positively effective and critical attitude toward the reform of his alienated society." Yet precisely these cogent words are likely to raise a

[3]On the component of heretical Christianity in Tolstoy and its political significance, Trotsky's essays on Tolstoy are far more illuminating than Lukacs's, perhaps because Trotsky writing under the Tsar was less inhibited in expressing his views than Lukacs under the reign of the Party. If, by the way, it is Marxist literary criticism that interests some young intellectuals these days, they will find it—to the extent that it can be said to exist—far more brilliantly, clearly, and elegantly achieved in Trotsky than in Lukacs. I sometimes suspect that the current fad of Lukacs has something to do with his imposing verbal opacity.

tremor of distrust among readers experienced in the politics of Marxism. For Lukacs is speaking not merely in the abstract about the need for theoretical vision and generality; he writes from his own version of Marxism-Leninism, and when he contrasts Solzhenitsyn's "plebeian" limitation with the largeness of "socialist" perspective, we can't avoid translating this into a contrast between Solzhenitsyn's "moral-social criticism of Communist society from the standpoint of freedom" and Lukacs's "criticism directed toward the resurrection of the Party within the framework of orthodox belief." What then becomes evident is that Solzhenitsyn's criticism of Russian society—even if limited by the "ignorant perfection" of the "plebeian" outlook—is far deeper, far more revolutionary, and far closer to the needs of a genuine socialism than that of Lukacs. Neither the dissident nor oppositionist label really fits Solzhenitsyn. Plebeian, yes. Plebeian, in that he has become the voice of all those who silently suffered through the decades of the terror and beyond. Brushing past the cant of Lukacs's world ("the leading role of the Party," "the Leninist heritage," etc.), Solzhenitsyn embodies in his fiction that empathy with the lowly and the mute which links him both to the great masters of the nineteenth century and the still-uncreated future of free men.

Solzhenitsyn: Art and Foreign Matter

BY DONALD FANGER

> Very significant and expressive use is made here of the word "abroad," as if it referred to some higher authority whose opinion was very much cherished. . . . I have never been abroad . . . I don't have time enough left in my life to learn about life there. I do not understand how one can be so sensitive to opinion abroad and not to one's own country, to pulsing public opinion here. For my entire life, I have had the soil of my homeland under my feet; only its pain do I hear, only about it do I write.
>
> —Solzhenitsyn, to the Secretariat of the Union of Soviet Writers, Sept. 22, 1967.

It is now ten years since Aleksandr Solzhenitsyn entered literature, six years since the last of his works was published in his homeland, and two years since the Nobel Prize recognized "the ethical force with which he has pursued the indispensable traditions of Russian literature." That this most anti-cosmopolitan of writers should continue to be publicly discussed only in the West is perhaps the central paradox of his career, and it has been predictably rich in giving rise to confusions of assessment.

Perhaps the clearest example of such confusion was provided by the *Times Literary Supplement* (London) in its editorial comment on the Nobel award. Solzhenitsyn's books, that journal

"Solzhenitsyn: Art and Foreign Matter." From *Problems of Communism* (May-June, 1972), 57-63. Reprinted by permission of the author.

complained, "have been received by minds vigorously massaged to read them in a way which intensifies their political meaning and focuses an unnatural [*sic*] attention on their author."[1] The ensuing controversy prompted an editorial "clarification": "What we were questioning was not the merit of Solzhenitsyn but the conditions under which the Nobel Prize is given and the way in which Solzhenitsyn has been continually implicated in the hypotheses of Kremlinologists." The editors' own wish was "to see Solzhenitsyn freed as far as possible from these dishonorable accretions and returned to the literary world." He is, they pointed out, "a writer of novels, not a pamphleteer, but the actual quality of his novels has been insufficiently examined in the rush to welcome him as an ideological friend."[2]

"Unnatural attention . . . ," "freed . . . and returned to the literary world . . . "—the perspective here is understandable but perverse. Solzhenitsyn's very entrance into literature shows why. *One Day in the Life of Ivan Denisovich* was not sensational; it avoided scenes of violence and brutality, as it avoided politics, to concentrate on "a truth that cannot be forgotten."[3] Yet for this very reason it provided—in the words of the *Novyi mir* reviewer—"that rare instance in literature when the publication of an artistic work rapidly became a *social and political event*" involving even "those who do not ordinarily read stories and novels."[4]

In other words, there could be no question of returning Solzhenitsyn to the literary world, because—like Tolstoy and his other predecessors in the tradition—Solzhenitsyn has never acknowledged a literary world separate or separable from the larger world of human experience. The 19th-century writers and critics who made this tradition in Russia regarded literature as one side of a dialogue with life, a response that would in turn elicit responses. Because artistic truth and the truth of experience—psychological, social, or religious—were deemed to coincide, either was testable against the other. Artistry as such was not much talked about. How could it be, when it was measured precisely by its effectiveness in transcending the

[1]Oct. 16, 1970, p. 1194.
[2]Jan. 15, 1971, p. 68.
[3]*Pravda* (Moscow), Nov. 23, 1962.
[4]V. Lakshin, "Ivan Denisovich, His Friends and Foes," translated from *Novyi mir* (Moscow), 1964, No. 11, in Priscilla Johnson, *Khrushchev and the Arts* (Cambridge, Mass.: M.I.T. Press, 1965), p. 275. (Emphasis added.)

boundaries of art?[5] "The hero of my tale," Tolstoy had written, "the one I love with all the power of my soul . . . is Truth."[6] Aside from Solzhenitsyn, it is hard to think of a major writer today who could use these terms without irony or extensive qualification.[7]

The *Times Literary Supplement* editorialist, while observing quite properly that Solzhenitsyn is a novelist and not a pamphleteer, failed to recognize how directly the principal values in Solzhenitsyn's novels translate into social terms. Yet it would seem impossible to miss, for example, the constant attention in Solzhenitsyn's writing to the nature of literature, good and bad; to the duties of the writer, the needs of the reader, to language itself. In the last case, his work offers an extensive gloss on Mandel'shtam's belief, voiced in 1921, that "social distinctions and class oppositions pale before the present division of people into friends and enemies of the word."[8] Characteristically enough, one of the criticisms of Stalin that led to Solzhenitsyn's arrest in 1945 was "that his language was primitive"—a point to which the author returned 20 years later in *The First Circle.*

Solzhenitsyn's sole article on the subject of language advocates healthy infusions of popular speech into literary style

[5]Lakshin, at the end of his long review, writes: "Someone may ask us: 'And where is your analysis of the author's craft, of the work's form?' Indeed, we have not spoken separately, as is usually done, about the story's 'distinguishing artistic features,' but we are confident that these were being discussed the whole time, with every mention of Ivan Denisovich, Tsezar, the Commander, of the atmosphere of the 'lucky day' itself, or of the scene at the power plant, because Solzhenitsyn's art does not lie in any external embellishment tacked on to the idea and content for effect. No, it lies precisely in the flesh and blood of the work, its soul. It may seem to the unsophisticated reader that he has before him a piece of life torn straight from its depths and left just as it is—alive, quivering. . . . But such is only the artistic illusion, which is itself the result of great mastery, the ability of the artist to see people as they live, to speak of them in unsullied—so to speak, newborn—words and in such a way that we can be sure that it could not have been said or written otherwise." *Ibid.,* p. 287.

[6]Leo Tolstoy, *Sebastopol,* Frank D. Millett trans. (Ann Arbor: University of Michigan Press, 1961), p. 110.

[7]The word *pravda* was strikingly frequent in published Soviet responses to Solzhenitsyn's work before the ban on him was imposed. Historically, it implies justice as well. See "Letter from Solzhenitsyn to Three Students" in Leopold Labedz, ed., *Solzhenitsyn, A Documentary Record* (New York: Harper & Row, 1971), pp. 125-126.

[8]"Slovo i kultura" ["Language and Culture"] in Osip Mandel'shtam, *Sobranie sochinenii v dvukh tomakh,* ed. by G. P. Struve and B. A. Filippov (New York: Inter-Language Literary Associates, 1966), Vol. II, p. 265.

and gives examples (as does his fiction) of lexical experimentation and new coinages.[9] The experimentation, however, bears little relation to what we think of as avant-garde practice, because Solzhenitsyn's fascination with the world of words has a goal in view: the transmission of experience as freshly and fully as possible to the broadest audience. So, even where he advocates the reintroduction of forgotten words, his purpose is the opposite of antiquarian, the underlying hope being that they may pass through successful literary use back into common speech. The ultimate test is always vividness, the ultimate aim to counter "the whole tendency of modern prose," which Orwell found to be "away from concreteness."[10]

Nadezhda Mandel'shtam has written that, from the point of view of the authorities, her husband's poem on Stalin was "a usurpation of the right words and thoughts that the ruling powers reserved exclusively for themselves"[11]—and this appears to be the attitude of the present Soviet authorities toward Solzhenitsyn's work as well.[12] From the author's point of view, however, what is in question is precisely the *reclaiming* of the right to words and thoughts which the ruling powers had reserved exclusively for themselves—that is, the reestablishment of a language whose only loyalty is to experience, and whose function is to render that experience communal. Solzhenitsyn's high seriousness in this respect recalls Gogol's dictum: "One must treat the word honestly; it is God's highest gift to man."[13] A very 19th-century attitude, and not Solzhenitsyn's only such.

His attitude toward language rests ultimately on a sense of moral responsibility—as does his larger view of the writer's

[9]"Ne obychai degtem shchi belit', na to smetana" ["It is Not the Custom to Lighten Cabbage Soup With Tar—For That We Have Sour Cream"], in his *Sobranie sochinenii* (Frankfurt: Posev, 1969), V, 261-267.

[10]Politics and the English Language," in *The Collected Essays, Journalism and Letters of George Orwell* (London: Penguin, 1970), Vol. IV, p. 163. *Cf.* Solzhenitsyn's statement to a Slovak interviewer: "I am convinced that in our literature the riches of the Russian language are insufficiently utilized. In the twentieth century languages are narrowing, are becoming standardized. We are losing many old values." "Odin den' u Aleksandra Isaevicha Solzhenitsyna" ["One Day with Aleksandr Isaevich Solzhenitsyn"], *Posev* (Frankfurt), June 23, 1967.

[11]*Hope Against Hope* (New York: Atheneum), 1970, p. 83.

[12]Khrushchev's attitude was more forthright. *The New York Times* of Nov. 22, 1970, quoted the late Soviet leader, who had just read *The First Circle,* as finding that "with the exception of a few details, Mr. Solzhenitsyn had 'told it like it was.' "

[13]N. V. Gogol', *Polnoe sobranie sochinenii,* Vol. VIII (Leningrad: Akademiia Nauk, SSSR, 1952), p. 231.

ideal role. "Talent," he told a Slovak interviewer, "involves duty." "The writer should be concerned, should be guided by his artistic memory, should write about what he sees and how he sees." "The basis of literature is the profound experiencing of social processes." One must, however, regard the writer's tasks "not only from the point of view of his duty vis-a-vis society, but also from the point of view of his *most important obligation,* vis-a-vis each individual," because "a human being is a physiological and spiritual entity before he is a member of society." In this connection Solzhenitsyn notes a "special obligation" of the writer at a time when religious influence is waning all over the world: "He must fill more than one vacated place."[14]

These views find a prominent place in Solzhenitsyn's large novels, in part through the attention given to literature in them. Already in his wartime diaries and letters he had written of "the artistic and ideological shortcomings of the works of many Soviet authors and *the air of unreality* that pervades many of them," and this—despite his explicit profession of faith in the victory of Marxism-Leninism—had become part of the case against him.[15] As a writer, he recurs continually and ironically to the banalities of standard Soviet literature. Demka, in *The Cancer Ward,* turns from geometry to lighter reading—specifically to

> *Water of Life* by one Kozhevnikov, recipient of a Stalin Prize. This was A. Kozhevnikov, but there was also an S. Kozhevnikov, and a V. Kozhevnikov besides. Demka was awed by how many writers there were. In the previous century there had been about ten, all of them great; in this one there were thousands: change one letter and you had another writer. There was a Safronov, and now there was a Safonov—more than one, apparently. And was Safronov the only Safronov? Nobody could manage to read all their books. And whichever you read, it did not seem to matter.[16]

Examples of this kind of satiric treatment could easily be multiplied. The point is that Solzhenitsyn does not stop at satire but goes on to provide portraits of both the producers and the consumers of such literature. The fullest portrait of the former is Galakhov in *The First Circle,* a writer of outstanding war

[14]"Odin den' u Aleksandra Isaevicha Solzhenitsyna," *loc. cit.* (Emphasis added.)

[15]See USSR Supreme Court Decision No. 4n-083/57 rehabilitating Solzhenitsyn, in Labedz, *op. cit.,* pp. 3-5. (Emphasis added.)

[16]*The Cancer Ward,* Chap. 10. Here and throughout, translations from the novels are my own.—D.F.

novels who slips into "spiritual paralysis" with the return of peace. Now

> each time he started some large new work, he would take fire, swear to himself and his friends that he would make concessions to no one, that this time he would write a real book. He would sit down to the opening pages with enthusiasm. But very soon he would become aware that he was not writing alone—that the image of the person for whom he was writing had arisen before him, looming more and more distinctly. No sooner would he finish a paragraph than he found himself reading it over with that person's eyes. And that person was not reader, brother, friend, or coeval. Nor was it some abstract literary critic. It was, for some reason, always that celebrated critic-in-chief, Zhabov. . . .
>
> And so, trying paragraph by paragraph to anticipate the counter-arguments of Zhabov and adapt to them, Galakhov would quickly weaken, remove the angularities, and the book itself would roll along cravenly, everything falling smoothly into place.[17]

As for the consumers, they are best represented by the odious Rusanov and his family in *The Cancer Ward.* Avieta, the daughter, brings her father a pile of recent books whose "very titles uplift the heart": the poems, *Baltic Spring* and *Kill Him!;* and the novels, *With Us It's Already Morning, Light Over the Earth, Toilers of the World, Mountains in Bloom, Youth is With Us.* And it is she who explains to the bemused Demka that "sincerity can by no means be the chief criterion" in judging a book, since if the ideas are "wrong" or "alien," sincerity only makes their expression more harmful. "Subjective sincerity can work against a truthful portrayal of life," she says—and that is "dialectics" (Chap. 21).

Solzhenitsyn includes such writers and readers, along with a host of others representing intermediate positions, in order to comprehend them in both senses of the word. And by so doing, he responds to the complaints expressed in both *The First Circle* and *The Cancer Ward* about "a kind of literature that dealt with everything on earth except what one could see with one's own eyes." Elizaveta Anatol'evna, in *The Cancer Ward* (Chap. 34), clearly speaks for Solzhenitsyn's ideal readership when, finding Anna Karenina's unhappiness enviable by comparison with her own, she protests: "Why should I read *Anna Karenina?* . . . Where can I read about us? Will that be only in a hundred years?" The explicit rationale for this kind of truth-telling—which I take to be a central feature of Solzhenitsyn's art—is set forth in the same novel:

[17]*The First Circle,* Chap. 57.

> If, decade after decade, no one is permitted to tell it as it is, human brains become irreparably skewed, until it becomes harder to comprehend one's own compatriot than a man from Mars. (Chap. 32)

Nadezhda Mandel'shtam's memoirs, which complement and corroborate Solzhenitsyn's fiction in so many ways, contain strikingly similar statements. For example, in her discussion of the "affliction of memory" from which former camp inmates suffer, she recalls her fear, in listening to them, that "there might be nobody who could ever properly bear witness to the past. Whether inside or outside the camps, we had all lost our memories."[18]

The goal of Solzhenitsyn's writing thus seems to be a kind of social therapy. The self-knowledge won in the fictional microcosm is intended to function actively in the macrocosm—which amounts to a rejoining of life and art in the way that the 19th-century Russian achievement made traditional.[19] All of Solzhenitsyn's major work may be seen as a *recherche du temps perdu,* an attempt to redeem time. It is this goal which explains and justifies the basic, old-fashioned realism of his writing (which even the cinematic and documentary devices of *August 1914* do not significantly alter). To a Western readership accustomed to judging a writer by the novelty he offers, reversion to such an outworn form must seem a drastic limitation in a writer of major gifts. But the Western reader is not the addressee of these works, nor can he be expected to understand the radical novelty they possess within the Russian context by virtue of the literary and cultural discontinuities that characterize it. Arkadii Belinkov summed up the matter at a meeting of the Moscow writers' organization in November 1966, when he acknowledged that "great art is never traditional" and—noting "the apparently traditional nature" of Solzhenitsyn's style—went on to say:

[18]*Hope Against Hope,* p. 379.

[19]Compare the picture of Soviet society drawn by an unnamed party official in conversation with K. S. Karol, a Franco-Polish journalist: "Beneath the flat surface of society in Russia, as presented by *Pravda,* a rich and complex life abounds, but it totally lacks any means of expression or communication. We are not a 'one-dimensional' society, as Westerners believe; on the contrary we are a fragmented society. Prevented from communicating with each other, we have almost no common criteria. Everyone takes hold of a piece of the truth from his daily experience and interprets it according to his own lights. The same words have a different meaning for each social group, almost for each individual. In such conditions we just can't make a serious analysis of the real state of affairs. . . ." "Conversations in Russia," *New Statesman* (London), Jan. 1, 1971, p. 8.

> Solzhenitsyn [in fact] creates a new system of Russian prose, because he introduces into the composition of his art new, unknown or forgotten ideas of good and evil, of life and death, and of the relationship between man and society.[20]

It was also Belinkov who observed:

> He has told us about what is important for all of us, what we come up against every day and therefore know ourselves. But the difference between him and other writers lies in the fact that the other writers did not write about it, while he did. He did what is possible only for a person of true talent and real courage. That is the significance and the sense of the art of Aleksandr Solzhenitsyn.[21]

Ivan Denisovich, as noted earlier, appeared at once as a literary text and a social event—which means that its author appeared simultaneously as an artist and as a potential moral and social force. More than a century before, Gogol had aspired to this role; Turgenev, Tolstoy, Dostoevsky, and (*mutatis mutandis*) Gorkii were later to fill it. All furnished examples, in Iurii Tynianov's words, of writers whose personalities were themselves literary phenomena. So, too, Solzhenitsyn: the unlikely permission that made him a public phenomenon could not, it turned out, be effectively withdrawn—the writer would not cooperate. His rare courage shows in the principled use he persisted in making of his fame and the literally unique position that fame gave him. The astonishing letter he addressed to the Union of Writers in 1967, asking discussion of his proposals that censorship be abolished and that the Union defend the legitimate interests of its members, was one such act of unprecedented civic courage, and its long-term effects cannot be gauged. He might well have borrowed for it the Tolstoyan title, "I Cannot be Silent!" But Solzhenitsyn's own emphasis, in a subsequent discussion of the letter at a session of the Secretariat of the Union of Writers, deserves attention. Those who think the letter is about censorship, he said, have understood nothing.

> This letter is about the destiny of our great literature, which once conquered and captivated the world but which has now lost its standing.[22]

Remove censorship, he suggested, and new Russian novels would once more dazzle the world—"the 'new novel' would die down and . . . 'neo-avant-gardists' would disappear." This faith

[20]Quoted in Labedz, *op. cit.,* p. 76. (Emphasis added.)
[21]*Ibid.,* p. 77.
[22]*Ibid.,* p. 123.

appears even more clearly in the author's letter itself, where he writes:

> If the world had access to all the uninhibited fruits of our literature, if it were enriched by our own spiritual experience, the whole artistic evolution of the world would move along in a different way, acquiring a new stability and attaining even a new artistic threshold.[23]

Solzhenitsyn is optimistic about what will follow the repossession of authenticity, but meanwhile repossession is his theme on every level. From Ivan Denisovich, who reflects that "the great thing about a penal camp was you had a hell of a lot of freedom," through the inmates of *The First Circle,* who discover with Gleb Nerzhin "the genuine grandeur of human beings . . . in prison," to the patients of *The Cancer Ward,* preoccupied with the discovery of what men live by, the dialectical lesson is the same: out of unfreedom can come the deepest existential freedom—the experience of integrity. This is the knowledge, as he remarks in *The First Circle,* of those "cleansed by the nearness of death"—a soldier's knowledge, ascetic, with no room for emotional luxuries and no use for the trivia of daily life. "In roadside ditches, in washed-out trenches, among the ruins of burned houses," the typical Solzhenitsyn hero learns "the value of a can of soup, an hour of quiet, the meaning of true friendship and the meaning of *life in general.*"[24]

It is the attainment of freedom and not its investigation that Solzhenitsyn writes about. Freedom in his books seldom issues in action. It is itself the goal, and he may more properly be seen as the poet of *liberation.* But the liberation, however profound, is inevitably local, Russian, Soviet. The dilemmas it may bring in its wake, the problematics of freedom, to which so much modern art is directed, are—understandably—beyond his scope. So are the problematics of truth. For him truth is no metaphysical riddle; it is what needs to be substituted for current lies. His area has been clearly marked out for him by the influential silences of the Galakhovs and the Shulubins, the vicious hypocrisies of the Rusanovs, the moral indifferences of the Podduevs.

Something similar can be observed in the area of character. Some fifty years have passed since D. H. Lawrence warned his readers not to look for the "old, stable ego of character," thus

[23]*Ibid.,* p. 84.
[24]*The First Circle,* Chap. 47. (Emphasis added.)

signaling an end to the ambiguity that fiction had by and large accepted between ontological status (*being* a character) and ethical status (*having* a character—good, bad or indifferent). Solzhenitsyn's work goes counter to the whole modern trend, in which Freud was a potent catalyst, if not instigator. But Freud may help us understand Solzhenitsyn. If we ignore the familiar scholasticism of Ego, Superego, and Id and think instead of Freud's more appropriately tentative designation of the psyche as consisting of a Self [*das Ich*], something incorporating external standards of conduct [*das Ueber-Ich*], and a darker instinctual component, the It [*das Es*], it becomes clear that Solzhenitsyn's treatment of character emphasizes the first two and pointedly slights the third.

This is why there is so little sex and violence in his books: what interests him is the achievement of authentic, moral selfhood. The obstacles to it are taken for granted; those who cannot surmount them are, in the only important sense, nonsurvivors. Solzhenitsyn's norm is made especially clear in *The First Circle,* where Nerzhin speculates on that sainted abstraction, the people [*narod*]. He has met them in the camps and, seeking to learn wisdom from them, reaped only another harvest of lost illusions:

> What was lacking in most of them was that individual point of view which becomes more precious than life itself.
>
> All that remained was—to be oneself.
>
> Having suffered through yet another enthusiasm, Nerzhin—whether definitively or not—understood the People in a new way which he had met nowhere in his reading: the People is not everyone who speaks our language, nor is it the elect, marked by the fiery stamp of genius. One joins the people not on the basis of one's birth or the work of one's hands, or on the wings of one's education.
>
> But through one's soul.
>
> Everyone forges a soul for himself, year by year.
>
> One must try to temper and fashion himself such a soul as will make him a *human being.*
>
> And thereby a particle of his own people.[25]

To be sure, the sexual urge plays a large role in *The First Circle* and *The Cancer Ward*—but as a problem in human relations, not a rebellious imperative of the "It." Solzhenitsyn evinces scant interest in the causes of human complexity, treating irrationality itself as a moral or logical absurdity—perhaps reprehensible, perhaps inevitable, but in either case capable of being transcended. And it is the difficult transcendence that he shows,

[25] *Ibid.,* Chap. 61. (Emphasis in the original.)

over and over again. The only fundamental distinction, his hero Vorotyntsev tells the militant Lenartovich in *August 1914,* is between decency and non-decency. Here is the crux of every portrayal in every one of Solzhenitsyn's works. As he himself put it in his letter to three students, "There is nothing relative about justice, as there is nothing relative about conscience."[26]

> The writer . . . is a teacher of other people; hasn't that always been our understanding? And a great writer—forgive my boldness, I'll lower my voice—a great writer is, so to speak, a second government in his country. And for that reason no regime has ever loved great writers, only minor ones.

These words, spoken by Innokentii Volodin in *The First Circle* (Chap. 57), clearly fit Solzhenitsyn's case and, properly understood, define his aspirations. The writer must not be confused with a preacher; he teaches by example, both in his works and outside them. What he teaches is personal responsibility, without which there can be no integrity. He can thus be likened to a second government only where government regards itself as sole source and arbiter of truth, in effect as the only audible public voice, obviating and suppressing individual testimony. In this situation—this Russian situation—Solzhenitsyn must be acknowledged a great writer; to argue whether he is a great novelist is another and lesser point.

It is also premature. The monumental work on which he is now engaged, of which *August 1914* is only the first installment, shows him turning for the first time outside his own experience to a non-Soviet theme, though one that joins his previous work as part of the "most fascinating and important task to be performed"—writing about "the fate of Russia."[27] Just as in his long novels of the Soviet period, which he depicts as detours from this original project cherished since 1936, his aim is "to resurrect those years," the better to understand the fate of Russia in the 20th century. As in his earlier work, the mode is documentary (though for the first time no enclosed society—camp, *sharashka* or hospital—serves as surrogate for the large world) and scenic; the point of view, what we might call ethical realism. Like his earlier work, too, *August 1914* displays high intelligence—a quality perhaps insufficiently remarked by commentators on his work—and bespeaks a particular admira-

[26]Labedz, *op. cit.,* p. 125.
[27]Interview with a Slovak journalist, in Labedz, *op. cit.,* p. 13.

tion for competence, particularly the competence of the soldier or engineer who knows how to deal, unbemused by abstractions, with the concrete problems of the practical world.

Some claim to see signs, in *August 1914* and elsewhere, of the isolation to which Solzhenitsyn has been subjected—isolation from sources, from honest criticism, from dialogue with his readers. This can hardly be surprising, any more than the defining signs—cultural, artistic and intellectual—of his Soviet Russian-ness. These are, after all, the grounds of his uniqueness and his particular heroism—which lie in his being free not *from* Soviet reality, but *in* it.[28] Born in 1918, Solzhenitsyn belongs to the first purely Soviet generation. Sharing that generation's central experiences of war, the camps, and eventual return to a changed Russia, he became its public witness and—with his talent and conviction that "no one can bar the road to truth"—the best hope of Soviet Russian literature. Edmund Wilson has complained of the monotony with which Solzhenitsyn returns to the theme of endurance but he fails to credit the way in which endurance is vindicated and transformed by the very existence of this testimony and of the man who bears it. "If, decade after decade, no one is permitted to tell it as it is, human brains become irreparably skewed, until it becomes harder to comprehend one's own compatriot than a man from Mars": Solzhenitsyn at least has lessened this danger, and that is no small service. Nor is it one which integrity or talent alone could have rendered. Aleksandr Tvardovskii's characterization of Solzhenitsyn's first published work could be applied to the sum of his work to date:

> . . . one of those literary phenomena after whose appearance it is impossible to talk about any literary problem or literary fact without measuring it against this phenomenon.[29]

[28]This point is developed in Father Alexander Schmemann's very interesting article, "O Solzhenitsyne" ["On Solzhenitsyn"], in *Vestnik russkogo studencheskogo khristianskogo dvizheniia* (Paris-New York), No. 98 (1970), 72-87. [The English translation of Fr. Schmemann's article appears in this volume. Eds.]

[29]Labedz, *op. cit.*, p. 44.

The Philosophical Foundations of Solzhenitsyn's Vision of Art

BY RICHARD HAUGH

Solzhenitsyn's writings prior to 1972 reveal a generally consistent pattern in his views on art. Nevertheless, it would have been difficult to speak with assurance of Solzhenitsyn's "philosophy of art," if only because a large proportion of these views was embedded in the pronouncements of fictional characters. With the publication of his Nobel Lecture in 1972 Solzhenitsyn's vision of art became unambiguous and explicit. The essential purpose of this article is to examine these views and to point to their philosophical roots and their theoretical implications. This article briefly looks at Solzhenitsyn's attitude toward socialist realism and his vision of the social role of the artist. Finally—but most importantly—it analyzes the philosophical foundations of Solzhenitsyn's vision of art and value.

I

In Solzhenitsyn's writings there is an almost total condemnation of both the theory and the practice of socialist realism, that officially prescribed dogma which demands of an artist "a truthful, historically concrete portrayal of reality in its revolutionary development."[1] An artist, according to this doctrine,

[1]This is the definition of the First Congress of Soviet Writers in 1934. Quoted from W.N. Vickery, *The Cult of Optimism* (Bloomington: University of Indiana Press, 1963), p. 70.

must not only portray that "reality" which does not contradict "ideological orthodoxy" but must also portray "reality" as it will be.[2]

What Solzhenitsyn objects to in socialist realism is quite clear. He is opposed to the censorious literary criterion of "ideological orthodoxy"[3] and rejects the theoretical principle that an artist must portray "the seedlings of the plants of the future,"[4] of that assumed "wonderful tomorrow."[5] The doctrines of socialist realism are shown to have had a baneful effect on the understanding of the Russian literary tradition; Dostoevsky, for example, is relegated to the level of an insignificant and unknown writer.[6] In Solzhenitsyn's novels the officially held literary views are portrayed as vapid, lifeless, and inane, as a distortion of reality and truth, and as a force opposed to conscience.[7]

In opposition to the theory and practice of socialist realism

[2]The distinction between present "reality" [*byt*] and the assumed certainty of the in-breaking socialist "reality" of the future [*bytie*] has remained a theoretical principle in Soviet literary theory since the 1920's. See Robert A. Maguire, *Red Virgin Soil: Soviet Literature in the 1920's* (Princeton: Princeton University Press, 1968), pp. 188-259.

[3]See *One Day in the Life of Ivan Denisovich,* tr. R. Hingley and M. Hayward (New York: Bantam edition, 1969), p. 93f. See also the specious defense of socialist realism by Avieta Rusanov in *Cancer Ward,* Ch. 21 (tr. N. Bethell and D. Burg [New York: Bantam edition, 1969], p. 281). At the meeting of the prose section of the Moscow writers' organization on November 17, 1966 Solzhenitsyn commented on Avieta Rusanov's defense of socialist realism: "I adopted here an impermissible device—there is not in the section about Avieta a single word of my own—she uses words spoken in the last fifteen years by our most important writers and literary critics... Yes, it is undisguisedly a farce, but it's not mine." (Quoted from Leopold Labedz, ed., *Solzhenitsyn: A Documentary Record* [New York: Harper & Row, 1971], p. 78f).

[4]See Demka's response to Avieta in *Cancer Ward,* Ch. 21; p. 284.

[5]Avieta Rusanov condescendingly explains this tenet of socialist realism to Demka in *Cancer Ward,* Ch. 21; p. 286. In *The First Circle* Gleb Nerzhin rejects a view of art which demands that art be concerned with the "becoming" reality. (See *The First Circle,* Ch. 53; tr. T.P. Whitney [New York: Bantam edition, 1969], p. 377). In his interview with the Slovak journalist Pavel Licko Solzhenitsyn stated: "We sometimes hear that literature should beautify the future. This is a falsification, and justifies lying." (Labedz, *op. cit.,* p. 15).

[6]See Klara Makarygin's evaluation of the views of literature promulgated in the lectures at school where Dostoevsky is regarded as "totally unknown." (*The First Circle,* Ch. 40; p. 273). In his letter to the Fourth Congress of Soviet Writers Solzhenitsyn wrote: "Even Dostoevsky, the pride of world literature, was at one time not published in our country (still today his works are not published in full); he was excluded from the school curriculum, made unacceptable for reading, and reviled." (Labedz, *op. cit.,* p. 83).

[7]See, for example, *Cancer Ward,* Ch. 10; p. 119 and *The First Circle,* Ch. 57; p. 414 and p. 418.

another vision of literature emerges from the pages of Solzhenitsyn's novels. Literature must "raise the right feelings,"[8] a phrase reminiscent of Tolstoy's theory of art.[9] Literature must not only "appeal to the heart"[10] but must also deal with those ultimate questions of existence which "tear and shake the human heart."[11] Before the Secretariat of the Union of Soviet Writers Solzhenitsyn declared:

> The task of a writer is to select more universal and eternal questions, [such as] the secrets of the human heart and conscience, the confrontation between life and death, the triumph over spiritual sorrows, the laws in the history of mankind that were born in the depths of time immemorial and that will cease to exist only when the sun ceases to shine.[12]

Literature must be rooted in the "conscience" and should assume the role of the "teacher of the people"[13] and the "teacher of life,"[14] confronting the people with the totality of truth and life.

Although he does not accept the principles of socialist realism, Solzhenitsyn has solemnly committed himself to "Russian Realism." When the writer Riurikov, at the meeting of the Secretariat of the Union of Soviet Writers on September 22, 1967, demanded that Solzhenitsyn renounce the title of "con-

[8]See *One Day in the Life of Ivan Denisovich,* p. 94.

[9]See *What Is Art?* (tr. A. Maude [London: Oxford University Press, 1962], p. 198f). Tolstoy's view that "true art" must evoke the "right feelings" in man is inextricably connected with his rather puritanical and restricted view of religion and "religious perception," a view not shared by Solzhenitsyn. "Art," wrote Tolstoy, "transmitting feelings flowing from the religious perception of our time . . . should be acknowledged, highly valued, and encouraged. . ." (p. 234). Tolstoy, who was so indignant about censorship in Russia ("I consider [it] to be an immoral and irrational institution" [p. 65]; "The Spiritual Censorship is one of the most ignorant, venal, stupid, and despotic institutions in Russia" [p. 67]), ultimately arrived at a view which was also censorious. All art which did not conform to Tolstoy's criteria of "right feelings" and "religious perception" "should be acknowledged to be bad art, deserving not to be encouraged but to be driven out, denied, and despised. . ." (p. 247). Tolstoy, explicitly consenting with Plato, wrote that "every reasonable and moral man" would rather see no art in the world than a world in which "some" good art must co-exist with bad art. (p. 261). Solzhenitsyn's vision of art does not push him at all in the direction of censorship. In his Letter to the Fourth Congress of Soviet Writers Solzhenitsyn wrote that "literature cannot develop in between the categories of 'permitted' and 'not permitted', 'about this you may write' and 'about this you may not'." (Labedz, *op. cit.,* p.84).

[10]See *Cancer Ward,* Ch. 21; p. 283.

[11]See *The First Circle,* Ch. 28; p. 194.

[12]Labedz, *op. cit.,* p. 121.

[13]See *The First Circle,* Ch. 57; p. 415.

[14]See *Cancer Ward,* Ch. 21; p. 285.

tinuer of Russian Realism,"[15] Solzhenitsyn replied: "Placing my hand on my heart, I swear that I shall never do it."[16]

"Realism," a most elusive term,[17] is here fortunately modified by the word "Russian." This helps in the sense that there is at least some agreement about the general characteristics of this literary tradition.[18] Solzhenitsyn's concern with the ultimate questions of human existence, with a professed commitment to truth and social justice, and with empathy for the suffering, the "insulted," and the "injured" are all recognizable elements of this tradition. The literature of the Russian nineteenth century, furthermore, inclined toward moral exhortation, considered itself a teacher of and servant to society, and assumed the inseparability of art and life. Solzhenitsyn clearly leans in the same direction.

Solzhenitsyn's "realism" is by no means restricted to a presentation of mere external reality. There is in his writing an idealistic, moral, and prophetic dimension. In a discussion on the nature of art with the artist Kondrashev-Ivanov in *The First Circle,* Rubin asks: "In other words, the painter doesn't simply copy?" Kondrashev-Ivanov's reply, quite probably echoing Solzhenitsyn's own view, is noteworthy:

> Of course not!... Externally there must be some resemblance . . . But isn't it rash to believe that one can see and know reality precisely as it is? Particularly *spiritual* reality?... And if, in looking at the model, I see something nobler than what he has up to now displayed in his life, then why shouldn't I portray it? Why shouldn't one help a man find himself and try to be better... Why must I undervalue his soul?... I will tell you something else: it is a major responsibility not only of

[15]Labedz, *op. cit.,* p. 116.

[16]Labedz, *op. cit.,* p. 122.

[17]Literary theorists and critics have discovered a mimetic realism, a naturalistic realism, a symbolic realism, a romantic realism, an idealistic realism, an intuitive realism, a mythic realism, an anecdotal realism, a grotesque realism, etc. The German literary historian Bruno Markwardt has discovered so many additional types of realism that, as René Wellek remarks, "one's head spins with the dance of bloodless categories." (René Wellek, *Concepts of Criticism* [New Haven: Yale University Press, 1963], p. 235).

[18]See Erich Auerbach, *Mimesis,* tr. W.R. Trask (Princeton: Princeton University Press, 1968), pp. 522-524. Dostoevsky distinguished his "realism" from that of his contemporaries. In a well-known passage he claimed he was a "realist in a higher sense" precisely because he described the "depths of the human soul." (See N. Strakhov and O. Miller, *Biografiia, pis'ma i zametki iz zapisnoi knizhki Dostoevskogo* [St. Petersburg, 1883], p. 373.) Dostoevsky explicitly stated that he had a totally different view of "reality and realism" than his contemporaries, claiming his "idealism" was "more real" than their alleged realism, for his was "fundamental, true realism." (See A.S. Dolinin, ed., *Pis'ma,* II [Moscow, 1930], p. 150 and 169).

portraiture but of all human communication for each of us to help everyone else discover the best that is in him.[19]

By accepting the view that it is a "major responsibility" of the artist to ennoble this "external reality" and to "discover the best" in man, art takes on an ethically inspired task, the ultimate purpose of which is to call mankind to seek moral perfection.

II

In his Nobel Lecture Solzhenitsyn asks: "What then, in this cruel, dynamic, explosive world which totters on the brink of destruction—what *is* the place and role of the writer?"[20] For Solzhenitsyn the answer is "obvious," and he acknowledges his agreement with Albert Camus' "brilliant statements on this theme."[21] Solzhenitsyn declares that he is "not ashamed to continue this tradition" of Russian literature which upholds the "concept that a writer can do much among his people—and that he must." For Solzhenitsyn there is no way an artist can escape from the real world precisely because an artist is first of all an organic member of society. Art and life are inseparable in Solzhenitsyn's view.[22] The artist who merely laments the human condition is essentially hypocritical, for—in words which seem to echo *The Brothers Karamazov*—Solzhenitsyn sees the writer as "an accomplice to all the evil committed in his country or by his people." The "stench" of all the evils of his society and nation mingles "with the breath of the writer."

Although Solzhenitsyn is clearly opposed to *l'art pour l'art,* he respects the freedom of an artist to reject the notion that

[19] *The First Circle,* Ch. 53; p. 375f.

[20] All quotations from Solzhenitsyn's Nobel Lecture are from the Alexis Klimoff translation which appears in this volume.

[21] In his Nobel Prize acceptance speech in 1957 Albert Camus asserted that a writer must accept the "two tasks that constitute the greatness of his craft: the service of truth and the service of liberty. Because his task is to unite the greatest possible number of his people, his art must not compromise with lies and servitude... The nobility of our craft will always be rooted in two commitments, difficult to maintain: the refusal to lie about what one knows and the resistance to oppression." See *Nobel Lectures: Literature 1901-1967,* ed. H. Frenz (Amsterdam-London-New York: Elsevier, Nobel Foundation, 1969), p. 525.

[22] Dostoevsky held the same view. See his remark about the inseparability of art and man in "Mr. -bov and the Question of Art" in *Dostoevsky's Occasional Writings,* tr. D. Magarshack (New York: Random House, 1963), p. 135.

art must serve society. With ironic seriousness Solzhenitsyn writes: "We shall not trample on the *right* of an artist to express nothing but his personal experiences and his self-observations while disregarding all that occurs in the rest of the world."[23] Insisting, however, that he too has the freedom and the right to attempt to shake such artists from a self-centered subjectivism to an encounter with total reality, Solzhenitsyn writes: "We shall not make *demands* on him,[24] but surely we can be permitted to reproach him, beg him, call him, or beckon to him."

For Solzhenitsyn the "great and blessed property" of true art [*istinno-khudozhestvennoe*] has a mission which is both *educational* and *prophetic*.[25] The educational mission of art allows both the individual and the nation the possibility of acquiring experience otherwise inaccessible.[26]

But for Solzhenitsyn art can do more than simply inform society. Its prophetic mission is to warn humanity, unify mankind, and work for the possible redemption of man. In his interview with the Slovak journalist Pavel Licko Solzhenitsyn asserted that everything which the artist's intuition perceives as "injurious or disquieting" must be revealed to society.[27] In his Letter to the Fourth Congress of Soviet Writers Solzhenitsyn wrote that

[23]In his Nobel Lecture Solzhenitsyn expresses astonishment that an artist can withdraw "into self-created worlds," into the "realms of subjective whim." He is dismayed that artists can "surrender the real world to others" and laments the fact that some artists only complain about "how hopelessly warped mankind is, how shallow people have become, and how burdensome it is for a lone refined and beautiful soul to dwell among them."

[24]Dostoevsky wrote similarly in "Mr. -bov and the Question of Art," (*Occasional Writings*, p. 96): "We repeat: . . . one cannot demand it, if only because one demands mostly when one wishes to compel by force, and the first law of art is freedom of inspiration and creation."

[25]Solzhenitsyn assumes that an artist must raise himself to the level of "true art." For Solzhenitsyn "true art" is not guided by considerations of the "market" nor by the principle of "relevance."

[26]For Solzhenitsyn only art can overcome the individual's "ruinous habit of learning only from his own experience, so that the experience of others passes him by without profit." Only art can bridge the gap between the transitory individual life and "timeless human nature," for art transmits between men "the entire accumulated load of another being's life-experience"; it "re-creates—life-like—the experience of other men, so that we can assimilate it as our own." In *What Is Art?* Tolstoy voiced a similar view, reducing experience to his own peculiar vision of "right feelings." ". . .It is on this capacity of man to receive another man's expressions of feeling and to experience those feelings himself, that the activity of art is based." (p. 121).

[27]Cited from a French version of the interview. See Georges Nivat and Michel Aucouturier, eds., *Soljénitsyne* (Paris: L' Herne, 1971), p. 117.

literature which "does not warn in time against threatening moral and social dangers—such literature does not deserve the name of literature; it is only a façade."[28] Solzhenitsyn envisions art as revealing the truth about the past and the present and as warning society of impending problems. In this prophetic function, art can unify and redeem mankind. This dimension of Solzhenitsyn's thought is inextricably bound up with the philosophical foundations of his vision of art and value.

III

If the mission of art is educational and prophetic, the source of art for Solzhenitsyn is spiritual and mystical, indeed of divine origin. Art, he states in his Nobel Lecture, is a "gift" which is "breathed into" the artist "ready-made at birth." Always bearing the "stamp of its origin," art has the capacity to reveal a "portion of its mysterious inner light" and to "warm even a chilled and sunless soul to an exalted spiritual experience." Through the "irrationality of art," through art's mystical encounter with reality, the artist conveys "revelations the likes of which cannot be achieved by rational thought," allowing man to glimpse the "Inaccessible" [*Nedostupnoe*]. Solzhenitsyn thinks that this revelatory aspect of art with its "unforeseeable

[28]Dostoevsky, maintaining a balance between "pure art" and art which is socially involved, gave an interesting example of unresponsive art in "Mr. -bov and the Question of Art." "Let us imagine that we are in the eighteenth century in Lisbon on the day of the great earthquake. Half of Lisbon's inhabitants are perishing; the houses are collapsing and crashing down... At that particular time a famous Portuguese poet was living in Lisbon. The next morning the Lisbon *Mercury* . . . appears. A paper published at such a moment naturally arouses a certain feeling of curiosity among the unhappy citizens of Lisbon... And suddenly on the most prominent place on the page they find a poem describing 'whispers, timid breathing and warbling of the nightingale', the 'silvery gleam and rippling of the sleepy brook', 'nocturnal shadows' . . . I don't know for certain how the Lisbon inhabitants would have reacted to this poem, but it seems to me that they would have lynched their famous poet there and then in the city square, and not because he had written a poem without a verb, but because instead of the warbling of the nightingale they had heard quite a different kind of warbling under the ground . . . even if the Lisbon citizens had lynched their favorite poet, the poem that had made them so angry . . . might have been excellent so far as its artistic perfection went... It was not art that was to blame, but the poet who abused art at a moment when the people were not in the mood for it. He sang and danced at the coffin of a dead man." (*Occasional Writings*, p. 94f; the poem in question is a famous lyric by Afanasii Fet, a defender of "pure art.")

discoveries" is too mystical to be "wholly accounted for by the artist's view of the world, by his intention, or by the work of his unworthy fingers."

Solzhenitsyn's vision of the source of art and value is ultimately rooted in his belief in the Absolute. In an unambiguous text from his Nobel Lecture Solzhenitsyn states that the artist has not "created this world, nor does he control it; *there can be no doubts about its foundations.*"[29] For Solzhenitsyn the world is a *created* world. It is a world which might not have existed at all and hence it points beyond itself to its spiritual source. The world, for Solzhenitsyn, is necessarily dependent and participatory, deriving its value and meaning from the uncreated and eternal. Implicit in his use of the word "eternal" is the vertical aspect of the transcendent Absolute. He believes it is the obligation of the artist to maintain a balance between the "eternal" and the "present." In his interview with Pavel Licko he stated:

> The writer must maintain the balance equally between these two categories. If his work is so taken up with the present that the author loses the perspective of the point of view *'sub specie aeternitatis'*, his work will not delay in perishing. Also, if he accords too much attention to eternity and neglects the present, his work will lack color, force, and expression. . .[30]

Solzhenitsyn is not a relativist. He is sharply critical of that attitude of the twentieth century which "drones into our souls that there exist no lasting concepts of good and justice valid for all mankind, that all such concepts are fluid and ever-changing. . ." Solzhenitsyn opposes and challenges such relativism with a belief in the "unshakeable nature of goodness, in the indivisible nature of truth. . ." Solzhenitsyn suggests that at the core of ultimate reality there exists a "tri-unity of Truth, Goodness, and Beauty [*eto staroe triedinstvo Istiny, Dobra i Krasoty*]."

> So perhaps the old tri-unity of Truth, Goodness, and Beauty is not simply the decorous and antiquated formula it seemed to us at the time of our self-confident materialistic youth.

It is significant that with this one sentence Solzhenitsyn

[29] "Zato: ne im etot mir sozdan, ne im upravliaetsia, *net somnen'ia v ego osnovakh. . .*" (My italics).

[30] See Georges Nivat and Michel Aucouturier, *Soljénitsyne,* p. 117. At the meeting of the prose section of the Moscow writers' organization on November 17, 1966 Solzhenitsyn stated that "in a work of art there must be a correlation between the present time and eternity." (Labedz, *op. cit.,* p. 78).

challenges one of the fundamental principles upon which Tolstoy built his theory of art. Solzhenitsyn's disagreement with Tolstoy on this issue is total. In evaluating the history of aesthetic theory in *What Is Art?,* Tolstoy devoted several pages to refuting the "trinity of Truth, Goodness, and Beauty."

According to Tolstoy, the 18th-century aesthetician Alexander Gottlieb Baumgarten (1714-1762) envisioned the "Perfect (the Absolute)" as existing in the "three forms of Truth, Goodness, and Beauty."[31] Dismissing as foolish those who try "to prove that this union of beauty and goodness is inherent in the very essence of things," Tolstoy explicitly states that "to this class belongs the astonishing theory of the Baumgartenian Trinity: Goodness, Beauty, Truth."[32] Tolstoy opposes this "mystical" view of beauty which merges beauty "into that of the highest perfection, God," asserting that this "mystical" view is a "fantastic definition . . . founded on nothing."[33]

> Learned people write long, cloudy treatises on beauty as a member of the aesthetic trinity of Beauty, Truth, and Goodness; *das Schöne, das Wahre, das Gute; le Beau, le Vrai, le Bon* are repeated with capital letters by philosophers, aestheticians, and artists, by private individuals, by novelists, and by *feuilletonistes;* and they all think when pronouncing these sacrosanct words that they speak of something quite definite and solid... In reality these words not only have no definite meaning, but hinder us in attaching any definite meaning to existing art.
>
> We only need escape for a moment from the habit of considering this trinity of Goodness, Beauty, and Truth presented to us by Baumgarten . . . to be convinced of the utterly fantastic nature of the union into one, of three absolutely different words and conceptions.[34]

"The notion of beauty," wrote Tolstoy, "not only does not coincide with goodness, but rather is contrary to it; for the good most often coincides with victory over the passions while beauty is at the root of our passions."[35] "But what," asks Tolstoy, "is there in common between the conceptions of beauty and truth on the one hand, and of goodness on the other?"

> Not only are beauty and truth not conceptions equivalent to goodness, and not only do they not form one entity with goodness, but they

[31] *What Is Art?,* p. 93. The idea is, of course, as old as Plato.

[32] *What Is Art?,* p. 140.

[33] *What Is Art?,* p. 112.

[34] *What Is Art?,* p. 141.

[35] *What Is Art?,* p. 141. It is remarkable that Tolstoy can present goodness as positive and present only the negative aspect, not of beauty in itself, but of man's perverted attitude to beauty. Truth can after all be distorted into the lie and goodness can be deformed into evil just as beauty can be subverted.

> do not even coincide with it... And lo and behold! the arbitrary conjunction into one, of these three conceptions which are . . . foreign to one another, has served as the basis for that amazing theory [*udivitel'noi teorii*].[36]

Solzhenitsyn affirms the existence in tri-unity of Truth, Goodness, and Beauty precisely because he accepts the existence of the "Absolute" or the "Perfect." Where there is perfection, truth and goodness necessarily co-exist, the "radiance" of which is Beauty. Truth, Goodness, and Beauty exist in tri-unity because perfection logically implies unity, a unity which is not merely restricted to numerical oneness but which is rather a unity of plurality—which the very idea of unity presupposes and implies.

For Solzhenitsyn the existence of the Absolute is intuitively obvious.[37] In his Letter to Three Students Solzhenitsyn approached the question of the Absolute from an interesting perspective. He wrote that justice is "obviously . . . a concept which is inherent in man, since it cannot be traced to any other source."

> There is nothing relative about justice, just as there is nothing relative about conscience... And please do not tell me that 'everybody understands justice in his own way.' No![38]

The meaning behind the statement that justice is "inherent in man" because it "cannot be traced to any other source" is quite significant for Solzhenitsyn's vision of value and art's prophetic mission. Solzhenitsyn has arrived at the conclusion that since the world of our experience contains only imperfection, the only possible basis for mankind's concept of and deeply rooted intuition of perfection (i.e. justice, truth, goodness, beauty) is precisely the existence—at some higher level—of perfection which grounds, sustains, and penetrates our world of imperfection and our inner consciousness.[39] Man, as it were,

[36]*What Is Art?*, p. 142.

[37]See, for example, Solzhenitsyn's 1962 prayer, published in English in Michael Bourdeaux, ed., *Patriarch and Prophets* (New York and Washington: Praeger, 1970), p. 344. In *The First Circle* even Stalin is portrayed as unable to escape the question of the Absolute. "Suddenly he stopped. 'And up there? Higher? He had no equals, of course, but if there, up there...' And he paced back and forth, but slowly. Now and again that one unresolved question crept into Stalin's mind." (*The First Circle,* Ch. 21; p. 131).

[38]Labedz, *op. cit.,* p. 125f.

[39]Solzhenitsyn would apparently agree with the view, both Platonic and Christian, that it is impossible to arrive at the concept of and intuition of perfection merely from the fact of imperfection. Truth, for example, can exist without the existence of the lie, but the lie can exist only in relationship with the positive reality of truth which the lie distorts and perverts.

bears the image of perfection within himself because the reality of perfection exists in the Absolute. In *The First Circle* Kondrashev-Ivanov states:

> A human being possesses from his birth a certain essence, the nucleus, as it were, of this human being. His "I." . . . he has in him an *image of perfection.*[40]

In *Cancer Ward* Solzhenitsyn writes that "the meaning of existence" is "to preserve unspoiled, undisturbed and undistorted the *image of eternity* with which each person is born. [*izobrazhenie vechnosti, zaronennoe kazhdomu*]."[41]

This "image of perfection" or "image of eternity," the internal link between man and the Absolute, is the basis of the intuition of the Absolute. It is the foundation of Solzhenitsyn's epistemology and teleology. Referring to an official tenet in Marxist epistemology, Kondrashev-Ivanov states in *The First Circle* that "truth is supposed to be the final result of long investigation." Disagreeing, he asserts: "But don't we perceive a sort of twilight truth before any investigation has begun?"[42] Kondrashev-Ivanov believes that man can intuitively grasp the truth.[43]

This revelatory aspect of epistemology is interconnected with Solzhenitsyn's teleology.[44] In this respect Solzhenitsyn's portrayal of Stalin as he attempts "to make his indelible contribution" to linguistics is significant. "Inspired, he wrote down several phrases: 'The superstructure was created by the basis *for the purpose of*... Language was created *for the purpose of*...'" Apparently Marxist teleology has missed the real purpose of human existence, for Solzhenitsyn writes: "and he did not see

[40]*The First Circle,* Ch. 42; p. 297. (My italics).

[41]*Cancer Ward,* Ch. 30; p. 428. (My italics).

[42]*The First Circle,* Ch. 53; p. 376.

[43]Even on a practical level intuition guides many of Solzhenitsyn's characters, especially in *August 1914.*

[44]The repeated use of certain words—"sight," "gaze," "vision," the "eye," the "heart"—links Solzhenitsyn, perhaps quite unconsciously and unintentionally, with that revelatory epistemology so common in the pre-scholastic Latin West and in the continuous epistemological tradition of Eastern Christianity. According to this view, man's inner being is interiorly illumined by the light of the Divine, allowing man to see and judge the temporal from the perspective of the eternal.

the *angel of medieval teleology* smiling over his shoulder."[45]

One of the aims of human existence for Solzhenitsyn is a genuine unity of mankind in Truth, Goodness, and Beauty. In his Nobel Lecture Solzhenitsyn writes that in the past few decades "humanity has imperceptibly and suddenly become united . . . humanity has become one." This unity, however, was achieved "not by means of gradually acquired experience, not from the eye..." Rather, it is a unity brought about by "international radio and the press" and it is therefore superficial, external, and fragile; it is not a spiritual, organic, and free unity of mankind. In fact, Solzhenitsyn claims that this superficial unity has brought about a divisive rather than a unitive vision of man, contributing to the spread of various "scales of values" which are now vying with each other for the heart of man. And yet, according to Solzhenitsyn, there was a time when "it was possible for the individual human eye to see and accept a certain common scale of values." At one time the "individual human eye" knew "what was cruel... what constituted honesty, and what deceit." But, writes Solzhenitsyn, "this twentieth century of ours," devoid of a single scale of values, "has proved to be crueler than its predecessors..."; it is a world which "upon seeing a slimy bog" exclaims: "What a charming meadow!"

"Who will reconcile these scales of values and how?" asks Solzhenitsyn. "Who is going to give mankind a single system of evaluation for evil deeds and for good ones...?" For Solzhenitsyn it is the prophetic mission of art to help "a troubled humanity to recognize its true self..." When Solzhenitsyn affirms the reality of the tri-unity of Truth, Goodness, and Beauty, he commits himself and art to absolute, universal values which are not "fluid and ever-changing" and which are "valid for all mankind" precisely because these values are rooted in that divine unity which is the source of all existence. It is only because of his belief in the Absolute that Solzhenitsyn is able to call mankind to embrace one scale of universal values.

[45]*The First Circle,* Ch. 19; p. 114. (My italics). The Middle Ages is favorably portrayed elsewhere in Solzhenitsyn's works. In *August 1914* Professor Ol'da Andozerskaia explains that "if you reject the Middle Ages, the history of the West collapses, and the rest of modern history becomes incomprehensible... the spiritual life of the Middle Ages is more important. Mankind has never known a time, before or since, when there was such an intense spiritual life predominant over material existence." See *August 1914,* tr. M. Glenny (New York: Farrar, Straus, and Giroux, 1972), p. 548f. See also *The First Circle,* Ch. 60; p. 442 and Ch. 42; p. 297f.

> Given six, four or even two scales of values there cannot be a unified world, a united humanity . . . We could not manage to survive on one Earth, just as a man with two hearts is not long for this world.

If the tri-unity of Truth, Goodness, and Beauty is of divine origin, and if the created world participates mystically in the uncreated spiritual world of this triad, then—in a world in which Solzhenitsyn sees truth and goodness mocked, trampled upon, and simply ignored—the only chance for humanity as a whole to regain the lost values of truth and goodness is through the mystery of beauty which still attracts mankind.[46] Art, as a reflection of beauty, has the capacity to reveal truth and goodness in a vivid way and thereby to arouse mankind to the cause of ethical concern:

> if the all too obvious and the overly straight sprouts of Truth and Goodness have been crushed, cut down, or not permitted to grow, then perhaps the whimsical, unpredictable and ever surprising shoots of Beauty will force their way through and soar up to *that very spot,* thereby fulfilling the task of all three?

Because of its organic relationship with Beauty, "true art" has the possibility of restoring universal sight and value to humanity. An artist must not necessarily share Solzhenitsyn's belief in the Absolute to produce "true art." An artist, if he is honest and true to his intuition, inevitably reveals that aspect of reality he depicts; this revelation is hence a reflection of the Absolute. But Solzhenitsyn believes that the prophetic task of true art can best be accomplished by the artist who "recognizes above himself a higher power and joyfully works as a humble apprentice under God's heaven." Solzhenitsyn thinks that it is difficult for a relativist or solipsist to "structure a balanced spiritual system" and hence their art does not consistently reflect either the "eternal" or the "present"; it fails because it does not reveal the foundations of existence.

> One artist imagines himself the creator of an *autonomous spiritual world;* he hoists upon his shoulders the act of creating this world

[46]In "Mr. -bov and the Question of Art" Dostoevsky wrote: "Art is as much a necessity for man as eating and drinking. The need for beauty and creation embodying it is inseparable from man and without it man would perhaps have refused to live in the world. Man craves it, finds and accepts beauty *without any conditions* just because it is beauty... Beauty is therefore inherent in everything that is healthy, that is to say, everything that is most of all alive and is a necessity of the human organism. It is harmony; it holds the promise of tranquillity; it is the embodiment of man's and mankind's ideals." (*Occasional Writings,* p. 124f).

> and of populating it, together with the total responsibility for it. But he collapses under the load, for no mortal genius can bear up under it, just as, in general, *the man who declares himself the center of existence is unable to create a balanced spiritual system.*[47]

The prophetic mission of art is to restore universal values and to arouse an ethical atmosphere in the world, the goal of which is convincingly expressed by Shulubin in *Cancer Ward.*

> We have to show the world a society in which all relationships, fundamental principles and laws flow directly from ethics, and from them *alone.* Ethical demands must determine all considerations: how to bring up children, what to train them for, to what end the work of grownups should be directed, and how their leisure should be occupied. As for scientific research, it should only be conducted where it doesn't damage morality, in the first instance where it doesn't damage the researchers themselves. The same should apply to foreign policy. Whenever the question of frontiers arises, we should think not of how much richer or stronger this or that course of action will make us, or how it will raise our prestige. We should consider one criterion only: how far is it ethical?[48]

"True art" has therefore an enormous task. Its educational mission is to teach individuals and nations. Its prophetic mission is to warn humanity of its precarious path and to call it to return to universal and absolute values. But when Solzhenitsyn quotes Dostoevsky's "enigmatic remark" that "Beauty will save the world [*mir spaset krasota*],"[49] the task of art seems to take on another dimension, almost messianic in scope. Is Solzhenitsyn's vision of the mission of art ultimately utopian? Does he seriously believe that art can and will ultimately save the world? Admitting that Dostoevsky's remark once seemed to him "simply a phrase," Solzhenitsyn writes that as time passed he came to realize that Dostoevsky's remark was "no slip of the tongue" but a "prophecy," one of Dostoevsky's "astonishing flashes of insight."

[47]My italics. In "Mr. -bov and the Question of Art" Dostoevsky wrote that "art deviates from reality because there really are mad poets and prose writers who sever all relations with reality." (*Occasional Writings,* p. 130); ". . .man can deviate from normal reality, from the laws of nature, during his life; art too will deviate with him" (p. 135).

[48]*Cancer Ward,* Ch. 31; p. 442. At Solzhenitsyn's meeting with the Secretariat of the Union of Soviet Writers on September 22, 1967 this moral vision expressed in *Cancer Ward* was attacked and denounced. One critic complained: "The philosophy of moral socialism does not belong merely to the hero. One senses that it is being defended by the author. This cannot be permitted." (Labedz, *op cit.,* p. 115). Another was more explicit: "The ideological and political sense of moral socialism is the negation of Marxism-Leninism. All these things are completely unacceptable to us, to our society, and to our people." (Labedz, *op. cit.,* p. 119).

[49]Ippolit attributes these words to Prince Myshkin in *The Idiot,* III, 5.

Several statements in the Nobel Lecture tend to support the interpretation that Solzhenitsyn seriously thinks that art can not only *help* humanity in its ethical warfare but that it can ultimately *win* the battle against evil. Writing that art and literature "hold the key to a miracle," Solzhenitsyn states: "We shall be told: what can literature do in the face of a remorseless assault of open violence?" He replies that "violence does not and cannot exist by itself: it is invariably intertwined with the *lie.* They are linked in the most intimate, most organic and profound fashion." "Lies," he writes, "can prevail against much in this world, but never against art." This is brought to a climax when Solzhenitsyn declares in a purely utopian spirit:

> And no sooner will the lies be dispersed than the repulsive nakedness of violence will be exposed—and age-old violence *will topple in defeat.*[50]

In the confrontation with evil Solzhenitsyn sees an enormous difference between the effective activity of the "ordinary brave man" and the Prophet-Artist. The only possible moral response for the "ordinary brave man" is not to participate in lies. "His rule: let *that* come into the world, let it even reign supreme—only not through me." But the effectiveness of the Prophet-Artist is seemingly unlimited.

> It is within the power of writers and artists to do much more: *to defeat the lie!* For in the struggle with lies art . . . shall always triumph!

The last sentence of the Nobel Lecture seems unambiguously utopian. Quoting the Russian proverb that "one word of truth shall outweigh the whole world," Solzhenitsyn declares that it is "on such a seemingly fantastic violation of the law of conservation of mass and energy that my own activity is based, and my appeal to the writers of the world."

If Solzhenitsyn ultimately envisions art as capable of redeeming the world, then his view is not only a "fantastic violation" of physical laws but also a "fantastic violation" of the very spiritual principles upon which his vision of art and value is

[50](My italics). In *What Is Art?* Tolstoy wrote similarly: "The task of art is enormous. Through the influence of real art . . . that peaceful co-operation of man which is now maintained by *external means*—by our law-courts, police, charitable institutions, factory inspection, and so forth—should be obtained by man's free and joyous activity. *Art should cause violence to be set aside.*" (p. 287; my italics).

based, a violation of the deepest aspect of human ontology—freedom. His view would then be more consistent with Tolstoy's sanguine utopian hopes than with Dostoevsky's thought.[51]

It would be unfair, however, to interpret Solzhenitsyn's statements on this subject too literally. Other statements in the Nobel Lecture support the interpretation that Solzhenitsyn sees in art only a powerful weapon with which to wage a vigorous battle against evil. "Could not then art and literature," he asks, "in a very real way offer succor to the modern world?" Believing that "world literature is fully capable of helping a troubled humanity," Solzhenitsyn calls on artists to "come out and join the battle."

The safest interpretation, and the one most consistent with his own personal life and his literary works, is that Solzhenitsyn views art as a most powerful weapon which can *help* but not save mankind. Solzhenitsyn has clearly exaggerated some of his expressions in order to emphasize his point: the prophetic potential of art.

Solzhenitsyn's view of evil is not naive. He is quite aware of the deepest dimensions of the problem of spiritual freedom. If man is spiritually free, then he is capable of "creating" evil simply by a perversion of the will. As long as man is spiritually free, there can be no earthly utopia. One well-known example of Solzhenitsyn's recognition of the depths of human evil is both striking and Dostoevskian.[52] At the end of *Cancer Ward* Oleg Kostoglotov visits a zoo and is astonished by "an announcement fixed to one of the . . . cages."

> The little monkey that used to live here was blinded because of the senseless cruelty of one of the visitors. An evil man threw tobacco into the Macaque Rhesus's eyes.[53]

Kostoglotov is "struck dumb," unable to comprehend it. This man "was not described as 'anti-humanist,' or 'an agent of American imperialism'; all it said was that he was evil. This was what was so striking: how could this man be simply 'evil'?" Kostoglotov, "obsessed with picturing the face of that blinded

[51]For an analysis of Dostoevsky's view of utopianism see my article "Dostoevsky's Vision of the Golden Age" in *Transactions of the Association of Russian-American Scholars,* VII (1973).

[52]For an analysis of Dostoevsky's view of evil see my article "Dostoevsky and Hawthorne?" in *Transactions of the Association of Russian-American Scholars,* V (1972), 38-59.

[53]*Cancer Ward,* Ch. 35; p. 506.

macaque monkey," repeats again and again that an evil man caused it—"just like that [*prosto—tak*]."[54] Evil, for Solzhenitsyn, is not the inevitable result of the economic and social order, but emerges from the depths of human freedom, rendering any utopia on earth impossible.[55]

Nevertheless Solzhenitsyn will not retreat into defeatism and pessimism. He believes a positive effort must be made to improve the moral climate of the modern world and he firmly maintains that art is inherently suited to engage in this effort. Artists, if they are genuinely interested in truth and goodness, can contribute enormously to the restoration of these lost values. Solzhenitsyn's ultimate vision of the mission of art is therefore neither naive nor utopian. It is profoundly idealistic, courageous, and noble.

[54]The last words of *Cancer Ward* are: "An evil man threw tobacco in the Macaque Rhesus's eyes. Just like that..." (*Cancer Ward,* Ch. 36; p. 532). For inexplicable reasons the Posev edition of *Cancer Ward* has omitted these last two lines.

[55]At the meeting of the Secretariat of the Union of Soviet Writers on September 22, 1967 the writer Abdumomunov was quite aware of the implications of this scene in *Cancer Ward.* See Labedz, *op. cit.,* p. 117.

Solzhenitsyn and New Realism

BY HEINRICH BÖLL

Efforts toward a new realism in Western Germany have not arisen by chance. But in our Western literature we have still not discovered the world of work, not to mention the working-class world—even though in our literature about war we have shown the worker estranged as soldier. The ignoble polemics about Max von der Grün[1] made clear how risky it is to have anything to do with the world of the worker; von der Grün was caught between unions and industry, the two powers which pretend they *want* to have the world of work described. As a third power one could name those who wish to see their world represented—one could even say ennobled—by the method of estrangement—and they are the workers who live in it. For decades we in the West (and I include myself) have regarded socialist realism with mild amusement. Now the backlash has set in and it will continue. The type of writers, theater directors, and graphic artists in Poland, Czechoslovakia, Yugoslavia, and the Soviet Union who are most sought after here proves, it seems, that socialist realism—even if only as a hated, dogmatic

Preface to the German translation of *Cancer Ward,* Part I (Neuwied & Berlin: Luchterhand, 1969). Copyright © by Heinrich Böll. Reprinted by permission. Translated by Marjorie L. Hoover.

[1]Member of the Dortmund "Group 61," whose novel *Stellenweise Glatteis* aroused controversy by its implicit accusation of both industry and the workers' union.—Tr.

opposite number—has not deprived writers of a voice in the lands where it holds sway. The only reprehensible thing about socialist realism which still remains today is the doctrinaire and dogmatic optimism imposed upon it; this is not just an approximate, but almost the exact equivalent of that cry for a healthy world which has by no means died down in the West. And yet the demand for a healthy world, for Christian art and literature, is only another variant of the wish for a Greek *deus ex machina* which would solve all problems easily and automatically. In such made-to-order Christian literature (as, for instance, in Claudel's work) grace assumed the role of *deus ex machina,* making on us nothing but an embarassing impression, quite as embarassing as the "happy-end" optimism of socialist realism approved by the Communist "establishment." The West, which still persists in calling itself "Christian," will yet experience its own breakdown; moreover (and this is more important) it will soon have to recognize and admit this. Only half a generation ago it outgrew "edifying" Christian literature, and the time may come very soon when an attempt will be made to include even Grass as a great "Westerner."

No doubt the development of art and literature in the world will make an about-face: the West, weary of "formalist" games, will seek a new realism. Pop, Op, and Happenings are intermediate stops on the way to upsetting all Western esthetic norms, which today still aspire to the Greek ideal. And that is as it should be: to bore from within is the prime function of artists and writers. Even the East will have to get over "formalist" games; it too must run the whole gamut. (Artists and writers who are spared this or try to avoid it are not true artists and writers.) The East will return, after all, to its great and marvelously broad narrative manner in the realist tradition. There will be—in West and East—many skirmishes. Everyone, every statesman basically desires that "healthy" literature which affirms his policy, be it in the form of a Western Christian literature laden with grace, or in the form of socialist-realist literature, a realism which one can permit to be critical as long as it responds in the end to the challenge of the good cause.

Solzhenitsyn's *Cancer Ward* could become the connecting link between the old and a renewed socialist realism, and it could become the model for our generally rather pitiful efforts toward a new realism here. The resentment which some Western writers (and soon surely some Eastern writers too) show at the continued survival of the novel is due only to a misconception of their own situation and potential: they do not realize that they are writing poems in prose, magnificent, poetic flashes of situation.

Translated by Marjorie L. Hoover

Lexical Peculiarities of Solzhenitsyn's Language

BY VERA CARPOVICH

It is widely acknowledged that Solzhenitsyn's language is peculiar and in certain respects puzzling. It differs from the literary language of classic and modern Russian writers. Various impressions and opinions reflecting readers' tastes have been published on the subject in recent years, many in passing, a few in a more detailed manner. However, no linguistic analysis has yet appeared. This article presents some results of an analysis of lexical peculiarities that make Solzhenitsyn's vocabulary idiosyncratic, difficult, unique, and even controversial.

In his programmatic article "Ne obychai degtem shchi belit', na to smetana" ["Cabbage Soup is Enriched With Sour Cream, Not With Tar"] which appeared in the Union of Writers' weekly *Literary Gazette* in 1965,[1] Solzhenitsyn states that the modern Russian language, particularly the written literary language, "has become impoverished." He explains the unhappy phenomenon by certain historical events and particularly by the fact that Russian writers "were too lazy to seek out and use worthy Russian words, or were ashamed by their 'rudeness,' or blamed them for their inability to express a modern lofty and subtle idea."

Other specific reasons which have contributed to the im-

[1]*Literaturnaia gazeta,* 4 November 1965. Reprinted in Solzhenitsyn, *Sobranie sochinenii,* V, 261-267.

poverishment of the contemporary Russian language Solzhenitsyn dares not mention. The lack of political and religious freedom in the Soviet Union, and the severe censorship have paralyzed the entire sector of the humanities. It is also a well-established historical fact that the Soviet period of Russian history has been characterized by the destruction of entire classes—intellectuals, "capitalists," clergy, merchants, military officers, prosperous peasants, and others. When those people perished, their specific language died too. Spiritually poor and materially squalid, Soviet life has thus contributed to the impoverishment of the vocabulary of modern Russian. As Baudouin de Courtenay once observed, a living language reflects first of all the real life of the people.

The dogma of Socialist Realism and the Soviet censorship created a climate for development of lexical clichés by Soviet writers (e.g. *v otnoshenii sena*—"with respect to hay"; *po voprosu sobaki*—"on the matter of the dog"; *dognat' i peregnat'*—"to catch up and surpass"). The stereotyped language has somehow alleviated the hard task of Soviet writers to adapt their work to the Party line and to the demands of the censor. Inevitably this situation led to a loss of a "lively narration" and consequently undermined the literary language. Although an anti-cliché campaign has been waged by Soviet periodicals for the last four decades, this did little to alleviate the situation, and even venerable Soviet masters of belles-lettres (A. Surkov, S. Mikhalkov, K. Simonov and others) were not free from this sin, according to the eminent scholar and academician V. V. Vinogradov. In 1965, Vinogradov wrote an article in *Literaturnaia gazeta,* in which he reluctantly recognized the fact that Soviet literature, while preserving much that is "meaningful and eventful," lacks sharp and graphic representation, colors, and aphoristic language. It was to this article that Solzhenitsyn responded with his "Ne obychai . . ."

To some extent this general process of impoverishment has been offset by the enrichment of modern Russian from two sources: (a) desultory borrowings from foreign languages, mostly from modern American, e.g. *dzhinsy* [jeans], *dizainer* [designer], *miniskert* [miniskirt], *shou* [show], *chipsy* [potato chips], etc.;[2] such words, as we see, are more or less distorted

[2]*Novye slova i znacheniia*: *Slovar'-spravochnik* [*New Words and Their Meanings*: *A Reference Dictionary*], ed. N.Z. Kotelova and Iu. S. Sorokin (Moscow: AN SSSR, 1971).

transliterations of American words; (b) revival of a few "prerevolutionary" Russian words like *soldat, ofitser, gvardiia, ministr,* etc.[3]

Apparently, foreign words borrowed today neither enrich the literary language nor solve the "cliché" problem. Solzhenitsyn's position on foreign borrowings (like that of Pushkin and Tolstoy) has been rather moderate: he accepts useful Russified foreign words (*energiia, nerv, protsess, dialog, problema, profil', futbol, khirurg*), but rejects words which might be replaced by valid Russian equivalents. Thus *konkretnost', ignorirovanie, gradatsiia* are avoided in favor of OSIAZAEMOST' [tangibility], NEZAMECHANIE [ignoring], NADVYSHENIE [gradation].[4] No foreign word has been found among the "peculiarities" in Solzhenitsyn's texts. Nor is Solzhenitsyn given to the other extreme—"Slavophilism." One of his protagonists in *The First Circle,* Sologdin, speaks what he calls the "Language of Ultimate Clarity" where all foreign words have been replaced with specially selected Russian or Church-Slavonic words. Thus, in Sologdin's usage, *inzhener* [engineer] becomes *zizhditel'* [builder], *istoriia* [history]—*bytiinoe vremia* [time past], *sfera* [sphere]—*osharie* [globoid], *kapitalizm* [capitalism]—*tolstosumstvo* ["moneybag-ism"], *reaktsioner* [reactionary]—*popiatnik* [backtracker] and so on. Solzhenitsyn ridicules this language.

In hopes of remedying these unfavorable conditions, Solzhenitsyn devised a sort of master plan for the enrichment of the literary language: (a) by introducing "worthy" old substandard Russian words undeservedly forgotten; these words are taken from the Dahl Glossary[5] and are not part of standard literary glossaries, and (b) by forming such neologisms as the natural flexibility of the language permits. Solzhenitsyn's borrowings from Dahl and his neologisms constitute his lexical "peculiarities." In his article "Ne obychai . . ." Solzhenitsyn asserted that "we are in the midst of the decisive decades when we are still able to correct the trouble" by using "a cautious lexical enlargement" of the modern Russian language. It should be noted that the writer does not impose his "peculiarities" on

[3]After the revolution of 1917 these words were replaced by *krasnoarmeets, komandir, armiia, komissar,* etc. Most of these, in turn, have become "historicisms" in the Russian literary language of today.

[4]Solzhenitsyn's lexical "peculiarities" are given in capital letters in this essay.

[5]Vladimir Dal', *Tolkovyi slovar' zhivogo velikorusskogo iazyka,* 4 vols. (Moscow: Inostrannye slovari, 1955 [Reprint of second edition of 1880-1882]).

the reader; rather, he gently suggests a "judicious use... of such words which, although they do not exist in the modern spoken language, are used so clearly by the author that they may meet with the approval of speakers... and in this way return to the language."

There is of course nothing new in Solzhenitsyn's attempts to enrich the literary language by borrowing from the popular language and from dialects. Most Russian writers (Lomonosov, Sumarokov, Krylov, Karamzin, Fonvizin, Pushkin, Gogol', Griboedov, Turgenev, Leskov, Mel'nikov-Pecherskii, Saltykov-Shchedrin, Tolstoy—the list is long) "recognized the right of the folk language [*narodnyi iazyk*] to be used in the speech of educated people and in books."[6] The great Russian writers of the past mastered not only the literary language but also the substandard language. Analyzing the language of Tolstoy in the 1850s and 60s, V. V. Vinogradov observed the introduction of new varieties of style in which the colloquial, popular, and peasant language were used. However, not a single Russian writer had devised a plan or a program for enriching the language. The idea of enriching the literary language was hardly a problem in the 19th century and up to the revolution of 1917. Only in the Soviet period did the literary language find itself in trouble, and Solzhenitsyn felt it necessary to come up with a remedy.

The principal points of this plan to enrich the literary language as formulated in his article "Ne obychai..." are:

1. To use whenever possible the short masculine and feminine verbal nouns (like Dahl's *peretask* [moving], *sokhran* [preservation], *nagromozdka* [heaping-up]) in lieu of the long neuter gerunds (*peretaskivanie, sokhranenie, nagromozhdenie*). Such short forms are regarded by Solzhenitsyn as "strong and maneuverable."

2. To use abstract nouns as little as possible.

3. To form new prefixed nouns (like Dahl's *predmestnik* [predecessor]) instead of commonly accepted long phrases (*moi predshestvennik na etom meste*).

4. To form new general Russian adverbs (*vpriporokh* [strewing or covering loosely (by snow or sand)]), *dotonka* [to the last detail], *odvukon'* [riding one horse while leading a

[6]V. I. Chernyshev, *Izbrannye trudy* [*Selected Works*], 2 vols. (Moscow: Prosveshchenie, 1970), I, 446.

second one beside it in reserve]) "which hold the main promise of brevity in our language."

5. To form new prefixed verbs (*ostegnut'sia* [to use the wrong button], *rasklonit'* [to bend apart], *vyshatnut'* [to pull out]) from the stems of generally used verbs (*zastegnut'*, *naklonit'*, *otshatnut'*).

6. "To search out and use worthy Russian words" (*osiazaemost'* [tangibility]) instead of wantonly borrowing foreign words (*konkretnost'*).

7. To use the Dahl Glossary as a fundamental source of substandard words for "cautious lexical enlargement" of the literary language.

All examples given above in parentheses were taken by Solzhenitsyn from the Dahl Glossary. Solzhenitsyn has carefully followed the same patterns in forming neologisms. Examples: 1. *short masculine and feminine verbal nouns*: ZAVIAZ—tie, NAVIS—overhang, OBSOKH—drying, KRIAKHT—crack (sound), ZAGOROZHA—shelter, ZATRAVA—bootstrap, NASTAVA—exhortation, ZAPUSHCH'—neglect, NADYM'—hanging smoke, etc.; 2. *new prefixed nouns*: OTDALENNIK—far-away man (instead of *chelovek zhivushchii v otdalenii*); 3. *adverbs*: VRAZNOKAP—by a few drops, DOKOSTI—down-to-the-bone; 4. *prefixed verbs*: VGOVARIVAT'—to persuade, POPRIGASNUT'—to dim; 5. *avoidance of needless foreign terms*: NEZAMECHANIE—ignoring (instead of *ignorirovanie*). In addition, Solzhenitsyn rather freely uses new compound nouns and adjectives in his works.

There is a substantial difference between Dahl and Solzhenitsyn in their views on using substandard language for enriching the literary language. Dahl proposed to break away entirely from the style of the literary language of his time, to reject the Church-Slavonic tradition, and to exclude borrowings from foreign languages. He considered a cultivated substandard Russian as the literary language. On the contrary, Solzhenitsyn tries only to enrich the existing vocabulary without changing the traditional system of the language.

In creating his new words, Solzhenitsyn has employed the traditional word-formation system. Nearly all of them have been formed according to the regular "productive patterns." Deviations (such as KOE-KAKSTVO—slipshod manner, ESHCHE-NE-BORODKA—a not-yet-beard) from the patterns are extremely rare. Solzhenitsyn has never used the unnatural breaking and joining of words so characteristic of Maiakovskii's creations. Many of Solzhenitsyn's neologisms show that he strives for semantic precision and effectiveness of the word, for its maximum expressiveness: VZGUL—start of rumbling, DORESHIT'—to reach a final decision, RASSKOROMNYI—far-from-fasting, SOLDIAGA—experienced soldier, RAZBITNIAGA—nimble, sprightly boy, IOTOCHKA—just a trifle, etc. As a result of this tendency, the synonymic groups have been enriched, and new antonyms have been added. Examples of *new synonyms*: NESPESHLIVYI—*netoroplivyi* [unhurried], SNAROSHKI—*narochno* [deliberately], OTRUBISTO—*otryvisto* [abruptly], NEMOCHNYI—*bessil'nyi* [powerless]; *new antonyms*: NEUMELETS [unskillful man]—*umelets* [skillful worker], NEDOBYCHNIK [unlucky man]—*dobychnik* [looter], RASSHCHURIT'SIA [to raise the eyelids]—*prishchurit'sia* [to squint], BEZUDACHLIVYI [hapless]—*udachlivyi* [lucky], etc. Solzhenitsyn also tries to augment lexical clusters. For example, the *new verbs* LUCHSHET' [to become better], NICHTOZHNET' [to become paltry], GROMCHET' [to become loud], MOLOCHNET' [to become milky] are derived from the existing adjectives *luchshii, nichtozhnyi, gromkii, molochnyi* (pattern: *krasnyi—krasnet'*). From the noun *doldon* [dolt] he derived an adjective DOLDONNYI, from *lezheboka* [loafer]— a verb LEZHEBOCHNICHAT', etc. The aspectal system of the Russian verb has also been enriched: ZASTANYVAT', ZASTYZHIVAT'SIA are iterative imperfective verbs added—among many others—by Solzhenitsyn to standard verbs *stonat',—zastonat'* [to moan, to groan], *stydit'sia—zastydit'sia* [to be ashamed].

Sometimes the polysemy of standard literary words or of words from Dahl is increased by Solzhenitsyn, e.g., the Dahl word RAZRESHETIT' [to use a grid pattern in wall painting] has acquired a new meaning "to take off the grid [bars]" as an antonym to a common word *zareshetit'* [to place a grid or bars in prison windows].

About 99 percent of Solzhenitsyn's neologisms have been formed morphologically, that is by affixation, by zero-suffix derivation, or by combining two words into one compound word. Only one percent of neologisms has been formed by semantic derivation.

In selecting words from Dahl, Solzhenitsyn has followed the same pattern as in the formation of his new words: he has searched for semantically rich and expressive words to enrich his language with new synonyms, antonyms, etc. Very rarely does Solzhenitsyn use words with figurative meanings. Sometimes he tries to uncover the primary, often forgotten, meaning of the word and uses it in a surprising way (as in NEUMELETS, DOBYCHNIK; see also NEUSTUPNYI—lacking a toe hold, NASMOTR—watch, vigil). In selecting words from Dahl, Solzhenitsyn does not hunt for "eccentric" or "queer" words (few Russian writers have been free from this temptation) to startle the unsophisticated reader. He has written: "Taking pride in words which have drifted far away and are therefore hopelessly lost is useless" in the task of enriching the language.

A careful examination of Solzhenitsyn's works published prior to 1973 has yielded close to 1350 peculiar words which have been identified as either neologisms (60%) or borrowed from Dahl (40%). Nearly all peculiar words occur in the author's narration [*avtorskaia rech'*]. In most cases they have been used once; only half a dozen neologisms occurred 4 to 6 times, a fact which might indicate that Solzhenitsyn regards them as particularly deserving promotion.[7] The largest group of "peculiarities" (393 words) are nouns; then come verbs (369), adjectives (259), adverbs (203), participles (101), and finally adverbial participles (22). Traced to their linguistic origin, about one-half (660) of the peculiar words have been found to stem from verbs.

The peculiar vocabulary of Solzhenitsyn may be assessed as experimental, and his entire linguistic venture may be termed a daring lexical experiment. There is no way to predict whether or not his peculiar words will be accepted into the literary language. Time alone will tell.

[7]Examples: GOTOVNO [readily, willingly], VPEREKREST [crosswise], IZBOKU [sideways, from the side], PEREKOSOBOCHENNYI [tilted (hut), uneven (cinder block)], UZHATOST' [squeeze], SHAROGOLOVYI [round-headed].

The "Language of Ultimate Clarity"

BY BORIS O. UNBEGAUN

Among the various political prisoners of an MGB-run research institute, described in Solzhenitsyn's *The First Circle,* there is an engineer called Sologdin whom his co-prisoners regard as a crank [*chudak*]. His harmless eccentricity consists in posing as a knight of ancient Russia and in arranging his moustache and beard in the way in which he thinks Aleksandr Nevskii did (on one occasion, however, the author describes his beard as a "neat little French beard" [*akkuratnaia frantsuzskaia borodka*], p. 158[1]). In addition—and this is certainly in keeping with his adopted attitude—he avoids using foreign words and tries hard to replace them by Russian expressions, sometimes of his own coining: this, after all, is not too difficult in a language with almost unlimited derivation potentialities. Foreign words are "bird-words" [*ptich'i slova*] to Sologdin, and Russian, once it has been purged of them, becomes the "Language of Ultimate Clarity" [*iazyk predel'noi iasnoti*].[2]

"The 'Language of Ultimate Clarity.'" From *Melbourne Slavonic Studies,* Nos. 5-6 (1971), 91-94. Reprinted by permission of the author and *Melbourne Slavonic Studies.* Adapted for inclusion in this volume by the editors.

[1]All quotations are from the edition of *V kruge pervom* published by Harper and Row at New York and Evanston in 1968. This, like all other editions of the novel, is not an authorized one. [The translation quoted here is based on Thomas Whitney, extensively revised.—Eds.]

[2]The term "bird words" is probably taken from the memoirs of Aleksandr Gertsen [Alexander Herzen], who recalls at one point that a well-known Moscow

We are introduced to Sologdin and his lexicomania in Chapter 24 ("Sawing Wood") during a conversation which he is having with his friend and co-prisoner, the mathematician Nerzhin:

> "You're not acting like a 'calculator' [*ischislitel'*] but like a 'versifier' [*piit*]."
> Nerzhin was not surprised. This was one of Solodgin's well-known eccentricities—to speak in what he called the Language of Ultimate Clarity, without using "bird words" or words of foreign derivation. It was impossible to tell whether he was playing a game or really believed in this fancy. With great diligence—sometimes resourcefully, and sometimes clumsily—he would dodge and evade trying to avoid in his speech even the most essential words like "engineer" [*inzhener*] or "metal" [*metall*]. Even in his shop-talk and in conversation with his superiors he tried to hold to this line and sometimes made his listeners wait while he tried to think up a word . . .
> And so he became for the zeks at the sharashka an acknowledged, unqualified, and irrevocable *crank.* (p. 122)

The last but one sentence must not be taken too literally: in fact, when Sologdin, in Chapter 73 ("Two Engineers"), is involved in a subtle, knife-edge dialogue with the MGB Colonel Iakonov—a dialogue on which his eventual release may depend—he entirely forgets about his Language of Ultimate Clarity (pp. 407-8). Or is it Solzhenitsyn, perhaps, who has forgotten about it?

This seems to suggest that Sologdin's lexical eccentricity is no more than a game or a pose. And his co-prisoner and friend, the staunch Communist Lev Rubin, was perhaps right in apostrophizing him in the heat of an otherwise abstract discussion:

> You're the one who is lying! That's just all one big act with you! That includes your idiotic "Language of Ultimate Clarity"! And your playing at chivalry and knighthood! And your make-up *à la* Aleksandr Nevskii! Everything's an act or a pose with you because in life you're a failure! (p. 359)

The words "calculator" [*ischislitel'*] and "versifier" [*piit*] at the beginning of the quotation of p. 122, stand for "mathematician" [*matematik*] and "poet" [*poet*]. In the ensuing conversation between Sologdin and Nerzhin we learn further expressions of the Language of Ultimate Clarity, such as "intense

astronomer, Perevoshchikov, used to call the jargon-ridden language of the Moscow intellectuals in the 1830's and 1840's—"bird language" [*ptichii iazyk*]. See Herzen's *My Past and Thoughts,* Part IV, Ch. 25. [The editors are grateful to Vera Carpovich for this information.]

doubt" [*usugublennoe somnenie*] for "scepticism" [*skeptitsizm*] (p. 123), "time past" [*bytiinoe vremia*] for "history" [*istoriia*] (p. 124), "globoid" [*osharie*] for "sphere" [*sfera*] (p. 124), "general view of the means of approach" [*obshchii ogliad na puti podkhoda*] for "methodology" [*metodika*] (p. 125).

A few examples of similar word-creations may be found in Chapter 30 ("Penalty Marks"), devoted to a casual love affair between Sologdin and the wife of an MVD officer, a free employee in the prison who is making tracing-paper copies: "transparency-tracer" [*prozrachno-obvodchitsa*] for "copier" [*kopirovshchitsa*] (p. 160), "constructor" [*zizhditel'*] for "engineer" [*inzhener*] (*ibid.*), "penalizing" [*penevyi*] for "punitive" [*shtrafnoi*] (p. 163), "moneybag-ism" [*tolstosumstvo*] for "capitalism" [*kapitalizm*] (*ibid.*), "to observe" [*dogliadat'*] for "to spy upon" [*shpionit'*] (*ibid.*).

Finally, in Chapter 60 ("A Duel Not According to Rules"), in a heated discussion with the Communist prisoner Rubin, Sologdin makes use of the following expressions: "backtracker" [*popiatnik*] for "reactionary" [*reaktsioner*] (p. 338), "crowned underling" [*uvenchannyi prisluzhnik*] for "certified lackey" [*diplomirovannyi lakei*] (*ibid.*), "one possessed" [*oderzhimets*] for "fanatic" [*fanatik*] (p. 339), "sign" [*titl*] for "theme" [*tema*] (*ibid.*), "ability to apply conclusions" [*umenie primeniat' vyvody na dele*] for "criterion of practicability" [*kriterii praktiki*] (p. 340), "material" [*veshchnyi*] and "applied" [*delovoi*] for "practical" [*prakticheskii*] (pp. 340, 341, 357), *fenia* for "jargon" [*zhargon*] (p. 341), the already mentioned *zizhditel'* for *inzhener* (p. 342), "reign of the workers" [*vladychestvo rabochikh*] for "dictatorship of the proletariat" [*diktatura proletariata*] (p. 359), "forward direction" [*peredovoe napravlenie*] for "progress" [*progress*] (*ibid.*).

However, not every foreign borrowing can be replaced by a Russian word—not even by the resourceful Sologdin:

> "That's right! In what direction will the . . . ah . . ."—he choked—"process [*protsess*] develop?" (p. 340)
>
> . . . "but deep inside you are really true to the motto [*deviz*]"—in the heat of the moment a foreign word escaped his lips, but at least it was one associated with chivalry—"that 'ends justify means.' " (p. 358)

In an article published in 1965,[3] Solzhenitsyn entered a mild

[3] "Ne obychai degtem shchi belit', na to smetana," *Literaturnaia gazeta*, November 4, 1965.

protest against the excessive use of foreign words, but there is no doubt that he does not share Sologdin's eccentricities. His own word-creations are of a different nature: strangely enough, he follows Dal' in believing that standard Russian may still be enriched by borrowings from dialects or by new words coined on the pattern of dialectal idioms, mainly adverbs.

Thus Sologdin's Language of Ultimate Clarity remains an isolated curiosity, a game—even a mania. To a philologist, however, it is unexpectedly revealing. As we have seen, it includes a few common Russian words and a few new creations formed with Russian elements. But the former, as one might expect, are only imperfect substitutes for foreign words, e.g. *dogliadat'* for *shpionit'* or *delovoi* for *prakticheskii,* or clumsy periphrases such as *obshchii ogliad na puti podkhoda* for *metodika,* or *umenie primeniat' vyvody na dele* for *kriterii praktiki.* The latter sound as implausible as his *osharie* for *sfera,* or *tolstosumstvo* for *kapitalizm* (both with a Church Slavonic suffix), or *popiatnik* for *reaktsioner.* However, the major, and one must admit, the most successful part of Solodgin's "Russianizations" ironically enough consist not of Russian but of Church Slavonic forms—this is not surprising since the foreign words which Sologdin wished to eliminate mostly refer to the higher strata of the vocabulary, which belong, in standard Russian, to the Church Slavonic area. Thus Sologdin's lexicomania furnishes additional proof to the well-known fact that, in word formation, modern standard Russian is still faithful to its initial Church Slavonic tradition.

Obviously Sologdin himself is completely unconscious of the fact that his Language of Ultimate Clarity turns out to be Church Slavonic rather than Russian. For him it represents the precious "Russian" treasure house, even though it includes such unmistakably Greek words as *piit* and *titl* as well as the strange *fenia* (probably derived from *ofenskii iazyk* ["itinerant peddlers' argot"]). But Solzhenitsyn? One wonders whether he is aware of this.

CRITICAL ESSAYS
II

Solzhenitsyn and the Grand Tradition

BY HÉLÈNE ZAMOYSKA

During the year 1956, Pasternak often remarked to his friends that with Stalin's death an entire era had come to an end, and that a new—and better—age in which our current dreams would be realized was already rising on the ruins of the old. It was the vision of a poet, directed towards the future, and of a man who had never ceased throughout all his torments to retain faith in the vitality of his people and in the creative energy of life; this was his security against the coming upheavals. To be sure, he was anticipating a little; but the ferment which has been taking place for several years now in the intellectual and artistic life of the Soviet Union does not belie his intuition. At the very least it denotes a period of transition. (. . .)

Significant in this context is the discussion in intellectual circles of "tradition and innovation," quite recently [1961-1963. Eds.] the subject of inquiry in the journal *Voprosy literatury.* This constitutes the fundamental question of the era itself. Is not the issue at stake the problem of how one can know, in the USSR, what tradition to break with in order to go forward and make a fresh start?

Let us point out immediately that not all Soviet writers grasp this problem in all of its dimensions. The conflict be-

Abridged from "Soljenitsyne et la grande tradition" by Hélène Zamoyska, in *La Table Ronde* [Paris], 185 (1963), pp. 61-81. Translated for this volume by David M. Halperin.

tween "tradition and innovation" signifies, for the majority of them, the struggle between "conservatism and progressivism" in literary or artistic forms. The spirit of innovation consists therefore of endowing the formula of "socialist realism" (rather looked down upon because of the mediocre level of "production" during the Stalin years, but impossible to attack directly) with such elasticity that it encompasses an infinite variety of forms, allowing for the most audacious probing. This is particularly the tendency of the young poets who wish to write new songs to old tunes. (. . .)

In this connection we would like to call attention to the subtle and profound response of the poet Evgenii Vinokurov to the question under discussion:

> The problem of innovation, to my mind, does not consist in searching for a new manner; it is contingent upon the conscience of the poet. Often we imagine that innovation in art amounts to changing mechanically certain "devices" and certain "formulae" and replacing them with others; the history of literature is seen as a straight line, something like an endless race course in which each literary event beats the preceding one and breaks a record.[1]

To this "sporting" conception of literature which he categorically rejects, Vinokurov opposes the essential task of the artist which is: "Above all to see, to acquire the vision of the inner eye. As for putting down on paper that which has been seen, seizing it, securing it—all that is a matter of artistic refinement, and innovation in this domain yields to freshness of feeling and thought."

Vinokurov does not underestimate formal expression *per se,* though he is not apparently seduced by other factors, such as the musicality of poetry; but citing Pasternak to support his view, he holds that the talent of a poet is "that of discovering and stating the truth." This is why he refuses to recognize any artificial distinction between "the new" and "the old," which are not labels arbitrarily pasted onto specific works, but are inextricably mingled categories. The bond between old and new is so organic that in his opinion any work detached from tradition is lifeless. Similarly, life, far from progressing with the successive abjurations of every passing generation, continues only because of the uninterrupted chain of generations which follow one another in mutual solidarity. According to this view, progress

[1]*Voprosy literatury,* 1963, No. 2.

is not effected by repeating the past, but by prolonging that part of it which remains alive.

Among his contemporaries, Vinokurov chose the name of Solzhenitsyn to illustrate his point: "[Solzhenitsyn is] an innovator," he writes, "because he reestablishes and extends one of the interrupted lines of the Grand Tradition."[2] This constitutes an entire program. The poet does not specify further what he means by this phrase, but the context and the other names which he had previously mentioned—Rublev, Pasternak, Zabolotskii—indicate it clearly: he signifies by this term a certain inner attitude towards life and mankind which has always and in every period characterized the best Russian artists dedicated to the discovery of truth.

In this sense the reference to Solzhenitsyn is perfectly justified. A reading of the three tales which he has published so far[3] does not, of course, warrant making any definitive judgment, but they are clearly sufficient to convince us of his fidelity to the Grand Tradition: that is why, if there is any writer at this very moment in the USSR who stands at the center of the psychological transformation which is sweeping over Russia, it is certainly he.

Solzhenitsyn is the witness of an era "not lacking in tears" (to use his own phrase),[4] and it is precisely the most tragic aspects which he describes: the concentration camps (*One Day*), the beginning of the war ("Incident at Krechetovka Station"), and contemporary life in a Russian village ("Matrena's Home").

In his choice of themes he is not a complete innovator, except for the first novel. And, if in fact he is an innovator in that respect, it still does not mean that others have not written

[2]*Voprosy literatury,* 1963, No. 2, p. 49.

[3]Mme. Zamoyska lists in a footnote the works of Solzhenitsyn which had appeared at the time of her essay [*One Day in the Life of Ivan Denisovich,* "Incident at Krechetovka Station" and "Matrena's Home"] and cites their French translations. The quotes used here are whenever possible drawn from the following published English editions of Solzhenitsyn's works presently available in the United States, with the appropriate page citations: *One Day in the Life of Ivan Denisovich,* trans. by Ronald Hingley and Max Hayward (New York: Bantam Books, 1972); "An Incident at Krechetovka Station" and "Matrena's Home" in *"We Never Make Mistakes,"* trans. by Paul W. Blackstock (New York: W. W. Norton & Co., 1971). The quotations used have been checked against the Russian by the editors and the more glaring errors of the Blackstock translation rectified. In these cases the page reference to the published English translation is prefaced by "cf."—Tr.

[4]"Matrena's Home," cf. p. 131.—Tr.

about the Stalinist camps.[5] According to the Soviet press, publishing houses are innundated with manuscripts devoted to this nightmare; but there is little chance that many of them will see the light of day. (. . .)

Solzhenitsyn has joined a current which seeks to reestablish the truth where it has been silent or distorted for so long; but he is better able than other writers to observe and describe what he sees. In this he remains faithful to the best traditions of what the Soviets call "critical realism."

Nothing escapes his penetrating vision. The conditions in which not only the inmates of labor camps live—but also the free wartime population and the peasants in the center of Russia ten years ago—are depicted with pitiless exactitude but without an overabundance of details. Their day-to-day existence unfolds, dominated by a ceaseless struggle against three enemies: cold, hunger, and exhaustion.

Hunger, the obsession of prisoners condemned to a maximum amount of work on a minimum of food ("But come to think of it, they ate four days for every five they worked" [p. 96]) is a constant and unrelieved torment.

> The prisoners were at their coldest and hungriest when they checked in through these gates in the evening, and their bowl of hot and watery soup without any fat was like rain in a drought. They gulped it down. They cared more for this bowlful than freedom, or for their life in years gone by and years to come (p. 151).

Once again it is hunger which drives a convoy of Russian soldiers, who have been evacuated in special cars to the interior of Russia, to hurl themselves like wild beasts upon a sidetracked trainload of flour during a stop at a station, in spite of the sentry who fires upon them ("Incident").

It is the cold against which each prisoner, forced to go to work outdoors all day in inhuman temperatures, tries vainly to protect himself by bundling up in all the rags he can manage to collect. The cold is no less fearful to the kolkhoz members, for whom no provision has been made to supply fuel in winter:

> Yes, that's the way it was. The frightening breath of winter was already beginning to blow. There were forests all around, but nowhere to take firewood. Excavators growled through the peat bogs, but did

[5] We deliberately omit the accounts of the painful subject which appeared quite early in the West (the excellent book by J. Czapski, *Souvenirs de Starobielsk,* for example, dates from 1944). We must confine ourselves to Soviet writers.

> not provide peat for the inhabitants, only for the authorities—the teachers, doctors, factory workers—everything for the authorities by the truckload. Fuel was not authorized for Talnov—and no one was supposed to inquire about it. The kolkhoz chairman walked through the village, looked at you either with demanding or ingenuous eyes, and talked about whatever you wanted except fuel, because he had already laid in a supply for himself. But winter wasn't in their plans.
>
> And so, just as wood had formerly been stolen from the landowners, peat was now hauled off from the Trust. (cf. p. 101).

Therefore the kolkhoz women take care of it themselves before winter comes by removing the peat in bricks:

> They would carry away in their bags some six peat bricks at a time if they were still damp, about ten if they were dry. One of these sacks was enough to stoke up the stove once; it had to be carried as far as three kilometers and weighed about two poods [one pood equals 36 pounds]. There were two hundred days of winter... (cf. p. 102).

Finally there is exhaustion, so persistent that one falls asleep at the slightest breath of warmth and fails to make roll-call, like the "real" Moldavian spy who gets himself beaten to a pulp by the guards and his fellow inmates for making them wait for him in the cold. In order to protect oneself from fatigue, one has to make the most economical use of one's strength. Thus Shukhov notes the transformation taking place in the newly-arrived Buinovskii "from a bossy, loudmouth naval officer into a slow-moving and cagey prisoner. He'd have to be like this if he wanted to get through his twenty-five years in camp" (p. 90).

These are forces which are at all times hostile to man—whether they are systematically exploited in camp to dehumanize him, triumph spontaneously in the cataclysm of war, or result from criminal neglect on the part of the authorities. Whatever the reason for which they are unleashed, they have to be put down. Only those who know the ropes manage to achieve this, either through theft or by using their wits (the way the kolkhoz women acquire their means of heating needs no comment). It is a question of life or death and even the most honest (Shukhov in the camp or Matrena in her village) have frequent recourse to such methods without scruple.

But such agonizing living conditions stem to a large extent from certain kinds of social or human relationships. And so the society described by Solzhenitsyn, or rather the segments of it he portrays, are regulated by cruel laws: the struggle for survival and the tyranny of the strong.

Shukhov's comrades, and Shukhov himself, are victims of the arbitrariness that condemned them to ten or even twenty-five years of forced labor, affecting Soviet citizens of all backgrounds and nationalities (peasants, officers, intellectuals; Russians, Ukrainians, Baltic peoples, and so forth) who are for the most part perfectly innocent; this has been done on the greatest variety of pretexts, with espionage being the charge most often cited. The worst oppressors are not the prisoners' guards, although they are brutal and paralyzed by their fear of a possible escape—the very thing which determines the character of their "humanism" ("The men meant more to a guard than gold. If there was one man missing on the other side of the wire, he'd soon be taking his place" [p.40]); rather, it is the prisoners themselves. (. . .) Such is the despicable manager of the mess hall whom Solzhenitsyn portrays with a few stark brush-strokes:

> A fat bastard with a head like a pumpkin and shoulders a yard wide. He had so much strength he didn't know what to do with it and he bounced up and down like on springs and his hands and legs jerked all the time . . . He didn't give a damn for anybody and all the men were scared of him. He had a thousand lives in the palm of his hand (p. 161-162).

In life outside the camps, the profiteers are mostly omnipotent bureaucrats—"as hateful as the fascists" (cf. p. 55) in the eyes of Zotov. He thinks of Samorukov, "a healthy, well-fed brute" (p. 54), the storekeeper and cashier of the rations office at Krechetovka Station. It matters little to Samorukov that troop trains arrive in the station after the store's closing time when no provision has been made for the men. We find the same egotism, the same indifference to the difficulties of one's neighbor among the employees of the Social Security Office who give the elderly Matrena the run-around from one office to another—miles apart—without the slightest regard for her age or poor health.....

Matrena is similarly exploited by her own kolkhoz, which does not pay her a pension or furnish her with any material assistance although she has worked on it for over thirty years. Even so, whenever they need an extra hand, they never fail to conscript her, of course without offering her any compensation. The wife of the chairman of the kolkhoz on such occasions deigns to bestir herself:

> She was city-bred and determined. Her short, gray jacket and threatening look made her seem military.
>
> She would enter the hut without a greeting and would look sternly at Matrena, who would become flustered.
>
> "So-o-o," the chairman's wife would say, dividing the word for emphasis, "Comrade Matrena, you've got to help the kolkhoz! You've got to go out tomorrow and haul manure!"
>
> Matrena's countenance would take on a half-apologetic smile—as if she were ashamed for the chairman's wife because she would not be able to pay her for the work.
>
> "Well, ah . . . ," she drew the words out. "After all, I'm sick, and I'm no longer officially a member of the kolkhoz." And right off she would hastily correct herself: "What time should I be there?"
>
> "And bring your own pitchfork!" the chairman's wife would admonish as she went out, her stiff petticoat rustling (cf. p. 104).

Nevertheless, the picture which Solzhenitsyn draws of societal relationships cannot be reduced to some formula—and a rather simplistic one at that—according to which superiors automatically become tyrants. For the peasant Shukhov, it is true, official authority is a sort of power that is foreign to his world, as his naive reaction (when Buinovskii informs him that the Soviet government has altered the daytime by decree) illustrates: "Did the sun come under their laws too?" (p. 74); but he is by no means an anarchist. He agrees without reservation to work under the command of capable and dedicated individuals. This is the case with his foreman Tiurin who protects his subordinates, arranges to obtain supplementary rations for them, and puts his shoulder to the wheel. "The higher-ups had a job to get a prisoner to work even in working hours, but your boss only had to say the word, even if it was the meal break, and you worked" (p. 103).

But above all it should be stressed that Solzhenitsyn's point of view is not that of a sociologist or of a politician. It is the attitude of a writer who is interested in the psychological source of human acts and of social systems. In this light, the forces of oppression appear complex and subtle, because they are rooted in man's nature and in the ideas which guide him.

Matrena's selfish neighbors almost naturally take advantage of her generosity; they ask her to give them a hand in digging up their own potatoes, with no thought of helping her in turn. She finally dies through the fault of her brother-in-law, Faddei, whose greed is the real cause of the accident which takes her life: Faddei wanted to tear down a part of Matrena's *izba* in order to procure the wood and use it elsewhere. (...) While they are transporting the wood during the night, the cable attached to the overloaded sled breaks, leaving the sled across the tracks. A train which is shunting without lights hits it, crushing Matrena. Solzhenitsyn makes of Faddei, this avaricious and heartless peasant, the very symbol of destruction. Observe him at work demolishing the *izba:* his "eyes flashed with business-like efficiency," as he was "furiously taking apart the *gornitza* board by board, in order to take it away from a property that was not his own" (cf. pp. 118-19).

But one can also be victimized by one's opinions and prejudices: such is the case of Zotov, the young lieutenant in charge of despatching convoys at Krechetovka Station, an ardent member of the Komsomol, and an idealist for whom the terrible setbacks of the war that devastate his country have not undermined his faith in Stalin, even though the military situation wracks his soul with despair. He burns to fight for his communist homeland, just as he once dreamed of going to Spain to crush fascism. He is pure through and through. He does not allow himself to touch Polina, a young woman to whom he is strongly attracted and who shares his views, "because of the sacred grief that united them" (p. 39). He is also a good, selfless man who strives to cut through as much of the bureaucratic tape as possible in order to provide transportation for the soldiers who come to him. However, his phobia about spies—common to all countries in time of war, but quite pronounced in Russia at all times—leads him to hand over to the police a conscripted actor, Tveritinov, who is trying to rejoin his echelon. In fact, he takes him for a disguised White army officer because the poor man had the indiscretion to ask what the name of Stalingrad was before it was debaptized. This question seems to Zotov to be highly suspect of anti-Sovietism, and his suspicions transform the irresistable attraction he had felt for this refined and cultivated individual into an equally violent repulsion.

Zotov is not only duped by his own vigilance; he is also the victim of an education which has accustomed him to think in slogans, although they have been adopted with complete conviction. His enthusiasm is conventional: his face is "flushed with pleasure" (p. 71) when he discovers that he is talking with an artist... He loves the theatre, and expresses himself in stereotyped phrases: "It's not merely entertainment but an education. Right?" (cf. p. 70) and, of course, he prefers Gorkii to all others: "He's our wisest, our most humane, our greatest writer!" (cf. p. 71). His aversions are equally typical: a hatred for officers has been inculcated in him since infancy—to tear off their shoulder boards had been one of the most symbolic gestures of the Revolution.[6] The thought that Tveritinov might be an officer "wounded him like the point of a bayonet" (cf. p. 78). Finally, what is most typical is the unconscious intolerance that animates him and leads him to consider anyone who departs from the established norm of the perfect citizen as an enemy, either actual or potential.

Solzhenitsyn does not tell the reader all this in so many words; in fact he hardly comments at all. It is with a complete impartiality that he enters into Zotov's consciousness and makes him come alive and perform before our eyes. It is up to the reader to interpret and to judge—the author does not condemn. Except perhaps for the bureaucrats and selfish profiteers, is anyone really guilty? The faults, the errors, the cruelties attain such phantasmagoric proportions that they exceed human understanding and seem to be the work of some mysterious evil force that makes a fool of man. For all is paradox and pure nonsense: Shukhov did not allow himself to be captured by the Germans and rejoined Soviet lines. That was sufficient to condemn him to forced labor as a spy. His only fault was to have been too patriotic... Buinovskii is another sort of "spy." He received a gift from a British admiral with whom he had served as a liaison officer during the war. The price of that gift: twenty-five years of hard labor! Before the war Zotov had been suspected of provocation by the military authorities because he begged them to send him to Spain to fight against the fascists (isn't it rather suspicious, really, to follow one's ideal to the letter without first having received an order?). But later, in a sinister reversal, Zotov in turn manifests such mistrust against the innocent Tveritinov and—supreme paradox—hands over a man who has just thanked him for his warm and gracious welcome and for whom he feels immense sympathy.

And what awful quirk of fate determined that Matrena, who had sacrificed a part of her *izba* out of sheer generosity, should be crushed in return by the very wood she had donated?

It is a cruel irony that makes use of words, formerly con-

[6]We personally had an opportunity to observe how sincere members of the Komsomol in the USSR were scandalized to see that shoulder boards, a detested symbol of the past, were reintroduced into the Red Army right after the war.

ceived as synonyms of freedom, to subjugate man: thus, the work site for the prisoners is called the "Socialist Community Development": "But so far it was nothing more than bare fields covered with snowdrifts, and before anything could be done there, holes had to be dug, posts put in, and barbed wire put up—by the prisoners for the prisoners, so they couldn't get out" (p. 4). Towards the end of the novel there is the following reflection: "The great thing about a penal camp was that you had a hell of a lot of freedom .... You could yell your head off about anything you liked ..." (p. 177).

What land is this where cruelty, misery, and suffering reign and from which an unspeakable sadness emanates, symbolized by this portrait of the camp: "The sky was as dark as ever, and the stars were blotted out by the camp lights" (p. 18). Is it not, to use the words of Zotov concerning the war, some "insensate oscillation of an ineluctable wheel"? (cf. p. 38). And is not man the plaything of an absurd destiny which strikes him blindly, without rhyme or reason, without regard for good or evil, guilty or innocent?

Solzhenitsyn perhaps may be tempted to believe it. In any case, he suggests it. But there are lighter and more cheerful notes in his stories as well: in the midst of this world of tears and injustices he is able to discover and appreciate that part of man which is truly worthy of respect and admiration—and in the black sky that blankets the earth, he kindles stars of hope.

The miracle is that man can keep from sinking to the level of animals, even under the appalling conditions to which he is subjected. Solzhenitsyn bears witness to this miracle; in fact, one could safely assert that it is the true theme of his stories. Not that he idealizes these prisoners, so much like the ones he himself has rubbed shoulders with, or these women, prey to the difficulties of their daily lives. He knows their weaknesses, but he appreciates their greatness.

How strong is man's basic sense of personal dignity, in spite of all his humiliations! This is apparent in his most humble gestures—his manner of eating, for example; despite the cold, Shukhov cannot bring himself to eat the scraps of food put before him without first removing his cap. And Iu-81, that tall, toothless old man, who has never been freed, doubtless a former noble whose "worn-out face was dark and looked like it had been hewed out of stone" (p. 172) is the only one to sit up straight, without hunching over his rations! Or again, the Ukrainians from the Carpathians who, before eating, make the sign of the Cross, whereas "the Russians didn't even remember which hand you cross yourself with" (p. 15), as Shukhov remarks.

This self-respect rules out certain kinds of behavior. In spite of the longing that grips him, Shukhov will never stoop to pick up a cigarette-butt, even though there are moments when he would rather have a cigarette "than his freedom" (p. 33). Never will he beg for a part of his more fortunate neighbors' food packages. And never in all his forty years has he learned to grease anyone's palm, no matter whose, even in camp.

One could hardly ask for more spectacular gestures from a prisoner: Buinovskii, a naval captain recently arrived in the camp, reacts with virulence against an order which seems to him outrageous: "You've no right to strip people in the cold!" he tells the guards during the frisking, "You don't know Article Nine of the Criminal Code! . . . You're not Soviet people," the Captain barks, "You're not Communists!" (p. 38). But he is a novice—such protests earn him ten days in the cooler, without heat or warm food, except once every three days. He will learn to his sorrow that in camp it is best to keep quiet.

The creative instinct, deeply rooted in man, persists with astonishing vitality. It is expressed by man's manner of working. Solzhenitsyn is free from a false pathos which would glorify labor as such and make it the meaning and purpose of existence. The simple men of his stories are not taken in by the glitter of fine phrases; the way these phrases have been used has served only to tarnish them. Did not the inmates of German concentration camps also hear the slogan *Arbeit macht frei* repeated? Shukhov doesn't fall for it: he does not at all appreciate the methods of "work therapy" practised by the camp doctor. ("What he didn't understand was that work has killed many a horse" [pp. 23-24], a reflection Matrena echoes: "Whatever you don't cart home on your back, you don't have" [cf. p. 102]). He knows all too well that work can be an instrument of enslavement which degrades man and virtually transforms him into a beast of burden: "There's work and work. It's like the two ends of a stick. If you're working for human beings, then do a real job of it, but if you work for dopes, then you just go through the motions" (p. 14).

But he knows the good end of the "stick" perfectly well. Once he is led by a foreman he respects, Shukhov puts all his energy into carrying out his job well. And the whole work gang acts the same way, each man revealing his character and his worth in their common labors, since work for Shukhov is an infallible test: Buinovskii, worn out as he is, goes at his work with courage: "To the Captain, camp work was like the navy. ('If you're told to do something, then get down to it!')" (p. 71). Fetiukov, the "slacker," always tries to "get out of it." Aleshka the Baptist is an ideal co-worker—a "lamb." Shukhov himself cannot stand to rush anything. He is so absorbed by his work on the wall that he loses track of time and nearly comes late to the roll-call. "Shukhov was kind of funny about these things . . . He still worried about every little thing and about all kinds of work" (pp. 124-125). A significant detail: Ivan Denisovich is the sort of man who, though he does not permit himself to steal anything for his own benefit, filches a trowel which he keeps carefully hidden, so that he will be able to do "a really fine job." You have to read those marvellous pages in which the author portrays Shukhov as possessed by the giddy joy of building, in such sharp contrast to the destructive frenzy of a Faddei. Matrena also takes a similar joy in the catharsis of labor. For her it is the sure way of recovering her good spirits, tranquillity, and "her kindly smile" (cf. p. 101).

Finally, one striking trait emerges from all these stories. Although the hardships of life encourage egotism in some, they also stimulate altruism in others. Often, it is true, the one and the other coexist or alternate, as is the case with the old woman Frosia who works at Krechetovka Station. Occasionally, she takes shameless advantage of the misfortunes of others, when, for example, she barters a basket of meager food for clothes from starving refugees. But the same Frosia houses and feeds without charge some Ukrainian refugees who have lost everything. The former, according to her, are rich and so have no need of pity, whereas the latter are in real misery.

Such mutual aid is powerfully evident in the camp. Those who have experienced total deprivation know the price of an additional hundred grams of bread, or a cigarette. Windfalls of this sort are a great occasion. Although Shukhov covets it for himself, he nonetheless approves of Pavlo's giving an extra serving to Buinovskii, who cannot believe his eyes. Should not one help him get accustomed to the place?

Such solidarity is also the bond which unites the work gang and makes it into a new family. Thus, Sen'ka waits for Shukhov, who was delayed at the power plant, and runs the risk of being seriously punished for the delay together with him, but "he wasn't the kind to leave you in the lurch" (p. 126). In the same brigade, Aleshka is always ready to do a favor, with an absolute selflessness that impresses Shukhov: "If only everybody in the world was like that, Shukhov would be that way too. If some one asked you, why not help him out? They were right on that, these people'" (p. 120).

Moreover, it is curious that such generosity should seem to be more frequent in camp than in normal life. Men who are free and yet intimately preoccupied with their neighbor's fortunes are rare. Zotov, the young lieutenant and member of the Komsomol, is haunted day and night by the misfortunes of his country, and he is scandalized to see that his staff is more concerned about food supplies or amorous intrigues. Polina is an exception, and that is why she is "the eye of his conscience and of his faithfulness" (cf. p. 39), to use the fine expression he employs to define her. In another milieu, Matrena is the only one never to deny her help spontaneously and freely, and the result of her cheerful self-abnegation is to be considered a fool by her neighbors and relatives.

These manifestations of pure altruism are difficult to discern, rare, and become exceptional when they are practised with the lack of self-interest of an Aleshka or a Matrena. But the very fact of their existence is sufficient to remind men that the law of the jungle where "big fish eat little ones" is opposed by another law which lifts man above bestiality: "Thou shalt love thy neighbor as thyself."

The Grand Tradition is first and foremost that of respect for Truth. It is in performing this demanding task that the greatest Russian writers have wielded their talent, and it is this very factor that makes them alive and close to us today. Like them, Solzhenitsyn does not invent life according to theoretical formulae; he describes it as he has known and felt it—violent, full of absurd and bloody misunderstandings, oppressive. His personal experience confers a poignant authenticity on his prose, and yet, it is not only personal impressions that he endeavors to convey to his readers; he also wants to share with us what he has discovered during his terrible years: namely, human beings who are worthy of the name. Thus, he disguises himself behind his characters in order to avoid serving as a screen between us and them. And we see them parade before our eyes, struggle, suffer, resist—each one different. Some are scoundrels, others drown in egoism, many help each other, some even achieve saintliness. The author condemns no one, except the "rapacious."

He manages to sustain this truthfulness in his portrayal of life and men by a form of narration purified of all superfluous commentary, of all emphasis. Solzhenitsyn writes only of what is essential, and the entire framework of life is carefully structured to bring out the character and the reactions of men. Their physical aspect is barely sketched in; on the other hand we see their gestures, perceive their attitudes, hear the crude and broken speech of the prisoners, the colorful language of the peasants; we distinguish the tone of their voices, their smiles, we witness their thoughts; in short, we know everything that reveals the quality of their souls. And then the narration continues—simple, laconic, almost dry because of its starkness, interrupted here and there by an image shot through with emotion; for example, when "the desperate face of King Lear in the burial chamber" (cf. p. 85) appears in the dim light of a lantern—Tveritinov delivered up by Zotov. This laconic quality and density of style are remarkable. They would recall the concise and inimitable simplicity of Chekhov were not the flavor of the words fully contemporary, sharper, and also harder, with a wealth of unsuspected tonalities. We must note in passing that such language corresponds precisely to the tastes and stylistic tendencies of the young contemporary Soviet prose writers.

The picture Solzhenitsyn paints is black, and many readers will turn away from it, protesting that it does not give a complete description of Soviet life. Solzhenitsyn, however, does not make any such claim; but he is not afraid to shake up the self-satisfied consciences of hypocrites and indecent optimists, whether the cause of their attitude be indifference or voluntary blindness. He remembers that a Russian writer in the service of Truth also serves Justice. Are not these two ideas closely linked in the Russian language, where the word *pravda* [truth] signified justice in former times? And to do justice to "the humiliated and the wronged" of our era, to those who, for so long now, have been systematically ignored or crushed in silence, is precisely to rejoin the grand, interrupted tradition of Tolstoy and Dostoevsky. Let us underscore that Solzhenitsyn is not content to have a clear and accurate vision of the past, armed with official blessings; he is lucid about more contemporary hardships—something far more rare and dangerous. Matrena died ten years ago. One might wish that she had taken with her to the grave the misery of her village for evermore...

Although Solzhenitsyn's pity is primarily directed towards victims, he is humane to all, without any illusions concerning humanity, but also without hatred. Every man, whoever he may be, is, he feels, worthy of respect. It is this open-heartedness that earned Turgenev, Tolstoy, Chekhov, Gorkii, and many others their universal reputation. Solzhenitsyn does not parcel out his understanding according to any particular hierarchy: all are equal in misery. This is brought to mind by the old railway employee, Kordubailo, who excuses the soldiers that attacked the flour car: "Everyone wants to eat..." (p. 27).

One's social origins are no guarantee of good or bad conduct: one finds a certain nobility of soul in Shukhov the peasant, Buinovskii the officer, Tveritinov the artist, etc.

Neither is there any chauvinism in this man who is Russian in every fibre of his being: Shukhov speaks with admiration of the Latvians, Estonians, and Ukrainians with whom he is thrown together. One could even say that all the non-Russians he portrays are models of dignity and courage.

No ideological sectarianism mars these tales. The author can portray with equal honesty Zotov the young member of the Komsomol, so sincere in his communist patriotism, with his ascetical purity, his faith in Stalin—and Aleshka the Baptist, the only man who is happy in camp because he suffers for Jesus Christ. Aleshka is nourished by the Gospel, and offers that rare example of a faith at once convinced and manifested through love of God and of one's neighbor.

True respect for others and for their convictions—here is a quality most rare in contemporary Soviet literature. Apart from Pasternak, it is difficult to mention any writer who, in alluding to believers, does not make them into caricatures or objects of our compassion. One might call it a kind of snobbery, and a rather cowardly one at that, but very widespread among the talented young, such as Tendriakov, Kazakov, and others. It is perhaps in this area, less often emphasized, that the "cult of personality" wreaked the greatest damage: Zotov is a striking and tragic example.

This return to a sense of the human, with all that it entails of respect for others, of tolerance in heart and mind for what is different from us (a tolerance which obviously has nothing to do with "non-resistance to evil") constitutes not a disavowal of that which is near and dear, but suggests rather a rootedness in one's own country. Solzhenitsyn gives proof of this. Disguised in the character of the math teacher, it is he who narrates the story of Matrena. His instinct drives him, after his imprisonment, to return to "the innermost heart of Russia" (p. 89) for which he had felt so nostalgic in camp. He hopes to rediscover in a remote village of Central Russia something indefinable, something immensely significant: is it the ancestral fragrance which Russian peasant life exudes and which permeates the ancient names of these hamlets—for example, *Vysokoe Pole* [High Field], "I felt good just hearing the name of the place" (p. 90)—next to which the nomenclature adorning its industrial neighbor *Torfoprodukt* [Peat Product] seems perfectly barbarous? Is it a certain musicality in the words and peasant intonation, or rather in the songs of days gone by which "people don't sing anymore in our mechanical age" (cf. p. 114)? Is it not also the poetic and imaginative manner of attributing natural phenomena to God: Shukhov, commenting on the phases of the moon, believes that "God breaks the old moon up into stars" (p. 128) because everybody knows that "the stars keep falling down, so you've got to have new ones in their place" (p. 129).

Solzhenitsyn loves the simple life that goes on in the village, because it is linked with nature and provides a source of joy. Matrena, this grandmother right out of a fairy tale (p. 98), finds a satisfaction in her work because "she doesn't bow to office tables, but to the bushes of the forest" (cf. p. 100). And in this life whose roots are sunk in time immemorial, men preserve the instinct of God and of fate which the city-dwellers have lost. To be sure, Matrena's faith is quite admixed with superstition. She is afraid of lightning and trains, but Solzhenitsyn does not make fun of her. Does not her fear express a muffled presentiment of the death that awaits her?

Solzhenitsyn is visibly taken with the charm of a country life whose colors are fading with the advance of industrialization; but he does not idealize it: although he appreciates popular traditions, they do not blind him when they are purely conventional. He prefers the spontaneous grief of Matrena's niece, "the plain sobbing characteristic of our age and so common to it" (cf. p. 131), to the funerary lamentations that veil the hypocrisy and cupidity of Matrena's relations. Solzhenitsyn is not a fancier of folklore; the tradition that moves him is brimful of life.

That part of the past which is not dead is a fundamental inner orientation which could be defined by the significant title Dudintsev chose for his novel *Not by Bread Alone.* Solzhenitsyn paraphrases it as follows: "I reconciled myself with this [the miserable food Matrena prepared] because life had taught me not to consider food the point of daily existence. I placed a higher value on the smile in her roundish face" (p. 99). From a man who has suffered the torments of hunger, this declaration possesses a singular forcefulness.

Without philosophizing or moralizing, Solzhenitsyn merely reminds us that man needs goodness and selflessness in order to grow. This is what Tveritinov senses when he thanks Zotov for his kind reception: "You have warmed me literally and figuratively. You are a good man. In hard times like these, that is especially priceless" (p. 76). These are the two qualities which give such beauty to the smile of those who embody them, "people who are at peace with their conscience" (cf. p. 120). Aleshka's smile, greeting the sunrise; Matrena's smile, as she returns exhausted by work . . . Neither one knows how to get along in life, and their total lack of egoism makes people regard them as simple-minded. And yet it is these despised, humble people whom Solzhenitsyn exalts. Giving free rein for once to his quickening feelings, he sets before us the true image of Matrena:

> Misunderstood and abandoned even by her husband, she buried six of her children but not her gregarious and friendly manner. She was considered "odd" by her sisters and her sisters-in-law, a laughable being who stupidly worked for others without pay. She never accumulated property against the time of her death: her only possessions were a dirty-white goat, a crippled cat, and rubber plants . . .
>
> We all lived beside her, and never understood that she was that righteous one without whom, according to the proverb, no village can stand.
>
> Nor any city.
> Nor our whole land. (cf. pp. 137-138).

It is striking that a simple Russian peasant woman should be chosen to personify the very image of embodied Justice. This homage paid to the humble and poor is directly inspired by no less than the most authentic Christian tradition, and this essential aspect of Christianity has always been particularly dear to Russian hearts. One has only to read any page of Dostoevsky to be convinced of this. Solzhenitsyn does not idealize his people, yet, deep within him, his country's secular traditions of true goodness and charity are maintained. Such ancient currents have a renewed freshness today, in this world of ours cruelly torn by hateful fanaticism, mutilated by sectarianism, fascinated by material productivity, and invaded more and more by a materialism which parches the heart and soul. These currents constitute, in fact, the very fountainhead of life. Shukhov and his comrades, Tveritinov and Matrena have all come to tell us that these qualities still well up within the Russian people, but they are concealed, and in order to discern them amid the struggles, bitterness, and agonizing injustices of our age, one must refine that "inner eye" mentioned by Vinokurov. It is thanks to such a vision that Solzhenitsyn has perceived and helped us to discover "the indelibly huge image of Russia,"[7] the pure smile of Aleshka, and the radiant goodness of Matrena. May the new era which is beginning in the USSR preserve, together with a horror for the senseless follies which "have set Russia alight like an expiatory candle for all the suffering and misfortune of men,"[8] the memory of this loving response.

Translated by David M. Halperin

[7]Boris Pasternak, *Doctor Zhivago,* Pt. XIV, Ch. 17.
[8]*Ibid.*

The Imprisoned World of Solzhenitsyn's *The First Circle*

BY HEINRICH BÖLL

"Attention!" he called out sharply, and seven guards turned in his direction. "You know the rules. You must receive nothing from your relatives. Anything which is to be turned over to you or to them must go through me. In your conversations you are not to mention work, work conditions, living conditions, the daily schedule, the location of the institute. You may not name any names. You may say of yourselves only that everything is all right and that you do not need anything."

"Then what can we talk about?" someone cried out. "Politics?"

Kliment'ev did not even deign to answer this, it was so patently absurd.

"Talk about your guilt," one of the prisoners advised somberly. "Talk about your repentance."

"No, you may not speak of your indictment. That is secret," Kliment'ev replied without a tremor. "Ask about your family, about your children. One more thing. There is a new rule: from now on, holding hands and kissing are forbidden." (p. 222.)[1]

The regulations did not specifically forbid tears, but, under a higher interpretation of the law, there was no place for them. (p. 264.)

Unfortunately for people—and fortunately for their rulers—a human being is so constituted that as long as he lives there is always something more that can be taken away from him. (p. 236.)

Solzhenitsyn's *The First Circle* has an enormous span, numerous girders, and several dimensions: literary, philosophical,

"The Imprisoned World of Solzhenitsyn's *The First Circle*." From *Merkur* (Stuttgart), No. 253 (May, 1969), 474-483. Translated and reprinted by permission.
 Translated from the German by Marjorie L. Hoover.

[1]Quotations from Solzhenitsyn's novel follow closely the English translation by Thomas P. Whitney (N. Y., 1968).—Tr.

political, and social. Its vault projects from many sides to many sides; it is a cathedral among novels with a stress precisely calculated to endure. That it withstands tension in the traditional sense is due not to novelistic devices, but rather to that balance for which one fears constantly in the course of one's reading—you wonder whether it will indeed support the several girders and the wide arch. Tension or suspense becomes here more like an architectural concept. The fact that the novel also contains information on contemporary history speaks merely of its subject matter, the material of which it is built, its unadorned plot.

The novel begins with a telephone call from State Counselor Second Rank Volodin, who wants to warn a professor friend against certain contacts abroad. This first break in the self-confidence of a gifted diplomat, whose career is secure with all its elegant appurtenances, marks the "entry" into the cathedral. The telephone call is made around Christmas 1949; the novel ends barely four days later with the description of a convoy of prisoners taken through Moscow. In a delivery truck labeled "Miaso-Viande-Fleisch-Meat" prisoners from the first circle of hell are being taken away, still not knowing which circle of hell will be their destination. The correspondent of the French newspaper *Libération,* on his way to a hockey game at Dynamo Stadium, reads the label on the truck, pulls out his notebook and writes with his Bordeaux-red pen: "On the streets of Moscow one often sees vans filled with foodstuffs, very neat and hygienically impeccable. One can only conclude that the provisioning of the capital is excellent."

The novel consists of 87 chapters and some 670 pages. To keep its cast of characters in mind is difficult even on second reading; it would be easier if the publisher could bring himself to add an exact index of characters,[2] indicating age, sex, function, job and political position—this last because there are so many nuances and involvements among both prisoners and non-prisoners (we shall say a word later about conceptions of free and unfree). They are all imprisoned, though not, of course, technically as criminals; their imprisonment is due to many causes, most of which are incomprehensible in the West. The fact that Solzhenitsyn has forbidden the publication of his

[2]Both the American and the British translations have such a list.—Tr.

novels in the West can be understood only in terms of this imprisonment, both in its real and metaphysical sense. That, by so doing, he became the victim (and the Soviet government along with him) of that lack of an agreement—and this alone could be sufficient reason for the Soviet Union to ratify the Bern Convention![3]—may be considered an ironic component in the game of mutual "freedom of publication."

It is this imprisonment which has made the Russians the nation on earth with the least joy in emigrating. In this sense I consider all the characters of the novel, prisoners and non-prisoners alike, imprisoned in the Soviet Union, even politically imprisoned; so as to exclude any misinterpretation or malicious distortions, let me say: I do not mean the kind of imprisonment imposed by the police; I mean the kind one imposes upon oneself: let semantics resolve the problem of the different implications of the words "imposed" and "self-imposed," "imprisonment" and "arrest." To my mind James Joyce remained thus the "prisoner" to the end of his days of Ireland and Catholicism.

The collective slap at the stupidity of the West at the close of the book doubtless refers to the fact that Western observers now and then see signs, and even recognize some of them. However, they never secure the key by which these signs could be decoded, perhaps because it changes daily, hourly, weekly and is subject to the enormous amount of chance usual in such a huge country. Nor have I secured the key. I am easily winded. Eastern Europe, though, has great endurance; it is not only experienced in the passion of suffering: it is at times hungry for it. The East is in the true sense of the word impassioned, and not just since the Revolution, and not just since Stalinism.

Not only several quite good Western novels, but also the entire results of decades of literature have become for me decorative side chapels or niches beneath the high vault of *The First Circle* with its many balanced supports, or when built outside this cathedral, auxiliary dwellings, or at best, elegant separate houses. Of course, the terrifying dialectics one senses in such a great work lies in the fact that it sums up and illumines an enormous amount of suffering and history. The form, the expression, the way in which Solzhenitsyn's prose composes and restrains itself, the composition which keeps its

[3]The Soviet government did so on May 27, 1973.—Tr.

own *balance*[4] to the last refinement, reveals that here not only a great author is at work, but also a mathematician, one at least familiar with scientific formulae. Here is the material of formulae in prose; here intellectual and epic lucidity conjoin in a parable of mathematical physics.

If I avoid the expression metaphysics, then it is only because I still have no name for *this* kind of writing. In any case, schemata are neither assumed nor super-imposed, and yet order is achieved. The process is "integration," as in the calculus in the mathematical-physical sense. Indeed, that new "materialistic metaphysics" has perhaps been born here which some physicists have sensed intuitively. Just as Western authors reject the dogma of security, so Solzhenityn, while not exactly rejecting the future, no longer includes it as an ideal goal, comparable to that heaven of the metaphysics we have lost. He sums up the present, and we must not forget that this is the present of the year 1949, four years before Stalin's death, and that this book was written in the years 1955-1964. In the Soviet Union of 1969 to be imprisoned and arrested meant something different from what it did in 1949.

Solzhenitsyn fortunately avoids "interpretation." He observes, notes, develops from elements he knows, from experiences and encounters, and since he need not *attack* schemata which have been assumed or super-imposed, need not dispute against them, he achieves a sobriety and dryness by which he shows himself superior both to the usual socialist realism, tailored into optimism, and also to the aims of the *nouveau roman.* This is not only because he has personally lived through the Stalinism which his Western colleagues have not experienced. It is also because the West has lost any sense of hidden suffering: the one and only use of suffering as a component of sexual joy represents possibly the great unrecognized transgression. I ascribe to Solzhenitsyn's work the character of revelation, an unpathetic revelation not only of Stalinism, the book's historical content, but also of mankind's history of suffering. To this extent Stalinism serves here as "only" a means, terrible enough in itself, yet only the means to a larger end.

Various tasks are imposed upon the prisoners in "the first circle of hell," as the Mavrino Institute near Moscow is called, all of which have the purpose of refining methods of detection

[4]The italics throughout are Böll's.—Tr.

and developing new ones, and thus turning in more prisoners. The inmates are caught up in the net; they are prisoners and yet as scientists they are free, while their guards are free and yet are prisoners of the permanent fear that they may be arrested. Nor is it at all certain whether the latter will be so fortunate as to get into the first circle of hell or whether they will have the misfortune of getting into the seventh. In order further to develop phonoscopy, which makes possible the identification of a person based on his electronic voice recording, five tape-recorded voices are given the prisoners to compare with among the five, Volodin's voice, as recorded from his telephone call. The prisoners' only triumph is that they are able to exclude three of the five suspects, and it is therefore their consolation that only two of the five are arrested, one of which is Volodin. His admission to prison at the Lubianka is described in detail in the next to last chapter. The long, pedantic, absurdly unreasonable initial humiliations to which the State Counselor Second Rank—already with an air ticket to Paris in his pocket—is subjected, vividly remind the reader of the process of arrest which the already familiar inmates of the "first circle" had undergone.

It is surely not by chance that this first circle of hell is a laboratory, a well-equipped and efficient laboratory. After all, I imagine that the space physicists, doctors, technicians and all their assistants are subject to strict supervision and constant observation by various security officers, or possibly remain under strict house arrest even for months at a time. Or that there are not only chemical, technical, and physics laboratories, but also those in the interest of the national economy and, above all, sales psychology laboratories in which new methods of influencing people are dreamed up and old ones analyzed and developed further. Or that probably even the dreams of those working in the innermost circle of hell must be supervised so that they will not divulge anything—then Solzhenitsyn's first circle of hell is very quickly de-Stalinized; the difference between imprisonment and freedom, the forebodings and fearlessness of prisoners and free men, of those under control and those in control becomes quite relative. I do not know the proportion of guards and free men, for example, at a space research center and in "the first circle of heaven," but I imagine the proportions and conditions differ in only minor ways from those in "the first circle of hell." There are enough secret worlds, even worlds of hidden suffering, which must prove to be not sexual suffering alone. In this sense, I consider "the first circle of hell" to be bound, of course, to the historical material of Stalinism, and yet to transcend it as a revelation.

The difference between being imprisoned in the transitive and intransitive sense could perhaps be the key to understanding the Soviet Union, a country which, however often that may be denied or however contrary to the constitution, is controlled by Russians and by Russia. This need not mean what it threatens more and more to become: imperialistic, nationalistic, and under Stalin even tsaristic again. Only upon reading Solzhenitsyn did I realize the meaning of Khrushchev's disclosures about Stalin in 1956. Among many other things, after all, they meant that Solzhenitsyn too was released, was able to write, was allowed to publish. That he is still writing, but is no longer allowed to publish, that, while living in the Soviet Union, he is a prisoner there, though he has not yet been imprisoned—all this can only mean it is still unclear whether the Soviet government will understand what politicians in the whole world never properly understand: that an author is sufficiently the prisoner of his language, that Solzhenitsyn as a person and an author, as one born in 1918 and wholly determined by the history of the Soviet Union, is not just typically and symbolically, but now and really a champion of the Soviet Union. The Soviet Union could, if he had not been repudiated and denounced as a heretic, be proud of him. After all, he goes no further politically than Khrushchev did in his famous speech; he has only taken de-Stalinization at its word and put it into words: he is the prisoner of the Soviet Union as much as one of the protagonists of the book, the convict Rubin, who remains the prisoner of socialism and the Soviet Union, who is wholeheartedly unnationalistic, though no cosmopolitan either, who, as a Marxist, accurately sees through his own situation, who, as one outwardly and inwardly imprisoned, is far superior to his guards. That those whom one accuses of dirtying their nest are mostly those who try to clean their own nest is a fact I have long found to be true of prophets to all nations.

Solzhenitsyn's book has great range; its vault is high, it is, besides, a revelation for Western literature's more or less helpless undertaking. It is descended from the great Russian tradition, has passed through socialist realism, overcome and renewed it. Contemporary in the daring of its construction, it yet proves secure in its equilibrium. It has the sweep of Tolstoy and the spirit of Dostoevsky, thus synthesizing the two minds which were thought to be antithetical both in the nineteenth century and on into present-day literary criticism, and it *is* unmistakably Solzhenitsyn. By way of Camus and Sartre and beyond, Solzhenitsyn concludes the age-old discussion of "imprisoned" and "free," not metaphorically, not philosophically, but within the material itself, which is not adulterated, and in which nothing is taken for granted, and nothing super-imposed. Take, for example, the encounter between the seemingly omnipotent minister Abakumov and the prisoner Bobynin: the trembling minister, who is well aware how many circles there are in hell, and Bobynin who is superior to him for having already endured several of them.

In such scenes, of which there are many examples, the unity of reality and symbol is not invented or imagined; it emerges from the existing material like the solution of a mathematical equation. It would be vain to list further examples. If I were a painter or graphic artist, I would try to visualize *The First Circle* as a classification system in the form of a giant rosette. I can conceive such a possibility as illuminating the written text and comprehensible at a glance, not with the overall validity of a criticism but as an aid. In any case, this prose does not flow with epic calm, it is no stream but rather a lake, fed by many springs, great and small. I am well aware of using here many and quite disparate comparisons: cathedral, lake, rosette; the reason is that this book has so many dimensions.

There is little that is novelistic in this novel: Volodin telephones on p. 4; the specialists in Mavrino are given their assignment of identifying his voice on p. 227; they request material for comparison, thus occasioning more wire-tapping; on p. 589 Volodin's voice is half identified; at the end of the novel he is arrested. About in the middle of the book the novel becomes most a novel: the material requested for comparison with Volodin's voice is recorded on the occasion of an evening party, given by the government prosecutor Makarygin with classically bourgeois luxury, at which several of the novel's few plot lines conjoin. Volodin is Makarygin's son-in-law. His wife Dotnara (called Dotty—note the very Western nickname, which reminds us, surely not by chance, of the same names customary among the aristocracy of Tolstoy's novels)—his wife is wholly absorbed in problems by no means typical of a classless society: servants and adultery. Simultaneously with her preoccupations, Volodin in his apartment slowly changes over from the class of carefree privilege to that of the anxious suspects. And it is that very phone conversation with his wife which is tape-recorded "in a very special intelligence center" and indeed "after Rubin at some time in the course of the afternoon had asked that the phone calls of all the suspects without exception be wire-tapped." Not only does the prisoner intervene at this point in the life of the State Counselor. A few more special, absurd "coincidences" conjoin at the time of Makarygin's party: Klara, Makarygin's unmarried daughter, a free officer with the rank of lieutenant in the state security service and a supervisor at the Mavrino Institute, who is in love with the prisoner Rostislav (and he with her), is the first to take up the receiver without realizing that in that very camp a few hours later this telephone call will lead to the arrest of her brother-in-law. Thus in two chapters several plot lines intersect, only to diverge again immediately. The conversation at Makarygin's party is, by the way, very witty; it is the conversation of the carefree, it is the small talk of the privileged members of the establishment. "None of the people gathered in the cozy little entrance hall could have imagined that in that harmless black telephone, in that light conversation about coming to a party, the ruin lay hidden which lies in wait for us all, even, as in Pushkin's poem, in the bones of a dead steed." (p. 392).[5]

Only in these two chapters, placed exactly in the middle of the novel—and surely this occurs not by chance in the work of a mathematician-author—is macabre tribute paid to the classical novel, only here does fate conjoin. The fate of all others, and they are many, is merely documented: Spiridon, Sologdin, Simochka and Myshin, Stalin and the prisoner Drysin, whose wife's letters are withheld so that he may read them only in Major Myshin's office. "No, read it here. I can't let you take a letter like that back to the dormitory. What will the other prisoners think of freedom on the basis of such letters. Read it." (p. 551). And Drysin reads, among other

[5]The reference is to "The Song of the Wise Oleg" (1825).—Tr.

things, "Dear Vania, You are offended because I seldom write. But I come home from work late and almost every day go into the woods for sticks, and then it's evening and I am so tired that I just fall into bed.... It's not a life, but prison labor.... If there were even a chance to sleep over holidays—but we have to drag ourselves to the demonstration...." (p. 552). Then the completely crushed Drysin is urged to write his wife a letter—"something in an optimistic tone—you know, encouraging." (p. 553). He continued: "Write an answer. A cheerful answer. I'll let it run more than four pages. You wrote her once that she should believe in God. Well, it's better she should believe in God—why not?" (p. 554).

The prisoner Drysin, whose fate in the novel is documented in but a few pages, has no "novelistic" function; he is only one of millions, and even from a prison camp he is supposed to sound the trumpet of optimism and cheerfulness into the free world. The mad absurdity of the arrest of those who are already prisoners, already magnificently documented for individual cases in the books of Lidiia Chukovskaia (*The Deserted House*) and Evgeniia Ginzburg (*Journey into the Whirlwind*), in a way which till now has found no comparable expression, is deepened, expanded, and universalized in Solzhenitsyn's novel elsewhere.

Along with everything else, it may be that our century is the century of camps, of prisoners, and whoever has never been imprisoned, whether he boasts or is ashamed of his good or bad fortune—has been spared *the* experience of the century, or—and one may view that as one likes—experience has escaped him. The survivors, and we are they, who read this or write it, yes all of us, can at best only recognize our imprisonment whether we have experienced it or not. Whoever has experienced it knows how relative luxury is: in the desert of a 100,000-man prison camp a piece of soap and a bowl of water are a more real, because available luxury, and so is five-twelfths of a cigarette, when a whole one costs 120 marks and one's whole fortune is only 50 marks—far more pleasure than that of the nabob who gambles away a few hundred thousands in one night because *he* feels nothing. This means *really,* not just symbolically, for the man who spends 50 marks for five-twelfths of a cigarette at least knows that with this banknote he could pay his month's rent at home. The idiocy of the affluent society in the West—and of its victims, the criminals who would like their share of it—lies in esteeming luxury as an absolute and seizing it as such. In this century you need to know that to a prisoner a tin of food and an empty bottle may *really* mean life or death; then you are able to esteem and enjoy luxury. This secret prisoners' philosophy (which includes a goodly share of theology) pervades *The First Circle,* invisible and yet tangible.

Another element is more tangible still: this is love, chastity and marriage. "Yes, yes, to love something," whispers the young prisoner Rostislav. "To love something, not history, not theory but a woman!" And he continues: "*What* have they really deprived us of? Tell me! The right to go to meetings or to subscribe to state bonds? The one way Stalin could really hurt us was to deprive us of women. And he did it. For twenty-five years! The bastard! Who can imagine . . . what a woman means to a prisoner?" (p. 79).

And who can imagine what it means for the prisoners' wives to have that "freedom" given them by their husbands with which they can in most cases do nothing. Who can accept "freedom" from a man condemned to at least twenty-five years? This calls into play something which possibly would never have come to pass in mutual freedom. Out of the material of imprisonment is born something so scorned in the West, not a virtue, but a quality: a wife's faithfulness to her husband. The sexual torment and the tormenting sex of Western literature only expresses an unconscious imprisonment and an absurdly misinterpreted freedom.

That both—sexual torment and tormenting sex—are wholly uninteresting not only to the Soviet censor, but also to the enlightened, socially conscious Soviet citizen, the citizen not without awareness, is surely one of the signs we find hard to interpret. Both would probably be interesting to the over-satisfied, bored class of the privileged and carefree in the Soviet Union, for whom servants too are a subject of conversation. A whole chapter long (Ch. 39), the girl lieutenant of the State Security, Klara Petrovna Makarygin, the daughter of a prosecutor, discusses Soviet society, privilege and ways of forging passports with the prisoner Rostislav in the laboratory at Mavrino. And it is the prisoner Rostislav who sows the seed of miraculous corruption. These two lovers are always putting their heads together. And what does the prisoner whisper to the highly privileged daughter from the class of the classless bourgeoisie?

"What was the Revolution against? Against privileges. What were the Russian people sick of? Privileges: some dressed in overalls and others in sables, some dragged along on foot, while others rode in carriages, some listened for the factory whistle, while others were fattening their faces in restaurants. True?"

"Of course," (p. 268) the dutiful prosecutor's daughter answers in her love for him, though she is to go, on the evening of that same day, to that luxurious party at the house of her transparently bourgeois mama where there will be crystal and silver, choice foods and wines, witty conversation and even servants on loan. And she will pick up the receiver and begin the conversation with her brother-in-law Volodin which, recorded on tape, that very night in that very lab in which she chats with the prisoner she has fallen in love with, Rostislav Doronin, will be used to unmask her brother-in-law. "Right," Rostislav says, "Then why is it that people now don't shun privileges but pursue them?" (p. 268). So they continue with the miraculous corruption of the girl lieutenant.

The many quotations and allusions could make it seem that here many novels and epics are united in one novel. It is hard to keep from quoting when one would like to quote most of the 670 pages. This novel is without that highly touted epic flow; it halts again and again, begins anew, halts again, has whole chapters full of bitter solitudes and elucidations, for example, on the theme of inspections by humanitarian committees, which it is easy to fool altogether, quite literally altogether deceive. Or the terrible half-hour-long visits of wives for which some prisoners receive permission once a year. The halting passages result from the broad sweep, not the narrow focus which may constitute the charm of the West-European novel. It is this broad sweep which reminds of Tolstoy, and the sarcasm and subtlety of psychological analysis which reminds of Dostoevsky. But it is Solzhenitsyn's book, unmistakably his nevertheless, now that one knows more of him.

Of course there are some experts at the Mavrino Institute who refuse to develop methods of detection further or who even skillfully sabotage their further development, since they alone, these experts who have been imprisoned uniquely for this purpose, know or would know how to develop such methods. They impress me as the true socialist scientists. Further, the women assistants, these lieutenants of the State Security, impress me as highly unreliable young girls, most of whom can only have been born after Lenin's death, whereas many a prisoner proves reliable. This insight makes one feel almost optimistic, despite the shattering evidence of suffering. Yet, after all, pensions are paid in the Soviet Union to the victims of Stalinism. In what may Solzhenitsyn's terrible crime consist, therefore? Of course, so much absurdity cannot be allowed to exist in a Marxist-structured and -conducted state: but will one be able in the long run to shut one's eyes to the fact of the mass imprisonment of prisoners under Stalinism when at the same time pensions are paid to the victims of Stalinism?

A hundred years after *Crime and Punishment* and after *War and Peace,* Solzhenitsyn's book has appeared—unfortunately only in the West for which it was not written. It was written to liberate socialism. We have no reason, not the slightest, to feel triumphant about *The First Circle* as a presentation of Stalinist misdeeds, absurdities and involvements. Instead, we have reason to ask whether a Western author could succeed in depicting so clearly the world of the carefree privileged and the world of those whose suffering is concealed, both in all the complication of their mutual involvement.

Translated by Marjorie L. Hoover

Limbo and the Sharashka

BY VADIM LIAPUNOV

> . . . Conscience dark
> with its own or another's shame
> will indeed feel thy words to be harsh;
> but none the less put away every falsehood
> and make plain all thy vision, —
> and then let them scratch where is the itch.
> For if they voice grievous
> at first taste, it will afterwards leave
> vital nourishment when it is digested . . .
>
> *Paradiso* XVII, 124-132
> (from Cacciaguida's charge to
> Dante in the John D. Sinclair
> translation)

The condition of the possibility of our beginning to understand Solzhenitsyn's *The First Circle* hinges on a recognition of the extent of our ignorance. We have to recognize what we don't know yet should know in order to read this novel with a measure of understanding.

The reference to Dante's *Divine Comedy* in the title—and let us keep in mind that a title is meant to be relevant for a text in its entirety—should be sufficient to call our attention to a pervasive narrative strategy of this novel: what is actually said in the text presupposes as a necessary part of its meaning the reader's familiarity with various kinds of information which are indicated without being set forth explicitly. Or to put it more comprehensively: what we are told in the novel is more often than not a particular part of an implied whole. What do we know concretely about the Soviet forced labor camp system (the "ramified penitentiary system," as Rubin calls it in Chapter 8, "without which no State can exist")?[1] What do we know concretely about Stalin, about Collectivization, about the Trials of the 1930's, about all that which is safely encapsulated in the term "Stalinism"? Etc., etc. The point here is not that we lack information on these matters but rather that we must make a conscious effort to absorb such information in our reading of Solzhenitsyn.

Thus, it is not enough to recognize that the title—translated literally as *Within the First Circle*—refers to the *Divine Comedy*. We must also know or, in any case, inform ourselves about what is being referred to. Otherwise we would choose to ignore that which the author counts on as understood. We would also choose to ignore that Solzhenitsyn counts on a reader willing to learn.

The vast distance in history and culture which separates us from Dante makes it unlikely that we would be able to ignore our ignorance when reading the *Divine Comedy*—if the *Divine Comedy* is to remain readable for us. But should we not be equally circumspect about the distance in history and culture which separates us from the context of Solzhenitsyn's novel—"Soviet Russia," where the abstruse term "Russia" is drastically complicated by the no less abstruse term "Soviet"?

Before I address myself to the job of exploring some of the possible meanings of the reference to the *Divine Comedy* in Solzhenitsyn's novel, let me demonstrate on an episodic example how a reference to presupposed information may work. Chapter 66, "A Keen Blade of Damask Steel," opens with an evocation of the *sharashka* immersed in sleep.[2] Rubin, unable

[1]All translations of Solzhenitsyn's text are my own. V.L.

[2]This opening section, incidentally, contains an allusion to Longfellow: "... That total and blissful oblivion of fetters which Longfellow had thought up in his 'Slave's Dream'—was not granted them ..." "The Slave's Dream" is the opening poem of a set of anti-slavery poems Longfellow published in 1842 under the title of *Poems on Slavery.* The last stanza of the poem reads as follows:

> He did not feel the driver's whip,
> Nor the burning heat of day;
> For Death had illumined the Land of Sleep,
> And his lifeless body lay
> A worn-out fetter, that the soul
> Had broken and thrown away!

to sleep after his decisive collision with Sologdin (Chapter 64, "With Clenched Fists"), is pacing the prison hallway, alone in the blank night:

> ...He was perfectly aware that things were far from pleasant for all of the prisoners—not just for those who had been imprisoned for nothing, but even for those who were the Enemy and had been imprisoned by their Enemies. His own situation, however, he saw as tragic in the Aristotelian sense. He had been struck down by the very hands which he loved the most. He had been put into prison by indifferent and bureaucratic men because he loved the common cause too deeply—to the point of indecency. Every day Rubin found himself compelled to stand up against the prison officers and guards whose actions expressed an entirely proper, just, and progressive *law;* he found himself compelled to stand up against them—owing to a tragic contradiction—in order to defend his own human dignity and that of his comrades. While his *comrades* were for the most part not his comrades at all and in every cell of the prison they reproached him, abused him, almost set upon him bodily—because they saw nothing but their own grief and were blind to the fact that everything was proceeding in accordance with Historical Law...

What we have in this passage is a third-person report of Rubin's view of his own situation. We are told that he saw it as "tragic in the Aristotelian sense" and in the sentences that follow we are given an explication of the tragic contradiction of his situation. Now the curious thing is that the tragic conflict described conforms not so much to Aristotle as to Hegel (Rubin's special field is German philology). The Tragic for Hegel is based on a conflict of ethical powers which confront one another as equally but non-reciprocally justified—leading to reciprocal violation and guilt:

> ...both sides of the opposition taken by themselves have their *justification,* yet at the same time each one of them can assert and establish the true and positive content of its purpose and character only as the negation and *violation* of the other, equally justified, ethical power, and as a result both sides find themselves equally *at fault* in and through their ethical essence.[3]

Applied to Rubin's situation, this means that Rubin's actions as well as the actions of the Party (or its representatives—the prison officers and guards) have an equal claim to ethical justification; that both sides are, in fact, *ethical* powers. The question is: on what basis does one decide the validity of such claims to ethical justification? On the basis of propounded theory? Or actual practice? (It is important to note that the

[3]Hegel's *Aesthetic,* Part III, Section 3, Chapter 3.

argument between Rubin and Sologdin in Chapter 64 centers precisely on the issue of theory and practice, or ends and means.) It is in connection with this implicit issue of judgment that the unexplicated reference to Aristotle gains its relevance for Rubin's situation. Aristotle's argument is that the change of fortune which occurs in a tragic action must be from happiness to misery, and that such a change must arise not from vice or depravity, but from some momentous *hamartia*—some momentous error or failure of judgment. At a critical point in the action, the moral agent turns out to have a "blind spot" and fatally misjudges the situation, even though otherwise he may be distinguished by keen and sympathetic insight. By leaving the concept of *hamartia* implicit, Rubin fails to bring it into effect in defining his own situation. This, in turn, betrays a want of critical-reflexive insight: for Rubin, to put the ethical validity of the Party into question is out of the question, and yet he is equally convinced that his own innocence is unquestionable. Rubin's peculiar blindness about his own "blind spot" is further dramatized by his criticism of his "comrades" (in the passage quoted above), and finally, at the end of Chapter 66, by his attempt to find consolation in the moral of Ivan Krylov's fable "A Blade of Damask Steel" (the first line of which provides the title of the chapter—"A Keen Blade of Damask Steel"). This fable is concerned with the fate of a sword which ends up in a peasant household and is misused for "menial tasks." The fable closes with the following six lines:

> "In a warrior's hands I would inspire dismay,"
> Answered the sword blade, "but here my gift is fruitless;
> True, the work I do here in this household is only menial:
>   But am I really free?
> No, it's not I who should feel shame, but only he
>   Who failed to understand what I am fit for!"

Of these six lines Rubin quotes to himself only four—omitting the third and fourth lines. Who is it that "fails to understand?" And what does it mean that Rubin conceives himself as a fighting *instrument?*[4]

[4]Devotees of Russian literature might also recall here that the fate of the sword blade in Krylov's fable is linked by tradition with the fate of General A. P. Ermolov, a hero of the Patriotic War of 1812; in 1827 Ermolov was compelled to give up his position as Commander-in-Chief in the Caucasus and to retire to his estate, because Nicholas I suspected him of sympathizing with the Decembrists. Krylov's fable appeared in 1830, and in that same year A. S. Khomiakov published his poem "The Blade" in which he speaks of the sound

The source of the title of Solzhenitsyn's novel is identified at the end of the chapter entitled "Dante's Conception" (Chapter 2). One of the new arrivals at the *sharashka* has the blissful feeling that he must be in paradise. Rubin corrects him:

> No, my friend, you are still in hell as before, but you have ascended to its best and highest circle—the first circle. You ask what the *sharashka* is? The *sharashka* was thought up, one might say, by Dante. Remember how Dante was torn as to where he should put the sages of Antiquity? The duty of a Christian commanded him to cast these heathen down into hell. But the conscience of a Renaissance man could not be reconciled to confounding these men of lucid intellect with the rest of the sinners and condemning them to bodily torments. And so Dante thought up a place apart for them. Let me see now . . . it's Canto IV and goes something like this . . .

Rubin then quotes lines 106-107, 110, 112-113, 84, 71-72, and 74-75 from Canto IV of Dante's *Inferno.*[5] In Canto IV Dante is led by Virgil into the First Circle of Hell—Limbo, the uppermost verge of the huge funnel of Hell—where the unbaptized souls of infants and virtuous pagans (in particular the poets, philosophers, and heroes of Antiquity) dwell "suspended" (line 45). They know no torment save exclusion from Salvation: "They did not sin," Virgil explains to Dante (lines 34-42), "but though they have merits, it is not enough, for they had not baptism, which is the gateway of the faith thou holdest; and if they were before Christianity they did not worship God aright, and of these I am one. For such defects, and not for any guilt, we are lost, and only so far afflicted that without hope we live in desire."[6]

Rubin's analogy is confirmed once more at the very end of the last chapter of the novel, Chapter 87, entitled "Meat." Khorobrov attempts to console himself and his companions (they are on their way back to the concentration camps proper) by arguing that the *sharashka* was pure hell. Nerzhin corrects

old Russian sword "forgotten in the scabbard by the hand of enervated generations." Khomiakov's poem later served as a source for another well-known treatment of the theme of the neglected sword—Lermontov's poem "The Poet," published in 1839.

[5]Rubin's quotations come from M. L. Lozinskii's Russian translation—which was awarded a First Order Stalin Prize in 1946.

[6]John D. Sinclair's translation. In Lozinskii's translation this passage is rendered with somewhat different emphases: "They did not sin; merits alone will not save, if there is no baptism—the pathway to the true faith; those who lived before the Christian teaching worshipped God not as we should. And I myself am one of these. For such omissions, and for nothing else, we are condemned, and here, sentenced by the highest will, we thirst without hope."

him: "No, Il'ia Terent'ich, that's not hell. That's not hell at all. The place we are going to is hell. We are on our way back to hell. While the *sharashka* is the highest, the best, the first circle of hell. The *sharashka* is almost—paradise . . ." Note that both Rubin's interpretation and Nerzhin's confirmation are each complemented by an interpretation from "ordinary life." Chapter 2 closes with Prianchikov's retort to Rubin's words: "Ah, Lev Grigor'evich, you're incorrigibly poetic. I'll explain to the comrade what the *sharashka* is much more intelligibly. One should simply read the editorials in newspapers: 'It has been established that high yields of wool from sheep depend on feeding and tending.' " Chapter 87 closes with the *Libération* correspondent's interpretation of the meaning of certain delivery trucks he had seen more than once in various parts of Moscow. These conflicting interpretations dramatize a recurrent issue throughout the novel: interpretation and misinterpretation, deceit and exposure, right and wrong.

There is, finally, one more explicit reference to the Inferno that should be mentioned. Chapter 82, in the course of which Volodin is arrested and brought to the Lubianka, takes its title from the inscription over the gateway into Hell (Canto III)—"Abandon Every Hope, Ye That Enter." (The Lubianka is that same State Security building at 2 Dzerzhinski Square that frightened Volodin when he was rushing off to warn Professor Dobroumov in Chapter 1.) The inscription upon the lintel of the gate of Hell constitutes the abrupt opening of Canto III of the Inferno:

> Through me the way into the woeful city,
> Through me the way to the eternal pain,
> Through me the way among the lost people.
> Justice moved my maker on high,
> Divine power made me and supreme wisdom and primal love;
> Before me nothing was created but eternal
> Things and I endure eternally.
> Abandon every hope ye that enter. (lines 1-9)

The inscription defines not only the meaning of the Gate itself, but also that of the "woeful city"—it is a part of the divine order of justice. The first three lines simply state the existence of an opening through which one can enter the realm of desolation, where one is awaited by the eternal pain suffered by the definitively lost. The following lines assert that this open entryway is a work of God's justice—just as Salvation is a work of God's *misericordia*. Dante's reaction to the words of the inscription—"Master, their sense is dreadful to me"—concerns primarily the point that the eternal pain suffered by the definitively lost goes back ultimately to a primal act of God's love. To come closer to understanding this point we must see "the eternal pain" as a function of the reality of a divine order of values, and Love as that primal act of the Creator which is directed at positing and realizing the divine order of values. Hell and Paradise are limit-states in which one's choice of fulfillment is fixed in its ultimate consequence: extermination or purification, definitive interment or transfigured life. By creating man as a being endowed with freedom of choice (and, therefore, with the ability to choose the contrary of God), the Trinity (Power-Wisdom-Love) created the possibility of Hell—the Gate of Hell.

In this sense, Dante's Hell is not a penal institution, but embodies the ultimate consummation of the life one chose to live. This radical significance of choice (within the *given conditions* of the created order of the universe) is immediately and savagely reinforced by what Dante encounters in the vestibule of Hell after passing through the Gate: the unbound whirl of those "who lived without disgrace and without praise" (III, 36). That is, those who avoided choice and, therefore, chose to avoid the risk of deciding for good or for evil.

The First Circle opens with a situation in which Volodin confronts the alternative of choosing to warn or choosing to abstain from warning Dobroumov. "It would be more logical—to wait a while. It would be more sensible—to wait a while," Volodin reflects. But later on—when he is already on his way—Volodin "all of a sudden felt perfectly calm: he felt unambiguously that there could be no other choice. Dangerous or not, but if one failed to do this . . . If we always take anxious precautions against something—do we remain human? . . ." Given the "order of justice" which sets the conditions of Volodin's choice, Volodin makes the "wrong" choice and suffers the fulfillment of its consequences: entry into "Hell" through the Lubianka.

Volodin's situation sets a fundamental pattern for the entire novel. The condition of every protagonist crystallizes at some point in the action into a limit-situation of radical choice, and these individual limit-situations come about as a result of the "chain reaction" set off by Volodin's decision. Volodin, it would seem, was free to choose and his choice leads from "freedom" into "bondage." Now the question that obtrudes itself here is how much choice did he have? In his formulation of Dante's problem in regard to the "sages of Antiquity," Rubin speaks of a conflict of "duty" and "conscience," and I would suggest that the choice of doing one's duty and ignoring one's conscience—or of breaking the *Law* and following one's conscience is, in effect, the alternative forced upon Volodin by the given "order of justice." In one case you cancel yourself as a moral agent and in the other—you end in "Hell." As a "freeman" Volodin is condemned to this alternative and he is freed from its constraint only when he is condemned. But if to be a "freeman" means to be faced with the problem of moral survival, then to be condemned and cast into the "abysmal valley of pain" (Canto IV, 8) means to be faced with the problem of sheer physical survival. In this context, the inmates of the *sharashka* lead a "suspended" existence. They live on the brink of "hell" and in this respect they resemble "the free." But since they inhabit "the best and the highest circle of hell," they are free from the constraint of the Duty-Conscience dilemma, and at the same time are raised above the brute struggle for physical survival. In effect, the Limbo in which they are "suspended" is the only space within the established "universe of values and justice" where the preeminent dilemma is how to define oneself as a moral agent; how to achieve a freedom the confirmation of which could be more than suicide.

Sologdin's entrapment of Iakonov in Chapter 73 ("Two Engineers") is one of the somewhat ambiguous exemplifications of how one can not only maintain oneself as a moral agent, but also prevail. Nerzhin's case is more paradoxical. He is a man who is *in search* of self-determination, and his refusal in Chapter 9 ("The *Rosenkreutzer*") is a decision to set out, like a knight-errant, on a "quest for the Holy Grail" (compare his talk with the painter Kondrashev-Ivanov in Chapter 42, "The Castle of the Holy Grail"). The direction, however, in which he sets out is downward. Juxtaposed with the model of order within which Dante enacts the Way to God,[7] Nerzhin's "upward descent" exposes a profound flaw in the "order" which defines the conditions of his choice: the spatial relations of Dante's theological cosmology appear to be radically inverted.

[7]Dante's own *passage* through the Inferno is a special Grace and is not to be conceived as a regular part of the order within which man has the *choice* of following the Way of God.

The cosmology is still "theological," one might say, except that Satan is "God." In such a cosmos the Way to God leads away from "God" to the ice-bound realm of "the guilty worm that pierces the world" (*Inferno,* XXXIV, 108).

The central locus of the novel's action—the Mavrino *sharashka*—is, like Dante's Limbo, a part of a total order of justice. That is to say: the *sharashka*/Limbo analogy we are asked to entertain calls for a juxtaposition of the total systems of which the two "establishments" are parts. The Limbo is a part of Hell which, in turn, is a part of the Cosmos: in the center is the Earth and in *its* center is "the guilty worm"; the Earth is encompassed by nine ever-widening concentric spheres, the outermost of which is the *primum mobile;* this, finally is encompassed by a metaphysical-mystical domain that can be no longer conceived in the categories of time and space—the Empyreum ("that which is on fire"), the "Place of God."

The primary similarity of the Limbo and the *sharashka* has its source in the radical question which the nature of these "establishments" raises concerning the justice of their respective universes: *the question of the innocently condemned.* For the Limbo, as the place to which Virgil is condemned, burdens Dante with a gnawing doubt from which he seeks relief throughout his journey: the impossible seems to be possible—the God of justice and mercy seems to condemn the innocent: ("... they did not sin, but though they have merits it is not enough ..."; "for such defects, and not for any guilt, we are lost ...", see Canto IV, lines 34-41). The answer Dante ultimately receives in the *Paradiso* draws its meaning from the source of the total order of justice and mercy of which the Limbo is a part. In the case of the *sharashka,* juxtaposed with the Limbo, we are left with the question: what could be the totality that confers moral sense upon the existence of the *sharashka?*[8]

In Russian the word "comedy" may be used in the derogatory sense of "a sham, an imposture of, a false show of; making

[8]The primary *similarity* of Limbo and the *sharashka* sets up a matrix of *divergences* between the two total orders of justice and mercy. In view of this I find V. I. Grebenshchikov's exclusive focus on the *Inferno* and his effort to discover *similarities* misguided in principle. See V. I. Grebenshchikov, "The Infernal Circles of Dante and Solzhenitsyn," *Transactions of the Association of Russian-American Scholars in USA,* Vol. VI (1972), pp. 7-20.

false pretenses." What in Dante's *Divine Comedy* is revealed as a total order created and moved by Power-Wisdom-Love, in *The First Circle* assumes the character of a historically enacted "*comedy*" of total order created and moved by . . . "Power-Wisdom-Love."

The Odyssey of A Skeptic: Gleb Nerzhin

BY JOHN B. DUNLOP

Gleb Nerzhin, who has been happily defined as an "unidealized positive hero,"[1] is the central protagonist of *The First Circle.* A quester, he dominates the novel through his desire to learn from the various zeks with whom he comes in contact and by his search for moral perfection. Although it would be unwise to claim that Nerzhin entirely represents the author's point of view—especially in light of the fact that Solzhenitsyn is a conscious writer of "polyphonic" novels[2]—it is certainly significant that the novelist has chosen to equip Nerzhin with many elements of his own biography.[3] It is also of interest that

[1]Viacheslav Zavalishin, " 'V Pervom Krugu': Roman Aleksandra Solzhenitsyna," *Novoe Russkoe Slovo,* 1 September 1968.

[2]"What do I mean by polyphony?" Solzhenitsyn once explained in an interview. "Each character becomes the central one while he is in the field of action. The author must thus speak through thirty-five heroes. He should not give preference to any one of them. He must understand and motivate all his characters." (From Georges Nivat and Michel Aucouturier, eds., *Soljénitsyne* [Paris: L'Herne, 1971], p. 118.)

[3]See Solzhenitsyn's "Autobiography" which also appears in this volume. Since name symbolism is important in *The First Circle,* it is highly probable that the name "Gleb" was not selected haphazardly for the novel's major character. The name recalls St. Gleb, the innocent eleventh century martyr-prince murdered by his ambitious brother Sviatopolk. See Serge A. Zenkovsky, ed., *Medieval Russian Epics, Chronicles and Tales* (New York: Dutton, 1963), pp. 87-91. Innokentii Volodin, who is in some ways Nerzhin's "double" in the novel, is even granted the name "innocent" with its connotations of religious purity. For

a character named Nerzhin appeared in an earlier unpublished Solzhenitsyn work.[4]

At first glance Nerzhin appears to resemble Iurii Zhivago, the idealistic poet-doctor and hero of Pasternak's *Doctor Zhivago.* Yet there are clear differences between them. Zhivago is unable to survive the horrors of the Stalin era; he is broken by the steely indifference of the times toward the human personality. Nerzhin, on the other hand, is tempered as in a furnace by Stalin's Russia; possessing all of Zhivago's spiritual depth, he is physically and psychologically tough. He has acquired the resourcefulness necessary to survive in a bleak and violent age.

Nerzhin was born, like Solzhenitsyn himself, in 1918. In the sole glimpse we are given of his childhood we see him as a "sharp, quick, tough fellow" standing in bread lines during the first Five-Year Plan.[5] From the time of his boyhood Nerzhin has had to depend on his wits and physical strength to get by. Shortly before the commencement of the Second World War we find him as a student of mathematics at R. University where he distinguishes himself in his studies and marries fellow student Nadia. A year later their marriage, still childless, is interrupted by the outbreak of war. Drafted into the army, Nerzhin begins as a horse driver of transport wagons and ends up as an artillery officer. As a captain of artillery, he sees action on the Northwest and Belorussian fronts where he, like Rubin, receives several decorations. Arrested for his "turn of thought"[6] by a SMERSH unit at the front he, like Rubin, is given a ten year sentence. After participating in the forced-labor construction of a "huge apartment house for the heads of the MVD" in Moscow,[7] he is transferred to the Mavrino sharashka as a

the name symbolism of Solzhenitsyn's female characters, see Jacqueline de Proyart, "La femme, l'amour et l'enfer" in Nivat and Aucouturier, *op. cit.,* pp. 436-90, passim.

[4]According to the June 26, 1968 number of *Literaturnaia gazeta,* "Captain Nerzhin" is a character in Solzhenitsyn's play *The Feast of Victors.* See Leopold Lebedz, ed., *Solzenitsyn: A Documentary Record* (London: Allen Lane, 1970), p. 138. Solzhenitsyn has renounced this play and attacked the Soviet authorities for reproducing and circulating it. (Labedz, pp. 82-83.)

[5]III, 94. Here and subsequently references to the only extant *Collected Works* of Solzhenitsyn, the six-volume *Sobranie sochinenii* (Frankfurt/Main: Possev Verlag, 1969-70), are indicated by the appropriate volume and page number. *The First Circle* occupies volumes three and four of this edition.

[6]III, 61.

[7]III, 292, Wh., p. 241. Here and elsewhere "Wh." refers to Thomas P. Whitney's capable translation of *The First Circle* (New York: Bantam, 1969). The first publication of this translation was by Harper and Row in 1968; the

mathematician and assigned to work with the linguist Rubin. His specific task is to "evaluate the fidelity with which speech characteristics were transmitted by various telephone circuits,"[8] a project of obvious practical use to the regime. Aware of the "customer" who will benefit from his research, Nerzhin is uneasy in his conscience.

Prison has left its mark on Nerzhin, "His reddish hair was neither thin nor gray, but there were already many deep wrinkles in his drawn face . . . His skin looked faded because of the lack of fresh air. But it was most of all his economy of movement that made him seem old—that wise economy with which nature husbands a prisoner's strength against the drain of a concentration-camp regime."[9] Realizing that he may very well have to return to the camps, Nerzhin keeps himself in good physical shape. He volunteers to saw wood. All winter long he rubs himself down with snow.[10]

Along with Nerzhin's physical strength goes a combative character which delights in making things difficult for his jailers, especially in cases where they arbitrarily stray from their own regulations. As he prepares for transport, the zeks "just as [people do] at funerals" remember "how he would stand up for their rights, and how often he had defended the prisoners' interests."[11] Through his expert knowledge of the regulations Nerzhin is even able to pry his treasured collection of Esenin's poems away from the intransigent Major Shikin. In the eyes of the head of the Mavrino guard, Colonel Kliment'ev, Nerzhin is "an insolent prisoner, always trying to find out what the law was."[12]

Yet Nerzhin is more than a scrappy "good fellow" of evident intelligence. He is also gifted with a power of spiritual perception distinguishing him from the vast majority of his fellow Soviet citizens. Even as a boy, we are told, he was sus-

pagination does not coincide with that of the Bantam edition. On a few occasions I have chosen to tamper with Whitney's translation.

[8]III, 40, Wh., p. 31.

[9]III, 29, Wh., pp. 21-22.

[10]III, 188.

[11]IV, 784, Wh., p. 656.

[12]III, 217, Wh., p. 179. Victor Louis, the KGB's best known roving international representative, had an opportunity to interview Solzhenitsyn and then wrote with cynical respect concerning the writer's legal knowledge, "Like any Soviet citizen who has spent time in a labor camp, he is his own lawyer . . . He uses his hard-earned knowledge of the law so that no one can blame him." (Labedz, p. 126.)

picious of the "cult of the personality" surrounding Iosif Stalin. He tells Rubin, "Listen, when I was a little boy, I started to read his [Stalin's] books after reading Lenin's, and I couldn't get through them. After a style that was direct, ardent, precise, suddenly there was a sort of mush. Every one of his thoughts is crude and stupid—he doesn't even realize that he always misses what's important."[13] From the time of his boyhood he has been hearing a mute alarm bell [*nemoi nabat*] ringing inside himself:

> There was a scene in Victor Hugo's *Ninety Three.* Lantenac is sitting on a dune. He can see several bell towers at once, and every bell is in motion. All the bells are sounding an alarm, but a gale wind carries the sound away and he hears nothing. In the same way, through some strange inward sense, Nerzhin had since adolescence been hearing a mute alarm bell—all the groans, cries, shouts of the dying, carried by a steady, insistent wind away from human ears . . . For Gleb Nerzhin the mute bell thundered through his entire youth. An inviolable decision took root in him: to learn and understand! To learn and understand.[14]

From the time of his youth Nerzhin has refused to allow the "gale wind" of the Stalin terror to prevent him from hearing the "groans" and "cries" of the persecuted and murdered. He feels innerly compelled to do combat with the lethal ruler of his country. In a moment of introspection he even wonders, "What *compulsion* drove him to grapple with the riddle of the inflated, gloomy giant who had only to flutter his eyelashes for Nerzhin's head to fly off?"[15] Secretly he records "in a needle-file" hand on tiny sheets of paper the history of Stalin's rule.[16] These writings, which he is later forced to burn, represent his "first coming of age in all his thirty years."[17]

Unlike his companions Rubin and Sologdin, both of whom believe they have "absolute truth," Nerzhin is a quester who believes that the men around him have something to offer. Although he reads widely in philosophy and religion, he deems his observation of his fellow men to be of equal importance. As he tells Rubin, "I draw my conclusions not from the philosophy I've read but from stories about real people I've heard in prison. And afterward, when I have to formulate my own conclusions . . .

[13]III, 53, Wh., p. 41.

[14]III, 284-86, Wh., pp. 234-36.

[15]III, 62, Wh., p. 49. Here and subsequently, all italics within citations are my own unless otherwise indicated.

[16]III, 35, Wh., p. 26.

[17]III, 62, Wh., p. 49.

I leaf through the ancient philosophers and find my newest discoveries there."[18]

What knowledge or wisdom does Nerzhin succeed in extracting from his fellow zeks? Let us deal with his close friend Rubin first. In his relations with his true-believer Communist colleague Nerzhin clearly distinguishes between Rubin's "mind" and "heart." The doctrinaire Rubin, the apologist for Stalinist orthodoxy, represents an opponent for verbal sparring. Nerzhin rejects his message entirely.[19] But the Rubin who can act from the heart is a different man. From him Nerzhin can and does learn. Thus Nerzhin is greatly impressed by Rubin's attitude toward the German POWs at the sharashka. As he tells Rubin, "I like your attitude toward them. You spend hours teaching Max Russian. Yet you have every reason to hate them."[20]

Nerzhin learns a great deal more from Sologdin. When on one occasion Nerzhin makes a philosophical pronouncement, Rubin mutters, "You certainly have everything worked out. Did you get it from Mitai [Sologdin]?" And Nerzhin answers, "Maybe. Idealism? Metaphysics? Yes? Go ahead and paste on the labels, shaggy beard!"[21] What Nerzhin acquires from Sologdin is the ability to discover and apply philosophical and moral maxims which will make prison life not only bearable but even rewarding. Thus, when Rubin remarks enviously that the free employees have left the sharashka for various places of amusement, Nerzhin ruminates, "But do they choose the right places? Do they get more satisfaction out of life than we do? That's the real question."[22]

From Sologdin Nerzhin learns the potential spiritual benefits of imprisonment. Shortly before his wife is permitted a visit, he reflects, "Seen from the outside it [his life] appeared an

[18]III, 50, Wh., p. 39.

[19]What I mean is that Nerzhin rejects the Soviet Marxist world-view. He is much closer to idealism than materialism; he is on the border of religious belief. It is true that Nerzhin does express some admiration for Lenin, though he does not divinize him, and in his "historical" writings he observes, "I remember a passage in Marx . . . where he says that perhaps the victorious proletariat can get along without expropriating the prosperous peasants. That means he saw some economic way of including *all* the peasants in the new social system." (III, 35, Wh., p. 26—A.S. italics.) But Nerzhin, unlike the "true believer" Rubin, considers Marx and Lenin as merely two of many world thinkers. He is drawn to the democratic, reforming pole of their thought and chooses to ignore the authoritarian pole.

[20]III, 28, Wh., pp. 20-21.

[21]III, 51, Wh., pp. 39-40.

[22]III, 33, Wh., p. 24.

unhappy one, but Nerzhin was secretly happy in that unhappiness. He drank it down like spring water. Here he got to know people and events about which he could learn nowhere else on earth, certainly not in the quiet well-fed seclusion of a domestic hearth."[23] And at his birthday party Nerzhin maintains, "Let's be fair! Not everything in our lives is so black. This happiness we have right now—a free banquet, an exchange of free thoughts without fear, without concealment—we didn't have that in freedom."[24] The philosophical benefits of imprisonment can be great, leading to self-knowledge and a knowledge of one's fellow men. Nerzhin's wife Nadia observes that prison has had a "good effect" on her husband, has "softened" him. It has also given him such a strong self-sufficiency that she wonders if he any longer needs a wife to look after him.[25]

Yet, despite the benefits of imprisonment which he discovers, Solzhenitsyn shows that the same zeks who hymn the philosophical fruits of incarceration are always fed by a hope that they will be freed. In moments of optimism Nerzhin may praise imprisonment, but in moments of depression he curses it. Remembering that five more years remain on his sentence, he thinks:

> Descriptions of prisons have always stressed their horrors. Yet isn't it even more appalling when there are no horrors? When the horror lies in the gray methodology of years? In forgetting your one and only life on earth has been shattered? . . . Your thoughts occupied with how you grab the heel of a loaf rather than the middle from the prison tray . . . One has to live through it; it cannot be imagined . . . Only endless, uninterrupted years can bring to fruition the true experience of prison.[26]

Solzhenitsyn's position, which is rendered even clearer by a reading of *One Day in the Life of Ivan Denisovich,* is unquestionably that imprisonment is an utmost evil. But, he asserts, those imprisoned against their will can derive some important spiritual benefits from their incarceration. At no point is Solzhenitsyn a preacher of morbid self-laceration. As Dan Jacobson has written, ". . . the paradoxical notion of an invaluable freedom which only prisoners can enjoy never lapses into a sentimentality . . . which might seem to threaten it: namely, a view of the tyranny as a power which, to adapt Goethe's words,

[23]III, 219, Wh., p. 181.
[24]IV, 448, Wh., p. 370.
[25]III, 292.
[26]III, 281, Wh., p. 232.

wills forever evil yet does forever good . . . Solzhenitsyn *never kisses the rod*."[27]

Although he develops his powers of introspection under Sologdin's tutelage, Nerzhin is in no sense a disciple of the proud engineer. For one thing, he is more earnest than his mentor. Whereas Sologdin pronounces his maxims half in jest, using them as an occasion to test his wit or intellect, Nerzhin is wholly serious. Furthermore, unlike Sologdin, whose ultimate value is himself, Nerzhin is led by his philosophical probings to a skepticism concerning all values and all absolutes. Sighing, Nerzhin asks Rubin Pontius Pilate's question, "And *what is truth,* peasant? Can anyone really know what truth is?"[28] In answer to Rubin's charge that he is is a "skeptic" and "young Montaigne," Nerzhin declares the "meaning of life" to be the following: "We live—that's the meaning of life."[29]

This is, of course, very good orthodox skepticism. Basing themselves on such passages, some critics have chosen to see Solzhenitsyn as a preacher of enlightened skepticism.[30] Such critics have missed the extreme dissatisfaction with skepticism which Nerzhin manifests in the course of the novel. It is my view that in its treatment of Gleb Nerzhin *The First Circle* presents us with the *odyssey of a skeptic.* In his dealings with his fellow zeks Nerzhin tests out his new-found philosophy of skepticism and finds it lacking.[31] Nerzhin admits to Rubin that perhaps skepticism represents only "a shed by the roadside

[27]Dan Jacobson, "The Example of Solzhenitsyn," *Commentary,* 47, No. 5 (1969), 83.

[28]III, 230, Wh., p. 190.

[29]III, 49, Wh., p. 38.

[30]See, for example, Natalie Rea, "Nerzhin: A Sartrean Existential Man," *Canadian Slavonic Papers,* 13, No. 2-3 (1971), 209-16.

[31]In similar fashion Nerzhin's "double," Innokentii Volodin, tests out a philosophy of skepticism, Epicureanism, before decisively repudiating it in Lubianka Prison:

> Another of Epicurus' thoughts—unrefuted and difficult to grasp yesterday in freedom—floated into his mind: "Inner feelings of satisfaction and dissatisfaction are the highest criteria of good and evil." That meant, according to Epicurus, that what one liked was good and that what one didn't like was evil. *The philosophy of a savage.* Stalin enjoyed killing—did that mean that for him killing was a virtue? And since being imprisoned for trying to save somebody did not, after all, produce satisfaction, did that mean it was evil? No! *Good and evil had now been substantively defined for Innokentii, and visibly distinguished from one another,* by that bright gray door, by those olive walls, by that first prison night. From these heights of struggle and suffering to which he had been lifted, the wisdom of the ancient philosopher seemed like the babbling of a child. (IV, 769, Wh., p. 643.)

where I can sit out the bad weather. But skepticism is a way of freeing the dogmatic mind, and that's where its value lies."[32] There can be little doubt that the main thrust of Nerzhin's "skepticism" is directed at Soviet Marxist dogma. Both in his reading and in his dialogues with the zeks he seeks for an alternative to the "absolutes" offered by Marxism.

In conversation with Ruska Doronin, for whom he serves as a kind of mentor, Nerzhin becomes painfully aware of the limitations of skepticism. Having imbibed Nerzhin's preaching, Doronin complains, "Everything bores me. Books and theories both. History is so monotonous it's repulsive to read. The nobler and more honest a man is, the more despicably his compatriots treat him . . . All history is one continuous pestilence. There is nowhere to appeal and nowhere to go."[33] Disturbed by this "quiver of skepticism" on "such young lips" (Ruska is twenty-three), and realizing that he has "planted" these thoughts in the youth, Nerzhin warns him, "No matter how clever and absolute the systems of skepticism or agnosticism or pessimism, you must understand that *by their very nature they doom us to a loss of will.* They can't really influence human behavior because people cannot stand still . . ."[34] Skepticism is therefore ultimately insufficient. "Look," Nerzhin continues, "I personally believe that people seriously need skepticism. It's needed to split the rockheads. To choke fanatical voices. But skepticism can never provide firm ground under a man's feet. *And perhaps, after all, we need firm ground.*"[35] Nerzhin's self-analysis and observation of his fellow man have convinced him that, while skepticism is necessary to puncture and destroy false dogmatism, it is inoperable as a world-view. It can only lead to spiritual stasis and death. Man has an organic need to believe in something which is absolute: he needs "firm ground."

In his relations with Valentin Prianchikov, Nerzhin the skeptic discerns the foolishness of a belief in mathematics or science. Prianchikov is a "priest [*zhrets*] of science," a man for whom science is a religion.[36] Unlike Valentin, Nerzhin has come to see higher mathematics as a near useless luxury, "Quantities solved, quantities not solved, quantities unknown—topology! The stratosphere of human thought! In the twenty-fourth century it

[32]III, 52, Wh., p. 41.
[33]III, 96-97, Wh., pp. 77-78.
[34]III, 97, Wh., p. 78.
[35]*Ibid.*
[36]III, 81.

might possibly be of use of someone, but as for now . . . 'I've nothing to say of the sun and world/I see only the torments of man.' "[37] Nerzhin elects not to remain within the fraternity of "rosicrucians,"[38] men for whom science and mathematics are an absolute value in themselves. Rather, he sees that his work in life must be anthropocentric, must relate to the "torments of man." As for Prianchikov, the vapidness of his world-view is underlined by his taste in music—"boogie-woogie."

Another zek comrade of Nerzhin's is Andrei Andreevich Potapov, a man like Prianchikov entirely absorbed in his work. Potapov had personally directed all the electrical calculations during the construction of the Dnieper Hydroelectric Station [*Dneprostroi*].

> No one who had known Potapov in his youth, and still less Potapov himself, would have dreamed that at forty he would be thrown in prison for *politics*. Potapov's friends, justifiably, called him a robot. Potapov's whole life was his work, and even the three-day holidays bored him . . . When there were shortages of bread, or vegetables, or sugar, he hardly noticed these external hardships at all. He punched one more hole in his belt, pulled it tighter and continued to concern himself with the only thing in the world that interested him: high-voltage transmission.[39]

Potapov so loves his work that, when he learns that the Germans have blown up his brainchild, the Dneprostroi, he forfeits his military exemption and volunteers for the army. Captured by the Germans and discovered to be the engineer who designed the Dneprostroi, he is offered "freedom, food rations, money" and, greatest temptation of all, "his own work" if he will reconstruct the station for them. "Without beating his chest and shouting proud words," Potapov demurs.[40] And so in a "mild, untheatrical way" he chooses "death over well-being."[41] For his heroism Potapov is given a ten year sentence by the Soviets for having allegedly betrayed the Dnieper Power Station (which had already been totally destroyed) to the enemy.

[37]III, 60, Wh., p. 47. The verses are from Goethe.

[38]Chapter nine of *The First Circle* is entitled "The Rosicrucians." Solzhenitsyn himself once made a decision similar to Nerzhin's. As he stated in an interview, "I had leanings toward mathematics, and it was proposed to me that I do my doctorate . . . but I did not want to consecrate my entire life to mathematics. Literature attracted me more . . ." (In Georges Nivat and Michel Aucouturier, eds., *Soljénitsyne,* p. 114.)

[39]III, 221, Wh., pp. 182-83. A.S. italics.

[40]III, 223, Wh., p. 184.

[41]*Ibid.*

Potapov is older than Prianchikov and has suffered more. Although he is religiously devoted to his work, he does not absolutize it. Nerzhin sees him as a pure spirit who unconsciously heeds the voice of conscience. In the argument at Nerzhin's birthday party over the permissibility of a "double standard" in love and marriage Potapov unerringly sides with the idealists. " 'Lev Grigorich, there's a simple way to achieve equality,' Potapov said firmly. 'Don't *you* make love to anyone except your wife!' "[42]

In his search for wisdom Nerzhin discovers that the sharashka janitor, the peasant Spiridon, has a great deal to offer. Nerzhin's "going to the people" [*khozhdenie v narod*] is one of the more significant "experiments"[43] carried out by the young mathematician in the course of the novel. We learn that his encounter with Spiridon has been preceded by considerable reflection on the nature of the Russian people. He has entertained and then rejected as "extreme" Rubin's view that "to look for life's loftiest meaning in the peasant class was a squalid and fruitless occupation, because only the proletariat is consistently purposeful to the end, and to it alone the future belongs."[44] He has similarly rejected Sologdin's tenet that " 'the people' is an over-all term for a totality of persons of slight interest, gray, crude, preoccupied in their unenlightened way with daily existence."[45] As an urban youth Nerzhin had encountered the "people," "haloed, silvery haired . . . embodying all wisdom, moral purity and spiritual grandeur," in nineteenth century Russian literature which "swooned" with compassion for the "suffering brother."[46] Believing that he lived not in "old Russia" but in the Soviet Union, Nerzhin left the people on the bookshelf and came to the elitist conviction that "the only people who matter are those who carry in their heads the accumulated culture of the world, encyclopedists, connoisseurs of antiquity, men who value beauty; highly educated many-sided men. One must belong to that elite."[47] Like Sologdin, he found himself attracted to a philosophy of the "elect," one holding the com-

[42]IV, 450, Wh., p. 372. A.S. italics.

[43]The term is Nerzhin's (IV, 558). His use of the word shows that he is consciously proceeding in a *scientific* manner, methodically eliminating false avenues.

[44]IV, 540, Wh., p. 449.

[45]*Ibid.*

[46]IV, 541, Wh., p. 449.

[47]*Ibid.*

mon people in contempt. His first experiences in the war served only to confirm this philosophy. Struggling to adjust to his work as a horse transport driver, he was disconcerted to find the "unshaven, profane, pitiless, and extremely disagreeable People" laughing loudly at his ineptitude.[48] Once he became an artillery officer, the People became "obedient, loyal, industrious, and, consequently, pleasant" but exhibited no more originality than previously.[49] Only in prison did he begin to reassess his views. The stimulus for this was a loss of faith in the "elite" Soviet intelligentsia. In prison these "delicate, sensitive, highly educated persons who valued beauty often turned out to be cowards, quick to cave in, adroit in excusing their own vileness. They soon degenerated into betrayers, beggars and hypocrites. And Nerzhin had barely escaped becoming like them."[50] Realizing that the "elite" all too easily degenerate into Artur Siromakhas, Nerzhin seeks to acquire from the simple working people "the wisdom of capable hands and their philosophy of life."[51]

Yet, though Nerzhin comes to believe in the relative superiority of the common people over the intelligentsia, he does not come "full circle" and place them on the same pedestal as did nineteenth century Russian literature. Tossed in among the people and ordered to work his "norm," Nerzhin did not have to "change his clothes and feel about for a staircase in order to go down to the people."[52] (A gentle dig at Lev Tolstoy.) What does Nerzhin discover among the People?

> Nerzhin saw clearly that these people were of no greater stature than he . . . They did not endure hunger and thirst any more stoically. They were no more firm of spirit . . . They were blinder and more trusting about informers. They were prone to believe the crude deception of the bosses. They awaited amnesties—which Stalin would have rather died than give them . . . And they were greedier for petty things . . .[53]

Nerzhin also comes to realize that the People lack that "personal point of view [*tochka zreniia*] which becomes more precious than life itself."[54] Nerzhin ultimately comes to the conclusion that to be *oneself* by forging and perfecting one's soul is to become a tiny particle of one's people.[55]

[48] IV, 541, Wh., p. 450.
[49] IV, 542, Wh., p. 450.
[50] *Ibid.*
[51] *Ibid.*
[52] IV, 542-43, Wh., p. 451.
[53] IV, 543, Wh., p. 451.
[54] *Ibid.*
[55] IV, 544.

It is clear that Solzhenitsyn does not idealize the Russian people in *The First Circle.* He does not claim that the common people are "super-human"; what he appears to maintain is simply that they have retained and not *perverted* their human nature, as much of the intelligentsia has done. Furthermore, although the People lack a world-view or "point of view," they do, Nerzhin discovers, possess a consistent world-sense (as opposed to world-view). This is brought out in Nerzhin's talks with Spiridon.

As he contemplates Spiridon's ruined life in which the only constants seem to be love of land and love of family, Nerzhin thinks, "Spiridon's complex life, his crossing and recrossing from one warring side to another, wasn't there more to it than simple self-preservation? Didn't it somehow relate to the Tolstoyan teaching that no one in the world is just and no one guilty? *Wasn't there a whole system of philosophical skepticism in the almost instinctive acts of the redheaded peasant?*"[56] Seeking an "alternative to the wisdom of his intellectual friends," Nerzhin expects to hear a "confirmation of skepticism" from the peasant to whom he feels so drawn:

> I've wanted to ask you something for a long time, Spiridon Danilych . . . Your life has been torn up, yes, and so have many others' too, not just yours . . . Why? I mean what standards . . . are we to use in trying to understand life? For example, are there people on earth who consciously want to do evil? . . . Probably not, don't you think? Maybe everyone wants to do good or *thinks* he wants to, but not everyone is free of guilt or error, and some are totally conscienceless . . . They convince themselves they are doing good, but it turns out to be evil. As you might say, they sow rye and grow weeds.[57]

When Spiridon does not get the point, Nerzhin tries a new tack:

> Let's say you make a mistake and I want to correct you. I speak to you about it, and you don't listen to me, you even shut me up. Well, what am I supposed to do? Beat you over the head? It's fine if I'm right, but what if I only think I am, if I have merely convinced myself that I'm right? Or maybe I used to be right, but now I am wrong. After all, life changes, doesn't it? *I mean, if a person can't be sure he is right how can he act?* Is it conceivable that any human being on earth can really tell who is right and who is wrong? Who can be sure about that?[58]

Having voiced a philosophy of pure relativism which, for

[56]IV, 558, Wh., p. 464.
[57]IV, 560, Wh., p. 466. A.S. italics.
[58]IV, 560-61, Wh., p. 466.

lack of any "absolute" guidelines, paralyzes one's ability to act, Nerzhin waits for the peasant's answer. When it comes, he is struck by its "simplicity and force," as well as by the burning conviction with which Spiridon utters his words: *"The wolfhound is right but the cannibal is wrong."*[59]

Spiridon, who has a consistent "world-sense," demolishes Nerzhin's relativism by affirming that man is not an animal—that the cannibal is guilty while the wolfhound is not. The cannibal is guilty because something distinguishes him from an animal, and that something is clearly *conscience.*[60] Stalin *is* guilty for his crimes in spite of his self-delusion, because Stalin is a man and not a wolfhound. It is noteworthy that for all his "skepticism" Nerzhin is unable to avoid employing absolutist terms in posing the problem ("they are doing *good,* and it turns out they are doing *evil*"). For a pure relativist there cannot, of course, be either a "good" or "evil." Although Spiridon cannot articulate the philosophy he unconsciously holds, he is nevertheless consistent in his moral "criterion." (The title of the chapter in which the discussion occurs is "Spiridon's Criterion.")[61]

If Nerzhin's "skepticism" receives a blow from Spiridon, it

[59]IV, 561, Wh., p. 466. Spiridon's maxim contains a feature common in Russian folksayings—rhyme: *"Volkodav—prav, a liudoed—net."* It is also worth noting that the Russian word *volkodav* [wolf-hound] literally means "wolf-killer" and the word *liudoed* [cannibal] means "people-eater." In *The First Circle* Stalin is depicted as a *liudoed* who treats human beings like "meat." Spiridon's dictum can be found in Vladimir Dal's *Tolkovyi slovar' zhivogo velikorusskogo iazyka* [Explanatory Dictionary of the Living Russian Language], where it is listed as a folksaying illustrating the word *volkodav.* Spiridon's near-blindness is also of symbolic importance—he has *inner vision.*

[60]In his "Answer to Three Students" Solzhenitsyn stresses that, "there is nothing relative about conscience . . . they can shout, they can take you by the throat, they can tear your breast, but convictions based on conscience are as infallible as the internal rhythm of the heart." (V, 269, Labedz, *op. cit.,* p. 101.)

[61]Irving Howe in a review of Georg Lukacs' study *Solzhenitsyn* takes the Marxist critic to task for attacking Solzhenitsyn's "plebianism." Howe's review appears elsewhere in this volume. The attraction exerted by the Russian peasant on Nerzhin is demonstrated by his favorite poet—Sergei Esenin, the gifted peasant poet who combined a chaotic life with deep spiritual yearning and who took his own life in 1925. A detailed discussion of Nerzhin's attraction to Esenin would fall outside the scope of this essay. It should, however, be mentioned that other major characters in the novel are characterized by their favorite writer or poet. Rubin's choice, for example, is Eduard Bagritskii (1895-1934), a poet who served as a Red guerrilla during the Civil War and whose most famous work celebrates a Bolshevik commissar who faced death at the hands of a peasant "without a flicker of an eyelash." (See Marc Slonim, *Soviet Russian Literature* [New York: Oxford University Press, 1967], pp. 128-29.) Sologdin's "author" is Dostoevsky; Potapov reveres only Pushkin.

is virtually annihilated in his talks with Ippolit Mikhailovich Kondrashev-Ivanov, the sharashka's "court painter." This philosophical idealist shares many of the ideas of Sologdin but, unlike Sologdin, lives in accordance with his views. It is undoubtedly of symbolic significance that Kondrashev's studio is at an altitude, located on a closed-off landing on the third floor. His involvement in the work of the sharashka is peripheral at best. His only task is to paint pictures for the lobbies and hallways of the ministry to which the sharashka belongs as well as for the private apartments of ministry officials such as Oskolupov. In the quiet meditative atmosphere of Kondrashev's studio Nerzhin finds it easy to reflect. As for Kondrashev, he speaks more through his paintings than in words.

The first painting which Nerzhin examines in the studio is a six-foot-tall canvas entitled "The Maimed Oak": "It showed a solitary oak which grew with mysterious power on the naked face of a cliff. What hurricanes had blown here! How they had bent that oak! And the skies behind the trees and all around were eternally stormswept . . . This stubborn angular tree with its clawing roots . . . refused to quit the battle and perilously clung to its place over the abyss."[62] Here is a depiction of the tenacity of the human spirit which refuses to capitulate despite unrelenting and perpetual attack; facing the ordeal of the camps Nerzhin can draw spiritual strength from such a picture.

A second painting he examines is entitled "Autumn Stream":

> A small stream occupied the center of the canvas. It seemed not to be flowing at all, and its surface was about to ice over . . . The first snow lay in patches on both shores, and yellowish-brown grass sprouted where it had melted . . . In the background was a dense forest of olive-black firs, before which flamed a single rebellious crimson birch. Beyond its lonely, tender fire the evergreen sentinels stood even gloomier, massed together, raising their sharp peaks to the sky. The sky was hopelessly skewbald, and the suffocating sun was sinking in the mottled overcast, powerless to break through with a single ray. But even that was not the most important element; rather it was the stagnant water of the settling stream. It had a feeling of being poured, a depth. It was lead-like and transparent and very cold. It held in itself the balance between autumn and winter. And some other kind of equilibrium.[63]

Here the "single rebellious crimson birch" plays the same role as the "maimed oak" of the previous painting—it symbolizes

[62]III, 350, Wh., p. 290.
[63]III, 356, Wh., pp. 294-95.

the human spirit "flaming" despite all obstacles (the evergreen sentinels and "skewbald" sky suggest imprisonment and persecution; the sun, symbol of light, truth and love, is "suffocating"). And the stream? It would seem that the slow freezing of the waters of the stream suggests the passage of time into eternity (i.e. what is termed "comprehension, peace, the unity of all things").[64] The drama of the individual spirit, seemingly so hopeless, takes place against a mystical background of eternity. And that, we are told, is what is "most important."

The final painting which Nerzhin views (it is actually a preliminary study for a painting) depicts the moment when Parsifal first glimpses the Holy Grail:

> The painting was twice as high as it was wide. It showed a wedgelike gorge between two mountain cliffs. On both cliffs . . . there was a forest, slumbering, primeval. Creeping ferns and clinging, hostile bushes had invaded the cliffs. At the top left, from out of the forest a light gray horse bore a rider in helmet and cloak. The steed was not frightened of the abyss, and had just raised its hoof, ready, at the will of its rider, to step back or to hurtle across. But the horseman was not looking at the abyss. Amazed, he was looking into the distance where a reddish-gold light, coming perhaps from the sun, perhaps from something purer than the sun, flooded the sky behind a castle. It stood on the crest of the mountain . . . vibrant, vague yet visible in its unearthly perfection: the aureate-violet castle of the Holy Grail.[65]

When confronted with "unearthly perfection"—the ideal—the horseman does not even notice the abyss or the "hostile" bushes. The sun and "perhaps something purer than the sun" is in the distance; danger is at hand. Yet for the horseman there is not even any question as to which direction must be taken.

Kondrashev does not preach; he bears witness. Through his paintings in which he tries to communicate the "highest synthesis of nature"[66] and through his words and actions he testifies to a mystical, other-worldly perfection which is within man's grasp if he desires it. Like Sologdin, Kondrashev admires the Middle Ages as a time when men willingly left home and family to serve the ideal. The painter serves as Nerzhin's mentor in much

[64] III, 357, Wh., p. 295. Cf. Solzhenitsyn's "sketch" entitled "Reflections in the Water" discussed in my essay "Solzhenitsyn's 'Sketches' " which appears elsewhere in this volume. As in the passage cited, Solzhenitsyn's sketch sees the arresting of the waters' motion as an intimation of immortality, of eternity.

[65] III, 360-61, Wh., p. 298.

[66] III, 357.

the way that Shulubin represents Kostoglotov's teacher in *Cancer Ward.*

For Kondrashev, with his eyes fastened on the Holy Grail of spiritual perfection, the very possibility of compromise with conscience is excluded. Nerzhin on one occasion complains to him, "In exchange for seven ounces of black bread they demand of us not only our spiritual harmony, but also the last remnants of conscience."[67] Rising to his full height and looking like a man "being led to execution," Kondrashev exclaims, "Never! Never! No camp must break a man's spirit."[68] Nerzhin replies cynically, "Perhaps it must not, but it does! You haven't been in camp yet, so don't judge. You don't know how they break us there . . . Yes it's well known: existence determines consciousness [*bytie opredeliaet soznanie*]."[69] Kondrashev refuses to accept this Marxist dogma which, of course, totally undermines human freedom, "No! No! No! That would be degrading. What is there to live for then? *And, tell me, why are people who love each other faithful when they're separated?* After all the circumstances dictate that they betray one another! And how do you explain the difference in people who have fallen into the same conditions, even in the same camp?"[70]

Kondrashev rejects the Soviet Marxist view of man as "degrading" and points to those who repudiate personal advantage for the sake of ideals as models. Although Nerzhin feels that the concepts of this "ageless idealist" (who, one might point out, is of "Decembrist" stock and bears the name of a famous idealistic Russian artist)[71] are "fantastic," he

[67] III, 358, Wh., p. 296.

[68] *Ibid.*

[69] III, 358, Wh., p. 297.

[70] III, 358-59, Wh., p. 297.

[71] The guards officers known as the "Decembrists," who unsuccessfully rose against Emperor Nicholas I in 1825, have come to symbolize men willing to sacrifice themselves for an ideal. The Russian painter A. A. Ivanov (1806-58) was renowned in the nineteenth century for his incredible self-sacrificial labors over his immense canvas "Christ Appears to the People." Nikolai Gogol' devoted an admiring chapter to him in his *Selected Passages from Correspondence with Friends* (1847). Gogol' writes, ". . . it is necessary, like Ivanov, to die to all the enticements of life; like Ivanov, to instruct oneself and consider oneself an eternal student; like Ivanov to refuse oneself everything, even an extra dish on feast days; like Ivanov, to wear a simple pleated jacket when at the end of one's resources and scorn vain conventions; like Ivanov, to endure all, despite one's lofty, delicate spiritual makeup . . ." (Cited from Nikolai Gogol', *Selected Passages from Correspondence with Friends,* trans. by Jesse Zeldin [Nashville, Tenn.: Vanderbilt University Press, 1969], p. 155.)

respects and draws strength from what Kondrashev says. The painter's view of man is the following:

> A human being possesses from his birth a certain essence, the nucleus, as it were, of this human being. His "I." And it is still uncertain which forms which: whether life forms the man or man, with his strong spirit, forms his life! Because . . . he has something to measure himself against, something he can look to. Because he has in him an Image of Perfection which in rare moments suddenly emerges before his spiritual gaze.[72]

Kondrashev refuses to accept all determinisms which attempt to deny or even belittle man's freedom and his duty endlessly to strive toward spiritual perfection. His words recall those of his counterpart Shulubin in *Cancer Ward:* "I feel so clearly that what is in me isn't all of me. There is something quite unconquerable, something very lofty! Some fragment of the World Spirit. Don't you feel that?"[73]

At Nerzhin's birthday party Kondrashev predictably sides with Nerzhin and Potapov in opposing the Sologdin-Rubin thesis that "a wife who has been unfaithful can't be forgiven but a husband can be."[74] And he exclaims, "What a blessed thing [*Kakoi sviatoi podvig*] constancy is!"[75] When the zek Adamson recites a "petty" verse of the poet Merzliakov ("All your friends, all your comrades/Last till the first black day"),[76] Kondrashev is appalled. "That's outrageous! How can anyone live one day with such a thought? One would have to hang oneself!"[77] In his theory of art, which he defends against Rubin, he develops similar views, but here is not the place for a discussion of this most interesting topic.

Kondrashev, a mouthpiece for a number of Solzhenitsyn's most precious ideas, is a mystic and idealist. There is no proof, however, that he is a theist. Another figure in the novel, who bears considerable resemblance to Kondrashev, definitely is—Dmitrii Dmitrievich Goriainov-Shakhovskoi, Nerzhin's professor of mathematics at R. University:

> Goriainov-Shakhovskoi! The little old man, slovenly in his great age, would sometimes smear his black corduroy jacket with chalk, at other times would pocket the blackboard rag instead of his handkerchief. He was a living legend, made up of a multitude of "absent minded profes-

[72]III, 359, Wh., p. 297.
[73]II, 534, Cited from Aleksandr I. Solzhenitsyn, *The Cancer Ward,* trans. by Rebecca Frank (New York: Dell, 1970), p. 559.
[74]IV, 449, Wh., p. 371.
[75]IV, 450, Wh., p. 372.
[76]IV, 451, Wh., p. 373.
[77]*Ibid.*

> sor" jokes. He had been the soul of the Warsaw Imperial University, having moved to industrial R. in 1915 . . . Half a century of scientific work brought congratulatory cables from Milwaukee, Capetown, Yokahama. And then he was purged . . . He went to Moscow and returned with a note from Kalinin: "Don't touch this old man!" It was rumored that Kalinin's father had been a serf of the professor's father. So they did not touch him. They did not touch him in a way that was awesome. He might write a research paper in the natural sciences containing a mathematical proof of the existence of God. Or at a public lecture on his beloved Newton he might wheeze from behind his yellow mustaches: "Someone just passed me a note: 'Marx wrote that Newton was a materialist, and you say he was an idealist.' I reply: *Marx was wrong. Newton believed in God like every other great scientist . . .*" It was absolutely impossible to understand his ideas while listening to his lectures, but when Nerzhin, working together with one of his comrades, succeeded in actually taking down what he said and figuring it out overnight, they were inwardly moved by the twinkling of starry heavens.[78]

That Nerzhin is moving toward similar beliefs is revealed during his supervized interview with his wife. When he hints that he may soon be sent away from the sharashka, Nadia, greatly disturbed, asks where. "Only God knows," he replies. "Don't tell me you've started believing in God?" she exclaims, shocked. Nerzhin "smiles" and answers, *"Pascal, Newton, Einstein."*[79] The three scientists Nerzhin names were, of course, all religious believers. When she reaches her dormitory room, Nadia tosses Gleb's disturbing words over in her mind, "And hadn't he said something about God—some phrase or other? Prison was crippling his spirit, leading him off into idealism, mysticism, teaching him submissiveness. He was changing; when he came back, she wouldn't know him any more."[80]

Gleb Nerzhin is a kindred spirit to Kondrashev and the

[78]III, 60-61, Wh., pp. 47-48.

[79]III, 312, Wh., p. 258.

[80]III, 385, Wh., p. 318. *The First Circle* gives a somewhat more detailed glimpse of the inner workings of another zek, radio engineer Dyrsin, who has come to religious belief. While being interviewed by Major Myshin of the security forces, Dyrsin "secretly prayed for his wife. He had learned to pray in camp." (IV, p. 658, Wh., p. 550.) The clearest expression of Solzhenitsyn's own theistic convictions is to be found in his well-known "Prayer":

> How easy it is for me to live with You, Lord! When my thoughts get stuck or my mind collapses, when the cleverest people see no further than this evening and do not know what must be done tomorrow, You send down to me confidence that You exist and that You will ensure that not all the ways of goodness are blocked. From the summit of earthly fame I look round with wonder at that road through hopelessness to this point from which even I have been able to shed abroad among men the refulgence of Your glory. And You will grant me to express as much as is necessary. And insofar as I am not able to

novel's other "idealists": Agniia, Muza, Innokentii Volodin's mother. It may be objected that he appears to be a man-of-action rather than a seraphic idealist barely touching earth. The truth is that Nerzhin is a kind of dual personality: half man-of-action and half mystic-contemplative. As he once tells free employee Simochka, "I am active because I hate activity." When she asks what he really likes, he replies, *"Contemplation."*[81] A word which prompts the narrator to add, "And indeed when the squall of work passed, he would sit for hours hardly changing his position. The skin of his face would turn gray and old and the wrinkles would appear. *Where had his self-assurance gone? He became slow and indecisive.*"[82]

On one occasion Nerzhin attempts to describe to Rubin the spiritual fruits of contemplation:

> If in camp—and even more so in the sharashka—there should be a miracle like a free, nonworking Sunday, then in the course of that day *the soul unfreezes* [*otmerznet i otoidet dusha*]. And even though nothing in my external situation has changed for the better, still the yoke of prison has let up on me a bit, and I have a real conversation or read an honest page and I'm on the crest of a wave. I haven't had any real life for many years, but I've forgotten about that. *I'm weightless, suspended, disembodied.* I lie there on my upper bunk and stare at the ceiling. It is very close, it's bare, the plasterwork is bad—and I tremble with the utter joy of existence! I fall asleep in perfect bliss.[83]

Like his kindred spirits Kondrashev, Agniia and the "reformed" Innokentii Volodin,[84] Nerzhin has the center of his existence elsewhere than in the mundane life of the body. Yet to a far greater degree than any of them, he is able to *act* out of his kernel of idealism. It is as if the idealist Kondrashev and man-of-action Khorobrov were combined into one. Rooted in the eternal, Gleb Nerzhin does not despise the temporal but strives to bring it into conformity with his eternal ideals.

---

do it, that means You have allotted the task to others.

(Cited from Michael Bourdeaux, ed., *Patriarch and Prophets* (London: Macmillan, 1969), p. 344. Russian text in *Vestnik RSKhD,* 81 (1966), 22.

[81] III, 41, Wh., p. 31.

[82] III, 41, Wh., p. 31.

[83] III, 50, Wh., p. 39.

[84] As I noted earlier, Volodin undertakes a spiritual "odyssey" similar to that of Nerzhin in the course of the novel. Nerzhin's odyssey, however, is conducted on a *deeper level* than Volodin's. Gleb's repudiation (or, rather, transcendence) of skepticism is the result of a long and philosophically sophisticated journey. The journey of the establishmentarian Volodin is swifter and as much due to moral sentiment as philosophical reflection. It is, however, a *valid* journey in Solzhenitsyn's eyes.

The Role of the Lie in *The First Circle*

BY DAVID M. HALPERIN

> Let us not forget that violence does not and cannot exist by itself: it is invariably intertwined with *the lie.* They are linked in the most intimate, most organic and profound fashion: violence cannot conceal itself behind anything except lies, and lies have nothing to maintain them save violence. Anyone who has once proclaimed violence as his *method* must inexorably choose the lie as his *principle.* (. . .) Lies can prevail against much in this world, but never against art.
>
> —Aleksandr Solzhenitsyn, "Nobel Lecture"

In an attempt to extinguish the human spirit in every area of society, Stalin transformed life into a living Hell during his reign: this is the central metaphor of *The First Circle.* The specific mechanism exploited by the demonic forces in the world of the novel is represented in turn by a single thematic structure: the role of the Lie.

Three basic levels of falsehood are depicted in *The First Circle*: empirical, psychological, and metaphysical; each recedes behind the next in a progression of deepening significance. What shall be called the *empirical* lie is the most obvious. It involves a variety of deceptions in the external order of society—mendacious newspaper articles, falsified production statistics, blatant propaganda, and so forth. All these, however, are products of a pragmatic or *psychological* lie whereby a new, warped code of moral conduct undermines and replaces the individual's ethical system. An example is Iakonov's expedient decision to sign a certain newspaper article: "It was not the complete truth, but it was not exactly a lie either. The facts existed, though there were other facts, too. Hesitation on Iakonov's part might have aroused suspicion, harmed his reputation. And, after all, whom could such an article hurt?" (XXIII, 149).[1] The psychological lie, in other words, refers to the specific rationale for men's actions; hence, it enables us to learn how each empirical fraud can be perpetrated. As for the abstract or *metaphysical* lie, it is the foundation on which the psychological lie rests. The metaphysical lie deforms the general world view of individuals or of an entire nation; it affects the very way people *think* and so ultimately accounts for every man's value system—and the actions which derive from it. Each level is portrayed in the novel according to its nature—the empirical lie by facts and occurrences, the psychological lie by personalities and actions, and the metaphysical lie by symbols and ideas. I shall take up the three types of lie in turn and show how Solzhenitsyn succeeds in exposing and refuting each. As the novelist has said elsewhere, "in the struggle with lies, art has always triumphed and shall always triumph."[2]

The society portrayed by Solzhenitsyn in *The First Circle* is held together by a vast network of lies extending from the very center of the social fabric and encompassing every facet of life. These lies are neither fortuitous nor spontaneous; rather, they are the purposeful expression of the will of the Master. But the aging Stalin is himself losing control, since he lives completely in the world of lies he has engendered. The cumulative effect of universal adulation has totally estranged him from reality and truth; this is illustrated by Stalin's acceptance of an incredibly distorted and slavish biography of himself: "The elemental, honest words of this book acted on the human heart with serene inevitability. His strategic genius. His wise foresight . . ." (etc.; XVIII, 100). Because he has become so insulated, both physically and morally, from truth and from what it entails, he has lost all respect for its power. Peering

[1]All references to the text include first the chapter and then the page number of the Bantam paperback edition, New York, 1969. All quotations are from the English translation by Thomas P. Whitney; all italics within the quotes are Solzhenitsyn's.

[2]"Nobel Lecture," trans. by Alexis Klimoff.

through the bulletproof window "in his guarded and fortified night office, Stalin did not fear [objective reality] in the least; he felt in himself the power to warp it, to bend it as he pleased" (XIX, 113). This is Stalin's most diabolical trait and it is precisely by exploring its implications that the novelist unites his vision of Soviet society as Hell to his specific image of Stalin as its Dark Prince.

As a serious student of Russian culture, Solzhenitsyn is of course familiar with the traditional depiction of the devil in Russian literature and folklore. Furthermore, being a deeply religious man (though perhaps not particularly well-versed in Christian theology), he is certainly acquainted with the devil's methods as they are described in the literary sources of Christianity. In the New Testament, although the devil is often referred to by his Old Testament name of Satan (Σατανᾶς, Σατανᾶ, or Σατᾶν), a Hebrew word meaning *adversary* or *enemy,* the Christian writers more often employ a different word of their own choosing: the Greek ὁ διάβολος (the diabolos, a cognate of the English "devil" and translated accordingly). The word itself is derived from the verb διαβάλλω—to accuse falsely—and denotes *slanderer* or *calumniator.* The significance of this term is elaborated by Christ Himself in John 8:44, which in the King James Version reads: "Ye are of your father the devil, and the lusts of your father ye will do. He was a murderer [ἀνθρωποκτόνος—"manslayer"][3] from the beginning, and abode not in truth, because there is no truth in him. When [ever] he speaketh a lie, he speaketh of his own: for he is a liar, and the father of it." A liar and the father of lies—what better description of Stalin ruling over oppressed subjects and victims? This is how the devil has been traditionally conceived; this is his primary function: to slander the goodness of God and of His creation, and to deny His love for man. With the passage of time the devil has also acquired many other attributes and characteristics, but mendacity has always been considered his quintessence.

In *The First Circle* Solzhenitsyn examines both the omnipresence of lying as a demonstrable feature of Soviet society and as a metaphysical, demonic device. By uniting these two aspects of the Lie, he has effectively forged his central metaphor—

[3]This particular aspect of Stalin both in *The First Circle* and elsewhere is all too clear.

Hell; for it is from Stalin just as from the devil that lies emanate to poison a whole society.

This process starts with Stalin's immediate subordinates. When Abakumov reports "successful developments . . . in the plot to assassinate Tito . . . he did not himself know whether they were real or illusory" (XX, 121). And it extends unabated to *their* subordinates: " 'When will the phones be ready?' And [Abakumov] added threateningly: 'Don't lie. I don't like lies' " (XV, 82). But the minister is equally powerless to affect the pervasive atmosphere of deception. The Leader's disregard for truth is infernally contagious and the "troika of liars" (Sevast'ianov, Oskolupov, and Iakonov) proceed to lie on schedule as they had planned.[4] The point is hard to miss: not even the government at its highest level can procure reliable information from its officials. The same is true in every other area of society. In the universities, Simochka and her peers graduate in total lack of proper training and with meaningless degrees. In the courts, judges mete out sentences for fictitious crimes. In the arts, critics have joined with artists in a patently false charade. As the critic Aleksei Lanskii solemnly explains, "Plays never fail here, and can't fail, because the playwrights and the public share the same vision, both artistically and in their general view of the world" (LVI, 406). Innokentii has no trouble seeing through this deception. "Your work [prose fiction] is the opposite of the work undertaken by the conscience" (LVII, 414), he tells his brother-in-law, the renowned writer Galakhov; he means that such work, since it invariably amounts to indiscriminate and dishonest praise of the existing order, is the reverse of the labor of conscience, which is always critical by nature.

In addition to the larger picture of a society founded upon deceit, the author shows us the inner world of the *sharashka* as a subset of the former. Filled not only with the customary preposterous lies—for instance, that the commonly available American electronics magazines which the prison contains are in fact top secret documents—the *sharashka* also has a false rationale for its very existence: that the intellectuals interned within it are supposedly working to benefit mankind in con-

[4]Incidentally, the use of "troika" here may have broader implications as a traditional symbol of Russian Statehood, conjuring up, perhaps, shades of Gogol' and recalling the "progressive" lawyer's liberal revision of that image at Dmitrii Karamazov's murder trial.

sonance with their professional ethics. In actuality, they have been made accomplices to oppression and murder. As Gerasimovich tells Oskolupov and Iakonov: "Putting people in prison is not my field! I don't set traps for human beings! It's bad enough that they put *us* in prison. . . ." (LXXIX, 583). Finally, the very word *sharashka,* construed[5] as "a sinister enterprise based on bluff or deceit," has broad implications for the general picture of Soviet society in *The First Circle.* If in fact the *sharashka* is not an *exact* metaphor for the whole, Solzhenitsyn's use of it is emblematic because it suggests an example of the sort of insidious deception taking place throughout the country.

Thus far, the tissue of lies has been viewed simply as the thematic background for the action of the novel. But the importance of falsehood explodes into the plot itself—at these two moments, for example: in the first chapter when the wife of the doctor whom Innokentii is trying to warn interrupts him at a crucial juncture in their conversation—shortly before the connection is broken off—with a jarring question: "Maybe it's all untrue. How can you prove you're telling the truth?" (I, 5). And towards the end of the novel, as Innokentii lingers in his office waiting for his time to be up, he remembers the woman's fateful words which recall the suspicion of a whole generation (LXXVIII, 571).

So far I have presented a sampling of the many lies depicted in the novel but without a single major theme or common denominator except for their frequency and falsity; consequently, there is no one philosophical truth to which Solzhenitsyn appeals in order to refute them. Rather, the novelist contents himself with pointing out in every instance the particular fact each lie attempts to conceal. Confronted with such empirical falsehoods, the reader probes for a deeper and more unified explanation of their origin.

About one third of the way into the novel Nerzhin, deeply disturbed by the conversation he has just had with his wife and depressed by the anxiety he feels about his future status, gives vent to embittered disillusionment and reacts cynically to Kondrashev-Ivanov's ideas (which, though naively expressed, still contain a good deal of truth and coincide fundamentally

[5]By Whitney in the Translator's Note to *The First Circle,* p. ix.

with Nerzhin's own deep-seated beliefs). At one point, thinking, perhaps, only of his wife's mention of divorce, Nerzhin remarks, "Yes, it's well known: circumstances determine consciousness" (XLII, 297). This basic premise, reflected on two levels, ethical and abstract, engenders two lies, psychological and metaphysical, that are related to each other like two sides of a coin. The dual nature of the Lie can be expressed schematically as follows. On the psychological level, this tag (which is of course not Nerzhin's own but an axiom of Marxism) means: "A person should act as his circumstances dictate"; on the metaphysical level: "Man *must* act as his circumstances determine." The metaphysical aspect will be examined later; the psychological, because it is depicted through the personalities and actions of people, emerges from the way the three major characters of *The First Circle* respond to truth and to falsehood.

Rubin has his own "absolute truth"—the false religion of Marxism-Leninism which allows no other competing truth and no other objectivity (LXI, 448). His is a collective, rather than a personal, moral system, rooted in the revealed "truth" about the flow of history. In his theory the Good is manifested by whatever and whoever represents the "progressive forces" of history. To these Rubin owes his personal faith and allegiance, a loyalty hardly shaken by how repulsive some of these forces appear in embodied form (XXXIII, 226-227). Rubin is, at the same time, a man of high ethical principles quite apart from the morality he favors for the State. But such "Party" morality nonetheless undermines his own and leads him to commit acts which he will later, inexplicably, regret (LXVI). While claiming complete objectivity in everything (VIII, 40; XXVIII, 190), he takes part, following Stalin's lead, in the falsification of what he knows to be true:

> Rubin was asked about today's news. But he was ashamed to review what had happened in December [the trial of Traicho Kostov]. After all, he could not behave like a non-Communist and abandon the hope of indoctrinating these people [the German prisoners]. And he could not try to explain to them, either, that in our complex age Socialist truth sometimes progresses in a roundabout, distorted way. Therefore he had to choose for them—for the sake of history, just as subconsciously he made selections for himself—only those current events which indicated the main road, neglecting those which obscured it (III, 14).

Thus, like his Master, Rubin deliberately falsifies reality both for others and for himself. (But the truth will out: the Germans listen to the BBC.)

Rubin's absolutist brand of "truth" is shown to lead to many dangers—not only to the atrocities in which he has already become implicated before his arrest, but also, for example, to apostasy from popular faith; an example is for in his willingness to attempt to channel sincere religious convictions into an officially palatable pseudo-religion complete with "Civic Temples." But his absolutist framework drives him to much more serious offenses. Working to unmask the "reckless fellow" [whom Rubin "likes" (XXXIII, 226)] who had tried to warn Doctor Dobroumov of an imminent provocation by the régime, he dreams of founding a new science of phonoscopy, in which a man could be identified by his voice print as easily and as surely as by his fingerprints. The attempt to develop such a science proves only partly successful within the novel, but already Rubin and his free supervisor Roitman have begun to envision "a consolidated audio-library with voice prints of everyone who had at one time or another been under suspicion. Any criminal conversation would be recorded, compared, and the criminal would be caught straight off . . ." (LXXX, 588). Rubin knows very well from his own experience and from that of the men around him what sort of people arouse the suspicion of the Stalinist government and what sort of use will be made of the device he hopes to invent.[6] No wonder Nerzhin says that Rubin is blindfolded (VIII, 40), and the Dostoevskian Sologdin calls him "possessed" (LX, 442). Rubin is a man whose personality is split between heart and mind. With all his intellect and conviction he believes in Marxism as if it were a religion—in fact it is a religion for him, as Sologdin implies when he calls Rubin "a Biblical fanatic" (*ibid.*); at another point Rubin uses an explicitly religious analogy to justify himself: Luther's *"'Hier stehe ich! Ich kann nicht anders'"* (VIII, 40). But in his heart Rubin knows differently; he is dragged along in spite of his misgivings. He does have a conscience, and he suffers for it.

With Sologdin we might seem to be approaching a bit closer to the truth about the life of the spirit, but we are eventually deceived; he is Rubin's exact opposite and represents the other

[6]Though less improbable, it bears a rather close resemblance to the "psychoscope," a machine designed to read men's minds dreamt up by Vitia and Tolia, the two secret agents in Andrei Siniavskii's *The Trial Begins*.

extreme from blind dedication to a Cause. Like Rubin, Sologdin believes in "Absolute Truth" but for him the truth resides in himself: he is the bearer of Truth. The truth is important because *he* is important and in effect he embodies his own truth: "Multitudes do not constitute the foundation of the colossus of the human spirit. Only unique personalities, shining and separate, like singing stars strewn through the dark heaven of existence, carry within them supreme understanding" (LXI, 449). In glaring contrast to Rubin's fanatical and utopian Marxist collectivism, Sologdin takes pride in his Nietzschean individualism. He is fond of talking about Good and Evil and claims to be an absolutist, but he does so out of pride and rebellion; he judges reality using himself as a standard. Despite the transcendency which he thinks he accords to philosophical abstractions, they seem in fact to have no objective reality outside of or apart from himself. Even when we first meet him, we are told that

> his chief quirk was to utter some nonsensical, utterly wild opinion on every question, such as that prostitution is a moral good or that D'Anthès was right in his duel with Pushkin; and he would defend that opinion with inspired enthusiasm.... When he was accused of absurdity, he laughed heartily.... "We can't all have the same views and the same standards. What would happen? There would be no more argument, no exchange of opinion. It would bore a dog!" (XXIV, 156).

It is clear that he is not particularly interested in receiving anyone else's opinion but merely in developing his own or in demonstrating his intellectual superiority. Truth is really a matter of profound indifference to him—he likes to play with it in order to keep from being bored or to sharpen his mind. On the grounds of "upholding the truth" he draws Rubin into a violent debate which, at the outset at least, he views essentially as an aristocratic game—a "duel" with words (LX, 440). This attitude exposes Sologdin's ultimate opportunism, of which Rubin rightly accuses him. Selflessly devoted to an overriding ideal (albeit a false one), Rubin sees through Sologdin's babble about the higher claims of the spirit—it amounts to a more refined egoism and eventually to individual license: the imperative of one's own personal right is masked beneath Sologdin's spiritual and moral élitism. When offered an ethically dubious opportunity to secure his release from incarceration (and to force the authorities to acknowledge his superior ability), Sologdin grabs it; basking in Iakonov's admiration for his strength of will, he pontificates: "*Sa Majesté le Cas!* His Majesty Opportunity! Opportunity rarely passes close to us; one has to jump on its back in time, and squarely in the middle of its back!" (LXXIII, 534-535). Sologdin had started out with "good" intentions (he wanted only to test his intellect) and with a firm will to see his project through the "Final Inch" from every dimension, including the moral one. But when Iakonov shows him the street from his window and offers him a chance to be free, Sologdin's will to resist crumbles, as it did when he allowed himself to be seduced by Larisa Emina in the Design Office. In general, relations with women and traffic with the authorities serve as Solzhenitsyn's criteria whenever the psychological lie is explored; for Sologdin, circumstances do determine his ethics—he does not act against his interests in the long run. This attitude leads to the unconscious abrogation of his highly-prized free will: as Rubin or any other religious person might have told him, and as Dostoevsky shows us again and again through such characters as Svidrigailov, Stavrogin, and Kirillov whom Sologdin so admires (LX, 442), for the proud man free will is certain to degenerate into self-will. Like Kirillov,[7] Sologdin is bound sooner or later to express his self-will.

Gleb Nerzhin, by contrast, owes his perception of truth not only to his will to know it, but also to a certain mysterious faculty for apprehending it:

> Through some strange inward sense, Nerzhin had since adolescence been hearing a mute bell—all the groans, cries, shouts of the dying, carried by a steady, insistent wind away from human ears.... From the very first, the boy did not believe what he read [in *Izvestiia*]. He did not know why—his reason could not grasp it—but he could clearly see that it was all a lie.... Gleb was only a ninth grader... when he... read that Kirov had been killed. And suddenly, like a blinding light, it became clear to him that Stalin and no one else had killed Kirov. Because he was the only one who would profit by his death! A feeling of aching loneliness seized him—the grown men, crowded near him, did not understand that simple truth.... It was so overdone, so crude, so excessive, that only a stone ear could fail to hear the lie (XXXIV, 234-235).

This almost mystical ability to understand links him with reality, in spite of his much-touted skepticism. Nerzhin's skepticism ("And what is truth...? Can anyone really know what truth is?" etc. XXVIII, 190 *et passim*) is by nature episte-

[7]See Dostoevsky, *The Devils,* Part Three, Book Six, Chapter 2; I will not reiterate Dostoevsky's reasoning here. Such bondage of the will is an important component of the traditional Christian concept of sin.

mological, *not* metaphysical; it derives from a profound respect for truth, and from the wish to avoid Sologdin's mistake of arrogating it to his own purpose. Nerzhin's epistemological uncertainly contrasts sharply with Ruska Doronin's authentic skepticism and cynicism: "All history is one continuous pestilence. There is no truth and there is no illusion. There is nowhere to appeal and nowhere to go" (XIV, 78). Even Nerzhin is disturbed by Doronin's remark, and feels obliged to caution him against undue skepticism on the ground that it entails a loss of will and renders action impossible.[8] Nerzhin, then, disbelieves not the existence of truth but the possibility of one man's grasping it in its totality without reducing it to an expression of his own personality. He is more properly a seeker in the grand nineteenth century Russian tradition; this is precisely the view of both Rubin and Sologdin (LXI, 448). Truth is so great, Nerzhin realizes, that it eludes man's attempt to say something definitive about it as a whole, except in aphorisms like those of Spiridon. It is this deep personal reverence for truth that allows him to approach it, whereas Rubin and Sologdin, in their proud certainty of possessing it, violate it utterly.

For Nerzhin, truth resides in one's conscience, in one's heart of hearts. He knows this by virtue of his mystical disposition as well as through grim experience.

> This is how I learned to behave in so-called normal life. I had no idea what good and evil were, and whatever was allowed seemed fine to me. But the lower I sink into this inhumanly cruel world, the more I respond to those who, even in such a world, speak to my conscience.... If you know when you die that you haven't been a complete bastard, that's at least some satisfaction (LXXXI, 600).

Conscience is what he has learned to refine in prison, and in prison is where he manifests it. When "he should have lied... he could not find the strength to lie" to Simochka (XII, 68). Nerzhin preserves his integrity in this most difficult of trials, exercising and maintaining his free will while Sologdin forfeits his. Similarly, he retains the strength not to lie, when he "should" have, and refuses Iakonov's offer of earning an early release by working in cryptography. In prison he discovers integrity, friendship, and (spiritual) freedom

[8]He need not have worried about the depth of Ruska's commitment—Ruska says he believes in being true not to a theory but to a woman (XIV, 79). Yet it is precisely the opportunity for romance that he forfeits (along with his life, presumably) by refusing to comply with the demands of the security officers.

(LIII, 370). No wonder Nadia tells him, "It suits you.... Everything. Here. All of this. Being here" (XXXVII, 257). Nerzhin comes to realize that truth is what is felt in the heart unalterably, irrevocably, eternally to be so. This is the "simple truth" (XXXIV, 235)—as Saint-Exupéry's Fox tells the Little Prince, *"Voici mon secret. Il est très simple: on ne voit bien qu'avec le coeur. L'essentiel est invisible pour les yeux.... Les hommes ont oublié cette verité."*[9]

We do not propose to recount Innokentii's long and tortuous journey from life to death and from illusion to truth. Let us just mention some of the truths he discovers, for in a short but intense period of suffering he duplicates Nerzhin's thinking process with regard to a few essentials, almost in the same way that he quickly learns to tie up his trousers with his shoelaces, unconsciously imitating many prisoners before him (LXXXIII, 623). First of all: "Up to then the truth for Innokentii had been: you have only one life. Now he came to sense a new law... : you also have only one conscience. And just as you cannot recover a lost life, you cannot recover a wrecked conscience" (LV, 399). Secondly: "He had had money, good clothes, esteem, women, wine, travel, but at this moment he would have hurled all those pleasures into the nether world for justice and truth... and nothing more" (LXXXIV, 630). Innokentii discovers that the most precious as well as ultimately the most pleasurable thing is truth, or as Khorobrov is fond of saying, "Better bread with water than pie with trouble" (LXXXVII, 669). He also learns that understanding entails sacrifices: one cannot always have every pleasure as well as truth, or a full life as well as an inviolate conscience. And he has finally realized that truth and conscience are more necessary to man than pleasure or even life itself. This realization is identical with Nerzhin's and sums up the central *ethical* theme of the novel; it constitutes what may be called Solzhenitsyn's psychological or pragmatic truth: Man should act as his conscience dictates, not as his circumstances imply or suggest. Only through voluntary and rigorous subjection of his desires or advantages to his own moral values can he achieve perfect freedom and purity of action. The mode of action is self-sacrifice; it is not only possible, but indispensable. The reality and practicality of self-sacrifice constitute complete denial of the psychological lie of Stalinism.

[9]Antoine de Saint-Exupéry, *Le Petit Prince,* XXI.

Just as practical freedom of action is the goal which the psychological lie obstructs, so the reality of free will is the philosophical category that the metaphysical lie denies. It is not surprising that a novelist concerned in part with depicting imprisonment should pay such close attention to the meaning of freedom. Metaphysical deceit deals with this very concept, vitiates it, and deforms the general world view of Soviet society.

In the last chapter of the novel several of the most conscientious zeks—including Gerasimovich, Nerzhin, Doronin, and Khorobrov—are loaded into a van marked MEAT in four languages and are removed from the sharashka. As the van moves through the city, a French journalist from a "progressive" newspaper notices it and accepts the label at its face value; he then decides to mention the truck in a forthcoming article. This entire episode portrays the Great Lie: it represents in a sense the source of all the other falsehoods revealed in the novel. As the greatest slander of Russia, socialism, and mankind, it is exactly what Solzhenitsyn sets out to refute in *The First Circle* by an ingenious use of symbols and ideas delineated in conversations scattered throughout the book.

On the most basic level, the meat truck loaded with living men merely suggests something we already know: that Stalin treats human beings like meat. The operation of the truck only confirms this impression: Nerzhin, after glimpsing what is written on the sides of the van,

> pushed through the narrow entrance door and the still narrower door beyond it, stepped on someone's feet, dragged his suitcase and bag past someone's knees, and sat down. . . . The rest of the space . . . was a single communal mousetrap, a low metal box into which, according to the norm, exactly twenty persons could be put. But if the steel door was forced shut with four jackboots, more than twenty could be jammed in. . . . When the Black Maria was full, other people and other people's possessions pressed against their wedged-in knees and their cramped, numb feet . . . the two guards escorting the prisoners . . . sat jammed in with their legs crossed beneath them (LXXXVII, 670-671).

The policy then is not limited to the prisoners; it is more general—applicable to the guards and hence (metaphorically) to free society as well. This universal contempt for humanity is apparent in the manhandling of Innokentii at the time of his arrest: "Having pulled back Innokentii's cheeks with dirty hands, as if he were a horse up for auction, and having looked under his eyelids, and thus determined that nothing had been hidden under his tongue, in his cheek, or in his eyes, the guard forced Innokentii's head back hard, in order to see inside his nostrils" (LXXXIII, 618). It is not necessary to continue this description of methodical dehumanization. It culminates in the concentration camps.

The meat truck may also reflect Solzhenitsyn's attitude toward Soviet Marxism. The four languages in which the word "Meat" is emblazoned on the sides of the van are mentioned twice (LXXXVII, 670, 673), beyond the demands of factual observation. There are several ways to interpret this. The van may be viewed as another instance of a Potemkin village (as in "Buddha's Smile," LIV) successfully staged for the benefit of the West, or as the familiar spectacle of Soviet Marxism masquerading under the guise of benevolent humanism. The latter aspect is the more important one. Communist food trucks rolling off to feed the hungry masses represent an ideologically powerful symbol, yet one that conceals the reality of monstrous crimes. Solzhenitsyn's concluding chapter recalls a similar and exactly parallel image from Dostoevsky. While interpreting the Apocalypse, Lebedev (the buffoon-cum-prophet in *The Idiot*) complains:

> [They say] "the rumble of carts bringing bread to starving humanity is perhaps better than spiritual peace."... But, vile man that I am, I do not believe in the carts that bring bread to humanity! For carts bringing bread to all humanity without a moral basis for that action, may quite deliberately exclude a considerable part of humanity from the enjoyment of what they bring, which has happened already.... A friend of humanity whose moral principles are shaky is a destroyer of humanity.[10]

There is hardly any need to dwell either on Stalin's amorality or destructiveness. But in *The First Circle* the significance of the quadrilingual sign on the meat truck extends further to encompass the international appeal of Soviet communism. What Solzhenitsyn attacks here is the very nature and essence of materialistic philosophy itself. This philosophy, to be sure, has supplanted the transcendent moral grounds upon which a Dostoevsky would have liked to see bread distributed and so, in his terms at least, caused moral principles to be shaky in the first place. But more important, the Marxist premises of dialectical materialism and economic determinism are under

[10]Dostoevsky, *The Idiot,* trans. by David Magarshack (Baltimore: Penguin Books, 1970), p. 413 (Part Three, Chapter 4).

attack in their own right for the harm they have brought about by denying free will. If defects in human society are due to the material environment rather than to profound flaws in man's nature, then any efforts to change man by forcibly altering his environment can be defended on the ground that they achieve greater happiness and harmony for the majority. It was Dostoevsky's lifework to expose this fallacy and so we shall not discuss it further; but it should be noted that Solzhenitsyn, like Dostoevsky, is showing that a conception of man and human society as materially determined is ultimately equivalent to reducing human beings to meat. He achieves this by endowing a realistic episode with symbolic value. It is Marxist deterministic materialism that stands discredited by the Stalinist meat van.

A note of caution is due here. To look upon man as meat is not a complete lie; he does have a body, after all. Furthermore, when the authorities rely exclusively on material means to mold and control men, they can at times manage to turn human beings into creatures whose lives are shaped solely by material needs. Such an outcome figures in Solzhenitsyn's portrayal of Soviet society; it is, after all, the avowed aim of the concentration camps, depicted in *One Day in the Life of Ivan Denisovich*. This is also the point of a highly important scene at the end of *The First Circle* when men about to be shipped off to the camps endlessly contemplate the quality of their food in anticipation of future deprivations.

> Here is a fat rich soup, a little thin to be sure, but with a meat flavor that one can taste; I am putting into my mouth this spoonful, and this one, and this one, with the speck of fat and the white fibers of meat; the warm liquid will pass down my esophagus into my stomach; and my blood and muscles are already celebrating in anticipation of new reinforcements and new strength (LXXXVII, 668).

The men continue to discuss their food virtually until they are loaded into the truck. Meat indeed. Can human beings really be transformed into wholly material creatures if a system seeks to control them solely through their material nature? Or is this possible only occasionally? The incident involving the soup is followed almost immediately by Doronin's shouts of defiance to his comrades. Thus, the author powerfully implies that the foregoing scene expresses only a half-truth about mankind.

This point is reiterated explicitly in Nerzhin's earlier argument with Kondrashev-Ivanov who is almost certainly speaking for the author:

> Kondrashev-Ivanov: Our Russian nature exults and rages and doesn't give way before the Tatar hoofs.
> Nerzhin: . . . And in camp? In exchange for seven ounces of black bread they demand of us not only our spiritual harmony, but also the last remnants of conscience.
> K-I: Never! Never! No camp must break a man's spirit.
> N: Perhaps it must not, but it does! You haven't been in camp yet, so don't judge. You don't know how they break us there. . . . Yes, it's well known: circumstances determine consciousness.
> K-I: No! No! No! No! That would be degrading. What is one to live for then? And, tell me, why are people who love each other faithful when they're separated? After all, circumstances dictate that they betray one another![11] And how do you explain the difference in people who have fallen into the same conditions, even in the same camp? (XLII, 296-297).

The perpetration of a false world view founded upon the denial of free will is only part of the damage wrought by the metaphysical lie. The meat truck's final and most sweeping insinuation signifies that man is a totally material being, that he has no spiritual nature and no immortal soul. It represents a denial of man's immortality, and this denial constitutes the fundamental metaphysical Lie on which all other lies are based. On this alone rests the elder Makarygin's "tobacco altar" and his "*Fumo, ergo sum*" (LVIII, 420);[12] this alone makes possible Galakhov's indifference to artistic immortality and this justifies his colleagues to whom "their present situations were what mattered, how things went for them during their lives. The hell with immortality, they said; isn't it more important to influence the course of events in the present?" (LVII, 417). Let not "immortality" here be understood in too narrow a sense; the passage quoted above is pervaded by religious overtones. For Pasternak, immortality was simply a stronger way of saying "life"; for the more orthodox Solzhenitsyn, it also signifies "spirit." The individual's contempt for his immortality—that is, for his spiritual nature—leads directly to *spiritual death* which is after all the desired end of materialism. For according to Nerzhin: "The

[11]Sologdin, happily married but bound by his own self-will, becomes (paradoxically for him) *determined* by exterior circumstance—that is, by Larisa's proposition and by his desire—in this most rigorous of personal tests; he loses in practice his free will. Nerzhin, on the other hand, will illustrate, by denying himself a relationship with Simochka, how people who are in love do not betray each other when circumstances seem to prescribe it.

[12]An amusing and provocative pun, especially in the context of infernal imagery. It is conceivably unintentional.

happiness of incessant victory, the happiness of fulfilled desire, the happiness of success and total satiety—*that* is suffering! That is spiritual death, a sort of unending moral pain" (VIII, 40). *Unending moral pain:* is not this precisely the Christian definition of Hell? In fact, from the viewpoint of Soviet society as presented in *The First Circle,* this is exactly what Stalin has endeavored to achieve. It is, of course, the central metaphor of the novel: a *living death.*

But the Great Lie is refuted by a multitude of things. First of all, by the mystical joy of existence:

> When I [Nerzhin] was free and used to read books in which wise men pondered the meaning of life or the nature of happiness, I understood very little of those passages.... But the meaning of life? We live—that's the meaning. Happiness? When things are going very well, that's happiness, everyone knows that. Thank God for prison! It gave me the chance to think. In order to understand the nature of happiness we first have to analyze satiety.... Satiety depends not at all on *how much* we eat, but on *how* we eat. It's the same way with happiness.... I have a real conversation or read an honest page and I'm on the crest of a wave. I haven't had any real life for many years, but I've forgotten about that.... I lie there on my upper bunk and stare at the ceiling. It is very close, it's bare, the plasterwork is bad—and I tremble with the utter joy of existence (VIII, 38-39).

When challenged, Kondrashev-Ivanov stresses the point that what is real is more than what can be perceived by the senses:

> But isn't it rash to believe that one can see and know reality precisely as it is? Particularly *spiritual* reality? Who sees and knows it? (LIII, 375).

In opposing the dictum that circumstances determine consciousness, he declares:

> A human being possesses from his birth a certain essence, the nucleus, as it were, of this human being. His "I." And it is still uncertain which forms which: whether life forms the man or man, with his strong spirit, forms life! Because he has something to measure himself against, something he can look to. Because he has in him an image of perfection which in rare moments suddenly emerges before his spiritual gaze (XLII, 297).

For Kondrashev-Ivanov, this perfection is symbolized by the Castle of the Holy Grail. The doctrine of the *immortality* of the *soul* signifies by a combination of these two ideas that a divine spirit is both eternally existent and yet personally present to each individual—it postulates freedom from matter, potency of conscience, and a higher spiritual reality. The concept of personal immortality, essential to respect for man, thus embraces every level of Truth that Stalinist society has rejected.

This is the message that emerges from Solzhenitsyn's epic account of the sufferings of political prisoners under Stalin: spiritual reality does exist, and not just in the abstract, but *within* the heart and conscience of each man. Man is decidedly not clay in the hands of those who have the power to mold him. He is not a wholly material being; he has a spiritual nature that exterior force cannot violate. And within the depth of his spiritual being, affected only by his conscience and his freely chosen system of values, supreme beyond the power of coercion, he is perfectly free to decide questions of moral conduct—and to realize his spiritual potential in its totality.

Cancer Ward: Of Fate and Guilt

BY HELEN MUCHNIC

The time is 1955. Stalin has been dead two years. There are rumors of important changes in the seat of government, of the possible liberation of political prisoners; it may be that for a man like Oleg Kostoglotov freedom is in sight. In his thirty-odd years he has experienced the most barbarous phases of Soviet history. Born in 1920, drafted into the army in his last year of school, he has gone through war, prison—for making disrespectful remarks about Stalin—a slave-labor camp, exile, and a painful illness from which he has not expected to recover. His family perished in the siege of Leningrad. In the slave-labor camp, he underwent a crude operation for cancer, the illness returned in his place of exile, and *Cancer Ward* is the story of his two-month stay in the hospital at which he arrived toward the end of January.

He is the most complex of Solzhenitsyn's heroes, as stubbornly courageous and independent as Gleb Nerzhin of *The First Circle,* as staunch and dignified as Ivan Denisovich, and more diverse in his interests than they, more curious, more contemplative. An intellectual by inclination, whose formal schooling was cut short by war and prison, he has an avid, alert, inquiring mind. In school he had had a year of geophysics; between soldiering and prison, a partial course in geodesy.

In prison he gathered bits of knowledge by listening to others, in labor camp managed to learn some Latin from a former classics instructor. Science is his major interest, but he is also sensitive to art, receptive to philosophic ideas, and concerned with policies of government. He is a humanist who trusts reason and has faith in the validity of experience. All doctrines, however loudly promulgated, all directives, however strictly enforced, all the beliefs that men profess are subject to his rational analysis and tested in the light of what he himself has learned to be true. "It's not education," he instructs the boy Demka, "but life that makes you smart." Read, by all means, learn all you can, but "trust your eyes, not your ears." His own eyes have given the lie to what his ears have heard, have seen great ideas falsified and debased, noble theories misused.

He is fearless, not because he has nothing to lose but because fearlessness is natural to him, an ingrained quality, a kind of habit to which his soul has grown accustomed. He has always said what he thought and done what seemed right. This accounts for his years of imprisonment and for the great scar that disfigures his face, earned in camp in defense of Japanese prisoners against the assaults of Russian hoodlums. "You see, Vera Kornil'evna, all I've suffered in life was mostly caused by my devotion to democracy. I tried to spread democracy in the army, that is, I was impertinent to my superiors." He speaks of himself half humorously, sardonically, neither boastfully nor in self-pity, quite unaware of his own heroism, the nobility and moral strength he takes for granted.

Like the heroes of Tolstoy's and Dostoevsky's novels, Kostoglotov is a rebel who questions and opposes what the majority of his countrymen accept, an independent spirit whose mind has retained its purity despite the inhuman callousness that has permeated his life, the perversions of elementary decency from which he has suffered. In the ward he incites men to question their assumptions and now and then succeeds in showing them what they really are. But his rebellion is both more perilous and more restricted than that of his nineteenth century predecessors, more perilous because it brands him not just as an eccentric, like Pierre Bezukhov or Konstantin Levin, but as a traitor; more restricted because it challenges palpable, immediate, existing evils, not like Raskol'nikov's or

Ivan Karamazov's, the root assumptions of ethics and religion. Tolstoy's and Dostoevsky's men defied the hypocrisies of privilege and the grounds of belief, Kostoglotov defies a specific political tyranny. He is up against a structure of absolutism that masquerades as freedom and a system of wily deception that locks the mind while pretending to give it scope, up against unprincipled acts represented as valor—confronted, in short, by barefaced lies to justify injustice, not by the mysteries and errors of belief. He belongs to Solzhenitsyn's world of twisted concepts whereby what once was vice is now called virtue, where to oppose crime is to be punished as a criminal, a world where men are officially encouraged, or even forced, to lie, spy, and denounce, so that even simple honesty requires exceptional courage. At great cost to himself, he struggles to break through the ambient deceit of propaganda and moral laxity. Truth is the pivot of his thinking, scrupulous honesty of his actions.

The debates he provokes have the heat and flavor, if not the subtlety, of medieval disputations about The True Faith, and are highly dramatic, carried on as they are by desperately sick men who argue bitterly, discussing the purpose and value of life, and the essence of whose argument is not politics but ethics. Tolstoy's short story, *What Men Live By,* finds its way to their ward. Kostoglotov reads it and urges it on the others. What do men live by? A problem so abstruse has never occurred to them before and under ordinary circumstances, with all they need to know and believe dinned into their heads, they would have thought it silly. Now, however, in their terrified, uncertain state, it appears neither unnatural nor irrelevant. And it is highly unsettling to these men who are enduring pain, thinking of their tumors, submitting to injections, blood transfusions, radium therapy, whose minds are almost wholly concentrated on their afflicted bodies. Laboriously, inadequately, they grope for answers. But to Solzhenitsyn they themselves are the answer. "Read? Why should I read? We'll all kick the bucket soon," grumbles Efrem Podduev, the most disconsolate and bitter among them. "That's why," retorts Kostoglotov, "Hurry or you'll have kicked the bucket before you've read it." This is the point. Set in the context of imminent death, *Cancer Ward* is a drama of mortality, a race with time, not for life but for an understanding of life, a drama played out by men in a state of enforced immobility, its action propelled by opinions, convictions, prejudices, emotions, in a struggle as gripping as physical combat, for the salvation of something more precious than life itself, something to be salvaged from grim existence and preserved beyond it.

Kostoglotov's opposite number is Pavel Nikolaevich Rusanov, with whose arrival at the hospital the novel opens, setting the tone of sly, impermeable meanness against which the story unfolds. At first his pompous shallowness, complaints, demands for special treatment seem only ridiculous, but presently as his past unfolds, they appear less innocuous, until one recognizes them as the traits of a thoroughly depraved character, who is not merely unpleasant but frightening and sinister. A bureaucrat of a particularly vicious kind, he has made his way in the service of Stalin's spying apparatus, devising elaborate methods to intimidate and entrap innocent people. He is enormously pleased with himself, delighted with his shrewdness and patriotism, proud of his whole "purposeful, vigorous and splendid" life. But suddenly, he is shocked and alarmed. A thankless country, on the evidence of newspapers, has forgotten Stalin's greatness; and it seems that the cases of political prisoners may be brought under review. Ten years earlier, Rusanov had managed to get a friend and neighbor of his imprisoned on trumped-up charges in order to get possession of his apartment. Now he fears a confrontation and possible disgrace. He even has a nightmare. But his daughter comes down from Moscow with the happy report that the new edict applies to offenses of only two years back and that her dear father is, therefore, safe, since his victim has been incarcerated a full decade and, most probably, is no longer alive. Rusanov's anxieties are laid to rest, he breathes more freely, and takes pleasure in describing to less fortunate men the luxurious appointments of his living quarters: they are a mark of his success and a fine illustration of the great Marxist principle that "being determines consciousness."

Rusanov is the type of greedy, self-satisfied little man one has met before in Russian literature; he strutted about in the shape of Gogol's grotesques and wormed his way around the great characters of Dostoevsky's novels. To Gogol' he was a figure of fun, to Dostoevsky a specimen of insidious evil. In Solzhenitsyn's unscrupulous and inhuman society his pettiness has greater objective power. The victims of Stalin's Rusanovs are in every corner of Russia, in every walk of life. And the worst of it is that this universal horror has become so customary as to pass unrecognized. A habit of non-thinking has obliterated truth and perpetuates the evil.

Of this habit Rusanov is a prime example. Unquestioning, ununderstanding, with visceral ardor, he supports the commonplaces of official dogma: "what is most important is to feel oneself a Man with a capital M. To be an optimist," "certain questions have been decided once for all" on the incontrovertible authority of Comrades Lenin, Stalin and Gorkii, and anyone who opposes them is guilty of "ideological sabotage." "Sheer religious rubbish!" he shouts at Efrem Podduev on whom Tolstoy's story has had a shattering effect. "You've read too much slush, Comrade Podduev, you've disarmed yourself ideologically. You keep harping on about that stupid moral perfection!" "What's so terrible about moral perfection?" Kostoglotov wants to know, and why keep a man from thinking about the meaning of life "when he himself is on the borderline between life and death?" As for Rusanov's vaunted ideology, Kostoglotov hammers away, "What does our philosophy of life boil down to? 'Oh, life is so good!. . . Life, I love you. Life is for happiness!'. . . Any animal can say as much without our help, any hen, cat, or dog." In his words, thoughts, actions—in his entire being, Kostoglotov epitomizes the struggle between the bestiality of Rusanov's official "ideology" and his own concept of what it means to be a man.

He receives support, in a somewhat grisly but eloquent fashion, from a patient who arrives toward the end of his stay at the hospital, a tall, stooped man who sits silently in his corner and, like a huge owl, fixes his big, swollen, round eyes on the others in the room. He moves with difficulty. "His walk was oddly unnatural . . . He hobbled away . . . reminding one of a large bird whose wings have been unevenly clipped to prevent it from taking off into the air." And this indeed is what Shulubin has become, a creature meant for flight, but, maimed and ungainly, weighed down by disease and a tormenting conscience, able only to limp and crawl on earth. A graduate of the foremost agricultural institute in Russia, the Timiriazev Academy, he lectured at the University of Moscow and when, on orders from above, professors, charged with propounding subversive doctrines, were arrested by the dozen, he saved himself by "confessing" and "renouncing" his "mistakes," changed his field to biology, descended from professor to assistant, from assistant to librarian and, as a librarian, burned books on official command. "Into the stove with all your genetics, leftist aesthetics, cybernetics, arithmetic. . . ." Why did he lie and debase himself? For the sake of wife and children and to save his own skin. His wife has died, his estranged children "spit on his soul," and he himself is about to undergo an operation which if he survives—and this is a big if—will leave him a loathsome cripple, unfit for human intercourse. But even if things had turned out differently, if his wife were still alive, his children loved him, and he was not smitten with a terrible disease, he has paid too high a price for what he thought was happiness. Happiness is a "mirage." To preserve it "he took books which were full of truth and burned them in the stove." And "as for the so-called happiness of future generations . . . who knows anything about it?"

For the sake of happiness, he, an old-time Bolshevik who fought in the Civil War, had turned traitor and, a cringing liar, applauded when his noblest comrades were condemned as "enemies of the people." Nor was he alone; the majority were like him. How was it that within ten years a whole nation changed from bravery to cowardice? Because, he answers, of "the herd instinct," to call it by its most "refined" term, "the fear of remaining alone, *outside the community*." It wasn't new. Francis Bacon, in the sixteenth century, had described it in his discourse on Idols. As he expounds them to Kostoglotov, Shulubin barely mentions the Idols of the Tribe and Cave but dwells on the more applicable Idols of the Theater and Market Place, "the voluntary acceptance," as he defines them, of the "authoritative opinions of others" and of "other peoples' errors." This, of course, is what Kostoglotov's own, untutored mind has already drawn from experience. "Voluntary acceptance," docility of spirit, swallowing whole and parroting "authoritative opinions" is what he has been denouncing with passion, and it is his championship of the right to skeptical and independent thought that has earned him Shulubin's confidence.

The quiet talk of these two men, perched like a pair of wounded birds on a hospital bench in the pale sunshine of early spring, is a recapitulation of the cardinal points at issue in the novel: the nature of truth, the place of the individual in Soviet society, the meaning of happiness, the value of life, the tragedy of guilt. He has never been in prison, says Shulubin, but his life has been harder than Kostoglotov's: "The people who drown at sea or dig the soil or search for water in the desert don't have the hardest lives. The man with the hardest life is the man who walks out of his house every day and bangs his head against the top of the door because it's too low."

Kostoglotov has not only escaped this fate in the past, he sees to it that he will not suffer it in the future. His final decision, unpolitical, wholly personal, involves more subtly and deeply than any action or decision of any other character, a sense of the values that men live by. It is the crux of the book, and it is centered on love and sex. Not only has Kostoglotov faced death in war and prison, he has known what it means to have died and been reborn. He was moribund when he came to the hospital, a hopeless shadow of a man who had been given but a few weeks to live. But, amazingly, he is on his way to recovery and he is not sure, he says jokingly, whether resurrection is what he wants. In death one is like a stone or tree, blessed with the indifference of matter; but life confronts one with passions, desires, and the necessity to choose.

He has discovered that the hormone therapy that is suppressing his tumor is also destroying his virility. Should he pay this price, he who does not ask for a long life, the limit of whose ambition is "to live just a little while without guards and without pain"? His doctors assume that there is nothing more precious than life, that "one should cling to life at any cost," but in camp Kostoglotov learned that the price of life can be too high, that it is not worth "betrayal or destruction of good and helpless people" nor "bootlicking and flattery." Injury to others and self-abasement are too much to pay for life. Now another price is asked of him. "To preserve his life, should a man pay everything that gives it color, scent and excitement? Can one accept a life of digestion, respiration, muscular and brain activity—and nothing more? Become a walking blueprint? Is not this an exorbitant price? . . . Should one pay?" Contradictory answers are given him by two women in the hospital to whom he has been strongly attracted, the nurse Zoia, who appeals to him physically and the doctor Vera

Gangart, Vega as he comes to think of her, who stirs him to more complicated and deeper emotions.

It is from Zoia he discovers the nature of the injections she has been instructed to give him; and she has asked herself whether he might not, after all, be the man to provide that stability and continuity she has hoped for in her sexually disordered life. A minor but significant episode defines Kostoglotov's feelings for Zoia. For the sake of being alone with her, he helps her fill the oxygen balloon required by a man in the last stages of lung cancer. The task means nothing to them; the secluded corner where they are at work is a trysting place and while the balloon is being inflated, he clasps her passionately to himself and they forget all about it, barely managing to turn off the tap before it bursts. Even then they delay, while Oleg proposes marriage and she reveals to him the nature of the prescribed injections. At last

> They walked up the stairs, holding not hands but the balloon, now inflated like a football. . . .
>
> On the landing the yellow, shrivelled patient . . . was sitting up in his folding bed. . . . He had stopped coughing and was beating his forehead against his raised knees as if they were a wall. . . .
>
> Today might be the day he was going to die, Oleg's brother and neighbor, abandoned and hungry for sympathy. Perhaps if Oleg sat by his bed and spent the night there, he could provide some solace for his last hours.
>
> All they did was give him the oxygen balloon and walk on. These last few cubic centimeters of air in the doomed man's balloon had been no more than a pretext for going off into a corner together and getting to know each other's kisses.

The rapt selfishness of physical desire could hardly be more impressively conveyed. Furthermore, since life without sex is meaningless to Zoia, she disobeys the doctor's orders and withholds the injections, choosing, that is, without compunction, a course that, for pleasure's sake, is bound to renew his suffering and shorten his life.

When a few days later Kostoglotov tells Vega how he feels about the treatment which she herself has approved, she is deeply shocked. To her a man is more than an instrument of sensual gratification, and although she too has dreamed of happiness with Kostoglotov, it is not in Zoia's way. Her ideal of life is opposed to Zoia's, and Kostoglotov has confirmed her in it, has seemed to justify her long years of solitude after the death of the boy she once loved who was killed in the war. And now to his cry "Why bother to save such a life as mine?

What use will it be?" she finds the strength to answer, "If everyone thought your way, who could we live with? What would we live for? Would we be able to live at all?" He cannot have spoken for himself, she exclaims, he must have borrowed someone else's notions. Her words have a momentous effect on Kostoglotov. "In a crazy parabola . . . high over the wastelands of his life, one wasteland after the other," they throw him back "to some land of long ago . . . the country of his childhood."

Their conversation takes place while Vega is giving Kostoglotov a transfusion of blood, and a small detail on this occasion is a telling contrast to the episode with Zoia. As he lies trustfully on the table—and for him, who for so long has had to be watchful and suspicious, "to be able to trust, to give himself to trust" is a great luxury—in the quiet room, so quiet that he can hear the faint ringing of the bubbles in the glass balloon from which the life-giving blood is entering his arm, Kostoglotov watches a bright patch of light on the ceiling above him. As Vega's indignant words send him flying back to his childhood, he remembers some popular books on the physiology of love he had read as a boy, books of "consistent, logical, irrefutable materialism," and discovers that she too has read them and that on her as on him they have had the same effect of vacuity and desolation. Oleg, still gazing at the ceiling, sees how "The strange patch of pale sunlight . . . suddenly began to ripple. A flashing cluster of silver spots appeared from somewhere. They began to move about," and realizes that this rippling, airy circle is none other than the reflection of a puddle outside the window. Bright and lovely, it is like his feeling for Vega or, for that matter, like the experience of any genuine human love, whatever its physiological basis might be, and indeed of any truly human relationship, and also of a man's conception of what he is and what he lives by.

The same distinction between "irrefutable materialism" and spiritual values or ideal aspirations holds true everywhere. It is implicit in Shulubin's discourse on his theory of "ethical socialism," a socialism not built on "an abundance of material goods" but on a society in which "ethical demands" would determine "all relationships": principles of government, education, scientific research. And it is most eloquent in the meditation of the wise old Doctor Oreshchenkov, whose aged body requires frequent periods of rest and whose mind craves moments of "silent immobility," of undirected "floating thoughts":

> At such moments an image of the whole meaning of existence—his own during the long past and the short future ahead, that of his late wife, of his young granddaughter and of everyone in the world—came to his mind. The image he saw did not seem to be embodied in the work or activity which occupied them, which they believed was central in their lives, by which they were known to others. The meaning of existence was to preserve unspoiled, undisturbed and undistorted the image of eternity with which each person is born.
>
> Like a silver moon in a calm, still pond.

Like the patch of light on Kostoglotov's ceiling. And like Shulubin's murmuring, between life and death after his operation, "not all of me shall die."

From the first, in appearance, manner, gestures, Vega has seemed to Kostoglotov an embodiment of light, grace, gentleness, and brightness. She revives his faith in something other than the reality of universal grossness that has been his lot, in the purity he has known in childhood and the beauty he has always found in art and nature. Zoia's fascination dissolves in his feeling for Vega. And Vega, for her part, is drawn to him by the very qualities he values in himself, qualities that Zoia can neither see nor appreciate. Each has roused energy and interest in the other, made his tasks absorbing, converted duty and endurance to delight. Why, then, does Kostoglotov renounce this enchanting woman who has transformed mere existence into life? The last two chapters, in which the steps to his difficult decision are traced, bring together the novel's major themes in a poignant resolution that is like the finale of a beautiful and sombre symphony.

Kostoglotov's last day in the story is a reversal of the first. As he walks out of the hospital before sunrise on a morning in early spring, everything speaks of life as on that night in January it had spoken of death. He had dragged himself there "hopeless, despondent . . . soaked by the January rain, expecting only to die." Now "he stood still" on the porch and "breathed in."

> It was young air, still and undisturbed. He looked out at the world—it was new and turning green. He raised his head. The sky unfolded, pink from the sun rising somewhere unseen. . . . It was the morning of creation. The world had been created anew for one reason only, to be given back to Oleg. "Go out and live," it seemed to say.

He smiles "at the sky and the trees," and decides to go off in search of a flowering apricot tree, just as on that January night he had trudged across town, hoping before he died to see a performance of *The Sleeping Beauty,* which was announced on a poster that had caught his eye. He did not see it, for the program had been changed. Now again he is in pursuit of beauty, but not in expectation of death but of life. And this time he is rewarded. He comes upon the "miracle" he had "planned on finding . . . pink and transparent . . . a rosy, weightless balloon." The whole spring day indeed, which he had never expected to see, is a miracle and a gift, "an extra portion of life like the piece of bread they used to pin onto the main ration with a pine twig to make up the weight; it was part of the ration, but a separate bit." Radiant with the joy of freedom, he makes the most of it. Passing from one precious adventure to another, he examines a photographer's display, goes into an old-fashioned wine shop, a pharmacy, a telegraph office, treats himself to tea, shashlick, ice cream, a glass of wine. Everything is new, everything is interesting: the passersby, the Oriental houses, the shops; and the thought that "there were many other joys in store for him" keeps ringing in his mind like a refrain.

He goes to the zoo. And this visit to the kingdom of imprisoned beasts is a summary of his life and an epitome of life itself. When in their first affectionate encounter, Zoia told him her name, she said that like "zoo" it came from the Greek word for "life." Now in Kostoglotov's reflective mood the zoo is a painful representation of humanity as he has known it: the squirrel running frantically to its death inside the wheel from which it does not have the sense to escape; the spiral-horned goat on a high rock, at the edge of a precipice, "like a continuation of the rock itself," motionless as a statue; the peacock and the pheasants, their brilliant plumage a feast of color; the vultures in a cage too low for flight, "great, gloomy birds . . . in torment, spreading their wings and beating them although there was nowhere to fly"; the grizzly bear with just room enough to turn round and round, and the black bear that hangs with its forepaws on the grilled cage, the white markings of its chest like a priest's chain with a cross. "What other way did it have," thinks Kostoglotov, "of showing its despair?" There are reptiles; and among beasts of prey, the hateful tiger with yellow eyes that, through a veiled but clear allusion, is recognizable as an image of Stalin; there is "a lonely, thoughtful chimpanzee with swollen eyes, hands dangling between his knees," like Shulubin. Worst of all, there is an empty cage marked "Macaque Rhesus," with a notice nailed to the plywood sign: "The little monkey that used to live here was blinded because of the senseless cruelty of one of the visitors. A wicked man threw tobacco into the Macaque Rhesus's eyes." Oleg is "struck dumb," sickened, and "as though the tobacco had been thrown into his own eyes," he wants to yell and roar across the whole zoo, "Why? . . . It's senseless! Why?" He makes for the exit to get away from these caged-in predators and victims, from this suffering and malice. And stops "in front of a miracle. After all that carniverous coarseness it was a miracle of spirituality: the Nilgai antelope, light brown, on fine, light legs, her head keen and alert but not in the least afraid. It stood close to the wire netting and looked at Oleg with its big, trustful and . . . gentle, yes, gentle eyes. The likeness was so true it was unbearable."

Throughout this day of gifts and wonders, there is one, Kostoglotov knows, that he desires above all others: to see Vega. She has invited him to come and he has waited for the appropriate moment. Now, impelled by the Nilgai antelope, he makes his way to her place, excited, fearful, delighted:

> It wasn't just those few blocks from the zoo that his heavy boots had tramped. He had walked the far-flung roads of his country for twice seven years. And now here he was, demobilized at last, at the very door where for those past fourteen years a woman had been silently waiting for him.

But Vega is not at home. A taciturn, suspicious woman barks out "She's gone . . . What are you waiting for, citizen?" On the veranda railing of her communal apartment, blankets, pillows, mattresses are hung out to dry in the sun. Oleg retreats from "this bastion of pillows . . . from this unassailable fortress" of bedding and gives away the bunch of violets he had bought for Vega to a pair of Uzbek schoolgirls. Pillows and mattresses are the reality of a world in which he has no place.

Earlier in the day he had already had an inkling of his estrangement from ordinary life. Propelled into a department store by a jostling crowd, he was stunned when a man requested a shirt not only by its own number but by the number of the collar too. His own world was one where men "rotted in trenches," were "thrown into mass graves," were "jolted from station to station in prison trucks," a world of men who "wore themselves out with picks, slaving away to be able to buy a patched-up quilt jacket," and here was one who remembered the number of his shirt collar, who would also know what to buy a woman in the section of costume jewelry, and before a full-length mirror would not, like Kostoglotov, be confronted by a worn, stooped, ragged tramp. The blankets and sheets are a more stern reminder of his alienation and deficiency, the realization that even the most spiritual, refined and ethereal woman, even Vega, must sleep in a bed, and that he does not belong there with her, that if she is proud of her fourteen years of loneliness, she has no conception of what torment a mere six months with him would be "together yet not together." He has no right to impose himself on her. So strong is the pull, nevertheless, that he makes one more pathetic, abortive attempt to return, then goes to the railway station, writes a note to Demka about the zoo, as he had promised, another one of grateful thanks to Zoia; and to Vega, a letter of renunciation in which he tells her for the first time that he loves and desires her and that this is the reason he is going away and will not come back.

Kostoglotov's decision is rational and magnanimous. It is a measure of his love and the crowning instance of the human ideal toward which the whole book has been directed, recalling all its discussions about the meaning of happiness and the purpose of life and all the dramatic examples of these. Kostoglotov himself in consenting at last to hormone therapy has already concluded that a man does not live primarily for sex. But to sacrifice another's happiness to his own inadequacy is another matter; and although it was Vega who had persuaded him, he cannot, in callous selfishness, take advantage of her generosity and inexperience; his conscience "forbids" him to see her again.

We last see Kostoglotov on the train, face down on the luggage rack where he has made himself comfortable for the journey "home" to Ush-Terek. His boots are dangling "toes down over the corridor like a dead man's," in the same position as on that first night when, in the passageway of the hospital, he had stretched out on a bench that was too short for him.

The similar posture brings the story around full circle. But between the beginning and the end, between the bench and the luggage rack, a whole society has passed through Oleg's mind, a whole world has been appraised, and although his boots are dangling down like a dead man's, he is far from dead. He has been resurrected both physically and spiritually, has come to a clear understanding of his role as a man in a miraculously beautiful and cruel world. On the bench in the hospital he was a helpless victim, prostrated by a blow of Fate. On the luggage rack in the train he is no longer merely pitiful; his posture now represents an act of will, a high-minded, responsible choice. He has become the hero of a characteristically Russian tragedy, low-keyed and noble.

More fully and clearly than any of his other heroes, Solzhenitsyn has created Oleg Kostoglotov in his own image, has made him live through his own most bitter experiences and given him his own voice and his own thoughts. Like his creator, Kostoglotov storms against the ways of a mendacious society where crimes are justified in the name of dubious laws, oppressions are sanctioned, obvious malpractices hypocritically vindicated, against all the glaring discrepancies between the theory of the Soviet State and the realities of Soviet life. His fury is directed not at his country but at the crimes against it, not at the principles on which it professes to stand, not at communism, but at the perversion of these principles, at willful misinterpretations of communism. With sickening clarity, time and again, Kostoglotov sees his own history repeated in the lives of others: mean denunciations, arrests, arbitrary evictions, imprisonments, humiliating physical privations, brutal assaults on the mind. He is angered by this savagery and horrified by men's blindness to it. The beasts in the zoo have grown so accustomed to captivity that were they given freedom they could not survive. But men are not beasts. How have they abdicated their humanity? What have they done with their minds and consciences, not only time-servers like Rusanov and his daughter but honorable souls like Vadim Zatsyrko, who is happy to sacrifice himself for his country but never wonders whether the science he idolizes and through which he serves, will ever free his country's slaves? Bacon's Idols classify and label the several categories of mental abnegation; they do not explain the spirit's atrophy.

Nor has Kostoglotov solved Shulubin's question, "how did it happen that within ten years a whole nation changed from bravery to cowardice," and only in *August 1914* does Solzhenitsyn, as a historian, begin to solve the problem. In *Cancer Ward,* and in his other works of fiction, Solzhenitsyn is not a historian but a witness. So is Kostoglotov. He endures, questions, wonders, observes, and once only hints at a solution. On the night before his departure from the hospital, in speaking with Elizaveta Anatol'evna, whom he has long noticed but never talked to before, he discovers that in 1935—(he was then fourteen years old)—when "a quarter of the city was deported," they were neighbors in Leningrad. "It's shameful," he says softly, "Why are we so calm? Why did we just wait quietly until it struck down our friends, our relatives and ourselves? Why is human nature like that?"—a reply to Shulubin, faintly suggested: at the heart of cowardice is the crime of indifference, of selfish unconcern for any suffering but one's own. But why "human nature is like that" remains unanswered.

Solzhenitsyn, as he himself has said in his speech accepting the Nobel Prize, belongs in the main stream of Russia's literature of "commitment," the old Russian literary tradition bent on elucidating human events in terms of human values, moral principles, theological doctrines. Oleg Kostoglotov, no less than the heroes of Tolstoy and Dostoevsky, is at once a unique individual and a figure in whom the nature of Man is tested, and if he differs from his predecessors both as a character and in the method of his portrayal, the measure of this difference—and it is immense—is the difference between the Soviet Union and nineteenth century Russia. For however similar he may be to nineteenth century writers, Solzhenitsyn turns their presuppositions upside down, even those of Tolstoy, whose name, works, thoughts are always cropping up like signposts for his own ideas, who is an inspiration and a touchstone and yet, intellectually, light years away. The nineteenth century mind could soar in an empyrean of freedom, experiment with concepts at the utmost reaches of the moral imagination. Raskol'nikov, Myshkin, the Karamazovs, Stavrogin, Pierre Bezukhov, Andrei Bolkonskii, Konstantin Levin and the other saints and criminals created by Dostoevsky and Tolstoy tried out human values at the extreme edge of human possibilities. Solitary, drastically individual, centered on the self, they worked out their "cursed" problems to invariably communal solutions, arrived at belief in universal peace, brotherly love, sympathy of man for man, at the cost of prolonged and agonizing introspection, madness, crime. In Solzhenitsyn's world such experiments must seem the indulgences of by-gone privilege. When a fantastic reality, more harrowing than even Dostoevsky's visions, cries out to be explained, when actualities have out-distanced the powers of fancy and forced the imagination to cope with their extravagance, speculative adventures cannot seem serious. Thought is drawn to earth; the problems that had been individual have become communal, and the solutions that were communal are now individual. "Brotherhood," not at all in the idyllic sense of love and sympathy but in the inescapable circumstances of day-to-day reality, is the condition of every man's life. It is no longer possible for anyone, either from the secure position of wealth, or the independence of monastic seclusion, or the detachment of an ivory tower, to be a spectator of human events; each one, in his words and actions, even in his silences, is ominously implicated in the fate of others; the "responsibility of each for all" is no longer the ideal doctrine of a holy Elder, like Dostoevsky's Zosima, but the inescapable condition of ordinary existence like that in which Shulubin has so tragically failed, or that of the doctors called up to testify in trials of their peers, even like Kostoglotov's in the innocence of boyhood, when he was persuaded in school that the deportations from Leningrad were "necessary" and "expedient." All men are responsible and all are guilty for the tyranny they endure, but most of them are neither conscious of their responsibility nor capable of recognizing their guilt. In an age of moral shabbiness, Kostoglotov's simple decency is exceptional, audacious, heroic.

Solzhenitsyn is a realist who takes for granted those ultimate questions that tormented Tolstoy and Dostoevsky: how justify the suffering of innocents in the light of God's beneficence, how apportion the forces of predestination and determinism, freedom and necessity in the progress of history, how apply the ideals of divine justice and forgiveness in the affairs of men. His heroes are confronted with the unambiguous wrongs of tyranny; their minds and spirits, as well as their bodies, are immured in actual prisons, not lost in labyrinths of their own devising; they must fight not themselves but a crushing power outside themselves. In short, they are less complex because in their morally brutish world philosophical problems are necessarily rudimentary.

But their linear simplicity is also a reflection of Solzhenitsyn's artistic and intellectual predilections. Kostoglotov picks up the sixteen year old Demka's textbook on stereometry, which he himself once studied in school. "Hell, what a book, Demka!" he exclaims. "Wouldn't it be fine if everyone wrote like that? Not fat at all, is it? But what a lot it contains!" Solzhenitsyn's enthusiasm, like Kostoglotov's, is given to the primary and irrefutable, the logic of a theorem, the beauty of a flowering apricot, the innate grace of Vega or the Nilgai antelope, the fortitude of Doctor Oreshchenkov or of the spiral-horned goat. Just as irrefutable is the ugliness of beasts and men, their rapacity, weakness, stupidity. There is no grasping the reality of which these are the visible signs, the covert reality of ultimate good and evil, that Solzhenitsyn accepts as the postulate of a theorem to be developed with mathematical precision and compactness—one day, a few weeks, a month or two. The problem set by the theorem is how to live in a way worthy of humanity within the malignities inherent in existence, the baneful, inevitable restrictions of time and Fate. All his novels are dramas of evil and adjudications of guilt. But in *Cancer Ward,* the most intricate of them all, structured like a symphony with themes that echo, repeat, and modify each other on various levels of meaning and emotional depth, the nature of evil is less obvious, responsibility less clear, and the whole ethical question more complicated than in the others. The matters primarily at issue in *One Day in the Life of Ivan Denisovich, The First Circle* and *August 1914* are here but aspects of a larger and more perplexing question. Men are judged by human standards, but relentless Fate looms back of them, implicated in their lives but unintelligible to their sense of right and wrong.

So Kostoglotov, in the narrow space he has preempted on the crowded train, meditates on his various blessings—(like Ivan Denisovich at the end of his day): he has not died, he may soon be free, and this train is better than the converted freight cars used to transport prisoners. Only when the train starts moving is he "seized with anguish," not the anguish of self-doubt nor even of regret for the happiness he has relinquished, but a painful sense of cruel irrationality at the heart of things, of inexorable, absurd injustice. The gentle, loyal, intelligent dog of the Kadmins, his good friends in exile, has been wantonly killed. His own youth has been wasted and his happiness taken from him. And an inoffensive little beast has been blinded by a wicked man. Of course, the wicked man should not have thrown tobacco into the monkey's eyes, but why did he throw it *just like that?* Who shall explain the *why* of man's wickedness?

Profoundly aware of the inexplicable—the thrilling wonder of ultimate good, the absurd and terrible reality of ultimate evil—Solzhenitsyn does not use this awareness to diminish his severe view of human responsibility, the responsibility "to preserve unspoiled . . . the image of eternity with which each person is born." This responsibility Kostoglotov has met.

Aleksandr Solzhenitsyn's *Cancer Ward*: The Failure of Defiant Stoicism

BY THOMPSON BRADLEY

With the considerable body of critical works on Aleksandr Solzhenitsyn from the mid-1960's and the veritable onslaught of publications following the Nobel Prize and the appearance of *August 1914* it might seem that all the major problems of his writing had been addressed if not resolved. Certainly, the official silencing and castigation of this most talented and fiercely honest writer and the unyielding repression of all intellectuals and rebels in the Soviet Union have contributed to an intensification of interest and discussion. Besides formal stylistic analyses, we have been presented with a wealth of comparative studies on Solzhenitsyn's indebtedness to Tolstoy, Dostoevsky, Leskov, Chekhov, and Dante, to cite but the most prominent, and with numerous other works stressing his Christian, Neo-Christian, Christian-Socialist, Populist, Slavophile, and even Anthroposophical orientation. Yet, for all that, one has rather the sense of viewing the author through a kaleidoscope and is left with the nagging feeling that some fundamental questions have been blurred or omitted. The fault well may lie in the approach of most of the studies.

An approach which opens up a more productive reading is found in Georg Lukacs' essay "Solzhenitsyn's Novels."[1] As a

[1]Georg Lukacs, "Solzhenitsyn' Novels," *Solzhenitsyn* (Cambridge, Massachusetts: M.I.T. Press, 1971), pp. 33-88.

Marxist, Lukacs admittedly represents for the West a decided minority, and for some, a discredited view, but there is a serious error in refusing to hear what he has to say for want of sympathy towards his political perspective. In any case, the merit of his essay lies not so much in a full realization of the implications he pursues as in the social, historical context and the philosophical framework he establishes. For the sake of brevity the following discussion will focus on Solzhenitsyn's *Cancer Ward,* although most of the points, it could be argued, would generally apply with equal validity to his other works, with the exception of *August 1914.*

After a lengthy and enthusiastic treatment of *The First Circle* and *Cancer Ward* Lukacs concludes with a provocative analysis of the limitations of the latter novel and the failure of its protagonist Oleg Kostoglotov. He emphasizes that Kostoglotov is "inwardly completely broken" at the end and has become "unable to continue with a life of his own."[2] Later, the critic notes "the transformation of his [Kostoglotov's] inwardness from a spirit of opposition to a state in which it is reduced to silence."[3] Here, as elsewhere in his concluding remarks, Lukacs fundamentally diverges from the more usual reading of *Cancer Ward* that with Oleg's departure the novel ends on a generally positive upbeat.

Although incomplete, Lukacs' analysis cuts to the moral and social center of the novel and provides the context for some new and useful questions. Unfortunately, the critic himself remains too restricted in his focus and, thus, fails to identify Kostoglotov clearly and overlooks the potential for a new future direction, which, though lacking in Oleg, is to be found elsewhere among the other characters. Two related questions, then, emerge from his essay: What does Kostoglotov represent and why does he falter? And, is there any positive alternative for the future in *Cancer Ward?*

The moral view which informs *Cancer Ward* (and most clearly *The First Circle* as well as *The Love-Girl and the Innocent*) is a contemporary version of Stoicism, which grew necessarily and organically out of the oppressive conditions from which Solzhenitsyn and his generation suffered deeply and which he confronts in his writing. One cannot help noting the critical similarities between the objective conditions under Stalin and

[2]*Ibid.,* p. 84.
[3]*Ibid.,* p. 85.

the repressive political and debased economic-social situation in the Roman Empire.[4] Precisely under these conditions in Rome, moreover, occurred the renascence of Stoicism, reflected in the works of Seneca, Epictetus, and Marcus Aurelius. Remarkable indeed are the correspondences between the exhortation to an austere self-discipline with its stress on inner freedom and moral strength of the Roman Stoics and the stark, exacting ethic of Solzhenitsyn's prisoner heroes. Such affinities are not ones of chance, but are born of similar conditions offering severely limited and determined moral alternatives. Without naming it as such and most probably without any direct influence, Solzhenitsyn has evolved a modern Stoicism.

In Oleg Kostoglotov we find one of the most realized and enduring defiant stoic heroes of contemporary fiction. His failings, noted, but not fully explored by Lukacs, are the limitations of stoic morality. For, though it was and remains the most human of responses to harsh tyranny in defense of individual freedom and the equality of all men, Stoicism, nonetheless, is an individual, inward defiance activated by conditions outside the individual's control. As a personal code it remains whole and viable only to the extent that the tyranny is total. It offers no guidance for change or for real or even potential freedom.

As several revealing moments disclose, Kostoglotov is a prisoner and casualty of the Stalinist past and of the moral identity he has forged in the struggle against the death, dehumanization, and terror wrought upon the entire society. Early in the novel he counsels a "practical" easier course with the young patient Demka and advises him to give up his plan of going to university in the search of truth and justice.[5] It is as if he considered Demka insufficiently strong to engage in this fight as he has. Yet, later, in his postcard written to Demka just before leaving Oleg writes—"Get well. Keep your ideals. I put my hopes in you!"[6] The sentiment strongly suggests that he recognizes his own insufficiency and the real, new promise of Demka. (There will be occasion to return to this point

[4]Michael I. Rostovtseff, *The Social and Economic History of the Roman Empire* (Oxford, 1926), pp. 177-179. See also, Stephen Usher, *The Historians of Greece and Rome* (London: Methuen, 1969), Chapters 7, 8; Gilbert Murray, *Five Stages of Greek Religion* (Garden City, New York, 1955), pp. 112-115; Tacitus, *Annals of Imperial Rome* (Harmondsworth: Penguin, 1969).

[5]Aleksandr Solzhenitsyn, *Rakovyi korpus* (Paris: YMCA Press, 1968), p. 330. [For translation in English see N. Bethell and D. Burg, translators, *Cancer Ward* (Harmondsworth: Penguin, 1971).]

[6]*Ibid.*, p. 442.

below.) In the department store and at the zoo Kostoglotov is able to perceive the present reality only through the prism of his lonely struggle in the war and the camps and comprehends what he sees in terms of his stoic moral code. Nowhere is this more apparent than in his special admiration for the immobile spiral-horned goat, of which he remarks—"That's the sort of character you need to get through life."[7] It is noteworthy that he admonishes Demka in his card to pay particular attention to this animal and think about what it means.[8] Here we have Solzhenitsyn's heavy emphasis on the necessary quality of noble endurance. It is revealing to compare that with the following from the stoic philosopher Epictetus, a Greek living in Rome in the first century A.D.:

> I must die. But must I die groaning? I am imprisoned. But must I whine as well? I must suffer exile. Can anyone hinder me from going with a smile, and good courage, and at peace? "Tell the secret." I refuse to tell, for this is in my power. "But I will chain you." What say you, fellow? Chain me? My leg you will chain,—yes, but my will,—no, not even Zeus can conquer that. "I will imprison you." My bit of body, you mean. "I will behead you." Why? When did I ever tell you that I was the only man in the world who could not be beheaded?[9]

Finally, in his decision to depart without seeing Vera, and particularly in the sentiment of his farewell letter, Oleg manifests

[7] *Ibid.*, p. 421.

[8] *Ibid.*, p. 442.

[9] Whitney J. Oates, ed., *The Stoic and Epicurean Philosophers* (New York, 1940), pp. 225-226. Compare with the political prisoner Bobynin's statement to one of the state security chieftains in *The First Circle; V kruge pervom* (New York: Harper & Row, 1968), pp. 77-78:

> I have nothing, you understand—not a thing! You can't get your hands on my wife and child—a bomb got them first. My parents are already dead. My entire property on earth is my handkerchief . . . You took my freedom away long ago, and you don't have the power to return it because you don't have it yourself. I am forty-two years old and you've given me a twenty-five year sentence. I've already worked at hard labor, gone around with a number on, in handcuffs, with police dogs, and in a strict regime brigade. What else can you threaten me with? What else can you take away? . . . And just get one thing straight and pass it on to *anyone higher up* who doesn't know that you are strong only so long as you don't take *everything* away from people. But a person from whom you've taken *everything* is no longer in your power, he's free again.

Compare further with the following passage from the semi-autobiographical account of his five-year imprisonment for political activity by the revolutionist and writer Victor Serge in *Men in Prison,* trans. Richard Greenman (Harmondsworth: Penguin, 1972), p. 151:

> The world I carry within me has a crystal sphere as its symbol: fullness, perfection. I am free because nothing more can be done to me. Chained to the wall by a circle of iron, I will know how to close my eyes, without

the noblest expression of the stoic ethic in its stern self-denial. The act is consistent, honorable, but it reveals by implication his inability to transcend himself and create a new life.

Both Kostoglotov and the complete Stalinist bureaucrat Rusanov are products of a particular period and shaped by its peculiar conditions, though each reflects an extreme of human response; some critics, properly, have viewed Shulubin as the norm. They share a peculiar relationship whereby one implies the other. Both lose their bearings, although in significantly different ways, with the changes in the defining conditions after Stalin's death. Rusanov has lost the legal, moral sanction of tyranny and collapses. Kostoglotov's integrity and dignity prevail, as they must, yet objectively they are insufficient for new development and hence irrelevant to the changing times. He falters and fails, for he can only endure: he cannot leap beyond. He must endure alone and away. He is too completely of that which he has defied, or as Kierkegaard characterized Stoicism in *The Sickness unto Death* in the section devoted to "the despair of willing to be oneself—defiance":

> . . . it does not even will in defiance to tear itself free from the Power which posited it, it wills to obtrude upon this Power in spite. To hold on to it out of malice . . . [it] must above all take care to hold on to that against which it is an objection.[10]

It has generally gone unnoticed that considerably before the novel's end the dramatic-moral concern gradually moves away from the older generation (Kostoglotov, Shulubin, Dontsova, and Rusanov). This process begins at that point in the first part of the novel when news of the external political changes filters into the ward with the contested issue of *Pravda.*[11] The central concern shifts to the younger generation and forces a new conception and rephrasing of the vital moral question drawn from Tolstoy, "What do men live by?" Most readers have recognized that this is the ultimate question which each of the patients and, finally, all of the characters must answer. But

---

a whimper. Let necessity run its course; I am all assent. I have divided the world into two parts: chains, things—and my very flesh, which is a thing—are in *your* power. The crystal sphere, my will, my lucidity, my freedom are irrevocably mine.

(Italics in original in both passages.) Note also Serge's reference to Marcus Aurelius later in the novel (page 165).

[10]Soren Kierkegaard, *Fear and Trembling. Sickness Unto Death* (Garden City, New York, 1954), p. 207.

[11]Solzhenitsyn, *Rakovyi korpus,* pp. 182-184.

this query attains an expanded meaning in its implied rephrasing in the latter half of the novel, wherein the emphasis is on the future,—"How *will* men live and what *will* they live by?" None of the older generation, especially Rusanov and Kostoglotov, hold the answer. Oleg himself seems to realize this as well as the need for a different way when he entreats Vera to spare the second half of her life.[12]

The potential answer resides with the novel's six young men and women,—Rusanov's two children Avieta and Iura, the nurse Zoia, and the three patients Vadim, Asia, and Demka. In their various ways they reflect the dynamic conflicting tendencies bodying out of the old to the new and raise the problem of continuity and change. As in Dostoevsky's *The Brothers Karamazov,* each individually must come to grips with a question of justice and truth. Their answers are crucial. Excepting Demka, all, furthermore, embody some distortion, some vestige from the Stalinist legacy, while they all hold a possible key to the future path of the society.

The neo-stalinism of Vadim, the elitest technocrat of the new bureaucracy, and of Avieta, the chameleon-like adept functionary, is transparent and has been sufficiently discussed elsewhere. As the heirs of Stalin's legacy they imply a continuity for a future Stalinism without Stalin. No mistake should be made in simply discounting them out of hand, however; they are the *best* realization of Stalin's rule, especially Vadim. Committed, energetic, self-assured they are not consciously, nor overtly, evil. Rather, it is in their appallingly callous responses to the questions of who shall live and who shall be set free that we recognize the future they portend. Through Asia—whom we have encountered before in the Volodins of *The First Circle* as well as in *Cancer Ward* in the varied figures of Chalyi and Podduev—all of whom Asia resembles with her philosophy of "you only live once"—Solzhenitsyn personifies the youthful product of Stalin's vulgar materialism and the cynical "socialism" of the elite. If only less actively destructive, her life implies a continuity of the stalinist past.

More hopeful, albeit timid intimations of discontinuity and change appear in the lives of Iura Rusanov and Zoia. Their doubts and actions express a re-affirmation of personal responsibility and individual justice in behalf of what Leonid Leonov

[12] *Ibid.,* p. 443.

once called the "human co-efficient." Zoia questions in her own life the superficial values espoused by her generation, those values dramatized in Asia. Concretely, on her own authority she stops Oleg Kostoglotov's sinestrol injections as a conscious human act. Out of a similar vague sense of justice Iura Rusanov protests and suspends the truckdriver's sentence and in another case personally intervenes to protect two young secretaries from harsh punishment. But, in this latter case and in Zoia's act as well, justice is served at the expense of truth. Both resort to deceit: Iura, by involving himself in the lives of the young women under false pretenses, and Zoia by shifting responsibility for the suspension of Oleg's shots to the other nurses. In these incidents Solzhenitsyn with a nice bitterness raises the problem of the continuing contradiction between ends and means. Appealing as they are by contrast to the others, Iura and Zoia offer a promising, but flawed break with the past.

No, the most hopeful future lies with Demka, the only one capable of overcoming his own sordid past and cruel illness and of breaking away from the stalinist hold. In him we re-discover the link with an older and nobler continuity, the quest for truth and justice, and the familiar figure of the *"pravda-iskatel'."* This he shares with Oleg Kostoglotov, which explains their immediate close affinity for one another. Demka's certain acts and responses, however, underscore important qualitative differences—most especially in his willingness and capacity to go beyond his present condition. It is Demka who raises the question of truth and sincerity in literature with Avieta and insists upon the obligations of the artist and art. To Oleg's advice that he get a safe job as a radio repairman and technician and forget about learning he retorts with the laconic, but powerful: "To hell with your radios—it's the truth I love."[13] Finally, and most significantly, Demka manifests precisely that human capacity to transcend his physical, subjective condition and find the human relationship, with Asia, before which Oleg falters.

The novel in no sense concludes with a rejection of Oleg Kostoglotov's profoundly moving struggle for personal dignity and freedom, but rather with an elucidation of the limits of defiance, of the Stoic code. His is the inner freedom of an unfree man, while Demka represents the potentially whole freedom of a man freeing himself. The hopes of the past and of

[13]*Ibid.*, p. 330.

the novel are concentrated in those parting words—"Get well. Keep to your ideals. I put my hopes in you."

Yet, no one, let alone Solzhenitsyn, could have foreseen or, at least, no one wanted to believe that the trial of Stalinism, now in his absence, would begin so soon and continue so long, even though in a somewhat more insidious and less wholesale manner. Those hopeful changes which had opened up and on which *Cancer Ward* is centered have been subverted and grievously retarded by the fearful inheritors of Stalin's legacy. Demka's leap into action will have been turned into direct but lonely opposition, leading to prison, and he will have to suffer as did Kostoglotov before him. What may save him is the critical dimension which qualitatively distinguishes him from the stoic prisoner-heroes manifest in his simultaneous expression and transcending of their opposition and defiance and embodied in the capacity and energy to learn and transform. He is the stuff of further radical change and in reality a greater threat. In this he combines the certainty of the peasant Spiridon's unconscious wholeness and the developing self-awareness of the imprisoned intellectuals.[14]

[14]It is necessary to point out that Demka represents in embryonic form only a most important possible departure and a development beyond the stoic heroes and the period which brought them into being. For that reason the significance of this character is emphasized here out of proportion to his much more modest role in the novel. As subsequent events and particularly *August 1914* have demonstrated Solzhenitsyn has emphatically rejected this avenue in his writing. One may speculate about the aura of resignation in this latest novel and wonder at the totally negative portrayal of all radicals and revolutionists, whereby each appears as a Rusanovite Stalinist before Stalinism. The implications are unsettling for what they suggest about the author's changed attitude. But the novel is still to be completed and the question beyond the scope of the present essay.

The Plays of Aleksandr Solzhenitsyn

BY GLEB ZEKULIN

Two plays by Solzhenitsyn have been published in the West: *The Love-Girl and the Innocent* and *A Candle in the Wind* (*The Light Which is in Thee*).[1] These plays have attracted much less attention than Solzhenitsyn's novels, but also less than his speeches, letters, and public pronouncements.[2] They are also practically unknown in the Soviet Union, even though one of them was accepted for production by the Moscow Sovremennik theatre in 1962 but stopped after the dress rehearsal.[3] And it seems that in contradistinction to the writer's novels, the plays are not circulating among the readers of *samizdat*.

Is the main reason for this apparent lack of interest simply

[1]*Olen' i shalashovka,* also translated into English as *The Tenderfoot and the Tramp* or as *The Prisoner and the Camp Prostitute;* and *Svecha na vetru.* (*Svet, kotoryi v tebe*). In this article references are made to the Russian edition: Aleksandr Solzhenitsyn, *Sobranie sochinenii,* 6 vols. (Frankfurt a.M.: Possev Verlag, 1969), V, pp. 7-124 and pp. 125-205. All translations from the Russian are mine.

[2]There exists little critical literature. See H. Muchnic "A Somber Theater," *The New York Review of Books,* 26 March 1970; *The New York Times,* 16 Nov. 1969 and 8 Feb. 1970; *The Times,* 17 Nov. 1969; *Time,* 23 March 1970; *N.Y. Herald Tribune,* 17 June 1970 and 20 Oct. 1970; my article on *A Candle in the Wind* in *Canadian Slavonic Papers,* XIII, 2-3, 1971, pp. 179-192. *The Love-Girl and the Innocent* was staged in Minnesota in October 1970.

[3]See Solzhenitsyn's "Autobiographical Note" submitted to the Nobel Foundation, as quoted in Leopold Labedz (ed.), *Solzhenitsyn: A Documentary Record* (Harmondsworth: Penguin, 1972), p. 27; and "Open Letter to the Fourth Soviet Writers' Congress," *ibid.,* p. 111.

due to their artistic or dramatic weaknesses? An attempt will be made in this article to give an answer to this question.

In his postscript to the Russian edition of *August 1914*,[4] Solzhenitsyn states the following about the origins of this work:

> The general conception of this work, of which the first part is presented here, arose in my mind in 1936, when I was finishing high school. From that time on I never parted with it, I understood it to be the main project of my life; being distracted—but only by the peculiar circumstances of my biography and by the density of contemporary impressions—into writing other books, I moved towards, I readied myself for, and collected materials for, only this one project.

It is possible to understand these words to mean that all his known works, with the exception of the announced *magnum opus* of which *August 1914* is the first part or "knot," are incidental, as it were, having been provoked more by outside pressures than by the inner necessity to create. They present, therefore, the author's analysis of topical problems which, in his opinion, needed to be explained and understood. Among these problems, one appears to have been paramount in his mind, namely, that of the *condition humaine et morale* of his contemporaries who lived under the rule of Stalin. To this problem he devotes a series of works in which he investigates the various stages through which men passed when exposed to the realities of life under Stalin.

Considered from this point of view, a group of "incidental" works could be considered as forming a chain where each link represents one stage through which Solzhenitsyn's contemporaries are made to progress. The works forming this chain, and arranged not chronologically according to the date of composition, the historical period used as their background, or their appearance in print, but rather in the order of progression, are the following: *The Love-Girl and the Innocent, The First Circle, One Day in the Life of Ivan Denisovich, Cancer Ward* and *A Candle in the Wind*. Taken in this sequence, these works chronicle vividly and in detail the life typical for a great many Soviet men after 1945, as well as providing an analysis of their state of mind and morals. The unity of this series is not dis-

[4]*Avgust chetyrnadtsatogo* (Paris: YMCA Press. 1971), pp. 572-3. The postscript has not been included, unfortunately, in the English translation of the novel published by Farrar, Straus, & Giroux, New York, 1972.

turbed by the fact that in each work a different protagonist is selected to be the carrier of the author's ideas and ideals; each of the main characters—Rodion Nemov, Gleb Nerzhin, Oleg Kostoglotov, Aleks Koriel—appears as the predecessor of the following, i.e. he is shown as having achieved the highest level of consciousness possible at the given stage of his development as a moral being.

There could be valid objections to the selection of works and to the order in which they have been arranged here. One could protest that *One Day in the Life of Ivan Denisovich* has no protagonist of the type mentioned; that Shukhov, as a peasant, does not qualify to follow Nerzhin or to precede Kostoglotov. The justification for including this novella in the sequence, and at the place indicated is found, first of all, in Solzhenitsyn's own words: "I spent the middle period of my sentence in such 'Special Prisons' (*The First Circle*). In 1950 I was sent to the newly established Special Camps which were intended only for political prisoners. In such a camp in the town of Ekibastuz in Kazakhstan (*One Day in the Life of Ivan Denisovich*) I worked as a miner, a bricklayer and a foundryman. There I contracted a tumor . . ."[5] But more importantly, the novella could also be regarded as necessary in the sequence for two reasons. First, it provides the "physical" feeling, the total awareness of the hellish life which Nerzhin is going to experience shortly and which Kostoglotov has experienced recently. Second, it vindicates Gleb Nerzhin's acceptance of folk values for his code of ethics by creating, in Ivan Denisovich Shukhov, the "ideal" folk hero [*narodnyi geroi*]. *One Day* can therefore be seen as being the central piece of the sequence, where the author shows that it is possible to live according to the moral code selected by him for his hero. Hence the clever, well-educated and intellectually refined Nerzhin merges with the natural, unspoiled and morally healthy Shukhov to produce Kostoglotov. It should also be noted that Solzhenitsyn uses for *One Day* a form which differs markedly from that of the novels which flank it, namely, a highly stylized form of narrative [*skaz*]. (Many consider this novella, and very rightly so, to be artistically the most successful of his works.) This, again, would emphasize the critical position of *One Day* in the sequence.

Another possible objection could be that Innokentii Volodin,

[5] "Autobiographical Note," quoted in Labedz, *op. cit.*, p. 26.

in *The First Circle,* is obviously intended by the author to be among his favorite characters, and that his experience—the arrest and the first hours of prison life—should have been placed at the head of the series. Since this is not the case, the argument would go, the proposed sequence is gravely affected. But this would be so only if one were not able to consider the Volodin episode—which serves as a frame for the novel—as a flashback.

The core of the sequence, consisting of the two novels with the novella between them, is then further extended on both sides by a play: *The Love-Girl and the Innocent* starts the series and *A Candle in the Wind* ends it.

As far as the remaining works, the short stories or the "miniatures" written before *August 1914,* are concerned, these can be considered either as "incidental" (e.g., "The Easter Procession") or as sketches—elaborate and beautifully finished ones but, nevertheless, sketches—for the large canvasses which the two novels are.

Considering the two plays separately from the remainder of the "sequence," one is first of all struck by the differences between them. *The Love-Girl and the Innocent* is "stageworthy": it has action, which is varied; it has dramatic tension; the characters have the chance to display their strengths and their weaknesses and to develop; they are "rounded," *A Candle in the Wind,* on the other hand, is a conversational play with little action; the play is allegorical and thus lacks dramatic tension; the characters personify ideas and are consequently rather flat.

The Love-Girl consists of four acts, divided into an unequal number of scenes, which the author calls "*kartiny.*"[6] The stage is very complicated, and extended into the auditorium in such a way as to force the audience to feel that it is, together with the actors, inside the prison camp: e.g., the guard towers, placed against the outside of the columns which hold the proscenium arch, are occupied by soldiers throughout the play; guards are changed during the intermissions, and if they find that the audience is in their way, the officer in charge shouts rudely: "Move away from the zone! Disperse!" (p. 58). The stage instructions are very long, very numerous and detailed, and require, for instance, that bronze be produced, a brick wall built and then

[6]Act I, scenes 1-4; Act II, sc. 5-6; Act III, sc. 7-9; Act IV, sc. 10-11.

demolished; that, during a long and violent fight between six people (of whom one is a woman) heads be bashed with an iron crow-bar and wooden planks, one of which is to break over the head of a fighter. There are eight different sets for eleven scenes: three sets depict the outdoors (two construction sites on which a tall building crane is operating, and one camp site with an arriving and departing truck in which prisoners are transported); five sets show various interiors of which one is a foundry in operation. When reading all these detailed instructions, set descriptions, and stage directions, the impression is mainly one of monumentality. This is stressed by the last printed words of the play—"*Konets spektaklia*" ["End of performance"], where *spetakl'* invites a comparison with Futurist "happenings" (*kartina* used instead of *stsena* has the same effect) rather than with a traditional play.[7] Also, the number of actors involved is staggering: there are 60 *dramatis personae* listed by names or professions, plus an unspecified number of prisoners, brigade leaders, warders, guards, etc.

A Candle in the Wind is divided into six scenes [*kartiny*] of irregular length. The stage sets are comparatively simple. All, with the exception of the set for scene 2, are interiors, of which only one (scene 4) is somewhat complicated, consisting of a large and a small drawing room, a hall and a view of a dining room. On only two occasions are slightly unusual requisites prescribed: in scene 1, the audience sees in the background the top of an arriving motorcar and hears the exhaust-pipe noises; in scene 2, the audience sees, but does not hear, trucks, cars, bulldozers and various other construction machines moving in the distance. Stage directions are precise but brief. The number of *dramatis personae* is limited to 15 (no list is given), of which 6 are episodic. The play could be classified as a *Kammerspiel* because of its quiet and subdued manner.

[7]As mentioned earlier, Solzhenitsyn's play had been accepted and rehearsed by the Moscow Sovremennik theatre. The Sovremennik is known to have attempted, in the late 1950s and in the 1960s, a return to the essentially Meyerholdian traditions of the 1920s. Their main aim seems to have been to achieve the fullest possible involvement of the audience in the play, resulting in the "totality" of theatrical experience. Thus it tried, on the occasion of a war drama presentation, to extend the play outside the theatre building by dressing the doorman and ushers in German SS uniforms and making them pretend to check the identity of the patrons along with their theatre tickets. Could it be that Solzhenitsyn has been influenced by this trend?

The main difference between the two plays lies, however, neither in the form nor in the mood, but rather in their intention.

There are two aspects of Solzhenitsyn's talent which complement each other and augment the tension which is specific to the works of this author. There is Solzhenitsyn the fighter for the cause, the intensely engaged man, who knows how to attack swiftly and mercilessly by means of a racy, colorful, energetic, and sometimes angry language. It is because of this quality that some Soviet critics have called him[8] a satirist (A. Borshchagovskii) and accused him of having a "caustic, topical-satirical style" (Salynskii), a "penchant for sloganeering and caricature" (Ozerov); of writing in a "journalistic" manner Borshchagovskii) and accused him of having a "caustic, topical-essayist, exposé nature" (Abashidze) and which "are more dangerous to us than those of Pasternak: Pasternak was a man divorced from life, while Solzhenitsyn, with his animated, militant, ideological temperament, is a man of principle" (Surkov); of writing caricatures (Novichenko); of suffering from "an abundance of naturalism, from a surfeit of all manner of horrors" (Kozhevnikov); of approaching "fundamental problems not in philosophical terms but in political terms" (Surkov).

What this criticism by his Soviet *confrères* means is that Solzhenitsyn's attacks are so effective that they cannot be answered by arguments which would prove him wrong, and that he is being dealt with along political lines since he refuses to conform to the "norm" adopted by the majority of members of the Writers' Union, i.e., since he insists on "seeing only the black" and is not prepared to "write only about joyful things."[9]

The defenders of the official policy in literature could possibly have tolerated the "publicist." It is the thinker, the moralist and the humanist in Solzhenitsyn that makes him totally unacceptable to them. This other aspect of Solzhenitsyn's talent led finally to his expulsion from the Writers' Union in November 1969, an act that turned him, from the official and legal point of view, into a "non-writer."

In the series of works mentioned earlier, both aspects—the

[8]See "Moscow Writers on *Cancer Ward*," in Labedz, *op. cit.*, pp. 83-105, and "Secretariat Meeting With Solzhenitsyn," *ibid.*, pp. 128-150.

[9]Kerbabaev, as quoted in Labedz, *op. cit.*, p. 144.

publicistic and the moralistic or philosophical—are present in varying proportions, but in the two plays under discussion these proportions are the least balanced. *The Love-Girl* contains hardly any moral discourse; *A Candle,* on the other hand, is almost totally devoid of publicistic invectives. If the plays are viewed, respectively, as the beginning and the conclusion of the writer's investigation of the condition of his contemporaries and, at the same time, as his attempt to suggest a remedy for this condition, then this imbalance is not surprising. It is the reflection of the evolution through which the author himself has passed: having started in anger, lashing out at the iniquities of life which he has experienced, he finishes by finding out not how to do away with the wickedness and gross injustice around him but by learning how to live with them while preserving the human dignity and values which make life worth living.

The plot of *The Love-Girl and the Innocent* can be summarized comparatively briefly. An army officer, Rodion Nemov, arrested at the front-line while fighting the enemy, arrives, in the autumn of 1945, in his first forced-labor camp. In spite of being a political prisoner, he is put in charge of the camp production at his own request. He is appalled by the exploitation of the prisoner-workers, by their unjust treatment at the hands of both the camp authorities and of the prisoners in privileged and leading positions, and he attempts to break the established and criminally unfair camp order. His clash with the camp establishment results in his demotion to a simple prisoner-worker and in his being designated for transport to a satellite camp where the work is so hard that prisoners have little chance of surviving. He is saved from this fate by a camp prostitute with whom he falls in love just at the time of his demotion: she manages, against his will and without his knowledge, to have the order for his transportation revoked by the camp doctor.

The interest of the play lies mainly in the character of Nemov. The strong, proud, self-assured, and honest front-line officer takes on the job of the production manager, the highest and the most privileged—but also envied—position a prisoner can occupy, a position which practically makes him the second-in-command in the camp.[10] He does it for two reasons. First,

[10]*Sobranie sochinenii,* V, 49.

he knows that as a rank-and-file prisoner-worker he might not survive (pp. 56, 86) to see the end of his sentence. Second, he thinks that by being honest, by obeying and seeing that all others obey the official rules for the treatment of prisoners, and by refusing to exploit his fellow-prisoners (p. 56), he can help them and make their life at least tolerable. His upright and correct attitude brings him into conflict with the privileged prisoners whose interests are threatened by Nemov and who manage, through intrigues and corruption, to have him dismissed. Nemov's innocent and naive honesty has no chance when it collides with the depravity of the camp establishment. The good, represented by Nemov, is easily and swiftly conquered by evil, represented by the camp authorities. Nemov's defeat is, on the surface, total. But instead of causing anger, envy, or anguish, this loss brings him peace of mind and soul, a satisfaction so strong that he feels free. (General Samsonov, in *August 1914,* has a similar experience of being free when he decides that he is no longer able to command his armies). Nemov says to Liuba, the love-girl: "In my fall from the high ladder, I wanted to cling to the lowest rung. I thought that by breaking the others I will not be broken myself . . . And it turns out that one is much freer as a simple navvy . . . See? I chip away at the slag and sing songs" (p. 84). Having lost all vestige of power, Nemov acquires, instead, "conscience" (p. 84). And, as if it were a reward for the change which occurred in him, he also acquires the ability to love. His beautiful, clean, and unselfish feeling for Liuba is reciprocated to such an extent that she sacrifices herself and even her love for him in order to save him from death.

In this first part of the "sequence," then, Solzhenitsyn takes his hero as far as the realization that only a moral life, lived according to the rules of one's conscience—and not according to the conventions of the society in which one finds oneself or according to someone else's commands—is worth living.

Apart from Nemov, two male characters are of particular interest. Pavel Gai, the brigadier of the masons, is also a front-line officer, a strong-willed and upright man who could develop, if he became a "seeker," into another Oleg Kostoglotov (Shchagov, in *The First Circle,* reminds one very much of him). The other, the orderly Kostia, is a character who reappears in all the novels: as Rus'ka in *The First Circle,*

Gopchik in *One Day,* and Demka (to a certain extent) in *Cancer Ward.* He is a basically good and clever youngster, full of vitality and not yet completely morally corrupted who, because of an unexpected and undeserved injustice done to him, has a good chance to be "saved."

The Love-Girl is, apart from "Matrena's Home," the only work where Solzhenitsyn has paid close attention to female characters. There is, first of all, the love-girl herself, Liuba Negnevitskaia. She appears episodically in Acts I and II, where her background is established more by her gestures and manner of speech than by her actual words. But beginning with Act III she takes a more prominent role in the play. Her camp experience tells her that Nemov, with whom she falls violently in love, will be sent away and that she can save him only by paying the highest price she can offer, namely herself (p. 112). And she does so without a trace of hesitation (p. 117). Liuba's main characteristics are kindness and the capacity to love to the degree of complete selflessness. She has preserved this capacity in spite of what life—through no fault of hers—did to her: as a small child during the collectivization she was exiled with her parents to the North, rescued on the way by her brothers who actually bought her from one of the guards; she was married off, at the age of fourteen, to a boor who beat her; her second husband was a drunkard who renounced her after she had been arrested; since then she moved from camp to camp, and survived by becoming a "love-girl" (p. 105).

The other female character, Grania Zybina, is more lightly sketched, which does not prevent her from being extremely interesting. As a young woman in Moscow she married "above her rank"; her husband was a university teacher. During the war she was mobilized and was at the front as a sniper, while her husband's conscription had been deferred. When she learned that he was unfaithful to her, she took a short leave, went to Moscow, entered her apartment, and, finding her husband in bed with a woman, shot him (p. 34). In camps she works hard and honestly, usually as a leader of a brigade. She once fell in love with Gai, saved his life when he was attacked by criminals who refused to be forced to work (pp. 92-98), but was sent to the satellite camp, on the transport which Nemov missed, because she refused the advances of the new production manager (p. 95). She belongs to Solzhenitsyn's positively portrayed and morally strong characters:

> What kind of a heart must one have to be able to cheat the working prisoners of even one gram of bread? I made the decision not to live the way people live in camps. I don't want to become like the rabble! And whether I live or not—what difference does it make? (p. 94).

There are in the play a great number of negative characters, all either members of the camp authorities or belonging to the privileged class of prisoners. Of these, the most prominent are Khomich, the new production manager, a black market operator who continues his deals in the camp, bribes the authorities and arranges a comfortable life for himself by exploiting his co-prisoners; and Doctor Mereshchun, former colonel and commanding officer of an army medical division, who manages, by various intrigues and shady deeds, to hold even the commandant of the camp at his mercy; even though he is a mere prisoner, he becomes the most powerful man in the camp. Mereshchun is possibly the most repulsive character created by Solzhenitsyn.

Another and very important aspect of *The Love-Girl* is the incredibly large amount of information provided about the administration and the day-to-day running of a labor camp. Unemotionally, using the same economy of words well known from his *One Day,* Solzhenitsyn piles detailed information upon detailed information (too numerous to be listed here), with the result that by the end of the play everything worth knowing about a camp is presented. Taken together, *The Love-Girl* and *One Day* form a complete encyclopedia of camp life.

By comparison, *A Candle in the Wind* gives practically no information at all about life. The play is set in the future, in a society that has reached a very high level of scientific and technological development. Solzhenitsyn's view of this life is somewhat naive and, interestingly enough, rather optimistic—in this respect he differs considerably from the majority of contemporary science-fiction writers. His projection into the future shows the life of our descendents to be very conformist but not fully regimented, governed by totally materialistic and utilitarian pursuits but able to appreciate beauty and art. The role of the military in this society is seen as very important (the latter seem to have taken over the function of the police, certainly as far as state and national security is concerned, and the concept "security" is extended to cover almost every aspect of human life) but there is enough leeway for individuals to think and even to act according to their own resolve. This last point is of particular importance to the author, for this is the area chosen by him for the development of the play's conflict. All in all, it would appear that Solzhenitsyn's projection is based on today's capitalist societies and not on socialist ones.

The plot line is thin and straight, without any deviations or "bulges." Aleks Koriel, a scientist, returns to the city after eighteen years of absence—three at the front in the war, almost ten in prison, accused of a crime which he has not committed, and five in voluntary exile.[11] He joins Filipp Radagais, his childhood friend and former co-prisoner, in the latter's bio-cybernetic institute and helps to "neuro-stabilize" the personality of his cousin Al'da. Horrified at what he helped do to his cousin, he leaves bio-cybernetics to work in socio-cybernetics where no interference with man's inner life is possible.

There is in the play only one small sub-plot—an intrigue among the institute research workers—which is very lightly sketched. A number of potential sub-plots connected with the private lives of the various protagonists are left undeveloped.

The conflict of the play lies on two planes. The first and more obvious is philosophical and is expressed in the clash between the world outlook of Aleks and that of the remaining characters. Aleks, who has learned during his years of imprisonment and exile to place ultimate value on the individuality of each human being, rejects the materialistic life which has developed in the technically advanced society: its utilitarian pseudo-values have come to dominate and determine all the actions, views, opinions and beliefs of the individuals who have accepted this code of ethics. The members of this "new" society have become slaves of their way of life rather than of a state, an ideology, or an economic system. Their enslavement is therefore voluntary; it is of their own doing, and they themselves carry the responsibility for it.

[11]The details of Aleks' biography and the placing in time of the action relative to his biography are so strongly autobiographical that one is tempted to see in Aleks more than a carrier of the author's ideas. A simple calculation shows that the action of the play takes place fifteen years after Aleks' arrest, i.e., the same period of time that elapsed between Solzhenitsyn's arrest and the year in which *A Candle* was written (1960), and at the time of the action, Aleks is almost exactly Solzhenitsyn's age—"about 40" (p. 124), vs. Solzhenitsyn's 42 in 1960.

The second and deeper plane on which the conflict develops is moral. It is an inner conflict that unfolds within each character. The "norms" of life as they have developed in this society clash with the uncontrollable intrusions of "fate" (e.g. illness) into the lives of the society's individual members, and upset what they consider the predictable "normalcy" of their lives. In these clashes and in the way they are resolved, the human worth of each individual is disclosed. Among the main characters of the play, only Aleks does not have to deal with this inner conflict since he went through this kind of struggle and worked out his own stand in prison and exile, i.e., before the action of the play begins.

As a character, Aleks is the last link in the chain connecting Nemov, Nerzhin, and Kostoglotov and as such is morally a fully developed being. Solzhenitsyn therefore makes him take the necessary next step, namely to re-enter life as it is actually lived by society. His first encounter with "real" life leaves him unperturbed, while all those with whom he comes into contact (his uncle Mavrikii, Mavrikii's wife Tiliia, Filipp) are shocked by his "eccentricity" (scene 1)[12]. He allows himself to be carried into their life, actively works on the neuro-stabilization project (p. 157) and is the initiator of the idea of trying out the new experiment on Al'da (p. 161, 164-5). He hopes to help her by letting her acquire artificially the strength and the determination that she lacks and that she is unable to draw from an experience similar to that of Aleks, making her acutely vulnerable in the rough and tough, ruthlessly indifferent world in which she lives. When he realizes, however, that Al'da has been transformed into a quietly determined, ideally balanced, dependable, and predictable, but utterly lifeless person (pp. 180-181, 186), he recognizes his dreadful mistake. The sinfulness, and at the same time the complete inadequacy of human interference with God's creation (p. 180), becomes apparent to him (p. 186). He leaves the bio-cybernetic institute with the recognition that his interference in "normal" life has been an utter failure, but he refuses to give up completely: he associates himself with Terbol'm's socio-cybernetic project which attempts to determine and optimize the man-made circumstances which govern man's social life without inter-

[12]The situation remotely reminds one of Dostoevsky's *The Idiot,* Part I: Prince Myshkin's return to Petersburg and his meeting with the Epanchin family.

fering with his inner life. But even then he decides to remain an observer and not an active performer, so that, if the need should arise sometime in the future, he could prevent socio-cybernetics from turning into "another Leviathan" (p. 203).

Aleks' main antagonist is Filipp, who went through the same experience (war and prison) without drawing from it the same conclusions. He is eager to "catch up" with what he understands to have missed during the ten wasted years of solitary, isolated life (p. 149). In the process he loses that which Aleks has acquired, namely his conscience.[13] Aleks and Filipp are conceived almost as doubles or twins ("We have completely swapped personalities. We have exchanged our world-outlooks," p. 142), with one—Aleks—possessing a conscience, while the other—Filipp—does not (pp. 159, 184-5, 190).

All the other characters, every one of them a carrier of an idea or attitude, are minor and serve only as foils to Aleks, and partly to Filipp. This applies also to Al'da, the "candle in the wind" of the title: "She is a candle, Filipp! She is a flickering candle in our dreadful wind! . . . Do not blow her out! Do not damage her!"—says Aleks before she undergoes the neuro-stabilization (p. 167). There is an element of the tragic in her. She is exploited—perhaps sacrificed would be a better word—by both sides (she is not the same Al'da even after the emotional shock occasioned by her father's unexpected death "de-stabilized" her), and this makes her stand out among the secondary characters.

A Candle in the Wind, due both to its form (long exchanges between characters which at times turn into short monologues) and content (a "morality play"), is better read than seen. It would have probably been more successful had it been written as a novel or a novella. There can be little doubt that the message which Solzhenitsyn tries to convey in this play is very important to him: and it seems possible to surmise that he needed to write it for his own sake, in order to find out where he himself stands as a man and a member of society. Aleks' attitude of an observer who will intervene in the life that surrounds him only in the case of real danger, his role, as it were, of a moral watchdog, could well be the role which Solzhenitsyn has assigned to himself.

[13]Filipp is strongly reminiscent of Colonel Iakonov in *The First Circle;* just as the latter, he is a moral villain almost in spite of himself.

What is, then, the answer to the question asked at the begining of this article? Why do Solzhenitsyn's plays seem to have attracted little interest? It would appear that as *pièces de théâtre,* neither is an outstanding success, with *The Love-Girl and the Innocent* having, however, a definite edge over *A Candle in the Wind.* But considered as integral parts of a sequence, or works which represent the author's masterful and timely analysis of the *condition humaine* of our contemporaries, the plays acquire importance and interest which go beyond the level at which artistic success or failure is judged. Both plays deserve to be known by all those who have read Solzhenitsyn's novels and found them, for one reason or another, important or outstanding works. They deserve, of course, to be studied closely by students of Solzhenitsyn's art. It seems impossible to acquire all the necessary background information on such characters as Gleb Nerzhin and Oleg Kostoglotov without knowing *The Love-Girl and the Innocent.* It is even less possible to understand the moral "message" Solzhenitsyn is trying to convey to the readers of *The First Circle, Cancer Ward,* and even *One Day in the Life of Ivan Denisovich,* without having thoroughly studied *A Candle in the Wind.* This work, though perhaps weak and not quite satisfactory as a play, acquires a stature of a key work if viewed in conjunction with the totality of Solzhenitsyn's creative output before *August 1914.*

Solzhenitsyn's "Sketches"

BY JOHN B. DUNLOP

In a rare interview granted in 1967 Aleksandr Solzhenitsyn remarked that he had completed sixteen stories of from fifteen to twenty lines each. These stories, he said, immediately acquired enormous popularity within the Soviet Union.[1] On another occasion he stated: "Barely had I given them [i.e. the stories] to people to read when they quickly reached various cities in the Soviet Union. And then the editors of *Novyi mir* received a letter from the West that these stories had already been published there."[2]

At present it is unclear when exactly Solzhenitsyn committed

"Solzhenitsyn's 'Sketches.'" From *Transactions of the Association of Russian-American Scholars in USA,* VI (1972), 21-28. Copyright © 1972 by *Transactions.* Reprinted (with minor changes) by permission of the author and *Transactions.*

[1]Pavel Licko, "Jedného Dna u Alexandra Isajevica Solzenicyna" ["A Day with Aleksandr Isaevich Solzhenitsyn"], *Kulturny zivot* (Bratislava), 13 (1967), 1-10. A French translation of this interview appeared in Georges Nivat and Michel Aucouturier, eds., *Soljénitsyne* (Paris: L'Herne, 1971), pp. 113-18. Licko's integrity has recently been called into question (*Time,* 28 December 1970, p. 18). There is, however, as yet no reason to doubt that most of the information provided by him is reliable. Where his information can be checked by other sources, it is usually proven accurate.

[2]From the "Proceedings" of a September 22, 1967 meeting of the Secretariat of the Union of Soviet Writers at which Solzhenitsyn was present. The Russian text is in Aleksandr Solzhenitsyn, *Sobranie sochinenii* (Frankfurt/Main: Possev Verlag, 1969-70), VI, 38. The English translation is from Leopold Labedz, ed. *Solzhenitsyn: A Documentary Record* (London: Allen Lane, 1970), p. 86.

his stories or "sketches" to paper.[3] What appears to be clear is that he was unable to find a Soviet publisher for them[4] and that he began distributing them in 1964.[5]

The "sketches" are prose poems[6] of a powerful lyric intensity. Language and, in particular, the rhythm of speech play a significant role in them, rendering all attempts at translation necessarily inadequate. Of the three extant English translations of which I am aware,[7] I would generally opt for the Harry Willetts version which appeared in *Encounter.* It is this translation which I shall be employing, with a few necessary alterations, in my quotations.

What are the "sketches" about? As I see it, they are primarily concerned with the spiritual inadequacy of modern life. The seedy, secular and arrogantly Promethean present is firmly and almost totally rejected by Solzhenitsyn. This rejection does

[3]Licko, *op. cit.,* states that Solzhenitsyn composed the sketches while in prison and committed them to memory. Only much later did he write them down. My suspicion is that some of the sketches were composed in prison and others, afterward, but this is only conjecture. Nivat and Aucouturier, *op. cit.,* p. 15, maintain that the sketches were written in 1961 but, unfortunately, adduce no evidence to support their date.

[4]Statement by Solzhenitsyn in his letter of May 16, 1967 to the Fourth Congress of Soviet Writers. In *Sobr. soch.,* VI, 12 and Labedz, p. 68. In his just-published study *Desiat' let posle "Odnogo dnia Ivana Denisovicha"* [*Ten Years After* Ivan Denisovich] Zhores A. Medvedev reveals that the "sketches" were actually accepted for publication by the obscure Soviet journal *Sem'ia i shkola* [*Family and School*]. The unexpected publication of the sketches by the émigré journal *Grani* in 1965, however, caused *Sem'ia i shkola* to abandon its plans. Medvedev is also of the interesting opinion that only one of the sketches, "Lake Segden," would have failed to pass the Soviet censorship (pp. 45-46).

[5]At the September, 1967 meeting of the Secretariat of the Writers' Union Solzhenitsyn stated that he began distributing the sketches "three years ago," i.e. in 1964. See *Sobr. soch.,* VI, 38 and Labedz, p. 86.

[6]The term is Solzhenitsyn's: "moi 'krokhotnye rasskazy' ili stikhotvoreniia v proze." See *Sobr. soch.,* VI, 38.

[7]The translations are by Harry Willetts in the March, 1965 *Encounter,* pp. 3-9, by Michael Glenny in Alexander Solzhenitsyn, *Stories and Prose Poems* (London: Bodley Head, 1970), pp. 225-42 and by anonymous in the January 18, 1965 *New Leader,* pp. 5-7. The *New Leader* contains a translation of only four sketches. *Encounter* contains fifteen sketches and the Glenny edition, sixteen. The sketch "The Old Bucket" [*Staroe vedro*] is missing from the *Encounter* edition. Fifteen of the sketches (minus "The Old Bucket") appeared in *Sobr. soch.,* V, 221-32. The 1971, No. 80 issue of *Grani* contains the Russian version of "The Old Bucket" and a *seventeenth* sketch entitled "The Means to Move" [*Sposob dvigat'sia*]. The Posev publishing house in Frankfurt has also issued a record with Solzhenitsyn reading from his own "sketches." The record is made from a tape-recording which is unfortunately of poor quality. The record contains sixteen of the sketches, lacking only "Starting the Day" [*Pristupaia ko dniu*].

not, however, lead him to nihilism because he espies two *alternatives* to the Soviet "now" which are capable of providing sustenance for the soul.

The first of these alternatives is Nature. In the initial sketch, entitled "Breathing" [*Dykhanie*], the narrator stands under an apple tree which is wet from a recent rain and in process of shedding its blossom. Transported by the tree's heady fragrance, he is spiritually detached from the modern world and announces joyfully, "I no longer hear the backfiring motorcycles, the howling radios, the crackling loudspeakers."[8]

Solzhenitsyn's attitude toward Nature appears to be both romantic and religious. He sees the quiet perfection of the Russian woods as a gateway leading from finitude to infinity. Thus, in the sketch "A Reflection in the Water" [*Otrazhenie v vode*] the narrator observes:

> On the surface of swift-running water you cannot make out the reflection of objects near or distant. Only when . . . the current has reached a placid estuary, or in small backwaters, or in small lakes with never a tremulous wave, can we see in the mirror-smooth surface of the water the smallest leaf of a tree on the bank, every fiber of a fine combed cloud, and the intense blue depths of the sky. *So it is with you and me.* If, try as we may, we never have and never shall be able to see and to reflect the truth in all its eternal, fresh-minted clarity, is it not simply because we are also still in motion, still living?[9]

Like the Russian poet Tiutchev, Solzhenitsyn passes from a short description of nature to a philosophical aphorism. His message in the "sketches" is quite close to that articulated by several of the protagonists of his novels—Agniia and the painter Kondrashev-Ivanov in *The First Circle* or Shulubin in *Cancer Ward*. Modern man, Solzhenitsyn seems to hold, is unable to penetrate to the essence of things because he, like a swift-moving stream, is in frantic motion.

In the sketch "A Storm in the Mountains" [*Groza v gorakh*] the narrator describes the awe he experiences upon viewing a wild thunderstorm from a campsite on a mountain side:

> There was nothing in the world but darkness—no above, no beneath, no horizon. Then there was a rending flash of lightning (and) the darkness was divided from the light . . . Just for a moment we half-believed that the land existed, when once again all was darkness and abyss . . . Like the arrows of the Lord of Hosts the lightning flashes fell from on high upon the Ridge and split into wriggles and dribbles

[8]Translation from Willetts, *op. cit.*, p. 3.
[9]Willetts, p. 5. My italics.

> of light . . . And we forgot our fear of the lightning, the thunder and the downpour. *We became insignificant and grateful particles of the world.* A world created today, from nothing, right before our eyes.[10]

Man, an "insignificant particle" in the immensity of Nature, looks with amazement on the lightning storm, a new creation *ex nihilo*. But his awed realization of his own limitation leads him not into despair or rebellion but, rather, to a humble "gratitude."

The modern Promethean refusal to accept the role of "particle" in the universe is touched upon in the sketch entitled "The Duckling" [*Utenok*]. The narrator picks up a "comical yellow duckling, wobbling on its thin yellow legs" and queries, "Who keeps body and soul together in this tiny creature? He weighs nothing at all, his little black eyes are like beads, his feet are like a sparrow's, *just one little squeeze and there would be nothing*."[11] The narrator marvels at the duckling's perfect formation, notes how different it is in character from its brothers and concludes: "We are the ones who will shortly be flying to Venus . . . But with all our atomic might, never, never shall we be able to synthesize in our test-tubes, nor even to assemble from bones and feathers ready-made—a weightless, puny and pathetic little yellow duckling."[12]

The first alternative to the cacophony and dissonance of modern life is, as we have seen, Nature. Unfortunately, it is no longer easy to take refuge in this alternative. In the sketch "Lake Segden" [*Ozero Segden*] the narrator discovers that the unearthly beauty of the lake has been taken captive by a "wicked prince"—the "new class" or bureaucratic elite—which rules the Soviet Union. All roads to the lake have been blocked off; no-trespassing signs and armed guards serve as additional deterrents. "The fishing and game," we are informed, "is kept up for *them* alone."[13] Having nevertheless somehow penetrated to the lake, the narrator thinks to himself, "There may be other things on earth, but who knows—nothing can be seen over the trees. And if there is anything else, it isn't wanted and will never be missed here. Here is a place to settle down for good . . . Your soul would flow, like the quivering air, between water and sky, and your thoughts would run pure and deep."[14] "Dear deserted

[10]Willetts, p. 6. My italics.
[11]*Ibid.*, p. 5. My italics.
[12]*Ibid.*
[13]Willetts, p. 4.
[14]*Ibid.*

lake," the narrator sorrowfully concludes, "Home [*rodina*]." The captive beauty of the lake symbolizes a captive people.

Fortunately, we are informed, Russia has not always been so grim and vulgar. "The Old Bucket" [*Staroe vedro*] presents World War II as a time when comradeship and selflessness were able to thrive, at least on the front lines. Further back in history there is the "alien magnificence" of Petersburg, the "window to the West" built by Peter the Great on the northern swamps. The narrator of the sketch "City on the Neva" [*Gorod na Neve*] is moved by the aesthetic harmony of the architecture of Petersburg and exclaims, "How fortunate that nothing else can be built here! No wedding-cake sky-scraper can elbow its way on to the Nevskii Prospekt, no five-storey box can ruin the Griboedev Canal."[15] Yet, though Petersburg exerts a powerful aesthetic attraction upon him, the narrator finds the city—as did Pushkin, Gogol' and Dostoevsky before him—morally ambiguous. "How delightful it is now to stroll along these avenues! But other Russians, clenching their teeth and cursing, rotted in sunless bogs to build all this beauty."[16] Was, he asks, this beauty worth the suffering which produced it?

The simpler and older beauties of rural Russia draw more unequivocal praise from the narrator. In the religious and aesthetic world-view of old Russia Solzhenitsyn finds a *second* alternative to the formlessness of modern life. The sketch "Travelling along the Oka" [*Puteshestvuia vdol' Oki*], which is perhaps the best known of all the prose poems, hymns the churches of Central Russia which are seen as representing the "secret of the pacifying Russian countryside." They "lift their belltowers—graceful, shapely, each one different" and "nod to each other from afar" as they "soar to the same heaven."[17] In another sketch, "A Poet's Ashes" [*Prakh poeta*], the narrator speaks of a monastery built along the river Oka by an ancient Russian prince:

> Ingvar' Igorevich, who was delivered miraculously from the knives of his brothers, built here, for his soul's sake, the monastery of the Assumption. On a clear day you can see a long way from here, over the rolling water-meadows, and more than twenty miles away on a hill . . . stands the tall bell-tower of the monastery of St. John the Divine. Batu Khan was superstitious and spared them both.[18]

[15]*Ibid.*, p. 5 and Glenny, p. 233.
[16]Willetts, pp. 5-6.
[17]*Ibid.*, p. 8.
[18]*Ibid.*, p. 4.

If Khan Batu, the grandson of Ghengis Khan who led the Mongol invasion of Russia in the thirteenth century, spared the churches and monasteries, the Soviets have acted otherwise. The Monastery of the Assumption, we are told, now stands virtually destroyed. The bricks of its two former churches have been carted off to construct a cow-shed at a nearby collective farm.

"Along the Oka" informs us that such is the normal plight of the Russian country churches. "When you actually get to the village, you find that *not the living but the dead* greeted you from afar. The crosses have been knocked off the roof or twisted out of place long ago . . . The murals over the altar have been washed by the rains of decades and obscene inscriptions have been scrawled over them."[19] Many of the churches have been put to menial use. Some serve as tractor garages, others, as workshops and others, as clubs which boast signs such as "Let Us Aim at High Milk Yields" on their walls. Solzhenitsyn views with subdued horror the mindless desecration of churches and other monuments of the past. He is not alone in his sentiments. One could also mention such talented contemporaries as Vladimir Soloukhin, author of the sketches "Black Boards" [*Chernye doski*] and "Letters from a Russian Museum," and Andrei Siniavskii, recently released from a camp. In Siniavskii's novel *Liubimov* a semi-ruined monastery, which the central protagonist wants to tear down in order to make room for a stadium, overshadows the entire plot.

The attachment of the narrator of the "sketches" to the religio-aesthetic world-view of old Russia is pronounced, as is his distaste for secularized and desacralized modern Soviet man. "People," he observes:

> were always selfish and often unkind. But the evening chimes used to ring out, floating over villages, fields and woods. Reminding men that they must abandon the trivial concerns of this world, and give time and thought to eternity. These chimes . . . raised people up and *prevented them from sinking down on all fours.* Our forefathers put all that was finest in themselves, all their understanding of life into these stones, into these bell-towers.[20]

Solzhenitsyn clearly subscribes to the Dostoevskian dictum that without God and eternity man becomes an animal for whom "all is permitted."

[19]Willetts, pp. 8-9. My italics.
[20]*Ibid.*, p. 9. My italics.

The traditional Russian, who lived close to Nature and joyfully accepted eternity, is in full contrast to modern Soviet man who is in terror of death. In the sketch "*We* Shall Never Die" [*My-to ne umrem*] the narrator muses, "Above all things we have begun to fear death and the dead."[21] Who would dare say, for example, that he was going to visit the graves of his family on a Sunday? "What sort of nonsense is that," Solzhenitsyn has modern man retort, "Visiting people who can't share a meal?"[22] In old Russia, on the other hand, death was not feared. "Once they used to go round our cemeteries on Sundays singing joyously and swinging sweet-smelling censers. The heart was at peace, and the scar which inevitable death had left on it throbbed less painfully . . ."[23] Now, if a cemetery has not gone completely to ruin, it bears signs like, "Grave Owners! You are liable to a fine if you fail to remove last year's litter." More often than not, according to the narrator, the cemeteries are leveled with bulldozers to make room for stadiums and parks of culture.

Modern man will hear nothing of death. He shouts at the dead, "Get lost, you pests, under your painted wooden obelisks . . . let us get on with the living. *Because we are never going to die* [*My-to, my-to ved' ne umrem*]."[24] This boastful and foolish claim is ironically defined by the narrator as "the summit of twentieth century philosophy."

Having lost the spirit, modern man has become hopelessly body-centered—this is the point of the bitterly humorous sketch "Starting the Day" [*Pristupaia ko dniu*]:

> At sunrise thirty young people ran out into a clearing, lined up facing the sun, and started bending, squatting, bowing, lying face downwards, stretching their arms outwards, raising their arms above their heads, and rocking backwards and forwards on their knees. This went on for a quarter of an hour. From a distance you might imagine they were praying . . . No, they weren't saying their prayers. They were doing their morning exercises.[25]

The narrator's conclusion: "No one in our time finds it surprising if a man gives careful and patient daily attention to

[21]Willetts, p. 8.
[22]*Ibid.*
[23]*Ibid.*
[24]*Ibid.*, p. 8.
[25]Willetts, p. 6.

his body. But people would be outraged if he gave the same attention to his soul."[26]

Solzhenitsyn, thus, rejects the Prometheanism and coarse materialism of Soviet man for the winds of eternity which he perceives in Nature and in the religious-based world-view of old Russia. Both Nature and Old Russia are in fact *one* for Solzhenitsyn—they both bear witness to the Divine Artist of the world.

The picture which Solzhenitsyn gives of contemporary Soviet life and mores is scarcely an optimistic one. Ineluctably the din of "back-firing motorcycles, howling radios and crackling loudspeakers" grows ever more audible. To escape for a moment to the forests and lakes of Russia is increasingly difficult; the "new class" has portioned off much of nature for itself. Churches have become tractor garages and clubs. Yet, despite all this, Solzhenitsyn feels powerfully drawn to his suffering, captive homeland. This would seem to be the point of the sketch "The Ants and the Fire" [*Koster i murav'i*]:

> I tossed a rotten log on the fire without noticing that it housed a dense colony of ants. As the wood began to crackle, the ants poured out and ran around in despair. They ran about the surface of the log, shrivelling and burning to death in the blaze. I took a grip on the log and rolled it to one side. Many of the ants escaped now . . . But, strangely enough, they did not run right away from the fire. As soon as they had mastered their dread, they turned back, ran around in circles, as though some force was drawing them back to their abandoned homeland—and there were many who even swarmed back on to the burning log and scurried about on it until they perished.[27]

Solzhenitsyn too is irresistibly drawn to the burning log. Few lands, the narrator of the "sketches" tells us, have suffered as Russia has in this century. "In three wars we have lost so many husbands, sons and sweethearts . . ."[28] "More men have died for us Russians than for any other people . . ."[29] Has the suffering Russia has endured been for nothing? "It is awesome to think," observes the narrator in "City on the Neva," "that perhaps our own shapeless and wretched lives, our explosive disagreements, the groans of the executed and the tears of their wives, will all be clean forgotten."[30] Or will purification and spiritual beauty emerge from the flames, just as the suffering of men

[26]*Ibid.*
[27]Willetts, p. 6.
[28]*Ibid.*, p. 8.
[29]*Ibid.*
[30]*Ibid.*, p. 6.

in northern bogs once produced the physical harmony of Petersburg? "Can this too [i.e. the hell of the Stalin experience]," the narrator asks, "give rise to perfect everlasting beauty?"[31] One could plausibly contend that Solzhenitsyn's "Sketches"—written by one who has endured the Stalin camps—are among the first fruits of such "everlasting beauty."

[31] *Ibid.*

Note on *August 1914*

BY ROMAN JAKOBSON

After the great era of Russian poetry in the early nineteenth century, it was in the first third of our century that Russian poetic art went through a second period of stormy growth. As to the novel, after its classical attainments in Russia of the late nineteenth century, a longer lull set in and until recently the novel lost its leading part in Russian literary development. This genre found its expression either in novelist experiments of poets from Sologub and Belyi till Pasternak or chiefly in rehashes of classical models. Solzhenitsyn is the first *modern* Russian novelist, original and great. His books, and among them especially *August 1914,* exhibit the unprecedented creative alloy of a cosmic epopee with tragic catharsis and latent homily. The ethos of life-long temporal distance amplifies all three constituents of this last novel, heightens its tension and novelty, and bewilders the sluggish reader.

Solzhenitsyn's greatness is the deepest reason not only for the dull and cruel persecution of the writer by red-tape underlings in his homeland but also for the defamatory squibs concocted by his countrymen here in America. We have been disgusted by captious and tasteless lists of imaginary anachronisms and linguistic blunders malignantly unearthed in the new

Extracted from an interview with Roman Jakobson conducted by Philip Rahv, "The Editor Interviews Roman Jakobson," *Modern Occasions,* Winter, 1972, pp. 19-20. Reprinted by permission of the author.

book of this sublime verbal master and precise portrayer, yet the record of morbid cavil is probably beaten in the same New York by another Russian periodical which announced that Solzhenitsyn is a mere hoax and that the books attributed to him are actually poor products of a perfidious trickery undertaken by the Moscow authorities!! As to native American critics who wave aside this writer's novels by proclaiming their topics too outlandish and alien to the American reader, such a lack of insight into the inmost universality of Solzhenitsyn's themes brings to my memory a review of the opera "The Golden Cockerel" in the *Herald Tribune* of the forties which admired Rimskii-Korsakov's music but found Pushkin's plot too Russian and thus too naive for the American public: the reviewer lost sight of its unmistakably American source, Washington Irving's tale borrowed by the Russian poet.

Indomitable Faith

BY MILOVAN DJILAS

If I remember correctly, it was sometime in 1963 that I read Solzhenitsyn's novel *One Day in the Life of Ivan Denisovich,* which was serialized in the Belgrade newspaper *Politika.* But even if my recollection of details is unreliable, I am sure that my introduction to Solzhenitsyn took place while I was in prison and that the weather, dreary and frightfully cold, fit the most banal descriptions of such places.

Since I had tasted years of loneliness in various prison cells many years before, and knew a great deal about Soviet, Nazi and, alas, Yugoslav labor camps, I did not expect to find anything new in Solzhenitsyn's work. And yet it turned out to be a revelation of such clarity as can only be found in art. Sitting in my prison cell, I began to understand through Solzhenitsyn the fate of people sentenced to the most terrifying vegetative existence but who, in spite of everything, managed to retain their humanity. Solzhenitsyn's indomitable faith in the Russian people, and their own immeasurable suffering are a devastating and total condemnation of a system founded on totalitarian ideology and concentration camps.

As I read *Ivan Denisovich* I also sensed that Solzhenitsyn had emerged whole and fearless from the horrors of death and still embodied the pure Russian spirit which I feared had

"Indomitable Faith." From *Book World,* VII, 38 (September 17, 1972), 1-2. © *The Washington Post.* Reprinted by permission of *The Washington Post.*

been distorted, frozen in dogma, mutilated by ideology, and numbed by violence. His later works and public behavior confirmed my belief in the immutability and indestructibility of this spirit. It is his deeply Russian poetic and prophetic qualities, as well as his social and ethical values, that make Solzhenitsyn's work of such fundamental importance for his country and the world.

There was once a belief among Serbian people that a vampire can be laid to rest only if his coffin is pierced by a dogwood stake. In such a way Nikita Khrushchev took it upon himself to combat totalitarian despotism. And it was Solzhenitsyn's work that made it clear Khrushchev's act was directed against an ideological vampire that sought to destroy people and nations. In making a concentration camp the protagonist of his novel and the model for Soviet society, Solzhenitsyn's skill as a writer and accuracy as a historian rendered the entire system utterly meaningless in spirit as well as structure. Although legalized violence and flouting of laws will continue, it is clear that after Solzhenitsyn the Soviet Union could not be turned again into a concentration camp.

By avoiding theorizing, by his impassioned portrayal of moral and ethical beauty, Solzhenitsyn typifies essential, traditional Russia, a Russia as inexhaustible and immense as her vast steppes and plains. He said recently, "I am serving Russia, and Russia is helping me," but he could have said: I represent Russia, that Russia which in mortal convulsions and death itself is overcoming oppression, invasions and dark furies. Rationally and intuitively, Solzhenitsyn knows that the totalitarian state and ideological camps are symbols of a more lasting and deep disfigurement of Russian life, which he is continuing to examine.

The beginning of this is *August 1914,* the "first knot," or fascicle, of a grand epic about World War I and the Revolution, both of which shook Russia to her foundations and diverted her from her centuries old course. Its setting is, of course, the Russian defeat at Tannenberg, at the very outset of the war. For Solzhenitsyn (and I think he is right), this represents the beginning not only of the final disintegration of the tsarist system but also of the decay of traditional humanist values. More objectively than anyone, Solzhenitsyn depicts the inefficiency and inexorable decline of the tsarist regime; but he also shows the unwavering sacrifices of Russian officers and soldiers. (Indeed, there is here a great deal of Tolstoy's boundless faith in Russia's strength; but for Tolstoy Napoleon's invasion in 1812 marked a time of national affirmation and of Russian entry into the European mainstream, while for Solzhenitsyn the defeats of World War I mark the beginning of national misfortunes and muddling of ancient hopes.) His main character, Colonel Vorotyntsev, is a symbol of the patriotism, courage and clear-headedness of the Russian officer corps against the background of the leaderless, intrigue-ridden and weak ruling clique.

Beyond the tsarist regime and the revolutionary ideology, Solzhenitsyn's Russia is healthy, dominated neither by church nor state and capable of enduring unimaginable suffering. That is the ancient spiritual Russia of goodness and justice reflected in his work. Like the Serbian poet and other creative spirits, Solzhenitsyn is more than a philosopher—he is a wise man.

In bringing to life pre-revolutionary Russia, *August 1914* refutes and grinds into dust all those "truths" and "scientific views" that, mercilessly crammed into the national consciousness of Russia and of other nations, have been perverting human life. After *August 1914* it will not be easy to dismiss history and life (as the official ideology did) with the phrase, "Those were the days of tsarism and capitalism."

Solzhenitsyn has begun to fill the emptiness superimposed on Russian culture and consciousness. He is returning Russia its soul—the very soul which had been revealed to the world by Pushkin, Gogol', Tolstoy, Dostoevsky, Chekhov and Gorkii. And by discovering this soul—this original Russia—in the frightful terror of Stalinist camps and in the bureaucratic grayness of post-Stalin days, Solzhenitsyn's work forecasts a renaissance in Russia.

By returning Russia to herself, by rejecting ideological Russia, Solzhenitsyn is returning her to the human community. Although ideology does not belong to any single people, and in one way or another all are suffering from it, only a spiritualized Russia—the true Russia, the one portrayed by Solzhenitsyn—can align itself with the rest of the world. Humanity is not perpetuated by disappearances and suppression of peoples but by affirmation of their qualities.

August 1914 is conceived in hope and suffering. We can only wish that Solzhenitsyn be allowed by health and circumstances to complete the work of returning Russia to her spiritual self and to the human community.

The Tolstoy Connection

BY MARY McCARTHY

For Western readers *August 1914* is a difficult book. The geography is unfamiliar; the logistics are bewildering to anybody but a military specialist; and the chronology is not easy to follow since the scene keeps shifting and many events overlap. Here the author has, in fact, been helpful, taking pains to scatter unobtrusive dates in each of the episodes (there are sixty-four chapters, which comprise fifty-five episodes told in direct narration, two flashbacks, four summaries, three montages of newspaper clippings) as they unroll, sometimes simultaneously, sometimes in sequence, during the fatal month of August 1914.

In the first chapter, laid in the remote steppes of the southern Caucasus, a young volunteer waiting for his train on the station platform buys newspapers reporting the Russian victory of Gumbinnen, which, as we later learn, took place August 7 in far-off East Prussia. Therefore the book must begin on August 8 or, more likely, 9. In Chapter 4, the following morning, a young woman on an estate in the northern Caucasus by which the volunteer's train has just passed has received "such a happy letter" from a lieutenant in the field who has not yet seen battle; this letter—as we discover 510 pages later, in Chapter 59—was postmarked August 5, at Ostrolenka, in eastern Poland.

"The Tolstoy Connection." From *Saturday Review* (September 16, 1972), 79-96.

Even if the passage of the volunteer's train had not told us what day it was, we would know that it was some time during the week before August 15, because the young woman's parents are keeping the fast preceding the Assumption of the Virgin, and there is no meat or milk on the breakfast table. On the previous Friday there has been an eclipse of the sun, which, for students of astronomy, will place the chapter celestially. Throughout the novel holy days and saints' days are imprinted in the characters' awareness, marking the calendar dates. The peak of the action is reached on the Day of the Assumption, August 15, which saw the disaster—for the Russians—of the battle of Tannenberg, recorded in history as the German Cannae (Hannibal's encirclement and annihilation of the Romans) but here shown less as a clear-cut battle than as a diffuse series of groping movements toward and away from the enemy on the part of Russian troops lost in a sandy forest and playing a nightmare game of blindman's buff.

The beautiful dovetailing of Solzhenitsyn's timetable, with its inlaid and often barely visible, almost watermark-like pattern, is clear enough to those who take the trouble to trace it. But the reader seeking light from Western sources will only become more confused unless he is warned that the author is using the old Julian calendar, in force in Russia until 1918. If, as I did, he tries consulting Winston Churchill's *The Unknown War* (1931) to make events tally, he should subtract thirteen days from Churchill's time-calculation or add thirteen to Solzhenitsyn's. The same for the *Britannica,* twelfth and thirteenth editions.

As for geography, the publisher has supplied a map in the form of end papers, but this is inadequate to the needs of a lay Western reader who really wants to understand what is going on in the novel. I am told that even for a Russian who was alive in 1914 the text is hard to follow, not because of any stylistic obscurity, but because of the dense thicket of military tactics and strategy he must work his way through. If ever a novel called for visual aids, this is it. What are wanted are military maps and diagrams showing troop positions and movements throughout the crucial days of mid-August, how the four-and-a-half corps of the Second (Samsonov's) Army were deployed, the placement of the cavalry divisions on the flanks, plus a table of the names of the five commanding generals, of the generals who served under them, and of those who commanded cavalry divisions. Footnotes or an explicatory preface describing the structure of a tsarist division, regiment, battalion, right down to company, would also be useful, and perhaps some identification of the historical persons in the novel.

I admit that at the beginning I took General Samsonov (partly because of his name) for a fictional character, a bemused, broad-browed, overweight, asthmatic Samson among the Philistines of his staff and Army Group Headquarters. Of course, no Russian would make that mistake, any more than we would about General Pershing or Joffre. But I should still like to be sure that Colonel Vorotyntsev, the novel's other hero and its searchlight intelligence, is imaginary (as the translator, Michael Glenny, declares in a *Life* article) or at least partly real. In the Grunfliess Forest, wounded and leading a small group of men to find a way out of the enchanted German ring of encirclement, Vorotyntsev abruptly tells one of them that he knows he will come out alive because an old Chinaman told his fortune when he was serving in Manchuria: He will not be killed in any war but will die a soldier's death at the age of sixty-nine—that is, in 1945. Does this riddle mean that we might find his name among those of officers shot by Stalin in that year—the date of Solzhenitsyn's own arrest? Such a gently dropped clue, a pebble in the forest, would be characteristic of this author's way of working. The reader might also like to know (a fact I found in the *Britannica*) that General Rennenkampf, commander of the First Army and one of the book's many high-placed villains, was shot by the Bolsheviks in 1918.

There is double reason to regret that the publisher has done almost nothing—beyond printing it in English—to make the book accessible to the ordinary American reader. It is in need of a pathfinder or friendly scout, because in other ways, having nothing to do with what corps the Kaluga regiment served in or who was General Sirelius, *August 1914* is going to be disorienting to current Western sensibility. It is likely to be put down in anger or dismissed as dated in its techniques (which is true, especially of the streamlined, "modernistic," silver-screen inserts when the author switches to film scenario), corny (true, too, sometimes: "mounted, as always, on his powerful stallion," "moving freely now at his full, magnificent height"), and, anyway, impossible to finish. To be fair to the book will not be easy for many readers, particularly those who like an author to conform to their own notions of political good manners. Solzhenitsyn himself, to say it straight out, is unfair in his novel to a whole category of society: the "liberals" and "advanced circles" of 1914, those who opposed the war and patriotic sentiments, who yearned, they thought, for revolution, despised religion, authority, tradition, anything respected and handed down. His standards are harsh and simple. There is one test he applies to each and all of his characters: What is their attitude to military service? Among men of draft age the bad are readily identifiable: They avoid conscription, they serve unwillingly, they have contempt for the colors and/or run away under fire. Among regular officers they are the ones who serve from ambition to get good marks in the rating book and promote their careers. Among the rest—mostly women and girls—the bad, who are more silly than wicked, reveal their trivial natures by denouncing patriotic demonstrations and doing everything in their power to deter their sons and schoolmates from joining up. The good serve their country, sometimes even at the cost of sacrificing principle—like the volunteer of the first chapter, who has been a practicing Tolstoyan, forgoing meat and sensuality—or, if too old to serve, defend it with their sympathy even when they are Jews and members of a liberal milieu deeply opposed to the reactionary tendencies of the government.

It is not a question of *approving* of the war; few of the good do, and to the more educated and wiser among them the war is a tragedy that will set progressive forces in Russia back ten years, twenty, a generation. Rather, it is a question of being willing to take one's part in the tragedy or not. The central ethic of the novel is one of sharing, and the characters are judged by whether, in their souls, they are sharers or hoarders. The prosperous draft-dodger on his "economy" in the Kuban hoards his worthless life; the enlightened liberal hoards his little store of second-hand ideas, which he regards as principles too valuable to sacrifice. From the author's point of view, they are both looking out for Number One, like the cowardly, self-serving generals; the difference is that the liberals and "advanced people" do not know it.

None of this can sit very well with American liberals and radicals, who have consistently sought to dissuade young men from sharing in the Vietnamese tragedy. Have we not used many of the same arguments advanced in *August 1914* by that highly unpleasant character, Ensign Lenartovich, and by a chorus of two Rostov students shrilly maintaining that the main enemy is capitalism? Unlike present-day American liberals, though, Solzhenitsyn does not seek to distinguish between justified war and unjustified war (the one to be supported, the other not). He is picturing a war that, unjustified on either side, was nevertheless endured and suffered by the masses, from whose blood sacrifice, in his opinion, nobody, once it began, should have held himself aloof.

He also seems to be saying that the Russian defeat, in which defeatist liberals played a part, led to the avoidable catastrophe of Bolshevism—a debatable proposition, since it is based not simply on an ethic but on a cause-and-effect sequence. Was October 1917 avoidable, in the long run, and was it inevitably and by definition a catastrophe? Did the Lenartoviches "cause" Stalin?

It is hard to read this volume without an eye nervously straying to current events and one's own responsibility in them. The temptation to do so has been put there by Solzhenitsyn himself, who clearly intends his reader to draw inferences from what he describes and apply the lesson to present-day life. Unlike the usual historical novel, far from offering escape into scenes of antique battle and undisturbed folkways, this book constantly, insistently brings one back to the present, as if the errors, sins, and follies of 1914 were still corrigible if one would only take them to heart.

Occasionally, on the strategic and tactical plane, the book seems merely to be refighting the Masurian Lakes campaign, and this time winning it—thanks to the clear-eyed Colonel Vorotyntsev, promoted in our imagination to full general. But the underlying engagement is for our contemporary hearts and minds. The author is urging us to turn away from the terrible encircling trap of revolutionary ideology and take the safer course of gradualism and inch-by-inch social progress. Yet to trust in progress today, when no cure for the body politic but surgery is visible, seems old fashioned, almost simple minded. It would take a Rip van Winkle still to hope for gradual betterment through reforms. Solzhenitsyn must be aware of this and aware also that "reformist" is a term of vilification in the Soviet Union and not a banner to fight under anywhere, unless perhaps in some crusade for simplified spelling or an intramural church struggle. It is as if his book had been designed to offend "advanced people" wherever they are to be found—revolutionaries, real and false, all those who wish, at least in thought, to be ahead of their time rather than behind it or in the middle of it.

Bravery is one of the highest values in *August 1914,* and the author exemplifies it in his own person to an almost alarming degree. He takes no protective measures whatever against the criticism he must have foreseen from Soviet literary officialdom and from many independent leftist writers in the outside world who have supported him up to now. Take, for instance, the question of class origins. The two principal figures, both deeply sympathetic, are a general and a colonel: Samsonov and Vorotyntsev. The great majority of the characters we come to admire or like belong to the gentry or the property-owning class: Colonel Pervushin, Colonel Kabanov, General Nechvolodov, General Martos, Colonel Kakhovskoi, the two Colonels Smyslovskii, Lieutenant Kharitonov, Colonel Krymov, the volunteer Isaakii and his friend Kotia, both students. A giant peasant, Arsenii, whom Vorotyntsev takes as his orderly, is simple, good, brave, and extremely capable. An artillery sergeant-major Terentii Chernega, a rough diamond, ranks high for competence and dauntless resolution. The peasant conscripts in the mass, "those trusting bearded men, those friendly eyes, those placid, selfless faces," are proved to have immense courage and endurance when put to the test—in particular the men of the Vyborg, Estland, Neva, and Dorogobuzh regiments—but few individuals stand out among them. On the negative side, there are scenes of Russian peasants looting the German towns, and the fact that officers are looting, too, in a genteel way that makes it look more like a leisurely shopping tour, does not equalize the picture, not at any rate to Soviet-style critics, who measure with a ruler. From a Soviet point of view, the amount of favorable space allotted to individuals of the officer class is utterly disproportionate. And why, these critics will ask, does Solzhenitsyn not show us a single proletarian?

Of course, in such a story, which is a story of leadership and its collapse, the chief actors will inevitably be officers. But hostile reviewers are unlikely to find the explanation there, in the most natural and obvious place; rather, they will look for it in Solzhenitsyn's "psychology." A frequent slur cast on him is that he comes from the officer class, which is both false and true. Solzhenitsyn's father was a lieutenant in the tsarist army and a Tolstoyan (like the boy Isaakii, who is evidently drawn from him—his last name is Lazhenitsyn); the family were well-to-do peasants forcibly settled by Peter the Great in Cossack territory. Yet, even if Solzhenitsyn is excused by his censors for extending sympathy to men like Samsonov, Vorotyntsev, and the various gallant colonels—who, after all, were patriots and have long ago passed into history—what about his unconcealed approval of "military" ideas of discipline, duty, command? Soviet Russians may not find much to object to here. But American liberals? And their children?

The generals in the book who send lying dispatches, disobey orders, cover up, and run away are held up to scorn, not for being militarists, but for being bad militarists who fail in their duty. Samsonov, who is no genius but honest and duteous, offers a touching contrast in his respect for the code of honor.

Still, courage, discipline, a high sense of duty both to those above and below, are not the unique property of men in the regular army who feel honor-bound by its rules. These qualities are also found in revolutionaries. And the bias of this opening volume of Solzhenitsyn's chronicle (the next will be *October 1916*) appears in the fact that the only so-called revolutionary we really get to know (and that one must say "so-called" tells a lot) is the despicable Ensign Lenartovich, who has not the slightest sense of duty and deserts his unit at a crucial moment with the excuse that his skin is too valuable to the workers to be left in the field. His cowardly desertion and striking out for himself (he wants to go over to the Germans and explain to them that he is a Socialist) is a breach of trust with the sole examples he knows of the oppressed masses he claims to be for—the men serving under him. He does not waste a thought on what will happen to them. Such a character is not basically implausible; there may have been many of him in the Tsar's army. Yet he is rather thinly realized and uninteresting. The shallowness of Lenartovich (even granting that he is conceived as a shallow person) shows a failure of justice on the author's part—understandable, God knows, humanly, after what he has suffered and seen others suffer because of the "ideas" of such embryo theorists, but in the author-as-novelist a shortcoming nonetheless. Tolstoy, one feels, would have gone deeper into Lenartovich, as he did with such a worldling as Vronskii, whose whole way of life he held in contempt and loathing. He would have probed, overcoming distaste, holding his broad nose if necessary, till he found a wretched fellow creature in the weak, complacent, sloganized young man. In Tolstoy's universe, cowardice in war is not so damning, i.e., so "revealing."

Nevertheless, when this is said, I have to remember that the scene of Lenartovich in the forest, with all its onesidedness, is magnificent. He has been found, sitting on a tree stump, by Vorotyntsev and his party, which at this point consists of only two—the giant peasant, Arsenii, and the young lieutenant from Rostov, Lieutenant Kharitonov, who has been released from a hospital with concussion and is trying to rejoin his unit. The opposite of Lenartovich, who does not have a scratch on him and is blubbering about having "nearly been killed" in a potato field by Germans. Lenartovich lies to Vorotyntsev about why he is not with his regiment, and Vorotyntsev sizes him up correctly as a deserter. Yet he takes him on as a responsibility. Lenartovich, sizing *him* up, decides to play along: Maybe this smart colonel can outwit the Germans and get the party through the line. Next they come upon a group of peasant soldiers from the Dorogobuzh regiment carrying two stretchers, one with the body of their dead colonel, which they are taking home for burial, and the other with a wounded lieutenant who is wrapped in the regimental colors. Carrying those heavy stretchers, these last survivors of a regiment that was cut to pieces covering the retreat of others in a heroic rearguard action have traveled more than twenty-five miles along forest paths, up and down hill, through the German lines. The opposite of Lenartovich.

At Vorotyntsev's invitation the two groups join up. Lenartovich is horror-struck. Is Vorotyntsev going to risk their own safety by taking on a dead body and a stretcher case? He cannot understand why "this clear-headed colonel was giving in to the ridiculous obscurantist notions of these peasant reservists from the darkest corners of Russia." He revises his opinion of Vorotyntsev sharply downward and becomes even more impatient and resentful when Vorotyntsev obliges him to take a front pole of the dead man's stretcher, he himself shouldering the other. Lenartovich has figured out that the wounded lieutenant, obviously a reactionary, has wrapped himself in the colors as a ruse to make those superstitious fools carry him: The whole procession is a disgusting, dangerous farce. But Vorotyntsev, when they come at last to a resting place, turns out to have a plan. He finds a sunny burial spot on a little hill and explains to the men that they are going to bury Colonel Kabanov now. They accept (the more willingly,

Lenartovich perceives, because he and the colonel have been sharing the burden of the body), and the grave is dug. There follows a funeral service, with Arsenii—who, it comes out, has sung in his church choir—intoning the prayers for the dead "in his strong diaconal voice" and leading the responses.

Lenartovich stands aside, with a twisted smile of condescension, not adding his voice to the responses, but his head is bared. Once the body is buried, there is still the problem of the wounded lieutenant they are carrying. Vorotyntsev makes no allusion to this, and they go forward with the stretcher till they are near the spot he has selected for them to try to cross the German-held main road. They wait for night. Then the reactionary lieutenant shows that he "knows his duty." Volunteering to stay behind, he invites the men to unwind the colors from his body, which they do; a peasant is wrapped in them. But, at the last minute, colors or not, they decline to accept his sacrifice. The strongest of the reservists, as they start to cross the road under machine-gun fire, picks up the lieutenant and hoists him onto his shoulder. The stretcher is left behind in the wood.

Now if you subtract Lenartovich from these happenings, which occupy three separate chapters, you see that the narrative is not the same without him—less forceful, less strangely moving. He, the deserter, is essential to that motley group in the woods, by no means all "good" men but sharing some natural wisdom he lacks. The ensign's very apartness from the others, his quality of onlooker, his coldness and self-satisfaction, his indifference to the colors, his irreligion, complete and sharpen the picture like the introduction of a shadow. If all this is a lesson, there must be someone present whom the lesson is aimed at—a heathen, in fact. Though perhaps not entirely irredeemable. Vorotyntsev thinks he has the makings of an officer in him—an estimate Lenartovich would angrily reject if he could see the thought running through the colonel's head. But if the potential for good in Lenartovich had been explored for the reader, in other words, if his creator had treated him more fairly, shown him to us "in the round," the very chiaroscuro of the effect I have just tried to describe would vanish. This novel is *not* the work of a liberal imagination, and its strong alternations of light and shade are essential to its particular vision, which is less close to the optics of *War and Peace* than to moralized myth whose beginning is the Separation of Light from Darkness.

The Masurian Lakes campaign is taken by Solzhenitsyn as the text for a sermon interspersed with cautionary tales and deriving much of its force from the natural setting of wilderness, menacing lakes, isthmuses, deep pine and oak woods. The failure of leadership to guide the men through the uneven, broken terrain, moral as well as topographical, is ascribed, though—and this is a surprise—more to plain stupidity than to any of the more familiar vices. The stupid generals of Army Group Headquarters, ignorantly directing the movements of Samsonov's and Rennenkampf's armies, issuing idiotic orders and insane counter-orders, neglecting the most elementary details of supply and transport, so that the men march five days beside a railroad track when they might have been sent by train and go into the attack hungry having received no bread rations and often not even hardtack; the stupid, lethargic corps commanders who order a retreat when their men are winning a battle, fail to send up reinforcements in a tight squeeze, do not notice a large gap in the defense perimeter, mistake two columns of advancing Germans for a Russian relief force and do not dispatch scouts to investigate, send out uncoded wireless messages, so that the amazed Germans are informed of their orders of the day and troop dispositions; and behind all these fools, the jackasses of the General Staff under the Tsar's uncle, the Grand Duke Nikolai, himself rather intelligent and alert but too fearful of court intrigues to use seriously his power as commander-in-chief to fire his incompetent and well-connected subordinates. All this massed and beribboned stupidity is seen as a kind of opaqueness, density, darkness of mind into which no thought can penetrate, no ray of truth or reason.

The primordial night of these men's minds is, in fact, the source of their cunning, lies, and incessant evasions, their adroitness in bureaucratic in-fighting, and avoidance of responsibility—an adroitness of maneuver and power of anticipation that they pitifully lack on the field. Stupidity is the mother of calculation; the task of covering up their incompetence stimulates their brain-power to an unremitting and feverish activity.

In contrast to the prevailing idiocy of the Russian command (an exception is General Martos, commander of XV Corps, a lively, intelligent man and brave as well), Solzhenitsyn sets the efficiency, good organization, and technical competence of the Germans. He admires German management, which he sees as progressive and enlightened, an example the Russians ought to have taken to heart. Yet, among the German generals he notes degrees and shadings of mental capacity. On the German side the outstanding brain is Hermann von François, too conceited to be respected as a man by Solzhenitsyn but, as a general, brave, brilliant, agile, resourceful. Solzhenitsyn attributes the victory of Tannenberg entirely to von François, and Churchill concurs, although, at the time he wrote, Ludendorff had been assigning himself the credit. Von François was successful, because (although, like Martos, he was a mere corps commander) he was not afraid to go over the heads of the cautious and pedantic Ludendorff, his wooden superior, Hindenburg and the General Staff itself to complain directly to the Kaiser when his projects were being thwarted. Nor did the Kaiser let protocol stop him from telephoning to von François in the field to hear his opinion on the correct deployment of his corps. That such a relation is possible is proof in itself of German superiority. Among the more pathetic documents cited by Solzhenitsyn are two Russian soldiers' jingles, one mocking the Kaiser, who is represented on a postcard as a miserable tomcat—"So who leads the German Army? Willy Whiskers—stupid cat!"—the other mocking von François—"O Hermann the German, you're wicked and silly! Almost as bad as that fool Kaiser Willy!" Von François also had the sense, when he did not get the orders he liked, to disobey the orders he got; in an intelligent man Solzhenitsyn excuses and applauds this.

As further contrast to the ponderous stupidity at the top of the Russian command, which was also top-heavy (there were too many generals in the Tsar's army), the author lets us see the intelligence and skill of many field officers, ranking down from colonel to captain, and the quick apprehension and perceptiveness of common soldiers like Arsenii, who cannot read and takes a German grand piano for a funny kind of black billiard table. The human resources and learning skills of the Russian people never cease to delight and astonish Vorotyntsev whenever he comes upon them. And whenever he meets intelligence, it goes hand and hand with bravery. In Solzhenitsyn's mind these qualities appear to be linked, as if in a holy marriage. No brave man can be wholly stupid, and no darkened mind venturesome. Whether this is true or not (which may depend on your definition of intelligence and of bravery), Solzhenitsyn, I think, loves intelligence because for him this faculty or its free exercise comes as much from the heart as from the brain. Lenartovich, whose judgments are almost infallibly wrong, illustrates the fact that nobody can be more stupid than a highly trained intellectual.

In any case there can be no doubt that in the present novel intelligence, whenever it shows itself, produces an effect of sheer joy comparable to the sensation of coming into a clearing in the woods. The circumstances of war, testing responses at every turn and with unexpected results in terms of rank and education, isolate this faculty and render it more valuable, more indispensable for survival than it is in ordinary life. At the same time, absence of it or momentary failures of it are much more conspicuous, taking the form of colossal blunders, for which somebody is going to be blamed.

In *August 1914* Colonel Vorotyntsev is the carrier of the precious quality. He has been sent as a sort of divine messenger by the Grand Duke, and his function is precisely to gather intelligence and report back to his commander in chief. Arriving on a Sunday (August 11), he finds Samsonov still in eastern Poland, comfortably installed in his headquarters and enjoying a predinner rest. He has in fact been lying down, in his stocking feet, with his military tunic off, the picture of unruffled tranquility, though his mind is uneasy because his superior, General Zhilinskii, at Army Group Headquarters, back in Bialystok, has been sending him impossible orders to keep pushing his troops ahead, though they have been nine days on the march already without the regulation day's rest, and they need a halt anyway for supplies to catch up with them; their rations are running out. Besides, it worries him that he has had no information about the enemy's whereabouts, nor about that of the First Army, to his right, nothing has come in from cavalry reconnaissance or from Army Group Headquarters. It is five days since his troops crossed the East Prussian frontier; the worn-out men have been advancing through an eerie, deserted countryside. For three days they did not see a German or hear a shot fired. Another irritation: Zhilinskii has taken two of his corps away from him, leaving him with three-and-a-half, while the invisible and, as it turns out, inactive Rennenkampf somewhere to the northeast has seven. Army Group Headquarters is confident that the German forces are up there facing Rennenkampf in the north, where they can be cornered and destroyed. Samsonov's instinct tells him that they are somewhere on his left, to the southwest of Rennenkampf: Why, after being defeated at Gumbinnen, would they just stand still in that marshy lake region waiting to be trapped? Zhilinskii will not listen and every day orders him to move his army farther right (i.e., to the northeast), while Samsonov, pursuing his instinct, is edging his forces left, where he is sure the Germans are. Sure enough, that day he has had confirmation. Contact has finally been made; yesterday a unit of General Martos's XV Corps, on the *left* of the left center, has wheeled *left* and caught the enemy, defeated him and forced him back. This has been the Battle of Orlau, August 10.

The sudden appearance of Vorotyntsev in his peaceful headquarters, on top of the news of this victory, galvanizes the corpulent Samsonov, who quickly orders his boots and tunic and places himself behind a desk. Soon he and the staff colonel are standing before a big wall map as he excitedly argues his case, pointing to the pins denoting troop positions, which Vorotyntsev has understood at a glance, and plunging the flag of XV Corps even more firmly into its place. Recognizing from Vorotyntsev's questions that here at last is an intelligence, even if a not uncritical one, Samsonov realizes that "in this man God had sent him the very person he lacked on his staff—someone he could talk to." Despite their disparities of endowment, visible in their bodily structures (Mercury to a somewhat out-of-training Hercules), it is a meeting of minds.

Samsonov is by no means a brilliant intellect; his mind works slowly, even heavily, unlike that of the fleet messenger, but they have understood each other at once. Here at Ostrolenka, surrounded by fools and human wolves, hurried on and reprimanded by those other fools and wolves at Bialystok, Samsonov's greatest yearning is to have time to *think;* there is an unpleasant buzzing in his head that disturbs his concentration, and he is aware that there is some vital factor in the situation that eludes him. And yet he is *right,* and Zhilinskii is wrong, and, behold, Vorotyntsev *agrees.* What is more, Vorotyntsev shows him where he is making a mistake; using his fingers as a compass, he indicates to the general that his headquarters are now six day's march from the front line—much too far away. Samsonov immediately feels himself blush; he had not noticed. Tomorrow he will move his headquarters to Neidenburg. Yes, God has sent this man. Moreover, the wonder-worker has brought an incredible message: Samsonov's prayers have been heard, and they are going to give him back I Corps, which has been immobilized at Soldau, when it ought to be moving up to make liaison with Martos in the center. Vorotyntsev will personally carry the order to General Artamonov so that there will be no chance of its miscarrying or being slyly ignored.

Thus at his first appearance the "clear-sighted" Vorotyntsev is placed for the reader squatting before a map and measuring with the compass of his spread fingers the distance between two points, i.e., using his body as a tool for understanding and instruction. From then on, he will rarely be separated from a map. The nadir of the action is reached when he awakes, with Arsenii, in the Grunfliess Forest in a condition of total despair, having lost his horse and his map case: "Arsenii was the only one left. Vorotyntsev had striven to help an entire army, and this single soldier was all that remained to him." Help arrives in the form of the dazed Lieutenant Kharitonov, who has with him a set of maps he has pinched from the German barracks at Hohenstein, while his men, turned loose like a force of nature on the products of German craft and industry, were grabbing macaroni, preserved veal, beer, sugar biscuits, cocoa, and his fellow officers were grabbing haberdashery, perfume, a child's bicycle, rugs, and ladies' coats. That is, only Kharitonov, one of the book's secondary heroes, has, by a sort of divination and hardly knowing why he does so, looted German property that has real value and is not just an article of consumption. His appearance in the woods is providential, the supply coming to meet the demand, and the superiority of the German maps to the Russian ones points the lesson once again. The map of the forest paths, glued together by Kharitonov in the hospital, is spread out on the ground by Vorotyntsev, who "hovered over it like a falcon over its prey." Thanks to the intelligence drawn from it, the party and the stretcher bearers who will soon join it are saved.

Maps, an improvised compass, binoculars, a Japanese flashlight—these attributes, denoting vision, belong to the half-mythic figure of Vorotyntsev as much as the caduceus and the winged sandals to Mercury. Science and the intelligent use of it are indispensable to practical wisdom. Before they meet Kharitonov, Arsenii proposes that, rather than try to break through, he and the colonel build a hut in the forest and hide in it till winter, staying alive on roots and berries. Hermits, he argues, have done it in the desert. "But we're not monks, we're soldiers!" succinctly retorts Vorotyntsev. General Nechvolodov, a somewhat senior but parallel figure to Vorotyntsev, with the same idea of usefulness, is repeatedly shown gazing through binoculars, and he makes use of a German flashlight, a trophy presented to him by a sergeant; he knows astronomy and astonishes an artillery colonel by being able to tell the time by the stars.

The application of science to the immediate problem of survival is not, though, the ultimate wisdom. The decisive moment in *August 1914* comes when Samsonov, having determined to share the fate of his army, moves his headquarters a second time, from the occupied town of Neidenburg up to Martos's advance post in the field, and disconnects the Hughes teletype. He wants relief from this chattering instrument carrying senseless orders from Zhilinskii and messages that demand reply. The move from civilization into the wilderness allows him to cut it off. Now, ignoring his staff, who are obliged by the rule book, and against their inclination, to stick with him, he can be alone with his thoughts. As he rides out at a trot from Neidenburg on that "red-letter day" of August 15, his mind is suddenly clear and confident. Yet, as the reader senses, he has taken his first direct step toward suicide. The decision to cut himself off has a double meaning that he is not yet aware of. The Hughes teletype has been bringing him only useless babble, static, because on the other end there is a group of idiots; so clarity is achieved by silencing it. Yet the gesture also means that he has put himself beyond communication: when Vorotyntsev, who has sent him an urgent letter by a dispatch rider telling him how he can still save the situation, comes to meet him in a field, to say that remnants of the Estland regiment are still holding out, Samsonov seems no longer to recognize him. The colonel too has become part of what is now a general irrelevant noise, like that buzzing in his head that has accompanied him from Ostrolenka and prevented him from thinking.

Has this mental activity, disconnected from any purpose, a significance or value of its own? Perhaps a higher value? Samsonov is a religious man, and the night before his fateful decision, on Assumption eve (*"die höchste Zeit,"* he has been murmuring to himself, ["the highest time"]), we have seen him at prayer. The notion of a peak of time has come to him as a clear thought piercing the darkness. A phrase from a

German school book, (*"es war die Höchste Zeit sich zu retten"*) ["it was high time to escape"], referring to Napoleon in burning Moscow, has floated back into his memory and fused, we suppose, with a holy image of the Virgin mounting upward borne by angels. There is a message for him in it, he feels; it is high time for him to do something, if he could only make out what. During the night he has waked up sweating with the word "assume" in his ears: "Assume command"? "I assume thee into my keeping"? In fact, his time is accomplished. The next morning, having disconnected the teletype, he will be with Martos, near Nadrau.

When Vorotyntsev hurriedly rides up on August 16, the Feast of the Uncreated Image of Christ, he finds Samsonov in a field near Orlau, saying farewell to the remnants of his army, taking off his cap and thanking them. He has moved his headquarters again during the night to get away from the advancing Germans; except for a few disciplined units, his troops are fleeing everywhere. Something might still have been salvaged, since the German encirclement is not yet complete. But Samsonov, to all intents and purposes, is no longer in command. That afternoon, he moves once more or, rather, is moved, like a bulky, powerless idol, jostling in a cart with his chief of staff, whom he can no longer even bother to despise. He is in a trance, buried in thought, which he emerges from to declare suddenly that he is going back, alone, to find XV Corps. His staff dissuades him. Next they are on foot; he is letting those men tear off his epaulets and bury them. Early the next morning, August 17, he slips away from them and hides in the woods. When they are gone, he kneels down in a clearing, and, begging God's forgiveness, he shoots himself.

These scenes of Samsonov mounting to his destiny while descending the staircase of power and authority are truly Shakespearean. There is nothing that I know of in Russian literature to compare them with. The closest is perhaps Mussorgskii's *Boris Godunov;* it is as if the slowly toppling Boris were merged with the fool in the snowstorm. But Boris has been a wicked man, and Samsonov is a good man, if not a very good general, who has done his best, given the circumstances, which are largely out of his control. His awareness of that, of a dimension in experience (not in generalship) that evades him and yet whose presence he senses, is what makes him a larger and even, yes, wiser being than Vorotyntsev, who so clearly sees what should be done at every juncture, how all may yet be saved if a hole in the line is plugged, how if I Corps can only be joined up to XV Corps, von François's encirclement can be smashed and the enemy, in turn, caught in a Russian pincers. . . . This precise, long-range vision, surveying all contingencies like a pair of binoculars sweeping over a distant slope, is limited by its own perceptions. It does not sense, as Samsonov dimly does, uncontrollable factors, i.e., the will of God, which has made everything just as it is and not otherwise: the fatal lakes, himself with all his shortcomings and oversights, the Grand Duke, General Zhilinskii.

Throughout the novel Solzhenitsyn is engaged in a polemic with Tolstoy. He disagrees with Tolstoy's contention in *War and Peace* that "great men" cannot influence the course of events but at best can only swim along with it and await a countercurrent or the turning of the tide. Solzhenitsyn holds that leadership is determining in war and uses examples from the tragic Eastern campaign to prove it. He is also angry with Tolstoy, or so it seems, because of the effect Tolstoy's doctrine of love and nonviolence had on young men of the war generation, persuading them that it was wrong to accept military service. In the first chapter Isaakii meets another Tolstoyan in the railroad station, a rather homely girl whom he has known in school and corresponded with. She reproaches him when she guesses that he is on his way to volunteer and, seeing that her words are making no impression, brings out her final argument: "What about Tolstoy? What would Lev Tolstoy say about it, have you thought of that?" Isaakii has. "I feel sorry for Russia" is his answer. In a more sarcastic vein the author portrays Roman Tomchak, the rich and useless draftdodger of several early chapters, as a great admirer of Lev Nikolaevich: he has had several oil paintings made of him by an artist in Rostov—Tolstoy scything, Tolstoy holding a plow, Tolstoy standing on his front steps—and has explained to his ignorant father that "to admire Tolstoy was the thing to do among educated people, that he was a count and great national figure. . . ."

Such rather low blows aimed at an author who had died in 1910 (and who would not have reciprocated Tomchak's admiration) seem puzzling, especially in view of the many Tolstoyan elements in Solzhenitsyn's own writing and general outlook, even if a desire to make clear his *differences* with

Tolstoy may help explain his sharpness. The real explanation, though, lies probably in the nature of these differences, which on examination turn out to be basic—something Solzhenitsyn himself may have discovered in the course of writing this novel. If there is a Solzhenitsyn faith unmistakably expressed here, it is opposed at every point to the doctrines preached by Tolstoy—on history, the role of leaders, technology and progress (Tolstoy held that in itself technology was morally neutral but that in a bad society machines only multiplied the existing potential for evil), the Orthodox Church, war. Assuming that the semi-mythic Colonel Vorotyntsev is a prototype or model, Vorotyntsev's idea of *usefulness,* the principle that guides him through the book, with his map case, binoculars, and torch, is in direct contradiction to the Tolstoyan view of the *uselessness* of any attempt to direct the movement of events. There can be no accommodation between these views. It has to be one or the other for, if Tolstoy is right, then the keen, bright-eyed colonel is just wasting his time galloping from point to point, measuring and asking questions.

But Vorotyntsev *is* just wasting his time and getting a lot of people needlessly killed. That is what the plot demonstrates from start to finish. When at the end he arrives at the Grand Duke's headquarters determined to report the *truth* of what has happened, he gradually discovers that he is wasting his breath: nothing will be changed. Vorotyntsev is only effective or useful when dealing with small, relatively humble matters, the kind that do not get recorded in history: sending some men to hold, for a few hours mistakenly thought to be precious, a thin line of defense, heartening the men during an artillery barrage, burying Colonel Kabanov, finding his way in the forest.... And it is only in this domain, of the small, "low," humble event that Tolstoy saw individual action as useful, capable of inducing change. Far from refuting Tolstoy, the novel confirms him. As Solzhenitsyn himself points out, General Martos's repeated victories not only accomplish nothing but even confuse matters further. Only on the level of colonel or below do we see leadership exercising a positive influence; but these brave, self-sacrificing officers are leading the pathetic remnants of a regiment or artillery brigade—not more than a handful of men. True, *August 1914* shows us a wealth of examples of *bad* leadership, mostly located at the top, and, on the German side, General von François' character and personality do seem to have been determining. Yet there was also the factor of luck, in which the Russian bungling and incompetence was a large component. We see the same thing, though, with Kutuzov in *War and Peace* taking advantage of the enemy's folly.

Yet, whoever is right—Solzhenitsyn or Tolstoy—about the course of history and the sense or lack of sense it makes does not matter so much here as the fact that the novel, as opposed to the novelist, seems to be so often on Tolstoy's side. On the plane of drama Samsonov achieves a grandeur of which Vorotyntsev, a model leader, is incapable. Samsonov's capacity for suffering and endurance, his eventual passiveness, as of a massive natural object, all of which show him as the opposite of a "great man," seem to be moving him to a supreme wisdom—the full acceptance of his fate. He bows to it, just as he takes off his cap to each of his demoralized soldiers, some of whom have served him badly. The marvelous realization of this character, though not in any way Tolstoyan (Tolstoy detested theater), nevertheless supports Tolstoy's view of what is important, finally, and what not. In creating Samsonov on the scale he does, Solzhenitsyn denies the ultimate interest of those cause-and-effect sequences he has been elaborating in order to pinpoint blame. It would be strange if he were not aware of this. Is the fact that Lenartovich is one of the men Samsonov lifts his cap to intended merely as an irony?

In using Vorotyntsev to draw the lesson of what ought to have been done to avert the Tannenberg disaster, it seems as though Solzhenitsyn has walked into a trap. To make this intelligent colonel effective he would have to write a different ending to the tale than the one history has provided. But if the colonel is not effective, then intelligence turns out to be a rather useless quality unless it is combined with power, which historically it rarely is—so that Vorotyntsev emerges more as a fantasy or dreamy wish fulfillment than an actual living possibility. We are left with the fleshly reality of Samsonov, one of the contributing causes, it could be said, of the Bolshevik Revolution. And whatever the novelist thinks about that, the novel disagrees. What the novel finds is the essential *Hercules furens* sitting on a tree-stump "throne" deep in reflection.

Solzhenitsyn's Quest

BY VICTOR ERLICH

August 1914, the first installment of Solzhenitsyn's broadly conceived historical trilogy, thus far has had a mixed reception. The publication of the Russian text of the novel in Paris has provided an occasion for another virulent Soviet campaign against its author. *Literaturnaia gazeta* has featured hostile articles by Finnish writer Martti Larni and by an obscure Polish journalist, Jerzy Romanowski, who managed to detect in Solzhenitsyn's portrayal of the Russian defeat at Tannenberg an insidious tendency to extol the "German militarists." These attacks by foreign nonentities were duly followed by irate letters from a standard assortment of native nonreaders.

Less predictably, the response of Solzhenitsyn's Russian-speaking admirers in the West has ranged from enthusiasm to uneasiness and disappointment. If the eminent Slavist Roman Jakobson hailed *August 1914* as Solzhenitsyn's most remarkable work to date, Roman Gul', editor of the Russian émigré journal *New Review,* in a sympathetic article, deplored the novel's alleged anachronisms and infelicitous neologisms.

Gul's strictures, though often picayune, are not entirely unwarranted. Solzhenitsyn's latest novel lacks the firmness of outline, the sureness of touch, in a word, the authority of *One*

"Solzhenitsyn's Quest." Revised from "Solzhenitsyn's New Novel" which appeared in *Dissent* (Fall, 1972), 639-641. ©1972 by *Dissent*. Reprinted by permission of *Dissent* and the author.

Day in the Life of Ivan Denisovich or *The First Circle.* The prose is not infrequently contrived and unwieldy. The account of the East Prussian campaign is overdocumented: in his determination to reproduce as accurately as possible the mechanism of the debacle, Solzhenitsyn weighs down his chronicle with operational detail. Now and then, in an apparent attempt to enliven the narrative, as well as to render directly the turmoil of battle, he resorts to a cinematic technique, oddly reminiscent of, though hardly derivative from, the "Camera Eye" sections of Dos Passos's *U.S.A.* But this self-conscious device proves less than effective.

Yet this is only part of the story. Though *August 1914* is a seriously flawed work, at its best it is as moving and vivid as any of Solzhenitsyn's previous creations. Some of the scenes, e.g., General Samsonov's farewell to his troops, belong among the most memorable passages in modern Russian fiction. Moreover, the occasional lapses of *August 1914* are, in a sense, a measure of how difficult is the task that Solzhenitsyn has set himself—a task especially exacting for a writer whose persuasiveness has often derived from a hard-earned first-hand knowledge of his materials. For what is attempted in *August 1914* is an imaginative repossession of a vanished world, a total reconstruction of Russian society on the eve of a great upheaval, and a searching inquiry into the causes of its disintegration. Clearly, Solzhenitsyn has embarked upon an enterprise of Tolstoyan proportions.

But if the scope of Solzhenitsyn's emerging epic makes one think of Tolstoy, its perspective is emphatically at odds with that of Solzhenitsyn's favorite Russian master. One of the most interesting aspects of *August 1914* is a polemic with Tolstoy's debunking of military science, with his insistence that no plans, however carefully laid, can significantly affect the actual outcome of a battle, shaped as it is by a myriad of unfathomable contingencies. *War and Peace* pits the slow, seemingly indecisive Kutuzov against the puffed-up narcissist Napoleon: while the latter suffers from the delusion of being in control of events, the former knows in his bones that no one can or ever will lead.

Solzhenitsyn has precious little use for these crotchety iconoclasms. He is deeply convinced that in war, as in any other realm, professional competence and dedication matter a great deal. The import of the evidence assembled in *August 1914* is unmistakable: the near-annihilation of General Samsonov's army at Tannenberg was eminently avoidable. The disaster was demonstrably a result of ineptitude, obtuseness, and irresponsibilty on the part of the Russian military leadership. The issue is joined in a passage where a top-level military careerist invokes Kutuzov's intuitive passivity as an alibi for incompetence:

> General Blagoveshchenskii was well aware of Kutuzov . . . like [the historic] Kutuzov, he was deliberate, cautious and sly, and like Tolstoy's Kutuzov he knew that it was never necessary to make any drastic or decisive moves, that a battle launched against its will would produce mere confusion . . . that there was an inevitable course of events and the best general was one who refused participation in these events.[1]

It occurs to one that in taking issue with Tolstoy's fatalistic philosophy of history, Solzhenitsyn might be aiming at a more proximate target, notably the Marxist-Leninist brand of historical determinism. By the same token, it stands to reason that to one who has fully experienced the horrors of Stalin's personal rule, Tolstoy's dogmatic denial of the individual's role in history must seem less than persuasive.[2]

At times the challenge to the Soviet ethos is quite explicit. One of the salient strands in *August 1914* is an impatience with the shibboleths of the radical intelligentsia. As the story gets underway, Sania Lazhenitsyn, a thoughtful young nonconformist inclined toward Tolstoyan pacifism, impulsively decides to enlist. An impressionable young girl who hitherto looked to him as her spiritual mentor is upset and baffled. She flings back at Sania the rhetoric of the radical protest as she reminds him of the vileness of the Tsarist establishment. "Where are your principles? Where is your consistency?" she cries indignantly. The usually voluble Sanya is reduced to incoherence; all he can do

[1]Quotations here are translated by the author.

[2]In her wide-ranging review of *August 1914* Mary McCarthy has some acute and some highly debatable things to say about what she calls the "Tolstoy Connection." She notes without visible pleasure Solzhenitsyn's polemical stance only to conclude that the actual dramatic emphasis of *August 1914* subtly undermines the author's intent. Far from refuting Tolstoy, she contends, the novel confirms him, as Samsonov's soulful passivity steals the show from Vorotyntsev's frenzied activism.

Miss McCarthy is both eloquent and persuasive about Samsonov's last moments, admittedly the highpoint of *August 1914*. Yet her argument appears to me far fetched. The failure of Vorotyntsev's mission does not really "confirm" Tolstoy. Rather than demonstrating the essential futility of planning, efficiency or professionalism, *August 1914* forcibly argues that these qualities were never given a chance by the Russian military establishment. [Mary McCarthy's article appears in this volume. Eds.]

is mutter apologetically: "I feel sorry for Russia." Does this imply that, when the chips are down, "gut reactions" take precedence over abstract principles? So it seems. But let us note the phrasing. Clearly, Sania's "patriotism" is a matter of compassion rather than national pride, of solidarity rather than flag-waving. It is not "my country—right or wrong," but a readiness to face the collective ordeal, to share the plight of millions of ordinary Russians.

Another relevant episode occurs at a later stage of the ill-fated campaign. A bedraggled band of survivors is trekking home through the East Prussian woods. Their leader, Colonel Vorotyntsev—a brave and independent-minded officer who comes as close as any character to being the hero of the novel—insists that the wounded comrades-in-arms be cared for and the dead be given a dignified burial. An articulate young Bolshevik, Sasha Lenartovich, balks at this exacting regimen. "Now you are forcing us to carry a corpse. Next thing you will order us to drag this [wounded] officer. And I can see just by looking at him that he is a reactionary." "Yes, I will," answers Vorotyntsev testily. "Party differences, lieutenant, are a ripple on the water." When Lenartovich asks "and which differences *are* important?" Vorotyntsev snaps: "the difference between decency and non-decency, lieutenant." Once again a basic moral code—that of courage, honor, solidarity—is given preference over political commitments and labels.

Some otherwise appreciative readers have noted with discomfort that this pervasive antipolitical bias asserts itself most frequently at the expense of the radicals. In fact, as various segments of the pre-1917 Russian society progressively enter the fray, the representatives of the Left, whether Marxist or otherwise, tend to come off somewhat worse than do non-ideological mining engineers bent on developing Russia's natural resources or religious thinkers playing down the importance of mere institutional change. As one who has had his fill of the spiritual aridities of a totally politicized culture, Solzhenitsyn knows only too well the cost of the doctrinaire narrow-mindedness that since the 1860s had been a persistent strain in the Russian radical tradition. (Needless to say, the phenomenon is not uniquely Russian: the scene in which radical girl students inveigh against the irrelevance of medieval studies has an uncomfortably familiar ring.) Yet in his recoil from the official Soviet travesty of that tradition, he runs the danger of doing less than justice to the liberating potential of the Russian revolutionary movement.

Such considerations may be a trifle premature: Solzhenitsyn's journey into the recent past has merely begun. In the meantime, let us wish him strength in the face of persistent harassment, and salute, whatever our misgivings, the stubborn courage of his dual quest—a quest for the roots of Russia's present plight and for the native sources of moral strength needed to overcome it.

In Dubious Battle

BY PHILIP RAHV

August 1914 is a long novel, it is only the first volume of a work of many parts. In his brief Foreword the author tells us that the whole work "may take as long as twenty years" to write and that he probably "will not live to finish it." We are obviously dealing here with an extremely ambitious project—an account in epical novelistic form of the events, including the October revolution and its aftermath, that have shaped Russia's destiny in the twentieth century.

Clearly, Solzhenitsyn has for many years been haunted by the question of how Russia had come to find itself in its present disheartening condition. A long inquiry into history was required to discover the answer, and he decided to start with the Russian defeat in the battle of Tannenberg, which occurred during the first month of World War I, and specifically with the encirclement and destruction of General Samsonov's Second Army, which invaded East Prussia at the beginning of August. Solzhenitsyn evidently regards this initial defeat as momentous, the decisive portent of the repeated Russian failure to halt the German advance, signifying the beginning of the disintegration of the Russian army, if not of the regime itself.

The defeat is the subject of this first volume which, freely

"In Dubious Battle." From *New York Review of Books* (October 5, 1972), 13-15. © 1972 by *NYREZ* Inc. Reprinted by permission of the author and the *New York Review of Books*.

mixing fictitious with historical characters, attempts at once to represent the battle in full detail and to elucidate the causes of its catastrophic outcome. Of course no complete judgment of Solzhenitsyn's immense undertaking can be formed until the novel as a whole becomes available. Still, this first volume does provide us with some indications (even if only provisional ones) of the novelist's approach to his material, his characteristic literary devices as well as his ideological position and outlook.

In spite of the efforts of the Soviet regime to stifle him we have for some time now been reading quite a bit of Solzhenitsyn, and this new novel only reinforces our conviction that he is by far the most gifted of living Russian writers and that he has the moral and intellectual stamina to continue to write powerfully in defiance of malevolent political persecution. The regime may yet kill him but so far it has been unable to silence him.

Critics have often compared him to Tolstoy, and rightly, for his manner is on the whole Tolstoyan. Yet his relationship with Tolstoy is complex and contradictory. Thus inevitably this new epic, even though unfinished, invites comparison with *War and Peace;* and, on the basis of my first impressions, I might as well say that Solzhenitsyn strikes me as superior to Tolstoy in his understanding of military strategy and tactics, quite as good as Tolstoy in his scenes of actual battle, but altogether inferior to him in his representation of private life (the theme of peace). Solzhenitsyn's students, young ladies, businessmen, and "deep thinkers" are not particularly memorable when measured against such Tolstoyan characters as Natasha, Sonia, Pierre Bezukhov, Prince Andrei and his father. In their private and inner lives Solzhenitsyn's people remain types whom he has not succeeded in converting into individuals. But the greater part of this novel, and certainly his most masterful scenes, of which there are many, pertain to war rather than to peace.

Solzhenitsyn's narrative of the war tells us what happens both from the viewpoint of the rank-and-file and from that of the higher-ups, the commanders in the field as well as the staff officers in the rear. The result is a highly comprehensive view of war, and in this respect he truly reminds us of Tolstoy, who also endeavored to understand war from the vantage point both of the commanders and of the common soldiers.

However, at a crucial point the paths of the two novelists

diverge very sharply. Whereas Tolstoy made every effort to idealize both the personality and the strategy of his commander-in-chief, General Kutuzov, Solzhenitsyn exposes nearly all of his generals, each of them based on the actual leaders of the Russian army, as incompetents and time-servers. His "ponderous and baffled" General Samsonov, who commits suicide after losing his troops, is treated sympathetically and is shown as the victim of the confusion and disorganization that prevail at General Headquarters.

Solzhenitsyn takes great pains to expose and analyze in depth the course of the catastrophe. Though undersupplied and underequipped, the Russian soldiers are shown to be brave enough, but time and again betrayed by the corruption, ineptness, and sheer lack of know-how of the military leadership. Because of outmoded methods of communication and confusing and contradictory orders, many divisions are needlessly sacrificed. Even as the Russian generals vainly seek to ascertain the disposition of the enemy forces, they are so stupidly incautious that they send uncoded wireless messages, which are of course regularly intercepted by the Germans. Sukhomlinov, the Minister of War, is a military ignoramus who owes his high position to intrigue and his flattery of the tsar. Some of the younger graduates of the Military Academy, known as the "Young Turks," have been preparing themselves for years to introduce military reform only to be frustrated and put down by their seniors, whose smugness and conceit are boundless.

For Solzhenitsyn, the inefficiency of the Russian command is in no sense a historical accident. It is a major symptom of the tsarist regime, which "granted no power or influence to anyone not fortunate enough to be close to the throne." Furthermore, as Solzhenitsyn sees it, the Russian invasion of East Prussia only a few weeks after the declaration of war was a grave strategic error, for the Russian army was ill prepared to carry through such a bold undertaking; the advance was much too precipitous and badly coordinated. Solzhenitsyn for the most part does not use generalizations to show what happened. In clear and vigorous narrative prose he describes dozens of vivid scenes taking place throughout the battlefield as the Russians stumble into the German trap, scenes that obviously have affinities with those in *War and Peace*.

But it soon becomes clear that the mentality of Kutuzov is anathema to Solzhenitsyn, and because of this he enters into a direct polemic against Tolstoy in passages of commentary as well as in the fiction itself. For example, in writing of the Russian defeat, he remarks that "there might appear to be some consolation in Tolstoy's conviction that it is not generals who lead armies, . . . not presidents or leaders who run states or political parties—were it not that all too often the twentieth century has proved to us that it *is* such men who do these things." And further on the polemic is continued in the sardonic portrait of General Blagoveshchenskii, who "had read about Kutuzov in Tolstoy's *War and Peace* and at sixty years of age, gray-haired, fat, and stiff, he felt himself to be just like Kutuzov. . . ."

> Like Kutuzov he was wary, cautious, and cunning. And like Tolstoy's Kutuzov he realized that one should never issue sharp, decisive instructions; that "nothing but confusion could result from a battle started against one's will"; that "military matters go their own way, which they are fated to follow whether or not it corresponds to what men propose"; that "there is an inevitable course of events"; and that the best general is the one who "declines to participate in these events." His long military service had convinced the general of the correctness of Tolstoy's views; there was nothing worse than sticking one's neck out by using one's initiative—people who did so always got into trouble.

This is clear enough, and of course Blagoveshchenskii's "wise" Tolstoyan passivity, his determination not to stick his neck out, contributes to the catastrophe at Tannenberg. In fact throughout the book Solzhenitsyn seizes every opportunity to expose Kutuzovism, the very qualities of mind and character of which Tolstoy was so enamored and into which he read the essence of Russianism. Solzhenitsyn, on the other hand, is a military activist, an exponent of intelligence, skill, organization, and modernization. He advocates a kind of technocratic efficiency in military as well as civilian afairs. Hence, if the novel can be said to have a single hero, it is surely Colonel Vorotyntsev, a staff officer who turns up at every important juncture of the action, who admires modern German military methodology, and who refuses "to sit at General Headquarters as a pen-pusher . . . at a time when a hazardous maneuver of the utmost boldness was being put into effect in Prussia."

Unlike the generals, Vorotyntsev appears to be Solzhenitsyn's own creation and he is the intelligence of the novel. Perfectly aware of the stodginess and sloth of the Russian generals, he is nevertheless a patriot who believes that Russia is "immeasurably strong, even if she is governed by a pack of fools." Convinced of that strength, the consciousness of defeat, far from demoralizing him, compels him openly to denounce his superiors at a conference presided over by the Grand Duke Nikolai Nikolaevich himself, with the result that his career is cut short when he is ordered by the grand-duke to leave the room for overstepping "the bounds of what is permissible." It is plain that this clear-headed colonel speaks for the author and that he will reappear in later volumes. Whether he will eventually join the Bolsheviks remains to be seen.

However, there is another side to the novel, which, in contrast to its bias toward the technocratic and the instrumental, is traditionally Russian and patently indebted to the Tolstoyan model. The peasant-soldier Blagodarev, whom Vorotyntsev chooses from the trenches as his orderly and who accompanies him on some of his most dangerous missions, is directly reminiscent of Platon Karataev, the peasant-soldier in *War and Peace* whom Pierre encounters in a French prison and from whom he absorbs the teaching that the supreme values of life are simplicity, truthfulness, and goodness. The very surname Blagodarev (the root-word is *blago,* which might be translated as gratitude or even beneficence) speaks for itself. He is cheerful, modest, and good, even when undergoing the worst trials. There is in him, we are told, "a great fund of simple humanity—a goodness that had nothing to do with rank, class, or politics but was the unspoiled simplicity of Nature herself."

Moreover, the sturdy ideal qualities of Karataev-Blagodarev are associated with Solzhenitsyn's admiration for another very Russian trait, as when he exultingly observes that "no disaster, no amount of bloodshed, is ever enough to galvanize Russians out of their passive endurance." In this admiration of suffering in passive endurance Solzhenitsyn is clearly at one with both Tolstoy and Dostoevsky. He fails to perceive the extreme ambiguity of this conspicuous Russian trait. It is by no means the purely positive quality that Solzhenitsyn, like his great predecessors, takes it to be. There is something about it which one can only regard as insidious. For, after all, did not this Russian compliance and acquiescence in passive suffering make possible the emergence of both the tsarist and Stalinist autocracy?

Another Russian writer, Vasilii Grossman, debates this question in his recent novel *Forever Flowing.* He ponders the paradox that runs throughout Russian history, the paradox that there exists in the same people a "meekness and readiness to endure suffering . . . unequaled since the epoch of the first

Christians" together with a "contempt for and disregard of human suffering" as well as a certain subservience to abstract theories on human welfare. Russian writers, the radicals no less than the reactionaries, idealized Karataevism as singularly Russian and noble and therefore vastly to be preferred to the mushy liberalism of the West.

Grossman concludes that in "the Russian fascination with Byzantine, ascetic purity, with Christian meekness, lives the unwitting admission of the permanence of Russian slavery. The sources of this Christian meekness and gentleness, of this Byzantine, ascetic purity" are also discernible in the "Leninist passion, fanaticism, and intolerance." It is clear that this trend of thought is completely alien to Solzhenitsyn, who sometimes seems to accept uncritically the Russian tradition even while contradicting it in advocating efficiency and modernization so forcefully. Looked at purely as a novelistic character, Blagodarev is truly admirable, but what he represents is a profound attachment to the Russian past, which is obviously at odds with the technocratic and practical bias that pervades the novel.

August 1914 makes plain that its author is above all a Russian rather than a Soviet patriot. His Russianism, as I have mentioned, is of a very traditional sort, so much so that at times one feels that his position might be described as quasi-Slavophile. In this sense he has really more in common with Dostoevsky than with Tolstoy. His manner and tone in this novel are Tolstoyan, to be sure; he in no way shares Dostoevsky's obsession with pathological and criminal states of mind, nor is he drawn to the famous Dostoevskyan "lacerations" [*nadryv*]. Yet ideologically, mainly because of his mystical, religious populism, he is closer to Dostoevsky than to Tolstoy, who, after all, was a stanch pacifist and whose version of the Christian doctrine transcended every form of nationalism. Solzhenitsyn is a Christian believer of the Orthodox variety but he is no pacifist. He is also a passionate nationalist. This fact emerges in many passages of the novel, as, for example, in the following speech of the engineer Il'ia Isakovich to a group of revolutionary young people:

> The country one lives in is in trouble. So which is right: to say, "Go to hell, I'll have none of you," or to say, "I want to help you, I belong here"? Living in this country, one must make up one's mind once and for all and stick to one's decision. Do I really belong to it heart and soul? Or don't I? If I don't, then I can smash it or leave it, it makes no difference which I do. . . . But if I *do* belong to it,

> then I must adapt myself to the slow process of history, by work, by persuasion and gradual change. . . .

Il'ia Isakovich and his guest the engineer Obodovskii are the civilian counterparts of Colonel Vorotyntsev, and they are rather more explicit than he is in declaring their contempt for the radical traditions of the intelligentsia. Obodovskii argues that

> . . . anyone who has created something with his own hands knows that production is neither capitalist nor socialist but *one* thing only: it is what creates national wealth. . . . Along come a bunch of arts students and they explain to the workers that they are earning too little, and that that little engineer over there in spectacles is earning God knows how much, and that it's sheer bribery. And these simple, uneducated people believe it and they are indignant . . .

"I believe," Obodovskii says, "the Union of Engineers could easily become one of the leading forces in Russia. It's more important and more constructive than any political party." He promises, "Give us ten years of peaceful development and you won't recognize Russian industry—or Russian agriculture for that matter." This technocratic mystique is one of the dominant motifs of the novel, and it is clear that the author is fully in sympathy with it.

To my mind there is something profoundly unpolitical in this mystique of technocracy. Where, in what country, have engineers ever seized power or even aspired to do so? In the United States as in all other Western countries of high technology the corporate elite is firmly in control and the engineers they employ knuckle under. They invariably carry out the decisions of their bosses, who are far more interested in financial manipulation than in the specific skills their engineers possess. After all, it is the communists who finally succeeded in industrializing Russia, while the Russian engineers worked under Lenin, Stalin, and now Brezhnev and Kosygin with the same docility that their Western counterparts exhibit in servicing the big corporations. His new book shows that Solzhenitsyn is in no sense a Marxist; he is a nationalist and a patriot, a belated *narodnik* whose mystic-religious populism oddly accords with his technological and pragmatic inclinations. There is an inherent contradiction, and a rather bizarre one at that, in trying to combine the two positions—of which, surprisingly enough, Solzhenitsyn appears to be quite unaware, at least in the first volume.

In addition to Vorotyntsev and the two engineers, there is another fictional character in the novel, Varsonof'ev, who is presented as a "deep thinker" and whose sole function seems to be that of voicing the author's philosophical views. In an argument with two radical students Varsonof'ev expresses approval of the war, for, as he puts it, "When the trumpet sounds, a man must be a man, even if merely for his own self-respect." Russia's backbone must not be broken, "and for that, young men must go to war." So much for Lenin's program of revolutionary defeatism! Varsonof'ev asserts, "Do not be so arrogant as to imagine that you can invent an ideal social order, because with that invention you may destroy your beloved 'people.'" In his view "history is *irrational*... It has its own, and to us perhaps incomprehensible, organic structure." The worst mistake one can make is to believe that history is "governed by reason."

The ideas expounded by Varsonof'ev, who is allotted only one scene in the novel, are crucial to Solzhenitsyn's view of the world. Once the premise that history is irrational is accepted, then not only Marxism but all other theories of history as well cease to make sense. Or does Solzhenitsyn suppose that only small, limited segments of history are open to rational analysis? Surely he must assume this, for otherwise I cannot see how he can reconcile the strenuous efforts of his hero Vorotyntsev to discover the causes of Russia's defeat with the assumption, which he seems to endorse, that the historical process is wholly irrational and incomprehensible. If that assumption were correct, it would be futile for Solzhenitsyn to concern himself so deeply and seriously with Russia's destiny, which, after all, cannot be exempted from the forces of history.

There is only one convinced Marxist among the many soldiers portrayed in this novel, and he is the young ensign Sasha Lenartovich, who is prepared to lay down his life any moment for the great cause of the revolution, and can think of nothing worse than "to die at the age of twenty-four defending autocracy." He looks forward to Russia's defeat, believing as he does in the Leninist policy of "the worse, the better." Lenartovich seeks to escape the war by surrendering to the Germans and in that aim he fails. He will probably turn up in later volumes as an officer of the Red Army. It is to Solzhenitsyn's credit that he manages to be scrupulously fair in his fictional rendering of this revolutionary type. But that he finds Lenartovich no hero is clear. The characters with whom he does seem to identify—Vorotyntsev, the engineers, and Varsonof'ev—are patriotic to the core.

Solzhenitsyn is a hero of Russian intellectual resistance to the vicious cultural policies of the present Soviet regime. He is also a very fine writer of fiction whose work will surely become a part of the canon of Russian literature. I do not think that the impression of confusion and turbidity conveyed by his more general ideas should count much against him. Tolstoy's ideas of history, presented so insistently in *War and Peace,* are equally open to criticism, yet we do not hesitate to accord that novel the very highest stature; nor does Dostoevsky's reactionary obscurantism prevent us from appreciating his great importance as an imaginative creator. I for one have never been prepared to judge works of fiction by subjecting them to a political-ideological test, for to do so is inevitably to lose oneself in a maze of considerations that are beside the point of literature. To be sure, ideological awareness and political attention are by no means to be eschewed by the literary critic, but in the last analysis he cannot afford to permit his own bias, whether radical or conservative, to overpower his judgment and perceptions.

In my opinion, *August 1914* is not Solzhenitsyn's *chef-d'oeuvre.* However, let us keep in mind the fact that it is only the first volume of a much longer work. When complete, it may indeed turn out to be the masterpiece we have every reason to expect of him.

On *August 1914*

BY MILTON EHRE

August 1914 is an impressive and important novel. It is not, however, a novel that will find easy acceptance among readers who like their fiction tidy and neat. It is rather one of those Russian "large loose baggy monsters" Henry James deplored. Characters are introduced and promptly forgotten, some do return but when we have forgotten them, others are there only to engage in intense intellectual arguments of the sort Russians have been unable to avoid inserting into their novels. When in the West "ambiguity" has become a major, and for some the sole, criterion of literary value, Solzhenitsyn is not shy about letting us know what he thinks. Where modernism in art has sought to distance itself from reality, to deform and "play" with the observed world, or shadow it with the mists of illusion, Solzhenitsyn loads his novel with all the messy details of actual experience. Like Tolstoy, he assumes an intimate relation between art and life, and the strength of his conviction gives his work the moral authority the great novels, particularly the great Russian novels, have always exerted.

Not that esthetic problems are trivial. In his first long fiction, the novella *One Day in the Life of Ivan Denisovich,* Solzhenitsyn set himself what has become his continuing task—to reveal the

"On *August 1914.*" From *Chicago Review,* XXIV, no. 3 (1972), 153-157.

social fabric of his nation. His procedure is to examine painstakingly a broad gallery of characters representative of its diverse social classes and groups. The concentration camps of *One Day...* and *The First Circle,* the hospital of *Cancer Ward,* besides serving as ready-made metaphors for Stalinist Russia, offered convenient locales where men and women otherwise unlikely to meet could be brought together. The view that a literary character must be socially representative or "typical" was widespread in nineteenth-century Russia and has achieved the status of dogma in the ideology of Socialist Realism. For gifted writers who adhered to it—and without talent no theory helps—the stress on typicality led to a grasp of the social dynamics underlying the vagaries of individual behavior. It also had its pitfalls. Typicality might be degraded into a schematism without anchor in the particularities of human personality. The work of fiction, in its effort to create a microcosm of the actual world and its characteristic features, might turn into a static gallery of types lacking formal cohesion.

Solzhenitsyn overcame these pitfalls, masterfully in *One Day ...,* which remains for me the most artistically satisfying of his novels, and with considerable success in *Cancer Ward,* by building his work around the perceptions and destiny of a single hero. Ivan Denisovich and Kostoglotov of *Cancer Ward* are characters so intimately experienced that they lend their novels substantiality and vividness from which occasional lapses into schematism (and there are none in *One Day ...*) cannot detract. They are important and their journeys, Ivan through a day in a concentration camp, which is all his days, Kostoglotov through illness and physical decrepitude, which is the fate of all of us, engrossed us. Nerzhin tried to do the same for *The First Circle,* but the ambitiousness of that project—it strove to do no less than incorporate all of Stalinist Russia—made a single character unequal to the task. The subject matter and the moral issues posed by the phenomenon of Stalinism seemed to have taken complete hold of Solzhenitsyn's mind and he lost interest in his hero and his story. I, for one, found those issues compelling enough to make the novel immensely readable. Indeed some of the digressions—notably, the portrait of Stalin—were so fascinating that the cumbersomeness of structure and the occasional intrusion of stereotypes were a small price to pay.

August 1914 is even more ambitious. Though a long novel, it is only the first in a projected series that presumably will treat Russia in Revolution and Civil War, as well as World War I. It begs comparison with Tolstoy's monumental epic *War and Peace,* and if we were dull enough to miss the analogy, Solzhenitsyn has pointed to it by invoking his great predecessor a good number of times. Solzhenitsyn is no match for Tolstoy as an architect of epic narratives or a psychologist of the human mind. Tolstoy was a master craftsman, who in *War and Peace* deftly blended personal destinies and historical events into an intricate weft of human experience. As a psychologist, he may have his equals, but no betters. Tolstoy possessed an uncanny, almost superhuman, knack of putting himself under another's skin—of feeling the "other" in all of his or her human fullness. Solzhenitsyn has given us several very interesting characters—the most memorable is an actual historical personage, General Samsonov, the commander of the Russian Second Army at the battle of Tannenberg, but there are no Natashas, Pierres, or Prince Andreis in *August 1914*—those unique Tolstoyan individuals whom we live with so long and come to know so well that they become part of the furniture of our minds. Essentially, Solzhenitsyn's *August 1914* is Tolstoy's "War" without the "Peace"—the historical novel minus the full rendering of the rhythms of social, familial, and private life. Several potentially interesting characters and families are introduced at the opening of the novel, but they are inexplicably abandoned once the War begins (they undoubtedly will return in later volumes). The fictional Colonel Vorotyntsev, whose special mission from General Headquarters permits him to roam freely about the scenes of battle, was obviously intended to perform the same function as Solzhenitsyn's previous heroes—to provide a perspective from which his microcosm of the world may be viewed, and a story on which to hang his material. But the material—the war—dominates, and Vorotyntsev remains too thin a character (though he may expand in future volumes in which he is destined to play a central role).

The war, however, rates with the best of Tolstoy. Here Solzhenitsyn is in full control. The writing is masterful. He has caught the drama of history in the making, the compelling intricacies of military strategy, the excitement of armies of men on the move and their collision in battle, and skillfully interspersed his historical account with scenes of individuals caught in the maelstrom of war and displaying all the courage, cowardice, hope, despair, stupidity, and nobility that is part of being human. The irony is savage and again Tolstoyan. However, where Tolstoy's scorn was directed mostly at a foreigner—Napoleon—Solzhenitsyn's target is his fellow Russians. Surely no soldiers have ever been so badly served by the commanding officers and heads of state who sent them out to fight and die. With a few exceptions, they are a pack of fools, cowards, and corrupt timeservers, and Solzhenitsyn tirelessly and relentlessly exposes them, while showing profound respect for the common soldiers whose unfortunate lot it was to have had such leaders. While the story of an individual passing through a social world provided the formal backbone of Solzhenitsyn's earlier novels, here it is the action of the war itself that stands at the center, and the worth of individuals is measured according to how they stand up to its demands. The progress of war, more than the story of any character, holds the novel together.

Solzhenitsyn looks back to Tolstoy not only to emulate him but to do battle with him. For Tolstoy, history was an endless chain of cause and effect which did not allow participants the perspective to comprehend it, much less control its direction. Napoleon is the villain of *War and Peace* precisely because he has the presumption to believe he can impose rational order upon history; his Russian counterpart, Field Marshal Kutuzov, is perhaps the true hero, at least of the "War," because he possesses the humility to surrender himself to its ceaseless flow, to follow his instincts instead of the seductions of rationalism. In *August 1914* Kutuzovism (or Tolstoyism) is a cardinal sin, and a distinctively Russian one. General Blagoveshchenskii is its caricature: letting "military matters go their own way" and observing from afar the "inevitable course of events" are merely pretexts for avoiding responsibility and indulging his cowardice. General Samsonov is also a disciple of Kutuzov (the Kutuzov of Tolstoy and not the quite different Kutuzov of history), and he is a brave, pious, and good Russian. Nevertheless, he is destroyed—for the very good reason that he does not know how to lead a modern army and wage a modern war. Instinct does not suffer: men require knowledge, technical skills, and a *rational* understanding of their circumstances. The story of Samsonov's disintegration has the ring of authentic tragedy about it—the scenes describing his suicide reminded me of Lear on the heath. Samsonov's tragedy is clearly the tragedy of Old Russia. He is granted all the attributes Russian writers have habitually given to exemplary representatives of traditional

Russia—piety, compassion, courage, nostalgia, love of the land, even "Russian melancholy"—and a reluctance to cope with practical problems. The latter failure is, for Solzhenitsyn, the height of irresponsibility.

Philip Rahv, who feels seriously enough about literature to confront its moral and social issues, has recently attacked Solzhenitsyn (*New York Review of Books,* October 5, 1972) for a "technocratic mystique" which coexists contradictorily with a "mystic-religious populism" and "quasi-Slavophile nationalism" reminiscent of Dostoevsky. The cult of technology is there—from Ivan Denisovich on Solzhenitsyn has favored the man who makes things, even if only a brick wall in a prison camp—and it gives him something in common with the Russian radical intelligentsia whom he otherwise repudiates. In Solzhenitsyn's case, however, his worship of technology is the product of his despair at Russian politics, which has always given much to despair at. He glorifies the man who quietly does a good piece of work, because he is filled with revulsion at the overblown rhetoric and unbending commitment to abstract ideological schemes that has too often passed for political discourse in Russia. As one of his characters, an engineer, laments: "On one side—the Black Hundreds; on the other—the Red Hundreds! And in the middle . . . a dozen people who want to pass through to get on with a job of work! Impossible!" One of the "dozen" is Colonel Vorotyntsev, who belongs to a group of younger officers calling themselves the "Young Turks" and who wish to get on with the job of modernizing the Russian army.

Rahv's charge of "mystic-religious populism" and "quasi-Slavophile nationalism" is based on the assertions of a single character, an obscure intellectual called Varsonof'ev, who appears in a brief scene in a cafe. Solzhenitsyn may or may not share his views, share them only in part, or, more likely, he has not yet fully resolved his own intellectual position. Whatever may be the case, Varsonof'ev's mysticism and insistence upon the irrationality of history are refuted by the major tendency of the novel. Rahv himself has noted that the attack upon Kutuzovism implies that at least slices of history are permeable to rational comprehension. Furthermore, though Solzhenitsyn is unequivocally a nationalist and feels much love for his Russian people, there is not a shred of chauvinism in his make-up which would deserve an epithet like "Slavophile" or comparison to

Dostoevsky. Indeed he consistently regards the German enemy with respect and even admiration. Nor is his love of the people mystical. Vorotyntsev takes as an orderly the common soldier and peasant Arsenii Blagodarev, in whom he finds "a great fund of simple humanity—a goodness that had nothing to do with rank, class, or politics but was the unspoiled simplicity of Nature herself." Blagodarev—the name means "thanks" or "gratitude" in Russian, but the word *blago* is a "blessing" or a "boon"; *dar* is a "gift"—epitomizes for Solzhenitsyn the extraordinary and "incorrigible" resilience of the Russian people, its capacity to endure suffering and injustice.

Blagodarev recalls Platon Karataev of *War and Peace,* and Solzhenitsyn may have had Karataev in mind in creating him. But where Pierre seeks and seems to find answers to the riddles of life in the example of the simple, "natural" Karataev, Vorotyntsev seeks nothing of the sort in Blagodarev. What *both* Vorotyntsev and Blagodarev, officer and common soldier, member of the gentry and peasant, do find is mutual respect and mutual responsibility—"an unspoken division of rights and duties . . ." Instead of mystical communion, Solzhenitsyn presents two otherwise very different men who share a strong sense of their individuality and self-sufficiency—his favored characters have always been extremely self-sufficient—and who are yet keenly aware of the responsibilities they owe to other men.

Vorotyntsev and Blagodarev are rare birds in the Russia of *August 1914.* Almost everybody else is absorbed in his private concerns—the court in its intrigues, officers in their ambitions, common soldiers in their allegiance to a single sector of Russia, so that Cossacks can leave their compatriots to die because they do not feel themselves to belong to the same nation. The Bolsheviks (Solzhenitsyn does not use the term) are at least candid about their hopes for the defeat of Russia under the principle of "the worse, the better." The constant backdrop for the separate concerns of individuals and classes is the brute fact of thousands dying. It is the ineluctable reality of death and suffering that leads Solzhenitsyn to place Leninist "revolutionary defeatism," Tsarist corruption, and the well-intentioned ineffectuality of the Samsonovs under the same rubric of gross irresponsibility. What happens to a nation when the fragile bonds of mutual responsibility and obligation which unite men and women, groups and classes, are broken is the true theme of the book. The result is national disaster, and we may expect

Solzhenitsyn to address himself to the consequences of that disaster in forthcoming volumes.

A word on the translation. Solzhenitsyn has complained about the "stylistic leveling" of his works, and the leveling continues in Michael Glenny's version of *August 1914*. Solzhenitsyn takes his inspiration and models from the great tradition of the Russian realistic novel. His language, however, is innovative and daring. Simon Karlinsky is correct and astute in tracing it back to Aleksei Remizov and other experimental writers of the years immediately before and after the Revolution, who tried to orient their literary language upon spoken Russian and were extremely sensitive to the nuances and emotive impact latent in words (*New York Times Book Review*, September 10, 1972). We would never know the kind of writer Solzhenitsyn is from the Glenny translation, as we may never know that Dostoevsky, for instance, was a master stylist, or that Russian writers don't all sound like each other. *Traduttore-traditore*, as the old saw has it, and until our translators begin to show some faith in the artists they are rendering, and until our publishers begin to regard books as something more than commercial ventures, we are likely to have many betrayals.

August 1914: Solzhenitsyn and Tolstoy

BY KATHRYN B. FEUER

August 1914[1] is a puzzling novel and the puzzle is somehow closely related to Tolstoy, to his continuing influence on Solzhenitsyn and to Solzhenitsyn's continuing debate with him. *War and Peace* is clearly a model for *August 1914* but it is also a subject of discussion by the author and his characters within the novel. Tolstoy's beliefs in his later years—ascetic Christianity, non-resistance to evil, non-recognition of state power, Love as the only law—are keys to Solzhenitsyn's conception of the work, but these beliefs are also subjects of discussion by the author and his characters; they are even personified within the novel when young Sania Lazhenitsyn meets and talks with Tolstoy. And as if to make sure that Tolstoy will hover over every page, Solzhenitsyn has given a name closely modeled on his own to Sania, has introduced Sania's Tolstoyanism into Chapter 1, has portrayed his meeting with Tolstoy in Chapter 2, and then counterpointed this with a reminder of fashionable Tolstoyanism in Chapter 3, through the many portraits scattered throughout the Tomchak home, "Tolstoys" which Roman Zakharovich has commissioned because:

> all the really cultured people have them; he was a great man of Russia and a Count. Roman esteemed and supported Tolstoy because of his rejection of confession and communion, which he himself despised. (p. 32)

[1]Page references to *August 1914* are to A. Solzhenitsyn, *Avgust chetyrnadtsatogo* (Paris: YMCA Press, 1971). I have also consulted the English translation by Michael Glenny published by Farrar, Straus and Giroux, New York, 1972.

After this initial emphasis one soon comes to fear that Solzhenitsyn has Tolstoy and *War and Peace* too much in mind and that the organic integrity of his own novel will consequently suffer. In Chapter 4 Ksen'ia is introduced, and from the first sentence she is *too* reminiscent of Natasha:

> No, there's no place so nice to be as at home! Such a comfortable bed, such a dear little blue room. . . . (p. 34)

And a little later, when told she'll probably marry a landowner:

> "Wha-at?? Ab-so-lute-ly never!!. . ." Ksen'ia leapt up as if she'd been stung, tore off the hair ribbon she wore for sleeping and flashed the whites of her laughing eyes like a little black girl. And—she burst out laughing, her mirth pealed forth, and she raised her arms to the ceiling, in a dancer's motion . . . There was the mirror, there she could see herself full-length! Singing to herself she gave a dancer's leap! A leap! How well she does it! She's like a bird! . . . Look, why she's almost an Isadora, she's second to none! And everything, everything still before her! (pp. 39-40)

Under the influence of such passages Irina begins to remind one of Princess Mary, her spiritual patriotism, her somewhat mystic religiosity (she has always dreamed of a pilgrimage to Jerusalem) and just beneath the surface her passionate sexuality, expressed in her musing as she stands holding a heavy bedspread:

> Behind just such a curtain, just such a covering, so most people dragged out their commonplace lives and for a whole lifetime, never knowing that blessing, that passion which in old age had come to her father, so that fearing neither the world's censure nor God's judgement he had shamelessly set out to bribe a bishop—just to be able to marry his mistress. (p. 74)

Then a few chapters later another major figure, Vorotyntsev, appears: a brilliant young officer who believes in military science, who is deeply ambitious but also totally committed to his code of honor and to his nation's cause. His staff appointment enables him to make a tour of military society, to move freely in the headquarters of generals and even of the High Command. Although he is an intellectual theoretician of war he is scornful of the military establishment and finds his greatest satisfaction when leading ordinary soldiers in a real field of danger. He is proud and yet he humiliates himself and endangers his career in order to tell the true military and human situation to the commanders who are remote from this reality; he has welcomed the war as a reason for leaving his wife whom he has causelessly ceased to love.

With Prince Andrei so firmly established in the novel the reader feels trapped; it seems almost inescapable that Sania Lazhenitsyn is about to gain weight and put on glasses and become a Pierre, for he is already a character of an open "Russian" nature and a spiritual seeker. Then, with Chapter 14, there is the sense that Iaroslav Kharitonov is to play Nikolai Rostov, the naive young man of good heart, common sense and ordinary sensibility who can experience the joys of combat and male comradeship and the disillusionments of pain and defeat and hero-worship-betrayed, all on a human, non-intellectual level.

The appearance, in a little more than a hundred pages of *August 1914,* of so many characters who seem deliberately to recall *War and Peace,* is a distracting feature of the novel, for it hinders the reader's appreciation of its originality. Most affected is one's apprehension of General Samsonov, whose portrayal is probably Solzhenitsyn's greatest triumph in this work. For too long one keeps expecting him to emerge as a twentieth-century Kutuzov, and his plump placidity, his religious devotion, his bouts of passivity all contribute to this anticipation. In fact Samsonov is a totally different character and he is presented in a totally different manner. One believes in Kutuzov's reverence when the Icon of the Smolensk Mother of God is shown to the troops but one cannot conceive of him, alone in his bedroom, kneeling on the bare floor to say his prayers. One can imagine Kutuzov committing suicide if, for instance, he had learned that he had a painful, incurable disease, but not from despair at his own or his country's failure. The reader resists but is reluctantly absorbed by Solzhenitsyn's massive, unrelenting insistence on every detail of Samsonov's hopeless position—by those dozens of chapters of confusing geography and difficult military detail in which Samsonov does not even appear as a familiar figure of concern. And slowly, the realization comes that Samsonov is not the Kutuzov of *August 1914,* that he could not be presented in Tolstoy's sharp swift moments of carefully stylized delineation, because he is not, like Kutuzov, the personification of the intellectual principle of passivity. Samsonov lives and dies and suffers an individual fate; his passivity is desperate and involuntary, a tragic fact of history, not an intellectual entity.

Of course it is true that for Solzhenitsyn Samsonov also has a representative role; he stands for all the good, decent, honorable, sane men who "feel sorry for Russia," who love her despite the fact that she is destroying them, crushing them between the historical past of autocratic privilege with its consequent immoral inefficiency and the now-known future of rebellious hatred with its subsequent immoral inhumanity. And in this sense it is Samsonov who offers the clearest key to the inescapable but elusive relationship between *War and Peace* and *August 1914.* Samsonov is above all a figure of defeat, the defeat of Russia as a nation by Germany in World War I and the Bolshevik defeat of the real Russia, the Russia whose countenance has vanished with "the gray heroes":

> Since then the look of our nation has changed, the faces have changed and the camera lens will never find again those trusting bearded countenances, those friendly eyes, those patient, selfless faces. (p. 355)

Solzhenitsyn seems to conceive of a chain of fellowship, a Russian chain, which extends from these peasant soldiers to Arsenii Blagodarev and Terentii Chernega, to Iaroslav and Sania and Tania and Kotia, to Vorotyntsev and Irina and Varsonof'ev, to Samsonov and to the Grand Duke Nikolai Nikolaevich. They are linked by love of God, love of country and love of their neighbor; indeed they are the true existence of the love which Tolstoy told Sania was the only means:

> "To serve the good. And through goodness, to create God's Kingdom on earth. . . ." [And this can be done] only by love. "Only by love!" (p. 23)

They were Russia's hope who might have built—if not God's Kingdom on earth—at least a decent commonwealth in her territory, and it is their defeat which Solzhenitsyn depicts when Samsonov shoots himself.

It is because he stands for all this that Samsonov emerges as the novel's central character despite the fact that he is portrayed in only nine of its sixty-four chapters.[2] Samsonov is present in the reader's thoughts in scenes in which he has no role, scenes in which even the war itself hardly figures: the lessons Madame Kharitonova teaches her pupils in Rostov and those Varsonof'ev tries to convey to Kotia and Sania in Moscow are all part of

[2]Or perhaps one should say 9 of 63 since Chapter 22 is omitted from the published versions. The chapters in which Samsonov appears are 10, 11, 17, 28, 31, 35, 39, 44, 48.

Samsonov's destiny, as is Roman's gold cigarette case from Paris which won't fit Russian cigarettes,[3] or the mills which Il'ia Isakovich has built and his daughter Sonia would tear down, or the notebook in Sasha Lenartovich's pocket.

Samsonov represents Russia's defeat, and this points to a great similarity between *War and Peace* and *August 1914* and also to a great difference. Like Solzhenitsyn, Tolstoy was writing about the past with his thoughts very much in the present, but where Tolstoy's original purpose was to voice a warning and a rallying cry, Solzhenitsyn's is to grope for an explanation. When he began *War and Peace* Tolstoy feared that the reforms and governmental reorganization being introduced by Alexander II would fatally transform Russia into an unauthentically "Westernized" nation. He saw the reforms as an invasion of Russia by the ideas of the French Revolution, and to portray them he wrote about the historical invasion of Napoleon whom he called "the representative of the Revolution." But although (in the first half of *War and Peace*) he depicts Napoleon's unwitting "allies" within Russia—the young Pierre who would not fight against the liberator of Europe, the Court nobility and Staff officers whose ambitious intrigues are for their own prosperity, not Russia's, the intellectual reformers like Speranskii (whom he called "a civic Napoleon")—nevertheless Tolstoy was writing about a victory. He could do full ironic or tragic justice to Russian losses at Austerlitz or Smolensk secure in the historical certainty that these were followed by Russia's triumph.[4] Whereas in Solzhenitsyn's perspective the external defeat of Russia by Germany is followed by the internal defeat, whose preparation, in 1914 and earlier, so much engrosses him. (The similarity of the terms of the two men's hostility to revolutionaries, by the

[3]There is a remarkable similarity here to an image Tolstoy introduced into *The Decembrists* where he described the food in a fashionable Moscow restaurant as "protected from flies by wire screening, utterly useless in Moscow in the month of December, but exactly like the ones they use in Paris." L. N. Tolstoi, *Polnoe sobranie sochinenii,* XVII, 17.

[4]As Tolstoy wrote, in a rejected preface to *War and Peace,* he found himself uncomfortable when he had begun the novel with the year 1812 and experienced "a feeling akin to embarrassment. . . . I was ashamed to write of our triumph in the struggle with Bonapartist France without also describing our failures and our shame. . . .If our triumph was not merely a matter of chance, if its cause lay in the realities of the character of the Russian nation and army, then that character must have been expressed even more sharply in the epoch of our failures and defeats." *Ibid.,* XIII, 54. Yet it is hard to imagine that the first part of *War and Peace* would be anything like it is, had 1805 not been followed by 1812.

way, whether Chernyshevskyite or Leninist, is vividly apparent if one compares *August 1914* with *The Decembrists,* the unfinished novel from which *War and Peace* evolved, or with the early drafts of *War and Peace* itself.[5] A whole range of their attitudes are in concert, as is their fundamental premise, that real and terrible abuses exist in Russia but that the progressives' remedies for these will bring about something worse, because of their scorn for national traditional values. And nowhere is this similarity more striking than in the outrage both express against those who considered Russia's defeat a victory for the just cause: a view expressed by Dobroliubov and many others after Russia's loss of the Crimean War and a phenomenon to which Solzhenitsyn constantly alludes in *August 1914.*)

But despite this kinship of attitudes, it is the novels' similarity of purpose—to comment on the present in terms of the past—which is most striking. It has opened Tolstoy and Solzhenitsyn to the same critical reproach, that their characters are intellectually and psychically men of the present and not of the historical era, a supportable criticism if one reads these as novels belonging to the school of Walter Scott. A more important point, however, then gets lost, that Tolstoy was the originator (or perhaps, with Victor Hugo, the co-originator) of a new genre, the historical-philosophical novel, the non-antiquarian historical novel, in which the past is used not for its exotic distance but to "distance" the present and in which the past is understood as organically part of the present while the present is sensed as inevitably implicit in the past. With all its flaws and difficulties *August 1914* is a distinguished addition to this Tolstoyan genre, and this despite the fact that Solzhenitsyn seems to believe in historical causation more than Tolstoy ever acknowledged that he did.

The question must then probably follow: why, with the advantage of *War and Peace* as a generic model, does *August 1914* seem so bulky and unwieldy, indeed such a "loose baggy monster"? Perhaps with time and familiarity it will not; certainly today we can condescend to James' condescension. But whatever our caution we cannot read with the eyes of posterity, and congenial as we are to experimentation, the structure of *August 1914* is troublesome. The introduction of engaging characters at the beginning of the novel who never (Irina) or barely

[5]See Kathryn B. Feuer, The Genesis of *War and Peace,* Ph.D. thesis (unpublished), Columbia University, 1965.

(Sania) reappear. The introduction of promising new characters, the Arkhangorodskiis and Engineer Obodovskii,—two chapters before the novel's conclusion! The nurse Tania, who has one very interesting scene, Varia and her provocatively enigmatic friend Veronika—will we ever see these people again? They seem to have been crowded out to the novel's edges by the endless portrayal of a hopeless battle, and just because they are individuals and not stock figures the reader tends to feel not gratitude for so varied a gallery of supporting characters but tantalized irritation. Tolstoy controlled his cast much better and he orchestrated his portrayals of war and peace, his many settings and themes, into a structure far more harmonious and satisfying, even if one assumes that *August 1914* is unfinished and ought to be read only as the first half or third of a novel.

The crucial difference seems once again to lie in the fact that Solzhenitsyn was describing not defeat followed by victory but defeat followed by defeat. In the first half of *War and Peace* Austerlitz is an important event but it can be kept in its place; the foreground can be occupied by the men and women who enact their private lives and there is even ample time and room for great chunks of the reproduction of life for its own joyous sake. So that when Tolstoy reached 1812 he could safely lose sight of these characters for long periods; no reader has ever had to turn back from the latter parts of *War and Peace* to check up on who Natasha is. And new characters could be introduced to play limited and specific roles; no reader expects or particularly feels the need to know more about Platon Karataev or Vereshchagin. But Solzhenitsyn cannot put the Battle of Tannenberg into any comfortable perspective. The defeat and despair and destruction of the good will only continue and grow and so they must be exhaustively explored and *understood.* If the effort sacrifices grace and symmetry, so be it, these are trifles compared to the goal of truth. It is a very Tolstoyan sentiment, and artist that he is, Solzhenitsyn may well achieve his own new symmetry which to future generations will have its own inevitable rightness.

Even the literary "experimentation," probably the least successful aspect of *August 1914* for contemporary readers, may come to redeem itself, though this is more difficult to foresee. The capitalized emphases are hard to accept from a writer elsewhere so subtle. The Dos Passos-like montages do not fall flat because they are old-fashioned; they fail because they are too long, too undifferentiated and too overbearingly ironic. The use of documents and chapters of historical information, each set off in special type, meets a problem which Tolstoy seems to have solved much better in the second half of *War and Peace,* where such material is at least subjected to the control of the historical narrator's voice. Two other stylistic devices of *August 1914* recall Tolstoy, but this does not (and why should it?) make them necessarily successful. The "Screen" segments ought to have the effect of endowing the novel with the same visual immediacy Tolstoy achieved in *War and Peace* by the carefully controlled use of characters' direct perceptions. (And the "Screen" technique reminds one also of what Tolstoy called his "lantern slide" or "peep-show" methods.) But Solzhenitsyn's Screen turns out not to be purely visual except in its first and shortest example (Chapter 25). Indeed in the longer sequences the narrator's deductions or reflections or interpretations intrude so often that the Screen effect is sometimes not as different as it should be from the "normally" related chapters.

It is in this realm of narration that Solzhenitsyn seems to encounter his most serious problems. In *War and Peace* Tolstoy rigorously separated his own commentary from the presentation of his characters' thoughts and feelings, while in *August 1914* the two are so much inter-mixed that the reader can resent the author's frequent moralizing.[6] Indeed, many times he cannot be sure whether it is a character's thoughts or Solzhenitsyn's that he is reading, and sometimes the difference in effect is great.[7] In the past Solzhenitsyn's genius has shown itself in the sustained tension he can create between a powerful, absolute moralism and

[6]I feel a fundamental difference here from *Cancer Ward* and *The First Circle,* although now, even in thinking of those books, I would not say, (as I did in my article "Solzhenitsyn and the Legacy of Tolstoy") that Solzhenitsyn's voice *never* takes on "the insistently didactic Tolstoyan accent."

[7]I cite just two examples although I found myself wondering about this again and again. At the end of Chapter 2, when Irina is seen by Sania from the train, through a break in the avenue of poplars, the closing sentences are "I zakrylos' opiat' topoliami. I ne uvidet' ee nikogda" (p. 26). Is this Sania's thought? Or is it, as the "I. . .I. . ." construction seems to suggest, the author's? Are we then to assume that we are receiving a hint about future developments in the novel? In Chapter 54 Vorotyntsev, trying to encourage Iaroslav, tells him that he knows he'll survive their danger because an old woman prophesied he'd live to be sixty-nine, that his death will come, "Well you don't even like to say it; that will be in 1945." All of this has been developed in direct conversation, but the next *un*quoted sentence is: "It's true, you don't like to say such a thing, it's like something from H. G. Wells" (p. 474). As Iaroslav's observation this is appropriate enough, but it seems to be Solzhenitsyn's and as such it is a distracting intrusion.

the immediately realistic depiction of moral ambiguities, of what Browning called "...the dangerous edge of things / The honest thief, the tender murderer / the superstitious atheist..." When the narrative voice is off-key as often as it is in *August 1914* this tension too often sags or stretches beyond the breaking point.

Intimately related to this problem of narrational voice is another of Solzhenitsyn's "experimental" usages, the ending of chapters with proverbs or songs.[8] It is difficult to understand why Solzhenitsyn, whose chapter endings are invariably effective and often brilliant, felt compelled to burden his text with his own commentary in this form. The songs are relatively less disturbing (although their irony is repetitious of that already expressed) but what is one to make of those proverbs? Their relevance to what has gone before is either mysterious ("There was a horn, but God knocked it down." p. 195) or too obvious ("You should not have searched in the village, you should have searched within yourself." p. 505). This is a Tolstoyan usage from the later moral tales and it epitomizes one's feeling that reading *August 1914* is like reading a *War and Peace* written by the Tolstoy of the 1890's.

Yet it is this same feeling which underlies much of the novel's enigmatic power. When Sania ventures to express his doubts to Tolstoy, they are based on his observation that there doesn't seem to be much universal love to rely on, at least in his part of the country. But we have already encountered his more important uncertainties: a pacifist, he *feels* (a most Tolstoyan basis for action) that he must fight; an anarchist—that he must serve his country. Solzhenitsyn's recurrent phrasing of this dilemma is surely one of the keys to his purpose; "I feel sorry for Russia" suggests that Tolstoy's principle of love can be extended to love of country, love of a spiritual entity which is not expressed by armies or governments or the trappings of state power but which nevertheless, in given historical circumstances, is inextricable from these distasteful external features.

[8]Chapters 14, 24, 38 and 57 end with the quotation of songs. Chapter 14 has an effective ending without this addition; the song ending of Chapter 24 (a Russian soldiers' boast about how easily they'll beat the Germans) distracts from the portrait of General von François in the chapter itself; the song at the end of Chapter 38 simply repeats the irony of 24. The song at the end of 57 is effective; it is not affixed as overt comment but is sung by a character. Chapters 6, 21, 31, 42, 58, and 64 end with proverbs. Chapter 55 ends with a Document followed by a proverb, Chapter 63 with a proverb followed by two Documents.

(The political implications of this view are, of course, fraught with ambiguity. One cannot help wondering if a Sasha Lenartovich of the year 1941 would be depicted with the same harshness. And yet, of all people Solzhenitsyn would seem capable of understanding the man who, just because he "feels sorry for Russia," refuses to fight for Stalin. Or even for Nicholas the Second. One must certainly wait for the sequel, but in this volume the wisdom of all the patriots, and the shallowness of all the oppositionists, is disquieting. In this perspective, *War and Peace* raises a further question. When Tolstoy wrote of the "national character" of the War of 1812 he created a massive image of all Russia joining together in a great upheaval, as spontaneous and natural as an earthquake, to cast the intruder from her soil. But the battles of *August 1914* take place on German territory and it is puzzling that so acute a moralist as Solzhenitsyn never seems to take this into account. The eerie absence of the German army is one of the novel's most powerful images, yet surely in so detailed and realistic a portrayal there were some burnt-out German civilians and some frightened German children to notice along the way.)

Still, *War and Peace* was not written by the Tolstoy of the 1890's and it is this Tolstoy, the philosopher of Love, who concerns Solzhenitsyn in *August 1914*. Tolstoyan moral doctrine is not introduced into the novel as a period detail, nor even as a fixed principle to be endorsed or refuted. "Only by love!" he tells Sania. "No one will ever think of anything better" (p. 23). Solzhenitsyn does not wish to dispute the view, in that he proposes nothing better. But he does explore, patiently and painfully, the insufficiency of love when the big guns belong to the enemy and the corrosions of love: how love for the people becomes hatred of their values and way of life, why love for the nation's possibilities becomes hatred for its actuality. If the protagonists of *August 1914* are recognizable descendants of *War and Peace* they are also recognizable progenitors of Vega and Kostoglotov and Rubin and Nerzhin.

A Lucid Love

BY ALEXANDER SCHMEMANN

I

Let specialists debate about what Solzhenitsyn wanted to say in his *August 1914,* and let historians confirm or refute his version, his evaluation of the military catastrophe which marked Russia's entry into the First World War. All I know is that several days have passed since I closed that remarkable book, so permeated with light, sadness, joy, anger, love—and still I have the same sensation in my soul of a feast, a celebration, and I have difficulty returning to mundane, earthly affairs. It is as if Solzhenitsyn has lifted me, and raised me on some sunlit height, where the air is so pure that only the essential is visible and it seems impossible to inhale ever again the poisoned air below. A mysterious consolation and promise seems to reverberate through the air:

> ...it was like the parish feast, but unusual, without the tolling of bells, without old women's gay kerchiefs. Sullen peasants gathered on the mountain from surrounding villages, and first a landowner on foot, then a local cleric on horseback circled them and promised either the world, or life in paradise, in exchange for suffering in this life... (*August 1914*).

If this book provokes such feelings here, where one is free,

First published in Russian in *Vestnik RSKhD* (Paris), No. 100 (1971), 141-152. Authorized translation by Serge Schmemann.

then what must be its impact there, in the dull and frightening grayness of Soviet monotony?

II

Why should I sense a feast? Solzhenitsyn is writing, after all, once again about suffering and death, evil and weakness. He wrings the reader's heart with sadness for Russia's fateful end and with horror for the senselessness of it—his book is, as someone has written, truly a "lamentation for Russia." Yet when I re-examine my impression and my mood, I know I sense a feast. Not a feast in the simple, earthly sense, but one that is given us so rarely, "not by law, but by grace" to know in the Church—a break out of narrow bounds, a touch of the hidden essence of things, a communion with that which is behind the visible, external and transient.

Above all I find in Solzhenitsyn a new feast in Russian literature, a new triumph for Russia. That at such a time Russia has such a writer—this alone is a call for rejoicing.

All my life I have read Western literature. French literature, for example, I have come to accept as my own from childhood, and I fully acknowledge that it has no equal in taste, measure, skill, style, or in its inherent order. Great writers, average, minor; eternal, transitory; but how well they all write, how well each knows his place and fulfills his function! What competence, quality and polish! This is culture, of course, and therefore should be loved and valued, and, indeed, "cultivated."

In comparison with this ordered culture, how flawed and primitively chaotic is Russian literature. Several indisputable giants, to be sure; several average writers—but beyond that, just countless Shiller-Mikhailovs and Boborykins, all with pretensions to profundity, prophecy, and pedagogy.

Why then is it always possible to lay down a Western work for dinner, a stroll, or a nap? Why is one so mindful that this is precisely "culture"—a vital, nourishing, enriching and delightful part of life but not life itself? And why is it impossible to interrupt reading Dostoevsky, Tolstoy, and now Solzhenitsyn? Why do the dinner, stroll, and nap now become burdensome and needless distractions?

It is literally impossible to lay their books down because all they have written really happens; to me, in me, in my life;

and having realized this, having communed with it, it is impossible to live or feel as before. What is the mystic power of these Russian writers, that they envelop one so totally, as if dismantling the very barrier between "culture" and "life"; that they batter the soul until the serious and learned Western literary scholarship begins to appear superfluous and empty (not to mention our own undernourished Russian criticism, meekly stumbling behind)?

Before *August 1914,* Solzhenitsyn's success and literary impact may have appeared simply a reaction to the acute urgency of his themes or to his tragic place and role in contemporary events. But now he has taken for his theme a long-forgotten episode, one thoroughly washed away, it would seem, by the waves of subsequent tragedies and catastrophes. And he has written a difficult novel, an almost technical work with no concession to the casual reader. Yet that distant, sunny August, those ancient pines, the mud and lakes of eastern Prussia, the movements of Corps and the wrangling of generals have all become our fate and our tragedy, and a timeless record of man, the world, and life. This is the work of a great writer.

I will not reiterate what I find to be Solzhenitsyn's indisputable literary merits—the remarkable flexibility and honesty of his prose, his gifts of personification and transformation, his freedom from current literary fetishes, from modish literary self-analysis. These gifts are even more evident in *August 1914,* just as his artistic reach, creative generosity, and resources have become firmer and broader.

I will note, however, that I do not find those cinematographic "screens" interspersed through the fabric of the novel, which many have criticized, unnecessary or affected. Solzhenitsyn, it seems to me, describes primarily what he sees. His writing is a sort of commentary on, almost a reaction to, that which he has visually absorbed; and so when a scene reaches a certain limit of complexity, it becomes necessary for him to transmit directly the images he sees, without literary intervention, and the "screens" are the viable and creatively justified result. What remains when the book is closed, after all, is precisely a *vision,* complete and indivisible, which transforms all the detail, all the action and time itself into one, unique, living image, forever illumined by that August sun.

III

I did not mention Tolstoy and Dostoevsky for a meaningless comparison, as tribute to the hackneyed custom of relating anything in the least noteworthy to these titans. I mentioned them because Solzhenitsyn, in his creative, human and (it is appropriate here) Russian conscience is turned toward them as toward no one else in Russia.

It is not by chance that Tolstoy's name appears throughout *August 1914*—which, in fact, almost begins with an appearance by the seer of *Iasnaia Poliana*—or that Dostoevsky, though not mentioned by name, is equally present and active through those mental states and that "tonality" which, correctly or not, have come to be associated with the prophet of the Pushkin speech and of *The Diary of a Writer.* In fact, that which Solzhenitsyn has used from Tolstoy and Dostoevsky is common to both, despite all their differences—it is a *myth of Russia.*

The *myth* was colored differently by Tolstoy and Dostoevsky but both based it on the same tonality, and, more importantly, both were heard and grasped in the same way by the Russian consciousness. It is precisely against this *myth* (that Russia had a peculiar, sanctified destiny, that she was governed by a unique spirit, that her natives were endowed with an unmatched and generally undefined spiritual perception) that Solzhenitsyn rebels in his novel. He exposes it as false and ruinous, as one about which both titans, for all their awesome and permanent truth about other and more important things, were *wrong.* The false *myth,* perhaps, did not originate with them, but developed gradually in the Russian consciousness. But because they are genuinely great, because they are inseparably merged with Russia—because they are the very essence of Russia—it is to Tolstoy and Dostoevsky that the Russian conscience must turn for the 50-year domination of Russia by all sorts of "demons."

The subject of *August 1914* is the beginning of Russia's doom, the merging of the threads of her fate, securing her collapse. But what are the forces active in the novel? It is not by chance, again, that the novel begins with the Tolstoyan student volunteering for the war. Volunteering too are the "pure Hegelian" Kostia, the populist Iaroslav Kharitonov, who yearns to meld with the people. At the universities, even talkative coeds, stuffed with the rhetoric of the intelligentsia, also babble about "purifying feats of war."

No, Russia is not yet decayed either by the Tolstoyan "non-violence," or by the "possessed" revolutionaries; the "composition of nations" has not yet been changed, and there are still "those trusting beards, those friendly eyes, those unhurried, unselfsatisfied expressions." Russia is alive and strong. Tolstoy, revolution . . . but still it's necessary to go; "I pity Russia" is enough to volunteer, and they go to war. But what do they meet at this fateful moment when all their powers are heightened? They meet that selfsame myth, which we cannot help but associate with the hallowed names of Tolstoy and Dostoevsky.

On the one side they meet other "Tolstoyans"—full generals, implanted with the Tolstoy-Kutuzov faith in the mysterious and ineffable spirit of Russian arms, a spirit which is supposed to somehow replace strategy, supplies and even basic concern for the soldier, by a faith in the ideal of Captain Tushin and Platon Karataev. They meet with a Tolstoyan scorn for Germans in general, and, for that matter, for initiative and action as something un-Russian; as antithetical to that hidden and primordial "something" by which Russia is supposed to live and which makes her, clearly, invulnerable.

On the other side they meet Tolstoyans in the grand duke who, stumbling upon a parish church of St. Nicholas Kochan (a blessed fool for Christ's sake), discerns in this a mystical omen and locates his headquarters there; or in the Imperial Court, firmly convinced that God cannot be other than "with Russia," and that the Mother of God would never allow L'vov to fall. And underneath all this religio-patriotic unction, the "nicest" and "kindest" courtiers and generals, either to please "higher-ups" or by conviction, question the soldiers not about whether they have rested or eaten, but about the parish feasts in their village. And as a result, they are fearfully and senselessly routed, and, in the tragic inevitability of that rout, they point to the inevitable end. This is the basic theme of *August 1914;* a terribly simple and bitter one.

And in that tragic defeat, in which no historian has perceived anything but a rout, the novel reveals a spiritual rout. The battle is probed to its deepest roots and divulges its spiritual ancestry; but the roots of that defeat are not where Tolstoy or Dostoevsky would have us look. No, Solzhenitsyn is not "against" Tolstoy—who can be against kindness, love, fairness?—nor does he contradict Dostoevsky when he rejects the demons of revolution; the cheap denial of heritage, roots, tradition, of all that constitutes the soul and fabric of one's native land. But Solzhenitsyn's "possessed" revolutionary, sublieutenant Sasha Lenartovich, cannot even subvert his own platoon. He can only follow powerlessly and passively, even during an attack, behind his own soldiers, and afterwards behind a band of heroes, bearing their slain colonel out of the German encirclement.

The revolutionary's hour would come later. But that hour is prepared, that platoon subverted, that rout—horrible, because militarily unjustifiable—is caused not by Sasha Lenartovich in that fateful August, nor by the "dark forces" personified in him, nor by the Duma (which, in fact, futilely demanded appropriations to strengthen Russian artillery), nor by the *intelligentsia,* nor even by the incompetent generals. The hour of revolution is prepared by that false myth, which had occupied the will and wisdom of Russia, paralyzing them; a myth dangerous because cloaked in the vestments of light, stuffed with pseudo-messianism and pseudo-mysticism, and with that spiritual deceit that authentic spirituality so fears.

It would be so immeasurably simpler if we could always put the blame for all tragedies on someone else or something "alien." There is nothing more frightening than to see the "abomination of desolation standing in the place of light." It is not surprising then, that the persecution of Solzhenitsyn by the Soviet government, so eminently predictable, is augmented by persecution from those still dwelling in deceit, who prefer myths to truth both there and here, in emigration. Already one malicious lie has entered circulation—that Solzhenitsyn is a collective creation of the KGB. We await a sequel, because so often we love not truth, but the inebriation of various myths. The external colorings of these myths are almost indistinguishable: the color of falsehood, the color of hatred for truth. They produce the same tonality, the same internal enslavement.

But Solzhenitsyn loves truth. He loves it as the most priceless and irreplaceable possession on earth, and precisely this love, almost miraculous in its sobriety, brought him to the theme of *August 1914;* to the events for which the blame could not be placed on the familiar, easy targets; the "dark forces." He is fated, apparently, to fill a tragically solitary place in Russian literature; that of an "exorcist" of the Russian consciousness, of its emancipator from all idols that had imprisoned it; from the idolatry that, alas, is peculiar to Russians, whether in the

Soviet Union, as a frightening press of a nightmarish regime, or here, as an eerie self-satisfaction and blindness among self-proclaimed guardians of righteousness.

With every work Solzhenitsyn grasps this indivisible truth more deeply and more broadly, and in *August 1914* he nears its primary and deepest knot. This is why this technical book on generals, encirclements and breakouts is again and anew a deeply Christian work; because there is no calling more important or necessary in Christianity than to discern whether spirits are from God—and there is nothing more dangerous than false or forged spirits.

IV

Again I have returned to that which is most important for me in Solzhenitsyn, the essence of that unexpected feast. This mysterious force I will name his "lucid love." I am convinced that Solzhenitsyn's soul, at its deepest, is determined by it, and so too the spiritual order of his creativity—that childishly simple, yet infinitely wise truthfulness which condemns incomprehension and persecution.

Lucid, seeing love. Not an un-Christian love, blind and passionate, which so often creates idols; not simply lucidity, which can coexist with falsehood, hate, and suspiciousness, and about which the Gospel says "you will look with your own eyes and will not see." No, precisely a lucid love, a mysterious combination of love and vision in which love is purified by clear vision of illusion, partiality and blindness; in which vision is deepened and cleansed by love and enabled to see all truth, rather than those pieces which pass for truth among idol worshipers of all types.

This lucid, seeing love lies at the foundation of Solzhenitsyn's creativity. It renders him free with a moral freedom which, unfortunately, has been lost by so many Russians of all ideologies. I mentioned the persecutions of Solzhenitsyn; but with a similar apprehension I await his "recognition," when he will be giddily adopted by adherents of some ideology, who will assert that as surely as two plus two is four, Solzhenitsyn is great and good because he says exactly what *they* always maintained. They will prove he was a monarchist, an anti-monarchist, a reactionary, a liberal, an orthodox, a modernist—they will, in other words, package and distribute the "thoughts" and "teachings" of Solzhenitsyn, stuffed with regurgitated and redigested "ideas" which, like gray clouds, will shut out the festal morning which finally promised, after a heavy and humid night, freedom, freshness, and happiness.

Solzhenitsyn can free us from "ideology." His is not another tract about healing; he is himself the medicine for which our bodies yearn. The power of his creativity is that he takes words that had long ceased to be words, but had become "slogans" and "problems," words filled with ideological narrowness and hatred, saturated with malice, serving only to divide and torture—"the people," "faith," "Russia"—and having washed them with his lucid love, returns them revived—new, whole, truthful, and alive.

V

"I pity Russia," says the Tolstoyan Sania, and he goes to war for her, so that the Germans "wouldn't break her backbone." Does he go because Russia has some special dimension or "essence"? Does he go because God and the Virgin Mary are necessarily and invariably "for" Russia and not "for" the Germans? Does he go because Russia is all that the prideful Russian fancy has made her, brightly glittering in cheap, spent mysticism? No, not at all, Solzhenitsyn seems to answer calmly, honestly and humbly. Sania goes because Russia *is,* and because she, and not another country, is his motherland, granted him like the sun and air; because she is his home and body, and no one can be without these. Of course it would be better to be at peace with Germany, rather than waging this unnecessary war. Russia would do better to learn some lessons from these same Germans about order, organization, production; but it's come to war, and, it follows, one must go to war. This "must," this "pity for Russia" is more convincing, more self-evident and more truthful than all the messianic rhetoric, and than the opposite rhetoric, that of revolution. And, because it is self-evident, Sania is mute—"he had nothing to answer." But Russia is as if returned to us, alive, complex, strong, weak, sinful, virtuous, wise, foolish—Russia as she is, not a Russia in which it is necessary to believe—since it is necessary to believe only in God—but a Russia which must live and for which, if necessary, one must die.

And if war, then it should be waged as well as possible. How refreshing in this age of hypocritical "pacificism" and "rejection of war," and of the equally repugnant "justification of war" with innumerable ideologies, is Solzhenitsyn's honest and personal interest in it! He neither rejects war nor justifies it, since both options are senseless. War is. His is not the curiosity of an expert, nor the fascination of a "buff"; rather it is the interest of a man who knows war as a heavy and fearsome undertaking, which demands from a man the concentration of all his powers—his mind, will, conscience and, in the end, his humanity. It is a test of the entire man, bringing out the best or the worst in him; it measures his relation to life, and his capacity for sacrifice and selflessness.

Hence the fine detail in the work, and Solzhenitsyn's almost technical battle descriptions. He rejects romanticizing war, positively or negatively. War, he says, is not waged or decided by miracles or omens, but by whether it will be possible to fill a gap on the left flank, whether Blagoveshchenskii's corps or Rennenkampf's cavalry will move, and whether generals, officers and soldiers will ably, intelligently and conscientiously do what circumstances demand. In this sense *August 1914* is a refutation of the "Tolstoy-Kutuzov" myth of *War and Peace,* the myth of wars heading their own fated way despite generals or strategies. If generals and officers are bad, Solzhenitsyn says, the battle collapses and the men run. If they are good, then everything holds, and there do occur miracles of heroism, and it is possible to win.

All this comes into focus in the tragic image of General Samsonov, the "250-pound lamb," doomed from without and from within. From without, by the weight of the myths which have paralyzed the army top to bottom. From within, by his inability to overcome them, to rid himself of the myths except by cutting all communication, abdicating all power, and, at the end, dying. The death of Samsonov, a pure, honest, knowing, intelligent and brave general, clearly aware why he was perishing and equally aware "he could not have done differently," is the height of Solzhenitsyn's lucid love.

Samsonov is the key symbol in *August 1914* because if the "kindest" and "nicest" people in headquarters can so calmly accept his loss, if everything can be excused, smoothed over and arranged through an invocation of "the will of God," then truly Russia's fate is sealed. "You won't raise dough with prayer," says Solzhenitsyn, but then he adds, "Untruth did not begin with us, and it won't end with us..." This is spoken by the writer-Christian, who does not allow the word God to be printed without the capital "G";[1] who derives from God and elevates to Him all fates, all creation and every man. And we approach now the final truth of Solzhenitsyn, which, however difficult, we must hear, or there is no point to *August 1914.*

VI

Solzhenitsyn holds God above all things and men. Reading Solzhenitsyn, one understands with trepidation why it was forbidden ancient Israel to utter the name of God. No, Solzhenitsyn's God is not one whose name can be declined into any case in military orders and regulations. His is not the God used to excuse human irresponsibility, or to obscure truth and justify senselessness; or the God in whose name one hates another while loving and lauding himself. His is not the God who can be always exploited to justify everything in a smooth and apparently humble, but in reality endlessly proud, "historiosophy." The God of Solzhenitsyn is the living and true God, "ineffable, incomprehensible, invisible and unfathomable." The endlessly distant God, All-surpassing and living and endlessly close to the unique, priceless soul of man. God, Who Is. And because He is, man stands before Him alive and unique, free and responsible; not a pawn in the hands of mysterious and elemental forces, "dark" or "light," not a slave of faceless idols, but a respondent to God for the life that is given him, for himself and for his brothers, and for the talents entrusted him. If only man would find the order of his soul, if only he would be true, not by word but by deed, if only he were humble, wise, truthful, free and conscientious, then in him and through him the rays of Divine glory and love would shine; then in him and through him, even in the torments of senselessness and death, concord would rule and light would shine, and he would be saved.

Why does Colonel Kabanov die? Why does the Dorogobuzh regiment perish? Solzhenitsyn does not reply with a ringing

[1]The reference is to Solzhenitsyn's May, 1971 "afterword" to the Russian edition of *August 1914.* [Eds.]

slogan about some "glory of Russian arms"; rather, calmly, almost methodically, he notes that "always, and in every army, there are those remarkable officers in whom the highest possible endurance of the human spirit seems to be concentrated." Then he says, "we are cut off; and others, men just like us, will leave for home, while we, under no obligation to them, not their relatives or blood brothers, will remain to die, so that they can live after us. . ."

Thus, without loud words, the one explanation and justification which is eternal and independent of this world, the one truth which triumphs over irrational history and over death, is enthroned over meaninglessness and hopelessness: as it is stated for eternity in the Gospels as the measure of all and the substance of all, and as the victory over all, "Greater love hath no man than this, that a man lay down his life for his friends." (Jn. 15:13).

When several abandoned soldiers bear the body of their commander, and on that sunny, peaceful morning, on a bright meadow under a high, festal sky, they hold that amazing service chanting "time-tried chants with one voice," we no longer ask why, for we are allowed to participate in a mystical celebration, "not *of* this world," but with the light, truth, beauty and joy without which it is impossible to live *in* this world.

Thus in the last analysis Solzhenitsyn "liberates" even religion from the petty human idolatry which has encrusted it, from its submission to oneself and to one's own, from everything essentially pseudo-religious and pseudo-Christian in it. Perhaps this is most important, since nothing has so obscured the visage of God in this world, or so hinders men from seeing Him, as all these "human, all too human" political, social, racial or ethnic reductions of religion. Purifying religion, Solzhenitsyn sets it again at the center of all. No, his book is not about religious "problems" or "searches for faith"; but his conscience, truthfulness, courage and freedom from idols can only be from God. His vision of the world, man and life comes from God. And his lucid love for the truly much-suffering Russia is from God. And because from God, a witness to Him.

Translated by Serge Schmemann

The Debate Over *August 1914*

BY NIKITA STRUVE

More than a year has passed since the appearance in the West—and subsequently in *samizdat*—of Aleksandr Solzhenitsyn's latest novel, the first fascicle ("knot") of a projected series of works devoted to Russia's fate over a span of more than forty years. In the short period since the appearance of this novel, many different and contradictory opinions have been expressed. Openly and sometimes in veiled fashion, a controversy has arisen around the novel both in Russia and in the West. From this controversy certain definite conclusions can already be drawn.[1]

The appearance of a literary genius is, for various reasons, always accompanied by a certain amount of uneasiness and distrust. There is in mankind, and perhaps in each individual man, a reluctance to acknowledge that which is superior; we fear that a phenomenon of a higher order will degrade us, and, therefore, something unquestionably low and sinful within us struggles against the recognition of such phenomena. But we also possess an opposite and conscientious desire to examine ourselves and

"The Debate Over *August 1914*." From *Vestnik Russkogo Studencheskogo Khristianskogo Dvizheniia,* 104/105 (1972), 197-210. Reprinted (in slightly abridged form) by permission of the author. Translated by Olga V. Dunlop.

[1]These remarks were written before an excellent *samizdat* collection of critical studies on *August 1914* reached the West. (N.S.) They have been recently published by YMCA Press in Paris as *Avgust chetyrnadtsatogo chitaiut na Rodine* [*How* August 1914 *Is Read in the Homeland*]—Eds.

make certain that we are not victims of self-delusion, illusion or infatuation, that we are not, in a fit of uncontrolled enthusiasm, elevating something which is really unworthy. Uneasiness and distrust, as well as enthusiasm and paeans of praise, have accompanied the appearance of each of Solzhenitsyn's works. When Solzhenitsyn's first two short works, *One Day in the Life of Ivan Denisovich* and "Matrena's Home" appeared, they immediately struck everyone by their close kinship, in terms of truthfulness and depth, to the great tradition of Russian classical literature (i.e. Dostoevsky, Chekhov, Turgenev). At the time readers remarked, "Yes, these are marvellous works, but they are only short narratives. Will the author be able to cope with the larger genre of the novel?" This legitimate question was answered in the affirmative when *The First Circle* and *Cancer Ward* made their appearance. But, although all now agreed that Solzhenitsyn had succeeded with both the long and short narrative form, new doubts arose. In his novels Solzhenitsyn describes what he has seen with his own eyes and has personally experienced. It was questioned whether he was capable of writing a novel not based on his own life; whether, like a true novelist, he could recreate through his imagination the heroes, mores, and life-style of another epoch and of other worlds. And, as if in answer to this no less legitimate question, there appeared *August 1914,* a novel written half a century after the historical events it describes, just as, incidentally, half a century separates the publication of Pushkin's *The Captain's Daughter* from the Pugachev rebellion and *War and Peace* from the Napoleonic wars.

Being, as it were, the final and supreme test of Solzhenitsyn's claim to recognition as a great writer, it is not surprising that *August 1914* has only served to sharpen those sentiments of approval and enthusiasm, on the one hand, and distrust and censure, on the other, which accompanied the appearance of all his works. (. . .)

The most basic objections which were expressed in the press, in private letters and in discussions concerned the following aspects of the novel: its literary form, which, in the eyes of some, was insufficiently rich in images; its formal structure with its preponderance of war over peace; an alleged inaccurate portrayal of the spirit of the times; an excessively mannered language. And, finally, many disliked the theme itself—the author's attitude toward Russia.

Some readers, especially in the Soviet Union (we know this from private letters and from the response of recent émigrés to Israel), were put off by the realistic manner of *August,* which they considered too akin to the notorious and detested method of socialist realism. Aside from the incorrectness of this judgment, it would seem that we are here dealing with an "overreaction," where a justifiable aversion to socialist realism has passed directly into a denial of realism as such. But it is of course quite obvious that socialist realism fails not because of its realism (there has never been a trace of realism in it) but precisely because of the absence or rather perversion and desecration of reality by political fiat. In this sense socialist realism is also a caricature of idealism. The "ideal" always has been and always will be the subject of art, including realistic art. In depicting a world compatible with Communist ideology, socialist realism has to describe that which does not exist in nature. Furthermore, even if such a world were actually to come into existence in the future, it would represent nothing but a gross reduction and distortion of man. Even without the presence of political demands, socialist realism, by denying the metaphysical foundation of existence, inevitably becomes philosophically flat, a false oversimplification of life. In other words, socialist realism fails because it is socialistic and materialistic. But realism as an artistic method is just as unchanging and eternal as the fantastic or other experimental forms of expression. It should also be obvious that the historical or historio-philosophical novel can only be realistic.

But there are different kinds of realism, different in the degree to which they encompass reality. While socialist realism perverts and impoverishes reality, its literary predecessor, naturalism, was satisfied merely to reflect nature, to copy its contours without stepping beyond its boundaries. Only a higher realism encompasses human existence in its fulness, from mundane details to the transcendent laws of life.

A perusal of the first few lines of *August 1914* is sufficient to convince us as to which of the three above-named types of realism this novel belongs. From the very start Solzhenitsyn uses this higher form of realism to describe his heroes and the action of the novel. The transcendent mountain range [*Khrebet*] which Sania Lazhenitsyn sees so clearly as he departs for the war is a many-sided symbol: on the historical plane it is a symbol of

Russia's highest hour before a fateful break;[2] on the metaphysical plane it symbolizes something higher and purer than man and his creativity. In this remarkably successful introduction, with its depth and variety of meaning, Solzhenitsyn defines from the outset both his perception of the world—unquestionably Christian—and his creative approach, which is not simply to reflect history, but an attempt to penetrate to its deepest meaning. It remains for us, however, to demonstrate to what extent Solzhenitsyn has been successful in carrying out his intentions, in embodying his perception of the world, and in sustaining his artistic approach.

One should first of all keep in mind that *August 1914* is only the first of several fascicles projected by the author. As Solzhenitsyn states in the foreword of his novel, he does not claim that the novel is complete, nor even that the characters are sufficiently developed. "Except for the military operation of Samsonov's army," the author explains, "this is only the preliminary layout." Since the majority of the characters are only barely outlined, we are not justified in making the same critical demands on them as we would on those of a completed novel. We are dealing here with a most difficult genre, the novel-in-many-parts, one which has no counterpart in Russian literature. Even in world literature few have successfully used this form (with the possible exception of Galsworthy). Moreover, such works usually trace the fortunes of one family through several generations rather than dealing with a variety of unconnected characters. On the basis of the first fascicle we cannot yet pass judgment on Solzhenitsyn's ultimate success or failure, but we must emphasize that he has taken upon himself a titanic task unprecedented in world literature.

Every great writer has his own unique approach to time and space, his own personal experience of these two dimensions of existence. In Gogol's works, for instance, time does not exist; his characters do not develop but are depicted in an immobile state, and Chichikov is not fated to be reborn. Space, therefore, is also illusory in his works; Chichikov travels extensively in *Dead Souls,* but he is only circling a monochromatic and undifferentiated area. In Tolstoy time unfolds smoothly. Despite the fateful events which are described, there are no discontinuities; time and space are unlimited; a landlord walks or drives the length and breadth of his estate for hours. In

[2]In Russian *khrebet* means both mountain range and backbone—Tr.

Dostoevsky time and space progressively build up in intensity, become concentrated, are brought to a climax and contract to a few fateful moments in a limited area (most often a room or staircase). Then comes an abatement or release in the form of a temporal-spatial lapse (Raskol'nikov's unconsciousness, the Idiot's journey which is not described to us, etc.). Just as Tolstoy's perception of time derived from the patriarchal way of life, so Dostoevsky's was a product of his experience of the last minutes before death on Semenovskii Square and of the momentary illumination preceding an epileptic seizure. Chekhov also has a unique experience of time: leisurely and slow, it changes pace only in extreme circumstances.

Solzhenitsyn has his own experience of time, one which, as far as I know, is unique in literature and which probably grew out of his extended concentration camp experience. Like Dostoevsky, although, as we shall see, in a somewhat different manner, Solzhenitsyn concentrates time to the utmost and maximally limits space. The camp life of Ivan Denisovich is described within the duration of one day, *Cancer Ward* lasts several weeks, and *The First Circle*—only four days. *August 1914* is compressed into eleven days. These telescoped time dimensions correspond to an increased density in space: a prison-camp, a railroad station, a home, a hospital, a sharashka or a small corner of Eastern Prussia . . . This constancy of vision and uniformity in the pattern of the temporal-spatial dimensions already attests and defines the imagistic nature of Solzhenitsyn's thought. This alone would make of him an important and original writer.

Following the laws of tragedy, Dostoevsky depicts his protagonists at a moment when their fate has already been internally determined and is building up for the denouement. With Solzhenitsyn it is different; his characters depend not so much on their own spiritual development as on external events and stimuli. They are part of a social and historical whole and come into conflict with each other and even with themselves as a result of external circumstances. The diverse representatives of Soviet society in the Tashkent hospital are brought together by illness. Technical training or plain chance has assembled the prisoners in the Moscow sharashka. The same is true of *August 1914;* war intrudes into the peaceful and mundane existence of the novel's future protagonists, catching them by surprise, making no distinction among them, and bringing some of them together on the first battlefield of the war. Obviously the author cannot fully develop his protagonists in the ten or eleven days which are described; they only begin to live. Therefore we shall be able to judge the final success or failure of each protagonist only after the completion of other volumes, if not at the end of the entire work. The one exception is General Samsonov, the chief and only fully developed hero in the first fascicle of the novel. *August* begins as a great and tragic epic about the history of the Russian people and state; in all probability, each subsequent volume of this epic will contain its own particular and completed tragedy. We may assume that the protagonists of the work will gradually become clearer and better defined against the background of these specific and self-contained tragedies.

In *August* the death of Samsonov and the destruction of his army is such a self-contained tragedy. It is on the basis of this tragedy that we must judge the whole work. And here, we believe, all must concur—both those who praise *August* and those who are critical of it. Piotr Rawicz, the literary critic of the French evening paper *Le Monde,* who published an enthusiastic review of Solzhenitsyn's novel, speaks of a "Shakespearian resonance" in the depiction of Samsonov. Even the harsh and unfair critic of *August,* Roman Gul', admits that "these scenes in the novel raise Solzhenitsyn to the summits of Russian classical literature."[3] Indeed, perhaps in no other of his novels was Solzhenitsyn able to penetrate so deeply into the secret depths of man's soul (except perhaps in the description of Volodin's arrest in *The First Circle*) and to unite so convincingly in one person the private with the corporate, the real and historical with the transcendent. Certainly no one can speak of "non-imagistic thought" here. General Samsonov is portrayed simultaneously on the psychological, historical, historiosophical and religio-ethical planes.

A conscientious, reasonable, modest, and honest general, he becomes by the will of Providence at once the perpetrator and victim of the catastrophe which will result in the fall of Russia. He is not directly responsible for the disaster since he did not conceive the absurd plan involving a premature offensive; nevertheless, as commander-in-chief, he carries responsibility for it.

[3]The reference is to Roman Gul's article "Chitaia 'Avgust Chetyrnadtsatogo'," ["Reading *August 1914*"] which appeared in the émigré *Novyi Zhurnal,* 104 (1971), 55-82.—Tr.

With extraordinary psychological insight Solzhenitsyn shows how Samsonov, sensing defeat, divests himself of everything he has accumulated during a long military career. He descends deeply into himself, to his childhood memories, and then rises upward in prayer, preparing himself for sacrifice. On this deep level Samsonov approaches a kinship with Christ, experiences his own Gethsemane. Like Dostoevsky, Solzhenitsyn was not afraid to superimpose the image of Christ onto a protagonist of his novel—and onto the fate of a Russian general at that. While kneeling in prayer, Samsonov wipes off a heavy sweat—compare this to the bloody sweat of Christ in the Gospel account. Like Christ in the Gospel, Samsonov experiences an hour of absolute isolation. When he rises from prayer, "no one had come for him either with a pressing question or with a cheering or bad report." And descending even deeper, Samsonov is granted a vision of his own impending death . . .

In comparing Samsonov with Christ, Solzhenitsyn has masterfully avoided any labored moments, any sentimentality or artificiality inherently possible in such a bold comparison. Colonel Vorotyntsev calls Samsonov a "seven-pood lamb." With this unusual word-combination Solzhenitsyn promptly defines the limits of his comparison and, at the same time, expands Samsonov's image to the dimensions of all Russia. This Shakespearian protagonist, having divested himself of all glory and earthly dignity, turns out to be a profoundly Russian hero, a symbol and sign of the approaching fate of Russia—at once guilty and innocent, sacrificed and self-sacrificing.

The days preceding Samsonov's death, his "pre-Petrine" and "pre-Muscovite" farewell to the army, become a singular rite of forgiveness and the high point of the novel. Nevertheless, the conclusion drawn by some critics (in particular Roman Gul') who think that this moment overwhelms the rest of the novel is wrong. On the contrary, Samsonov's monumental and in-depth portrait does not stifle but rather elevates the entire body of the novel to an appropriate height. In the light of Samsonov's death, we can understand the real significance of the army's prolonged and senseless advance and of its staunch resistance even to death. Between the tenth and twenty-first of August, through the fault of its obdurate leadership and partly through no one's fault, but according to the mysterious laws of inscrutible destiny, all Russia was going to the slaughter amid the sands and lakes of Eastern Prussia. The movements of the many different regiments are described in precise detail, and Solzhenitsyn forces us to march with them over the sandy roads of Prussia because he wants us to witness and to participate in Russia's national Golgotha.

In the light of what has been said, the objections of those who complain that the chapters describing the military maneuvers are not well integrated with the rest of the work, that they stand alone and are written for the military specialist rather than the average reader, pale to insignificance. Furthermore, in addition to their image-creating, unifying function, the military chapters also have other qualities. Solzhenitsyn is an unsurpassed portrayer of battle. He succeeds as few others in simultaneously showing both the mass nature of modern war and its deeply personal character. Despite the detailed description of the planned or disorderly movements of the troops, they never create confusion or swallow up the individual and personal aspects. Following Stendhal, Tolstoy described a small section of the battle through the eyes of one of his protagonists or ascended with the army command to some observation point from which he observed the battlefield. Solzhenitsyn, on the other hand, is always in the very thick of movements, skirmishes or battles. I am not aware of any other work in Russian or world literature in which the personal and the corporate are so harmoniously combined, or which gives such a complete picture of a military operation, from the high command down to the innumerable and nameless soldiers.

It is appropriate here to touch upon the question of Solzhenitsyn's insertion of special chapters into the fabric of the novel—the montages of newspaper items of the time, the "survey" chapters which exclude the fictional characters and, finally, the "screen" chapters. These chapters, which stand out both graphically and stylistically, seemed to many to be an unnecessary tribute to the literary modernism which was the rage in the Western novel of the twenties. Solzhenitsyn, they said, included these chapters in order to disarm those critics who accused him of excessive traditionality. It seems improper, however, to pose the question this way. Solzhenitsyn had need of these chapters not in order to answer his critics but to encompass as fully as possible that reality which he had undertaken to describe. The newspaper clippings allow him, in an unusually concise way, to throw light on those aspects of Russia which remain outside the scope of the narrative, i.e. beer-hall patriotism, a banal belief in progress, the general smugness which reigned on the eve of the fateful catastrophe, the lack of mutual understanding between the home front and the army, etc. Furthermore, the newspaper clippings introduce an element of healthy and objective humor, which every tragic epic needs like a safety vent.

The survey and screen chapters expand the panorama of the war. The survey chapters, which are, incidentally, not obligatory for the indolent reader, allow the author to single out in an impartial fashion high-lights of the advance and the defeat which would otherwise be lost in the course of the narrative. They serve as a kind of bird's-eye view of events—distant in both time and space. The screen chapters, on the other hand, offer a close-up view; they direct the eye to details and heighten the emotion of the moment. The alternation of different kinds of chapters adds a rhythmic movement to the novel: the survey chapters slow down the rhythm, the screen chapters accelerate it. We are not then dealing with an antiquated modernism or the employment of devices allegedly rendered illegitimate after their use by Dos Passos. It is true that Solzhenitsyn did not invent these devices, although it would be difficult to find in world literature an exact analogy to the screen chapters, with their distinct focus on sound, long-distance shots, details, and direct speech. Moreover, is the criterion for accepting a literary device merely its originality and not its appropriateness? Surely not only that which is novel is worthwhile and justified but also that which finds an appropriate and organic function. Why should one hold that Dos Passos discovered a literary device suitable only for himself? Like all major writers, Solzhenitsyn has absorbed the novelistic techniques of many different eras . . .

The military chapters stand out in still another, no less important way—by their remarkable and almost scientific precision. Perhaps nowhere did *August* elicit such approval as among the veterans of World War I in the Russian emigration. In the opinion of these eyewitness-specialists this military operation of some fifty years ago is described with unimpeachable exactitude. Here we encounter one of the peculiarities of Solzhenitsyn's genius: his scientific cast of mind. We should observe, however, that in this respect Solzhenitsyn has only brought to perfection a quality possessed by all true novelists. Since Pushkin had no historical materials which he could easily draw upon, he became a historian to write *The Captain's*

Daughter; he recreated the Pugachev period solely on the basis of carefully collected and meticulously examined materials. Tolstoy also studied the era of Alexander I for several years, although in the long run his poetic and polemical talent overcame the historian in him. Solzhenitsyn has a similar approach. He did not need to write the history of the Prussian campaign (there were already many such studies), but he did study the existing materials with great thoroughness. Therefore the reproach of some critics who accuse him of inaccuracy is comical. We must distinguish here between reproaches for specific factual errors and a more general charge of an inaccurate grasp of the spirit of the time. Pushkin's *The Captain's Daughter* was also reproached for containing a number of anachronisms, but does this in any way diminish its literary worth? After more than a century not a single reader can any longer notice these anachronisms. It is also a fact that the veterans of the campaign of 1812 were indignant at the inaccuracies in Tolstoy's descriptions of military operations in *War and Peace,* but this has not the slightest significance for us. Therefore the question, raised by one critic, as to whether Varsonof'ev could have lured two young students into a beer-hall and drunk beer with them is of little importance. This may now seem like an anachronism to some, but in twenty years not a single reader will notice this detail. Moreover, if one must accuse Solzhenitsyn, I would rather reproach him for having an insufficient number of anachronisms, for reproducing the period too exactly . . . Perhaps every work of art needs a little poetic fantasy . . .

The question as to whether the author has faithfully reproduced the spirit of the time described is more substantial, since it touches upon matters of aesthetics. We know that *War and Peace* was widely criticized for showing the epoch it depicts in a false light. Konstantin Leont'ev wrote that Natasha Rostov is more characteristic of the spirit of the eighteen-sixties than of 1812. That may well be true. But the mistake lies in the way the question is posed. All historiosophical novels throw light simultaneously on two historical periods—the period they describe and that in which they are written. Pushkin undertook *The Captain's Daughter* in an attempt to illumine and rethink the socio-political relations between the gentry and the people in the light of the Pugachev rebellion. The rather unlikely friendship and mutual respect between Grinev and Pugachev reflect the hope for harmony between the classes prevalent in the eighteen-thirties. Similarly, the starting point for Tolstoy's *War and Peace* was the return of the Decembrists from exile and the writer's desire to return to the epoch which gave them birth.

Solzhenitsyn has the same approach. Like his great predecessors he sees the past through the present. It is not by chance that the same time span of half a century separates the three novels we have mentioned from the events they describe. The historical novel is born naturally of a gap in time in order to reestablish a lost connection. There was little of Catherine's epoch left in the reign of Nicholas I and little of the Alexandrian era in post-Emancipation Russia. Much more awesome is the gap between pre-revolutionary and contemporary Russia. Solzhenitsyn himself emphasized this break when he said in the novel that one no longer meets the same smiling, trusting faces as before. The events described in *August* are not only interesting in and of themselves but even more as a key to the understanding of the present. A dialogue with the present is an important element of the novel.

When Roman Gul' writes that no one in 1914 would have said, as Sania Lazhenitsyn does in the novel, "I feel sorry for Russia," he is wide of the mark. "No one would even have entertained such an idea," Gul' maintains. In the first place, I would like to ask the critic how he can be so omniscient. Perhaps the war did awake uneasy presentiments in some Russians (one person experiencing such presentiments was, for example, Rasputin), if only because of its analogy with the defeat in the recent Japanese war. But that is not really the point. "I feel sorry for Russia," is more than just another point in the controversy between pro-war and defeatist factions. It has a more general, trans-temporal significance. It is one of those threads that bind eras together. What is appropriate in a work of art is not that which seems most plausible to the average reader but that which can raise the moment above the flow of time, without contradicting the essence of the epoch which it describes. The statement "I feel sorry for Russia," especially in reference to 1914, may express not only Sania Lazhenitsyn's feelings but also the author's and even our own, since we know the events which followed. Konstantin Leont'ev once remarked that Pierre Bezukhov is not a man of 1812 but of a later era, since one can discern echoes of Gogol' and Dostoevsky in his thoughts. Certainly Pierre is not believable from the point of view of pedestrian realism; but from the artistic point of view he embodies that mutual penetration of different historical epochs which is a sine qua non of any true historical novel. Konstantin Leont'ev also stated that Tolstoy made the psychology of the generation of 1812 more complex than it actually was, since he was viewing it through the prism of his own time. It is possible that the opposite has occurred with Solzhenitsyn: he may have somewhat simplified the psychology of prerevolutionary Russia by viewing it through the prism of the nineteen seventies. It could not be otherwise and to complain of this is in vain. (. . .)

Equally unjustified are those who reproach Solzhenitsyn for using a modernized form of the Russian language. It is obvious that Solzhenitsyn could not and should not have written in the language of 1914; the result would have been an archaeological, and hence artificial, reproduction of the past and not a novel. Pushkin used a contemporary rather than eighteenth-century language in *The Captain's Daughter,* and only occasional lexical archaisms remind us that the narrative is dealing with the past. From the artistic point of view it is important for the author to capture, both in his language and his concrete details, the spirit of the period he describes in what is basic and most important, not in minute details. A historical novel is not a photographic reproduction but an artistic recreation in which many levels of language play a role. The reader of the work must be aware of a distance in time, but, at the same time, this distance must to some extent be capable of being disregarded; otherwise one is left with a dead copy and not a living narrative. Despite their differences the time which the novel describes and period in which it is written become one. A historical novel must also not be too contemporaneous. Perhaps this will help us to understand why Solzhenitsyn's quest for a language peculiarly his own is more noticeable in *August* than in his other works.

However, it is precisely this distinctive language of the novel which has been criticized so strongly for being pretentious and mannered. This view ignores the problem of language which confronts the contemporary Russian writer. The Russian language has become gray, impoverished, and faded in the Soviet period. The degeneration of the language is only a reflection of the general degeneration of the country. In all of his works

Solzhenitsyn has taken up the difficult task of returning vitality, verve, and color to the Russian language. This was especially needed in *August;* it was unthinkable for the author to describe pre-revolutionary Russia in his contemporary language. And so Solzhenitsyn evolved a language of his own. *August* is striking in its dynamic use of syntax. There has probably never been such select, terse, tense speech used in Russian prose, with the possible exception of Marina Tsvetaeva. At the same time Solzhenitsyn, like Leskov, has expanded the lexical pool of the language. It is difficult to determine at present whether all the words that Solzhenitsyn has picked up from actual speech or culled from dictionaries are successful. (. . .) It is difficult to dispute about language with a great writer possessing a sharper instinct for words than his critics. Besides, whether Solzhenitsyn's every lexical innovation is justified is not vitally important. What is important is that the Russian language in *August* appears renewed, shines with new color, acquires new strength and power.

Solzhenitsyn's language expresses one of the particularities of his literary genius: his overwhelming will-power. Russian literature has never known a writer of such forceful will. Pushkin and Lermontov were first of all poets, and their will-power was therefore of necessity weakened. Tolstoy also did not express a forceful will in his fiction; again and again his poetic gift overcame his will. Thus *War and Peace* gradually changed from the pacifistic novel that the author had originally intended into a poetic apology for war. Dostoevsky did manifest will-power, but it was limited by his illness. Goncharov, Turgenev and Chekhov were all in their own way devoid of will. But Solzhenitsyn's fate, life and work are characterized above all by will. To survive four years at the front, live through the Soviet concentration camps, overcome serious illness, struggle to become a writer, gain a world reputation against inhuman odds, and finally unswervingly to follow his path—all this is a miracle of rare will-power. Ivan Denisovich, Matrena, Nerzhin, Kostoglotov, Vorotyntsev are characters of supreme will-power whom Solzhenitsyn presents as examples to his readers. And to some extent this volitional element somewhat overcomes the poetic element in Solzhenitsyn, or, rather, it adds a peculiar and, on occasion, somewhat brusque nuance to his work.

We have already stated that Samsonov's death is the high

point of the novel. But there is another high point in the book which parallels it and is no less important—the breakthrough of the small group led by Vorotyntsev through the Grunfliess forest. Just as the decay and the foredoom of Old Russia are graphically depicted in Samsonov's death, so the breakthrough serves to offer us hope for a better future. All is lost, all is destroyed, but there is still action, even if on the most insignificant scale. Vorotyntsev, who at one point traversed the entire front in an effort to save the situation, can now save only himself and the handful of men left to him. Thus Solzhenitsyn shows that in all circumstances, in the words of his prayer, "not all the paths of goodness are closed." Vorotyntsev's breakthrough embodies the author's philosophy of the will, one relevant for all periods of time but especially appropriate for the present. Even when confronted with total destruction one must continue to act wherever possible. The conditions necessary for a successful result of such activity are also indicated—a close bond to the soil and to heaven. The exhausted Vorotyntsev, upon awakening from sleep, feels "the grass, so pristine, uniform, silky, from which purity flowed into him." And the same Vorotyntsev takes part in a memorial service under the open sky before the body of the heroically fallen Colonel Kabanov. Downward, to the earth, to childhood, to the past, and upward, to what is higher, toward the future and the eternal, and between them, supported by and nourished by both—there remains an effort of will and action in the present. Such is the philosophy of the will in *August* and to it both the structure of the novel and its imagery and language are subordinated.

We have not yet touched upon the last of the disputed questions listed at the beginning of this essay: the author's attitude toward Russia. The essence of this has already been admirably expressed by A. Schmemann.[4] Solzhenitsyn disappoints those who have lost all hope for Russia, seeing her as a land of perpetual slaves and masters, as well as those who blindly and thoughtlessly extol her in the face of all evidence. Solzhenitsyn's "lucid love" (in A. Schmemann's phrase) knows that Russia has been both great and petty, holy and sinful, and also that she must be formed in the image of the free and

[4]The reference is to Alexander Schmemann's article "A Lucid Love" which also appears in this volume—Eds.

wilful men who will recreate her. Solzhenitsyn does not give a final, conclusive judgment concerning the past and supplies no recipe for the future. But he does not turn away from the reality of Russia and calls on all to achieve the task set before her.

August 1914 will enter into the corpus of Russian literature as one of its most tonic works. The dispute which has broken out over the novel represents a first testimony to this fact.

Translated by Olga V. Dunlop

August 1914: Historical Novel or Novel History

BY DOROTHY ATKINSON

O, say, can you see
by the dawn's early light—
the debris of a battlefield. Dead horses rupturing space with upturned legs. Corpses. The wheeling benediction of birds of carrion, still wheels, silent guns.
What so proudly—
"God. . . help us."

It is quite possible that more people will see the battle of Tannenberg through the pages of Aleksandr Solzhenitsyn's *August 1914* than will be brought to witness by all the textbooks of history. The situation is not unique. Scott's historical novels were considered by a well-known English historian to have done more for history than the work of any modern professed historian.[1] In the dedication of *Ivanhoe* Scott admitted no pretense to complete accuracy. Comparing his writing with the art of the painter, he acknowledged responsibility for realism only in his outline and general coloring; the details, the lights and shadows, were subject to his artistic discretion.

Most readers of Solzhenitsyn's work will assume some similar correspondence between the picture so vividly detailed in *August*

[1]George Macaulay Trevelyan, "Influence of Sir Walter Scott on History," *An Autobiography and Other Essays* (London, 1949), p. 200.

1914 and "real" history, but will allow considerable latitude for what Scott called "fair license." A portrayal that takes us into the innermost thoughts, the feelings, even the dreams, of men clearly owes something to the author's imagination. Where is the line here between fiction and fact, between the novel and history? Unlike Scott, Solzhenitsyn has not defined his parameters, but one of his characters provides a key: "The material of history," according to a scholar in the book, "is not *viewpoints,* but *sources* and the conclusions that derive from them."[2]

Since war is an eminently historical phenomenon, sources for *August 1914* are not lacking. For this is not a "war story"—a romance set in war; it is a story of war. Only the introductory chapters and a few later segments are set beyond the range of military operations. This is just the first part of a larger work projected by the author since youth and intended to illuminate the historical significance of the first world war and its aftermath.

Attention here centers on the first major Russian collision of the war. As Solzhenitsyn indicates, the German war plan called for an initial concentration of forces against France, with only a minimal defensive screen to be left facing Russia. While slow-moving Russian forces mobilized, France was to be defeated and the main strength of the German army then redirected east. The Russians, however, honoring military commitments and responding to French appeals, launched an early offensive in East Prussia. In the first encounters they met with success. German troops pulled back and refugees flooded into Berlin, creating a panic. The eastern front command was replaced and units of the German army in the west were sent to help block the Russian advance. Before they arrived, the battle had been decided. The victorious Germans gave it the name of Tannenberg—a village unimportant in the fighting but marked in history as the site where Teutonic Knights were defeated by Slavs in 1410.

Solzhenitsyn's account focuses on the military action as it unfolded in the critical week beginning with Sunday, August 10,

[2]Aleksandr Solzhenitsyn, *Avgust chetyrnadtsatogo* (Paris: YMCA Press, 1971), p. 503. Footnotes refer to this edition unless the English title is cited. Page references given parenthetically in the text are to the translation by Michael Glenny, *August 1914* (New York: Farrar, Straus, and Giroux, 1972).

1914.[3] In a postscript to the Russian language edition the author indicates that he assembled materials for some time though denied access in his own country to collections available to others. Inviting the criticisms and corrections of his readers, he requests additional information on specific military figures and *unpublished* materials on certain cities for the subsequent volumes of his work. All of this suggests a serious use of historical material, but since his sources are not identified, confirmation calls for some probing among historical stockpiles.

In addition to the many Russian strategical analyses, documentary materials, memoirs, and war studies dealing with Tannenberg, there are of course many in German which Solzhenitsyn reads. Material originally from the works of Generals Ludendorff, von François and Hoffmann appears in *August 1914.* The British General Knox is among the many characters portrayed here who left a record of experiences with the Russian 2nd Army in East Prussia. Since much of the same material appears in many works, evidence that corroborates information or scenes presented in *August 1914* often reappears in different places. As a result, it is rarely possible to conclude with assurance that a particular source was actually utilized. However, in one case a positive identification seems justified and this turns out to be of considerable importance.

In a discussion of the short-lived "military renaissance" that followed Russia's defeat in the Japanese War in 1905, Solzhenitsyn refers enthusiastically to the group of progressive officers at the General Staff Academy known as the "Young Turks." Among them was a brilliant young professor at the Academy, Nikolai Golovin. When a change in military leadership brought the group into disfavor, Golovin—"a strategist the equal of any in Europe," according to Solzhenitsyn (p. 113)—was sent to command a minor cavalry unit. Though not involved in the military operations described in *August 1914,* and not in Solzhenitsyn's cast, his name reappears later as an authority ("In Golovin's opinion..." p. 393), and again at the end of the book (p. 620) when a leading character, Vorotyntsev, is described as a former student in his class at the Academy.

[3]Dates are given here in the old style Russian calendar in use at the time, and used by Solzhenitsyn in *August 1914.* Add 13 days to bring these into conformity with the western calendar.

These scattered references lead to an arresting figure. A colonel of cavalry early in the war, Golovin was decorated for bravery and distinguished service; rising rapidly, he was to become chief of staff for a group of six armies. Following the February revolution in 1917 he was elected Director of the General Staff Academy. With the help of his students Golovin managed to gather many documents during the war. Later he collected archives abandoned by the disintegrating Russian army, solicited memoirs and compiled extensive war bibliographies. Uniquely well informed, Golovin was also endowed with a broad perspective: among his technical military publications are studies on the psychology of combat and on sociological aspects of war.

A post-war article written by the former head of the French General Staff but based entirely on German sources prompted General Golovin—then in exile—to undertake a full account of the East Prussian campaign. This extraordinary work—highly detailed and documented, judiciously reasoned, animated by a restrained patriotism, insistent on the force of both logistical and psychological factors in warfare, sprinkled with references to Tolstoy—is an invaluable source on Tannenberg.[4] Though Solzhenitsyn uses much material not supplied in Golovin's text, he makes much use of what is there.

Both authors stress the blunder made by the Russian military command at the conference table with France before the war: acceptance of a commitment to begin an offensive on the 15th day of mobilization. Both criticize the decision to conduct offensive operations simultaneously on two fronts. Both convey a dismal impression of military leadership where seniority and favoritism stifled talent and initiative. Both complain of general unpreparedness, of technical inadequacies that compounded problems in transport, communications and supply. Both point to the difficulties faced alike by the commander in chief and the head of the 2nd Army as last-minute appointees compelled to carry out plans they disapproved with staffs they had not chosen.

These points are by no means confined to Golovin's book. Yet in the presentation of data, in matters of interpretation,

[4]Nikolai N. Golovin, *Nachalo voiny 1914 g. i operatsii v Vostochnoi Prussii* (Prague, 1926). Translated as *The Russian Campaign of 1914*, (Fort Leavenworth, Kansas, 1933). The author's name appears as Golovine in the English edition to which all citations here refer.

in the choice of detail, and at times even in phraseology, a repeated similarity can be remarked. As an example illustrating a major theme, in Golovin's text (p. 67) we read: "In promising decisive assistance, Russia did not promise to commit suicide." The final pages of *August 1914* echo the protest as Vorotyntsev hurls a reproach at Supreme Command Headquarters: "... Russia promised 'decisive assistance,' but not suicide!"[5]

Colonel Vorotyntsev is a fictional character. As a General Staff officer sent out to collect information for General Headquarters, he moves across different scenes of military operations, lacing the narrative together and serving on occasion as spokesman for the author. Vorotyntsev, the same age and rank as Golovin at the beginning of the war, reports that a fortuneteller has predicted he will not be killed in any war he fights in, but will nonetheless die a military (war) death at the age of 69. Golovin died in exile during the second world war at 69.

Of the numerous military figures (close to 100) identified by name in *August 1914,* only a handful appear to be fictional. Apart from Vorotyntsev, most of these are common soldiers or men of low rank. Some even here may be historical persons, but this could not be authenticated. Others—described but unnamed by Solzhenitsyn—are historically identifiable (e.g., Colonel Zhil'tsov who was appointed to replace the commander of the Kopor regiment, p. 378). The small fictional group includes several fairly prominent characters: the socialist Lenartovich, young Lt. Kharitonov, the peasant Blagodarev. Each of these individuals is placed in a specific military unit and participates in authentic military events that are described in accurate detail. Lenartovich, for example, fights at Waplitz. Later he joins a group (with Vorotyntsev, Blagodarev, and Kharitonov) carrying the body of Col. Kabanov in an episode based on a true incident.[6]

All of the higher-ranking military personnel (including all

[5]Solzhenitsyn, *Avgust chetyrnadtsatogo,* p. 570.

[6]This dramatic story (and many others) can be found in the account of a general staff officer of Samsonov's army, P. N. Bogdanovich, *Vtorzhenie v Vostochnuiu Prussiiu v avguste 1914 goda* [*The Invasion of East Prussia in August 1914*] (Buenos Aires, 1964), p. 213. The feats of other heroes described or mentioned in *August 1914:* Pervushin, Kakhovskoi, and Alekseev among them, are recounted in various sources.

German officers mentioned) are historical persons. In his high-key portraits of some of these men Solzhenitsyn might be thought to be exercising the prerogative claimed by Scott: to be shading an historical outline at his own artistic discretion. Yet he explicitly denies this. Keeping closer to historians than to novelists, as he states, he has been forced to sacrifice artistic balance in portraying the Russian generals. "We would not have dared to invent such unrelieved blackness; light and shadow would have been distributed within the limits of plausibility."[7]

Assessment of the personality of historical characters is a legitimate concern of any historian, whether traditionalist or psychohistorian, and wherever he stands in the large debate on the role of the hero in history. Solzhenitsyn's credo that "men make history" has been spelled out with emphasis in *August 1914*. Since "leaders do lead," the role of military commanders is critical here, and comparison of personal profiles with historical records provides a touchstone for Solzhenitsyn's use of sources.

The most harshly drawn portrait in the book is that of the hapless commander of the 1st Corps on the left flank of the 2nd Army, General Artamonov. According to Golovin, Artamonov became the whipping boy of the higher command after the defeat of the army. Yet, though he advises caution in accepting the view that Artamonov's premature retreat was responsible for the entire disaster, Golovin himself concludes that the destruction of the army was due to the outflanking of the left.[8] He presents Artamonov as an incompetent who had no control of his corps or grasp of the battle plan. In line with his outmoded concept of leadership, and in place of more vital functions, states Golovin, the general motored about visiting troop positions. Another account substantiating a scene in *August 1914* reports that Artamonov had a reputation "even before the war for his visits to the troops in which the main attention

[7]Solzhenitsyn, *Avgust chetyrnadtsatogo,* p. 350.

[8]Golovin, pp. 299, 324; see also: RSFSR, Komissiia po issledovaniiu i ispol'zovaniiu opyta mirovoi i grazhdanskoi voiny, *Strategicheskii ocherk voiny 1914-1918 gg., Chast' I* [Commission on the Investigation and Utilization of the Experience of the World War and Civil War, *Strategical Outline of the War of 1914-1918. Part I*] (Moscow, 1922), p. 93.

was directed to whether there were enough ikons in the barracks and whether the soldiers knew their prayers."[9]

Informed writers confirm that Col. Krymov had been sent from 2nd Army headquarters to keep an eye on Artamonov, "always known as a man easily carried away." Krymov is said to have warned the 2nd Army staff about 2 o'clock on August 14 that Artamonov seemed about to pull out. Army headquarters checked with Artamonov and was reassured with a phrase that was to become notorious: the 1st Corps was holding "like a rock." Minutes later Artamonov ordered communications taken out and gave orders for retreat.[10] Solzhenitsyn's portrayal does, in fact, reflect the sources, but even here "unrelieved blackness" is softened by understanding: there is something all-too-human in the figure of the self-deluding general standing erect in his retreating phaeton like some epic hero, framed in the flaring red wings of his coatskirts.

General Blagoveshchenskii whose withdrawal opened the right flank of the army is treated with little ceremony in *August 1914* or elsewhere. Though equally critized by military analysts, he commands somewhat less attention. An officer involved in the operations of the 6th Corps (more accurately, his division was unaccountably *not* involved when it might have saved the day) described Blagoveshchenskii as a paper-shuffler who knew nothing and cared less about military science.[11] The general was removed from his position after the campaign.

The case of General Kliuev may be somewhat less obvious. While still a prisoner-of-war, Kliuev managed to send back his own version of events, a document of particular importance since all staff correspondence and field records of the encircled army core (the 13th, 15th, and part of the 23rd Corps) were lost in battle. In drawing up this account, which Solzhenitsyn

[9] I. Patronov, "Deistvie VI korpusa i glavnye prichiny neudachi II armii v Vostochnoi Prussii" ["The Operations of the VIth Corps and the Main Reasons for the Failure of the IId Army in East Prussia"], *Voennyi sbornik* [*Military Writings*] (Belgrad), IV (1923), 172.

[10] Bogdanovich, pp. 113, 144, quoting Postovskii and the report of a special commission under Gen. Panteleev that held an investigation after the defeat; see also Golovin, p. 227, and *Kratkii strategicheskii ocherk voiny 1914-1918 gg., vyp.* 1 [*Short Strategical Outline of the War 1914-1918,* I] (Moscow, 1918), p. 101n.

[11] Patronov, p. 163. This account (p. 169) confirms that a captured map showing German plans was sent to Blagoveshchenskii's Corps headquarters on the night of August 15-16. The *Short Strategical Outline,* p. 124, seconds Patronov's judgment of Blagoveshchenskii.

says "he managed to slant, color and blur," (p. 382) Kliuev had the assistance of staff members captured with him. His report provides a defense against some of the criticisms raised against him in *August 1914,* but it justifies others—and gives ground for more.[12] Kliuev may have had a greater capacity for military reasoning than for military action; it may be, too, that his defense was reasoned in the light of hindsight and of what Gen. Brusilov described as a "characteristic self-conceit."[13]

The one unforgiveable crime laid on Kliuev's head by Golovin, and undoubtedly a factor influencing Solzhenitsyn's outlook, was his surrender when he still had a large group of men and many guns. According to Golovin the German forces facing these men were no larger, therefore the surrender was the result of a psychological collapse, a broken will. Yet he grants that of the troops under Kliuev "the majority were non-combatants, and a large percentage of the combatants were wounded."[14] Solzhenitsyn's surrender scene is close to the description of a witness who heard Kliuev give the order "to avoid useless bloodshed." This observer does not record a protest of the troops to the surrender order. On the contrary, when the order was carried out and the mob became aware of what was going on, "white handkerchiefs and shirts began to gleam in the air."[15] Yet there is ample evidence here and else-

[12]See A. R.-P. "Prichiny neudach II arm. gen. Samsonova v Vost. Prussii v avguste 1914 (po zapiske gen. Klieva)" ["Reasons for the Failures of Gen. Samsonov's IId Army in East Prussia in August 1914 (according to Gen. Kliuev's memorandum)"], *Voennyi sbornik,* IV (1923), 154-162. Cf. the account of one of Kliuev's staff officers: V. Fuks, "*Kratkii ocherk operatsii Narevskoi armii gen. Samsonova v Vost. Prussii v avguste 1914 g.* [Brief Outline of the Operations of Gen. Samsonov's Narva Army in East Prussia in August 1914]," *ibid.,* pp. 120-153.

[13]Aleksei A. Brussilov, [Brusilov], *A Soldier's Notebook 1914-1918* (London, 1930), p. 28.

[14]Golovin, pp. 321-322, estimates 20,000 in the immediate group and 11,000 more in the area. Solzhenitsyn (*Avgust chetyrnadtsatogo,* p. 463) makes it "up to 30,000, the majority unwounded." In general, the figures cited by Solzhenitsyn tally with the sources. When sources disagree, there seems to have been some preference for "sympathetic" data—e.g., the 2200 German prisoners said taken at Waplitz (*August 1914,* p. 353) was the highest of several figures found in different sources.

[15]Bogdanovich, p. 244. Kliuev's retreat, incidentally, involved passage through a tight spot which Solzhenitsyn's soldiers call "Schlaga-M" from a map abbreviation (for Schlaga-Mühlen). The passageway here was actually about 14 feet (2 sazhens) wide, not 7 feet (Fuks, p. 141). Solzhenitsyn (*Avgust chetyrnadtsatogo,* pp. 384, 405) gives the equivalent of both, and the translator chose the latter (pp. 418, 441).

where of the resistance to surrender shown in *August 1914*.[16]

Turning to the remaining important Corps commander, Solzhenitsyn's portrait of General Martos fits other accounts so well that almost every detail could be footnoted. It may be sufficient to mention that two contrasting views—Martos studying the battle on a hilltop with Samsonov while German prisoners are led away, and Martos auditing the battle the next day as a prisoner of General von François—are both historical scenes which include some recorded dialogue.[17]

Martos, "utterly unlike the other. . . Russian generals" in Solzhenitsyn's view (p. 279), emerges from the sources as the Russian commander most widely respected for his role in the campaign. His own account of his experiences contains a dramatic description of his capture which does not appear in *August 1914*—most likely because it is counter-climactic to Samsonov's final scene. Details from this description though, appear in the authentic episode in which a hospitalized Cossack is shown reporting Martos' death to General Sirelius (pp. 525-527). The incident was reported to Krymov by Sirelius in explanation of his retreat.[18]

One other omission concerning Martos is worth noting. The reader is informed that "there had been no fighting at all," (p. 280) when Martos occupied Neidenburg. Yet describing Samsonov's later entry into the smoldering, damaged town Solzhenitsyn comments, "Before the fighting it had been a neat, well-built town. . ." (p. 164). What happened to Neidenburg? Solzhenitsyn provides no explanation and thereby is lost a tale. According to one account, when Martos approached the town he was met by a deputation which turned over the keys to the city and assured him all German forces had left. Martos' record confirms only that an advance party of Cossacks sent in to reconnoiter were fired upon, and reported troops and barricades in the town. He therefore ordered it shelled,

[16]*Short Strategical Outline,* p. 107; Golovin p. 320. Golovin also quotes a German source here, Max Schwarte, *Der Grosse Krieg 1914-1918* (Leipzig, 1921; page reference should read "I: 317"), which gives a brief description of the battlefield at dawn following surrender similar to Solzhenitsyn's final screen scene (Ch. 56).

[17]Martos left an account of the operations of his 15th Corps in East Prussia; the manuscript was in Golovin's possession and is quoted extensively by him. See pp. 263ff and 317-318, as well as Hermann von François, *Marneschlacht und Tannenberg* (Berlin, 1920), p. 231.

[18]Panteleev report, Bogdanovich, p. 240.

destroying much of it, but the artillery fire was not returned. Later, as a German prisoner, he was accused of bombarding undefended centers of habitation and—harbinger of Nuremberg—threatened with a death sentence. Solzhenitsyn might be thought to be skirting an awkward topic here, but his description of Russian looting elsewhere suggests no intent to side-step. Nor does the record suggest any need: after investigation, the charges against Martos were dropped.[19]

The central historical figure in *August 1914* is the head of the 2nd Army, 55-year old Aleksandr Samsonov. Solzhenitsyn presents a generally sympathetic portrait of the general. There is reason for sympathy. As correctly reported in the book, Samsonov had been abruptly transferred from his position as Governor-General of Turkestan to direct a partially mobilized army ordered to plunge into an immediate offensive. Unfamiliar with the regional plans, provided with a second-rate staff, and with understrength, poorly-supplied forces, Samsonov faced formidable difficulties. Not the least of these was the superior command of the Northwest Army Group.

To the north of Samsonov's advancing troops the Russian 1st Army under General Rennenkampf had successfully engaged German forces. The Army Group command, responsible for the coordination of the two armies, ordered Samsonov to move north-northeast to cut off the anticipated line of German retreat. Samsonov, however, for both strategical and logistical reasons, wanted to direct his forces northwest. His proposal was rejected by Group Commander General Zhilinskii, as were his repeated requests for a rest period to restore the hard-pressed troops.

Stretching his orders, Samsonov managed to deflect the direction of advance somewhat, and Zhilinskii reluctantly acceded to a compromise axis when German forces appeared in the west. The compromise, though, involved a dangerous lengthening of the front, and at the same time Samsonov was deprived of freedom to deploy the two corps on his flanks. With arms nailed open by the higher command, the 2nd Army extended the line of its fan-shaped front as it advanced; units became isolated, communications deteriorated, supplies disappeared. Despite the heroic efforts of the troops and of many field commanders, disorganization and lack of direction led to disaster.

[19]Martos ms. cited in Golovin, pp. 186-188. Cf. Bogdanovich, p. 78.

The flanking corps were knocked back, the center was encircled, and Samsonov—overwhelmed by catastrophe—perished with his army.

Samsonov's role in the catenation of events in *August 1914* is a pivotal one. He stands at the neck of an hour glass, under the burden of the higher command, over a spreading mass of militarized humanity, as time runs out. The general, who recalls at one point (p. 423) a legend of an Uncreated Image wiped on the canvas of a frustrated artist, appears himself on Solzhenitsyn's pages in an eidetic image absorbed from sources. Countless scattered details have been culled from historical records to reflect a lifelike Samsonov. The reconstruction of his mental universe has necessarily called on the artist's creative ability, but elements even here suggest an historically informed imagination.

A hero of the Japanese War, Samsonov was known as a gallant cavalry officer and a man of personal bravery. The effect of Zhilinskii's accusation of cowardice when he proposed a northwest move is not difficult to picture. Solzhenitsyn reports Zhilinskii's language literally and joins other writers in pointing to the incident in explanation of Samsonov's reluctance to abandon the offensive and retreat in time.[20]

The tug-of-war in which Zhilinskii dragged the army to the right while Samsonov pulled it to the left is discussed at length by all strategical analysts. Some blame Samsonov for not obeying orders, some for not disobeying more radically. Though most support Solzhenitsyn's view that Samsonov was strategically correct, the implication that he stood alone in his opinion is open to question. Both Postovskii (Samsonov's Chief-of-Staff) and Kliuev had worked on plans for the region, were familiar with German war games under similar conditions, and had warned Samsonov of the danger of an attack from the west. At any rate both claimed later to have done so.[21]

If Solzhenitsyn has been on the whole generous in his treatment, he has balanced it with criticism. Samsonov is shown

[20]Golovin, p. 204, 254; Bogdanovich, pp. 145-148. Since the news about Artamonov's retreat reached headquarters about 6 p.m. on August 14, the conclusion of some writers that Samsonov continued with the offensive only because of poor communications seems questionable. Cf. A. M. Zaionchkovskii, *Mirovaia voina 1914-1918. Obshchii strategicheskii ocherk* [*The World War 1914-1918. A General Strategical Outline*], 2nd ed. (Moscow, 1931), p. 100.

[21]Postovskii, quoted in Golovin, p. 182; "Kliuev Memorandum" (see Note 12 above), p. 155.

under "a cloud of guilt" (p. 430): for inadequate reconnaissance, for breaking communications, for the loss of central control, and other failings for which he is reproached in historical literature. He "made mistakes," grants Vorotyntsev, "but they were tactical mistakes" (p. 619).

Why he accepted a compromise which involved such risk remains an open question. He has been blamed for too narrow a concept of discipline (he took orders, complained a critic, "as a soldier, not as a general"), for the outlook of a divisional commander of cavalry who could see no solution but to take to his saddle in a pinch. All this is conveyed in *August 1914,* According to one report, Samsonov was told by the Northwest Army Group command that he would be relieved of his command if he did not carry out his orders.[22] As one of his officers observed, "Generals who can contend simultaneously with the enemy, with their superiors, and with their own staff are rarely met in military history."[23]

Samsonov's last hours provide a dramatic highpoint in the book. Here again, there is impressive historical back-up, not only of the essential outline but also of detail. Wherever Solzhenitsyn's account shows any discrepancy with the sources consulted, the deviation tends toward a somewhat heroicized portrait. For example, a witness of Samsonov's last morning describes him as a man already "physically infirm and spiritually crushed," who had to be helped down from his saddle and spent the morning in a peasant cottage with his staff.[24] Solzhenitsyn provides a strikingly similar description of this spot near Orlau (the glowing disc of the sun rising on cue over woods to the left, mist swirling below, etc.), but shows Samsonov leaving his staff behind and riding out among the troops.[25] Though this episode (which serves to interweave fictional characters) appears to have been fabricated, the appearance, the dazed mannerism, even the fact that he had been thinking of Kuropatkin—a Russian general defeated in the Japanese

[22]Fuks, p. 132. Martos, on the other hand, invited replacement (as Solzhenitsyn shows) when confronted with unreasonable orders. See his ms., Golovin, p. 225.

[23]Bogdanovich, p. 113.

[24]Bogdanovich, p. 220.

[25]Solzhenitsyn, *Avgust chetyrnadtsatogo,* pp. 390-392; cf. Bogdanovich, p. 217. Glenny's translation (pp. 425-427) omits the direction.

War—comes from the reports of observers.[26] A sagging shoulder that made the same eyewitness wonder if Samsonov might have had a stroke becomes in Solzhenitsyn's description "heroic shoulders weighed down by an invisible burden." (p. 429).

Solzhenitsyn curiously does not mention that Samsonov was on sick leave when called in July to take over the 2nd Army. References to his asthma are not particularly stressed. One might deduce from the way Vorotyntsev subjects himself to unnecessary wear that the author views the burdens of the flesh as constraints on manliness, best ignored. In any case, during the night of August 16-17 Samsonov, as Solzhenitsyn indicates, seems to have reached the limits of his strength. Postovskii's memoir, unlike *August 1914,* states that he had spoken of suicide earlier in the day and had been dissuaded by his officers. Here and in other reports there is no record of protest from Samsonov to the decision to tear off identifying insignia. He is said to have collapsed and pushed away his orderly, Kupchik, who ran to inform the others. Or, alternately, merely to have fallen behind. The group advancing in the darkness heard a shot, according to Postovskii, but were forced to move on without locating him. The next morning the body was found and buried by the Germans. Identification was made later from his medallion and watch.[27]

Many writers present Samsonov's personal tragedy as symbolic of the larger one that engulfed it. What may have been the most telling epitaph was omitted by Solzhenitsyn. Referring to the suicide, Sukhomlinov wrote Ianushkevich: "About Samsonov—His Majesty said there was no point to what he did."[28]

"What he did," remains somewhat uncertain. Most accounts accept Postovskii's conclusion that a suicide occurred, but a few suggest that Samsonov was shot by German troops firing through the woods. Gurko, who attributed a weak heart to the general, feels it may have given out. He reports the tale of an artilleryman who said he ran into Samsonov wandering alone in the night. The *Soviet Historical Encyclopedia* states

[26]Bogdanovich, pp. 219-221; on p. 149 Postovskii is cited on Kuropatkin. Another description of Samsonov among the troops (*August* 1914, p. 376) and the fact that his attempt to rouse the men fell flat, are corroborated by Bogdanovich, p. 192.

[27]Postovskii's report, Golovin, p. 301. Cf. Bogdanovich, p. 236; Fuks, p. 146; Vasilii I. Gurko, *War and Revolution in Russia, 1914-1917* (New York, 1919), pp. 77-78.

[28]Bogdanovich, p. 238.

that the commander "perished under unclear circumstances (apparently he shot himself)." Apparently. But we never hear the shot in *August 1914.*

The final major historical personality introduced in *August 1914* is the Commander-in-Chief of the Russian Army, Grand Duke Nikolai Nikolaievich. Solzhenitsyn's portrayal of this generally well-regarded figure is somewhat ambivalent. The description of the Grand Duke's reforming role in the Council of State after 1905 corresponds with widespread favorable appraisals, but the later personal portrait of a man of intelligent dignity dissolves at times under sardonic strokes. The ambivalence appears to stem from the author's inability to reconcile historical approval of the Grand Duke with the policies emanating from General Headquarters. Golovin tackled the problem by attempting to distinguish between the views of the Grand Duke and those of his staff. But he admits that throughout the critical week of August 10-17, any distinction that may have existed left no mark on events.

As in all the cases discussed, Solzhenitsyn's depiction of the remaining high-level military figures (Sukhomlinov, Ianushkevich, Danilov, Zhilinskii, Oranovskii, Postovskii, Filimonov) finds support in the records. Every historical sifting, of course, involves matters of evaluation and interpretation. Beyond the "facts of history" the conclusions that derive from sources represent judgments based on evidence. Some points in Solzhenitsyn's appraisals may thus be open to debate, but historical evidence substantiates his claim: the men who make history here are men taken from history.

Having found so much of Solzhenitsyn's text reinforced by both the hard and soft data of the sources, it could be anticipated that the more obvious source material incorporated into *August 1914*—the six numbered documents[29] and two chapters of newspaper excerpts (Ch. 7 and Ch. 60)—would prove authentic. The first five documents are readily traceable, and it seems reasonable to assume that the sixth, said to be a German leaflet dropped to Russian troops, could be located with further probing.[30] A scanning of Russian newspapers for July and

[29]*August 1914,* pp. 270, 422, 531, 537, 599, 600.

[30]The first document, quoted by Golovin, is from Maurice Paléologue, *An Ambassador's Memoirs* (London, 1923) I, 82; others are in *Pravitel'stvennyi vestnik* [*Government Herald*] of the appropriate date, and/or in *God voiny* [*A Year of War*], a documentary collection published in Moscow in 1915.

August, 1914 turned up a substantial number of newspaper items (some were spliced fragments of separate articles) and a few interesting sidelights to boot. Among the latter: Kerenskii's Duma speech, *accurately* reported in at least some papers despite the complaints of Solzhenitsyn's Mme. Kharitonova (p. 540); large ads for (Major General) A. D. Nechvolodov's *Tales from Russian History* bearing the official endorsement "approved for all libraries" (cf. pp. 201, 509); articles discussing the eclipse of August 8 and the coincidence of past Russian wars and eclipses (mentioned by Irina, p. 40); premature obituaries for Martos (see Document 4, p. 537).

Several times in *August 1914* Solzhenitsyn breaks his narrative to inject a brief historical description of the progression of military events through the critical week of the battle. His resort to this unliterary device, or to what is at least an unconventional literary device, clearly stems from a determination not to lose the framework or sequence of developments in the shifting episodic nature of the presentation. Strategy, decision-making, and personal roles on both sides are outlined and appraised here; no fictional character appears. Though the writer's judgments are—as always—strongly expressed, these sections reflect a variety of sources. Much of the presentation here accords with Golovin, but one point of variance is worth noting. Repeatedly in these sections, as well as at other points in the work, Solzhenitsyn attacks General Rennenkampf for failing to advance energetically. Though conceding that Zhilinskii's orders played a role here also, he joins the broad ranks of historians who quote German General Ludendorff's statement that Rennenkampf's inaction made the encirclement of the 2nd Army possible. Thus, he is in agreement with contemporary Soviet historical opinion that Zhilinskii and Rennenkampf are to be faulted for Samsonov's defeat.[31] Golovin, however, along with Gurko, disputes the notion of the "criminal immobility of Rennenkampf's army" as a myth inspired by Ludendorff's "facile pen."[32]

[31]*Sovetskaia istorischeskaia entsiklopediia* [*Soviet Historical Encyclopedia*], XII (1969), article on Samsonov.

[32]Golovin, pp. 159-165, 314-315. Glenny has suggested (*Survey,* Spring, 1973, pp. 115-116) that Solzhenitsyn may have been unaware of a quarrel between Samsonov and Rennenkampf at the time of the Russo-Japanese war. He conjectures that the memoirs of German General Max Hoffmann who "witnessed" it and linked it later with Rennenkampf's failure to advance are probably unavailable in the Soviet Union because they discuss Trotskii's role in 1918 peace negotiations.

Though Solzhenitsyn echoes Golovin's assessment of Ludendorff as a well-trained mediocrity who lacked the "intuition" of genius (p. 393; cf. Golovin, p. 288), his few comments suggest a clockwork commander and he passes over Golovin's observations on Ludendorff's state of nerves, which the German general confesses in his memoirs. General von François, in contrast, appears with the zesty panache evident in all accounts and nurtured by his own. Solzhenitsyn gibes at the general's careful tailoring of his own historical image, but makes use of it to enliven his narrative.[33]

On the whole, the external enemy comes off well in *August 1914*. German efficiency, whether in General Staff organization or in peasant farms, draws admiration. "Look at the clever way these Germans do things!" (p. 300). A respectful attitude for things German and especially for German military science was widespread in pre-war Russia.[34] German military repute rode high everywhere after the defeat of France in 1871. A writer trained as a mathematician might well appreciate the methodical German approach to the "mathematically exact" rules of warfare. But an appreciation of German military science is not an apology for German militarism as hostile critics have implied. That a work so transparent in its love of country should have been called anti-Russian only serves as a reminder that history does indeed involve viewpoints. Solzhenitsyn's contention that "history is not politics" (p. 549) stands in direct contradiction to the much-publicized view of a former dean of Soviet historians, M. Pokrovskii, who insisted precisely that "history is past politics."

August 1914 has not been permitted publication at home, yet it has been reported, oddly enough, that a popular western

However, Hoffmann also records the incident in a work confined to the campaign, his *Tannenberg, wie es wirklich war* (Berlin, 1926, pp. 74-75), and in the following paragraph provides unrelated material which Solzhenitsyn makes use of on p. 392 ("The Russians are coming!"). This is not conclusive evidence, of course, but since it opens the question of why Hoffmann's speculations might have been passed over it should be noted that he was not present at the Mukden quarrel which he reports only at second hand, and that some of his other information on Rennenkampf is patently incorrect.

[33]E.g., cf. von François, p. 229 with *August 1914,* p. 473. Von François may have helped provide less obvious detail also: he recorded the weather regularly in his diary.

[34]See, for example, Brusilov (pp. 37-42) who discusses the high level of German prestige in the country and concedes that even he is forced to respect Germans, though he dislikes them.

history recently issued in the Soviet Union may have been circulated to discredit Solzhenitsyn's book.[35] Before publication in the USSR, Barbara Tuchman's *The Guns of August* had been favorably compared with *August 1914* in the Soviet press.[36] It is undoubtedly the case that the Tuchman book is "more objective" insofar as it reflects no special feeling for Russia or any sense of national identification. Presumably, though, its appeal for Soviet critics lies elsewhere.

Dealing only in part with the eastern front, *The Guns of August* is more critical throughout of the German military. Its lively and adept description of Tannenberg, necessarily less detailed, is in some matters less accurate.[37] It is also highly critical of Russians. As in *August 1914,* Russians are shown with a high opinion of the enemy: Russian soldiers fired at any airplane, writes Tuchman, "convinced that such a clever invention as a flying machine could only be German."[38] Both books credit German success in large measure to factors beyond German talent or control: to Russian incompetence, to Rennenkampf's failure to advance, to such incredible blunders as the open Russian dispatch of uncoded wireless messages. Solzhenitsyn, though less involved with the German side of events, brings out many of the same failings in German leadership at Tannenberg—confusion, indecisiveness, quarrels, insubordination.

Noting that both works present the war as a product of statesmen's miscalculations (rather than more properly as a

[35]*New York Times,* Jan. 8, 1972, p. 2.

[36]In an article reprinted from a Polish journal and appearing in *Literaturnaia Rossiia* [*Literary Russia*] and *Trud* [*Labor*] April 7, 1972. An English translation is available in *The Current Digest of the Soviet Press,* May 3, 1972, along with translations of other articles attacking *August 1914* reprinted from Swedish and German sources by the Soviet *Literaturnaia gazeta* [*Literary Gazette*] Feb. 23, 1972. It has been charged that critical articles reprinted from foreign journals were implants actually prepared for the Soviet press. See *The New York Times,* Jan. 8, 1973, p. 2; *Washington Post,* May 15, 1973, pp. 1, 3.

[37]E.g., Dushkevich, not Sirelius, succeeded Artamonov; the Russian army was scheduled to be only one-third, not half ready on the 15th day of mobilization; it was the 13th Corps that lacked the key to the 6th Corps cipher, not vice-versa; Samsonov was not responsible for Blagoveshchenskii's position, nor did he have confidence in Artamonov, etc. The point is not to disparage Tuchman's work, but merely the fact that it was described (in the *Literaturnaia Rossiia* article cited above) as "accurate" in contrast to Solzhenitsyn's book. Following its publication in the Soviet Union, *The Guns of August* was reviewed in *Pravda* (Feb. 9, 1973; translation in *The Current Digest of the Soviet Press,* March 7, 1973) by an historian who found much to commend despite "quite a few factual errors" which were not specified.

[38]Barbara W. Tuchman, *The Guns of August* (New York, 1962), p. 269.

product of imperialism), the Soviet press remarked on the large role credited to chance in *The Guns of August.* Accident, luck, an accumulation of "ifs," help shape events here during a month that caught the nations, the book concludes, in "a trap from which there was, and has been, no exit." In *August 1914* it is not Fate that forms history's trap, but human hands. Not only is Tolstoyan fatalism explicity rejected, but Marxian historical determinism is challenged here. Hands that make traps can break them.

Or rather, can build exits, for Solzhenitsyn's work decries the destructive violence of revolution. Such a disavowal can only be disquieting to authority basing its legitimacy, its world position, and its view of history, on revolution. On this score, *The Guns of August,* which does not involve itself in considerations of revolution, is more acceptable to Soviet critics.

Despite different approaches, both works meet on the common ground of historical factualism. *The Guns of August,* drawing for its account of Tannenberg largely from German memoirs and from Golovin, reflects essentially the same historical contours as *August 1914.*

The many sources that confirm those contours suggest the answer to why Solzhenitsyn has chosen to write at such length about one battle. From the voluminous literature on Tannenberg two distinct interpretations emerge. Weighed in the larger balance of history Tannenberg is seen as a tragic necessity—or as a needless tragedy. According to one assessment—shared by the German chief of state Moltke, his French counterpart Foch, by many of their contemporaries, and by later writers—the Russian advance into East Prussia, by disrupting German war plans and causing a transfer of two corps from the western front, determined the outcome of the battle of the Marne.[39] By saving France at this critical point, Tannenberg made possible the ultimate allied victory. Though the cost was high, the decision was justified.

In the alternate appraisal, the East Prussian campaign was a blow, an act of self-mutilation, from which Russia never recovered. Whatever advantages it brought to her allies were bought at too high a cost. Golovin (p. 59) considered the battle an outright mistake, based on a "fatal decision" (Vorotyn-

[39]See Helmuth von Moltke, *Erinnerungen, Briefe, Dokumente, 1877-1916* (Stuttgart, 1922), pp. 434-435; Foch's preface to Golovin's book; Brusilov, pp. 27-28; Bogdanovich, pp. 8-9, 261.

tsev borrows a phrase again, p. 621). Many military analysts agree. A. A. Svechin, who appears as Vorotyntsev's friend at Headquarters (p. 601 ff.), wrote that "Russia exceeded reasonable limits in subjecting her own interests to those of France."[40] Others suggested that charity should begin at home, that a healthier dose of political egoism was in order. How long, asks Vorotyntsev (p. 116), will Russia's ally remember her sacrifice?

Foch credited Russia with France's survival but others have been less generous. Russians have long felt that their contribution to allied victory went unrecognized or "was very soon forgotten."[41] One allied general, as noted, wrote of Tannenberg using only German sources. Another suggested that the campaign was the typical, rather untidy, large gesture to be expected from an unbusinesslike people.[42] His compatriot Knox, portrayed unsympathetically in *August 1914,* went so far as to complain, "Russia's allies had to pay dearly for the low mental development of the mass of the Russian population. From the very commencement of the war the Russians surrendered in thousands, and Russian prisoners freed hundreds of thousands from agriculture and industry to man the trenches in the west."[43] Despite the possible inference that one Russian prisoner was worth a hundred German workers, the passage offers slight consolation. The recognition that *August 1914* seeks, however, is of a different sort.

In addition to irreplaceable losses in men and materials, Tannenberg inflicted irreparable psychological damage. Writers of many outlooks maintain, along with Solzhenitsyn, that the "psychic shock" of the first battle "reflected on the entire course of the war."[44] Demoralization and continued stress paved

[40]Aleksandr Andreevich Svechin, *Strategiia* [*Strategy*], 2nd ed. (Moscow, 1927), p. 83. Cf. Golovin, p. 59; Fuks, p. 151.

[41]R.S.F.S.R., *Trudy voenno-istorichiskoi komissii, Snosheniia s soiuznikami po voennym voprosam vo vremia voiny 1914-1918 gg. Chast'* 1. [*Works of the Military-Historical Commission, Relations with the Allies on Military Problems During the War 1914-1918. Part 1*] (Moscow, 1920), p. 13; Bogdanovich, p. 260.

[42]Edmund Ironside, *Tannenberg* (London, 1925), p. 282.

[43]Alfred Knox, *With the Russian Army, 1914-1917* (London, 1921), I, xxxiv.

[44]Phrases quoted from Iu. N. Danilov, *Rossiia v mirovoi voine,* 1914-1915 [*Russia in the World War, 1914-1915*] (Berlin, 1924), p. 194; cf. Solzhenitsyn, *Avgust chetyrnadtsatogo,* p. 381; Patronov, p. 170. Soviet sources have stressed Tuchman's conclusion that Tannenberg may have determined the outcome at the Marne, and that it was quantitatively overshadowed by the Russian victory in Galicia. *Literaturnaia Rossiia* quotes her as saying of the latter battle, "It

the way to what modern Soviet historiography describes as "The Great October Revolution." All later Russian history, and much of world history, have taken shape under its influence.

In Solzhenitsyn's view there was a great deal wrong, out of phase, in pre-War Russia. But practical constructive work in society, however constrained between forces of conservatism and impatience, offered the most reasonable path to improvement. That option was a forfeit of war. It is likely that Solzhenitsyn's later work will present the events of 1917 as a vital assertion of a right to national survival. In Vorotyntsev's view the war could lead to "a great rebirth of Russia or be the end of her altogether" (p. 112). Yet revolution is a harsh midwife. It entails senseless destruction, warns another character in *August 1914,* and the greater its cost to a country, "the more likely the revolution is to be dubbed 'great' " (p. 582). If, in making their own history, men have made tragic errors then they must recognize them for what they are or be condemned to repeat them. The "historical lesson" implicit in *August 1914*—the lesson of a man who spent years in prison for criticizing a leader—is that leadership must be open to scrutiny, subject to criticism, and responsible for its acts. But responsibility does not end there.

In the concluding pages of *August 1914,* Svechin attempts to dissuade Vorotyntsev from giving a full report on Tannenberg that is likely to get him into trouble.[45] "You might have convinced me," replies the hero, "if this were purely a military matter... But this is a *moral* issue." (p. 603). The moral of the fable involves not only the responsibility of leadership, but the responsibilities of the led. "Don't the people have any *obligations?*" asks another character (p. 407), "Or do

crippled Austria." Tuchman's sentence actually reads, "It crippled Austria but could not restore the losses or heal the effects of Tannenberg" (p. 308).

[45]Svechin himself was unable to avoid trouble. Though he held high military positions after 1917, he and his "reactionary" military views were attacked at a special session of a section of the Communist Academy in 1931. Among the charges: a "hatred of revolution," said to be evident in his writings. Among the attackers: M. Tukhachevskii who was soon to become the most prominent military victim of Stalin's purges. See *Kritika strategicheskikh i voennoistoricheskikh vzgliadov prof. Svechina. Stenogramma otkrytogo zasedaniia plenuma sektsii. . . 25 aprelia 1931 g.* [*Criticism of the Strategical and Military-Historical Views of Prof. Svechin. Stenographic Record of the Open Session of a Plenum of the Section. . . of April 25, 1931*] (Moscow, 1931). Svechin, d. 1938, was subjected to repression without justification, according to the *Soviet Historical Encyclopedia,* but has been posthumously rehabilitated.

they have only *rights?*" Elsewhere Solzhenitsyn has stated that "the study of Russian history" has shown him "how important it is that authority, no matter how autocratic and unlimited, should listen with good will to society, and that *society should assume the position of real power.*"[46] The peasant who accepts the war as an inevitable act of God or nature, the intellectual who accepts it as the inevitable outcome of deterministic "laws" of history, are fated only to be victims of their own resignation.

Solzhenitsyn's aim is clearly far from Scott's, his technique far "closer to historians than novelists." Why then has he chosen to communicate "the meaning of history" through a historical novel? Truth, he well knows, is not only stranger than fiction, but stronger than fiction. Yet problems of communication may obscure meaning. In his Nobel Lecture Solzhenitsyn stressed the transcendent value of literature. We learn from experience—not only our own, but each other's. Through the universality of art and literature countries, too, can learn from one another: "Despite the differences of language, customs, and social structure we are able to communicate life experiences. . . a difficult national experience," and save others "from a path which is dangerous or mistaken or destructive."

In writing *August 1914* Solzhenitsyn relied substantially—at times astoundingly—on historical sources. But history in full dimension can never be encapsulated in records. Every historian, like every writer attempting to understand other men, other times, must extrapolate from his own experience. In his reconstruction of the ambience of August 1914 the author has tapped the source of personal history: school days in Rostov, artillery service in East Prussia in the second world war, family background. Young Lazhenitsyn who opens the story is patterned on Solzhenitsyn's father, a university student when he volunteered for the army in World War I. Ksen'ia (Xenya) Tomchak represents the author's mother, Zakhar—his grandfather, Irina and Roman—an aunt (still living) and uncle.

All such complementary material fleshing out the narrative can only enhance its historical validity. Just as the "new journalism" has broadened literary license with the adoption of such conventions as composite characters and time telescoping in order to convey a greater degree of reality, Solzhenitsyn might

[46]*New York Times,* April 3, 1972, p. 10, quoted from an interview. Italics added.

be said to have taken similar license with the same aim (and far more justification) in writing "novel history."

The author's references to the book at the time of publication suggest that he himself may view *August 1914* as essentially a work of history. Though the jacket of the English translation quotes him as describing it as a "novel," the passage from which this is taken actually refers to it only as "this book" and "this first part of my work." The distinction, however, may be without real significance. A contemporary mutation in the evolution of Russian realism, Solzhenitsyn sees literature not just as a mirror of reality, but as a potential molder of reality. History is that same reality, composed by men in the dynamic of time, and reflected in records.

Some years ago a scholar discussing historical novels wrote, "The historian and the novelist work on parallel lines which never meet, the former telling us what happened and the latter helping us to see it happen."[47] In *August 1914* the lines converge.

[47] G. P. Gooch, "Historical Novels," *Studies in Modern History* (New York, 1931), p. 358.

Behind the Front Lines: On Some Neglected Chapters in *August 1914*

BY GLEB STRUVE

In reading the critical appraisals of Solzhenitsyn's *August 1914*—both by Russian émigré critics, and by a few foreigners familiar with the Russian language, after the publication of the Russian original of the novel, and by many Western European and American critics after the appearance of it in several translations—one might have received the impression that Solzhenitsyn's new novel was devoted almost entirely to a description and interpretation of the military operations in East Prussia in the late summer of 1914 which ended in the tragic debacle of General Samsonov's army and his suicide. Some critics, both Russian and non-Russian, thought the novel was "overloaded" with military details.

True, it was also pointed out that Solzhenitsyn was concerned with both "war" and "peace" and that his conception of the novel was therefore somewhat similar to Tolstoy's famous work. But, quite apart from the fact that it would be rather premature to draw any parallels on the basis of the first volume of what was planned as a many-volumed novel, such statements were factually inaccurate: in *August 1914* there is no real division into "war" and "peace"; all the action in it, as the author's sub-title emphasizes, unfolds between August 10 and August 21 (by the Julian calendar)—in other words, entirely at the time when Russia was already in the war. One can distinguish only between "front" chapters and "rear" chapters, not between chapters of "war" and "peace." Nor are there very many flashbacks into the pre-war period; most of them are concerned with personal biographies of some of the characters and serve to elucidate their backgrounds.

For his story of the twelve days in August, 1914—twelve days which he seems to regard as crucial, if not fatal, as far as Russia's part in World War I (the war which he apparently views as a great historical disaster) is concerned—Solzhenitsyn needed over 550 pages (the Russian edition has 571 pages) of which only some 120 are given to "the rear," as distinct from "the front" (not counting the movie screen chapters and the "documents," which are interlarded in the narrative and in which the events in the rear alternate with military information).

In the present article I am concerned only with those chapters of the novel in which the action is set in the rear and concerns the characters who live there. These "behind-the-lines" chapters have so far attracted much less critical attention than the military ones, especially among the non-Russian critics. The action in them is set in the Northern Caucasus (Mineral'nye Vody spa), on the Tomchak family estate, or ranch, in the steppes, in Moscow, in St. Petersburg, and in Rostov-on-the-Don. There is also a chapter describing what was going on, after the defeat at Tannenberg, at the Russian Army Headquarters in Mogilev, immediately behind the front line.

The novel begins in Mineral'nye Vody where Solzhenitsyn introduces us to a young Moscow student Sania (Isaakii) Lazhenitsyn[1] who has decided to volunteer for the army and is returning to Moscow, before the summer holidays are over, to enroll in a military school. Later this Sania Lazhenitsyn reappears in the short Chapter 42, with his friend Kotia who is also volunteering for the service. In the same chapter we also meet a very interesting character whose name is Varsonof'ev but who is known under the nickname "Zvezdochet" ("Stargazer," or "Astrologer"). The two boys know him from having seen him in the Moscow Public Library. They help him with his books and he invites them to a meal in a beerhouse, which becomes the scene of a typical Russian "philosophical" conversation. It is impossible to guess what role will be assigned

[1]This is a more than transparent pseudonym for the author's father, Isai Solzhenitsyn.

to Varsonof'ev in the later volumes, but it is not unlikely that he has a prototype in real life.[2]

It is in connection with Sania Lazhenitsyn that we have—much earlier, in Chapter 2, a description of his meeting, in the woods near Iasnaia Poliana, with Leo Tolstoy—one of the few flashbacks into the pre-war period. It is to be presumed that this Sania is called upon to play an important role in the subsequent development of the novel.

The initial chapters about Sania Lazhenitsyn are followed by chapters about the rich Tomchak family, describing the life on their vast steppe estate. The role of the family in the general scheme of the novel is not yet clear, but even at this early stage the author establishes several important connections for us: Tomchak's daughter Ksen'ia went to a private boarding school in Rostov-on-the-Don run by a Mme. Kharitonov whose son Viacheslav-Iaroslav[3] the reader will meet soon at the front and who is obviously meant to play a prominent part in the novel, and perhaps also in the life of Ksen'ia. She herself reappears towards the end of the novel in the chapters set in Rostov. In the Tomchak chapters (Chapters 3-6 and 8-9) an important part is played by Tomchak himself, his son and his daughter-in-law, and they are all very colorfully drawn, but after that they fade out for the rest of the volume.

The St. Petersburg chapters (57-58) are only twelve pages

[2]This article was already written when I read (in No. 110 of the New York *Novyi Zhurnal* [March, 1973, 296-299] a short article by Aleksei Kiselev which argues quite convincingly that in portraying Varsonof'ev Solzhenitsyn must have had in mind the philosopher Nikolai Fedorovich Fedorov (1828-1903) who was associated with the Rumiantsev Museum Library in Moscow. He was personally known to, and greatly respected by, Dostoevsky, Tolstoy, and Vladimir Solov'ev. His reputation as a philosopher was mainly posthumous and was based on his book *Filosofiia obshchego dela.* In support of his identification Mr. Kiselev adduces a number of quotations from various writings about Fedorov. He also shows that Solzhenitsyn's description of what Fedorov looked like may have been based on Leonid Pasternak's sketch of Fedorov made by him in the Rumiantsev Library for a group portrait which showed Fedorov together with Leo Tolstoy and Vladimir Solov'ev. Mr. Kiselev points out that the ideas developed by Varsonof'ev in his conversation with Sania Lazhenitsyn and his friend Kotia resemble those of Fedorov. It is true that Fedorov had long since been dead when World War I broke out.

[3]The name Iaroslav, which the parents wanted to give the boy, was objected to by the ecclesiastical authorities; hence, his two names. The objection to Iaroslav was made on the ground that this was a pagan name and that there was no such saint. One of its early bearers was an 11th-century Prince of Kiev who became George in holy baptism. I knew of a similar real-life case, when a boy had to be named Daniel, instead of Iaroslav. Solzhenitsyn's Iaroslav Kharitonov continued to be called Iaroslav by his family.

long. Here we meet mostly representatives of the younger generation, students of the University and of the Higher Courses (College) for Women. One of the girls, a friend of Sania's, had appeared earlier, at the very beginning of the novel. Some of the others are connected with the young man called Lenartovich whom the reader knows already from the "front" chapters as a revolutionary-minded wartime officer. He is strongly opposed to the War and one can easily discern in him the makings of a future Bolshevik.

In Chapter 58 Solzhenitsyn introduces briefly one of the faculty members of the Women's College, Professor Ol'da Andozerskaia, a specialist in medieval history. She expounds some of her views in a conversation with the students in the corridor of the College. The way her views and interests are presented made me think of Professor Ol'ga Dobiash-Rozhdestvenskaia, although some of her former students pointed out to me that there was little *outward* resemblance between her and the woman as described by Solzhenitsyn. It was, however, her ideas about History in general, and about the Middle Ages in particular, that called to my mind Professor Dobiash-Rozhdestvenskaia. It would be interesting to know whether Solzhenitsyn had ever heard of her or read any of her writings.[4]

In Chapters 59 and 61-62 (interrupted by the "montage" in Chapter 60) Solzhenitsyn takes the reader to Rostov-on-Don, after which the novel ends with two chapters set at the Grand

[4]Ol'ga Antonovna Dobiash-Rozhdestvenskaia (1874-1939) graduated from the Women's College in St. Petersburg in 1899. Later studied in Paris where she obtained a doctoral degree. She began teaching Medieval History at the Women's College in 1911 and was the first Russian woman teacher with a doctor's degree in General History. In 1929 she became a Corresponding Member of the Soviet Academy of Sciences. Her publications in French include: *La Vie paroissiale en France au XIIIe siècle* (1911), *Le Culte de St. Michel et le Moyen Age latin* (1922), *Les Poésies des goliards* (1931). In Russian she published *History of Writing in the Middle Ages* (1923, 1936). She was one of the pioneers in the teaching of Latin Palaeography in Russia. An entry in the *Great Soviet Encyclopaedia* describes her standpoint as "idealistic" and says that she "viewed spiritual life as an independent factor, not conditioned by the social-economic development of society." It is interesting to juxtapose this with the words which Solzhenitsyn puts into the mouth of his Andozerskaia in the conversation with the students: ". . . what is more important [than the Western Enlightenment] is the spiritual life of the Middle Ages. Mankind has not known such an intensive spiritual life, with a predominance over material existence, either before or since." Solzhenitsyn slightly altered Mme. Dobiash's first name, giving her one that does not exist in Russian (she explains it as "perhaps" Scandinavian, a "whim of her father"), and changing her patronymic to "Orestovna." Solzhenitsyn mentions that his Andozerskaia received her doctorate in France.

Duke Nicholas's Army Headquarters in Mogilev. These last two chapters are not, strictly speaking, "rear" chapters—even though no military operations are described in them—but they should be briefly mentioned here. A prominent part is played in them by Colonel Vorotyntsev, one of the important characters in the earlier "front" portions of the novel and presumably one of its future "heroes," who, at the same time, may be the author's military *porte-parole.* Some real-life prototypes have been suggested for Vorotyntsev, but it is more likely that he is a composite figure.

The portrayal of the Grand Duke by Solzhenitsyn is not what one might have expected it to be, considering his generally critical attitude to the Russian conduct of the war. It is, in fact, very "objective." His actions as Commander-in-Chief are presented critically—mostly through the eyes of Vorotyntsev who has seen the war in East Prussia at first hand. His unquestioning loyalty to the Emperor, bordering on a cult, which makes him give way and act against his own better judgment (or instinct) is duly emphasized (one wonders how Solzhenitsyn is going to portray the Emperor himself, if he does so in the next volume), but his chivalrousness is also shown quite clearly.

But of all the "rear" chapters I have found the two Rostov-on-Don ones, towards the end of the book (Chapters 61 and 62), to be the most rewarding and interesting. In Chapter 59 we see Ksen'ia Tomchak visiting her former headmistress, Mme. Kharitonov, and learning about the complicated relations that have arisen within her family. In the two other Rostov chapters Ksen'ia appears again, but this time as a dinner guest in the house of Il'ia Isaakovich Arkhangorodskii. These chapters are dominated by two men who appear here in the novel in the flesh for the first time. Both of them are very interesting and throw an interesting light on some of the processes in the Russian society at the time. They are Arkhangorodskii himself and his guest of honor, Sviatoslav Iakinfovich Obodovskii.

Arkhangorodskii had been fleetingly mentioned in the novel much earlier, almost at its very beginning. He was then referred to as "a most intelligent Jew"[5] and "an honorable man." This is, in any case, how he is thought of by Ksen'ia Tomchak's father who goes to Rostov to seek advice about his daughter's school-

[5]Although the word *"zhid"* [Yid] is used here, there is no justification for translating it that way, for in the South of Russia (as in both Polish and Ukrainian) this was the normal and non-pejorative equivalent of "Jew."

ing. It is Arkhangorodskii who suggests to Tomchak that he should send Ksen'ia to Mme. Kharitonov's boarding school where his own daughter is boarded. This leads to a personal friendship between them.

In this early chapter Arkhangorodskii was characterized not only as "a most intelligent Jew," but also as "a first-rate specialist in flour mills, even the most modern ones, be they electric or anything you may wish." Not a single mill as far as Baku on the Caspian Sea was said to have been built without him and when "the great Paramonov" (a real-life personage) decided to erect a five-storied one in Rostov, it was again Arkhangorodskii who constructed it for him.

In Chapter 61 we see Arkhangorodskii at close quarters. He represents a type more or less new in Russia at the time—that of an entrepreneur and a high-calibre engineer in one. He tells his guest Obodovskii that he was one of the first alumni of the Kharkov Technological Institute who specialized in flour milling. There were five of them in the year he graduated, and great opportunities opened before each of them. To the great indignation of his father, a small broker, he spurned those opportunities and decided to begin at the very bottom of the ladder, as a simple workman, gradually learning from experience what was what in the milling business. Now he was one of the biggest in it, particularly proud of two of his achievements: the new city grain elevator and the Paramonov mill with a million-ruble turnover. He was also representing, in the South-West of Russia, several major national industrial concerns.

His guest, Obodovskii, is no less interesting, and his career even more unusual. A former anarchist, a follower and admirer of Prince Petr Kropotkin, "but yesterday an émigré, and the day before, a political criminal and a haunted revolutionary." Amnestied in 1913 in connection with the tercentenary of the Romanov dynasty, he returned from abroad, whither he had fled earlier from his Siberian exile, and threw himself into a feverish activity as an engineer interested in the development of Russia's productive forces. He saw almost unlimited economic possibilities opening up before Russia, the prospect of an unheard-of industrial expansion, and was now on an extensive trip across the country, studying the situation and marvelling at what he saw.

This is how Solzhenitsyn writes about him:

> He no longer recalled his anarchist past which had led to two trials, imprisonment, exile, and flight abroad. He talked more about his recent experiences abroad: he had been to America; had studied mining in Germany; had worked on labor insurance in Austria and written a book about it... But above all he was fascinated by his present trip. Russian mines and pits could have been so easily accessible to a graduate of the Mining Institute! But at that time he was concerned about making the revolution, and he very nearly managed to get into a Siberian mine in handcuffs. Later, as an émigré, he worried himself out by thinking how he would get to the Donets Basin and try out mining work there. And now he was carrying on with enthusiasm about what one could do here in ten or twenty years' time... "Why, the calm is over! The calm is over in Russia! And given the wind, one can sail even against the wind!" Obodovskii kept exclaiming excitedly.[6]

Speaking of his trip across Russia, Obodovskii tells Arkhangorodskii that he feels "like a samovar with many faucets: anyone who opens for me one or two faucets and lets a little steam out does me good. Had I stayed abroad a little longer I would have burst...." After completing this trip, he wants to "unload" himself and fling himself "into the thick of life" ("to use Gorkii's words," as he says). He is fed up with trying to enlighten his countrymen by writing from abroad things which Russia cannot even read. He is anxious to tackle the task of building Russian life with his own hands, and is quite willing to reduce his sleeping hours to four in twenty-four. "On this trip I don't sleep at all," he adds.

Mentioning a number of attractive jobs he was offered upon his return to Russia, Obodovskii says that he has turned them all down, agreeing only to give some lectures at the Mining Institute. It is difficult, he says, for him to make up his mind about the priorities: there are the students, there is the insurance business, there are labor exchanges, there are ports, commerce, banks, technical associations—Russia needs everything, you must find time to be everywhere. "To put it succinctly," sums up Obodovskii, "two equally important tasks face us, and we must succeed in both of them: the development of our productive forces and the development of public initiative."

Arkhangorodskii is obviously impressed by Obodovskii's dynamism and agrees with his general views, but he strikes a note of caution: all this would be very fine, he says, were it not for the war. Obodovskii retorts that it is not the war that matters but the people at the top who do not know how to run

[6]All the quotations from *August 1914* in this article are given in my own translation from the original Russian YMCA Press edition.

it. The old state mechanism is rusty, and those who run it are no good. They look upon Russia as their patrimony: "If such is their whim, they will make peace; if not, they'll go on fighting as they did with Turkey in the last century. And they think that they will always get off scot-free." Not one of the grand dukes, says Obodovskii, has ever even heard the expression "productive forces." The Imperial court will never experience any shortages. What is more, they attach too much importance to jubilees, "chewing over Susanin, arranging celebrations in Kostroma, coining medals . . ." These references to the Romanov jubilee celebrations in 1913 provoke from Arkhangorodskii a sly rejoinder: "Well, were it not for that jubilee, your samovar would have burst somewhere in the Ruhr Basin." Obodovskii laughs, but cannot help agreeing. However, he immediately goes on, quite serious again: "No, honestly, if only we could have ten years of peaceful development, we would not recognize either our industry or our countryside. And what an agreement we could conclude with Germany . . ."

There can be no doubt that behind Obodovskii's picture of Russia's dynamic potential on the eve of World War I is Solzhenitsyn's own view of the state of things in 1914. It is also clear that he sees the war itself (as did many Russians, mostly in retrospect) as the starting point of all the disasters. In his novel he will undoubtedly develop this thesis. Whether he will touch upon the problem of avoidability of that war is another matter.

The conversation between Obodovskii and Arkhangorodskii begins after their visit to the mills. It is continued during dinner. Obodovskii speaks of the role which the Association of Engineers may be called upon to play in the economic development of Russia. In his view it could easily become one of the major factors of Russian life, outweighing in importance all political parties. "And take part in governing the country?" asks Arkhangorodskii. To this Obodovskii replies that he has remained true to Kropotkin, whom he came to know well while living abroad, and does not attach much importance to government as such. "Businesslike and intelligent men do not govern—they create and transform," he says, adding, however, at once that if the government should get in the way of the country's development—"well, then perhaps we shall have to replace it." After this remark the reader would be perhaps justified in visualizing Obodovskii as sympathizing with the February Revolution of 1917 and even taking some part in it.

Obodovskii also voices his surprise at the fact that all the branches of Arkhangorodskii's enterprises are known as "South-Eastern." To him, Rostov and the entire Don Region are the South-*West.* Arkhangorodskii explains that the term "South-West" usually refers to Little Russia (that is, the Ukraine), and that even their railroad is known as "South-Eastern." At this Obodovskii explodes:

> Where are you standing then? What is your vantage point? You just can't see Russia then! At Russia, my dear man, one must look from a distance, from far away—from the moon I daresay! Then you will see the Northern Caucasus at the extreme south-western tip of this body. And all that is spacious and rich in Russia, our entire hope for the future lies in the North-East. Not the Straits, not the Mediterranean—this is sheer stupidity!—but precisely the North-East. From Pechora to Kamchatka—the whole northern part of Siberia. Oh, what couldn't we do with it! Lay across it circular and diagonal roads, railways and automobile roads, warm up and dry up the tundra. What a lot can one extract there from underground, what a lot can one plant, grow, build! How many people can one settle there!

Arkhangorodskii reminds Obodovskii that in his revolutionary days he wanted to found a Siberian Republic—probably with the idea of seceding from the Russian Empire. "No, not seceding," protests Obodovskii laughingly, "but starting to liberate Russia from over there." The real conquest of Siberia lies still ahead, he adds, and says that even Dostoevsky, towards the end of his life, came to believe in Siberia and gave up his dream about Constantinople. He also recalls how the great Russian scientist Mendeleev, who was keenly interested in the problem of developing Russia's natural resources and productive capacity, prophesied once that by the middle of the 20th century the population of Russia would exceed 300 million, while in the opinion of a contemporary Frenchman it may reach the figure of 350 million by 1950.[7]

The first of the two significant "rear" chapters in the book

[7]The Frenchman referred to by Obodovskii, but not named by him, must be Edmond Théry who, not long before World War I, published a book in which he predicted a great economic upswing for Russia in the next few decades. The book was entitled *La Transformation économique de la Russie* (1914). It did not attract particular attention at the time, and in any case the war that broke out that year, and the revolution that came in its wake, did away with all the premises on which Théry's prediction was based. There were, however, some Russians who were inclined to share Théry's views, and Solzhenitsyn portrays Obodovskii as one of them.

(Chapter 61) ends again on a note of caution sounded by Arkhangorodskii. His words can also be read as a grim prophecy: "All this, Sviatoslav Iakinfovich," he says, "provided we don't start cutting each other's throats."

At one point during the dinner the conversation turns into a hot debate between the two older men and the younger generation as represented by Arkhangorodskii's daughter Sonia and her friend Naum Galperin, son of a well-known Rostov Menshevik, who did not follow in the footsteps of his father and joined the Socialist-Revolutionaries. Ksen'ia Tomchak does not take part in the conversation: she listens to it, but is occupied with her own thoughts, and the reader remains in the dark as to where her sympathies lie. She does not seem to be interested in the subject.

Sonia and Galperin had decided in advance to challenge Arkhangorodskii: both were quite incensed by his participation in the patriotic manifestation of the Rostov Jews which had taken place late in July. They thought it "disgraceful." After prayers in the synagogue for the victory of the Russian arms, speeches were made by the rabbi and the chief of police, and the national anthem was sung. Then some twenty thousand Jews, carrying flags and patriotic posters, marched through the city and held a meeting under the monument to Emperor Alexander II. They also sent a telegram to the Emperor, professing their loyalty. Sonia and Naum could neither understand nor accept Arkhangorodskii's participation in all this: not a believer, he normally attended the synagogue only on great holidays ("by tradition") and could very well have abstained doing so on this occasion.

Sonia had no chance of talking to her father at the time, for she had to go to Moscow. But now that a documentary film of the manifestation was being shown in the two local movie-theaters, she and Naum felt revolted even more by its "sentimental falsity." The presence at dinner of a guest, a well-known ex-anarchist, at first put them off and made them think of postponing their attack on Arkhangorodskii, but then they saw some advantages in the situation: if there were still some relics of conscience left in this anarchist, he might support them; if not, it will be all the more thrilling.

Obodovskii himself was by no means anxious to become involved in a debate: he still had some business to do after dinner and would have preferred to enjoy the rest of the meal in peace. Besides, he was more interested in expounding his views to a sympathetic audience than in arguing with those young people. Nevertheless, when Naum asked him a question that was meant to "provoke" him—"And what kind of production are you going to promote? Capitalistic?"—he took the bait.

Here, with some cuts and some interpolations of mine, is Solzhenitsyn's account of this dinnertime argument:

> I recognize this question (says Obodovskii). It is some twenty years old. At the student parties at the end of the Nineties this was the sort of thing we asked each other. It was then that this split among the students was revealed: a division into revolutionaries and engineers. To destroy or to build? I also thought that building was out of the question. I had to visit the West in order to begin to marvel. How neatly the anarchists lived, how tidily they worked. Whoever has had anything to do with work, whoever has made something with his own hands, knows that there is no such thing as capitalist or socialist production, that there is only *one* kind of production—that which creates national wealth, the common material basis without which no people can live.

Naum, his dark eyes burning, retorts that under capitalism the people will never even set eyes on this "national wealth," that it will slip past them, and into the hands of the exploiters. "And who are the exploiters?" asks Obodovskii with a grin. To Naum the question is "ridiculous" and he says that Obodovskii should be ashamed of asking it. In reply, Obodovskii tells him of their earlier visit, that day, to the grain elevator and the new mill, and says:

> I cannot even tell you what an amount of intelligence, knowledge, foresight, experience, and organizing ability has been invested in it. Do you know what all this, put together, amounts to? To *ninety per cent* of the future profits! As for the labor of the workers who laid the stones and installed the machinery, it represents only ten per cent, and even that could have been done by cranes. And they did get their ten per cent. But here come young people, humanitarians . . . who come along and explain to the workers that they did not get enough, whereas some wretched bespectacled engineer who did not move a single piece of iron—goodness knows what they are paying *him* for, it's sheer bribery!

When Galperin asks what does the owner of the mill, Paramonov, get his share of the profits for, Obodovskii answers that even that is not all for nothing, that there is the organizing ability, that not all of it is unearned, and what is must be gradually, through reasonable public measures, channelled elsewhere and "not taken away with bombs, as we used to do."

Galperin and Sonia are, of course, unimpressed; they see in

it a capitulation before capitalism, a renunciation of revolutionary methods. And when Obodovskii says that he used to attach great importance to the distribution of wealth, but is now mainly concerned with *creating* things, they exchange ironic glances and snort: "Creating! Tsarism will not allow you to create." When, in reply to a question from Obodovskii about his political affiliation, Naum says that he is a Socialist-Revolutionary, Obodovskii seems to lose his interest in the discussion, and from then on the main brunt of it is carried by Arkhangorodskii. He taxes the young people with impatience, warns them not to expect much from the revolution because the latter "implies long and insane destruction":

> Any revolution ruins a country, instead of renovating it, and this for a long period of time. And the bloodier it is and the longer it lasts, the higher is the price which the country has to pay for it, and the more likely is it to be called "great" . . .

Upon Sonia's remark that it is impossible to live any longer "with that stinking monarchy," her father warns her:

> Don't imagine that without the monarchy everything will at once become so good . . . Don't imagine that a republic is a pie to gorge on. A hundred lawyers will gather together—and aren't they great gabblers?—and will try to outdo each other in talking. The people will never govern themselves.

Sonia and Naum shout: "They will! They will!" and bang their fists on the table. They still hope that the ex-anarchist will come out on their side, but he is now engaged in a conversation with his hostess and seems to be taking no interest in the argument.

Finally, Sonia shouts out hysterically her question about the Jewish patriotic manifestation. Arkhangorodskii answers her calmly, without raising his voice. He tries to explain to her the complexity of the problem and says:

> . . . when your country is in trouble you must help it. If you live in this country, you must decide once and for all whether you belong to it heart and soul. If you don't, then you can let it go to the dogs or you can leave it, there is no difference. But if you do belong to it, you must become part of the patient process of history, you must work, try to persuade people, and gradually help things move along.

Sonia refuses to subscribe to this "evolutionary" attitude, she makes a passionate diatribe against antisemitism and accuses her father of ignoring it and joining in the singing of the national anthem before the monument of Alexander II, and of bowing to the "Black Hundred." Her father appeals to her to rise above all this, to "see in Russia something else beside the Union of the Russian People."[8] Here Obodovskii rejoins the conversation and says: "For instance, the Union of Russian Engineers."

Arkhangorodskii predicts the future when the few reasonable people who are bent on constructive work will be trapped between the "Black Hundred" and the "Red Hundred," and on this the last "rear" chapter of the novel ends.[9] It will be interesting to learn the subsequent fate of the two main protagonists of those chapters.

When I first read *August 1914,* I thought that in what Arkhangorodskii and Obodovskii say about revolution and in the contrast which they draw between the creative processes of life and the destructive elemental force of the revolutionary upheaval, in their faith in Russia's renovation and bright future, one can feel echoes of the ideas which inspired the authors of *Vekhi [Landmarks],* the famous collection of essays, published in 1909, which soon became a bestseller. This slender volume, of a little over 200 pages, containing essays by seven eminent Russian intellectuals (philosophers, economists, political scientists, publicists), was at the time received critically on the Left (including many traditional Liberals, such as Pavel Miliukov) and was particularly vehemently, even viciously, denounced by Lenin who kept returning to it and attacking it in later years. But it soon became something of a bestseller—rather unexpectedly for a book of that sort—and went through several editions. It was recently reissued outside Russia, with three denunciatory articles from Soviet encyclopaedias appended by the new editors.[10]

[8]This was the name of the political organization of the extreme Right. Its members and other ultra-rightists were also known as "Black Hundred" [*chernaia sotnia*].

[9]We know now that Solzhenitsyn's *August 1914,* as distinct from his earlier work, has aroused some very negative reactions among certain elements of the so-called "Democratic Movement" in the Soviet Union. It is possible that some of them have read into those "compromise" arguments of Arkhangorodskii a topical, present-day meaning. Whether such a procedure is justifiable is highly questionable. In any case, it seems to go counter to Solzhenitsyn's "sense of history."

[10]*Vekhi. Sbornik statei o russkoi intelligentsii.* Reprinted by Possev Verlag, Frankfurt/M, 1967. The three appended articles are taken from the 1928 edition of the *Great Soviet Encyclopaedia, The Philosophical Encyclopaedia* (vol. I, Moscow, 1960), and *The Soviet Historical Encyclopaedia* (vol. 3, 1963). In

It is certainly significant that earlier in Solzhenitsyn's novel, where we learn about Sania Lazhenitsyn's reading in the years preceding the war of 1914, *Vekhi* is mentioned as a book which made an enormous impression on him. In Chapter 2 of the novel we read:

> For a long time he still felt that he was backward, underdeveloped, that he could not think things through, to their very core. He got mixed up in a multitude of truths, he was tormented by the convincingness of each of them. So long as he was holding but a few books in his hands Isaakii felt to be on a firm ground. When he was a junior in high school, he regarded himself as a Tolstoyan. But then he was given Lavrov and Mikhailovskii to read—they seemed to be right, very true. He was given Plekhanov—true again, and everything fitted in so neatly, so smoothly. Kropotkin—also true, goes to the very heart. But when he opened *Vekhi,* he trembled: everything went counter to what he had been reading previously, but how true! priercingly true!

Whether this little detail is biographically accurate, whether Solzhenitsyn's father was one of the many enthusiastic readers of *Vekhi,* we do not know. But that Solzhenitsyn himself is familiar with the book, and that *he* may have "trembled" reading it, is more than likely. We do not know *when* he read it, but he could have read it only as "forbidden fruit": to this day its very title, as well as the names of most of its contributors (of whom five died as political emigres after the October Revolution), are more or less terms of opprobrium in the Soviet Union. Most Soviet mentions of *Vekhi* are accompanied by references to Lenin's vituperative attacks on the volume.

The seven authors of *Vekhi*—Nikolai Berdiaev, Sergei Bulgakov, Mikhail Gershenzon, Aleksandr Izgoev, Bogdan Kistiakovskii, Petr Struve, and Semen Frank—were very dissimilar men. Their antecedents and their main fields of interests were also different, though several of them had passed through the Marxist stage in their youth, and one of them, like Obodovskii, had been a political émigré (before 1905). But there was one common underlying thesis in all of their essays—the stress they laid on the need to re-assess the traditional values of the Russian intelligentsia, with its emphasis on philosophical positivism, on political dogmatism, and on revolution. It is this attitude that we see reflected, at least in some of its aspects,

volume V of *The Philosophical Encyclopaedia,* brought out quite recently (1972), we find longish and relatively objective entries about such major contributors to *Vekki* as Petr Struve and Semen Frank, mentioning most of their prerevolutionary writings. Of course, here too, there are inevitable references to Lenin's denunciation of *Vekhi.*

in the views advanced on that evening by Arkhangorodskii and Obodovskii. These two approach the problem from their own point of view, in a purely practical way, as economists and technologists, but some of the underlying premises are the same. Perhaps their closest counterparts in *Vekhi* are to be seen, *mutatis mutandis,* in the essays by Petr Struve and Semen Frank.

It would also be interesting to examine to what extent Solzhenitsyn may have been influenced by the ideas of Aleksandr Ėrtel' (1855-1908) in whose writings (especially in his *Letters,* published in 1909, almost simultaneously with *Vekhi*) one of the *Vekhi* authors (Petr Struve) found great affinity with *Vekhi.* In one of his articles about Ėrtel', Struve described him as "an embodiment of the idea of *lichnaia godnost',*" while in an earlier article, which had preceded *Vekhi,* he had related the word and concept *godnost'* to the English *efficiency* and German *Tüchtigkeit* and characterized it as one of the cardinal "bourgeois" virtues.[11] Closely allied to it, and also represented in Ėrtel's "philosophy of life," he saw the notion of "compromise," in opposition to the traditional "maximalism" of the Russian intelligentsia. There is no mention of Ėrtel' in Solzhenitsyn's novel, but the idea of *lichnaia godnost'* is certainly close to his heart.[12]

But when I read the Rostov-on-Don chapters of *August 1914* I was struck even more by the resemblance between the ideas developed by Obodovskii and some of the views briefly set forth on more than one occasion by another Russian ex-revolutionary and erstwhile companion of Lenin in his Swiss exile, who wrote a very interesting book about their meetings and conversations there.[13] His name was Nikolai Vladislavovich Vol'skii (1879-1964), but most of his writings were published under two pseudonyms: N. Valentinov and E. Iur'evskii.

Vol'skii was not influenced by *Vekhi.* At the time of its publication he had no sympathy with it: he was then still a

[11] Petr Struve's two articles on Ėrtel', originally published in *Russkaia Mysl'* in 1909, will be found in his volume *Patriotica: Sbornik statei za piat' let* [1905-1910 gg.] (St. Petersburg, 1911), pp. 423-465. The earlier article (about *godnost'* = efficiency) appeared also in *Russkaia Mysl'* and was also reprinted in *Patriotica* (pp. 362-369). It was called "The Intelligentsia and National Economy."

[12] It is possible that some echoes of Ėrtel's ideas will be found in Varsonof'ev in *August 1914.* Ėrtel himself was, of course, no longer alive at the time.

[13] N. Valentinov, *Vstrechi s Leninym* (New York, 1953). There is an English translation: *Encounters with Lenin* (London: Oxford University Press, 1968).

Socialist, though no longer a Leninist. Its religious-philosophical orientation was, and remained, alien to him. And if, in later years, he came to advocate some ideas that were very close to those of the "vekhists," this was not due to any direct influence of that volume but, rather, a fruit of his own experiences, both before and during the Revolution.

In the period preceding World War I—and especially after 1908—Vol'skii saw Russia as being on the eve of an unheard-of economic revival, heading for unprecedented prosperity. He mentioned this, in retrospect, more than once, but never had a chance to develop his views at any length, as may be seen from the letter he wrote me on January 28, 1956, from a suburb of Paris where he spent the last years of his life. What Vol'skii wrote in that letter bears a striking resemblance to Obodovskii's harangues in Arkhangorodskii's apartment. This resemblance is enhanced by the fact that, as in the case of Obodovskii, the picture drawn by Vol'skii was based on the impressions received by him during his trips across the wide expanse of Russia in the years preceding World War I. Here is the relevant portion of Vol'skii's letter to me:

> Yes, Gleb Petrovich, the period 1908-1914, extremely interesting in the history of Russia, has so far failed, alas, to find an historian. Many people, let alone the Bolsheviks, see it as standing under the sign of "dark reaction" and of court-martials. This is a complete distortion of reality. This period saw a remarkable growth of industry (had there been no interruption, its level would be equal to that of Soviet industry today!); housing in the cities was growing on an enormous scale; land was passing, in huge chunks, into the hands of thrifty peasants; all forms of cooperation, and especially in the villages, were developing in a remarkable way. In 1907-1914, desirous to see with my own eyes what had become of the country after it had been swept by the storm of the revolution of 1905 (which, despite its many excesses, I still regard as a positive factor), I visited a great number of cities: Kazan', Nizhnii-Novgorod, Samara, Syzran', Vol'sk, Saratov, Tambov, Morshansk, Suzdal', Romanovo-Borisoglebsk, Vladimir, Kostroma, Khar'kov, Odessa, the Crimea, Tuapse, Novorossiisk, Vladikavkaz, Rostov [on the Don], Batum, Tiflis, Kamyshin, the German colonies on the Volga, etc., etc. Everywhere I saw turmoil, upswing, even "Gründerei," a growth of cultural demands, a craving for education among the popular masses. Many times have I considered describing this interesting time, but every time the need of earning money, and of doing, because of that, something else, distracted me from my task...

Vol'skii's letter to me was printed as an appendix to another book of his, the subject of which was remote from his main interests.[14] It would be interesting to find out whether, by any chance, Solzhenitsyn had an opportunity of seeing that book, or whether he had heard anything about Vol'skii and his views. It is more likely, however, that in Obodovskii we have simply a case of meeting of the minds: *les beaux esprits se rencontrent.* And it is also probable that Vol'skii's and Obodovskii's travels are a sheer coincidence. In any case, Vol'skii was certainly not the only man at the time to see Russia's future in 1913 in very bright colors, though in all probability he was the only orthodox Socialist (which he then still was) to do so.

[14]N. Valentinov, *Dva goda s simvolistami* [*Two Years with the Symbolists*] (Stanford, California, 1969), pp. 236-237.

Questions

BY CZESLAW MILOSZ

Question. One of the most important documents of our time, the acceptance speech sent by Aleksandr Solzhenitsyn to the Nobel Prize Committee, has received in America a very limited press coverage. To my knowledge, a "nearly complete version" (as the caption calls it) appeared in *The Washington Post* of August 27, 1972, and another, much better, translation by Thomas Whitney, was published by *The New York Times,* in two installments—of September 30, 1972 and of October 7, 1972. Yet readers of other newspapers learned at best vaguely about its subject. In his speech, directly addressing his Western audience in the name of all his fellow writers who had perished, the Russian writer spoke "accompanied by the shadows of the fallen," and said: "In exhausting camp marches, rows of lanterns lighting the columns of prisoners in the darkness of subzero nights, more than once we felt in our throats what we would have liked to shout to the whole world, if only the world could have heard some spokesman from among us."* Why has the American press proved to be so unresponsive to that profound and desperate message?

Commentary. Several explanations are possible. Long speeches are rarely reproduced by the American press in their entirety. Moreover, Solzhenitsyn, though famous, is only a novelist, i.e.,

*I quote from the speech in Thomas P. Whitney's translation.

by American standards, a figure somewhere between a producer of commodities and a clown; writers have always been ranked here much lower than in the Slavic countries and they can hardly claim moral authority. There is also the policy of newspapers. If the press proudly wages war against any interference by the government, the editor's pencil every day cuts out whole pages of news and articles, leaving what suits the needs of the moment—as appraised by people at various levels in the hierarchy of a given editorial office. One may surmise that neither the tone nor the contents of Solzhenitsyn's speech were to the taste of the editors. The average American cocktail party where a man speaking his mind would be avoided as insane provides a clue as to why the tone of the speech might have discouraged more than one editor, while the contents showed that Solzhenitsyn's attitude was, unfortunately, not liberal enough. The following passages might even sound offensive:

"Dostoevsky's *Devils* who seemed a provincial, nightmarish fantasy of the last century, are crawling under our very eyes through the whole world, even in countries where they could not have been imagined."

"Youth—at an age when it has had no experience other than sexual, when it does not have behind it years of its own suffering and its own understanding—rapturously repeats our discredited Russian bywords of the nineteenth century while imagining it has discovered something quite new."

"And those who have lived their lives and who understand—many of them in any rate—those who are able, if they wish, to refute the young *do not dare* to refute them, but even flatter them and fawn upon them, will do anything so as not to seem to be 'conservative'—and this again is a phenomenon of the Russian nineteenth century. Dostoevsky called it *'enslavement to progressive fads.'* "

Or what Solzhenitsyn has to say about "the spirit of Munich":

"The spirit of Munich has by no means retreated into the past. It was not a brief episode. I would even be so bold as to say that the spirit of Munich dominates the twentieth century."

Whatever explanations we choose, the fact remains that American editors, with two exceptions, did not see fit to acquaint the public with Solzhenitsyn's message.

Question. Does the Western reader of Solzhenitsyn's stories, novels, and pronouncements understand him in the same way that a Russian reader does? In other words, is there not a possibility of misinterpretation which undermines the concept of "world literature"?

Commentary. The answer probably would be: yes, there is a possibility of misinterpretation. The Western reader is living at the end of the twentieth century, Solzhenitsyn is a writer of the nineteenth century. This should not be taken as a judgment of value. To maintain that that which bears a later date is better would be absurd. Besides, what comes earlier is not necessarily a step to what comes later, because it may give rise to a completely different "later." What I mean is that Russian literature achieved greatness in the nineteenth century, but for many decades of our century it has been artificially restricted to the forms and techniques of the past; they were codified and deprived of their previous spontaneity by "socialist realism." At the same time Western literatures have been carried forward by a rapid movement of successive artistic revolutions, the result of which we observe today. Just as in painting the human face and the human form disappeared, the novel got rid of a hero who would move us or enrapture us, with whom we could identify, introducing instead of characters nothing more than drifting receptacles of perceptions and reflexes. In this sense Western art and writing are growing dehumanized. As a consequence they have lost their grasp of surrounding reality, since only a clearly delineated human form enables us to distinguish between the real and the unreal. It is possible that no novel other than a realistic one is possible, i.e., it must always deal with *zoon politikon.* Georg Lukacs seemed to see in Thomas Mann the last Western representative of the venerable novelistic tradition and, shortly before his death, he drew a parallel between the microcosm mirroring society at large in Mann's *The Magic Mountain* and those of Solzhenitsyn's novels: Mann's sanitarium in Davos, a prison in *The First Circle,* a hospital in *Cancer Ward.* One is tempted here to think of the provincial town in Dostoevsky's *The Devils* or of the even more provincial Skotoprigonevsk in *Brothers Karamazov.* The social panorama, however, disintegrates into a sociological novel in the absence of unforgettable heroes endowed with individual destinies, such as Dostoevsky's characters, Thomas Mann's Castorp or, to mention only the most convincing protagonists created by Solzhenitsyn, Matrena and Kostoglotov.

Paradoxically, Solzhenitsyn owes everything to the "freeze" in Russia, which forced him to oppose a parody of realism by going back to his great Russian predecessors. He is relatively uncontaminated by Western influences. A possible misinterpretation may blur his very concept of art. When he quotes Dostoevsky: "beauty will save the world" and invokes the trinity of the true, the good and the beautiful, the Western reader smiles cynically, for he knows that the sly aestheticism of Flaubert paved the way for the disintegration of "beauty" in works of fiction. Let us not forget, though, that while Dostoevsky saved pathetic and miserable Stepan Verkhovenskii because the old man had always loved beauty, this salvation was conceived in Christian and moral terms, something which is alien to the Western idea of artistic discipline for its own sake. A Russian reader, provided he has access to Solzhenitsyn's works, will ask: "Is he telling the truth?" A Western reader lacks his own approach to the reality of Soviet society (all sovietological analyses miss the point), therefore he will be inclined to view Solzhenitsyn's stories and novels *qua* stories and novels, finding them wanting in many respects and often bearing too many marks of the nineteenth century. There is a basic difference of rhythm between the two parts of our planetary civilization. Is it not surprising that perhaps the only "positive" hero offered us by Western literature in recent decades is the fairy-tale creature, Frodo Baggins, in I. R. R. Tolkien's *The Trilogy of the Rings?*

Question. Is Solzhenitsyn a conservative?

Commentary. Solzhenitsyn's is the case of a peculiar rebel who shares the proclaimed values of the majority of people in his country: patriotism, military valor, self-sacrifice for the sake of others, discipline, a belief in the unique destiny of Russia. If he rebels, it is against the distortion of these values. Like the Russian masses, he, we may assume, has strong authoritarian tendencies. As we learn from many sources, the average Russian reacts with distaste when he hears about the rioting youth in Western countries and wonders why their actions against administrators go unpunished; this indicates that he is unable to grasp the complexities of the Western world. Solzhenitsyn's indictment of the young people in the West should not be taken lightly, and yet the analogy with the revolutionary group in *The Devils* brushes aside the structural differences between the Russia of the past century and the America or Western Europe of today. His views are not far different from those of many a Russian: if they have freedom of speech and of assembly, what more do they want? Such a reaction from a people deprived of many rights—and commodities—is understandable, especially in view of the fact that the distorted image of the capitalist countries in the official Soviet press leads its readers to exaggerations in the opposite direction. Whatever the reasons, Solzhenitsyn's perspective is much more like that of a blue-collar worker in America than that of liberal or radical intellectuals. Besides, it is they who bear the brunt of connivance with the oppressors of Russia, and a visit by a highly placed American liberal to the Butyrskaia prison at the peak of the terror is described in *The First Circle* with savage irony.

If by conservatism is meant an attachment to tradition, then Solzhenitsyn is a conservative. On page after page he deplores the terrible loss brought about by the Revolution, not only in terms of millions of human victims, but also in terms of the destruction of so many precious things: community ties, kindness, respect, piety, architectural beauty—and the sound of bells without which Russia is not Russia.

If, however, by conservatism is meant a defense of the status quo, then Solzhenitsyn is a rebel, for he presents the situation of a man in his country as unbearable. To ask him about his vision of the future would be unfair. It is doubtful whether there is even one person in the Soviet Union knowledgeable enough to cope with *the* problem of the State as sole owner, master, distributor, judge, legislator and overseer.

Question. After *August 1914* appeared, many critics saw Solzhenitsyn primarily as a Russian nationalist. In his Nobel Prize speech he raises a fundamental objection to superficial internationalism:

"In recent times there has been much talk of the levelling of nations, of the disappearance of peoples in the cauldron of contemporary civilization. I do not agree with this, but discussion of this point is a separate matter. At this juncture it is merely appropriate to say that the disappearance of nationalities would impoverish us no less than if all people were to become identical, to possess one single, identical personality, one identical face. Nationalities are the wealth of humanity; even the smallest among them has its own special coloration, hides within itself a particular facet of God's design."

A nation is united by the language it speaks and therefore poets, novelists, playwrights are its voice and conscience: "But woe to that nationality whose literature is cut short by forcible interference. This is no mere simple violation of 'freedom of the press.' This is a closing, a locking up, of the national heart, amputation of the national memory. That nationality has no memory of its own self. It is deprived of its spiritual unity. And even though compatriots apparently speak the same language, they suddenly cease to understand one another. Whole speechless generations are born and die off who do not tell each other about themselves, nor speak about themselves to their descendants."

What is the meaning of that stress laid by Solzhenitsyn upon the nation and its memory?

Commentary. This is a most difficult issue and, one may suspect, inaccessible to an American, unless he has been exposed for a long time to cultures other than his own. The concept of the nation as distinguished from the State and endowed with a special spirit of its own as well as with a special destiny goes back to Johann Gottfried Herder and has a long history in Europe. It has been appropriated by the foes of the established order and, in turn, by its defenders. Associated in the first half of the nineteenth century with democratic and republican aspirations, it moves later on from the left to the right of the political spectrum. Crucial for the student of Slavic literatures, this concept is at the very core of Polish romanticism, which strengthens it with borrowings from the Jewish messianic movements, while in Russia it provides fuel for the protracted feud between the Slavophiles and the Westernizers. It can be said without risk of exaggeration that both what is most sublime and what is most objectionable in the Slavic literature is linked to the shifting contents of that idea which escape clear-cut definition. Basic ambiguities result from the appraisal of the role of a State which violates the nation but at the same time, at least in the case of Russia, appears as its protector, securing its might and glory, albeit through a policy of conquests.

The Communists, though internationalists in their original

program, have been contributing to a new variety of ambiguity. The goal of popular literacy and a school curriculum based to a large extent on the study of native history (even if falsified for propaganda purposes) and on native "classics" contribute to an increase of national feelings seasoned with pride among the dominant, Russian, nationality and with resentment among the nationalities dominated. As the State lacks legitimacy, a sort of alliance between the governing and the governed is achieved primarily through appeals to nationalism, which is, however, a double-edged weapon in a multi-national empire.

Solzhenitsyn is a descendant of the Slavophile line, as was his avowed spiritual master Dostoevsky, but without the latter's tortuous justifications of the State's imperial aims: "The writer," he says in his Nobel Prize speech, "is no sideline judge of his compatriots and contemporaries. He is guilty along with them of all the evil committed in his native land or by his people. And if the tanks of his fatherland have shed blood on the asphalt of a foreign capital, the brown stains have for all eternity spattered the writer's face."

Thus, every nation, even the smallest, has its own angel before the throne of God, and a writer is held responsible before that angel: Solzhenitsyn's thought is curiously reminiscent of European romanticism ca. 1848. The Italian followers of Garibaldi, the Polish democrats, the Hungarian rebels fought then in the name of the peoples of Europe against the so-called Holy Alliance; the monarchs in the Alliance, after the defeat of Napoleon, had concluded a mutual agreement over the heads of their peoples at the Congress of Vienna. Similarly, Solzhenitsyn has bitter words for the present equivalent of the Holy Alliance: "It is not a United Nations Organization but a United Governments Organization, in which governments freely elected are equated with those which have imposed themselves by force, which seized power by force of arms. With self-seeking partiality, the majority in the UN concerns itself jealously with the freedom of certain peoples and carelessly neglects the freedom of others."

Question. The heroes of Solzhenitsyn's stories and novels are confronted with a choice between good and evil. He is in complete disagreement with his age which proclaims "that there are no stable and universal concepts of justice and good, that all values are fluid, that they change"—to quote from his Nobel speech. The distinction between good and evil in his works is not only metaphysical but clearly Christian. Why is it that a major Christian writer has appeared in Russia where the Christians have been oppressed for decades, while in the West, where there is complete freedom of religious practice, literature is nearly synonymous with agnosticism and moral relativism?

Commentary. The safest answer to this question would be to say that this is an enigma. Another answer would be to appropriate Solzhenitsyn's contention that the Western intelligentsia is following the road once taken by the Russian intelligentsia who, however, condensed in a few decades some two hundred years of Western intellectual experience; in consequence, a Russian writer knows something his Western colleague does not know. It is also possible to argue that faith and lack of faith, good and evil remain for men vague notions unless they have spent a few years in a labor camp. But to find an answer one should probably have to dedicate many pages to the slow erosion of religious beliefs as contrasted with the sudden eradication of beliefs by means of an edict; the latter leaves a trace, just as the blood of martyrs resists dry-cleaning: "On one side of the scale, amid persecutions which yielded nothing to those of ancient Rome, hundreds of thousands of silent, unheard Christians sacrificed their lives for their faith in God"—says Solzhenitsyn in his speech. Yet the measures applied by the government proved to be effective, resulting, on the one hand, in the dechristianization of the masses and, on the other, in total subservience of what remained of the structure of the Orthodox Church. Thus the defense of religion fell to the isolated individual—if any—and to the sectarian. All this should be placed against the background of international politics where the old cooperation between the Churches and autocratic rulers seems to take shape under a new guise. The zeal of Church hierarchies to be progressive does not necessarily announce a departure from their habit of compromising with the powers of this world; it may as well testify to their groping towards an accommodation with the new centers of temporal power. Solzhenitsyn's attitude is characterized by a double resistance—against the *anomia* of the masses and against Church officialdom.

There is a functional link between Solzhenitsyn's Christian orientation and the technique of his works. The hero as a subject endowed with free will was in European literature intimately related to the whole Christian heritage, whether writers were believers or sceptics. In a sense he always incarnated the Sinner of the morality plays, situated between Heaven and Hell. The moment man as a free agent was supplanted by man as a tangent of psychological or social forces, the art of the narrative was stricken at its core. Let us note that Soviet socialist realism has attempted to preserve the model of the Sinner hesitating between good (the Party) and evil (the class enemy), and that artistic failures of the doctrine should probably be ascribed to its internal contradictions, just as a deterministic Weltanschauung relativizing good and evil clashes with the postulated freedom of the hero. Solzhenitsyn is indebted to the narrative technique of socialist realism, but he also liberated himself from its contradictions.

Question. Must truth be reactionary?

Commentary. Among the many definitions of truth, one deserves to be recalled here: truth is an escapee from the camp of the victors. Thus it often happens that truth is on the side of the reactionaries, as the very word re-action implies. But it would be wrong to forget that we live in a Tower of Babel under construction and that the signs we use do not signify the same thing in different parts of the building. To be progressive may in one country denote advocating State ownership of the means of production; in another it may denote searching for a way out of the impenetrable bureaucratic tangle which grows where such ownership is a reality. In one country a reactionary is a man who praises decency, while in another the very appeal to decency is subversive and nearly a call for revolution. To stay constantly in the lead in formal experimentation may be a prerequisite for an artist and a writer in one geographical zone, while in another it would mask a betrayal of the most urgent moral duties. And so on. The question is not without validity, as it forces us to meditate on the phenomenon of a solitary man who rejects any conformity. A fool. Any derogatory epithets thus apply to him.

DOCUMENTARY MATERIALS

Statements by Solzhenitsyn

TRANSLATED BY ALEXIS KLIMOFF

ALEKSANDR SOLZHENITSYN

Autobiography[1]

I was born on December 11, 1918, in Kislovodsk. My father, a student in the Department of Philology at Moscow University, failed to complete his studies because he volunteered for the armed forces in the war of 1914. He became an artillery officer on the German front, served for the duration of the war, and died in the summer of 1918, six months before I was born. I was brought up by my mother. She was a typist and stenographer in Rostov on the Don, where I spent my entire childhood and youth. It was there I finished secondary school in 1936. From childhood on I experienced an entirely unprompted inclination toward writing and produced a great deal of the usual adolescent nonsense. During the 1930's I made attempts to get my writings published, but my manuscripts were not accepted anywhere.

I had intended to acquire a literary education, but the kind I desired was unavailable in Rostov, and our modest means, together with the fact that my mother was ill and alone, did not permit me to depart for Moscow. I therefore enrolled in the Department of Mathematics at Rostov University. I had considerable aptitude for mathematics and mastered it with ease, but did not feel it to be a life-long vocation. Yet mathematics was to play a beneficial role in my fate, saving my life on at

 Translation by Alexis Klimoff.

TRANSLATOR'S NOTES

[1]Solzhenitsyn submitted this autobiography to the Nobel Foundation soon after he was awarded the Nobel Prize for Literature in 1970. The Russian text appeared in the Nobel yearbook, *Les Prix Nobel en 1970* (Stockholm: Nobel Foundation, 1971), pp. 131-133.

least two occasions: I would probably not have survived the eight years of camps, had I not, as a mathematician, been removed for four years to a so-called *sharaska.* And later, in exile, I was permitted to teach mathematics and physics, which made my life more bearable and made it possible for me to pursue writing. Had I received a literary education, I could scarcely have survived my trials: I would have been subjected to greater deprivations. Later on, it is true, I did take up literary studies as well: between 1939 and 1941, and concurrently with my studies in physics and mathematics, I took courses at the correspondence division of the Institute of History, Philosophy, and Literature in Moscow.

I graduated from the Department of Physics and Mathematics at Rostov University in 1941, a few days before the outbreak of the war. On medical grounds, I was assigned at the beginning of the war as a driver in a horse-drawn transport unit, remaining there throughout the winter of 1941-42. Only later, once again thanks to mathematics, was I transferred to an artillery school, where I completed the abridged course of studies in November of 1942. I was immediately placed in command of an observation battery;[2] in this capacity I served continuously without leaving the front line right up to the time of my arrest in February of 1945. This occurred in Eastern Prussia, a region that has been strangely linked to my fate: back in 1937, as a first-year university student, I had picked the "Samsonov Debacle" of 1914 in Eastern Prussia as a topic for an essay and had studied materials bearing on this subject; in 1945 I came by foot to these very places. (And just now, in the fall of 1970, my book on that theme, *August 1914,* has been completed).

The grounds for my arrest were passages extracted by the censor from my correspondence with a school friend during 1944-45, mainly certain disrespectful remarks about Stalin, although we referred to him by a pseudonym. Further evidence for the "charge" was provided by the drafts of stories and of reflections found in my field bag.[3] Nevertheless this was insuf-

---

[2]This unit was engaged in determining the location of enemy artillery by means of sound ranging.

[3]A brief description of those passages in Solzhenitsyn's letters and diary which attracted the investigators' attention is given in the official Soviet document which certifies his rehabilitation. See Leopold Labedz, ed., *Solzhenitsyn: A Documentary Record,* Enlarged Edition (Bloomington: Indiana University Press, 1973), p. 22.

ficient for a "trial," and in July, 1945 I was "convicted" and sentenced in absentia—a procedure in wide use at the time—by a decision of the OSO (the "Special Commission of the NKVD")[4] to eight years in the camps. (This was then considered a mild sentence.)

At first I served my sentence in corrective-labor camps of a mixed type (as described in the play *The Love-Girl and the Innocent*). Later, in 1946, I was summoned from there as a mathematician into the system of scientific research institutes of the MVD-MGB[5] and in such "special prisons" (see *The First Circle*) spent the middle part of my sentence. In 1950 I was sent to the newly-established *special* camps for political prisoners only. In such a camp in the town of Ekibastuz in Kazakhstan (see *One Day in the Life of Ivan Denisovich*) I worked as a common laborer, a bricklayer, and a foundryman. There I developed a malignant tumor which was operated on but not cured: its true nature was discovered only later.

With a delay of one month past the end of my eight-year term there arrived—without any new sentence or even a "resolution of the OSO"—an administrative order: I was not to be freed but sent into PERPETUAL EXILE in Kok-Terek (southern Kazakhstan).[6] This was not a special measure directed at me but a very common procedure at the time.

From March, 1953 (on March 5, the day that Stalin's death was made public, I was let out of the camp for the first time without an escort) until June, 1956, I served this sentence of exile. Here I rapidly developed cancer and by the end of 1953 I was already on the brink of death, unable to eat or sleep and incapacitated by the poisons of the tumor. Released for treatment in Tashkent, however, I was cured over the course of 1954 in the oncological clinic there (see *Cancer Ward* and "The Right Hand"). All these years of exile I taught mathematics and physics at a rural school, and, thanks to my strictly solitary way of life, could write prose in secret. (In the camp I could write only poetry—for memorization.) I was able to

[4]OSO, an acronym for *Osoboe soveshchanie* [Special Commission], was a quasi-judicial organ of the NKVD, instituted to speed up the disposal of "counterrevolutionary" cases by imposing summary sentences.

[5]MVD and MGB stand respectively for "Ministry of Internal Affairs" and "Ministry of State Security."

[6]Solzhenitsyn has on several occasions commented on the metaphysical implications of the adjective "perpetual" [*vechnyi*] in this context. See, for example, *Cancer Ward,* Ch. 20.

preserve these prose writings and to bring them from my place of exile to the European part of the country. There I continued in the same manner to pursue teaching openly and writing in secret, at first in the Vladimir *oblast'* (see "Matrena's Home") and later in Riazan'.

Throughout these years and up to 1961 not only was I CONVINCED that I would never in my lifetime see a single line of my writing in print, but I scarcely dared to allow even my close acquaintances to read anything I had written for fear of disclosure. Finally, when I had attained the age of forty-two, such secret authorship began to weigh upon me. The most burdensome aspect was the impossibility of testing my work on readers of literary sophistication. In 1961, after the 22nd Congress of the CPSU and the speech of Tvardovskii at this Congress,[7] I decided to emerge: to offer *One Day in the Life of Ivan Denisovich* for publication. Such self-disclosure then seemed to me—and not without reason—to be very risky: it could lead to the destruction of all my manuscripts and to my own death. Things turned out happily then: after protracted efforts A. T. Tvardovskii managed to publish my novel a year later. But the printing of my works was stopped almost immediately; my plays and (in 1964) my novel *The First Circle* were blocked, and in 1965 this novel was seized together with my files going back many years. During those months I believed it an unpardonable mistake that I had revealed my work prematurely and would thus not be able to carry it to completion.

Even those events which we have already lived through we can rarely comprehend and evaluate at once, immediately after their occurrence. All the more unpredictable and astounding proves to be the ongoing course of events.

Translated by Alexis Klimoff

---

[7]The 22nd Party Congress opened in Moscow on October 17, 1961. Khrushchev's outspoken attacks on the "cult of personality" at this Congress included his suggestion that a memorial be constructed to the "leading figures of the Party and government" who died in Stalin's purges. On October 30 the Congress unanimously voted to remove Stalin's body from the Lenin-Stalin mausoleum. In his address to the Congress, Aleksandr Tvardovskii called on writers to abandon the blithe and self-congratulatory depiction of Soviet life typical of Stalinist literature. As in Tolstoy's famous dictum, said Tvardovskii, the hero must be truth. See *XXII S"ezd Kommunisticheskoi Partii Sovetskogo Soiuza 17-31 oktiabria 1961 goda. Stenograficheskii otchet* (Moscow: Gospolitizdat, 1962), vol. 2, pp. 528-539.

ALEKSANDR SOLZHENITSYN

Letter to the Fourth Congress of Soviet Writers[1]

To the Presidium and Delegates of the Congress
To the Members of the Union of Soviet Writers
To the Editors of Literary Journals and Newspapers

Not having access to the rostrum at this Congress, I request that the Congress bring up for discussion:

1) that no longer tolerable oppression to which our literature has been subjected by the censorship for decades on end and which the Writers' Union cannot continue to accept.

Unstipulated by the [Soviet] Constitution and hence illegal, this censorship—nowhere publicly identified as such and provided with the obfuscating label of "Glavlit"—weighs heavily

TRANSLATOR'S NOTES

[1]The Fourth Congress of Soviet Writers was convened in Moscow on May 22, 1967. According to the official report, it was attended by 515 delegates representing 6608 writers, as well as by a number of sympathetic foreign guests (including Pablo Neruda). Since 1967 was the 50th anniversary year of the Bolshevik Revolution, special efforts were made to insure a façade of complete ideological solidarity. Solzhenitsyn was not invited. With the help of friends, he prepared some 250 copies of his open letter, about 150 of which he mailed to members of the Presidium and to selected delegates. Some 70 copies went to writers not in attendance, 30 more were addressed to editors of various literary periodicals. The letters were mailed to arrive just before the opening of the Congress. (See Zhores A. Medvedev, *Desiat' let posle "Odnogo dnia Ivana Denisovicha"* [London: Macmillan, 1973], p. 80.) The text of the letter quickly reached the West, with an early translation appearing in *The New York Times* on June 5. The translation here follows the text as printed in Aleksandr Solzhenitsyn, *Sobranie sochinenii,* 6 vols. (Frankfurt/Main: Possev Verlag, 1970), VI, 7-13.

on our literature and permits individuals unversed in literary matters to hold unchecked power over writers.[2] A relic of the Middle Ages, censorship is managing to stretch its Methusalah-like existence almost into the twenty-first century! Of ephemeral value, it strives to take over that which is the task of deathless time: to separate worthy books from unworthy ones.

The right of our writers to voice judgements which are ahead of their time concerning the moral life of man and society, their right to an independent elucidation of social problems or of the historical experience of our country, gained at the cost of such great suffering—these rights are neither presupposed nor recognized. Works that might have given expression to a national sentiment whose time had come, which might have exerted a timely and salutary influence within the realm of spiritual values or which could have fostered the growth of social consciousness—such works are banned or mutilated by the censorship out of considerations that are petty and selfish, as well as shortsighted from the national point of view. Many members of the Union and even the delegates to this Congress know well how they themselves have buckled under pressure from the censors and how they have made concessions in the structure and spirit of their books, replacing chapters, pages, paragraphs, and phrases, supplying drab titles—all for the sake of seeing their works in print—and thereby irremediably distorting them. It is characteristic of literature that such distortions are disastrous for gifted works and imperceptible for inept ones. It is precisely the best of our literature which appears in print in mangled form.

At the same time the censors' labels—"ideologically harmful," "corrupt," and so forth—are themselves volatile and fluid, changing before our eyes. Even Dostoevsky, the pride of world literature, was at one time not published in our country (and even today his works are not published in full); he was excluded from school curricula, made unavailable to readers, and reviled.[3] For how many years was Esenin considered "counter-revolu-

[2]*Glavlit* is an acronym for "*Glav*noe upravlenie po delam *lit*eratury i izdatel'stv" [Main Administration of Literary and Publishing Affairs]. For a recent discussion of Soviet censorship, with an extensive bibliography, see *Studies on the Soviet Union,* N.S. XI, No. 2 (1971).

[3]For an account of the situation up to 1950, see Marc Slonim, "Dostoevsky under the Soviets," *Russian Review,* X, No. 2 (April, 1951), 118-130. Dostoevsky was "rehabilitated" in 1956 and the first *Complete Works* was launched in 1972.

tionary"?[4] (Prison sentences were even meted out for the mere possession of his books.) Was not Maiakovskii once considered a "quasi-anarchistic political hooligan"?[5] For decades the ever-vibrant poetry of Akhmatova was deemed anti-Soviet.[6] The first timid printing of the dazzling Tsvetaeva was declared a "gross political error."[7] Only after a lapse of twenty or thirty years were Bunin, Bulgakov, and Platonov returned to us.[8] Mandel'shtam, Voloshin, Gumilev, and Kliuev must inevitably follow.[9] The "recognition" of Zamiatin and Remizov will also unavoidably come some day.[10] There is a decisive moment in this process: the death of the objectionable writer, sooner or later after which he is returned to us with an "explanation of his errors." Only a short time ago Pasternak's very name could not even be spoken aloud; but then he died, and his books are now being published and his verse is even quoted at public ceremonies.[11]

Truly Pushkin's words have come to pass:

They are capable of loving only the dead![12]

But the belated publication of books and the "sanctioning" of names compensates neither for the social nor the esthetic

---

[4]Sergei Esenin (1895-1925) fell into official disfavor soon after his suicide for his alleged "*kulak* ideology." See Gordon McVay, "Yesenin's Posthumous Fame," *Modern Language Review*, vol. 67, No. 3 (July 1972), 590-602.

[5]Vladimir Maiakovskii (1893-1930) was viewed with suspicion and hostility by the doctrinaire ideologues of RAPP [Russian Association of Proletarian Writers].

[6]This charge is prominent in Zhdanov's 1946 attack on Anna Akhmatova (1889-1966). See Andrei I. Zhdanov, *Essays on Literature, Philosophy, and Music* (New York: International Publishers, 1950), pp. 21-26.

[7]Marina Tsvetaeva (1892-1941) emigrated in 1920 and returned to Russia in 1939, where she committed suicide. On the reception of her poetry in post-Stalin Russia, see Simon Karlinsky, *Marina Cvetaeva: Her Life and Art* (Berkeley: Univ. of California Press, 1966), pp. 111-120.

[8]The first separate edition of the works of the émigré writer Ivan Bunin (1870-1953) appeared in the Soviet Union in 1956. Mikhail Bulgakov (1891-1940) and Andrei Platonov (1899-1951) both faced serious obstacles in the publication of their works, especially after 1930. Their works began reappearing in print in the post-Stalin period.

[9]Osip Mandel'shtam (1891-1938), Maksimilian Voloshin (1878-1932), Nikolai Gumilev (1886-1921), and Nikolai Kliuev (1887-1937) are each major poets. None has had a separate edition of his poetry published in the USSR since the 1920's.

[10]Evgenii Zamiatin (1884-1937) emigrated in 1931 and is considered "anti-Soviet" for his novel *We*. Aleksei Remizov (1877-1957) emigrated in 1922. Neither writer has been published since the time of his emigration.

[11]Boris Pasternak died in disgrace in 1960. A small book of his verse was published in Moscow in 1961, followed by a major collection in 1965.

[12]See Aleksandr Pushkin, *Boris Godunov*, Scene 7, line 24.

losses suffered by our people as a consequence of such hideous delays and from the suppression of our literary consciousness. (In particular, one might mention several writers of the 1920's—Pil'niak, Platonov, Mandel'shtam—who very early pointed to the beginnings of the personality cult and to certain peculiar traits of Stalin, but they were destroyed and silenced instead of being listened to.[13]) Literature cannot develop within the categories of "they [the censors] will pass this, but they won't pass that," or "you can write about this but not about that." A literature that is not the very breath of the society of its time, one that dares not transmit its pains and apprehensions to society or to warn it, in times of need, of threatening moral and social dangers—such a literature does not even deserve the name: it is merely cosmetics. Such a literature loses the respect of its own people, and its output is used not as reading matter but as material for recycling.

Our literature has forfeited the leading position in world literature that it occupied at the end of the last century and the beginning of the present one; lost, too, is the brilliant experimentation that distinguished it in the 1920's. To the entire world the literary life of our country appears immeasurably more pallid, bland, and inferior than it is in reality, and than it would have become, had it not been constricted and isolated. The loss is to our country in world public opinion, and to world literature: were the latter to avail itself of the unhampered fruits of our literature, and were it to be enriched by our spiritual experience, then the entire evolution of the arts would not be proceeding along its present course; art would have attained a new stability and would even have risen to a new artistic level.

I propose that the Congress adopt a resolution to demand and secure the abolition of all censorship—open or concealed—of works of art, and that it ensure the liberation of publishers

---

[13]Boris Pil'niak (1894-1937) in 1926 published a story called "Povest' o nepogashennoi lune" ["Tale of the Unextinguished Moon"], subtitled "Murder of the Army Commander," which alludes to the rumors that the death of Mikhail Frunze had been engineered by Stalin. In 1937 Pil'niak became a victim of the Purge. Mandel'shtam, who is known to have abhorred Stalin, was arrested in 1934 for writing an anti-Stalin epigram. Released and then re-arrested, Mandel'shtam died in a camp in 1938. (For the text of the epigram, see Osip Mandel'shtam, *Sobranie sochinenii,* 3 vols. [Washington: Inter-Language Literary Associates], I [Second Edition, 1967], 202.) Platonov criticized Stalin's policies of collectivization in *Vprok* (1931) and *Kotlovan.* He was accused of being a "*kulak* agent" and reduced to almost total silence.

from the legal obligation to obtain clearance for each printer's sheet;[14]

[I further request that the Congress discuss:]

2) the responsibilities of the Union toward its members. These responsibilities are not clearly formulated in the Statutes of the Union of Soviet Writers ("protection of authors' rights" and "measures to safeguard other rights of writers,") even though it has been the sad experience of a third of a century that the Union has defended neither these "other" rights nor even the authors' rights of those being persecuted.

Many authors have been subjected during their lifetime to abuse and slander in the press and in public speeches without being accorded the physical possibility of replying. Beyond this, they were subjected to harassment and persecution on a personal level (Bulgakov, Akhmatova, Tsvetaeva, Pasternak, Zoshchenko, Platonov, Aleksandr Grin, Vasilii Grossman).[15] Not only did the Writers' Union fail to make its periodicals available to these writers for rebuttal and self-justification, not only did it refrain from coming to their defense, but the leadership of the Union invariably proved to be first among the persecutors.[16] Names which will be the glory of our twentieth-century poetry appear on the list of those expelled from the Union or of those not even accepted![17] Moreover, the leadership of the Union cravenly abandoned in misfortune those writers for whom persecution was to end in exile, labor camp, or death (Pavel Vasil'ev, Mandel'shtam, Artem Veselyi, Pil'niak, Babel', Tabidze, Zabolotskii,

[14]A "printer's sheet" [*pechatnyi list*] is a typographical unit equal to sixteen pages of printed text. Akin to English "signature."

[15]Some of these writers were publicly attacked as "anti-Soviet" (Akhmatova, Pasternak, Zoshchenko), others accused of sympathies for the Whites (Bulgakov) or for *kulaks* (Platonov), still others of exhibiting questionable patriotism (Grossman), and so on. The personal consequences of such charges in the Soviet context are incalculable. Furthermore, a number of these writers were subjected to acute suffering on a different level: Tsvetaeva's husband was shot and her daughter imprisoned, Akhmatova's only son was held for many years in a prison camp on unspecified charges.

[16]Since its inception, the Union has slavishly adhered to the Party line on every issue. As the *Brief Literary Encyclopedia* puts it: "The presentation of the Order of Lenin to the Union of Soviet Writers in May, 1967 was an expression of the Soviet Government's deep appreciation of the activities of the Union." (See *Kratkaia literaturnaia entsiklopediia,* vol. 7 [Moscow, 1972], p. 111.)

[17]Among those expelled were Akhmatova (1946) and Pasternak (1958); Mandel'shtam was never accepted.

and others).[18] We are forced to cut short this list with the words "and others": after the twentieth Congress of the CPSU we learned that there were *over six hundred* such completely innocent writers whom the Union obediently handed over to their fate in prisons and labor camps.[19] But the scroll is even longer; its curled-up end cannot and will never be read: on it are listed the names of those young poets and prose writers whom we came to know only by chance through personal encounter. Their talents perished in the camps before they had a chance to blossom, and their writings got no further than the offices of the state security agencies in the days of Iagoda, Ezhov, Beriia, and Abakumov.[20]

There is no historical necessity why the newly-elected leadership of the Union should share a responsibility for the past with the previous governing body.

I propose that all guarantees of protection which the Union grants to members subjected to slander and unjust persecution be formulated in unmistakable terms in Section 22 of the Statues of the Union of Soviet Writers, in order that a recurrence of the lawlessness of the past be rendered impossible.[21]

Should the Congress not remain indifferent to my statement, I request that it give consideration to the interdictions and persecutions which I myself am experiencing:

1. My novel *The First Circle* (35 author's sheets[22]) was confiscated nearly two years ago by the KGB and this impedes open editorial promotion of this work.[23] Instead, in my lifetime,

---

[18]Of the writers listed, only the poet Nikolai Zabolotskii (1903-1958) survived imprisonment.

[19]Robert Conquest cites statistics which indicate that the impact of the Purges on the ranks of writers was more devastating than on any other Soviet professional group. See Robert Conquest, *The Great Terror: Stalin's Purge of the Thirties* (New York: Collier, 1973), p. 437.

[20]Heads of the secret police under Stalin.

[21]Section 22 of the Statutes reads: "The Board of Directors of the Union of Soviet Writers takes upon itself the protection of authors' rights within the USSR and abroad, through the appropriate Soviet agencies; it undertakes all necessary measures to safeguard the other rights of writers who are members of the Union; it provides legal aid for writers and speaks on their behalf in state and social organizations."

[22]An "author's sheet" [*avtorskii list*] is a unit measure of textual length used in the Soviet Union. It is equal to 40,000 typographical characters.

[23]A. T. Tvardovskii made determined efforts to publish *The First Circle* in *Novyi mir.* Announcements of a serial publication in 1965 were printed in the summer of 1964 and an advance payment was even made to Solzhenitsyn. See Zhores Medvedev, *Desiat' let posle "Odnogo dnia Ivana Denisovicha,"* pp. 42-45.

against my will, and even without my knowledge, this novel has been "published" in an unnatural "restricted" edition meant for an unnamed select circle. My novel has been made available to literary officials, but it is being withheld from the majority of writers. I cannot obtain an open discussion of the novel in writers' conferences and I am powerless to avert misuse or plagiarism.

2. Confiscated together with my novel were my literary papers dating back some fifteen or twenty years—items which were not intended for publication. One-sided excerpts from these papers have now been "published" in "restricted editions" and are being distributed in the same circles. The play *The Feast of the Victors* which I composed in verse and committed to memory while in camp—at a time when I wore a four-digit prison number and when, condemned to death by slow starvation, we were forgotten by society and *no-one* stood up against the repressions—this play, abandoned long ago, is being ascribed to me as my latest work.[24]

3. For three full years an irresponsible campaign of slander has been directed against me, a man who served throughout the war as a battery commander and who received battle decorations: it is alleged that I served a term as a common criminal or that I surrendered to the enemy (I was never a prisoner of war), that I "betrayed my country" and "collaborated with the Germans."[25] Such is the interpretation given to my eleven years spent in camps and exile for criticizing Stalin. This slander is conducted at closed briefing sessions and meetings by people in official positions. My attempts to stop this slander by appealing to the Board of Directors of the Writers' Union

---

After Khrushchev's fall from power in October of 1964 the chances of obtaining the necessary clearance were reduced to nil. The manuscript of the novel was seized in September of 1965.

[24]Despite this protest, the play was distributed to officials of the Writers' Union later in 1967. See Leopold Labedz, ed., *Solzhenitsyn: A Documentary Record,* Enlarged Edition (Bloomington: Indiana University Press, 1973), pp. 128-129.

[25]Solzhenitsyn's official military record is cited in the document certifying his rehabilitation: "Solzhenitsyn . . . fought courageously for his homeland, more than once displayed personal heroism and inspired the devotion of the section he commanded. Solzhenitsyn's section was the best in the unit for discipline and battle effectiveness." See Leopold Labedz, *op. cit.,* p. 23. Allegations that Solzhenitsyn had been a POW and that he had been sentenced for a criminal offense were instrumental in blocking his otherwise strong chances of winning the Lenin Prize in 1964. See Zhores Medvedev, *Desiat' let. . . .* pp. 36-37.

of the RSFSR and to the press were in vain. The Board did not even respond, and not a single [Soviet] newspaper printed my reply to the slanderers. On the contrary, the slander against me that is being spread from rostrums has increased in quantity and vehemence over the past year; use is being made of distorted materials from my confiscated papers, while I have been deprived of the possibility to reply.

4. My novel *Cancer Ward* (25 author's sheets), Part I of which was cleared for publication by the prose section of the Moscow writers' organization, cannot be published in selected chapters (it was turned down by five magazines) to say nothing of a full publication (rejected by *Novyi mir, Zvezda* and *Prostor*).[26]

5. The play *The Love-Girl and the Innocent,* accepted for production by the Sovremennik Theatre in 1962, has thus far not been cleared for performance.[27]

6. The screen play *The Tanks Know the Truth,* the play *A Candle in the Wind* (*The Light Which is in Thee*), a group of short stories—"The Right Hand," and the series of "micro-stories" or "sketches"—can find neither a producer nor a publisher.

7. My short stories which appeared in *Novyi mir* have not once been reissued in book form and are rejected for republication everywhere (by [the publishing houses] *Sovetskii pisatel', Gospolitizdat,* and *Biblioteka "Ogon'ka."*) They are therefore inaccessible to the general reader.[28]

8. At the same time I have been prohibited from all other contact with readers. This includes public reading of selections from my works (in November, 1966, for example, nine of eleven scheduled appearances were cancelled at the last moment) as well as readings on the radio. In fact, merely to give a manuscript to someone for "reading and copying" is now pro-

[26]Tvardovskii continued his efforts to publish *Cancer Ward* in *Novyi mir* even after this letter was written. In the fall of 1967 he was given an oral assurance that he could proceed to set the manuscript into type. The novel was to be serialized in *Novyi mir* beginning with the December, 1967 issue. But the novel was stopped in the galley stage. All further hopes for a Soviet publication vanished with the appearance of the novel in the West in 1968. See Zhores Medvedev, *Desiat' let. . . ,* pp. 86-91.

[27]The play was actually being rehearsed when it was stopped.

[28]The only work by Solzhenitsyn that has appeared in the Soviet Union in book form is *One Day in the Life of Ivan Denisovich.*

hibited on pain of criminal prosecution (ancient Russian scribes were permitted this liberty five centuries ago!).

My work is thus totally silenced, isolated, and reviled.

In view of such a gross violation of my author's as well as of my "other" rights, will the Fourth Congress undertake to defend me or will it not? It would seem that this choice is not devoid of significance for the literary future of a number of the delegates as well.

I am of course secure in the belief that I shall fulfill my task as a writer under any conditions, even more effectively and irrefutably from the grave than during my lifetime. No-one can obstruct the movement of truth; to advance it I am ready to accept even death. But perhaps the many lessons of history will teach us, at last, not to halt a writer's pen during his lifetime.

Never yet has this insight graced our history.

A. SOLZHENITSYN

May 16, 1967.[29]

Translated by Alexis Klimoff

[29]Solzhenitsyn's letter was not openly discussed at the Fourth Congress, even though an airing of the issues raised by Solzhenitsyn was demanded by numerous members of the Union. One petition to this effect was signed by 80 writers, including such respected figures as K. Paustovskii, V. Kaverin, and Tvardovskii. See Leopold Labedz, *op. cit.*, pp. 112-113.

ALEKSANDR SOLZHENITSYN

To Patriarch Pimen of Russia[1]

Lenten Letter

Your Holiness!

The substance of this letter is like a tombstone crushing down upon the head and breast of the yet surviving Russian Orthodox people. It is known to all, and it has been shouted aloud, and again a doomed silence reigns. And to this stone one needs add but a single pebble to make further silence impossible. Such a pebble pressed down on me when I heard your epistle on Christmas Eve.[2]

I was especially pained by that passage where you spoke at last about *children*—perhaps for the first time in half a century from your high office—whose parents, together with love for their country, are to foster in their children love for the Church (and apparently, for the Faith as well?), and are to strengthen this love by their own good example.[3] I heard these words, and

An earlier version of this translation appeared in *Diakonia,* VII, No. 2 (1972), 101-107. Reprinted with permission.

TRANSLATOR'S NOTES

[1]Several somewhat differing versions of the Russian text of the "Lenten Letter" have reached the West—a fate common for *samizdat* documents. This translation follows the text as printed in *Russkaia mysl'* (Paris), No. 2888, March 30, 1972, which appears to be the most complete. Solzhenitsyn's use of capitals for emphasis has been rendered by italics.

[2]An English translation of Patriarch Pimen's "Christmas Message" appears in *One Church,* 1972, No. 1, pp. 4-5. It is addressed to "the Archpastors, Pastors, and all faithful Members of the Russian Orthodox Church and Fellow Communicants living beyond the borders of our Motherland."

[3]Patriarch Pimen writes in his "Christmas Message," p. 5: "Fellow Com-

my early childhood arose before me, a childhood of attending many church services, and it was that uniquely fresh and pure first impression which could not later be obliterated by any of life's hardships or by any abstract intellectual theories.

But what is this? Why is your forthright appeal directed only to Russian émigrés? Why do you call for *those* children to be raised in the Christian faith, why do you admonish only the distant flock to "discern slander and falsehood" and to be strengthened in truth and righteousness? And should not *we* discern it? And in *our* children, should we foster love for the Church or should we not? True, Christ did command us to seek the one sheep in a hundred which is lost, but only when the ninety-nine are safely in the fold; however, when those ninety-nine have strayed, should not the first concern be for them?[4]

Why, on coming to church to christen my son, did I have to present my passport? For what canonical purposes does the Moscow Patriarchate require the [civil] registration of the newly baptized? One can only be amazed at the spiritual strength and deeply ingrained psychological tenacity of those parents who go through with this denunciatory registration, only to be later victimized at work or publicly mocked by fools. But this is as far as their perseverance can go, since all the ties of the child with the Church usually end after baptism. Subsequent opportunities for growth in the faith are completely barred: participation in the church service is prohibited, sometimes Communion as well, or even church attendance itself. We are robbing our children, we are depriving them of the inimitable, purely angelic experience of the church service, which in adulthood can never be recaptured, and the loss of which one does not even realize. Extinguished are the right to continue the faith of our fathers, and the right of parents to raise their children in their own beliefs, while you, hierarchs of the Church, have made your peace with this and support it, interpreting it as an authentic example of the *freedom of religion.* You find evidence of religious freedom in the fact that we are forced

municants living beyond the borders of our Motherland, we now appeal to you with these words of sincere felicitation. May your spiritual bonds with the Mother Church be strengthened. Inculcate this love in your children and strengthen it by giving a good example (. . .) carefully discern that which is false and a lie, and may God strengthen you in truth and righteousness."

[4] "If a man has a hundred sheep, and one of them has gone astray, does he not leave the ninety-nine on the hills and go in search of the one that went astray?" (Matthew 18:12).

to turn over our children—defenseless—not into neutral hands, but to a domination by atheistic propaganda of the most primitive and unscrupulous kind, as well as in the fact that adolescents torn away from Christianity—(they should under no circumstances get infected by it)—have been left with no room for moral growth except the narrow gap between the handbook of the political agitator and the Criminal Code.

One half century of the past has already been lost, it is too late to rescue the present, but how can the future of our land be saved? The future which will consist of today's children? In the final analysis, the true and ultimate fate of our land depends on whether the concept of *"might makes right"* will once and for all take root in the conscience of the people or whether the *power of truth* will come out of eclipse and shine anew. Shall we be able to restore in ourselves at least some Christian traits, or shall we lose the few that are left and give ourselves over to calculations of self-preservation and profit?

A study of Russian history of the last centuries convinces one that it would have proceeded incomparably more humanely and harmoniously had the Church not renounced its independence and had the people heeded the Church's voice, as for example occurred in Poland. Alas, it has not been so with us for a long time. Step by step we have lost that radiant ethical Christian atmosphere which for a thousand years shaped our mores, our way of life, our beliefs, our folklore, and the very fact that the Russian word for the people—*krest'iane* [peasants]—was derived from "Christians." We are losing the last traces and signs of a Christian people. Is it possible that this should not be the *main* concern of the Russian Patriarch? The Russian Church has its agitated opinion on every injustice in far-away Asia and Africa, but on misfortunes at home—never a word.[5] Why are the communications which come down to us from the highest level of the Church so conventionally serene? Why are all church documents so beningly placid, as if published among the most Christian of peoples? While one serene epistle follows another, might not the very need to write them vanish in some stormy year: there will be no one to address them to, no flock will remain outside the Patriarchate's Chancellery.

[5]Recent pronouncements of the Moscow Patriarchate on foreign affairs are collected in the mimeographed study by John B. Dunlop, *The Recent Activities of the Moscow Patriarchate Abroad and in the USSR* (Seattle: St. Nectarios Educational Series, 1970), pp. 1-44. See also William C. Fletcher, *Religion and Soviet Foreign Policy, 1945-1970* (London: Oxford U. P., 1973), pp. 117 ff.

It will soon be seven years since the two righteous priests Iakunin and Eshliman wrote their celebrated letter to your predecessor, confirming, by their sacrifice and example, that the pure flame of Christian faith has not been extinguished in our land.[6] They fully and convincingly described to him that voluntary inner enslavement—unto self-destruction—to which the Russian Church has been brought. They asked that any untruth in their letter be pointed out to them. But their every word was *true,* and not one of the bishops took it upon himself to refute them. And how were they answered? In the most simple and brutal manner: they were punished for the truth—and prohibited from serving in church. And you have not remedied this to this very day. And the terrifying letter of the twelve from Viatka also remained without an answer and resulted only in the persecution of the signers.[7] And to this day, Ermogen of Kaluga is still exiled and confined to a monastery, the only fearless archbishop who did not permit the forces of a late-blooming and frenzied atheism to close his churches, to burn icons and books, as had so frequently occurred in the years before 1964 in other dioceses.[8]

Seven years will soon have passed since this was loudly proclaimed, and what changes have occurred? For every functioning church there are twenty which have been levelled or ir-

---

[6]The letter from Frs. Nikolai Eshliman and Gleb Iakunin (also spelled Yakunin) to Patriarch Aleksii is dated November 21, 1965. Two complete English translations are available: in *St. Vladimir's Seminary Quarterly,* vol. 10 (1966), No. 1-2, and in the booklet *A Cry of Despair From Moscow Churchmen* (New York: Synod of Bishops of the Russian Orthodox Church Outside of Russia, 1966). Very extensive excerpts from the letter are published in Michael Bourdeaux (ed.), *Patriarch and Prophets: Persecution in the Russian Orthodox Church Today* (New York: Praeger, 1970), pp. 194-221. For further documentation bearing on Frs. Eshliman and Iakunin, see Bordeaux, pp. 221-238.

[7]Viatka, renamed Kirov in 1934, is a city some 500 miles northeast of Moscow and the administrative center of a large *oblast'*. In 1966 twelve believers of the Kirov diocese sent a letter to the Patriarch protesting against the calamitous situation prevailing in the diocese. A short excerpt from their statement can be found in Bourdeaux, pp. 60-61. Shortly thereafter the same situation was described in detail by Boris Talantov. See Bourdeaux, pp. 125-152.

[8]The most brutal phase of the religious persecutions under Khrushchev occurred in 1959-64. Archbishop Ermogen (also spelled Yermogen) of Kaluga is singled out for praise by Frs. Eshliman and Iakunin for his courageous defense of the Church. See the "Appendix" or "Supplement" to the priests' letter to the Patriarch, which appears in each of the sources cited in Note 6. Archbishop Ermogen was retired against his wishes and assigned to the Assumption monastery in Zhirovitsy in 1965. In 1967 he wrote a letter to the Patriarch demanding his reinstatement. For his statements and the response of the Patriarchate, see Bourdeaux, pp. 239-254.

reparably wrecked and twenty more abandoned and desecrated; is there a sight more soul-wrenching than a church-skeleton left to the birds and to warehouse-keepers? How many population centers are there in the country, to which no church is closer than 100 or even 200 kilometers? And the churches are completely gone from our Northlands, the age-old repository of the Russian spirit and, foreseeably, Russia's greatest assurance for the future. But every attempt by concerned individuals, by donors, and by testators to *restore* even the smallest church is blocked by our one-sided laws of the so-called *separation* of Church and State. We dare not even ask about the ringing of churchbells—but why has Russia been deprived of her ancient adornment, her most beautiful voice? Would that it were only churches: in our country we cannot even get hold of the Gospels. Even the Gospels are brought in to us from abroad, just as our missionaries once used to take them to the Indigirka.[9]

Almost seven years have passed, but has the Church upheld and defended anything whatever? The entire governance of the Church, the appointment of priests and bishops (even of disreputable ones, so that the Church might more easily be mocked and destroyed) is conducted as secretly as before by the Council for Religious Affairs.[10] A Church ruled dictatorially by atheists—this is a spectacle unseen in two thousand years. Given over to the atheists' control is also the entirety of the operational management of the Church and the allocation of Church funds—those coppers dropped into the collection by pious hands. Five million roubles at a time are contributed with magnanimous gestures to various extraneous funds, while beggars are chased from the church steps and there is no money to repair a leaking roof in a poor parish. Priests have no authority in their own parishes, only the service itself is still entrusted to them, and that only within the confines of the church; to venture beyond the door to a sick parishioner or to a cemetery requires permission from the town council.

By what reasoning could one convince oneself that the cal-

[9]The Indigirka is a large river in northeastern Siberia.

[10]The Council for Religious Affairs was formed in January, 1966, by merging the Council for the Affairs of the Russian Orthodox Church with the Council for the Affairs of Religious Cults (which had supervised all other religious bodies). For an example of an important secret circular, see Richard H. Marshall, Jr., Thomas E. Bird, and Andrew Q. Blane (eds.), *Aspects of Religion in the Soviet Union, 1917-1967* (Chicago & London: Chicago U. P., 1971), pp. 459-462.

culated *destruction*—one directed by atheists—of the body and spirit of the Church is the best method of *preserving* it? Preservation, but *for whom?* Certainly not for Christ. Preserved, but *by what means?* By *lies?* But after falsehood, with what hands is the Eucharist to be performed?

Your Holiness! Do not entirely disregard my unworthy appeal. It may not be every seven years that even such an appeal as this will reach your ears. Do not let us suppose, do not make us think, that for the bishops of the Russian Church temporal power is higher than the heavenly one, that earthly responsibility is more awesome than accountability before God.

Let us not profess falsely before the people—and all the more so in prayer—that external fetters are stronger than our spirit. It was no easier in the early days of Christianity, which nevertheless prevailed and flourished. It showed us the way: *sacrifice.* He who is deprived of all material strength always achieves victory in *sacrifice.* Such martyrdom, worthy of the first centuries, was accepted by many of our priests and fellow believers within our living memory.[11] But at that time they were thrown to the *lions,* today one can only lose one's well-being.

During these days, as you kneel before the Cross which has been brought out into the center of the church, ask of the Lord: what else could be the purpose of your ministry to a people which has nearly lost the spirit and likeness of Christianity?

ALEKSANDR SOLZHENITSYN

Great Lent
The Week of the Veneration of the Cross[12]
1972

Translated by Alexis Klimoff

[11]We have definite information concerning 130 bishops who were martyred for their faith between the years 1918 and 1941. See Nikita Struve, *Christians in Contemporary Russia* (New York: Scribner, 1967), pp. 393-398. There is no equally reliable estimate of the number of priests exiled and killed in the same period, but the figure must certainly run into the tens of thousands. The number of ordinary believers who suffered imprisonment, exile, or death for their faith will probably never be precisely known, since it has been common Soviet practice to couch religious persecution—and hence the specific accusations against individuals—in totally political terms.

[12]In 1972, this fell on March 12-18. Solzhenitsyn's letter elicited several responses in defense of the Moscow Patriarchate. The best known is an open letter from Fr. Sergii Zheludkov, dated Easter 1972. (It is published in *Vestnik Russkogo Studencheskogo Khristianskogo Dvizheniia,* No. 103 [1972], pp. 156-158). Zheludkov defends the accommodation of the Moscow Patriarchate with the atheist state, asserting that historically there simply was no other

choice if the Church were to survive at all. He calls Solzhenitsyn's letter "an amazingly pretentious document" (p. 158) which would further harm the Church by discrediting its helpless hierarchy. He accuses Solzhenitsyn of attempting to coerce the Church leaders into sacrifice and martyrdom, and concludes: "We must accept *reality:* the hierarchy of the Russian Church cannot, within the given system, influence this system in any tangible way. It is very easy and safe, Aleksandr Isaevich, to criticize the bishops, but truly difficult is genuine work for the Lord. The fate of the Russian Church is inseperably tied to the fate of the people. 'If there will be a future,' then there will be—there will be without fail—a rebirth of Russian Christianity" (p. 158).

Solzhenitsyn's response to Zheludkov is dated April 28. It is quoted here in full:

> Dear Fr. Sergii:
>
> You also surprised me. "If there will be a future," you say. And we ourselves, are we to do anything? Is that what Christ taught? It is precisely *inner* upholding of the faith that is lacking. That women after the age of 50 come to church is a virtue of women and not a merit of the Church. It is precisely *inner* steadfastness that has been lost, that's what is so ruinous. It has been lost most of all by the hierarchs, and the higher up—the more irretrievably.
>
> In this dilemma you missed the principal way out, the one to which I call: through *personal sacrifice* visibly to reeducate the surrounding world. "One person can do nothing," you say? Untrue. Everyone can, one person can. Did you know anything about me nine years ago? And now you lean in the opposite direction and assert that for me everything is "safe." How did this come about? That means there is a way, doesn't it? You may say that I was surrounded by the silent sympathy of many of my countrymen. But does the Church have less sympathy? Does not the Patriarch still have millions of believers?
>
> To *coerce* people into making sacrifices is of course wrong. But can't one *call* them to sacrifice? Why should you forbid *that* also?
>
> Respectfully,
>
> Solzhenitsyn

(Translated from *Vestnik* RSKhD, No. 103 [1972], p. 159).

ALEKSANDR SOLZHENITSYN

Nobel Lecture[1]

Just as the savage in bewilderment picks up . . . a strange object cast up by the sea? . . . something long buried in the sand?. . . a baffling object fallen from the sky?—intricately shaped, now glistening dully, now reflecting a brilliant flash of light—just as he turns it this way and that, twirls it, searches for a way to utilize it, seeks to find for it a suitable lowly application, all the while not guessing its higher function . . .

So we also, holding Art in our hands, confidently deem ourselves its masters; we boldly give it direction, bring it up to date, reform it, proclaim it, sell it for money, use it to please

---

TRANSLATOR'S NOTES

[1]The Nobel Prize for Literature was awarded to Solzhenitsyn on October 8, 1970. The citation reads: "For the ethical force with which he has pursued the indispensable traditions of Russian literature."

In a letter to the Swedish Academy in which Solzhenitsyn explained why he would be unable to attend the banquet held in his honor—there was a grave risk that he might not be allowed to return to his homeland—the writer promised to prepare his Nobel Lecture within six months from December 10, 1970. The text of the Lecture was released by the Nobel Foundation in August of 1972.

The translation follows the official text as published in *Les Prix Nobel en 1971* (Stockholm: Nobel Foundation, 1972), pp. 129-140. Solzhenitsyn's use of capitals for emphasis has been rendered by italics.

The translator gratefully acknowledges the helpful suggestions made by several friends and colleagues. Special thanks are due to John Dunlop and Michael Nicholson, who read the entire translation in draft form and offered numerous constructive criticisms. The responsibility for any errors or infelicities that remain is mine alone.

the powerful, divert it for amusement—all the way down to vaudeville songs and night-club acts—or else adapt it (with a muzzle or stick, whatever is handy) towards transient political or limited social needs. But art remains undefiled by our endeavors and the stamp of its origin remains unaffected: each time and in every usage it bestows upon us a portion of its mysterious inner light.

But can we encompass the *totality* of this light? Who would dare to say that he has *defined* Art? Or has enumerated all its aspects? Moreover, perhaps someone already did understand and did name them for us in the preceding centuries, but that could not long detain us: we listened briefly but took no heed; we discarded the words at once, hurrying—as always—to replace even the very best with something else, just so that it might be new. And when we are told the old once again, we won't even remember that we used to have it earlier.

One artist imagines himself the creator of an autonomous spiritual world; he hoists upon his shoulders the act of creating this world and of populating it, together with the total responsibility for it. But he collapses under the load, for no mortal genius can bear up under it, just as, in general, the man who declares himself the center of existence is unable to create a balanced spiritual system. And, if a failure befalls such a man, the blame is promptly laid to the chronic disharmony of the world, to the complexity of modern man's divided soul, or to the public's lack of understanding.

Another artist recognizes above himself a higher power and joyfully works as a humble apprentice under God's heaven, though graver and more demanding still is his responsibility for all he writes or paints—and for the souls which apprehend it. However, it was not he who created this world, nor does he control it; there can be no doubts about its foundations. It is merely given to the artist to sense more keenly than others the harmony of the world, the beauty and ugliness of man's role in it—and to vividly communicate this to mankind. Even amid failure and at the lower depths of existence—in poverty, in prison, and in illness, a sense of enduring harmony cannot abandon him.

But the very irrationality of art, its dazzling convolutions, its unforeseeable discoveries, its powerful impact on men—all this is too magical to be wholly accounted for by the artist's view of the world, by his intention, or by the work of his unworthy fingers.

Archeologists have yet to discover such an early stage of human existence when we possessed no art. In the twilight preceding the dawn of mankind we received it from Hands which we did not have a chance to see clearly. Neither had we time to ask: *why* this gift for us? how should we treat it?

All those prognosticators of the decay, degeneration, and death of art were wrong and will always be wrong. It shall be we who die; art will remain. And shall we even comprehend before our passing all of its aspects and the entirety of its purposes?

Not everything can be named. Some things draw us beyond words. Art can warm even a chilled and sunless soul to an exalted spiritual experience. Through art we occasionally receive—indistinctly, briefly—revelations the likes of which cannot be achieved by rational thought.

It is like that small mirror of legend: you look into it but instead of yourself you glimpse for a moment the Inaccessible, a realm forever beyond reach. And your soul begins to ache...

2

Dostoevsky once let drop an enigmatic remark: "Beauty will save the world."[2] What is this? For a long time it seemed to me simply a phrase. How could this be possible? When in the blood-thirsty process of history did beauty ever save anyone, and from what? Granted, it ennobled, it elevated—but whom did it ever save?

There is, however, a particular feature in the very essence of beauty—a characteristic trait of art itself: the persuasiveness of a true work of art is completely irrefutable; it prevails even over a resisting heart. A political speech, an aggressive piece of journalism, a program for the organization of society, or a philosophical system can all be constructed—with apparent smoothness and harmony—on an error or on a lie. What is hidden and what is distorted will not be discerned right away. But then a contrary speech, journalistic piece, program, or a differently structured philosophy comes forth to join the argument, and everything is again just as smooth and harmonious, and again everything fits. And so they inspire trust—and distrust.

In vain does one repeat, what the heart does not find sweet.[3]

[2]These words are ascribed to Prince Myshkin by Ippolit in Dostoevsky's novel *The Idiot* (1868), Part III, Ch. 5.

[3]Russian proverb.

But a true work of art carries its verification within itself: artificial and forced concepts do not survive their trial by images; both image and concept crumble and turn out feeble, pale, and unconvincing. However, works which have drawn on the truth and which have presented it to us in concentrated and vibrant form seize us, attract us to themselves powerfully, and no one ever—even centuries later—will step forth to deny them.

So perhaps the old tri-unity of Truth, Goodness, and Beauty is not simply the decorous and antiquated formula it seemed to us at the time of our self-confident materialistic youth. If the tops of these three trees do converge, as thinkers used to claim, and if the all too obvious and the overly straight sprouts of Truth and Goodness have been crushed, cut down, or not permitted to grow, then perhaps the whimsical, unpredictable and ever surprising shoots of Beauty will force their way through and soar up to *that very spot,* thereby fulfilling the task of all three?

And then no slip of the tongue but a prophecy would be contained in Dostoevsky's words: "Beauty will save the world." For it was given to *him* to see many things; he had astonishing flashes of insight.

Could not then art and literature in a very real way offer succor to the modern world?

Today I shall attempt to set forth those few aspects of this problem which I have been able to discern over the years.

3

To have mounted this rostrum from which the Nobel Lecture is delivered—a platform placed at the disposal of but few writers and then only once in a lifetime—I have climbed not the three or four attached steps, but hundreds and even thousands of them, with almost no toe hold, steep, and covered with ice, leading out of the darkness and cold where it had been my fate to survive while others—perhaps more gifted and stronger than I—perished. Only a few of them did I meet in the "Gulag Archipelago," scattered as it was into a multitude of islands.[4] But under the burden of surveillance and mistrust I could not say much to most of them; of some I only heard;

[4] "Gulag" is an acronym for "*G*lavnoe *u*pravlenie ispravitel'no-trudovykh *lag*erei" [Main Administration of Corrective-Labor Camps]. The image of an archipelago is suggested by the huge empire of dispersed and isolated prison-camps, united under a single administration.

of still others I could only guess. Those who vanished into this abyss when they had already earned a literary reputation are at least known; but how many there were who had not yet been recognized, who had never been publicly named! And almost no one managed to return. An entire national literature remains there, buried without a coffin, even without underwear—naked, with only an identifying tag on one toe. Not for a moment did Russian literature cease! Yet from the outside it seemed a wasteland. Where a congenial forest might have stood there remained after all the felling but two or three trees overlooked by chance.

And today, accompanied by the shades of the fallen, as with bowed head I permit others who were worthy earlier to precede me to this platform—how am I today to surmise and to express what *they* would have wished to say?

This duty has long weighed upon us and we knew it all along. In the words of Vladimir Solov'ev:

> Even in chains we must ourselves complete
> That orbit which the gods have traced for us.[5]

In the midst of exhausting prison-camp relocations, marching in a column of prisoners in the gloom of bitterly cold evenings, with strings of camp lights glimmering through the darkness, we would often feel rising in our breast what we would have wanted to shout out to the whole world—if only the whole world could have heard any one of us. It all seemed very clear then: just what our fortunate messenger would say and how the world would at once respond in turn. Our field of vision was then filled with distinct physical objects and clear psychological motivations; an unambiguous world seemed to contain nothing which could prevail against this vision. These thoughts came not from books and were not borrowed for their appearance's sake: they were forged in prison cells and around bonfires in the forest, in conversation with people now dead; they were tested by *that* life and it is *from there* that they arose.

But when the external pressures had fallen off, our field of vision grew broader, and gradually, even if only through a tiny crack, that "whole world" became visible and understandable. To our amazement the "whole world" turned out to be quite different from what we had hoped, it was not living by the

[5]See Vladimir Solov'ev, *Stikhotvoreniia i shutochnye p'esy,* 7th ed. (Moscow, 1922; Reprinted, Munich: Wilhelm Fink, 1968), p. 61.

"right" values, nor was it headed in the "right" direction; it was a world which upon seeing a slimy bog exclaimed: "What a charming meadow!" and of a concrete pillory said: "What an exquisite necklace!" Where some were shedding tears that could not be wiped away, there others danced to the tune of a carefree musical.

How did this happen? Why this yawning chasm? Were we insensible? Or is the world? Or is this due to a difference in languages? Why are people who address each other sometimes incapable of making out distinct speech? Words ring out and fade away, they flow off like water—leaving no taste, no color, no smell. No trace.

As I came to understand this more and more over the years, a succession of changes was introduced into the structure, meaning, and tone of my projected speech. Today's speech.

And it now bears little resemblance to the one first conceived on those icy evenings in the prison camp.

4

Man has from the beginning been so constituted that his view of the world (if it is not induced by hypnosis), his motivations and scale of values, his actions and his intentions are all defined by his experience as an individual and as a member of a group. In the words of the Russian proverb: "Your brother, he might lie; trust instead your own bad eye." This is the soundest of bases for understanding one's environment and for acting in it. And for many long centuries, while our world was completely and mysteriously dispersed—before it was interlaced by unbroken lines of communication and turned into a single feverishly throbbing mass—people were unfailingly guided by their own experience within their own circumscribed locality, within their community, within their society, and finally within their national territory. At that time it was possible for the individual human eye to see and accept a certain common scale of values: what was considered average, what unbelievable; what was cruel, what was beyond villainy; what constituted honesty, and what deceit. And even though the scattered nations lived quite differently, and the scales of their social values could diverge as strikingly as their systems of measurement, these discrepancies astonished only the infrequent wayfarer or turned up as curiosities in magazines. They held no danger for humanity, which was not yet united.

But in the course of the last few decades, humanity has imperceptibly and suddenly become united—a unity fraught with hope and with danger—so that shocks or inflammations in one part are instantly passed on to the other portions—some of which may well lack the appropriate immunity. Humanity has become one, but it is not the stable undividedness of a former community or even that of a nation. It is a unity achieved not by means of gradually acquired experience, not from the *eye,* affably referred to as "bad" in the proverb, not even through a common native language; but rather—surmounting all barriers—this is unity brought about by international radio and the press. Onrushing waves of events bear down upon us: half the world learns in one minute of what is splashed ashore. But lacking are the scales or yardsticks to measure these events and to evaluate them according to the laws of the parts of the world unfamiliar to us. Such scales are not, nor can they be, carried to us through the ether or on sheets of newsprint: these scales of values have been settling into place and have been assimilated for too long a time and in too unique a fashion in the particular lives of specific countries and societies; they cannot be transmitted on the wing. In each region men apply to events their own particular hard-won scale of values; intransigently and self-confidently, they judge by their own scale and by no other.

There are perhaps not multitudes of such different yardsticks in the world, but certainly several: a scale for close-by events and a scale for far-off ones; the scale used by old societies and that used by new ones; the scale of the well-off and that of the unfortunate. The gradations on the various scales diverge drastically, their kaleidoscopic variety makes our eyes smart. To prevent discomfort, we dismiss all alien scales out of hand, as if they were madness and error, and we confidently judge the whole world according to our own homegrown scale. Thus we perceive as more significant, more painful and more intolerable not those conditions which are indeed all of these things—but those which are closer to us. But everything that is far away and does not threaten—today—to surge up to our doorsill, we accept—with all its groans, stifled shouts, destroyed lives, and even its millions of victims—as being on the whole quite bearable and of tolerable dimensions.

In one region not so long ago hundreds of thousands of voiceless Christians laid down their lives for their faith in God amid a persecution that yielded nothing to that of ancient Rome.[6] In another hemisphere a certain madman (and he is undoubtedly not alone) speeds across an ocean in order to *free* us from religion with a blade-thrust aimed at the Pontiff. He deduced this from his own scale of values for the benefit of us all.[7]

What according to one scale—from afar—seems an enviable and contented freedom, is perceived according to another scale—close at hand—as galling coercion which calls for buses to be overturned. What in one land would be dreamed of as an improbable level of well-being—in another land provokes resentment as a barbaric exploitation demanding an immediate strike. Different also are the scales for evaluating natural disasters: a flood with two hundred thousand victims seems less important than a minor incident in our home town. There are different scales for assessing personal insult: in one place an ironical smile or a disdainful gesture can humiliate, in others even a cruel beating can be forgiven as a bad joke. There are different scales for punishment and for wrong-doing: according to one, a month-long detention, a banishment to the countryside, or "solitary" with white rolls and milk—all stagger the imagination and fill columns of newsprint with wrath. But according to another scale it is both commonplace and forgiveable to have prison sentences of twenty-five years, punishment cells with ice on the walls where the prisoners are stripped to their undearwear, insane asylums for normal persons,[8] and shootings at the border of countless unreasonable people who for some reason keep trying to flee somewhere. Our heart is

[6]For a detailed scholarly account of the massive persecution of religion in Soviet Russia, see Nikita Struve, *Christians in Contemporary Russia* (New York: Scribner, 1967).

[7]On November 27, 1970, Pope Paul VI was attacked at the Manila airport by Benjamin Mendoza y Amor Flores, a Bolivian national. Disguised as a priest, Mendoza lunged at the Pope with a long knife, but was disarmed and arrested. In an interview after his arrest, Mendoza said he had attempted to "save the people from hypocricy and superstitution." See *The New York Times,* Nov. 27, 1970, p. 1.

[8]On the practice of confining Soviet political dissenters to psychiatric prison-hospitals, see *The Abuse of Psychiatry for Political Repression in the Soviet Union,* a collection of materials assembled for a hearing of a subcommittee of the U.S. Senate Committee on the Judiciary, held on September 26, 1972. (Available from Superintendent of Documents, U.S. Government Printing Office, Stock No. 5270-01653).

especially at ease about that exotic land about which we know nothing whatsoever, from which no tidings ever reach our ears with the exception of some belated and hackneyed conjectures from a few correspondents.

This double vision, this torpid inability to understand someone else's distant grief should not be blamed on human eyesight: man is simply built that way. But for mankind as a whole, compressed as it is into a single mass, such a mutual lack of understanding threatens to bring on quick and violent extinction. Given six, four or even two scales of values there cannot be a unified world, a united humanity. We shall be torn apart by this difference in rhythm, the divergence in frequency of oscillation. We could not manage to survive on one Earth, just as a man with two hearts is not long for this world.

5

But who will reconcile these scales of values and how? Who is going to give mankind a single system of evaluation for evil deeds and for good ones, for unbearable things and for tolerable ones—as we differentiate them today? Who will elucidate for mankind what really is burdensome and unbearable and what merely chafes the skin due to its proximity? Who will direct man's anger toward that which is more fearsome rather than toward that which is closer at hand? Who could convey this understanding across the barriers of his own human experience? Who could impress upon a sluggish and obstinate human being someone else's far-off sorrows or joys, who could give him an insight into magnitudes of events and into delusions which he has never himself experienced? Propaganda, coercion, and scientific proof are all equally powerless here. But fortunately there does exist a means to this end in the world! It is art. It is literature.

They both hold the key to a miracle: to overcome man's ruinous habit of learning only from his own experience, so that the experience of others passes him by without profit. Making up for man's scant time on earth, art transmits between men the entire accumulated load of another being's life experience, with all its hardships, colors, and juices. It recreates—life-like—the experience of other men, so that we can assimilate it as our own.

But even more, much more than this: countries and entire

continents continually repeat each other's mistakes with a time-lag—occasionally one of centuries—when, it would seem, everything is so very clear. But no: what one people has already endured, appraised, and rejected, suddenly emerges among another people as the very latest word. Here once again the sole substitute for an experience which we have not ourselves lived through is art and literature. Both are endowed with the miraculous power to communicate—despite differences in language, custom, and social structure—the experience of the entire nation to another nation which has not undergone such a difficult decades-long collective experience. In a fortunate instance, this could save an entire nation from a redundant, or erroneous, or even destructive course, thereby shortening the tortuous paths of human history.

It is this great and blessed property of art to which I resolutely wish to call attention today from this Nobel platform.[9]

There is one other invaluable direction in which literature transmits incontrovertible condensed experience: from generation to generation. In this way literature becomes the living memory of a nation. It sustains within itself and safeguards a nation's bygone history—in a form which cannot be distorted or falsified. In this way does literature together with language preserve the national soul.

(It has lately been fashionable to speak of the levelling of nations, of the disappearance of individual peoples in the melting-pot of modern civilization. I disagree, but a discussion of this problem would be a theme in itself. It is here appropriate to say only that the disappearance of nations would impoverish us not less than if all men should become alike, with one personality and one face. Nations are the wealth of mankind, its generalized personalities; the least among them has its own unique coloration and harbors within itself a unique facet of God's design.)

---

[9]Solzhenitsyn's ringing assertion of the role of art in helping to create a common scale of values for mankind may have been intended—at least in part—as the writer's response to an international conference (sponsored by the Nobel Foundation) devoted to the problem of values in the modern world. See *The Place of Value in a World of Facts: Proceedings of the Fourteenth Nobel Symposium, Stockholm, September 15-20, 1969,* ed. Arne Tiselius and Sam Nilsson (New York: Wiley; Stockholm: Almqvist and Wiksell, 1970). The summarizing statement of the conferees to the Nobel Foundation begins: "A human society without a system of values shared by its members is highly unstable . . ." (p. 493).

But woe to that nation whose literature is cut short by the intrusion of force. This is not merely interference with "freedom of the press" but the sealing up of a nation's heart, the excision of its memory. A nation can no longer remember itself, it loses its spiritual unity, and despite their seemingly common language, countrymen cease to understand one another. Mute generations live out their lives and die, without giving an account of their experiences either to themselves or to their descendants. When such literary masters as Akhmatova or Zamiatin are walled up for their entire lives, condemned till the grave to create in silence and unable to hear any echoes to their work—then this is not only their personal misfortune, but a calamity for the whole nation, a menace to it.[10]

And in some cases this could even be a grievous misfortune for the whole of humanity: whenever such silence causes all of *history* to become incomprehensible.

6

At various times and in various countries there have been heated, angry, and refined polemics about whether art and the artist should live for their own sake or whether they must always keep in mind their duty towards society and serve it, albeit without bias. For me the answer is obvious, but I shall not once again rehearse the long train of arguments. One of the most brilliant statements on this theme was Albert Camus' Nobel lecture, and I happily join in his conclusions.[11] Indeed, Russian literature has for decades been disinclined to engage in

[10]Anna Akhmatova (1889-1966), one of the finest Russian poets of the twentieth century, was viciously denounced in a notorious policy speech by Andrei Zhdanov in 1946. She was expelled from the Writers' Union and slowly made her way back into literature only in the post-Stalin era. Akhmatova was a warm admirer of Solzhenitsyn's early works.

Evgenii Zamiatin (1884-1937), prose writer, dramatist, and master stylist, is best known as the author of the brilliant anti-Utopian novel *We* (1921), which remains unpublished in the Soviet Union. Subjected to increasingly hostile criticism in the Soviet press and eventually deprived of the ability to publish, Zamiatin resigned in protest from the All-Russian Writers' Association in 1929. In 1931 he successfully petitioned Stalin for the right to emigrate. Zamiatin's works have not been published in the Soviet Union since 1930.

[11]Camus received the Nobel Prize for Literature in 1957. In his acceptance speech, Camus thus formulated the obligations of the writer: "Whatever our personal weaknesses may be, the nobility of our craft will always be rooted in two commitments difficult to maintain: the refusal to lie about what one knows and the resistance to oppression." See *Nobel Lectures: Literature (1901-1967)*, ed. by Horst Frenz (Amsterdam: Elsevier, 1969), p. 525.

excessive self-contemplation, or in flitting about in too carefree a manner—and I am not ashamed to continue this tradition to the best of my ability. Through Russian literature we have long ago grown familiar with the concept that a writer can do much among his people—and that he must.

We shall not trample on the *right* of an artist to express nothing but his personal experiences and his self-observations while disregarding all that occurs in the rest of the world. We shall not make *demands* on him—but surely we can be permitted to reproach him, beg him, call him, or beckon to him. After all, an artist develops his gift only partially by himself; the greater part has been breathed into him ready-made at birth. And together with this talent, a responsibility has been imposed upon his free will. Granted, an artist does not *owe* anything to anyone, but it is painful to see how, by withdrawing into self-created worlds or into the realms of subjective whim, he *can* surrender the real world into the hands of profit-seekers, of non-entities, or even of madmen.

This twentieth century of ours has proved to be crueler than its predecessors, and its horrors have not been exhausted with the end of its first half. The same old atavistic urges—greed, envy, unrestrained passion, and mutual hostility—readily picking up respectable pseudonyms like class, race, mass, or trade union struggle, claw at and tear apart our world. A primitive rejection of all compromise is given the status of a theoretical principle and is regarded as the high virtue which accompanies doctrinal purity. This attitude creates millions of victims in ceaseless civil wars, it drones into our souls that there exist no lasting concepts of good and justice valid for all mankind, that all such concepts are fluid and ever-changing—which is why you should always act in a way that benefits your party. Any professional group, at the first opportunity to *get their hand on something extra*—though unearned and even unneeded—grabs it, and the rest of society be damned. As seen from the outside, the careening fluctuations of Western society seem to be approaching that amplitude beyond which a system becomes metastable and must disintegrate. Less and less restrained by the confines of long-established legality, violence strides brazenly and triumphantly through the world, unconcerned that its futility has already been demonstrated and proven many times in history. It is not even brute force alone that is victorious, but also its clamorous justification: the world is being flooded by the brazen conviction that force can do all, and righteousness—nothing. Dostoevsky's *Devils,* who had seemed part of a provincial nightmarish fantasy of the last century, are now infesting the world before our eyes, reaching lands where they could not earlier have even been imagined.[12] And now, by the hijacking of airplanes, by the seizing of *hostages,* by the explosions and conflagrations of recent years, they signal their determination to shake civilization to its roots and to bring it down. And they may well succeed. Today's youth, at an age when they have not yet had any experience except sex, before they have lived through their own years of suffering and reached their own personal understanding—these young people enthusiastically mouth the discredited clichés of the Russian nineteenth century, thinking that they are uncovering something new. The recently-manifested degradation of human beings into non-entities as practiced by the Chinese Red Guards is taken as a joyous model by the young. What shallow lack of understanding of timeless human nature, what naive confidence of inexperienced hearts: "We'll just oust *these* vicious, greedy oppressors and rulers, and those next in charge (that's us!), having put aside grenades and submachine guns, will be compassionate and just." Some chance indeed! . . . And yet among those who have seen life, who do understand, and who could refute these young people—many *do not dare* to do so. They even assume fawning attitudes, just so as not to seem "conservative." This once again is a Russian nineteenth-century phenomenon; Dostoevsky called it *subservience to progressive little notions.*

The spirit of Munich has by no means retreated into the past, it was no short-lived episode. I would even dare to claim that the spirit of Munich dominates the twentieth century. A timorous civilized world, faced with the onslaught of a suddenly revived and snarling barbarism, has found nothing to oppose it with except concessions and smiles. The spirit of Munich is a malady of the will of affluent people; it is the chronic state of those who have abandoned themselves to a pursuit of prosperity at any price, who have succumbed to a belief in material well-being as the principal goal of life on earth. Such people—and there are many in today's world—choose passivity and retreat, just so long as their accustomed life can be made to last a little longer, just so long as the

[12]Dostoevsky's 1871 novel *The Devils* (the title is frequently translated as *The Possessed*) depicts a group of fanatical and morally corrupt revolutionaries.

transition to hardship can be put off for another day; and tomorrow—who knows?—everything may turn out to be all right . . . (But it never will! The price paid for cowardice will only be the more exorbitant. Courage and victory come to us only when we are resolved to make sacrifices.)

We are also threatened by destruction from another quarter: our physically compressed and cramped world is restrained from merging spiritually; molecules of knowledge and sympathy are prevented from leaping from one half to the other. This *blockage of information flow* between parts of the planet is a mortal danger. Modern science knows that the blockage of information is the way of entropy and of general destruction.[13] Information blockage renders illusory international agreements and treaties: within the *isolated* zone there is nothing easier than to reinterpret any treaty or simply to forget it as if it had never existed (Orwel understood this well[14]). This isolated zone seems to be inhabited not by earthlings but by some expeditionary force from Mars; these people know nothing about the rest of

---

[13]Entropy in the physical sciences is a measure of the degree of disorder or randomness in a given system; it also measures the energy of a system which has permanently ceased to be available. In any process that involves the exchange of energy, entropy increases. Thus it is said that entropy measures the "running down" or "decay" of any closed system.

This concept is also applied in information theory. Information is ordering—the opposite of randomness and entropy. Solzhenitsyn is saying that the cut-off in the influx of new information into a system will lead to an increase of disorder and entropy. Solzhenitsyn has touched on the theme of the vital necessity of unrestricted communication at some length in his play *A Candle in the Wind* (1960). In Scene IV, the scientist Terbol'm demonstrates to the hero an electronic machine that serves as a socio-cybernetic model:

TERBOL'M. Take the brain, for example. *(The lights dim. A model becomes visible: it is a sphere covered with glowing pin-points of light which are constantly varying in intensity. The interior of the sphere is dark.)* Between the cells there is communication. *(Lively threads of light flicker on and off, cutting across the interior space of the sphere.)* This unrestrained communication alone permits an organism to survive—to resist external destructive phenomena and to recuperate after injury. But if this communication flow is cruelly restricted *(on the model all the pin-points and threads of light freeze in one position),* then all development stops and life itself is threatened. *(The model falls dark. Lights.)* In the same way a society must be able to survive destructive events: droughts, epidemics, earthquakes, economic stagnation, financial collapse, war . . .

GENERAL. . . . Revolution . . .

TERBOL'M. From all this one must emerge restored and capable of further development. For this, society needs only unimpeachable information, coordination, and feedback. (Translated from Solzhenitsyn, *Sobranie sochinenii* V, 173.)

[14]See for example Orwell's description of the way the past is manipulated in Oceania: *1984,* Part I, Ch. 3-4.

the Earth and are ready to trample it underfoot in the solemn belief that they are "liberating" it.

A quarter of a century ago the United Nations Organization was born amid the great hopes of mankind. But alas, in an immoral world it too grew up without morality. It is not a United Nations Organization but a United Governments Organization, where governments freely elected are equated with regimes imposed by force or with those that have gained control by an armed seizure of power. By dint of the self-interested bias of the majority of its members, the UN jealously guards the freedom of certain peoples and completely neglects the freedom of others. Through an obeisant vote it has rejected the investigation of *private grievances*—the moans, cries and entreaties of humble individual *mere people,* who were judged entities just too miniscule for such a great organization.[15] Its best document in the twenty-five years of its existance—the Universal Declaration of Human Rights—the UN has not taken the trouble to make *mandatory* for its member governments, a *condition* of membership—and has thereby abandoned little people to the mercy of governments they did not elect.

One might have thought that the structure of the modern world be entirely in the hands of scientists, since it is they who decide all the technical steps of mankind. One might have thought that the direction in which the world is to move would

[15]Solzhenitsyn is undoubtedly referring here to a series of incidents that occurred in 1969. In May, a group of Soviet citizens wrote an appeal to the UN Commission on Human Rights, protesting the imprisonment and persecution of Soviet dissidents. The employees of the UN Information Center in Moscow refused to accept the letter on the grounds that they could not accept appeals from private individuals. The petition reached the West by other channels and received world-wide publicity. A great number of the signers were subsequently arrested. Nevertheless, a new appeal was handed to the UN Information Center in Moscow on September 26. It was again refused, first on a technicality, and then on the grounds that the center "was not competent" to forward a petition that was in violation of Paragraph 7 of Article 2 of the UN Charter. (This paragraph reads, in part: "Nothing contained in the present Charter shall authorize the United Nations to intervene in matters which are essentially within the domestic jurisdiction of any state . . .")

On October 2, the UN Office of Public Information ruled that the Moscow office had been correct in its action; an internal memo directed the UN's information centers around the world to henceforth refuse to accept private appeals. See *The New York Times,* Oct. 4, 1969, p. 1, which reported that "it is general knowledge that the order was given to avoid possible friction with the Soviet government over forwarding of unauthorized messages."

This series of events was reported in detail in the clandestine Soviet periodical *The Chronicle of Current Events,* Nos. 8-11. See Peter Reddaway, ed., *Uncensored Russia* (New York: American Heritage, 1972), pp. 150-170.

be determined by a world-wide concord of scientists, not of politicians. All the more so since the example of individuals demonstrates how much ground they could gain if only they joined forces. But no, scientists have made no explicit attempts to become an important independently-motivated force within mankind. Entire congresses of them back away from the suffering of others: it is cozier to remain within the limits of science. The same spirit of Munich has spread its enervating wings over them.

What, then—in this cruel, dynamic, explosive world which totters on the brink of destruction—what *is* the place and role of the writer? We do not, after all, send up rockets, we don't even push the meanest of supply carts. Indeed, we are held in total contempt by those who respect material might alone. Would it not be natural for us also to retreat, to lose faith in the unshakable nature of goodness, in the indivisible nature of truth? Should not we merely recite to the world our bitter but detached observations about how hopelessly warped mankind is, how shallow people have become, and how burdensome it is for a lone refined and beautiful soul to dwell among them?

But even this escape is not open to us. Once we have taken up the *word,* it is thereafter impossible to turn away: a writer is no detached judge of his countrymen and contemporaries; he is an accomplice to all the evil committed in his country or by his people. And if the tanks of his fatherland have bloodied the pavement of a foreign capital, then rust-colored stains have forever bespattered the writer's face. And if on some fateful night a trusting Friend is strangled in his sleep—then the palms of the writer bear the bruises from that rope. And if his youthful fellow citizens nonchalantly proclaim the advantages of debauchery over humble toil, if they abandon themselves to drugs, or seize *hostages*—then this stench too is mingled with the breath of the writer.

Have we the insolence to declare that we do not answer for the evils of today's world?

7

But I am encouraged by a vivid sense of *world literature* as one great heart which beats for the cares and woes of our world, though each of these is manifested and perceived in its own way in its separate corner of the globe.

Apart from the well-established tradition of national literatures, there has long existed the concept of world literature. It was traditionally seen as a curve enveloping the peaks of the national literatures and as the sum total of all literary influences. But there were time-lags: readers and writers discovered foreign authors with a delay, occasionally one of centuries. As a result, mutual influences were held back and the curve encompassing the national literary high-points was discerned only by posterity, not by contemporaries.

But today there exists an interaction between the writers of one land and the writers and readers of other lands which, though not immediate, is close to it; I can vouch for this myself. My books—unpublished, alas, in my own country—have in spite of hasty and often poor translations rapidly acquired a responsive world readership. Such outstanding Western writers as Heinrich Böll have devoted critical analyses to them. Throughout these last years, when my work and my freedom did not collapse, when they seemed to hang in mid air in violation of the laws of gravity, seemingly supported by *nothing at all*—except the invisible and mute tension of the cohesive film of public sympathy—all those years I have gratefully and quite unexpectedly come to know the support of the world-wide brotherhood of writers. On my fiftieth birthday I was astounded to receive congratulations from well-known European writers. No pressure upon me could any longer pass unnoticed. In the hazardous weeks when I was being expelled from the Union of Writers, the *protective wall* erected by the writers of the world saved me from worse persecution, while Norwegian writers and artists hospitably readied a shelter for me in case the threatened banishment from my homeland should occur. Finally, my very nomination for the Nobel Prize was initiated not in the country where I live and work, but by François Mauriac and his colleagues. And more recently still, entire organizations of national writers have expressed their support for me.

And so I came to understand through my own experience that world literature is no longer an abstract enveloping curve, no longer a generalization coined by literary scholars, but a kind of collective body and a common spirit, a living unity of the heart which reflects the growing spiritual unity of mankind. Borders of states continue to turn crimson, heated to a red glow by electrified wire and by bursts of machine-gun fire. Certain ministries of internal affairs continue to believe that literature too is an "internal affair" of the countries over which they claim jurisdiction. Newspapers continue to display banner headlines: "They have no right to interfere in our internal affairs!" But in the meanwhile—all *internal affairs* have ceased to exist on our crowded Earth! The salvation of mankind lies only in making everything the concern of all. People in the East should without exception be concerned with what people are thinking in the West; people in the West should without exception care about what is happening in the East. Literature, one of the most sophisticated and sensitive instruments available to human beings, has been one of the first to pick up, to assimilate, and to join in expressing this feeling of the growing unity of mankind. And I here confidently address myself to the world literature of today—to the hundreds of friends whom I have never met in person and whom I perhaps may never see.

Friends! Let us try to help if we are worth anything at all! Who in our various countries—torn as they are by the tumultuous discord of parties, movements, castes, and groups—who is it that from the beginning has been not a divisive force but a unifying one? That, in essence, is the role of writers: they are the articulators of the national tongue (that main tie which holds a nation together) and of the very land inhabited by a people; in fortunate instances, they give expression to the national soul.

I believe that world literature is fully capable of helping a troubled humanity to recognize its true self in spite of what is advocated by biased individuals and parties. World literature is capable of transmitting the concentrated experience of a particular region to other lands so that we can overcome double vision and kaleidoscopic variety, so that one people can discover, accurately and concisely, the true history of another people, with all the force of recognition and the pain that comes from actual experience—and can thus be safeguarded from belated errors. And at the same time we ourselves shall perhaps be able to develop a *world vision:* focusing on what is close at hand with the center of our eye—just like everyone else—we shall begin to use our peripheral vision to take in what occurs in the rest of the world. And we shall proceed to make correlations, adhering to a world-wide standard.

Who else but writers shall condemn their incompetent rulers (in some states this is in fact the easiest way to earn a living; it is done by anyone who feels the urge), who else shall censure their respective societies—be it for cowardly submission or for self-satisfied weakness—as well as the witless excesses of the young and the youthful pirate with knives upraised?

We shall be told: what can literature do in the face of a remorseless assault of open violence? But let us not forget that violence does not and cannot exist by itself: it is invariably interwined with *the lie.* They are linked in the most intimate, most organic and profound fashion: violence cannot conceal itself behind anything except lies, and lies have nothing to maintain them save violence. Anyone who has once proclaimed violence as his *method* must inexorably choose the lie as his *principle.* At birth, violence acts openly and even takes pride in itself. But as soon as it gains strength and becomes firmly established, it begins to sense the air around it growing thinner; it can no longer exist without veiling itself in a mist of lies, without concealing itself behind the sugary words of falsehood. No longer does violence always and necessarily lunge straight for your throat; more often than not it demands of its subjects only that they pledge allegiance to lies, that they participate in falsehood.

The simple act of an ordinary brave man is not to participate in lies, not to support false actions! His rule: let *that* come into the world, let it even reign supreme—only not through me. But it is within the power of writers and artists to do much more: *to defeat the lie!* For in the struggle with lies art has always triumphed and shall always triumph! Visibly, irrefutably for all! Lies can prevail against much in this world, but never against art.

And no sooner will the lies be dispersed than the repulsive nakedness of violence will be exposed—and age-old violence will topple in defeat.

This is why I believe, my friends, that we are capable of helping the world in its hour of crisis. We should not seek to justify our unwillingness by our lack of weapons, nor should we give ourselves up to a life of comfort. We must come out and join the battle!

The favorite proverbs in Russian are about *truth.* They forcefully express a long and difficult national experience, sometimes in striking fashion:

One word of truth shall outweigh the whole world.

It is on such a seemingly fantastic violation of the law of conservation of mass and energy that my own activity is based, and my appeal to the writers of the world.

Translated by Alexis Klimoff

DOCUMENTARY MATERIALS

Bibliographic Surveys

Aleksandr Solzhenitsyn: A Bibliography of Responses in the Official Soviet Press from November 1962 to April 1973

BY MICHAEL NICHOLSON

The following bibliography comprises:

1. A numbered, chronological list of references, briefly annotated to indicate theme and length. Books and annuals appear at the end of the list for the appropriate year. In the case of longer articles, the pages referred to are, wherever possible, those on which Solzhenitsyn is actually mentioned.
2. An alphabetical index of authors of articles, or of statements within articles.
3. A brief subject index, giving a selection of items on individual works by Solzhenitsyn, and on episodes in his career.

Many of the articles from the provincial press which are included here are unobtainable outside the Soviet Union, and sometimes even within it. The designation [*Letopis'*] indicates an item taken from standard Soviet listings of periodical articles (see List of Abbreviations) which it has proved impossible to check against the original. Items marked [*Slovo*] were published in the Soviet press, usually in obscure publications; they appear, in whole or in excerpt, in the *samizdat* collection of materials on Solzhenitsyn, *Slovo probivaet sebe dorogu* [*The Word Carves Its Own Way*], copies of which have reached the West. Such items could not be checked against their originals, but the compilation has proved itself to be generally reliable in the case of articles which can be cross-checked. It has not yet been published, although individual items have appeared in print, and it was evidently used in the preparation of the volume, *Soljénitsyne,* edited by G. Nivat and M. Aucouturier (Paris: L'Herne, 1971). A very few items have been included which, while not published in the Soviet Union, bear directly upon the Soviet press treatment of Solzhenitsyn.

The listing of English translations is not meant to be exhaustive, but is restricted to items published in *Current Digest of the Soviet Press, Current Abstracts of the Soviet Press,* and *Digest of the Soviet Ukrainian Press.*

I should like to express my gratitude to Nick Anning, Martin Dewhirst, G. S. Smith and Victor Swoboda for their generous assistance in the compilation of this bibliography, and also to A. Artemova, who kindly permitted me to use item No. 71, which appears in her bibliography for the forthcoming expanded edition of volume VI of Posev's *Sobranie sochinenii.*

List of Abbreviations

CDSP	Current Digest of the Soviet Press
Current Abstracts	Current Abstracts of the Soviet Press
Izv.	Izvestiia
Kom.	Kommunist
Koms. pr.	Komsomol'skaia pravda
Letopis'	Letopis' gazetnykh statei Letopis' retsenzii Letopis' zhurnal'nykh statei
LG	Literaturnaia gazeta
LR	Literaturnaia Rossiia
NM	Novyi mir
Okt.	Oktiabr'
Pr.	Pravda
Slovo	Slovo probivaet sebe dorogu (*samizdat* collection of materials on Solzhenitsyn)
SR	Sovetskaia Rossiia

1962

November

[First publication of *One Day in the Life of Ivan Denisovich, NM* 11/1962.]

1 A. TVARDOVSKII, Vmesto predisloviia [In Place of a Foreword].
—Preface to *One Day.*
NM 11/1962, pp. 8-9.
Soviet Literature 2/1963, pp. 4-5 [as "By Way of Introduction"].

2 V. KOZHEVNIKOV, Molodye sily nashei literatury [Youthful Forces in Our Literature].
—Brief reference to *One Day.*
Kom. 17/1962, pp. 75-76.

3 K. SIMONOV, O proshlom vo imia budushchego [Concerning the Past in in the Name of the Future].
—On *One Day.*
Izv. 18 Nov. 1962.
CDSP XIV, No. 46.

4 G. BAKLANOV, Chtob eto nikogda ne povtorilos' [May This Never Happen Again].
—On *One Day.*
LG 22 Nov. 1962.
CDSP XIV, No. 45.

5 V. ERMILOV, Vo imia pravdy, vo imia zhizni [In the Name of Truth, in the Name of Life].
—On *One Day.*
Pr. 23 Nov. 1962.

6 P. KOSOLAPOV, Imia, novoe v nashei literature [A New Name in Our Literature].
—Biographical.
SR 28 Nov. 1962.

7 A. DYMSHITS, Zhiv chelovek [Man Survives].
—On *One Day.*
Literatura i zhizn' 28 Nov. 1962.

8 I. KASHNITSKII, "Odin den' Ivana Denisovicha" [*One Day in the Life of Ivan Denisovich*].
Sovetskaia Litva 30 Nov. 1962.

December

9 G. SKUL'SKII, Vsia pravda [The Whole Truth].
—On *One Day.*
Sovetskaia Estoniia 1 Dec. 1962.

10 I. KASHKADAMOV, Uchitel' s ulitsy Revoliutsii [A Teacher from Revolution Street].
—Biographical.
Uchitel'skaia gazeta 1 Dec. 1962.

11 E. BROIDO, Takomu bol'she nikogda ne byvat' [Such a Thing Will Never Happen Again].
—On *One Day.*
Poliarnaia pravda (Murmansk) 2 Dec. 1962. [*Slovo*]

12 N. KRUZHKOV, Tak bylo, tak ne budet [Thus It Was, Thus It Will Not Be].
—On *One Day.*
Ogonek 49/1962, pp. 28-29.

13 I. CHICHEROV, Vo imia budushchego [In the Name of the Future].
—On *One Day.*
Moskovskaia pravda 8 Dec. 1962.

14 V. LITVINOV, Da budet polnoi pravda [Let the Whole Truth Be Told].
—On *One Day.*
Trud 12 Dec. 1962.

15 L. AFONIN, Chtob vdal' gliadet' naverniaka . . . [To Look Unerringly into the Distance . . .]
—On *One Day.*
Orlovskaia pravda 14 Dec. 1962. [*Letopis'*]

16 A. SOFRONOV, Reflections on Alexander Solzhenitsyn's Story.
—On *One Day.*
Moscow News 15 Dec. 1962.

17 N. ZORIN, Pravda gor'kaia, no neobkhodimaia [A Bitter Truth, But an Essential One].
—On *One Day.*
Kuznetskii rabochii (Novokuznetsk) 15 Dec. 1962. [*Slovo*]

18 V. KAGAN, Da budet polnoi pravda [Let the Whole Truth Be Told].
—On *One Day.*
Kirovskii rabochii 16 Dec. 1962. [*Slovo*]

19 A. MAZUREVSKAIA, Surovaia pravda [The Grim Truth].
—On *One Day.*
Tuvinskaia pravda 16 Dec. 1962. [*Letopis'*]

20 L. TERAKOPIAN, Vremia, sobytiia, liudi [Time, Events, People].
—On *One Day.*
Gudok 16 Dec. 1962 [*Letopis'*]

21 A. ASTAF'EV, Solntsu ne prikazhesh' [The Sun Does Not Take Orders].
—On *One Day.*
Ul'ianovskaia pravda 18 Dec. 1962. [*Slovo*]

22 L. IL'ICHEV, Tvorit' dlia naroda, vo imia kommunizma [To Create for the People in the Name of Communism].
—Speech of 17 Dec. 1962 to a meeting of Party and Government leaders with representatives of the cultural world, including a brief reference to *One Day.*
LG 22 Dec. 1962.

23 V. ERMILOV, Besslavnyi polet "Slavik rev'iu" [Ignominious Flight of the *Slavic Review*].
—Brief reference to *One Day.*
Izv. 25 Dec. 1962.
CDSP XV, No. 1.

24 V. IL'ICHEV, Bol'shaia pravda [A Great Truth].
—On *One Day.*
Ural'skii rabochii 26 Dec. 1962. [*Letopis'*]

25 M. NOL'MAN, Schet tiazhkikh dnei [The Reckoning of Hard Days].
—On *One Day.*
Severnaia pravda (Kostroma) 29 Dec. 1962. [*Slovo*]

1963

January

["Incident at Krechetovka Station" and "Matrena's Home" published in *NM* 1/1963. Extracts from "Incident at Krechetovka Station" had previously appeared in *Pr.* 23 Dec. 1962].

26 F. KUZNETSOV, Den', ravnyi zhizni [A Day Equal to a Life].
—On *One Day.*
Znamia 1/1963, pp. 217-221.

27 G. BROVMAN, Traditsii i novatorstvo v literature nashikh dnei [Traditions and Innovation in the Literature of Our Times].
—Brief discussion of *One Day.*
Moskva 1/1963, p. 205.

28 F. CHAPCHAKHOV, Nomera i liudi [Numbers and People].
—On *One Day.*
Don 1/1963, pp. 155-159.

29 I. DRUTSE, O muzhestve i dostoinstve cheloveka [On the Courage and Dignity of Man].
—On *One Day.*
Druzhba narodov 1/1963, pp. 272-274. [*Slovo*]

30 M. KUZNETSOV, Chelovechnost'! [Humanity!]
—On *One Day.*
V mire knig 1/1963, pp. 26-27.

31 TVORIT' DLIA NARODA—VYSSHAIA TSEL' KHUDOZHNIKA [To Create for the People Is the Artists' Highest Goal].
—Brief reference to *One Day.*
Kom. 1/1963, p. 93.

32 F. SAMARIN, Tak ne budet! [Such a Thing Will Not Happen!]
—On *One Day.*
Penzenskaia pravda 5 Jan. 1963. [*Letopis'*]

33 L. IL'ICHEV, Sily tvorcheskoi molodezhi—na sluzhbu velikim idealam [The Power of Creative Youth in the Service of Great Ideals].
—Speech of 26 Dec. 1962 to a meeting of the Central Committee's Ideological Commission with young writers and artists, including a brief discussion of *One Day.*
LG 10 Jan. 1963.
Sovetskaia kul'tura 10 Jan. 1963.
CDSP XV, No. 2.

34 L. FOMENKO, Bol'shie ozhidaniia [Great Expectations].
—On *One Day,* with an editorial note.
LR 11 Jan. 1963.

35 G. LOMIDZE, Neskol'ko myslei [A Few Thoughts].
—On *One Day.*
LR 18 Jan. 1963.

36 V. SHCHERBINA, Geroicheskaia nravstvennost' [Heroic Morality].
—Brief reference to *One Day.*
Pr. 20 Jan. 1963.

37 G. MINAEV, V redaktsiiu "Literaturnoi gazety" [To the Editors of *Literaturnaia gazeta*].
—Letter on *One Day.*
LG 22 Jan. 1963.

38 V. BUKHANOV, U Solzhenitsyna v Riazani [Visiting Solzhenitsyn in Riazan'].
—Biographical.
LR 25 Jan. 1963.
Kommunist Tadzhikistana 30 Jan. 1963.
Sovetskaia Kirgiziia 31 Jan. 1963.
Sovetskaia Litva 31 Jan. 1963.
Moscow News 16 Feb. 1963, p. 12.

39 V. ERMILOV, Neobkhodimost' spora. Chitaia memuary I. Erenburga "Liudi, gody, zhizn'" [The Need for Debate. On Reading I. Erenburg's Memoirs, *People, Years, Life*].
—Brief discussion of *One Day.*
Izv. 30 Jan. 1963.
CDSP XV, No. 5.

February

40 E. VINOKUROV, Iskusstvo prinadlezhit narodu. Pisateli o traditsiiakh i novatorstve [Art Belongs to the People. Writers on Tradition and Innovation].
—Reply to a questionnaire, including a reference to Solzhenitsyn and the "Great Tradition."
Voprosy literatury 2/1963, p. 49.

41 A. EL'IASHEVICH, Vechnaia molodost' realizma [The Eternal Youthfulness of Realism].
—Brief reference to *One Day.*
LG 12 Feb. 1963.

42 L. VARLAMOV, Liudi bol'shoi sovesti [People of Great Conscience].
—On "Matrena's Home" and "Incident at Krechetovka Station."
Penzenskaia pravda 15 Feb. 1963. [*Letopis'*]

43 V. NOVIKOV, Sila pravdy [The Power of Truth].
—On *One Day.*
Kalininskaia pravda 27 Feb. 1963. [*Letopis'*]

March

44 V. BUSHIN, Nasushchnyi khleb pravdy [The Daily Bread of Truth].
—On *One Day.*
Neva 3/1963, pp. 180-185.

45 N. GUBKO, Chelovek pobezhdaet [Man Triumphs].
—On *One Day.*
Zvezda 3/1963, pp. 213-215.

46 V. KOZHEVNIKOV, Tovarishchi po bor'be [Companions in the Struggle].
—On "Matrena's Home."
LG 2 March 1963.

47 I. TROFIMOV, Den', kotoryi ne povtoritsia [A Day Which Will Not Recur].
—On *One Day.*
Tambovskaia pravda 3 March 1963. [*Letopis'*]

48 N. KHRUSHCHEV, Vysokaia ideinost' i khudozhestvennoe masterstvo . . . [High Ideological Content and Artistic Mastery . . .]
—Speech of 8 March 1963 to a meeting of Party and Government leaders with representatives of literature and the arts, including a brief reference to *One Day.*
Pr. 10 March 1963.
LG 12 March 1963.
CDSP XV, No. 10.

49 K. LAGUNOV, Vekhi v puti [Landmarks on the Way].
—On "Matrena's Home" and "Incident at Krechetovka Station."
Tiumenskaia pravda 17 March 1963. [*Slovo*]

50 S. BABAEVSKII, Partiia i literatura [The Party and Literature].
—Brief reference to "Matrena's Home."
Sovetskaia Kuban' (Krasnodar), 19 March 1963. [*Slovo*]

51 V. TEVEKELIAN, Speech reported under the heading: Sobranie aktiva pisatelei stolitsy [Gathering of the Vanguard of the Capital's Writers].
—Brief discussion of *One Day* and "Matrena's Home."
LG 19 March 1963.

52 V. PANKOV, Ot pervoi knigi—tol'ko vpered [From the First Book, Ever Onward].
—Unambiguous indirect reference to Solzhenitsyn as having been undeservedly praised by A. Makedonov at a meeting of literary critics.
Koms. pr. 21 March 1963.

53 S. PAVLOV, Tvorchestvo molodykh—sluzheniiu velikim idealam! [The Creativity of the Young Should Serve Great Ideals!]
—Brief reference to "Matrena's Home."
Koms. pr. 22 March 1963.

54 V. CHALMAEV, Ia est' narod . . . [I Am the People . . .]
—Brief discussion of *One Day.*
LG 26 March 1963.

55 V. POLTORATSKII, Matrenin dvor i ego okrestnosti [Matrena's Home and Its Environs].
Izv. 30 March 1963.
CDSP XV, No. 12.

56 A. DYMSHITS, Rasskazy o rasskazakh, zametki o povestiakh [Stories about Stories, Notes on Novels].
—On "Matrena's Home."
Ogonek 13/1963, p. 30.

April

57 A. KONDRATOVICH, In the Name of Truth.
—On *One Day.*
Soviet Literature 4/1963, pp. 169-171.

58 N. SERGOVANTSEV, Tragediia odinochestva i "sploshnoi byt" [The Tragedy of Solitude and the "Daily Grind of Life"].
—On all three stories.
Okt. 4/1963, pp. 198-207.

59 ZA IDEINOST' I SOTSIALISTICHESKII REALIZM [For Ideological Content and Socialist Realism].
—Editorial article, including discussion of *One Day.*
NM 4/1963, pp. 4-5.

60 M. SOKOLOV, Partiia uchit trebovatel'nosti [The Party Teaches Exactigness].
—Speech at 4th Plenary Session of the Board of the Soviet Writers' Union, including a brief reference to stories by Solzhenitsyn.
LG 2 April 1963.

61 A. SEMENOVA, Fal'shivym golosom [In a False Voice].
—Brief reference to "Matrena's Home."
Sovetskaia Klaipeda 9 April 1963. [*Slovo*]

62 V. KOLESOV, Deistvitel'no, vokrug da okolo [Round and About, Indeed].
—Letter, with a brief reference to "Matrena's Home."
SR 13 April 1963.

May

63 V. BUKIN, Chitaia Solzhenitsyna . . . [On Reading Solzhenitsyn . . .]
—On *One Day.*
Nauka i Religiia 5/1963, pp. 90-91.

64 S PARTIEI, ZA KOMMUNIZM [With the Party, for Communism].
—On "Matrena's Home."
Don 5/1963, p. 163.

65 A. TVARDOVSKII, Literatura sotsialisticheskogo realizma vsegda shla ruka ob ruku s revoliutsiei [The Literature of Socialist Realism Has Always Gone Hand in Hand with the Revolution].
—Interview with the Moscow correspondent of UPI, including a brief discussion of Solzhenitsyn.
Pr. 12 May 1963.
CDSP XV, No. 19.

66 V. PANKOV, Den' begushchii, stremitel'nyi! [A Racing, Impetuous Day!]
—On *One Day* and "Matrena's Home."
Izv. 19 May 1963.

67 M. MIKHAILOV, Sozdavaite proizvedeniia, dostoinye nashei epokhi! [Create Works Worthy of Our Epoch!]
—A meeting of kolkhoz workers discusses "Matrena's Home."
Volgogradskaia pravda 21 May 1963. [*Slovo*]

June

68 P. ZHURAVLEV, Letter on "Matrena's Home."
Leninskoe znamia (Gus'-Khrustal'nyi) 25 June 1963.
[Reference and excerpt in V. LAKSHIN, Pisatel', chitatel', kritik, *NM* 8/1966, p. 230.]

July

["For the Good of the Cause" published in *NM* 7/1963.]

69 I. MOTIASHOV, Vremia romantiki i vremia analiza [A Time for Romanticism, a Time for Analysis].
—On "Matrena's Home."
Pod"em 4/1963 (July-August), pp. 126-133.

70 I. MOTIASHOV, "Pravda" i "pravdochka" ["Truth" and "Petty Truths"].
—On "Matrena's Home."
LG 4 July 1963.

August

71 Z. KEDRINA, Chelovek—sovremennik—grazhdanin [Man—Contemporary—Citizen].
—Brief discussion of "Matrena's Home."
Voprosy literatury 8/1963, p. 29.

72 A. TVARDOVSKII, Ubezhdennost' khudozhnika [The Artist's Conviction].
—Speech at a session of the governing council of COMES, including a brief discussion of *One Day* and "Matrena's Home."
LG 10 Aug. 1963.

73 K. CHUKOVSKII, Vina ili beda [Guilt or Misfortune].
—Mentions Solzhenitsyn as a difficult writer to translate.
LG 3 and 10 Aug. 1963.

74 Iu. BARABASH, Chto est' spravedlivost'? [What is Justice?]
—Discussion of "For the Good of the Cause."
LG 31 Aug. 1963.
CDSP XV, No. 36.

September

75 V. BUSHIN, Geroi—zhizn'—pravda [Hero—Life—Truth].
—On first three stories.
Pod"em 5/1963 (Sept.-Oct.), pp. 112-121.

76 A. NALDEEV, Pravda mnogogranna [Truth Is Many-Sided].
—Brief reference to *One Day*.
Ogonek 39/1963, p. 24.

October

77 V. CHALMAEV, "Sviatye" i "besy" ["Saints" and "Devils"].
—On "For the Good of the Cause."
Okt. 10/1963, pp. 215-217.
CDSP XV, No. 44.

78 O RASSKAZE A. SOLZHENITSYNA "DLIA POL'ZY DELA" [On A. Solzhenityn's Story, "For the Good of the Cause"]:
E. IAMPOL'SKAIA, I. OKUNEVA and M. GOL'DBERG, Udacha avtora [A Success for the Author].
L. REZNIKOV, Otkrytoe pis'mo Iu. Barabashu [An Open Letter to Iu. Barabash].
V. SHEINIS and R. TSIMERINOV, Tak nado? [Is This How Things Should Be Done?]
NM 10/1963, pp. 193-198.
CDSP XVI, No. 4.

79 I. ATADZHANIAN, Letter to *Literaturnaia gazeta.*
—On Solzhenitsyn's stories.
LG 1 Oct. 1963.

80 A. GUDZENKO, My ostavalis' liud'mi . . . [We Remained Human . . .]
—Letter on *One Day*.
Kazakhstanskaia pravda 6 Oct. 1963.
CDSP XV, No. 41.

81 M. SINEL'NIKOV, Pravda bez "priprav" [The Truth Without Any "Dressing"].
—On "For the Good of the Cause" in response to No. 74.
LG 8 Oct. 1963.

82 D. GRANIN, Prav li kritik? [Is the Critic Right?]
—Letter on "For the Good of the Cause."
LG 15 Oct. 1963.
CDSP XV, No. 44.

83 N. SELIVERSTOV, Segodniashnee—kak pozavcherashnee [Today's Is Like the Day before Yesterday's].
—Letter, with an editorial note;
and
N. PUZANOVA, Letter.
—Both on "For the Good of the Cause."
LG 19 Oct. 1963.
CDSP XV, No. 44 (Seliverstov only).

November

84 T. MOTYLEVA, V sporakh o romane [Arguing about the Novel].
—Quotes V. Aksenov (at the COMES meeting in August 1963) on Solzhenitsyn's technique.
NM 11/1963, p. 225.

85 VNIMANIIU CHITATELEI [Notice to the Readers].
—Announcement of forthcoming publications including a story by Solzhenitsyn.
NM 11/1963, back cover.
CDSP XVI, No. 5.

86 V. KOCHETOV, Ne tak vse prosto [Things Are Not So Simple].
—Unambiguous indirect references to "Matrena's Home."
Okt. 11/1963, pp. 217 and 221.

87 A. OVCHARENKO, Zhizneutverzhdaiushchaia sila sotsialisticheskogo realizma [The Life-Asserting Force of Socialist Realism].
—On *One Day.*
Druzhba narodov 11/1963, pp. 247-249.

88 V. PERTSOVSKII, Sila dobra [The Power of Goodness].
—On "Incident at Krechetovka Station."
Voprosy literatury 11/1963, pp. 21, 36-38, 40.

December

89 PAFOS UTVERZHDENIIA, OSTROTA SPOROV. REDAKTSIONNYI DNEVNIK [Enthusiastic Affirmation, Pointed Arguments. Editor's Diary].
—Accuses *Novyi mir* of biased selection of readers' views on "For the Good of the Cause."
LG 12 Dec. 1963.
CDSP XVI, No. 4.

90 A. MAKAROV, Chitaia pis'ma . . . [Reading the Mail . . .]
—Quotes from an anonymous letter on Solzhenitsyn's stories.
LG 14 Dec. 1963.

91 V REDAKTSIIU "LITERATURNOI GAZETY" [To The Editors of *Literaturnaia gazeta*].
—A reply from the editors of *Novyi mir* to *Literaturnaia gazeta's* criticism (see No. 89);
and
OT REDAKTSII [From the Editors].
—An answering statement.
LG 26 Dec. 1963.
CDSP XVI, No. 4.

92 V KOMITETE PO LENINSKIM PREMIIAM . . . [In the Lenin Prize Committee . . .]
—Announcement of the nomination of *One Day* for a Lenin Prize.
LG 28 Dec. 1963.

93 V. IVANOV, Ne priukrashen li geroi? [Hasn't the Main Character Been Embellished?]
—A letter on *One Day* and the Lenin Prize.
Izv. 29 Dec. 1963.
CDSP XVI, No. 3.

---

94 S. ARTAMONOV, O povesti Solzhenitsyna [On Solzhenitsyn's Novel *One Day*] *Uchenye zapiski Literaturnogo instituta imeni Gor'kogo* No. 2 (1963, annual), pp. 51-61.

95 V. BUSHIN, *Pust' zvezdy stanut blizhe* [*Let the Stars Draw Closer*], Moscow, 1963, pp. 14-17. [*Slovo*]
—Pamphlet, "Znanie" series, with discussion of *One Day.*

96 V. KOZHINOV, *Proiskhozhdenie romana* [*The Origin of the Novel*], Moscow 1963, p. 401.
—Brief reference to Solzhenitsyn's language.

97 N. MASLIN, Geroi i siuzhet. Zametki o proze 1962 goda [Hero and Theme. Notes on the Prose of 1962], pp. 171-2.
and
A. KHVATOV, Iazyk i kharakter [Language and Character], pp. 299-302.
—On *One Day.*
Both in N. Gubko (ed.), *Geroi sovremennoi literatury. Stat'i.* [*The Hero of Contemporary Literature. Essays.*] (Moscow-Leningrad, 1963.)

1964

January

98 A. DREMOV, Deistvitel'nost'—ideal—idealizatsiia [Reality—Ideal—Idealization].
—On "Matrena's Home."
Okt. 1/1964, p.206.

99 V. LAKSHIN, Ivan Denisovich, ego druz'ia i nedrugi [Ivan Denisovich, His Friends and Foes].
NM 1/1964, pp. 223-245.

100 G. BROVMAN, Pravda istoricheskogo optimizma [The Truth of Historical Optimism].
—On "For the Good of the Cause."
Moskva 1/1964, pp. 186-188.

101 V. SURGANOV, A nado pomnit' [But One Must Remember].
—On *One Day* and "Matrena's Home."
Moskva 1/1964, pp. 202-205.

102 L. ZHUKHOVITSKII, Ishchu soavtora! [Co-Author Wanted!]
and
G. BROVMAN, Obiazatel'no li byt' soavtorom? [Is It Necessary to Be a Co-Author?]
—Letters on "Matrena's Home."
LR 1 Jan. 1964.
CDSP XVI, No. 5.

103 M. GARIN, A. SOSKIN, O chem rasskazali posetiteli [What the Visitors Had to Tell].
—A real-life parallel with "For the Good of the Cause."
Izv. 10 Jan. 1964.

104 V. BUSHIN, Snova i snova: zhizn'! [Again and Again: Life!]
—Letter on "Matrena's Home."
LR 10 Jan. 1964.
CDSP XVI, No. 5.

105 NASHE MNENIE [Our Opinion].
Letters from M. LEZINSKII and from N. MOLCHANIUK.
—Lenin Prize discussion.
LG 11 Jan. 1964.
CDSP XVI, No. 5.

106 V. PANKOV, Istoricheskii parol' [A Historic Watchword].
—On "For the Good of the Cause."
Ogonek 2/1964, p. 25.

107 V. PALLON, Zdravstvuite, kavtorang! [Greetings, Commander!]
—Interview with a character from *One Day.*
Izv. 15 Jan. 1964.
CDSP XVI, No. 3.

108 V. PANKOV, Nositeli sveta [Bearers of Light].
—Lenin Prize discussion.
LG 18 Jan. 1964.
CDSP XVI, No. 5.

109 A. STAVITSKII, Za malym—mnogoe [A Great Deal Concealed in a Little].
—Lenin Prize discussion, a letter.
LG 23 Jan. 1964.

110 S. MARSHAK, Pravdivaia povest' [A Truthful Story].
—Lenin Prize discussion.
Pr. 30 Jan. 1964.
CDSP XVI, No. 5.

111 V. TRUFANOVA, Politik, grazhdanin, khudozhnik [Politician, Citizen, Artist].
and
R. GAZIZOV, Glubina i svezhest' kriticheskoi mysli [Depth and Freshness of Critical Thought].
—Letters on "Matrena's Home."
LR 31 Jan. 1964.
CDSP XVI, No. 6.

February

112 V. SKUIBIN, Glubinnoe postizhenie zhizni [A Profound Grasp of Life].
—Brief discussion of *One Day.*
Iskusstvo kino 2/1964, p. 56.

113 GDE I KOGDA? [Where and When?]
—Short bibliography of reviews of *One Day.*
LG 4 Feb. 1964.

114 G. BROVMAN, Dialog o geroe [Dialogue about the Hero].
—On "Matrena's Home."
LR 7 Feb. 1964.

115 VZYSKATEL'NOST' [Exactingness].
—Report of Moscow Writers' meeting to discuss Lenin Prizes, including V. KAVERIN, D. EREMIN, L. KOPELEV et al. on *One Day.*
LG 8 Feb. 1964.

116 G. MITIN, Izderzhki spora [The Costs of Debate].
—On "Matrena's Home."
LR 14 Feb. 1964.

117 OT KOMITETA PO LENINSKIM PREMIIAM V OBLASTI LITERATURY I ISKUSSTVA [From the Committee for Lenin Prizes in the Field of Literature and Art].
—Announcement that *One Day* is among the works from which the final selection will be made.
Pr. 19 Feb. 1964.

118 OBSHCHII TRUD KRITIKI. REDAKTSIONNYI DNEVNIK [The Common Tasks of Criticism. Editor's Diary].
—On *One Day* and Lakshin's article.
LG 20 Feb. 1964.

March

119 OTVETSTVENNOST' [Responsibility].
—Report of combined meeting of Moscow and RSFSR Writers' Unions, at which D. EREMIN, B. D'IAKOV, A. TODORSKII et al. discussed *One Day.*
LR 6 March 1964.

120 V. OZEROV, Dukhovnoe zdorov'e, tvorcheskaia smelost' [Spiritual Health, Creative Boldness].
—Brief reference to *One Day.*
Izv. 8 March 1964.
CDSP XVI, No. 10.

121 N. GUBKO, Zhivye traditsii [Living Traditions].
N. SERGEEV, Preddver'e . . . [The Threshold . . .]
S. SAVIN, Odnostoronnost' [One-Sidedness].
—Letters on *One Day* and the Lenin Prize.
LR 27 March 1964.

April

122 BOL'SHOI RAZGOVOR O KRITIKE. DNEVNIK [A Major Discussion of Criticism. Diary].
—Report of a Writers' Union meeting at which B. D'IAKOV and A. TODORSKII spoke on *One Day* and Lakshin's article.
Okt. 4/1964, pp. 188-189.

123 M. LAPSHIN, Dostoinyi vklad v sovetskuiu literaturu [A Worthy Contribution to Soviet Literature].
—On *One Day.*
Politicheskoe samoobrazovanie 4/1964, pp. 54-60.

124 K. BUKOVSKII, Ekonomicheskaia replika literatoram [A Reply to the Litterateurs from the Point of View of Economics].
—On *One Day.*
LG 2 April 1964.

125 V. POLTORATSKII, V poiskakh "pruzhiny." Otvet K. Bukovskomu [In Search of the "Driving Spring." A Reply to K. Bukovskii].
—On *One Day.*
LG 9 April 1964.

126 VYSOKAIA TREBOVATEL'NOST'. IZ REDAKTSIONNOI POCHTY [High Exactingness. From the Editors' Mailbag].
—Discussion of letters on *One Day* and the Lenin Prize.
Pr. 11 April 1964.
CDSP XVI, No. 16.

127 L. GREKOV, Dostoina! [It Is Worthy!]
—Report of a local meeting to discuss *One Day* and the Lenin Prize.
Za meditsinskie kadry **(Rostov-na-Donu) 14 April 1964. [*Slovo*]**

128 DOBRAIA STROGOST' [Benevolent Severity].
—Report of mail on *One Day* and the Lenin Prize.
Trud 19 April 1964.

[The Lenin Prize Committee announced its awards in *Pr.* 22 April 1963. *One Day* was not mentioned.]

May

129 L. KRIACHKO, Pozitsiia tvortsa i besplodie meshchanina [The Position of the Creative Artist and the Sterility of the Philistine].
—On "Matrena's Home" and "For the Good of the Cause."
Okt. 5/1964, pp. 210-212.

130 E. SEREBROVSKAIA, Opekunsha iz FRG [The Guardian from West Germany].
—On the stories, particularly "Incident at Krechetovka Station."
LR 8 May 1964.

131 Iu. BARABASH, "Rukovoditeli," "rukovodimye" i khoziaeva zhizni [The "Leaders", the "Led" and the Masters of Life].
—On *One Day* and Lakshin's article.
LG 12 May 1964.

June

132 SPOR IDET . . . [The Debate Is On]:
V. LAKSHIN, V redaktsiiu "Literaturnoi gazety" [To the Editors of *Literaturnaia gazeta*].
—Letter on *One Day.*
OT REDAKTSII [From the Editors].
LG 4 June 1964.

133 A. PERVENTSEV, Vysokaia missiia literatury [The Lofty Mission of Literature].
—Brief reference to "Matrena's Home."
Sovetskaia Kuban' 7 June 1964. [*Slovo*]

July

134 D. STARIKOV, Real'naia nravstvennost' [Real Morality], pp. 29-31.
V. SARNOV, Eto bylo nevozmozhno desiat' let nazad [This Was Impossible Ten Years Ago], pp. 32, 35.
A. KOGAN, Geroi i vremia [The Hero and Time], pp. 36-37.
—On "Incident at Krechetovka Station."
Voprosy literatury 7/1964.

135 V. BARANOV, Za zhanrovuiu opredelennost' [For Clear Distinctions of Genre].
—Brief reference to "Incident at Krechetovka Station."
LR 3 July 1964.

136 ISKUSSTVO GEROICHESKOI EPOKHI [Art of the Heroic Epoch].
—Brief reference to "Matrena's Home."
Kom. 10/1964, p. 33.

August

137 V. IVANOV, Ne prostoe eto slovo [This is Not Said Lightly].
—Defends his earlier letter on *One Day.*
Izv. 20 Aug. 1964.

September

138 Iu. KARIAKIN, Epizod iz sovremennoi bor'by idei [An Episode from the Current Battle of Ideas].
—On *One Day.*
NM 9/1964, pp. 231-239.
(reprinted from *Problemy mira i sotsializma* 9/1964.)
Soviet Review VI (1965) No. 3, pp. 21-31.

139 N. VOLGIN, Vsegda v stroiu soldaty revoliutsii [The Soldiers of the Revolution Are Always at Their Posts].
—On *One Day.*
Krasnoiarskii rabochii 27 Sept. 1964. [*Slovo*]

October

140 A. TVARDOVSKII, "Novyi mir" v 1965 godu [*Novyi mir* in 1965].
—Announcing a "big novel" by Solzhenitsyn.
LG 27 Oct. 1964.
NM 10/1964, p. 287, headed: Ot redaktsii [From the Editors].
CDSP XVI, No. 45.

November

141 I. ZOLOTUSSKII, Podvodia itogi [Summing Up].
—On *One Day.*
Sibirskie ogni 11/1964, p. 163. [*Slovo*]

December

142 A. VLASENKO, Trud—poeziia! [Labour Is Poetry!]
—On *One Day.*
Okt. 12/1964, pp. 200-201.

143 VYSOKII DOLG PISATELIA [The Lofty Duty of the Writer].
—With N. SHUNDIK'S comments on Solzhenitsyn at a meeting of Riazan' writers.
Priokskaia pravda 17 Dec. 1964. [*Slovo*]

144 POETY KHODIAT PO ZEMLE [Poets Travel the Land].
—With a brief comment on Solzhenitsyn's works by V. SOLOUKHIN.
Sovetskii uchitel' (Leningrad) 17 Dec. 1964. [*Slovo*]

1965

January

145 G. BROVMAN, Nravstvennaia trebovatel'nost' i istorizm [Moral Exactingness and Historicism].
—Brief reference to *One Day.*
Okt. 1/1965, p. 200.

146 G. BROVMAN, Obraz sovremennika [The Image of Our Contemporary].
—Brief discussion of "Matrena's Home."
Nash sovremmenik 1/1965, p. 111.

147 A. TVARDOVSKII, Po sluchaiu iubileia [On the Occasion of an Anniversary].
—On *One Day.*
NM 1/1965, pp. 10-11.
CDSP XVII, No. 11.

148 Iu. KUNGURTSEV, Solzhenitsyn v Kazakhstane [Solzhenitsyn in Kazakhstan].
—Biographical.
Leninskaia smena (Kazakhstan) 10 Jan. 1965. [*Slovo*]

February

149 N. EGORYCHEV, Vospitanie molodezhi—delo partiinoe [Education of Youth Is the Business of the Party].
—Brief reference to *One Day.*
Kom. 3/1965, p. 18.

March

150 NA ZEMLE KUBANSKOI [On the Soil of the Kuban'].
—Report of speech at 2nd Congress of RSFSR Writers' Union, including a brief reference to "Matrena's Home" by V. LAPIN.
VYSOKII DOLG KHUDOZHNIKA [Lofty Duty of the Artist].
—Further speeches, including a reference to *One Day* by N. EGORYCHEV.
LG 5 March 1965.
CDSP XVII, No. 10 (Egorychev only).

151 S. GAISAR'IAN, Prizvanie literaturnoi kritiki [The Calling of Literary Criticism].
—Brief reference to works of Solzhenitsyn.
Pr. 28 March 1965.
CDSP XVII, No. 13.

April

152 E. VUCHETICH, Vnesem iasnost': nekotorye mysli po povodu odnogo iubileinogo vystupleniia [Let Us Clarify Matters. Some Thoughts About an Anniversary Article].
—Brief reference to *One Day.*
Izv. 15 April 1965.
CDSP XVII, No. 15.

August

153 OT REDAKTSII [From the Editors].
—Editorial comment appended to a letter from V. PORTNOV et al., S kogo vy pishete portrety? [From Whom Do You Draw Your Portraits?], with a brief reference to "Matrena's Home."
Izv. 14 Aug. 1965.
CDSP XVII, No. 33.

November

[Publication of an article by Solzhenitsyn, "Ne obychai degtem shchi belit', na to smetana" ("It Is Not Customary to Whiten Soup with Tar; Sour Cream Is Used for That") in *LG* 4 Nov. 1965.]

December

154 S. PAVLOV, Vystuplenie na 8 plenume TsK VLKSM [Speech at the 8th Plenum of the Komsomol Central Committee].
—Brief indirect reference to *One Day.*
Koms. pr. 29 Dec. 1965.

155 L. VLADIMIROV, Planeta zemlia—strana khimiia [The Planet Earth, the Land of Chemistry].
—Opens with a paraphrase of Solzhenitsyn's prose poem "Utenok" ["The Duckling"].
Znanie—sila 12/1965, page preceding p. 1.

156 T. VINOKUR, O iazyke i stile povesti A. I. Solzhenitsyna "Odin den' Ivana Denisovicha" [On the Language and Style of A. I. Solzhenitsyn's story *One Day in the Life of Ivan Denisovich*].
Voprosy kul'tury rechi No. 6 (1965, annual), pp. 16-32.

157 Iu. BARABASH, *"Za" i "protiv"* [*"Pro" and "Contra"*], Moscow, 1965, p. 34. [*Slovo*]
—Pamphlet, izd-vo "Pravda", with discussion of *One Day.*

158 V. BARANOV, Za zhanrovuiu opredelennost' [For Clear Distinctions of Genre], pp. 280-281.
—Expanded version of No. 135. Brief reference to "Incident at Krechetovka Station."
A. KOGAN, Prodolzhaia razgovor . . . [Continuing the Discussion . . .], pp. 296-300, 313.
—On "Incident at Krechetovka Station," *One Day* and "Matrena's Home." Both in *Literatura i sovremennost'. Sbornik 6. Stat'i o literatura 1964-1965 godov* [*Literature and Contemporaneity. 6th Collection. Essays on Literature 1964-1965*] (Moscow, 1965).

159 ISTORIIA RUSSKOGO SOVETSKOGO ROMANA [History of the Soviet Russian Novel], in 2 vols., Moscow-Leningrad 1965, vol. 2, pp. 311-12.
—On "For the Good of the Cause."

1966

January

["Zakhar-Kalita" published in *NM* 1/1966.]

160 E. PASHNEV, Dvizhenie russkogo iazyka. Eshche odno mnenie v spore [The Movement of the Russian Language. A Further Opinion in the Debate].
—On Solzhenitsyn's article "It Is Not Customary . . ."
Pod"em 1/1966 (Jan.-Feb.), p. 142.

April

161 I. BODIUL, Speech at XXIII Congress of CPSU.
—Brief reference to *One Day.*
Pr. 3 April 1966.
CDSP XVIII, No. 17.

162 M. ALEKSEEV, Etapy bol'shogo puti [Stages on the Great Journey].
—Brief discussion of *One Day.*
LR 22 April 1966.

May

163 V. KOZHEVNIKOV, Za Davydovykh i Korchaginykh nashikh dnei [For the Davydovs and Korchagins of Our Day].
—Brief reference to *One Day.*
LR 6 May 1966.

July

164 TIP—IAVLENIE EPOKHI [The Type is a Phenomenon of the Epoch].
—"Oktiabr' " Club discussion, including:
P. STROKOV, Vstuplenie v temu [Introduction to the Theme], p. 200.
—Brief discussion of Solzhenitsyn with a reference to "Zakhar-Kalita";

S. MOZHNIAGUN, "Literatura fakta" i naturalizm [The "Literature of Fact" and Naturalism], pp. 206-207.
—On "Zakhar-Kalita";
G. BROVMAN, Ne "fiziologiia byta" a chelovekovedenie! [Not the "Physiology of Life" but the Study of Man!], p. 208.
—Brief reference to "Matrena's Home."
Okt. 7/1966.

August

165 V. LAKSHIN, Pisatel', chitatel', kritik. Stat'ia vtoraia [Writer, Reader, Critic. Second Article].
—On "Matrena's Home."
NM 8/1966, pp. 219-231.
CDSP XVIII, No. 46.

166 G. PETELIN, Razdum'ia nad metodom i stilem [Reflections Upon Method and Style].
—On *One Day.*
Don 8/1966, pp. 167-169.

October

167 N. ABALKIN, Na dobruiu pamiat' [Fondly Remembered].
—Brief account of S. MARSHAK reading *One Day;* Lenin Prize.
Znamia 10/1966, p. 241.

168 L. KRIACHKO, Pravdu nel'zia razryvat' [The Truth Cannot Be Divided].
—Brief references to "Matrena's Home."
LR 28 Oct. 1966.
CDSP XVIII, No. 46.

1967

March

169 I. MOTIASHOV, Logika bor'by [The Logic of the Struggle].
—On "Matrena's Home."
Moskva 3/1967, pp. 201-202.

April

170 A. METCHENKO, O literaturnoi kritike [On Literary Criticism].
—Brief discussion of "Matrena's Home."
Kom. 6/1967, p. 118.

---

171 T. MOTYLEVA, *Glazami druzei i vragov. Sovetskaia literatura za rubezhom* [*Through the Eyes of Friends and Foes. Soviet Literature Abroad*] (Moscow, 1967), p. 32.
–Brief discussion of *One Day.*

1968

April

172 G. MARIAGIN, Vmeste s partiei, s narodom [Together with the Party, with the People].
—Brief references to "Matrena's Home."
Krasnaia zvezda 24 April 1968.

June

173 IDEINAIA BOR'BA. OTVETSTVENNOST' PISATELIA [The Ideological Struggle. The Responsibility of the Writer].
—Letter from Solzhenitsyn with an extensive editorial article on his works and behaviour.
LG 26 June 1968.
CDSP XX, No. 26.

November

174 E. MIKULINA, Zhizn', kak ona est' [Life As It Is].
—Personal attack on Solzhenitsyn.
Okt. 11/1968, pp. 149-150.

175 ZHIZN' I POZITSIIA GAZETY. OBZOR PECHATI [Life and the Newspaper's Position. Press Survey].
—Briefly supports *Literaturnaia gazeta's* attack on Solzhenitsyn of 26 June.
Pr. 25 Nov. 1968.
CDSP XX, No. 47.

December

176 P. STROKOV, O narode-"Savrasushke," o "zagadkakh" russkogo kharaktera i iskaniiakh "pri svete sovesti" [On the "Savrasushka"-People, on the "Enigmas" of the Russian Character and on Strivings "by the Light of One's Conscience"].
—Brief reference to *One Day* and "Matrena's Home."
Okt. 12/1968, p. 197.

1969

January

177 A. METCHENKO, Sovremennoe i vechnoe [The Contemporary and the Eternal].
—Brief reference to Solzhenitsyn's works.
Moskva 1/1969, p. 201.

February

178 A. ELKIN, Zakat vifleemskoi zvezdy [The Setting of the Star of Bethlehem].
—Brief reference to the journal *Osteuropa's* support for Solzhenitsyn.
Moskva 2/1969, p. 209.

March

179 I. DEDKOV, Stranitsy derevenskoi zhizni [Pages of Rural Life].
—Brief reference to "Matrena's Home."
NM 3/1969, p. 242.
Current Abstracts II, No. 2.

180 I. DROZDOV, Zakat bezdukhovnogo slova [Decline of the Spiritless Word].
—Brief reference to *One Day* and "Matrena's Home".
Zhurnalist 3/1969, p. 53.

181 A. GREBENSHCHIKOV, Poka ne pozdno [Before It Is Too Late].
—Briefly criticizes planned encyclopedia treatment of Solzhenitsyn.
Okt. 3/1969, p. 201.
Current Abstracts II, No. 2.

April

182 V. FEODOS'EV, O chem shumit iugoslavskaia pressa [What the Yugoslav Press Is Shouting About].
—Brief discussion of Yugoslav publication of *The First Circle.*
SR 5 April 1969.
CDSP XXI, No. 14.

May

183 A. METCHENKO, "Aktual'nye retrospektivy" ili reaktsionnye mify ["Topical Retrospects" or Reactionary Myths].
—On the Yugoslav critic, P. Broz's exploitation of Solzhenitsyn's letter to the IV Writers' Congress.
Okt. 5/1969, pp. 191-192.

November

184 V SOIUZE PISATELEI RSFSR [In the Russian Republic Writers' Union].
—Solzhenitsyn's expulsion from the Writers' Union.
LG 12 Nov. 1969.
LR 14 Nov. 1969.
Priokskaia pravda (Riazan' oblast') 16 Nov. 1969. [*Slovo*]
CDSP XXI, No. 46.
(The texts are not all identical.)

185 OT SEKRETARIATA PRAVLENIIA SOIUZA PISATELEI RSFSR [From the Secretariat of the Board of the Russian Republic Writers' Union].
—On the expulsion and Solzhenitsyn's open letter of protest.
LG 26 Nov. 1969.
CDSP XXI, No. 47.

December

186 V SEKRETARIATE PRAVLENIIA MOSKOVSKOI PISATEL'SKOI ORGANIZATSII [In the Secretariat of the Board of the Moscow Writers' Organization].
and
OTCHETNO-VYBORNOE SOBRANIE PARTIINOI ORGANIZATSII LENINGRADSKOGO OTDELENIIA SOIUZA PISATELEI RSFSR [Meeting of the Party Organization of the Leningrad Branch of the Russian Republic Writers' Union to Hear Reports and Elect Officers].
—Unanimous approval of the expulsion at both meetings.
LG 3 Dec. 1969.

187 M. SHOLOKHOV, Schast'e zhit' sredi takogo velikolepnogo naroda! [It Is a Joy to Live Amongst Such a Magnificent People!]
—Unambiguous allusion to Solzhenitsyn as a "pest".
LG 3 Dec. 1969.

188 G. MARKOV, Sud'ba narodnaia, sud'ba chelovecheskaia [The Destiny of the People, the Destiny of Mankind].
—Briefly approves of expulsion.
Sovetskaia kul'tura 11 Dec. 1969.

189 S. MIKHALKOV, Pozitsiia khudozhnika [The Artist's Position].
—Description of Solzhenitsyn as a "talented foe of Socialism."
Koms. pr. 14 Dec. 1969.
Reprinted in slightly different form as:
Vystuplenie Sergeia Mikhalkova [Sergei Mikhalkov's Address].
LG 17 Dec. 1969;
and
Tvorchestvo—eto bor'ba [Creativity Is a Struggle].
LR 19 Dec. 1969.

190 G. MARKOV, Literatura, kotoraia sluzhit millionam [Literature in the Service of Millions].
—Briefly approves of expulsion.
LG 17 Dec. 1969.

---

191 CHITATELI "TRUDA" [The Readers of *Trud*].
—Reports on the popularity of *One Day* among readers.
Informatsionnyi biulleten' No. 20 (35) [Seriia: Materialy i soobshcheniia. Chitatel' i gazeta. Itogi izucheniia chitatel'skoi auditorii tsentral'nykh gazet. Vypusk I] (Moscow, 1969), pp. 76 and 80.

1970

January

192 S. MIKHALKOV, Podlinnaia literatura—vyrazhenie narodnogo dukha [True Literature Is an Expression of the Spirit of the People].
—Interview with a Canadian journalist including a brief justification of the expulsion.
LG 7 Jan. 1970.

193 N. RYBAK, Pid praporom internatsionalizmu [Beneath the Banner of Internationalism].
—Brief reference to Ukrainian writers' approval of the expulsion.
Literaturna Ukraina 20 Jan. 1970.
Digest of the Soviet Ukrainian Press March 1970.

194 M. ALEKSEEV, Tsel'—vozvyshennaia i blagorodnaia [The Goal Is a Lofty and Noble One].
—Brief discussion of *Samoizdat* (sic.) and Solzhenitsyn.
LG 28 Jan. 1970.

February

195 N. GRIBACHEV, Slezy na eksport. Otkrytoe pis'mo general'nomu sekretariu Evropeiskogo soobshchestva pisatelei [Tears for Export. Open Letter to the Secretary-General of COMES, the European Association of Writers].
—Justifies the expulsion.
and
V BIURO SOVETSKOI SEKTSII ESP [In the Bureau of the Soviet Section of COMES].
—Brief reference to the alleged persecution of Solzhenitsyn.
LG 18 Feb. 1970.
Current Abstracts III, No. 5.

March

196 M. VLADIMOV, Perebezhchik [The Turncoat].
—Poem, unmistakably alluding to the expulsion.
SR 4 March 1970.

April

197 S. MIKHALKOV, Speech at III Congress of Russian Republic Writers' Union.
—Repeats earlier attacks, but without naming Solzhenitsyn.
LG 1 April 1970.

May

198 Iu. KOSACH, Taka vona, pravda, panove! [That's the Truth of it, Gentlemen!]
—On Heinrich Böll's intercession for Solzhenitsyn.
Literaturna Ukraina 29 May 1970.

199 I. SAIANSKII, Zasluzhennoe nakazanie [A Well-Deserved Punishment].
—Letter from Australia supporting the expulsion.
Golos Rodiny 42/1970 (May).

October

200 NEDOSTOINAIA IGRA. PO POVODU PRISUZHDENIIA A. SOLZHENITSYNU NOBELEVSKOI PREMII [An Unseemly Game. On the Occasion of the Award of the Nobel Prize to A. Solzhenitsyn].
Izv., Pr., Koms. pr. 10 Oct. 1970.
CDSP XXII, No. 41.

201 S. MIKHALKOV, Slovo pisatelia—na sluzhbu sovremennosti [The Writer's Word at the Service of the Times].
—Brief discussion of the Nobel award.
SR 14 Oct. 1970.
CDSP XXII, No. 41.

202 NEDOSTOINAIA IGRA [An Unseemly Game].
and
KOMMENTARII "LG": K VOPROSU O PRIORITETE [*Literaturnaia gazeta's* Commentary: On the Question of Priority].
—On Western machinations behind the Nobel award.
LG 14 Oct. 1970.
CDSP XXII, No. 41.

203 GDE ISHCHET PISATEL'SKII TALANT I SLAVU NOBELEVSKII KOMITET? [Where Does the Nobel Committee Look for Literary Talent and Glory?]
Koms. pr. 17 Oct. 1970.
CDSP XXII, No. 41.

204 SOLZHENITSYN'S PRIZE: POLITICS NOT LITERATURE.
Soviet Weekly 17 Oct. 1970.

205 NOBELEVSKAIA PREMIIA I KHOLODNAIA VOINA [The Nobel Prize and the Cold War].
—Press responses from the USA and Sweden.
Pr. 21 Oct. 1970.
CDSP XXII, No. 41.

206 PROVOKATSIIA V DUKHE "KHOLODNOI VOINY" [A Provocation in the Spirit of the "Cold War"].
and
STOKGOL'MSKAIA GAZETA OSUZHDAET RESHENIE SHVEDSKOI AKADEMII [A Stockholm Newspaper Condemns the Decision of the Swedish Academy].
—Expanded version of the article in *Pravda* 21 Oct. 1970.
LG 21 Oct. 1970.

207 PROVOKATSIONNAIA AKTSIIA V DUKHE "KHOLODNOI VOINY" [A Provocative Action in the Spirit of the "Cold War"].
—On responses in the Bulgarian and W. German press.
LG 28 Oct. 1970.

November

208 V. MAEVSKII, Koe-chto o zoologii [Something About Zoology].
—Feuilleton, linking Solzhenitsyn and a giant panda, Chi-Chi.
Pr. 2 Nov. 1970.

209 "ZA SOTSIALIZM, MIR, LITERATURU!" ZAIAVLENIE SOIUZA NEMETSKIKH PISATELEI ["For Socialism, Peace, Literature!" Statement from the German Writers' Union].
—East German writers condemn the Nobel award to Solzhenitsyn.
LG 4 Nov. 1970.

210 LITERATOR [Litterateur], Dzhankarlo Vigorelli, chelovek-fliuger [Giancarlo Vigorelli, a Human Weathercock].
—Brief reference to the Nobel award.
LG 18 Nov. 1970.

211 S. PILOTOVICH, O rabote partiinykh organizatsii respubliki po dal'neishemu uluchsheniiu marksistsko-leninskogo obrazovaniia kommunistov i komsomol'tsev [On the Work of the Republic's Party Organizations in Further Improvement of the Marxist-Leninist Education of Communists and Young Communists].
—Report to the Plenum of the Belorussian Central Committee linking Solzhenitsyn with Siniavskii and Daniel'.
Sovetskaia Belorossiia 18 Nov. 1970.
CDSP XXII, No. 46.

212 ZAIAVLENIE BOLGARSKIKH PISATELEI [Statement by Bulgarian Writers].
—Deploring the Nobel award.
Pr. 28 Nov. 1970.

December

213 V. VOROB'EV, V. I. Lenin o mirovozzrenii pisatelia [V. I. Lenin on the Weltanschauung of the Writer].
—Brief discussion of *One Day* and Solzhenitsyn's "betrayal" of the traditions of Soviet Literature.
Don 12/1970, p. 168.

214 U RYTMAKH LENINS'KOHO ROKU [In the Rhythms of Lenin's Year].
—Report of a meeting of Kiev writers, with a brief reference to foreign acclaim for Solzhenitsyn's "anti-Russian" writings.
Literaturna Ukraina 1 Dec. 1970.

215 PROTEST BOLGARSKIKH PISATELEI [Protest by Bulgarian Writers].
—Open letter to the Nobel Committee criticizing the award to Solzhenitsyn.
LG 2 Dec. 1970.

216 I. POPOV, Bolgarskie pisateli nakanune s"ezda BKP [Bulgarian Writers on the Eve of the Bulgarian Communist Party Congress].
—Brief reference to the Nobel award.
LG 9 Dec. 1970.

217 ZAIAVLENIE A. LUNDKVISTA [A Statement by A. Lundquist].
—A Swedish writer criticizes the Nobel award.
Pr. 12 Dec. 1970.

218 A SUD'I KTO?... [But Who Are the Judges?...]
—Reprint of an article from the German press on the Nobel selectors, with an editorial note referring to Solzhenitsyn.
LG 16 Dec. 1970.

219 I. ALEKSANDROV, Nishcheta antikommunizma [The Poverty of Anti-Communism].
—Includes a wide-ranging attack on Solzhenitsyn.
Pr. 17 Dec. 1970.
CDSP XXII, No. 49.

220 CHTO UDRUCHAET SIN'ORA MATTEOTTI [What Is Depressing Signor Matteotti].
—Response to a statement in support of Solzhenitsyn by an Italian Minister.
LG 23 Dec. 1970.

221 M. SINEL'NIKOV, Po kompasu kommunisticheskoi partiinosti [Following the Compass of Communist Party-Mindedness].
—Brief reference to Solzhenitsyn as an anti-Soviet writer.
Krasnaia zvezda 26 Dec. 1970.
CDSP XXII, No. 52.

---

222 K. ZELINSKII, *Soviet Literature: Problems and People* (Moscow, 1970), p. 227.
—*Cancer Ward* and *The First Circle* as frankly anti-Soviet works.

1971

January

223 V. BOL'SHAK, Na khvyliakh Baltyky [On the Waves of the Baltic].
—On Western editions of *Cancer Ward* and *The First Circle.*
Zhovten' (Lvov) 1/1971, p. 102.

224 V. SAPUNOV, Literatura i iskusstvo—ideologicheskii front bor'by [Literature and Art—the Ideological Front of the Struggle].
—Brief discussion of the Nobel award and Solzhenitsyn's betrayal of his people.
Kommunist vooruzhennykh sil 2/1971 (Jan.), p. 21.
CDSP XXIII, No. 4.

225 D. RID (Read), Oktrytoe pis'mo A. Solzhenitsynu [Open Letter to A. Solzhenitsyn].
—American folk-singer criticizes Solzhenitsyn's protest against his expulsion.
LG 27 Jan. 1971.
Ogonek 5/1971, pp. 26-27 [With an introductory article and extracts from one of Read's poems].

February

226 G. MARKOV, Vsegda s narodom, s partiei [Always with the People and the Party].
—Brief reference to the Nobel award.
Pr. 12 Feb. 1971.

227 G. EVDOKIMOVA, Retsidiv "kholodnoi voiny" [A Recurrence of the "Cold War"].
—Survey of letters on the Nobel award from Russian émigrés, and an American press response.
Golos Rodiny 16/1971 (Feb.).

March

228 LITERATURA PATRIOTICHESKOI VERNOSTI I INTERNATSIONAL'NOGO BRATSTVA [Literature of Patriotic Loyalty and International Brotherhood].
—Klub "Oktiabr' " discussion including a reference by I. BALANDINA to Solzhenitsyn's works as retrogressive and anti-Soviet.
Okt. 3/1971, p. 201.

229 A. OVCHARENKO, Sotsialisticheskii realizm v svete mezhdunarodnykh sporov [Socialist Realism in the Light of International Controversy].
—Very brief reference to *The First Circle.*
Molodaia gvardiia 3/1971, p. 291.

April

230 O. NOSENKO, Efirni dyversii [Sabotage via Radio].
—Very brief reference to Solzhenitsyn.
Literaturna Ukraina 20 April 1971.
Digest of the Soviet Ukrainian Press July 1971.

May

231 V. SHCHERBINA, Put' sotsializma, puti iskusstva [The Path of Socialism, the Paths of Art].
—Brief reference to Solzhenitsyn's reception in the West.
Nash sovremennik 5/1971, p. 122.

232 PROMOVA NATANA RYBAKA [Speech of Natan Rybak].
—Very brief reference to the "nobelization" of Solzhenitsyn.
Literaturna Ukraina 23 May 1971.
Digest of the Soviet Ukrainian Press July 1971.

October

233 E. MARKIN, "Belyi bakan," "Nevesomost' " ["The White Buoy," "Weightlessness"].
—Poems referring in veiled form to Solzhenitsyn and Markin's part in the expulsion from the Writers' Union.
NM 10/1971, pp. 96-98.

December

234 M. IOVCHUK, Sovremennye problemy ideologicheskoi bor'by, razvitiia sotsialisticheskoi ideologii i kul'tury [Contemporary Problems of the

Ideological Struggle, the Development of Socialist Ideology and Culture].
—Brief reference to "Matrena's Home" and Solzhenitsyn's "slanders" of Soviet reality.
Kom. 15/1971, pp. 100, 111.

1972

January

235 ZHURNAL "SHTERN" O SEM'E SOLZHENITSYNYKH [The Magazine *Stern* about the Solzhenitsyn Family].
—Reprint of a German article, with editorial comment, including discussion of *August 1914*.
LG 12 Jan. 1972.
CDSP XXIV, No. 1.

February

236 V. OZEROV, Literaturno-khudozhestvennaia kritika i sovremennost' [Literary and Artistic Criticism and the Present].
—Very brief reference to "Matrena's Home."
LG 2 Feb. 1972.

237 V. PROLETKIN, U pozornogo stolba [At the Pillory].
—Brief reference to Solzhenitsyn as a "degenerate".
Kommunist (Saratov oblast' newspaper) 4 Feb. 1972. [Reference in the *samizdat* journal *Khronika tekushchikh sobytii* No. 24].

238 NA PEREDOVI RUBEZHI SUCHASNOSTI [To the Front Lines of Contemporaneity].
—Report of a Kiev writers' meeting with a brief reference by Iu ZBANATS'KYY to Solzhenitsyn as a "poisonous weed."
Literaturna Ukraina 8 Feb. 1972.
Digest of the Soviet Ukrainian Press March 1972.

239 M. LARNI, Kogda istoriiu staviat v ugol [When History Is Stood in the Corner].
and
M. STIUTS (Stütz), V krivom zerkale [In a distorting Mirror].
—On *August 1914*.
LG 23 Feb. 1972.
Bulletin édité par le Bureau Soviétique d'Information (Paris), Nouvelle série, No. 4, 331, 22 Feb. 1972.
CDSP XXIV, No. 14.
[Larni's article also appeared in Czech as: Zfalsovaná historie v literárním hávu (Falsified History in Literary Garb) in *Rudé právo* 11 Feb. 1972].

April

240 E. ROMANOVSKII (J. Romanowski), "Avgust Chetyrnadtsatogo" Aleksandra Solzhenitsyna ili pravda o knige i mife [Aleksandr Solzhenitsyn's *August 1914* or the Truth about the Book and the Myth].
—Reprinted from a Polish journal.
Trud, LR 7 April 1972.
CDSP XXIV, No. 14.

241 L. PROKSHA, Po kakoi Rossii plachet Solzhenitsyn? [Which Russia Does Solzhenitsyn Weep For?]
D. MAMEDOV, Istoki ozlobleniia [The Source of the Hatred].
M. MKRIAN, Dostoinaia otpoved' [A Worthy Rebuttal].
Then under a general title "Stroki is pisem" [Extracts from Letters], letters by:
N. ZHARKANBAEV
I. SAVCHENKO, I. DAN'KOV, Zh. BESHUK, N. KONOVALOVA and G. MAZUR (one letter)
G. ORDIAN
A. MIKHALEVICH
S. ROZENFEL'D and L. OLIANDER (one letter)
G. RYKUNOV
A. IAKSHIN
—Letters on *August 1914,* with editorial comment.
LG 12 April 1972.
CDSP XXIV, No. 14.

242 M. TANK, M. LYN'KOV, I. SHAMIAKIN, I. MELEZH, A. KULAKOVSKII, V odnoi upriazhke s nedrugami [In Double Harness with the Enemies].
—Letter on *August 1914* from Belorussian writers.
and
E. FERRARI, Kto zakazyvaet muzyku . . . [He Who Calls the Tune . . .]
—Wide-ranging attack, reprinted from an Italian journal.
LG 19 April 1972.
CDSP XXIV, No. 17.

November

243 A. IAKOVLEV, Protiv antiistorizma [Against A-historicity].
—Includes a discussion of *August 1914.*
LG 15 Nov. 1972.

1973

January

244 A. METCHENKO, Neotsenimaia pomoshch' [Invaluable Aid].
—Brief reference to *One Day* and "Matrena's Home."
LR 19 Jan. 1973.

February

245 A. CHAKOVSKII, Chto zhe dal'she? [But What Next?]
—Brief indirect reference to American offers of financial help to Solzhenitsyn.
LG 14 Feb. 1973.

246 N. FORSBLUM, O patriotizme [On Patriotism].
—Strong attack on *The First Circle, August 1914* and the Nobel award, reprinted from a Finnish journal.
Golos Rodiny 12/1973 (Feb.).

April

247 V. OZEROV, "Dukhovnaia elita" ili boitsy partii? Zametki o mezhdunarodnoi literaturnoi zhizni ["Spiritual Elite" or Soldiers of the Party? Notes on International Literary Life].
—Brief reference to Solzhenitsyn as a "renegade" and to his "anti-social" behaviour.
Znamia 4/1973, pp. 199 and 202.

248 A. SHILKIN, Staryi antisovetizm v novom pokolenii [The Same Old Anti-Sovietism in a New Generation].
—Brief reference to praise of Solzhenitsyn et al. in the émigré journal *Vestnik RSKhD*.
Nauka i religiia 4/1973, p. 73.

ALPHABETICAL INDEX OF AUTHORS

(Numbers refer to items listed in the bibliography)

SUBJECT INDEX

Solzhenitsyn in English: An Evalution

BY ALEXIS KLIMOFF

Some hold translations not unlike to be
The wrong side of a Turkey tapistry.
—James Howell (1594?-1666).

To any reader of Solzhenitsyn's works in the original, the writer's concern with language is as obvious as the moral and social thrust of his narrative. More consistently and more imaginatively than any other contemporary Soviet writer, Solzhenitsyn has attempted to eschew the ubiquitous clichés that have long ago spilled over from the pages of *Pravda* and *Izvestiia* and inundated Soviet writing. Solzhenitsyn's fiction represents a conscious endeavor to offer an alternative. For this purpose he has mobilized the full resources of the Russian language; especially bold use has been made of what the grammar books call "popular" or "substandard" speech [*prostorech'e*]. His syntax is dense, elliptical, and will appear innovative and thorny to those accustomed to urbane commonplaces. The vocabulary range is so great that a recent seventeen-volume dictionary of the Russian language is of no help for many hundreds of items. With few concessions to his readers, Solzhenitsyn makes use of technical terminology, prison-camp slang, rare words culled from Vladimir Dal's famous glossary, as well as large numbers of neologisms.

These qualities alone make the task of Solzhenitsyn's translators extremely difficult. But the caliber of the translations has also been affected by two external factors. To begin with, there is the problem of textual uncertainty. The manuscripts of many of Solzhenitsyn's works (including *Cancer Ward* and *The First Circle*) came to the West by indirect channels, and there are significant differences between the various Russian-language editions of his works. Certain of these variants can be attributed to revisions made by the author; others seem to be corruptions resulting from what has been called the "neo-scribal" process of *samizdat* distribution. Translators and publishers have been forced to make choices and compromises, some of them unfortunate.

But much greater damage has been wrought by the unseemly haste with which many of the translations were produced. Before Solzhenitsyn retained a Swiss attorney, Dr. Fritz Heeb, to defend his interests in the West (1970), each new work by the author was liable to set off a race—not to say a free-for-all—between competing translations. Considerations of quality were all too obviously subordinated to the single-minded aim of "cornering the market" by appearing on the bookshelves before a rival edition. The publishing history of *One Day in the Life of Ivan Denisovich* gives an inkling of the tempos involved. The novel appeared in the Soviet Union in mid-November of 1962, and the first reviews of *two* different English translations had already been published by the second half of January, 1963. If one subtracts the time needed for the technical production of the book, it is evident that the translators were accorded no more than a few weeks to render a text of enormous stylistic subtlety and complexity. Such deadlines are as unrealistic as they are intolerable: the publishers who impose them should bear a large share of the responsibility for the inevitable flaws of the end product.

In this review essay I offer an evaluation of the major English translations of Solzhenitsyn's fiction. My list does not aspire to bibliographic completeness: the principal aim has been to examine critically those translations which have had the greatest impact on the English-speaking world in the course of the past decade. For this reason all translations of Solzhenitsyn published in periodicals and in various literary anthologies have been excluded from consideration; my review is limited to books or book-length collections consisting entirely of works by Solzhenitsyn. Even this more manageable list has had to be restricted to the author's best-known works. The present survey does not include a discussion of the English renditions of "For the Good of the Cause" (separate edition, trans. by David Floyd and Max Hayward, 1964) or of the plays (*The Love-Girl and the Innocent,* trans. by Nicholas Bethell and David Burg, 1969; *Candle in the Wind,* trans. by Keith Armes, 1973).

In each case I have examined a recent edition of the translation in question, frequently a paperback. The analysis is concerned solely and exclusively with the quality of the translation per se. No mention is made of the various introductions, appendices, or afterwords which enhance the value of several of the editions reviewed. I have also avoided all consideration of the legality or propriety of the various editions, some of which have provoked sharp controversy and even litigation.

The criterion in my evaluation has at all times been accuracy: the degree to which the translation communicates the content, spirit, and manner of the original. Defined in this way, accuracy goes far beyond "basic meaning" to include stylistic level, imagery, tone, and "flavor." I shall note further that I have assumed at all times that these translations are addressed to non-readers of Russian. This excludes considering their worth as a crutch or "pony" to help the reader who is partially familiar with the language of the original. Literal, word-by-word translations have their proper place and function but they can never be appropriate for a general audience. As Pushkin observed about Chateaubriand's earnest but misguided attempt to reproduce Milton in French with absolute literal fidelity:

> There can be no doubt that in his endeavor to render Milton *word for word,* Chateaubriand was, at the same time, unable to maintain a faithfulness to meaning and expression. An interlinear translation can never be accurate. (*A.S. Pushkin o literature* [M., 1962], p. 474).

I should add, finally, that I do not claim to have checked every word of the translations discussed against the original. My judgment is based primarily on a close scrutiny of selected chapters or passages in each of the works reviewed. At least ten percent of the translated text has been checked against the Russian in the case of the major novels; a considerably greater proportion was examined in each of the shorter works.

A. *One Day in the Life of Ivan Denisovich*

All presently existing translations of *One Day* were rendered obsolete upon the publication of the authorized and unexpurgated Russian version in Paris in May of 1973. (See entry No. 28 in John Dunlop's "A Select Solzhenitsyn Bibliography" which appears in this volume). The translations reviewed here are all based on the censored text which was published in *Novyi mir* in 1962. Five different English translations of this novel have appeared in print up to 1973:

1. *One Day in the Life of Ivan Denisovich.* Translated by Max Hayward and Ronald Hingley. New York: Frederick A. Praeger, 1963. [My references are to the Bantam paperback edition, 1969.]
2. ——————————. Translated by Ralph Parker. New York: Dutton; London: Gollancz, 1963. [My references are to the Signet paperback edition, 1971.]
3. ——————————. Translated by Thomas P. Whitney. New York: Fawcett [Crest paperback], 1963.
4. ——————————. Translated by Bela Von Block. New York: Lancer, 1963. [My references are to the Lodestone paperback, 1973.]
5. ——————————. Translated by Gillon Aitken. Revised Edition. New York: Farrar, Straus and Giroux, 1971.

One Day presents a formidable challenge to the translator. The greater part of this short novel is expressed in the idiom of the protagonist, a man of peasant origin and no formal education. To achieve this effect, Solzhenitsyn has made use of a narrative style far removed from standard literary Russian. Folksy colloquialisms are combined with vivid slang and prison-camp jargon into a pungent and original but nevertheless entirely credible mixture. In addition, the dialogue contains some of the earthiest language ever to appear in print in the Soviet Union.

Only Hayward and Hingley (No. 1) have faced up to this challenge in a systematic fashion. As they state in a prefatory note, the translators have attempted to capture the stylistic flavor of the original by turning to the speech forms of uneducated American English. While this is not the only possible solution (surely Cockney English is at least as rich), it is certainly a legitimate one. The translators have evidently found this approach productive and they have been able to render many difficult passages with imagination and striking success.

But they have not always followed their own prescription, especially in the second half of the novel. All too many colorful phrases have been pruned to bare and unremarkable English prose. I will cite only a few typical examples. *Ocheredi ne bylo . . . Zakhodi* is translated with the almost neutral: "there wasn't a big crowd lined up . . . So he went straight in" (p. 15). If American slang is to be used, several expressions come easily to mind for *zakhodi* in this context, including "in you go" or perhaps even "waltz right in." *Ekh, da i povalili zh! Povalili zeki s kryl'tsa!* is toned down to "They were all pouring out down the steps now" (p. 191). The visual immediacy of the original is almost entirely erased in the process. A more accurate rendering—once again in accordance with the translators' own program—might be: "Just look at 'em pour out! The zeks are just pouring down the steps." *Zagnat' v dereviannyi bushlat* means literally "to drive into a wooden jacket" and is a jocose euphemism for causing death. Hayward and Hingley have chosen the conventional "to finish off" (p. 50), while there are numerous expressive possibilities in American slang which would reproduce the tone if not the image of the original (e.g. "to put to bed with a shovel").

Many of the abusive epithets have also been unnecessarily reduced in variety and expressiveness. *Obaldui, spina elovaia,* "numskull, clumsy ox" is clipped to "dope" (p. 14); *fitil'*, a term for a weakling or someone on his last legs, becomes simply "old bastard" (p. 5). In general, "bastard" serves with monotonous regularity for a whole series of epithets, including *padlo, gad, svoloch', chert, chuma,* and *sterva.* Alternative translations can easily be found for at least some of these. (At other times, Hayward and Hingley have added abusive terms where none are to be found in the original [e.g. p. 191].)

Apart from such stylistic inadequacies, the Hayward-Hingley version of *One Day* is not entirely free of "ordinary" mistranslations. *Kum* is prison slang for "chief security officer," and *kumu stuchat'* is therefore much more specific than "to squeal to the screws" (p. 2). *Grazhdanin nachal'nik* is decidedly not "Comrade Warder" (p. 13) but "Citizen Warder" (prisoners were forbidden to use the term "comrade"). *Serzhant prikladom karabin povorachivaet* does not mean the sergeant "was twisting the butt of his rifle" (p. 136) but rather that the sergeant was turning his rifle over in order to strike butt-first. Several more errors of this type were noted, most of them quite minor. Apart from the regrettable tendency toward stylistic reduction noted earlier, this translation rates quite high for general accuracy.

Parker's translation (No. 2) appeared simultaneously with the Hayward-Hingley version. (It is of interest that Parker's text as printed in *Soviet Literature* [February, 1963] differs considerably from the text published by Dutton.) Parker has frequently followed the syntactic structure of Solzhenitsyn's Russian more closely than Hayward and Hingley. But this is a questionable virtue, especially when combined with Parker's lack of regard for stylistic levels. Thus *Fetiukov, shakal, podsosalsia* is rendered by "Fetiukov, the jackal, had come up closer" (p. 40). At least two things are wrong here. First of all, a strongly marked slang term with derisive overtones, *podsosat'sia,* has been transformed into the neutral paraphrase "to come closer." Second, though *shakal* does indeed literally mean "jackal," the figurative sense of this word does not coincide in the two languages. In Russian, it implies primarily a greedy person, someone on the prowl; in prison-camp usage it means "scrounger, scavenger." In English, according to both OED and Webster, "jackal" is used primarily to describe a person who does base work for his superiors. Parker's quasi-literal approach is conducive to such questionable renderings and examples can be cited from practically every page. In some cases this method has been carried to unacceptable extremes. In an apparent attempt to retain the sound of the Russian interjection *ukh,* Parker translates *Ukh, kak litso brigadirovo perekosilo* by "Ugh, what a face Tiurin made" (p. 99). (The Hayward-Hingley version is clearly preferable here: "God, the way the boss's face twitched all over.")

There are a number of other translation problems. To name but a few, *Volkovomu ustupka* means "a concession to Volkovoi," not "thanks to Volkovoi" (p. 130). *Balanda,* a derisive term for the watery gruel fed to prisoners—the use of this word was a punishable offense in some camps—is euphemistically christened "stew" (p. 28). Even less plausibly, *magara,* the grass-like mush which they receive, is labelled "oatmeal" (p. 27). *Zona* [compound] is translated as "zone" (p. 29), a term which would be puzzling to most readers. Another minor, but irritating point: the Gospel passages quoted by Aleshka are given in Parker's own and definitely uninspired translation from the Russian (pp. 36, 155). The first of these, besides, contains an error: *zlodei,* a common word rendered as "wrongdoer" or "evildoer" in the standard translations of this passage (I Peter 4:15), is unaccountably construed as "[one guilty of] sorcery."

lated correctly by Hayward and Hingley as "Must have been a Western Ukrainian and new to the place." Von Block expands this to read "Must be from the Western Ukraine, we didn't liberate it 'til '39, so they've still got the old habits. A new prisoner, too, by the looks of things" (p. 20). Since the narrative voice here is Shukov's, this inexcusable addition makes him mouth a Soviet cliché about "liberation." Nothing could have been further from the author's intention. Several other "improvements" of Solzhenitsyn were noted.

Gillon Aitken's translation (No. 5) was first published in Great Britain in 1970. Apart from introducing unmistakably British slang ("that was a mug's game" for *durakov, mol, net* [p. 163]; "old sod with a mustache" for *bat'ka usatyi* [p. 152], etc.) this rendition breaks very little fresh ground. It is frequently similar to the Parker or the Hayward-Hingley versions—to the point of repeating their mistakes and inaccuracies—or else it tends to be a cut below either of these two earlier translations. The passage below, one of many possible examples, illustrates each of these points (P stands for Parker, HH for Hayward and Hingley; the emphasis has been added by me throughout):

AITKEN	*COLLATION OF HH AND P*
Inside it was as steamy	It was like a steam bath
as in THE bath-house—	inside—
what with the frosty air	what with the frosty air
coming through the	coming in through the
doors and the steam	doors and the steam
from the gruel.	from the thin camp gruel.
MEMBERS OF THE GANGS	The men
were sitting at tables	were sitting at tables
or crowding in the	or crowding in the
areas between them,	spaces between them,
waiting for places.	waiting for places (HH, 15) . . .
Yelling to each other	*Shouting to each other*
across the crush,	*across the crush,*
two or three workers	two or three men (P, 27) . . .
from each gang were	from each gang were
carrying bowls of	carrying bowls of
gruel and porridge on	gruel and mush on
wooden trays and	wooden trays and
trying to find places	looking for a place
for them on the tables.	for them on the tables.
And even so, *they don't*	And even so, *they don't*
hear you, the dolts,	*hear you, the dopes,*
and UPSET your tray	they bump into your tray (HH) . . .

—and splash, splash! IF you have a free hand —then give it to *them* in the neck! That's the way! Don't stand there in the way, looking for something to LICK UP (p. 16).	Splash, splash! You've a hand free (P) . . . let *them* have it in the neck (HH) . . . That's the way. Don't stand there (P) . . . in the way (HH) . . . looking for something to swipe! (P)

The capitals indicate significant words and phrases in Aitken's text that do not have any analogous constructions in earlier translations. Of the five instances so designated in this passage, only "to lick up" (for *podlizat'*) is an improvement over both HH and P. "Members of the gangs" is an indifferent alternative translation for *brigady*. The three other instances are less than satisfactory. The definite article in the opening sentence implies—wrongly—that the camp had a steam-bath; "to upset" is a poor rendering of *tolknut'* [to bump; to shove]; there is no "if" in the phrase where Aitken has placed it.

The italics point to constructions which are inaccurate in both Aitken and an earlier version. *Proklikat'sia* is a neologism formed by analogy to a verb such as *prodirat'sia* [to fight one's way through a crowd]. Both Aitken and Parker have misread it as *pereklikat'sia.* (Hayward and Hingley have it right: "Shouting their way through the mob . . .") "They don't hear, the dolts" closely resembles the HH version. But this is an altered and incomplete translation of [*on*] *ne slyshit, obaldui, spina elovaia* [(he) doesn't hear, the blockhead, the clumsy ox].

This is not to maintain, of course, that Aitken's entire text could be dealt with in this fashion. Nor is the resemblance noted here meant to imply any impropriety whatever. After all, there are only so many ways to translate any given passage. The point is rather that Aitken brings few improvements to "the state of the art": he has learned little from the mistakes of his predecessors. Since the text chosen here is not unique, it seems safe to say that Aitken's translation does not represent an important addition to the literature.

If one were to grade the relative merits of the five translations, Hayward and Hingley would unquestionably take first place. Parker and Whitney each have their strong points but are frequently marred by stylistic dissonance. The two others are not recommended.

B. Collections of Short Works

There have been two English collections of short prose works by Solzhenitsyn. They are:

6. *"We Never Make Mistakes": Two Short Novels.* Translated by Paul W. Blackstock. Columbia, S.C.: U. of South Carolina Press, 1963. [I refer to the Norton paperbound edition, 1971].
7. *Stories and Prose Poems.* Translated by Michael Glenny. New York: Farrar, Straus & Giroux, 1971. [References are to the Bantam paperback, 1972].

The Blackstock collection (No. 6) contains "Incident at Krechetovka Station" and "Matrena's Home." Two excellent short stories are here presented in a blurred and inadequate form. The following is a sample of the kind of errors which fill this book. *Beloemigrant* [White Russian émigré] is stood on its head to become "White Russian immigrant" (p. 77); *goluboi, belyi i zheltyi* [blue, white and yellow] is recolored "deep white and yellow" (p. 114); trains are said to have "slowed their march" (p. 89), a curious rendition of *zamedliali svoi khod* [slowed down]; *dobraia ulybka* [kindly smile] becomes "pleased smile" (p. 101); *za god do togo* [a year earlier] is translated "for a year afterward" (p. 89); *dazhe elektrikom na poriadochnoe stroitel'stvo menia by ne vziali* [they would not even have hired me as an electrician on a decent construction job] turns into "already after considerable construction work had been completed, they had turned me down as an electrician" (p. 90). Matrena's account of her fateful decision concerning the missing Faddei is completely misrepresented. *Poshel on na voinu—propal* [He went off to the war—and disappeared] has been twisted into "He went off to war—and fell" (p. 114). The reader is left to puzzle out the best he can why then Matrena should have waited for Faddei for three years thereafter (as Blackstock has correctly translated in the very next sentence). Nearly every page of this collection yields several mistakes of this type.

Under the circumstances, there is no point in discussing Blackstock's success at rendering stylistic levels. I might note only that he has attempted to provide "local color" by popping Russian words into the narrative (e.g. "Da, Comrade Sergeant" [p. 14]).

Some sentences are missing (e.g. on p. 101). Total chaos reigns in the transcription of Russian names and words. Russian *kh* appears in at least four guises: "*Kh*arkhov" (p. 18), "MXAT" (p. 70), "Dyachi*ch*in" (p. 13), and "Ber*h*ova" (p. 18). (The last of these, incidentally, is Blackstock's version of "Verkhov'e.") Russian *ch* and *ts* appear either in this form (Kre*ch*etovka," "Lipe*ts*k" [p. 13]) or else acquire a quasi-Germanic look ("Vasili*tch*" [p. 36], "gorni*tz*a" [p. 93]). It is "Varnakoff" on p. 13, but "Varnakov" on p. 14. Other unlikely transcriptions include "Rtistchev" for Rtishchev (p. 25) and "nanya," an aberrant variation on *niania* [nanny] (pp. 10, 129).

This woeful inability to cope with Russian sounds leads directly to the most spectacular blunder of all. Blackstock's title for his collection, *"We Never Make Mistakes,"* is drawn from the ending of Solzhenitsyn's "Incident at Krechetovka Station." The phrase is part of the curt answer given by an NKVD officer to Zotov's inquiry about the fate of Tveritinov. In his translation of this passage, Blackstock has missed the key point. The NKVD man in his response to Zotov garbles Tveritinov's name, pronouncing it "Tverikin": *Raz-berutsia i s vashim Tverikinym. U nas braka ne byvaet* [They'll sort out your Tverikin all right. We never make mistakes]. Blackstock, confused by all those Russian names, substitutes the correct "Tveritinov" in this sentence, with one stroke depriving the story of its grimly ironic punchline. No mistakes, indeed.*

The Glenny collection (No. 7) contains all of Solzhenitsyn's short works published in *Novyi mir* with the exception of *One Day in the Life of Ivan Denisovich.* This includes "Incident at Krechetovka Station," "Matrena's Home," "For the Good of the Cause," and "Zakhar-Kalita." In addition, the book contains several works not published in the USSR like "The Right Hand," "The Easter Procession," and sixteen "prose poems" or "sketches."

Although it is on the whole less helpless than Blackstock's translation in rendering the basic meaning of the original,

*When the present volume was already in proof stage, it came to my attention that Donald Fiene's recent bibliography of Solzhenitsyn (see entry No. 1 in John Dunlop's "A Select Solzhenitsyn Bibliography") states that a *revised* edition of Blackstock's translation was published by the University of South Carolina Press in 1971 (Fiene, p. 36). A check revealed that the 1971 U. of S. C. edition has added an "Afterword" but is otherwise identical to the 1963 edition. Not a single one of the innumerable mistakes in this translation has been corrected. Blackstock has not even bothered to rectify the misprints of the 1963 edition and the first page of the preface still thanks several persons for assistance "with unclean [*sic*] and difficult words."

Glenny's translation is also unacceptably marred by serious errors. At the beginning of "Matrena's Home" the narrator, who has just returned from the hot wastelands of Central Asia, speaks with deep feeling about his love for the Russian heartland. To him this is tied directly to language and he is moved by the sing-song speech of a woman who sells milk in the market: *slova ee byli te samye, za kotorymi potianula menia toska iz Azii* [her words were the very ones which nostalgia had drawn me out of Asia to hear]. Glenny has reversed the meaning, introducing a jarring discord with all that comes before: "her words made me feel nostalgic for Asia" (p. 3).

Glenny disregards context in this fashion on a number of other occasions; I give two examples from "Matrena's Home." To the narrator's chagrin, Matrena disapproves of Fedor Shaliapin's singing: *Chudnó poiut* [It's a strange way of singing]. In spite of the accent (provided in the original) and in the teeth of context, Glenny translates: "He sings beautifully" (p. 18). A little earlier in the story, Solzhenitsyn tells us that Matrena had gone to church for the blessing of water [*vodosviatie*]. We are told, furthermore, that this is a holiday in December or January. *Kreshchen'e,* therefore, could only be "Epiphany," a holiday that falls on January 6 (O.S.) and at which the Christian East commemorates the Baptism of Jesus. Undeterred by such considerations, Glenny translates *kreshchen'e* as "christening party" (p. 17). (It must have been at this fancied occasion, incidentally, that Glenny re-baptized Faddei, Matrena's fiancé, into "Ilya" [p. 22 ff]. No explanation is offered for this strange decision.)

A depressingly long catalogue of other mistakes could be listed, and I shall give only a sample. *V poltysiachi let* [in the course of five hundred years] becomes "for fifteen hundred years" (p. 107); *khorosho dogadalis' my v loshchinke u kolodtsa napit'sia* [we had the good sense to drink our fill at the well in the valley] turns into "we guessed rightly that we would be able to quench our thirst . . . at the well in the valley" (pp. 107-108); *izbu Matreny do vesny zabili* [Matrena's house was boarded up till spring] is given as "Matrena's cottage was handed over before winter was out" (pp. 40-41); *v ogorode—slepoi saraichik* [in the garden there is a windowless shed] is translated as "outside is a little fenced-in yard" (p. 209); an allegorical sculpture of Victory [*Pobeda*] is transformed into one of "History" (p. 205). An especially farfetched translation occurs in "Matrena's Home." In a halfhearted effort to get her illness diagnosed, Matrena agreed to undergo some tests. The results were sent to the district hospital for analysis, *da tak i zaglokhlo. Byla tut vina i Matreny samoi* [but nothing more was heard of it. Matrena was herself partly to blame here]. The point is that Matrena should have tried again. In his translation of this passage, Glenny would have us believe that Matrena was sent to the district hospital, "where the illness just subsided. Matrena, of course, was blamed for wasting their time" (p. 15).

At other points Glenny's rendition is unintelligible rather than merely wrong. In the sketch which describes a visit to a desecrated monastery where the poet Polonskii had been buried, the narrator is told the following bit of local tradition: *Monastyr' tut byl, v mire vtoroi. Pervyi v Rime, kazhetsia, a v Moskve—uzhe tretii* [There was a monastery here, the second biggest in the world. The largest is in Rome, I think, and the one in Moscow is already third]. Glenny's translation is completely opaque: "There was a monastery here, in the second world. They say the first world was Rome, and Moscow is the third" (p. 201).

There are omissions: several were noted in "Matrena's Home" alone. An entire paragraph which relates the narrator's first impression of Matrena is absent (p. 5), a sentence in the description of her struggle to get a pension has been left out (p. 10), and one of the geographic units (*selo* [village]) which make up Solzhenitsyn's credo-like ending of the story has been cut (p. 42).

Solzhenitsyn's stories have undergone much stylistic leveling. *Mnogopudovaia tsarstvennaia svin'ia* [an enormous and majestic pig] is refashioned into simply "pig" (p. 209); *sapozhnik-dezertir* [the deserter-shoemaker] becomes plain "shoemaker" (p. 40); *rychali vokrug ekskavatory na bolotakh* [excavators roared around us in the bogs] is typically—and needlessly—changed into "excavators were digging peat out of the bogs all around us" (p. 11). The narrator's faintly amused comment about the custom of singing the hymn "Eternal Memory" just before eating *kisel'* at a wake is deprived of its light touch of irony: *tak i ob"iasnili mne, chto poiut ee—pered kiselem obiazatel'no* [that's just how they explained it to me: it had to be sung before the *kisel'* without fail]. This comes out as "they explained to me that traditionally this had to be sung before the *kisel'* " (p. 39).

It is clear that neither the Glenny nor the Blackstock collection can be safely recommended. To get a more reliable idea of the quality of Solzhenitsyn's short fiction, the English reader is directed to a competent translation of "Matrena's Home" by Harry T. Willets, which appeared first in *Encounter,* May, 1963. (It has been reprinted in *Halfway to the Moon: New Writings from Russia,* ed. Patricia Blake and Max Hayward [New York: Holt, 1964] and in *Fifty Years of Russian Prose: From Pasternak to Solzhenitsyn,* ed. K. Pomorska [Cambridge: MIT, 1971], vol. 2.)

C. The First Circle

As in the case of *One Day,* the existing translations of *The First Circle* are based on an incomplete text. Unlike *One Day,* however, the full and authorized text has not yet appeared anywhere. Furthermore, there are certain differences between the Russian versions of *The First Circle* published so far in the West. In an interview with Western newsmen on March 31, 1972, Solzhenitsyn stated: "I worked for many years on that novel. I started it while I was in exile. There are indeed different versions (. . .) I continued to work on that novel after it was published in the West, and the latest version is the one I prefer." (See *The New York Times,* April 3, 1972, p. 10.) As this book goes to press, Solzhenitsyn has announced that he has begun *samizdat* distribution of two additional chapters belonging to a "rewritten version" of his novel. These are Chapters 44 and 88, entitled, respectively, "In the Open" and "Dialectical Materialism." (See *NYT,* September 22, 1973, p. 2.)

In the remarks that follow, I have systematically eliminated all references to passages which were not identical in the principal Western Russian-language editions of *The First Circle* (I have checked those published by Flegon, Harper and Row, Posev, and YMCA Press).

The two extant translations are:

8. *The First Circle.* Translated by Thomas P. Whitney. New York: Harper and Row, 1968. [I refer to the Bantam paperback, 1969].

9. ——————————. Translated by Michael Guybon [pseud.]. London: Collins and Harvill, 1968. [References are to the Fontana paperback, 1972].

Whitney's translation (No. 8) has a consistent tendency to simplify Solzhenitsyn. Modifiers and sometimes whole subordinate clauses have been simply cut. For example, *nezatumanennye dvoinye stekla vysokogo okna, nachinaiushchegosia ot samogo pola* which means, "the mist-free double panes of a tall window which reached to the floor" has been "streamlined" by Whitney to read: "the double panes of the tall window" (p. 1). *Nerzhin rezko pokachal rukoi i golovoi* [Nerzhin shook his head and hand sharply] is abridged to "Nerzhin shook his head" (page 39); *tomishche* [huge tome] is demoted to just plain "volume" (p. 76); *golova kak budto eshche molodogo, no uzhe lyseiushchego Poskrebysheva* [a head belonging to a still seemingly young but already balding Poskrebyshev] is shorn of its qualifiers to become "the young balding head of Poskrebyshev" (p. 104). Dozens of other examples were noted. In some cases an image is destroyed, as when Rubin describes Nerzhin's philosophical eclecticism in the following terms: *ty vydiraesh' otovsiudu po tsvetnomy peru i vse vpletaesh' v svoi khvost* [you pluck out colorful feathers everywhere you go and add them all to your own tail plumage]. This has been stripped of the peacock image to read, "You pluck bright feathers from everywhere" (p. 39). More damaging still is the transformation of *kriterii praktiki v gnoseologii* [practicality as a criterion in epistemology] into simply "gnoseology" (p. 443). This renders part of the argument between Rubin and Sologdin incomprehensible. Although the majority of cases do not involve such a radical injury to the meaning, at the very least such reductions impoverish Solzhenitsyn's style.

Whitney also has some difficulty with prison and underworld slang. His most serious blunder in this regard is the translation of *Pakhan,* an epithet used repeatedly for Stalin, by the puzzling "Plowman" (p. 26, etc.). The Russian word means "head of a gang of thieves," and might be rendered for an American audience by "the Boss." Other instances noted include *rvite kogti* [get lost] rendered as "you're wasting time" (p. 17); *kurochit'* [to steal blind; to rob] translated by "to fool around" (p. 9), and *shalashovka* [camp prostitute], by "female prisoner" (p. 36). *Na tsyrlakh,* an expression which Solzhenitsyn has defined elsewhere as "simultaneously on tip-toe, at great speed, and with the greatest diligence," is left out entirely (p. 7).

A substantial number of other mistakes could be cited. To quote only a few of the more serious ones, [*trubka*] *plavilas' v ruke* means the receiver "was melting in his hand," not "swimming" in it (pp. 6-7). *Poslushnik* is "novice" in the religious sense, not "obedient pupil" (p. 132). *Na pomin dushi* is not "for the good of one's soul" (p. 132) but "for the remembrance of [their] souls." Abakumov, in his fit of rage at the "troika of liars" is said in Whitney's version to have "stamped on their feet" (p. 137), a misreading of *nastupal na nikh,* which in the given context means rather that he threatened or menaced them.

There are irritating errors in the verse citations. In Chapter 2, Rubin recites several lines from Dante interspersed with comments. Quotations from Canto IV of the *Inferno* are given in the following order: lines 106, 107, 110, 112-113, 84, 71-72, 74-75. Whitney, who quotes Dante in John Ciardi's translation, has managed to scramble this sequence completely. Line 108 is substituted for 110, making Rubin's subsequent remark incomprehensible. Instead of lines 112-113, he cites line 83; lines 71-72 are not translated at all. A similar fate befalls the hackneyed war correspondents' songs quoted in Chapter 59: in two of the four examples cited by Solzhenitsyn, the essential meaning has been completely altered in the translation (p. 435).

Michael Guybon's translation (No. 9) appeared in print a short time after Whitney's. It suffers from a different set of problems. Although Guybon has not engaged in the stylistic "streamlining" so evident in Whitney's version, he has by no means refrained from cutting deeply into the text. In fact, Guybon's omissions are if anything more irresponsible and damaging. A particularly serious instance is his exclusion of all chapter titles. This represents a wanton excision of information that is important for a proper understanding of the text (e.g. such headings as "Abandon Hope, All Ye Who Enter Here" which is the only explicit connection to the Dante theme in the chapter describing Volodin's arrest).

The majority of the quotations of poetry have been simply dropped by Guybon. In some cases they have been transformed into a brief paraphrase, frequently without any indication that verse has been cited. For example, Chapters 53 and 54 contain a total of six poetic passages, each of which is closely integrated into the narrative. Four of these have disappeared without a trace in Guybon's translation, one is given in paraphrase, and only one has survived as a recognizable verse citation (p. 392).

This proportion is not untypical. Other types of cuts involve entire sentences. Thus when Potapov prepares to tell the story entitled "Buddha's Smile" he takes a dig at Rubin by asserting with mock earnestness that no literary work can be understood without knowing the social conditions that determined it. Potapov is complimented for this observation by Nerzhin in the same mock-serious tone: *Vy delaete uspekhi, Andreich* [You're making progress, Andreich]. For inscrutable reasons, this line has been replaced by three dots in Guybon's translation (p. 398). Later on the same page, at the very end of Ch. 53, Guybon has left out four entire lines of the original. Several other instances of this type were noted.

Mistranslations abound as well. One occurs in the very first line of the novel, where *piat' minut piatogo* [five past four] is translated as "five to five" (p. 11). Some mistakes are hard to explain, as in the case of *zhir* [fat] rendered by "milk" (p. 48). Others are grotesque, as when *lobok* [pubic region] has been misconstrued as the diminutive of *lob* [forehead] and is repeatedly translated by "head" (pp. 403, 411). Guybon has not fared much better than Whitney with prison slang; most of the errors and omissions cited in my comments on Whitney's translation are repeated in Guybon's version. (*Pakhan,* however, is translated more or less correctly as "Big Chief" [p. 36].) And Guybon, like Whitney, has scrambled the quotations from Dante. But he adds a characteristic twist: since one of Rubin's interpolated comments no longer fits the disarrayed sequence, it is simply cut (p. 20).

But perhaps the most disastrous aspect of this rendition is Guybon's apparent inability to cope with irony and parody. Chapter 54 ("Buddha's Smile") is a case in point. In a manner that seems almost perversely methodical, phrase after phrase of Potapov's brilliant improvisation is stripped of its irony and reshaped into doggedly neutral style. *Opekuny Butyrskogo sanatoriia* [the legal guardians of the Butyrki health resort] becomes "the men in charge of Butyrki Prison" (p. 399). *Vragi naroda* [enemies of the people], a Soviet cliché deliberately employed for ironic effect, appears simply as "prisoners" (p. 400). *Tartar* [Tartarus], a mock-heroic metaphor used to describe the sterilization room, is transformed humorlessly (and inaccurately) into "fumigation chamber" (p. 402). When Mrs. R. wonders whether the prisoners might be hungry, her reasonable question is reported with the following scandalized comment by the narrator: *vyskazala nelepoe predpolozhenie vstrevozhennaia gost'ia* [the alarmed lady guest made the absurd suggestion]. Guybon translates this as "suggested the anxious lady guest" (p. 410), thereby neutralizing the narrator's voice. The list goes on. One is tempted to conclude that Guybon has either consciously tried to edit Solzhenitsyn or else that he simply does not understand irony.

In spite of all my strictures it should be said that both translations are "readable." On the whole, Whitney has a better style and transmits the spirit of Solzhenitsyn's novel more effectively than Guybon. (Among other things, Whitney has captured the irony very well.) But it is clear that both versions would benefit from revision.

D. *Cancer Ward*

This novel shares the fate of *The First Circle* in that no authorized Russian text has been published to date. In compiling the remarks that follow, I have checked two Russian editions (YMCA Press, and Posev) and have refrained from commenting on translations of passages where variant readings exist.

Several independent English translations of the novel were planned in 1968. In view of Solzhenitsyn's vigorous protests against foreign publication of *Cancer Ward,* two of the publishers involved withdrew from the project. The two English translations that were brought to completion are:

10. *Cancer Ward.* Translated by Nicholas Bethell and David Burg. 2 vols. London: Bodley Head, 1968 and 1969. Published as one volume, New York: Farrar, Straus and Giroux, 1969. [My references are to the Bantam paperback, 1969].
11. *The Cancer Ward.* Translated by Rebecca Frank [pseud.]. New York: Dial Press, 1968. [My references are to the Dell paperback, 1973, which has the same pagination].

The Bethell-Burg version of *Cancer Ward* (No. 10) is uneven in quality. The translators have made a genuine effort to make their English style rich and full-blooded. Unfortunately, their imagination has on more than one occasion exceeded their discipline in this regard. To give a relatively harmless example, Solzhenitsyn writes that Efrem Podduev *ostanovilsia kak byk* [stopped like a bull]. Bethell and Burg write "stopped dead like a thwarted bull" (p. 12). While this may sound like "good English," one is left wondering whether "thwarted" does not impose an unwanted dimension on this image. It is generally true that adding gratuitously to a translation is more damaging than suppressing an equal amount of information: new variables with potentially significant relationships are superimposed on the original text, often with far-reaching implications. An example of this is the rendition of Kostoglotov's appellation for Zoia, *pchelka s chelkoi,* by "Teddy bear with the golden hair" (p. 36). The Russian means literally "honeybee with bangs," with *pchelka* being an affectionate term for a girl. The word falls somewhere mid-range in terms of emotional weight, and carries connotations of praiseworthy industriousness. Since no exact equivalent seems to exist in English, the translators have evidently decided to imitate the rhymed-jingle quality of the Russian phrase. It was this consideration ("bear": "hair") that has presumably led to their decision to use "teddy bear." But their choice injects strong "cuddly" associations into the text which are simply absent in the original. The fact that subsequent developments in the novel confirm this "cuddly" image is precisely proof of the highly misleading nature of such a rendition. A conscientious reader of the novel in the Bethell-Burg translation would naturally assume that Solzhenitsyn has meant Zoia's appellation to be prophetic or otherwise symbolic in a way not intended by the author. (It should be pointed out that the word *pchelka* gets more than passing mention. Among other things, it is the title of Chapter 3).

The translation has its share of more conventional errors. I give only a representative sample here. When Nellia announces she will catch up on her sleep on the sofa *v zasedaniiakh,* this is merely her way of saying "in the conference room" (*Komnata vrachebnykh zasedanii* is mentioned two lines later). Bethell and Burg have translated this as a joke, "[I shall be] in session" (p. 27). Kostoglotov's blunt accusation, *v blokade vinovat kto-to drugoi* [someone else is to blame for the (Leningrad) blockade], has been softened to read "there was someone else responsible for the blockade too" (p. 30). *V karuseli zhe bylo i spasenie ot karuseli* [the merry-go-round was in itself a means of salvation from the merry-go-round] is completely misinterpreted as "a merry-go-round that didn't even protect him from other merry-go-rounds" (p. 328). *Zhuravl' dolgonogii* [long-legged stork] is rendered "long-nosed stork" (p. 323), possibly due to a misprint in the Russian; an ordinary brown bear [*buryi medved'*] is transformed into a "grizzly" (p. 505). A particularly unfortunate mistranslation occurs in Chapter 24. In the course of Kostoglotov's blood transfusion, just after he has flung his accusations at Vega, she makes a desperate attempt to communicate her beliefs to him: *Golosom izlomivshimsia, sverkh sily, ona peretiagivalas' cherez rov* [With a broken voice, she was making a supreme effort to reach across the chasm]. Bethell and Burg have not understood this image: "Her voice was shattered. She was trying to pull herself up out of the ditch, but it was beyond her strength" (p. 333). A few lines later, when Solzhenitsyn tells us that Vega has indeed succeeded in reaching across the gulf that separates her from Kostoglotov [*peretianuvshis'*], she is shown instead by Bethell and Burg to be clambering out of the ditch into which they so unfairly placed her: "she had pulled herself up and over the edge." Another significant error of this type was noted in the novel's last chapter. Kostoglotov is riding an unbelievably jampacked streetcar and thinking: *Tak stiskivalo, byvalo, tol'ko v voronkakh* [Only in the Black Marias had there ever been a crush like this]. Bethell and Burg write: "Only in the shell holes had he ever been as close to people as this" (p. 521). The translators have implausibly interpreted *v voronkakh* as the locative plural form of *vorónka* [shell hole], whereas the context of all that comes before makes clear that the reference is to *voronók* [Black Maria; paddy wagon]. It is in fact an important point which emphasizes how Kostoglotov's mind continues to operate in images determined by his prison experience (cf. his manner of viewing the animals in the zoo in the preceding Chapter 35).

The Bantam edition of *Cancer Ward* also contains a substantial number of misprints, certainly more than any of the other translations of Solzhenitsyn reviewed. Some occur in sensitive spots; for example, the date of the letter that begins Part II is given as March 3, 1956; the correct year should have been 1955. The date as printed would (among other incongruities) place the action after the Twentieth Congress of the CPSU.

No embroidering on Solzhenitsyn's style was noted in the much more sober Rebecca Frank translation (No. 11). This rendition suffers, instead, from the more usual sin of flattening and impoverishing the original. The first sentence is typical. *Rakovyi korpus nosil i nomer trinadtsat'*, translated correctly by Bethell and Burg as "On top of everything, the cancer wing was Number 13," is reduced by Frank to "The cancer wing was Ward No. 13" (p. 1). Needless to say, this is not a unique instance. But perhaps more serious is the high number of mistranslations uncovered; I shall cite only a few here. In the first paragraph of the novel, Rusanov continues to object to the numeration of the cancer ward: *Vot uzhe takta ne khvatilo nazvat' trinadtsatym kakoi-nibud' proteznyi ili kishechnyi* [They might have had the tact to assign number thirteen to some prosthetic or intestinal ward]. Frank twists this into "they should have had the tact to call it something like 'prosthetic' or 'intestinal,' not '13' " (p. 1). When Kostoglotov says to Efrem: *nadoel bol'no, skulish'*, he means something like "I'm sick and tired of your whining" and not Frank's strange "you're sick and tired of things, you go around whining" (p. 15). Many errors concern simple words or constructions. *Kaznit'* is "to execute," not "to jail" (p. 501). *Ves' vek ia proboialsia* [I've lived my entire life in fear] is unaccountably rendered "All my life I lived in fear of your fate" (p. 504). *Stolik dlia pisem* means "table for writing letters" not a "mailbox" (p. 609). *Vy razreshili mne prikosnut'sia gubami—k zhizni nastoiashchei*, an important phrase from Kostoglotov's letter to Zoia, which means "you have permitted me to touch my lips—to genuine life," is deprived of much of its meaning and virtually all of its force: "[you] let me come close to your lips, to real life" (p. 610). The most amusing gaffe noted concerns the description of two Uzbek girls whom Kostoglotov presents with the flowers originally intended for Vega. They had their hair done in the same manner: *s odinakovymi chernymi kosichkami, zakruchennymi tuzhe elektricheskikh shnurov* [with identical little black braids, twisted more tightly than electric cords]. Frank translates: "with identical black braids, tied tightly at the ends with bits of electric-wire cord" (p. 595).

There are also omissions. For example one of the obscene ditties quoted by Chalyi to Rusanov has been censored out by Frank. We are left with: "He recited a bawdy verse and slapped Rusanov on the knee" (p. 371).

As in the case of *The First Circle,* neither of the two English translations of *Cancer Ward* can be recommended without certain reservations. In terms of relative merit, the Bethell-Burg version is written in a more attractive style than Frank's; it also seems to have somewhat fewer errors. But this advantage is offset by the more serious nature of the mistakes noted.

E. *August 1914*

There is one English version of this novel:

12. *August 1914*. Translated by Michael Glenny. London: Bodley Head, 1972; New York: Farrar, Straus and Giroux, 1972. [My references are to the American edition].

The story of this translation is particularly disheartening. Solzhenitsyn had taken special pains to see this novel into print properly: he had not released the text "for reading and copying" and his newly-acquired Western agent successfully prevented the appearance of a pirated Western edition. With an authorized Russian text available and under Solzhenitsyn's full legal control, the stage seemed to be set for a careful and unrushed translation of what is undoubtedly his most complex and difficult work.

But things went wrong from the beginning. During the negotiations among the several publishers who were undertaking translations into the major European languages, a singularly shortsighted proposal was made and adopted. It was decided that "because of the title [of Solzhenitsyn's novel] . . . it would be nice to publish in August [1972]." To meet this arbitrary deadline, Michael Glenny was cajoled and pressured into producing an English translation in a period of some eight months. (See Glenny's embittered interview, as reported in Roger Jellinek's "*August 1914:* The Last Word," *The New York Times Book Review,* September 24, 1972, p. 63). Not surprisingly, the translation shows every sign of haste.

But much more distressing is the attitude of the translator toward the work entrusted to him. With a total lack of sympathy for Solzhenitsyn's linguistic goals, Glenny has characterized *August 1914* (in the interview cited above) as a book written in "pseudo-vernacular" and "would-be-conversational" style. The novel exhibits, he contends, "insecure verbal control" and is stylistically "very regressive in Solzhenitsyn's development"; in short, "no one has yet dared to say how badly written the book is." Glenny's conclusion follows naturally. In order to make the novel acceptable to readers of English, "the whole tone had to be altered and much had to be smoothed out." Only one thing is indisputable in this harangue: Glenny is defending his role as an actively hostile editor of Solzhenitsyn.

Since a detailed and reliable account of Glenny's attempts to "smooth out" Solzhenitsyn's prose has already appeared in print—I refer to Simon Karlinsky's perceptive review of *August 1914* in *The New York Times Book Review,* September 10, 1972, esp. pp. 49-51—there is no need to go over the same ground here; I shall cite just one typical example. Among Solzhenitsyn's favorite devices in *August 1914* (as well as in all his preceding works) is the technique of shifting back and forth between third-person narrative and a direct transcription of the unuttered thoughts of his protagonists. The following example is drawn from Chapter 3. Irina Tomchak has just woken up: *Raspakhnula stavni v park—a utro kakoe! a vozdukh s tenevym kholodkom!* [She flung open the shutters facing the park—what a morning! what air with its touch of shady coolness!]. Glenny has changed the narrative structure—and the tone—in his translation of this passage: "She threw open the shutters giving onto the park. It was a wonderful morning, with just a touch of coolness in the air from the shade..." (p. 22). Perhaps the most annoying aspect of this revision (which stands for scores of similar cases) is its needlessness. Modern readers would hardly have been confused by the more accurate rendering, let alone devotees of Joyce or Faulkner. Glenny's fastidiousness is at least half a century out of date.

Other stylistic tampering includes omissions (e.g. on p. 432) and the reduction of complex sentences to their simplest components. One can only agree with Simon Karlinsky's severe conclusion in his review of the book: "In fairness to the reader, the English version of the novel should have been labeled by the publishers 'adapted' or 'paraphrased' by Michael Glenny, rather than translated by him."

With the manner and form of Solzhenitsyn's novel betrayed, one has the right to expect at least the content to have been grasped properly. Not so. Numerous mistakes in basic meaning were found in every chapter checked; the following list is but a brief selection. When *med* is blessed after the Transfiguration service, this is "honey," not "mead" (p. 22); *inoi god* means "in other years," not "one year" (p. 63); *bumaga okazalas' ser'eznaia* should be "the document turned out to be important," not "the paper appeared to be important" (p. 77); *tut i nemtsy podzhigali* means "the Germans set fires here as well" not "it was set on fire by the Germans" (p. 145). *Bral gorod. Ne vzial* is a classic example of Russian aspect usage that should read "He tried to take a town. He didn't succeed," not Glenny's "Took a town, but lost it again" (p. 150). When Samsonov contemplates his lack of rapport with the rest of the top command he puts it in the following terms: *i Rennenkampf i Zhilinskii byli luidi kakoi-to chuzhoi dushi* [both Rennenkampf and Zhilinskii were men of an alien cast of soul]. It is clear that they are alien *to Samsonov,* not to each other as Glenny would have it: "Rennenkampf and Zhilinsky were temperamentally ill-matched" (p. 80). In the course of the remarkable burial service for Kabanov, Blagodarev chants a supplication that the soul of the departed be granted refuge in "a place of light and of peace." Solzhenitsyn continues: *otchasti uzhe sbyvalas' molitva* [the prayer was already being answered in part]. Glenny's translation of this phrase is unrelated to the correct meaning: "the prayers for the dead man's soul were almost over" (p. 492). A number of errors bespeak carelessness and haste, as when *nevestka* [daughter-in-law] is mistaken for *nevesta* and is translated as "fiancée" (p. 64).

To summarize: Glenny's translation of *August 1914* is exceedingly mediocre, and Solzhenitsyn's novel must not be judged by it.

* * *

The reader who has stayed with this cheerless survey to the end is entitled to wonder whether it is even worth the effort to read Solzhenitsyn in English. The answer must be yes, for in spite of the countless infelicities, mistakes, revisions, and "corrections," the prose of this verbal master still produces a powerful and sometimes overwhelming effect. This is not because a poor translation does little damage—the opposite is surely true—but because Solzhenitsyn's work is so rich in thought, imagery, and texture, that even an imperfect or partial rendering retains abundant literary worth. But that Solzhenitsyn deserves better treatment than he has received—of this there can be little doubt.

A Select Solzhenitsyn Bibliography

BY JOHN B. DUNLOP

The following bibliography does not aim at exhaustiveness; it attempts, rather, to offer a selection of the more valuable and important contributions to a literature which has experienced a rapid expansion over the past decade. Apart from a listing of the most reliable editions of Solzhenitsyn's works, this bibliography concentrates mainly on publications in the English language. Exceptions to this rule include several book-length studies and compilations devoted to Solzhenitsyn in languages other than English and a number of articles of outstanding merit. Many of the items listed are supplied with a brief annotation. The compiler wishes to acknowledge the helpful suggestions which he has received from colleagues Alexis Klimoff and Michael Nicholson.

I BIBLIOGRAPHICAL MATERIALS ON SOLZHENITSYN

1. Fiene, Donald. *Alexander Solzhenitsyn: An International Bibliography of Writings By and About Him, 1962-1973.* Ann Arbor, Michigan: Ardis, 1973.
   The most complete bibliography to date.

Other useful compilations include:

2. Artemova, A. "Bibliografiia proizvedenii A. Solzhenitsyna" ["A Bibliography of the Works of A. Solzheni-

tsyn"]. In: Aleksandr Solzhenitsyn, *Sobranie sochinenii.* Frankfurt/Main: Possev Verlag, 1970, VI, 367-85.
Lists the editions of Solzhenitsyn's works in Russian and in translation. Has been updated in an expanded edition of this volume, 1973, which also includes a bibliography of Solzhenitsyn criticism.

3. D'Argent, François. "Essai de bibliographie d'Alexandre Soljénitsyne." In: Georges Nivat and Michel Aucouturier, eds. *Soljénitsyne.* Paris: L' Herne, 1971, pp. 493-511.
Strongest on French items.

4. Havrlant, Ludmila. "A.I. Solzhenitsyn: Selected Bibliography, December 1962-October 1970." *Canadian Slavonic Papers,* 13, No. 2-3 (1971), 243-52.

5. Radio Liberty Library (Munich). "A.I. Solzhenitsyn: A Bibliography." 24 November 1969.

6. Rothberg, Abraham. "Bibliography." *Aleksandr Solzhenitsyn: The Major Novels.* Ithaca: Cornell University Press, 1971, pp. 203-210.

II SOURCES FOR "L'AFFAIRE SOLJENITSYNE"

The term "L'Affaire Soljenitsyne" or "Delo Solzhenitsyna" has come to denote: (1) the debate between Soviet "liberals" and "hardliners" over the political implications of Solzhenitsyn's fiction, (2) Solzhenitsyn's public statements (e.g. his protests against censorship, police harassment, etc.), (3) the campaign against him by the regime, (4) *samizdat* statements in his defense by Soviet intellectuals and common citizens, and (5) the controversy surrounding honors accorded him or positive opinions about him in the West (e.g. the Nobel Prize controversy).

A. *Collections of Documents:*

The fullest compilation of source materials in English is:

7. Labedz, Leopold, ed. *Solzhenitsyn: A Documentary Record.* Enlarged Edition. Bloomington: Indiana University Press, 1973.
An enlarged and updated version of a book originally published by Harper and Row in 1971.

For the Russian texts see:

8. "Delo Solzhenitsyna." In: Aleksandr Solzhenitsyn, *Sobranie sochinenii.* Frankfurt/Main: Possev Verlag, 1973, VI (Expanded edition).

Other collections include:

9. Brumberg, Abraham, ed. *In Quest of Justice: Protest and Dissent in the Soviet Union Today.* New York: Praeger, 1970, pp. 245-94.
   Many of the documents in this volume also appear in the more complete Labedz collection.

10. *Les Droits de l'écrivain: Alexandre Soljenitsyne.* Paris: Seuil, 1969.

11. Floyd, David and Hayward, Max, compilers. "Appendix." In: Alexander Solzhenitsyn, *For the Good of the Cause.* Trans. by David Floyd and Max Hayward. New York: Praeger, 1964, pp. 95-134.
    An interesting collection of Soviet press reactions to the publication of Solzhenitsyn's short novel in *Novyi mir.*

12. Guttenberger, Elena, ed. *Bestraft mit Weltruhm: Dokumente zu dem Fall Alexander Solzhenizyn.* Frankfurt/Main: Possev Verlag, 1970.

13. Markstein, Elisabeth and Ingold, Felix Philipp, eds. *Über Solschenizyn. Aufsätze, Berichte, Materiälen.* Neuwied and Berlin: Luchterhand, 1973.

14. Nivat, Georges and Aucouturier, Michel, eds. *Soljénitsyne.* Paris: L'Herne, 1971, pp. 101-324.
    Contains the complete texts of some important materials not included in the Labedz or the Russian "Delo" compilation (No. 8).

14a. *Solzhenitsyn: Press Comment.* Moscow: Novosti Press Agency Publishing House, 1972.
    The preface states the purpose of this volume in unambiguous terms: "This book presents material . . . from the Soviet and foreign press concerning A. Solzhenitsyn's 'writings' and the anti-Soviet campaign conducted in connection with his name by certain circles in the West." This is an 81 pp. English-language compilation of hostile and defamatory press reactions to Solzhenitsyn's works and activities. Virtually all materials included were published in *Literaturnaia gazeta* between 1968 and 1972.

B. *Book-Length Studies Discussing "L'Affaire Soljenitsyne":*

15. Björkegren, Hans. *Aleksandr Solzhenitsyn: A Biography.* New York: The Third Press, 1972.

A thin commentary woven around unevenly translated documents. The work suffers from hasty translation and editing and incorrect transliterations. It also contains several factual errors.

16. Burg, David and Feifer, George. *Solzhenitsyn.* New York: Stein and Day, 1972.

An ambitious but untrustworthy study to be used with caution. The book lacks documentation and is seriously marred by extravagant hypothesizing and a tendency to invent Solzhenitsyn's thoughts and feelings. See the review by Zhores Medvedev entitled "Getting Solzhenitsyn Straight," in *The New York Review of Books,* 17 May 1973, pp. 32-34, and the subsequent Feifer-Medvedev exchange in the 19 July 1973 *NYRB.*

17. Daix, Pierre. *Ce Que Je Sais de Soljenitsyne.* Paris: Seuil, 1973.

An appreciative account of Solzhenitsyn's activities by a noted French Communist.

18. Grazzini, Giovanni. *Solzhenitsyn.* New York: Dell, 1973.

A wide-ranging "life and times." The book lacks focus, contains some factual inaccuracies and a distressing number of garbled transliterations. The names of Solzhenitsyn's characters are often misspelled. One suspects hasty translation and editing.

19. Hegge, Per Emil. *Mellommann i Moskva* [*Go-Between in Moscow*]. Oslo: J.W. Cappelens Forlag, 1971.

An intriguing account by the Norwegian journalist who acted as "middleman" in Solzhenitsyn's unsuccessful attempts to obtain the awarding of his Nobel Prize medal. For an abridged English translation see: *Survey,* 18, No. 2 (1972), 100-111. Extracts also appear in the Labedz volume (No. 7).

20. Medvedev, Zhores A. *Desiat' let posle "Odnogo dnia Ivana Denisovicha."* [*Ten Years After* Ivan Denisovich] London: Macmillan, 1973.

A valuable study of the Solzhenitsyn "affaire" by a close friend of the writer. The book corrects some fallacies in earlier accounts. English translation is due for publication in the U.S. (by Knopf) in late 1973 or early 1974.

C. *Related Studies:*

21. Johnson, Priscilla, ed. *Khrushchev and the Arts: The Politics of Soviet Culture 1962-1964.* Cambridge, Mass.: The M.I.T. Press, 1965.

Contains an informative discussion of the Solzhenitsyn "affaire" during the last two years of Khrushchev's reign.

22. Reddaway, Peter, ed. *Uncensored Russia: Protest and Dissent in the Soviet Union.* New York: American Heritage Press, 1972.

Contains an absorbing account of the view of Solzhenitsyn held by Soviet dissident intellectuals.

23. Rothberg, Abraham. *The Heirs of Stalin: Dissidence and the Soviet Regime, 1953-1970.* Ithaca: Cornell University Press, 1972.

Includes a detailed and valuable discussion of the impact of Solzhenitsyn's personality and writings on Soviet Russia during the nineteen sixties.

24. Tatu, Michel. *Power in the Kremlin: From Khrushchev to Kosygin.* New York: The Viking Press, 1970.

Expertly relates the Solzhenitsyn "affaire" to the struggle for power within the Soviet leadership.

III RUSSIAN EDITIONS OF SOLZHENITSYN'S FICTION

The most textually reliable editions to date are the following:

25. *Rakovyi korpus* [*Cancer Ward*]. Paris: YMCA Press, 1968.

26. *V kruge pervom* [*The First Circle*]. Paris: YMCA Press, 1969.

27. *Avgust chetyrnadtsatogo (10-21 avgusta st. st.)* [*August 1914*]. Uzel I [Part I]. Paris: YMCA Press, 1971. Vtoroe ispravlennoe izdanie [Second, Corrected Edition].

This second edition rectifies the numerous misprints in the first edition.

28. *Odin den' Ivana Denisovicha. Matrenin dvor.* [*One Day in the Life of Ivan Denisovich.* "Matrena's Home."] Paris: YMCA Press, 1973.

This important edition, issued with Solzhenitsyn's imprimatur, is the only complete and unabridged publication of these works. Words, phrases, and entire passages cut or altered in the official Soviet editions are here restored to their original form.

29. Solzhenitsyn, Aleksandr. *Sobranie sochinenii.* Frankfurt/Main: Possev Verlag, 1969-1970. 5 volumes.

The Posev edition of Solzhenitsyn's *Collected Works* has the advantage of being an almost complete edition. It includes, however, the *Novyi mir* (i.e. censored) version of *One Day* and "Matrena's Home."

The works are arranged as follows:

VOLUME I: (a) *Odin den' Ivana Denisovicha* [*One Day in the Life of Ivan Denisovich*].
(b) "Sluchai na stantsii Krechetovka" ["Incident at Krechetovka Station"].
(c) "Matrenin dvor" ["Matrena's Home"].
(d) "Dlia pol'zy dela" ["For the Good of the Cause"].
(e) "Zakhar-Kalita" ["Zakhar the Pouch"].
VOLUME II: *Rakovyi korpus* [*Cancer Ward*].
VOLUME III: *V kruge pervom* [*The First Circle*]. Chapters 1-47.
VOLUME IV: *V kruge pervom.* Chapters 48-87.
Note: The Posev editions of *The First Circle* and *Cancer Ward* differ on a number of small points from the YMCA editions of these novels, but their relative textological merit is difficult to establish with certitude.
VOLUME V: (a) *Olen' i shalashovka* [*The Love-Girl and the Innocent*].
(b) *Svecha na vetru* [*A Candle in the Wind*].
(c) "Pravaia kist' " ["The Right Hand"].
(d) "Krokhotnye rasskazy" ["Sketches"].
(e) "Paskhal'nyi krestnyi khod" ["Easter Procession"].
Not included in the *Collected Works* are *August 1914* and the following two "sketches" or "microstories":

30. ——————. "Staroe vedro" ["The Old Bucket"] and "Sposob dvigat'sia" ["The Means to Move"]. *Grani,* 80 (1971), 8-9.

IV CRITICISM OF SOLZHENITSYN'S FICTION

A. *Books and Complete Issues of Journals:*

31. *"Avgust chetyrnadtsatogo" chitaiut na rodine* [*How* August 1914 *Is Read in the Homeland*]. Paris: YMCA Press, 1973.
A collection of Soviet *samizdat* reactions to Solzhenitsyn's latest novel. The contributions are of varying worth, with the piece by "L.O." clearly being the most significant.

32. *Canadian Slavonic Papers,* 13, No. 2-3 (1971).
An entire double-issue devoted to Solzhenitsyn.

33. Lukacs, Georg. *Solzhenitsyn.* Cambridge, Mass.: The M.I.T. Press, 1971.
A plodding study somewhat redeemed by occasional flashes of insight. See the review by Irving Howe in this volume.

34. Markstein, Elisabeth and Ingold, Felix Philipp, eds.

Über Solschenizyn. Aufsätze, Berichte, Materiälen. Neuwied and Berlin: Luchterhand, 1973.

35. Nivat, Georges and Aucouturier, Michel, eds. *Soljénitsyne.* Paris: L'Herne, 1971.
    Includes a large selection of Solzhenitsyn criticism. Of particular note is Jacqueline de Proyart's important study of Solzhenitsyn's women, "La femme, l'amour et l'enfer."

36. Pletnev, R. *A.I. Solzhenitsyn.* Munich: Author Publication, 1970.
    A disorganized study containing, however, some useful information. An updated edition of the book has been published by YMCA Press, 1973.

37. Rothberg, Abraham. *Aleksandr Solzhenitsyn: The Major Novels.* Ithaca: Cornell University Press, 1971.
    While not devoid of interest, this study suffers from the author's pronounced insensitivity to the artistic level of Solzhenitsyn's writing.

38. Rzhevskii, Leonid. *Tvorets i podvig: ocherki po tvorchestvu Aleksandra Solzhenitsyna* [*Artist and Exploit: Essays on the Art of Aleksandr Solzhenitsyn*]. Frankfurt/Main: Possev Verlag, 1972.
    A solid survey of Solzhenitsyn's fiction but with little that is particularly new in Solzhenitsyn criticism.

B. *Articles:*

39. Atkinson, Dorothy G. "Solzhenitsyn's Heroes as Russian Historical Types." *The Russian Review,* 30, No. 1 (1971), 1-16.

40. Bayley, John. "The Guns of Tannenberg." *The Listener,* 21 September 1972, pp. 573-74.

41. Blagov, D., pseud. "A. Solzhenitsyn i dukhovnaia missiia pisatelia" ["A. Solzhenitsyn and the Writer's Spiritual Mission."] *Sobranie sochinenii,* Aleksandr Solzhenitsyn. Frankfurt/Main: Possev Verlag, 1969-1970, VI, 287-355.
    An extravagant but suggestive essay by a personal friend of Solzhenitsyn's.

42. Bradley, Thompson. "Alexander Isaevich Solzhenitsyn." *Soviet Leaders.* Ed. George W. Simmonds. New York: Crowell, 1967, pp. 329-39.
    A good survey of Solzhenitsyn's short works published in *Novyi mir.*

43. Brown, Deming. "Cancer Ward and First Circle." *Slavic Review,* 28, No. 2 (1969), 304-13.

Contains a somewhat controversial evaluation of *The First Circle.*

44. Brown, Edward J. "Solzhenitsyn's Cast of Characters." *Slavic and East European Journal,* 15, No. 2 (1971), 153-66.

Excellent analysis of works prior to *August 1914.* Reprinted in Edward J. Brown, ed., *Major Soviet Writers: Essays in Criticism* (New York: Galaxy, 1973), pp. 351-66.

45. Erlich, Victor. "Post-Stalin Trends in Russian Literature" and "Reply." *Slavic Review,* 23, No. 3 (1964), 405-19, 437-40.

Suggestive discussion of Solzhenitsyn's early works.

46. Esslin, Martin. "Solzhenitsyn and Lukacs." *Encounter,* 36, No. 3 (1971), 47-51.

47. Fanger, Donald. "Solzhenitsyn: Ring of Truth." *The Nation,* 7 October 1968, pp. 341-42.

Excellent discussion of *The First Circle.*

48. Garrard, J.G. "The 'Inner Freedom' of Alexander Solzhenitsyn." *Books Abroad,* 45, No. 1 (1971), 7-18.

49. Glenny, Michael. "Alexander Solzhenitsyn." *Studies in Comparative Communism,* 2, No. 1 (1969), 160-67.

Good.

50. ——————. "A New Russian Epic: Solzhenitsyn's 'August 1914'." *Survey,* 18, No. 2 (1972), 112-22.

51. Grebenshchikov, Vladimir I. "The Infernal Circles of Dante and Solzhenitsyn." *Transactions of the Association of Russian-American Scholars in USA,* VI (1972), 7-20.

52. Gul', Roman. "A. Solzhenitsyn, sotsrealizm i shkola Remizova" ["A. Solzhenitsyn, Socialist Realism and the School of Remizov"]. *Novyi zhurnal,* 71 (1963), 58-74.

Reprinted in Roman Gul', *Odvukon'* (New York: "Most," 1973), pp. 80-95.

53. ——————. "Chitaia 'Avgust chetyrnadtsatogo' " ["Reading *August 1914*"]. *Novyi zhurnal,* 104 (1971), 55-82.

Contains a controversial criticism of Solzhenitsyn's lexical innovations. Reprinted in *Odvukon',* pp. 5-32.

54. Harari, Manya. "Solzhenitsyn's 'Cancer Ward'—Part II." *Survey,* 69 (1968), 145-49.

55. Hayward, Max. "Solzhenitsyn's Place in Contemporary Soviet Literature." *Slavic Review,* 23, No. 3 (1964), 432-36.
On Solzhenitsyn's early works.

56. Hingley, Ronald. "The Evil That Men Do." *Spectator,* 15 November 1968, pp. 698-99.

57. Howe, Irving. "Predicaments of Soviet Writing—I." *The New Republic,* 11 May 1963, pp. 19-21.

58. Jacobson, Dan. "The Example of Solzhenitsyn." *Commentary,* 47, No. 5 (1969), 81-84.
Suggestive.

59. Karlinsky, Simon. "August 1914." *The New York Times Book Review,* 10 September 1972.

60. Koehler, Liudmila. "Alexander Solzhenitsyn and the Russian Literary Tradition." *The Russian Review,* 26, No. 2 (1967), 176-84.

61. Kovaly, Pavel. "Problems of Anti-Humanism and Humanism in the Life and Work of Alexander Solzhenitsyn." *Studies in Soviet Thought,* 11, No. 1 (1971), 1-18.

62. Lakshin, V. "Ivan Denisovich, ego druz'ia i nedrugi" ["Ivan Denisovich: His Friends and Foes"]. *Novyi mir,* 1964, No. 1, 223-45.
Also in Aleksandr Solzhenitsyn, *Sobranie sochinenii,* VI, 243-86. Partial English translation in Priscilla Johnson, ed. (No. 21), pp. 275-88.

63. Luckett, Richard. "Solzhenitsyn and the Battle of Tannenberg." *Spectator,* 23 September 1972, pp. 466-67.

64. Luplow, Richard. "Narrative Style and Structure in 'One Day in the Life of Ivan Denisovich'." *Russian Literature Triquarterly,* Fall (1971), 399-412.

65. McCarthy, Mary. "A Guide to Exiles, Expatriates, and

Internal Emigres." *New York Review of Books,* 9 March 1972.

Brief but suggestive discussion of Solzhenitsyn.

66. Mihajlov, Mihajlo. "Dostoevsky's and Solzhenitsyn's 'House of the Dead'." *Russian Themes.* New York: Farrar, Straus and Giroux, 1968, pp. 78-118.

67. Monas, Sidney. "Ehrenburg's Life, Solzhenitsyn's Day." *Hudson Review,* 16, No. 1 (1963), 112-21.

68. Muchnic, Helen. "Aleksandr Solzhenitsyn." *Russian Writers: Notes and Essays.* New York: Random House, 1971, pp. 400-450.

Excellent survey of Solzhenitsyn's works. The section dealing with *The First Circle* appeared in an earlier form in *The Russian Review,* 29, No. 2 (1970), 154-66.

69. Nicholson, Michael. "Solzhenitsyn's *The Right Hand.* An Early Variant?" *Scando-Slavica,* XVIII (1972), 97-109.

A careful analysis demonstrating the knotty textological problems which arise from *samizdat* distribution.

70. Pervushin, N.V. "The Soviet Writer Solzhenitsyn, His Critics and the Classical Russian Literature." *Slavic and East European Studies* (Montreal), 10, No. 1-2 (1965), 3-19.

71. Pritchett, V.S. "Hell on Earth." *The New York Review of Books,* 19 December 1968.

72. ——————. "War and the Futility of War." *New Statesman,* 22 September 1972, pp. 391-92.

73. Rossbacher, Peter. "Solzhenitsyn's 'Matrena's Home'." *Slavic and East European Studies* (Montreal), 12, No. 2-3 (1967), 114-21.

74. Rzhevskii, Leonid. "Obraz rasskazchika v povesti Solzhenitsyna 'Odin den' Ivana Denisovicha' " ["The Image of the Narrator in Solzhenitsyn's Tale *One Day in the Life of Ivan Denisovich*"]. *Studies in Slavic Linguistics and Poetics in Honor of Boris O. Unbegaun.* Ed. R. Magidoff et al. New York: New York University Press, 1968, pp. 165-78.

75. Salisbury, Harrison E. "The World as Prison." *The New York Times Book Review,* 15 September 1968.

76. Scammell, Michael. "Introduction." *Russia's Other Writers: Selections from Samizdat Literature.* New York: Praeger, 1971.
Useful background information.

77. Steiner, George. "Georg Lukacs and Solzhenitsyn." *East Europe,* 20, No. 4 (1971), 31-32.

78. Toynbee, Philip. "Heavy Artillery: 'August 1914'." *Observer* (London), 17 September 1972, p. 36.

79. Tvardovskii, Aleksandr. "Vmesto predisloviia" ["Instead of a Foreword"]. *Novyi mir,* 11 (1962), 8-9.
Tvardovskii's foreword to *One Day in the Life of Ivan Denisovich.* English translation in the Signet, Bantam and Praeger editions of *One Day.*

80. Vinokur, T.G. "O iazyke i stile povesti A.I. Solzhenitsyna 'Odin den' Ivana Denisovicha' " ["Concerning the Language and Style of A.I. Solzhenitsyn's Tale *One Day in the Life of Ivan Denisovich*"]. *Voprosy kul'tury rechi,* 6 (1965), 16-32.
A seminal study of Solzhenitsyn's language and narrative technique.

81. Weissbort, Daniel. "Solzhenitsyn's 'Cancer Ward'." *Survey,* 68 (1968), 179-85.

82. Wilson, Edmund. "Solzhenitsyn." *The New Yorker,* 14 August 1971, pp. 83-87.
Controversial but insightful.

83. Windle, Kevin. "The Theme of Fate in Solzhenitsyn's 'August 1914'." *Slavic Review,* 31, No. 2 (1972), 399-411.

84. Zaitsev, Boris. "Pis'mo A.I. Solzhenitsynu" ["A Letter to A.I. Solzhenitsyn"]. *Vestnik russkogo studencheskogo khristianskogo dvizheniia,* 94 (1969), 97-99.

85. Zekulin, Gleb. "Solzhenitsyn's Four Stories." *Soviet Studies,* 16, No. 1 (1964), 45-62.
On Solzhenitsyn's first four stories published in *Novyi mir.*

86. Zissermann, Nicholas. "The Righteous Ones: A Study in Figural Interpretation." *Landfall,* 18, No. 2 (1964), 140-51.

Interesting but extravagant.

V MISCELLANEOUS

87. Galler, Meyer and Marquess, Harlan E. *Soviet Prison Camp Speech: A Survivor's Glossary, Supplemented by Terms from the Works of A.I. Solzhenitsyn.* Madison: University of Wisconsin Press, 1972.

A useful aid for anyone intending to read Solzhenitsyn in the original.

VI FORTHCOMING

Solzhenitsyn is currently working on two volumes which continue the account begun in *August 1914.* They will be entitled *October 1916* and *March 1917.* He recently announced that he has also completed a "non-fiction study" of Soviet concentration camps in the Far East during the period 1918-1956 called *Arkhipelag Gulag* [*The Labor-Camp Archipelago*]. A number of other significant—but so far unnamed—works by Solzhenitsyn have yet to see publication. In a late-August, 1973 interview the writer asserted, "my death will not make happy those who count on it to stop my literary activities. Immediately after my death or immediately after I have disappeared or have been deprived of my liberty, my literary last will and testament will irrevocably come into force and then the main part of my works will start being published, works I have refrained from publishing all these years." (*New York Times,* 29 August 1973, p. 8.)

Major new studies of Solzhenitsyn's life and works are being prepared in the United States by Patricia Blake and in Britain by Michael Scammell. Both are due for publication in 1974. In October, 1973 Possev Verlag is due to publish Dimitrii Panin's *Zapiski Sologdina* [*The Memoirs of Sologdin*]. Panin, now residing in the West, was the prototype for Solzhenitsyn's Dimitrii Sologdin in *The First Circle.* This book is also scheduled to appear in English translation.